D0481265

Case problems in management accounting

The Willard J. Graham Series in Accounting

Consulting Editor **Robert N. Anthony** *Harvard University*

Case Problems
in
MANAGEMENT
ACCOUNTING

Edited by

M. EDGAR BARRETT, Ph.D.

Professor and Director of Maguire Oil and Gas Institute
Edwin L. Cox School of Business
Southern Methodist University

and

WILLIAM J. BRUNS, JR., Ph.D.

Professor of Business Administration
Graduate School of Business Administration
Harvard University

1982

R I C H A R D   D .   I R W I N ,   I N C .
Homewood, Illinois   60430

© RICHARD D. IRWIN, INC., 1982

All rights reserved. No part of this publication may be
reproduced, stored in a retrieval system, or transmitted,
in any form or by any means, electronic, mechanical,
photocopying, recording, or otherwise, without the prior
written permission of the publisher.

Case material of the Harvard Graduate School of
Business Administration is made possible by the
cooperation of business firms who may wish to remain
anonymous by having names, quantities, and other
identifying details disguised while basic relationships
are maintained. Cases are prepared as the basis
for class discussion rather than to illustrate either effective
or ineffective handling of administrative situations.

ISBN 0-256-02724-2

Library of Congress Catalog Card No. 81–80225

Printed in the United States of America

2 3 4 5 6 7 8 9 0 MP 9 8 7 6 5 4

Acknowledgments

A wide variety of people contributed to the development of the case materials contained in this book. Perhaps the most important of these were the business managers who contributed both time and material to the development of the cases. These managers were gracious in their hospitality, supportive in their comments and, in most cases, made available to the case writers a wide range of factual data.

Many of our colleagues, at the Harvard University Graduate School of Business Administration, the Edwin L. Cox School of Business at Southern Methodist University, and at other institutions, offered their support and counsel. Prominent among these colleagues were Robert N. Anthony, Stanley Baiman, Neil C. Churchill, George Foster, Thomas R. Hofstedt, F. Warren McFarlan, James S. Reece, John K. Shank, and Richard F. Vancil. The effect of their support, often provided in the form of insightful comments, is obvious in many of the cases included in this volume.

The cases in this edition were written or supervised by 27 different faculty members. Most of the cases were developed by faculty members in the employ of the Harvard University Graduate School of Business Administration. A significant number, however, were developed elsewhere, with the Edwin L. Cox School of Business at Southern Methodist University and the Management Development Institute known as IMEDE serving as sites for multiple case development.

We would like to expressly thank Professors Hawkins, Shank, Shillinglaw and Vancil, who gave us permission to reproduce more than one case written or supervised by them.

We also wish to express our appreciation to IMEDE for permission to reprint the Azienda Vinicola Italiana, Crans–Mon S.A., A/S Dansk Minox, Galvor Company (R–3), and the AB Thorsten (A) cases in this volume.

We also wish to extend our thanks to the many research assistants at both the Harvard University Graduate School of Business Administration and the Edwin L. Cox School of Business at Southern Methodist University who wrote or assisted in the writing of many of the cases in this volume while under the supervision of senior faculty members.

We would also like to express our special appreciation to Kathryn Murdoch, Norma Murdoch, and Susan Swearingen for their forbearance and support as they helped us to nudge this project toward completion.

Despite the above acknowledgments, the editors assume full responsibility for the contents of this volume.

M. Edgar Barrett
William J. Bruns, Jr.

Contents

————◦◦◦◦————

PART THREE: MANAGEMENT ISSUES IN THE FINANCIAL REPORTING PROCESS

Foreign currencies

Inflation and price changes

PART FOUR: COMPREHENSIVE CASES

APPENDIX

Introduction

———⚬———

Although the case method is not new to accounting instruction, this book will provide a different experience for many students and teachers who use it. For those whose prior study of management accounting has been based in other methods of teaching/learning, initial exposure to the case method may be somewhat frustrating. In contrast to methods which focus on teaching solutions to accounting problems, where there is often a single acceptable solution based upon the application of well-known techniques and procedures, the case method is characterized by incomplete information, a variety of possible approaches, and quite frequently no clear "right" answer. In most cases, major amounts of analysis are left for the reader, and a variety of frameworks, techniques, or methods might be appropriate.

The essence of the case method of learning lies in the fact that students are left to develop and practice ways of thinking about and analyzing information and problems. Using cases such as those in this book, management accounting techniques can be practiced and theories can be developed and tested. Less effective approaches can be compared directly to approaches which seem more effective, at least in the case at hand. Learning occurs in the process of trying to apply methods and techniques to available information in order to reach conclusions. If errors are made, they are much less expensive than similar errors might be in a real-world management situation. If good results are obtained, they can be remembered and applied to similar problems that will confront the student in the future.

Most of the cases in this book are descriptions of actual decision situations managers have faced. The authors of cases try to capture and include as much information as they can so that the student has the same information a manager had when actually trying to solve the problem. The case description includes information about the environment, the organization, and the situation, and usually gives some hints about the objectives or need for a decision. Student and teacher are then left to analyze the situation and choose a course of action.

For students of accounting, we can compare cases and the case method to accounting problems and the lecture-review method so frequently used in teaching accounting techniques. In most situations cases go well beyond the kind of information that is usually included in the problems. Environmental data and information about the organization, about managers, and about alternatives that may not be relevant to the "solution" of the case are often included. Students must decide which information to analyze and how to weigh and use conflicting data and information. Knowing accounting techniques alone usually will not suffice to solve a case. It is not unusual for students using the case method to reach very different conclusions. As they do so and share these with each other in class discussion, they practice and develop skills in presenting their analyses and conclusions and in evaluating the different conclusions reached by other members of the class.

In selecting cases for this textbook, the editors have attempted to include cases that will be useful as a basis for three kinds of courses. First, the text is designed to be the basis of a course in management accounting. Such a course will go beyond accounting techniques alone. Students will quickly learn that managers must work with accountants and accounting information to develop analyses to use in making decisions that will allow the organization to achieve its goals and objectives. We believe the topics raised by the cases in this book are appropriate for a management accounting course, and that through study of these cases, students will learn techniques for measuring and reporting financial information and cost data to managers.

This textbook is appropriate also in an advanced-level course for students who have already studied management accounting using the problem-lecture method. In attempting to apply the techniques, practices, and procedures learned in such a course, students will discover much about the disparity between the manager's task and the limited information so many accounting techniques and methods provide. They will be better accountants or more effective managers from the insights they will acquire.

A third use of this text is for students of management who will spend their working lifetimes solving problems with limited information. In most organizations, accounting systems provide the best information that is available. But such information is always incomplete at best, and rarely leads to simple answers to the complex questions with which management decision makers must deal.

The reader who wishes to survey the topics covered in this text is invited to review the table of contents, where we have tried to provide a hint of the major topics covered in each of the cases included in the book. Three major kinds of topics are included: (1) cost measurement and analysis; (2) management accounting and management control systems, which are used to control and plan activities in firms; and (3) cases on problems managers frequently encounter as they work with accounting systems and accountants. In many cases the manager must understand the difficulty of accounting before being able to effectively cope with the inadequacy of accounting information.

In the case method, three kinds of preparation are appropriate. A student should work alone when first reading a case. During this reading, alternative courses of action should be considered, information should be analyzed, and a conclusion should be reached. After thorough individual preparation, most students find it advantageous to discuss their conclusions with a small group of other students before their class meets. This discussion clarifies students' understanding of the case and usually sharpens their reasons for feeling one way or another about the appropriate action to take. The small group discussion also makes every student a teacher of others in the group. Finally, the majority of class time should be devoted to a discussion of the case. There students present their analyses to each other, defend their positions, sharpen their understanding of the positions of others, and learn from what others saw in the case or were able to develop from it. It is not necessary that the class agree on a "solution" to the case—and in most cases that will be impossible, anyway.

In preparing to teach a class using the case method, an instructor has a somewhat more difficult job than in the lecture method, because control of the pace of the class and its conclusions is yielded to students to a large degree. It is essential that the instructor develop, in his or her mind, clear objectives for the class. Preparation for the class itself will also include analysis of the case not unlike that which will be done by students. Along with this analysis, instructors develop plans for classtime use of visual aids such as the blackboard, transparencies, or films, or for clarifying comments to interject at certain points of the discussion. Instructors who effectively use this method think continually about how to best implement the student discussion so that the class objectives can be realized.

To many first-time users, the case method seems harder than traditional teaching/learning methods. Preparation time for both students and instructors is usually somewhat longer than for other methods. But students inevitably report that they feel the case method is more fun and results in exceptionally positive feelings about themselves and their ability to deal with real business problems. The learning students will get from using this book will seem more real than the learning that comes from a textbook and a set of lecture notes, because in searching for decisions in case situations, they are dealing with the same issues that people in the organizations described in the cases were dealing with. They are learning from others' experiences and are creating experiences for themselves which will never be forgotten.

M. Edgar Barrett
William J. Bruns, Jr.

—·◄P A R T O N E►·—

Developing and using cost information

───CASE I–1───

Prestige Telephone Company

In April 1972, Daniel Rowe, president of Prestige Telephone Company, was preparing for a meeting with Philip Bradley, manager of Prestige Data Services, a company subsidiary. Under a special agreement with the state Public Service Commission, Prestige Telephone had been permitted to establish a computer data services subsidiary to perform data processing for the telephone company and to sell computer service to telephone customers. Mr. Rowe had told the commission in 1969 that a profitable computer services subsidiary would reduce pressure for a telephone rate increase. However, by the end of 1971 the subsidiary had yet to experience a profitable month. Mr. Bradley felt only more time was needed, but Mr. Rowe felt action was necessary to reduce the drain on company resources.

Prestige Data Services had been created for three reasons. First, Prestige Telephone needed computer services to plan, control, and account for its own operations in the metropolitan region it served. Second, the company knew that other businesses in the metropolitan region needed similar services and felt that centralized serviced provided over telephone circuits had several advantages which could be used in selling computer time not needed by Prestige itself. Finally, the state Public Service Commission had encouraged all public utilities under its jurisdiction to seek new sources of revenue and profits to reduce the need for rate increases which higher costs would otherwise bring.

Because it operated as a public utility, the rates charged by Prestige Telephone Company for telephone service could not be changed without the approval of the Public Service Commission. In presenting the proposal for the new subsidiary, Mr. Rowe had argued for a separate but wholly owned entity whose prices for service would not be regulated. In this way, Prestige could compete with other computer service organizations in a dynamic field; in addition, revenues for use of telephone services might also be increased. The commission accepted this proposal subject only to the restriction that the average monthly charge for service by the subsidiary to the parent not exceed $20,500, the estimated cost of equivalent services used by Prestige Telephone company in 1969. All accounts of Prestige Data Services were

---

This case was prepared by Professor William J. Bruns, Jr.

separated from those of Prestige Telephone, and each paid the other for services received from the other.

From the start of operations of Data Services in 1970 there had been problems. Equipment deliveries were delayed. Personnel had commanded higher salaries than expected. And most important, customers were harder to find than earlier estimates had led Mr. Rowe to expect. By the end of 1971, a time when income of Prestige Telephone was low enough to necessitate a report to shareholders revealing the lowest return on investment in over 10 years, Mr. Rowe felt it was time to reassess Data Services. Mr. Bradley had asked for more time, as he felt the subsidiary would be profitable by March. But when the quarterly reports came (Exhibits 1 and 2), Mr. Rowe called Bradley to arrange their meeting.

Mr. Rowe received two reports on operations of Data Services. The Summary of Computer Utilization (Exhibit 1) summarized the use of available hours of computer time. Service was offered to commercial customers 24 hours a day on weekdays and 8 hours on Saturdays. Routine maintenance of the computer was provided by an outside contractor who shut the machine down for eight hours each week for testing and upkeep. The reports for the quarter revealed a persistent problem; available hours, which did not provide revenue, remained high.

EXHIBIT 1
Prestige Data Services (summary of computer utilization, first quarter 1972)

Revenue hours	January	February	March
Intracompany	206	181	223
Commercial	123	137	141
Total revenue hours	329	318	364
Service hours	32	32	40
Available hours	175	162	180
Total hours	536	512	584

Revenue and cost data were summarized in the quarterly report on results of operations (Exhibit 2). Intracompany work was billed at $100 per hour, a rate based on usage estimates for 1972 and the Public Service Commission's restrictions that cost to Prestige Telephone should not exceed an average of $20,500 per month. Commercial sales were billed at $200 per hour.

While most expenses summarized in the report were self-explanatory, Mr. Rowe reminded himself of the characteristics of a few. Space costs were all paid to Prestige Telephone. Data Services rented the ground floor of a central exchange building owned by the company for $2,000 per month. In addition, a charge for custodial service based on the estimated annual

EXHIBIT 2
Prestige Data Services (results of operations, first quarter 1972)

	January	*February*	*March*
Revenues			
Intracompany sales	$20,600	$18,100	$22,300
Commercial sales			
Computer use	24,600	27,400	28,200
Other	2,311	2,296	3,172
Total revenue	$47,511	$47,796	$53,672
Expenses			
Space Costs			
Rent	2,000	$ 2,000	$ 2,000
Custodial services	310	310	310
	2,310	2,310	2,310
Equipment costs			
Computer lease	23,750	23,750	23,750
Maintenance	1,350	1,350	1,350
Depreciation			
Computer equipment	6,375	6,375	6,375
Office equipment			
and fixtures	170	170	170
Power	411	400	460
	32,056	32,045	32,105
Wages and salaries			
Operations	7,374	7,308	7,584
System development and			
maintenance	3,000	3,000	3,000
Administration	2,250	2,250	2,250
Sales	2,800	2,800	2,800
	15,424	15,358	15,634
Materials and supplies	2,258	2,185	2,579
Sales promotion	1,985	1,760	2,021
Corporate services	3,856	3,839	3,908
Total expenses	$57,889	$57,497	$58,557
Net income (loss)	($10,378)	($ 9,701)	($ 4,885)

cost per square foot was paid by Data Services, as Telephone personnel provided these services.

Computer equipment had been acquired by lease and by purchases; leases had four years to run and were noncancelable. Owned equipment was all salable but probably could not bring more than its book value in the used equipment market.

Wages and salaries were separated in the report to show the expense of four different kinds of activities. Operating salaries included those of the nine persons necessary to run the center around the clock as well as amounts paid hourly help who were required when the computer was in operation. Salaries of the programming staff who provided service to clients and maintained the operating system were reported as system development and maintenance. Sales personnel, who called upon and serviced present and prospective commercial clients, were also salaried.

Because of its relationship with Prestige Telephone, Data Services was able to avoid many costs an independent company would have. For example, all payroll, billing, collections, and accounting was done by Telephone Company personnel. For these corporate services, Data Services paid Prestige Telephone an amount based on wages and salaries each month.

Although Mr. Rowe was discouraged by results to date, he was reluctant to suggest to Bradley that Prestige Data Services be closed down or sold. The idea behind the subsidiary just seemed too good to give up easily. Besides, he was not sure that the accounting report really revealed the contribution that Data Services was making to Prestige Telephone. In other cases, he had felt that the procedures used in accounting for separate activities in the company tended to obscure the costs and benefits they provided.

After examining the reports briefly, Mr. Rowe resolved to study them in preparation for asking Mr. Bradley to estimate the possible effects on profits of increasing the price to customers other than Prestige Telephone, reducing prices, increasing sales efforts and promotion, and of going to two-shift rather than 24-hour operation.

QUESTIONS

1. Appraise the results of operations of Prestige Data Services. Is the subsidiary really a problem to Prestige Telephone Company? Consider carefully the differences between reported costs and costs relevant for decisions that Mr. Rowe is considering.

2. Assuming company demand for service will average 205 hours per month, what level of commercial sales of computer use would be necessary to breakeven each month?

3. Estimate the effect on income of each of the options Mr. Rowe has suggested if Mr. Bradley estimates as follows:
   a. Increasing the price to commercial customers to $250 per hour would reduce demand by 30 percent.
   b. Reducing the price to commercial customers to $150 per hour would increase demand by 30 percent.
   c. Increased promotion could increase sales by up to 30 percent. Mr. Bradley is unsure how much promotion this would take. (How much could be spent and still leave Prestige Data Services with no reported loss each month if commercial hours were increased 30 percent?)
   d. Reducing operations to 16 hours on weekdays and 8 hours on Saturdays would result in a loss of 20 percent of commercial revenue hours.

4. Can you suggest changes in the accounting and reporting system now used for operations of Prestige Data Services which would result in more useful information for Mr. Rowe and Mr. Bradley?

⸺·◄CASE I–2►·⸺

Atherton Company

Early in January 1975, the sales manager and the controller of the Atherton Company met for the purpose of preparing a joint pricing recommendation for Item 345. After the president approved their recommendation, the price would be announced in letters to retail customers. In accordance with company and industry practice, announced prices were adhered to for the year unless radical changes in market conditions occurred.

The Atherton Company was the largest company in its segment of the textile industry; its 1974 sales had exceeded $12 million. Company salespersons were on a straight salary basis, and each salesperson sold the full line. Most of Atherton's competitors were small. Usually they waited for the Atherton Company to announce prices before mailing out their own price lists.

Item 345, an expensive yet competitive fabric, was the sole product of a department whose facilities could not be utilized on other items in the product line. In January 1973, the Atherton Company had raised its price from $3 to $4 a yard. This had been done to bring the profit per yard on Item 345 up to that of other products in the line. Although the company was in a strong position financially, it would require considerable capital in the next few years to finance a recently approved long-term modernization and expansion program. The 1973 pricing decision had been one of several changes advocated by the directors in an attempt to strengthen the company's working capital position so as to insure that adequate funds would be available for this program.

Competitors of the Atherton Company had held their prices on products similar to Item 345 at $3 during 1973 and 1974. The industry and Atherton Company volume for Item 345 for the years 1969–74, as estimated by the sales manager, is shown in Exhibit 1. As shown by this exhibit, the Atherton Company had lost a significant portion of its former market position. In the sales manager's opinion, a reasonable forecast of industry volume for 1975 was 700,000 yards. He was certain that the company could sell 25 percent of the 1975 industry total if it adopted the $3 price. As many consumers were convinced of the superiority of the Atherton product, the sales

---

This case was prepared as a basis for class discussion rather than to illustrate either effective or ineffective handling of an administrative situation.

EXHIBIT 1
Item 345, prices and production, 1969–1974

| | Volume of production (yards) | | Price | |
| | | | | |
Year	Industry total (000)	Atherton (000)	Charged by most competitors	Atherton company
1969........	610	213	$4	$4
1970........	575	200	4	4
1971........	430	150	3	3
1972........	475	165	3	3
1973........	500	150	3	4
1974........	625	125	3	4

manager reasoned that sales of Item 345 would probably not fall below 75,000 yards, even at a $4 price.

During the pricing discussions, the controller and sales manager had considered two other aspects of the problem. The controller was concerned about the possibility that competitors would reduce their prices below $3 if the Atherton Company announced a $3 price for Item 345. The sales manager was confident that competitors would not go below $3 because they all had higher costs and several of them were in tight financial straits. He believed that action taken on Item 345 would not have any substantial repercussions on other items in the line.

The controller prepared estimated costs of Item 345 at various volumes of production (See Exhibit 2). These estimated costs reflected current labor and material costs. They were based on past experience except for the estimates of 75,000 and 100,000 yards. The company had produced more

EXHIBIT 2
Estimated cost per yard of Item 345 at various volumes of production (000)

	75	100	125	150	175	200
Direct labor..............	$0.800	$0.780	$0.760	$0.740	$0.760	$0.800
Material..................	0.400	0.400	0.400	0.400	0.400	0.400
Material spoilage	0.040	0.040	0.038	0.038	0.038	0.040
Department expense						
Direct*	0.120	0.112	0.100	0.100	0.100	0.100
Indirect†	0.800	0.600	0.480	0.400	0.343	0.300
General overhead‡	0.240	0.234	0.228	0.222	0.228	0.240
Factory cost..............	2.400	2.166	2.006	1.900	1.869	1.880
Selling and administrative						
expense§	1.560	1.408	1.304	1.236	1.215	1.222
Total cost...........	$3.960	$3.574	$3.310	$3.136	$3.084	$3.102

  * Indirect labor, supplies, repairs, power, etc.
  † Depreciation, supervision, etc.
  ‡ 30 percent of direct labor.
  § 65 percent of factory cost.

than 100,000 yards in each of the last 10 years, and earlier experience was not applicable because of equipment changes and increases in labor productivity.

QUESTIONS

1. How, if at all, did the company's financial condition relate to the pricing decision?

2. Should $3 or $4 have been recommended? (Assume no intermediate prices are being considered.)

3. What information not in the case would you like to have in making this pricing decision? (Do not let the lack of information prevent your answering Question 2!)

─◄CASE I-3►─

Azienda Vinicola Italiana

Azienda Vinicola Italiana produced and sold bottled wines. A large percentage of its sales were of a special table wine. Most of its clients, located in the principal Italian cities, were contacted through local representatives. Its prices were in line with those of competitors.

In 1974 the firm sold 704,000 liters of wine, in 871,850 bottles.[1] In recent years demand had been increasing, and the firm had approached the limit of its productive capacity, which was estimated to be 900,000 bottles a year.

The production process was not complicated since the firm did not buy grapes but rather bought either mosto or bulk wine.[2] This had the disadvantage that the firm could not assure itself of a consistently high-quality product. Moreover, it was estimated that if grapes were purchased, the price of raw material would be reduced by about Lit. 55 per bottle.[3] On the other hand, the purchase and installation of equipment needed for pressing

---

Copyright © 1957 by l'Institut pour l'Etude des Méthodes de Direction de l'Entreprise, (IMEDE), Lausanne, Switzerland. Reproduced by permission.

[1] One liter is slightly more than one U.S. liquid quart.

[2] Mosto is the juice of grapes before the fermentation process takes place. The fermentation process takes about one month. During this process carbon monoxide develops, and the sugar is converted into alcohol. Therefore, mosto is an unstable product, and wine is a stable product.

[3] In 1974, 100 Italian Lira (abbreviated "Lit.") equaled approximately U.S. 15 cents.

grapes would require an additional investment of about Lit. 275 million. No significant increase in labor costs was anticipated under such a practice.

In the production department there were 40 workmen who worked a total of about 90,000 hours in 1974 and whose average wage per hour, including fringe benefits, was Lit. 2,000. The administrative manager was of the opinion that 40 percent of this labor expense should be considered as being fixed, while the remainder could be considered as varying proportionally with production volume.

In 1974, production had required 700,000 liters of mosto and bulk wine, purchased at a total cost of Lit. 301,136,000. The average cost incurred for auxiliary materials (bottles, stoppers, neckbands, labels, etc.) was about Lit. 225 per bottle.

The income statement for 1974 is shown in Exhibit 1.

EXHIBIT 1

AZIENDA VINICOLA ITALIANA
Income Statement
For 1974 in Lira (000)

Sales		960,685
Costs		
Labor	178,568	
Raw materials	301,136	
Auxiliary materials	196,757	
General manufacturing expenses (including pay of two cellar foremen)	26,372	702,833
Gross margin		257,852
General administrative expenses (including salary of person skilled in art of making and preserving wine)	92,098	
Depreciation	57,970	
Interest	41,250	
Advertising	43,450	234,768
Net profit		23,084

The administrative manager wished to reorganize the firm in order to exploit its productive capability to the utmost and, above all, to increase the net profit, which was not considered as being satisfactory by the owners. They were of the opinion that a net profit of 8 percent or 9 percent of sales could be realized.

The administrative manager intended to use for this purpose, charts of costs and revenues which he had seen being used by other firms and which he considered useful. The first step in this graphic analysis was a study of costs, separating fixed costs from variable costs. For that purpose, he examined the income statements of preceding years and came to the conclusion that the figures for 1974 were representative. He also noticed that the different types of wine had been sold in more or less the same relative proportions each year, despite large fluctuations in the total volume of business, and this confirmed his belief that the figures for 1974 were representative. He therefore prepared the following analysis (in thousands of lire):

    a. Fixed costs

40 percent of labor cost.............	71,427
Staff salaries	59,098
General manufacturing expenses	26,372
General administrative expenses	33,000
Advertising expenses	43,450
Interest	41,250
Depreciation.....................	57,970
	332,567

    b. Variable costs

60 percent of labor cost.............	107,141
Raw materials	301,136
Auxiliary materials	196,757
	605,034

The administrative manager assumed a maximum capacity of 900,000 bottles a year. At current prices he estimated this would produce sales revenue of Lit. 990 million.

With the present structure of costs and revenue, the profits resulting from an annual production of 900,000 bottles would be small. The administrative manager decided, therefore, to try to discover a way to change costs and revenue so as to obtain a profit of Lit. 88 million per year, which would be 9 percent of sales of Lit. 990 million.

QUESTIONS

1. Accepting the distribution between fixed and variable elements as estimated by the administrative manager, prepare a chart of costs and revenues. Determine the volume of production at which the firm reaches its break-even point and the profit at capacity operation.

2. Draw three other charts, each constructed so that a production of 900,000 bottles will produce a profit of Lit. 88 million, one in which selling price is assumed to increase, another in which fixed costs are assumed to decrease, and a third in which variable costs are assumed to decrease. What are the break-even points in each of these situations?

3. What are the most likely alternatives to consider so as to achieve a profit of Lit. 88 million?

Cotter Co., Inc.

In preparing its profit plan for 1968, the management of the Cotter Co., Inc., realized that its sales were subject to monthly seasonal variations, but expected that for the year as a whole the profit before taxes would total $240,000, as shown below:

	1968 budget	
	Amount ($000)	*Percent of sales*
Sales	$2,400,000	100
Standard cost of goods sold:		
Prime costs	960,000	40
Factory overhead	840,000	35
Total standard cost	1,800,000	75
Gross profit	600,000	25
Selling and general overhead	360,000	15
Profit before taxes	$ 240,000	10

Management defined "prime costs" as those costs for labor and materials which were strictly variable with the quantity of production in the factory. The overhead in the factory included both fixed and variable costs; management's estimate was that, within a sales volume range of plus or minus $1 million per year, variable factory overhead would be equal to 25 percent of prime costs. Thus, the total factory overhead budgeted for 1968 consisted of $240,000 of variable costs (25 percent of $960,000) and $600,000 of fixed costs. All of the selling and general overhead was fixed, except for commissions on sales equal to 5 percent of the selling price.

Mr. Cotter, president of the company, approved the budget, stating that, "A profit of $20,000 a month isn't bad for a little company in this business." During January, however, sales suffered the normal seasonal dips, and production in the factory was also cut back. The result, which came as some surprise to the president, was that January showed a loss of $7,000.

12

Operating Statement
January 1968

Sales		$140,000
Standard cost of goods sold		105,000
Standard gross profit		35,000
Manufacturing variances:	Favorable or (unfavorable)	
Prime cost variance	$(3,500)	
Factory overhead:		
Spending variance..........	1,000	
Volume variance	(12,500)	(15,000)
Actual gross profit		20,000
Selling and general overhead.....		27,000
Loss before taxes		$ (7,000)

ASSIGNMENT

1. Explain, as best you can with the data available, why the January profit was $27,000 less than the average monthly profit expected by the president.

2. What is Cotter's monthly break-even volume?

3. What was Cotter's January production level?

4. How much did finished goods inventory change in January?

5. What were actual factory overhead costs in January?

CASE I–5

Wayland Publishing Company

In June 1979, the three officers of the Wayland Publishing Company were trying to decide which of three directions their new company should move. For almost a year, Tom Riley, president, and two friends had been investigating opportunities in publishing and taking the legal steps necessary to form their new company. In May they had successfully offered and sold stock to 30 investors, thereby obtaining the $200,000 which they felt they needed to begin operations.

Tom Riley had great plans for Wayland Publishing Company, and he hoped that eventually it would become an important publisher of magazines, books, and other educational materials. While limited capital would restrict the scope of operations initially, he hoped that fresh ideas would lead to success which would ensure rapid and profitable growth. Using his ideas as the principal selling point, he had convinced the 30 stockholders to buy shares in hopes of participating in the success of the new venture. In addition, he had secured a line of credit from a local bank, which would provide by loans at 10 percent interest up to two times the stockholders' investments.

The officers of the firm had decided to begin with a single major project, but each preferred a different one. Because little financial analysis had been done, they agreed to study all three in detail before making a final choice. In particular, they were concerned about whether they would have sufficient income to be reported each year, and the return that would be earned on the stockholders investment.

THE HIGHLAND QUARTERLY

As Tom Riley had been building toward the start of operation, another publisher had met with him to discuss the possibility that the firm purchase *The Highland Quarterly*, a quality specialty magazine devoted to travel. The magazine was sold only on newsstands and it had never done well financially. Nevertheless, Mr. Riley felt it had high potential if editorial quality was improved and if sold by subscription only. The rights to use the name, some material ready for publication, and an address list of high potential subscribers would be purchased for $100,000.

Mr. Riley estimated that it would take three years to get the magazine started. He estimated that in each year Wayland could sell 100,000 new subscriptions at a $4 introductory rate, and that half of those would renew and remain as permanent subscribers at an annual rate of $6. The costs to print and deliver four issues each year to subscribers were estimated at an average cost of $2 per subscriber. While advertising would be limited, Mr. Riley was sure that $50,000 would be collected from advertisers each year.

The annual expenses of publishing *The Highland Quarterly* were estimated at $360,000. Principally salaries, those costs would cover circulation, editorial services, production, and advertising sales. In addition, Mr. Riley estimated that first year start-up costs would total about $30,000. In projecting cash flows in this and other projects, Mr. Riley decided to assume all receipts and expenditures would take place at the beginning of each year.

TEXTBOOKS

A second course of action open to the firm was to enter the industry as a publisher of textbooks. The plan which another officer had developed called for the firm to develop a list of high quality, high volume texts based upon work to be purchased from expert authors and consultants. Initially, the firm would develop one text at a cost of $450,000. Books would be printed at a cost of $4 a copy, distributed at an additional cost of $1 per copy, and sold at net revenue to Wayland of $12 per copy. Annual costs for sales and administration would be $100,000.

Sales targets for each text would be set initially at 50,000 copies in the first year of publication and 40,000, and 30,000 in subsequent years respectively. After the third year, each text would be revised and updated.

EDUCATIONAL FILMS

A third course of action appeared promising also. Potential use of multimedia teaching stations, video cassettes, and other experimental teaching devices appeared to provide great opportunities for firms with film production capabilities. While none of the officers had experience in film production and distribution, they estimated that they could secure help necessary to produce eight films the first year at an average cost of $50,000 per film. If sales and rentals of each film could return $30,000 in the first year, $30,000 in the second year, and $30,000 in the third, films appeared an attractive investment. Mr. Riley had estimated that annual sales expenses of $100,000 would be necessary to obtain sales of these amounts. Of the three alternatives, Mr. Riley considered films the most risky because of the unsettled state of the market for quality educational films. Nevertheless, another officer felt that films were the key to media of the future and was strongly supporting their selection as the first project of Wayland Publishing.

QUESTIONS

1. Analyze each of the three alternatives being considered by Wayland Publishing. How well, over a three year planning period, does each promise to meet the criteria of feasibility, profitability, and return to stockholders.

2. If the firm chooses one project to begin operations, it could select another at a later date. What are the implications for profits and resource requirements of choosing another similar project (a second magazine, a second text, or a second set of films) compared to choosing another kind of project?

————◄CASE I–6►————

Crowe Chemical Division

————◄∞►————

Michael Demming, executive vice president of the Crowe Chemical Division of Majestic Tool Company, Inc., was sitting in his Beaumont, Texas, office. It was late in the evening on a midweek day in July 1976. Demming had stayed late at the office in order to be able to spend some time assessing the ramifications of a recently announced price cut by a major competitor.

The competitor, Cajun Chemical Corporation, was the industry leader in the region of the country and the market segment served by Crowe Chemical. The Louisiana based firm was both larger and more profitable than Crowe.

THE COMPANY

Crowe Chemical was a wholly owned subsidiary of Majestic Tool. It was a small concern, with manufacturing and administrative facilities located in or near Beaumont, Texas. The firm was engaged in the production of industrial chemicals which were used primarily in the oil refining process.

This case was written by Charles T. Sharpless, research assistant, and Professor M. Edgar Barrett. Copyright © 1978 and 1979 by M. Edgar Barrett.

Although it was far smaller than most firms in the chemical industry, Crowe had managed to survive and, in fact, stay quite competitive.

Crowe's divisional strategy was built upon the premise that the firm would concentrate its efforts in the marketing, manufacturing, and distribution of specialty chemicals. The manufacturing process for each of the firm's products was nearly identical. With a few minor exceptions, the productive plant and equipment could be used for the manufacture and packaging of all three products.

The firm's three products were also closely related in that they required similar raw materials. One of the raw materials used to produce one of the three products (Sa 11) was itself a by-product resulting from the manufacture of another of the firm's products (Sa 10). The amount of this by-product which resulted from the manufacture of Sa 10 at the current level of production was well in excess of the firm's current and projected needs as an input to the Sa 11 production process. The excess amount of by-product was sold on the open market and treated as a reduction in Sa 10's overall raw material costs.

The sales and marketing efforts of the Crowe Chemical Division were concentrated in three Gulf Coast states. The salaried salesmen were assigned to specific geographic regions in Texas, Louisiana, or Mississippi. Price was a major consideration for the smaller refineries with which the Crowe Chemical Division often dealt. However, some degree of brand loyalty had been created as a result of long-standing customer relationships developed by the regional salesmen. The management of Crowe Chemical estimated that they held an average market share of 16 percent for Sa 10, 14 percent for Sa 11 and 8 percent for Sa 12 within the three-state region served by the firm.

SOME HISTORY

Crowe Chemical Company was founded in 1939 by John Lewis Crowe. The firm benefited handsomely from the wartime economic boom. By 1946, annual sales had reached the level of $5 million. The firm continued its pattern of gradual, but steady growth over the next three decades. Record sales of nearly $42 million were recorded in 1974.

J. L. Crowe resigned from his management position in mid-1973. The resignation had been planned for some time as a result of Mr. Crowe's explicit desire to free most of his time for use in family-related interests and personal real estate ventures. The presidency of the firm was handed to Mr. Crowe's son-in-law, George Thompson.

Mr. Crowe, however, did not totally withdraw from the ongoing activities of the firm. He had, for example, played an important role in the merger negotiations that took place during 1975.

ACQUISITION BY MAJESTIC TOOL

Due in large part to spiraling production costs, 1975 was not a very profitable year for either Crowe Chemical or the industry as a whole. In fact, 1975 was an exceptionally poor year for the entire chemical industry. Raw material prices rose considerably. Rising labor costs and sharply higher utility rates took their toll in terms of reduced levels of profit. Finally, it was widely acknowledged that production capacity had recently grown in a manner disproportionate to increases in demand.

Crowe's common stock, traded over the counter, fell considerably in price during the year. After being the target of two unannounced takeover bids, Crowe's management sought out a friendly partner. Majestic Tool, a Louisiana-based supplier of high technology products and services to the energy sector, ultimately entered into merger discussions with the firm.

The acquisition talks centered, at one point, on what role George Thompson would play in the emerging subsidiary. It was finally agreed that he would remain in his present capacity as chief executive officer, with responsibility for planning and personnel. The agreement stipulated, however, that one of Majestic's own men was to be brought in as executive vice president. This man, Michael Demming, had had extensive experience in industrial products and was to be in charge of day-to-day operations.

ANALYSIS OF OPERATING RESULTS

Demming assumed his new position in early 1976. Several days after his arrival, he and Thompson met to review the firm's 1975 operations. The two men inspected the income statement for the year just ended (Exhibit 1), as well as several other documents recently computed by the controller's department. One of these other documents was a product line profitability analysis for the calendar year 1975 (Exhibit 2). Another document provided information about the particular characteristics of individual product costs,

EXHIBIT 1
CROWE CHEMICAL DIVISION
Income Statement
For the Year Ended December 31, 1975

Gross sales	$37,985,788
Less: Discounts	690,343
Net sales	37,295,445
Cost of goods sold	19,655,641
Gross margin	17,639,804
Operating expenses	16,980,765
Operating income	659,039
Less: Interest	357,143
Divisional profit (before tax)	$ 301,896

EXHIBIT 2
Product line profitability analysis (for the year ended December 31, 1975)

	Sa 10		*Sa 11*		*Sa 12*	
	$000	*Per unit*	**$000**	*Per unit*	**$000**	*Per unit*
Gross sales	$15,514	$7.7500	$13,517	$9.0000	$8,954	$9.5000
Discounts	194	.0969	304	.2024	192	.2037
Net sales	15,320	7.6531	13,213	8.7976	8,762	9.2963
Cost of goods sold						
Direct labor	2,035	1.0165	3,352	2.2319	1,579	1.6753
Direct material[1,2]	1,919	.9586	1,701	1.1326	1,439	1.5268
Indirect labor	1,087	.5430	1,189	.7917	907	.9623
Fringe benefits	81	.0405	134	.0892	64	.0679
Insurance	104	.0519	79	.0526	49	.0519
Repair service	336	.1678	254	.1691	157	.1666
Power	124	.0619	94	.0626	58	.0615
Property taxes	204	.1019	154	.1025	94	.0997
Supplies	507	.2533	1,109	.7384	845	.8965
Total	6,397	3.1954	8,066	5.3706	5,192	5.5085
Gross margin	8,923	4.4577	5,147	3.4270	3,570	3.7878
Operating expenses						
Administrative	970	.4846	628	.4181	534	.5666
Advertising	1,706	.8522	1,213	.8076	797	.8456
Depreciation	2,396	1.1969	1,906	1.2690	1,089	1.1554
Interest	164	.0819	116	.0772	77	.0817
Research and development	1,745	.8717	1,241	.8263	814	.8636
Allocated overhead	892	.4456	634	.4221	416	.4413
Total	7,873	3.9329	5,738	3.8203	3,727	3.9542
Divisional profit (before tax)	$ 1,050	$ .5248	($ 591)	($ .3933)	($ 157)	($ .1664)
Unit sales (in barrels)	2,001,842		1,501,885		942,512	

Notes:

[1] The sale of the excess by-product resulting from the production of product Sa 10, as well as the internal transfer of by-product to product Sa 11, resulted in a reduction in the recorded direct materials cost for product Sa 10.

[2] The Sa 10 by-product used in the production of Sa 11 was charged to Sa 11. It was valued at the market price of the by-product in the outside (of Crowe Chemical Division) market.

EXHIBIT 3
Controller's analysis of manufacturing costs

Variable costs

Direct labor:	Direct labor costs have been historically treated as varying with volume of production. An identifiable number of workers, however, are paid their full weekly wages regardless of units produced.
Direct materials:	Purchased at market price. The market is highly susceptible to the relative forces of supply and demand, but prices tend to change on a quarterly basis. See also the notes to Exhibit 2.
Fringe benefits:	Included are compensation insurance, group health plan, and group life insurance. These programs are mandatory and the amount paid is most directly related to the amount of direct labor costs.
Supplies:	Supplies are purchased from company offering most favorable terms. Cost is net of discounts.
Repair service:	Has historically varied with level of production. Repairmen are available on short notice in case of unforeseen downtime.
Power:	Charged industrial rates. The total bill tends to be directly related to production volume.

Fixed costs

Indirect labor:	This consists largely of supervisory labor. A few laborers available to relieve workers or substitute for those on holiday and sick leave are also included.
Depreciation:	This represents a fixed amount assigned to each product.
Interest:	Total interest charges are divided among the products on the basis of a formula largely derived from expected unit sales.
Administrative:	These costs represent salaries paid to executive and office personnel.
Advertising and research and development:	The total amount of expenditures is fixed at yearly budget meetings. They may be augmented during the year at management's discretion. The total is allocated to specific products based on the same formula used for interest.
Insurance and property taxes:	Fire, property, and vehicle insurance charges are assigned to each product line. Property taxes are based on assessed values and are considered to be fixed. They do, however, tend to rise slightly each year.
Allocated overhead:	Other overhead costs. This category includes such things as heat, water, and janitorial services.

---

including some written comments regarding their projected behavior (Exhibit 3).

While no action was taken as a result of the discussion that took place between the two men, Mr. Thompson did express his concern about the loss shown on Sa 11. Excerpts from the conversion are included below.

George Thompson: It looks to me like we're losing our shirt on Sa 11. The results have never been great on this product, but now they've really turned bad. I wonder if we shouldn't cut back on our production and sales efforts on this one.

Michael Demming: According to the records, we've never shown a very substantial profit on this product. With the disaster of a year we've had, the loss may have been unavoidable.

George Thompson: You may be right, Mike. But, I just don't see any feasible way to lower manufacturing costs by 39 cents a barrel. We also ought to look at Sa 12. We're off-budget on that one as well.

Michael Demming: Let's hang on for another quarter, George. Making drastic changes may well do us more harm than good. If things don't improve with time, we'll have to address the issue head-on later during this year.

First-quarter results. Around the middle of April, Demming received an income statement for the first three months of 1976 (Exhibit 4). Much to his satisfaction, the division had managed to earn a modest profit. A week or so later, Demming received the first quarter's version of a new product line profitability analysis form that he had specifically requested from the divisional controller (Exhibit 5). Demming inspected the report and compared the results to the previous year's operations.

EXHIBIT 4
CROWE CHEMICAL DIVISION
Income Statement
For the Quarter Ended March 31, 1976

Gross sales	$9,913,923
Less: Discounts	180,309
Net sales	9,733,614
Cost of goods sold	4,985,357
Gross margin	4,748,257
Operating expenses	4,343,212
Operating income	405,045
Less: Interest	89,124
Divisional profit (before tax)	$ 315,921

CAJUN CHEMICAL'S PRICE ANNOUNCEMENT

During the second quarter of 1976, the Gulf Coast chemical industry suffered from the results of circumstances quite similar to those that had existed in 1975. The Crowe Chemical Division managed to keep a tight grip on their market share. Nonetheless, profits for the three-month period declined.

Even before the release of the second quarter operating data, events took what Demming perceived to be an even more somber tone as Cajun Chemical announced a price decrease. This decrease, to be effective immediately, meant that Cajun's version of product Sa 10 would carry a net list price of $7.15 a barrel. It was this price cut that Demming had now focused upon for analysis.

Demming recalled that he and George Thompson had speculated several weeks ago that a price cut by Cajun was a possibility that they should consider. At that time, Thompson had stressed that he did not wish to sell Sa 10 below cost. He had based his view on the fact that the product was currently the division's major source of profit.

EXHIBIT 5 Product line profitability analysis (for the quarter ended March 31, 1976)

Majestic Tool, Inc.: Form 64Q

Copies to: _____ / _____ / _____

		Product Sa 10				Product Sa 11				Product Sa 12		
	Standard per unit	Total at standard cost and actual units (000)	Total at actual (000)	Variance (000)	Standard per unit	Total at standard cost and actual units (000)	Total at actual (000)	Variance (000)	Standard per unit	Total at standard cost and actual units (000)	Total at actual (000)	Variance (000)
Revenue (net sales)	$7.6533	$3,973	$3,973	—	$8.7975	$3,265	$3,265	—	$9.2957	$2,495	$2,495	—
Variable costs												
Direct labor	1.0775	559	545	$14	1.6754	622	764	$(142)	1.6752	450	453	$(3)
Direct materials	.9585	498	509	(11)	.9486	352	366	(14)	1.5268	409	409	—
Fringe benefits	.0405	21	19	2	.0670	25	29	(4)	.0678	18	18	—
Repair service	.1680	87	88	(1)	.1680	62	60	2	.1666	45	51	(6)
Power	.0620	32	33	(1)	.0626	23	23	—	.0615	17	17	—
Supplies	.2535	132	131	1	.7384	274	273	1	.8965	241	231	10
Total variable costs	2.5600	1,329	1,325	4	3.6600	1,358	1,515	(157)	4.3944	1,180	1,179	1
Fixed costs												
Indirect labor	.5430	282	272	10	.7919	294	297	(3)	.9045	243	227	16
Depreciation	1.1969	621	599	22	1.2690	471	476	(5)	1.0888	292	272	20
Interest	.0819	43	41	2	.0772	29	29	—	.0771	21	19	2
Insurance	.0519	27	26	1	.0526	19	20	(1)	.0495	13	12	1
Administrative	.4846	252	243	9	.4180	155	157	(2)	.5430	146	137	9
Research and development	.8717	453	436	17	.8260	307	310	(3)	.8139	218	203	15
Advertising	.8522	442	437	5	.8165	303	308	(5)	.7986	214	201	13
Property taxes	.1019	53	51	2	.1025	38	38	—	.0940	25	23	2
Allocated overhead	.4456	231	224	7	.4221	157	158	(1)	.4135	111	103	8
Corporate overhead	.0720	37	36	1	.0693	26	26	—	.0681	18	17	1
Total fixed costs	4.7017	2,441	2,365	76	4.8451	1,799	1,819	(20)	4.8510	1,301	1,214	87
Divisional profit (before tax)	.3916	203	283	80	.2924	108	(69)	(177)	.0503	14	102	88
Unit sales (barrels)		519,140				371,185				268,413		
Expected sales (barrels)		500,000				375,000				250,000		

Demming also recalled a conversation held earlier in the same day with the divisional sales director. The director, Mr. Sharpless, predicted that the sales volume for Sa 10 during the second half of 1976 would approximate 1 million barrels. When pressed, however, he admitted that this estimate was based on an assumption of price parity with the Cajun Chemical product. He said that sales would probably fall to around 875,000 barrels if the Cajun price cut was not met.

QUESTIONS

1. What impact, if any, would the dropping of product Sa 11 have had on the firm's income statement for the quarter ended March 31, 1976?

2. Should Crowe match Cajun's price decrease?

———◄ C A S E   I – 7 ►———

Richardson Paints

Peter Gearin, production manager of the Richardson Paints Corporation, was sitting in the den of his North Dallas home. It was mid-July 1978 and it had been another hot day at the plant. The cool, quiet solitude of the den seemed to make it easier for him to get things straight in his mind. The question of whether Richardson should enter into a proposed subcontract arrangement as a means of expanding capacity was the issue on his mind at the moment.

Due in large part to a very fast moving local real estate market, Richardson had been operating at or near its practical production capacity for better than 90 days. One suggestion for dealing with this problem involved, in essence, farming out some of the production to a company based in Kansas City, Missouri.

THE COMPANY

Richardson Paints Corporation was founded by John R. Maguire shortly after World War II. In its early years, the firm had focused its primary marketing efforts on the contract paint business. The firm had concentrated

---

This case was prepared by Professor M. Edgar Barrett. Copyright © 1978 by M. Edgar Barrett.

its production efforts on paint consistently throughout its 30-year history. In the mid-1960s, however, the firm began to offer paint-related and home decoration products in its list of products. These latter items were all purchased from other manufacturers.

In the early 1970s, the company opened its first retail paint store. The venture was an immediate success. The firm had 15 such stores by late 1977. Seven were in the Dallas-Fort Worth area, three in San Antonio, two in Austin, and three in Houston. Five sites had been selected for new stores to be opened during 1978.

Despite the growth of the retail business, Richardson Paints' total sales volume was still heavily weighted toward contract sales. For 1976, such contract (direct to specific customers) paint sales represented some 60 percent of the firm's sales. Also, 1976 saw the phasing out of the firm's oil-based paint line. Several recent advances in latex paint technology had rendered the oil-based business both small and marginally profitable for Richardson.

In early 1977, Maguire was approached by a representative of Majestic Tool Company. Majestic, a Louisiana-based supplier of high technology products and services for the energy sector, had been active as of late in the mergers and acquisitions market. Among their recent acquisitions had been a specialty chemicals company and a chain of home improvement centers. They hoped to add Richardson to their stable and thus integrate backwards from the retail market. After several months of negotiations, an acquisition based on the issuance of convertible preferred shares of Majestic Tool was worked out. Richardson became a wholly owned subsidiary of Majestic on July 1, 1977.

THE PAINT PRODUCTION PLANT

Peter Gearin had joined Richardson Paints in 1972 as a production worker. He was promoted to supervisor of the night shift in 1975. Shortly after Majestic assumed ownership, Peter was named production manager.

The fall of 1977 saw Richardson's paint plant operating at about 75 percent of capacity. It also saw the introduction of a new simplified weekly cost report (Exhibits 1 and 2). This report was issued on Tuesday of the week following production.

In the spring and early summer of 1978, the demand for Richardson's paint products rose to unprecedented levels. The weekly cost report for the week ending July 15, 1978 reflected the 12th straight week of capacity production (see Exhibit 3).

Peter, ever mindful of the potential for advancement in a large organization, had solicited bids from two potential paint suppliers. Only one of them, a firm based in Kansas City, Missouri, had responded with a bid. The firm, Midwest Paints, submitted a bid of $5.10 per gallon, FOB Dallas,

EXHIBIT 1
Weekly cost report (for the week ending 8 October 1977)

	Cost per gallon of product			
Item	*Exterior enamel*	*Exterior undercoat*	*Interior enamel*	*Interior undercoat*
Direct labor	$ 0.80	$0.68	$ 0.71	$ 0.60
Raw materials	3.04	2.55	2.72	2.31
Packaging	0.42	0.35	0.37	0.30
Prime cost	4.26	3.58	3.80	3.21
Overhead	1.97	1.67	1.75	1.48
Total cost	6.23	5.25	5.55	4.69
Production (gallons)	1,710	865	2,580	1,262 (6,417 total)

EXHIBIT 2
Derivation of data for weekly cost report

1. Direct labor. Each production worker kept a record of the time spent working on each variety of paint. The total amount of time spent on each variety was totaled and costed at the direct labor rate of $5.10 per hour. The per-gallon cost was derived by dividing the total cost by the number of gallons produced.

2. Raw materials. Raw materials were carried as a separate inventory item until such time as they were used in the production process. The amounts used, including waste, were totaled for each variety of paint. The per-gallon cost was a matter of division.

3. Packaging. Packaging, which included the paint containers, the labels, and the shipping boxes, was also costed on an "inventory consumed" basis. The amounts used, including waste, were totaled for each paint variety and the result was then divided by the number of gallons produced.

4. Overhead. The total of all supervision, maintenance, and other plant overhead was divided by the amount of direct labor cost incurred. The resulting figure was then multiplied by the direct labor cost per gallon to arrive at an overhead charge per gallon.

EXHIBIT 3
Weekly cost report (for the week ending 15 July 1978)

	Cost per gallon of product			
Item	*Exterior enamel*	*Exterior undercoat*	*Interior enamel*	*Interior undercoat*
Direct labor	$ 0.79	$ 0.67	$ 0.71	$ 0.59
Raw materials	3.06	2.58	2.74	2.32
Packaging	0.43	0.36	0.38	0.31
Prime cost	4.28	3.61	3.83	3.22
Overhead	1.57	1.32	1.41	1.17
Total cost	5.85	4.93	5.24	4.39
Production (gallons)	2,280	1,150	3,480	1,724 (8,634 total)

for the delivery of 1,000 gallons of exterior undercoat paint per week. The price was valid for all shipments sent during the remainder of 1978. One week's notice would be required to cancel the contract. The quality standards specified in the bid equaled those now used by Richardson.

Peter knew that Richardson could use the freed capacity to step up production (on a gallon-for-gallon basis) of exterior enamel paint. He thought that a majority of this possible new production could be sold by the company at its current sale price.

The contract sales price of Richardson's paint products, FOB Dallas, was as follows:[1]

Exterior enamel	$7.20
Exterior undercoat.....	6.16
Interior enamel........	6.50
Interior undercoat	5.48

QUESTIONS

1. What was the total overhead expense for the week ending October 8, 1977? Does it differ from that of the week ending July 15, 1978? Why?

2. Should Peter Gearin recommend the acceptance of the Midwest Paints bid?

---

[1] This represents, in essence, the sales price of the paint to contract customers. It was also used as the transfer price to Richardson's and Majestic's retail stores.

⸺◂CASE I–8▸⸺

A/S Dansk Minox, Copenhagen:

"Costing the cabbage"

A/S Dansk Minox in Copenhagen, specialized in branded vacuum-packed meat and other food products. For many years it had sold vacuum-packed sliced pork in gravy, a very popular dish in Denmark. In 1965 the product represented about 15 percent of the firm's total sales. The Danish housewife very often served this dish together with a red cabbage salad. This salad is rather time-consuming to prepare at home and certain competitors of A/S Dansk Minox had recently introduced red cabbage salad in either vacuum-packed, canned, or frozen form. However, A/S Dansk Minox estimated that the major part of the red cabbage sold was still prepared at home. Although sales of ready-made red cabbage salad had expanded rapidly, it was felt—and consumer research confirmed—that there was still untapped potential for such a product.

Since it was so often eaten together with sliced pork, the company management was considering the production of red cabbage salad. A/S Dansk Minox had recently considered the introduction of a specialty line of complete meals, which were to be sold in an attractive carton containing vacuum-sealed bags with the different ingredients for the meal. The management decided that the first product in this specialty line was to be "sliced pork in gravy with red cabbage." The product was to be packed in a carton containing the standard vacuum-sealed bag with sliced pork plus another bag with the red cabbage. Cost allocation problems arose in this connection, leading to long discussions between the marketing and finance departments of the Danish company.

The standard product "sliced pork in gravy" was sold in a 450-gram bag at a consumer price of DKr4.85. This was the "ideal" quantity for an average family, giving between three and four servings. The marketing department did not wish to change the quantity of sliced pork in gravy. Extensive testing showed that the average family consumed between 500 and 600 grams of red cabbage salad with 450 grams of sliced pork in gravy. It was decided to sell the "complete meal" product in a 1-kilogram pack,

Copyright © 1967 by l'Institut pour l'Etude des Méthodes de Direction de l'Entreprise (IMEDE), Lausanne, Switzerland. Reproduced by permission.

containing the standard 450-gram bag with sliced pork in gravy plus another vacuum-sealed bag with 550 grams of red cabbage salad.

PRICE CALCULATIONS

The marketing department received the following preliminary selling price calculation from the finance department, based on the assumption that the new product should produce approximately the same profit per kilogram as the standard sliced pork in gravy. For comparison, the selling price calculation for standard sliced pork in gravy was also given, both for 1 kilogram and for 450 grams. This showed that the raw material costs and labor costs for sliced pork in gravy were exactly the same in both the existing standard pack of this product and in the new 1 kilogram "complete meal" pack.

	"Complete meal" 1 kilogram	Sliced pork in gravy 1 kilogram	Sliced pork in gravy 450 gram
Consumer price	8.20*	10.78	4.85
Less turnover tax (12.5% of consumer price before tax)	.91	1.20	.54
Consumer price before tax	7.29	9.58	4.31
Retailer's margin (27.5% of price to retailer)	1.57	2.07	.93
Price to retailer	5.72	7.51	3.38
Raw material, sliced pork	1.67	3.71	1.67
Raw material, red cabbage	.50	—	—
Labor, sliced pork	.25	.56	.25
Labor, red cabbage	.25	—	—
Packaging material	.26	.24	.11
Transport and storage	.20	.20	.09
Margins and discounts to wholesalers (8% of price to retailer)	.46	.60	.27
Sundry variable costs	.10	.10	.04
Total variable costs	3.69	5.41	2.43
Marginal contribution	2.03	2.10	.95
Production fixed expenses	1.20	1.20	.54
Other product-related fixed expenses	.30	.30	.14
General selling and administrative expense and overhead (4% of price to retailer)	.23	.30	.14
Total fixed expenses	1.73	1.80	.82
Net operating profit	0.30	0.30	.13

* All amounts are in DKr.

The difference in consumer price between the two packs as proposed by the finance department meant that the consumer would have to pay DKr3.35 (8.20 − 4.85) for the red cabbage salad, since the sliced pork in gravy content of the two packs was the same. The marketing department protested that this price difference was prohibitive. They noted that the ingredients for making the red cabbage salad at home could be bought for approximately DKr1.10 and the labor costs at home (if counted at all) would not amount to more than approximately 0.70. They further argued that A/S Dansk Minox could not expect the consumer to pay more than DKr2.00 for the red cabbage salad and the added convenience. This would leave a consumer price for the new pack of 4.85 + 2.00 or 6.85. The marketing department contended, furthermore, that the selling price calculation showed that the raw material and labor costs amounted to only 0.75 for the red cabbage salad. They thought that it was unreasonable that the other cost elements should result in a consumer price difference of 3.35.

Since the only difference between the standard pack and the "complete mean" pack was the red cabbage and a more elaborate package, the marketing and finance departments listed those cost elements which varied between the 1,000-gram "complete meal" pack and the 450-gram standard pack with sliced pork in gravy. These elements were the following:

	"Complete meal" 1 kilogram	*Sliced pork in gravy* 450 gram	*Difference*
Raw material, red cabbage salad	.50	—	.50
Labor, red cabbage salad	.25	—	.25
Packaging material	.26	.11	.15
Transport and storage...................	.20	.09	.11
Margins and discounts	.46	.27	.19
Sundry variable costs	.10	.04	.06
Production fixed expense	1.20	.54	.66
Other product-related fixed expenses	.30	.14	.16
General overhead	.23	.14	.09
Totals	3.50	1.33	2.17

The difference in the retail margins and the turnover tax plus the difference in operating profit of DKr0.17 were added to the cost difference of DKr2.17 to arrive at the previously mentioned selling price difference of DKr3.35. As an approximation, the consumer price was computed by multiplying the retail price by 1.45. This meant that if the marketing department wished a new price of DKr6.85 for the "complete meal" pack (DKr2.00 more than the standard pack with sliced pork in gravy), the difference in the price to the retailer could not exceed approximately DKr1.38. Thus, with a consumer price of DKr6.85 and an unchanged net operating profit per pack, the difference in the cost elements in the selling price calculation would have to be reduced from DKr2.17 to 1.38 (a reduction of 0.79).

There was no disagreement between the marketing and finance departments with regard to the raw material, labor, packaging material, transport and storage, and sundry variable costs. The item "other product-related fixed expenses" covered mainly advertising; consequently, the marketing department did not argue with the finance department about this item. The two items "margins and discounts" and "general overheads" were calculated as fixed percentages of the price to the retailer (8 percent and 4 percent, respectively). The marketing department was satisfied that the cost would decrease automatically if a lower selling price could be agreed upon.

PRODUCTION FIXED EXPENSES

After internal agreement on the sales budget every year, the total production fixed expenses were divided by the total sales quantity, expressed in kilograms. This computation resulted in a rate of DKr1.20 per kilogram for the year under consideration. This rate was then applied to all products from the company's factory. There was no need to buy any new equipment for making the red cabbage salad and there was spare capacity available for the estimated production of the new "complete meal" product. The estimated sales of the new product were included in the budgeted sales quantity.

The finance department claimed that any departure downward from the rate of DKr1.20 per kilogram for production fixed expenses would result in an underabsorption of fixed expenses. The marketing department replied that a strict application of this rule would lead to unreasonable consequences in this case. The finance department stated that it would be impractical to use different burden rates per kilogram for different products. It was supported in this view by the managing director, who said that the product should not be introduced if a normal selling price calculation did not show an operating profit.

The marketing department responded that selling the new product at DKr8.20 per pack was out of the question; therefore, only two alternatives remained:

a. Abandon the whole project.
b. Establish a consumer price of DKr6.85 and a price to the retailer of DKr4.78. The 8 percent margins and discounts to wholesalers and the 4 percent general overhead would then amount to 0.38 + 0.19 instead of 0.46 + 0.23, a reduction of 0.12. If the production fixed expense were then reduced from 1.20 to 0.54, the same amount as for one standard pack of sliced pork in gravy, expenses in the selling price calculation would then be reduced by a total of 0.78. This is almost exactly the necessary reduction of 0.79 mentioned earlier.

The managing director decided to introduce the new product at a consumer price of DKr8.20. The sales budget was set at 85 metric tons. (A metric ton is equal to 1,000 kilograms.) This was about 45 percent of the budgeted sales of the standard pack of sliced pork in gravy. The company did not expect that the new "complete meal" product would steal sales from the standard pack. Some customers would certainly switch over from the old product to the new, but these losses were expected to be offset by the added sales resulting from greater consumer awareness of Minox products due to the planned advertising campaigns for the "complete meal" item.

In the months that followed, a number of complaints about the high price of the new product were received from retailers and consumers. Sales for the first year amounted to only 30 tons in contrast to the budgeted 85 tons. Sales of the standard pack, on the other hand, exceeded the budgeted amount by a small percentage.

QUESTIONS

1. How much would the company's net operating profit have differed from the actual results (assuming that all costs behaved as expected) if:
    a. The proposal to see the "complete meal" pack had been abandoned?
    b. The consumer price had been DKr6.85 and the budgeted volume of sales had been achieved?

2. At what sales level would a consumer price of DKr6.85 give the same total net operating profit as 30 tons at a consumer price of DKr8.20?

3. What gave rise to this problem? How might the situation have been avoided?

———◄CASE I-9►———

Industrial Grinders NV

———◄∞►———

In late May 1974, Mr. Bridgeman, the general manager of the German plant of Industrial Grinders (IG) NV was considering what he should do at a meeting he was to attend that afternoon with his sales manager, accountant, and development engineer. The meeting was to discuss the introduction by Henri Poulenc, a French competitor, of a plastic ring to take the place of a steel ring presently used in certain machines sold by the company. The new ring, which had been put on the market recently, not only had a much longer life than the IG steel ring but also apparently had a much lower cost. Mr. Bridgeman's problem stemmed from the fact that IG had a large quantity of the steel rings on hand and had a substantial inventory of special steel for their manufacture. After a thorough survey, he had found that the special steel could not be sold even for scrap. The total book value of these inventories was in excess of $93,000.

For nearly 70 years Industrial Grinders had manufactured industrial machines which it sold in a number of countries. The particular machine involved in Mr. Bridgeman's decision was made only at the German plant situated in Cologne which employed several thousand people. The different models were priced between $4,500 and $6,820 and were sold by a separate sales organization. Parts which in total accounted for a substantial part of the company's business were sold separately. As in the case of the steel rings, these parts could often also be used on similar machines manufactured by competitors. The company's head office was in Holland. In general the separate plants were allowed considerable leeway in administering their own affairs. However, the executives in Holland could be approached easily for advice either by correspondence and telephone, or during their visits to the individual plants.

In recent years, competition had become fairly strong. Japanese manufacturers had had more than a little success in entering the field with low-priced spare parts. Other companies had appeared with lower quality and

This case was adapted from the Stardust Grinder Company case (9-104-057), which was written by J. Taylor and E. Hohl and copyrighted by IMEDE. It was adapted by Rohan Weerasinghe, Research Assistant, under the supervision of Associate Professor M. Edgar Barrett. Copyright © 1974 by the President and Fellows of Harvard College.

lower priced machines. There was little doubt but that in the future competition would become more intense.

The steel ring manufactured by IG had a normal life of about two months, depending upon the extent to which the machine was used. A worn-out ring could be replaced in a few seconds and, although different models of the machines required from two to six rings, the rings were usually replaced individually as they wore out.

The sales manager, Mr. Greiner, had learned of the new plastic ring shortly after its appearance and had immediately asked when IG would be able to supply them, particularly for sale to customers in France where Henri Poulenc was providing the strongest competition faced by Industrial Grinders. Mr. Ericsson, the development engineer, estimated that the plastic rings could be produced by mid-September. The additional tools and equipment necessary could be obtained for about $1,800. At this point Mr. Ericsson had raised the question about the investment in steel ring inventories which would not be used up by September. Mr. Greiner said that if the new ring could be produced at a substantially lower cost than the steel ones the inventory problem was irrelevant. It should be sold for whatever could be obtained or even thrown away if it could not be sold. However, the size of the inventory caused Mr. Bridgeman to question this suggestion. He recalled that the size of the inventory was the result of having to order the highly specialized steel in large amounts in order to find a mill willing to handle the order.

Mr. Greiner emphasized that as Henri Poulenc was said to be selling the plastic ring at about the same price as the IG steel ring, and as the cost of the former would be much less than the latter, the company was refusing profits as well. Finally, it was decided that the company should prepare to manufacture the new ring as soon as possible but they would only be sold in those markets where they were offered by competitors until the inventories of the old model and the steel were exhausted. No one expected that the new rings would be produced by any company other than Henri Poulenc for some time. This meant that no more than 10 percent of the company's markets would be affected.

Shortly after this, Mr. Van Boetzalaer of the parent company in Holland visited Cologne. During a review of company problems the plastic ring case was discussed. Although the ring was a small part of the finished machines, Mr. Van Boetzalaer was interested in the problem because the company wanted to establish policies for the production and pricing of all such parts which, in total, amounted to a substantial portion of IG's revenues. Mr. Van Boetzalaer agreed that the company should proceed with plans for its production and try to find some other use for the steel. He then said "if this does not seem possible, I would, of course, expect you to use this material and produce the steel rings."

Within a few days after Mr. Van Boetzalaer's visit, both Mr. Ericsson and Mr. Greiner came in to see Mr. Bridgeman. The former came because he felt that the plastic ring would completely destroy demand for the steel ring as tests had indicated that it had at least four times the wearing properties. However, because he understood that the price of the competitive ring was very high (perhaps even higher than the IG steel ring) he felt that the decision to sell the plastic ring only in the market areas where difficulties existed was a good one. "In this way we would probably be able to continue supplying the steel ring until stocks at least of processed parts were used up."

Mr. Greiner, the sales manager, was still strongly against selling any steel rings after the new ones became available. If steel rings were sold in some areas, while plastic rings were being sold elsewhere, customers in the former would eventually find out. The result would affect the sale of machines, the selling price of which was many times that of the rings. He produced figures to show that if the selling price of both rings remained at $320.40 per hundred, the additional profit from the plastic rings, which would cost $66.60 per hundred as contrasted with $263.85 per hundred for the steel, would more than cover the so-called investment in the steel inventory within less than a year at present volume levels. Mr. Bridgeman refused to change the decision of the previous meeting but agreed to have another discussion within a week.

In anticipation of the meeting and also having in mind Mr. Van Boetzalaer's concern Mr. Bridgeman obtained the following data from the cost department on the cost of plastic and steel rings:

	Plastic rings	Steel rings
Material	$ 4.20	$ 76.65
Direct labor	15.60	46.80
Overhead*		
Departmental	31.20	93.60
Administrative	15.60	46.80
Total (per 100 rings)	$66.60	$263.85

* Overhead was allocated on the basis of direct labor dollars. It was estimated that the variable overhead costs included in the above summary were largely fringe benefits related to direct labor and amounted to about 40 percent of the departmental amounts.

Mr. Bridgeman also learned that the inventory of special steel had cost $26,400. This steel consisted of a large enough quantity to produce approximately 34,500 rings. Assuming that sales continued at the current rate of 690 rings per week, some 15,100 finished rings would be left on hand by mid-September without any further production taking place. It then occurred to him that during the next two or three months the plant would not be operating at capacity. The company had a policy of employing its excess labor during slack periods at about 70 percent of regular wages on various make-work projects rather than laying the men off. He wondered if it would be a good idea to convert the steel inventory into rings during this period and use some of this labor productively.

QUESTIONS

What action should Mr. Bridgeman take? Why?

⟶ CASE I–10 ⟵

The Liquid Chemical Company

The Liquid Chemical Company sells a range of high-grade products which, because of their chemical properties, call for careful packing. The company has always made a feature of the special properties of the containers used. They had a special patent lining made from a material known as GHL, and the firm operated a department specially to maintain its containers in good condition and to make new ones to replace those which were past repair.

Mr. Walsh, the general manager, had for some time suspected that the firm might save money and get equally good service by buying its containers outside. After careful inquiries, he approached a firm specializing in container production, Packages, Inc., and obtained quotations from them. At the same time he asked Mr. Dyer, the controller, to let him have an up-to-date statement of the cost of operating the container department.

Within a few days, the quotation from Packages came in. They were prepared to supply all the new containers required—at that time running at the rate of 3,000 a year—for $120,000 per annum, the contract to run for a term of five years certain and thereafter to be renewable from year to year. If the number of containers required increased, the contract price would be increased proportionately. Additionally, and irrespective of whether the above contract was concluded or not, Packages undertook to carry out purely maintenance work on containers, short of replacement, for a sum of $35,000 per annum on the same contract terms.

Mr. Walsh compared these figures with the cost figures prepared by Mr. Dyer covering a year's operations of the container department, as follows:

This case was prepared by Professor David Solomons of the University of Pennsylvania.

Materials		$ 40,000
Labor		70,000
Departmental overheads:		
Manager's salary	$16,000	
Rent	3,000	
Depreciation of machinery	12,000	
Maintenance of machinery	2,700	
Other expenses	12,600	46,300
		156,300
Proportion of general administrative overheads		13,500
Total cost of department for year		$169,800

Walsh's conclusion was that no time should be lost in closing down the department, and in entering into the contracts offered by Packages. However, he felt bound to give the manager of the department, Mr. Duffy, an opportunity to question this conclusion before he acted on it. He therefore called him in and put the facts before him, at the same time making it clear that Duffy's own position was not in jeopardy, even if his department were closed down. There was another managerial position shortly becoming vacant to which he could be moved without loss of pay or prospects.

Mr. Duffy looked thoughtful, and asked for time to think the matter over. The next morning he asked to speak to Mr. Walsh again, and said he thought there were a number of considerations which ought to be borne in mind before his department was closed down. "For instance," he said, "what will you do with the machinery? It cost $96,000 four years ago, but you'd be lucky if you got $16,000 for it now, even though it's good for another four years at least. And then there's the stock of GHL we bought a year ago. That cost us $60,000, and at the rate we're using it now, it'll last us another three years or so. We used up about a quarter of it last year. Dyer's figure of $40,000 for materials probably includes about $15,000 for GHL. But it'll be tricky stuff to handle if we don't use it up. We bought it well—$300 a ton we paid for it, and you couldn't buy it today for less than $360. But you wouldn't have more than $240 a ton left if you sold it, after you'd covered all the handling expenses."

Walsh thought that Dyer ought to be present during this discussion. He called him in and put Duffy's points to him. "I don't much like all this conjecture," Dyer said. "I think my figures are pretty conclusive. Besides, if we are going to have all this talk about 'what will happen if,' don't forget the problem of space we're faced with. We're paying $5,500 a year in rent for a warehouse a couple of miles away. If we closed Duffy's department, we'd have all the warehouse space we need without renting."

"That's a good point," said Walsh. "Though I must say, I'm a bit worried about the men, if we close the department. I don't think we can find room for any of them elsewhere in the firm. I could see whether Packages can take any of them. But some of them are getting on. There's Walters and Hines, for example. They've been with us since they left school 40 years ago. I'd feel bound to give them a small pension—$2,000 a year each, say."

Duffy showed some relief at this. "But I still don't like Dyer's figures," he said. "What about this $13,500 for general administrative overheads. You surely don't expect to fire anyone in the general office if I'm closed down, do you?" "Probably not," said Dyer, "but someone has to pay for these costs. We can't ignore them when we look at an individual department, if we do that with each department in turn, we shall finish up by convincing ourselves that general managers, accountants, typists, stationery and the like, don't have to be paid for. And they do, believe me."

"Well, I think we've thrashed this out pretty fully," said Walsh, "but I've been turning over in my mind the possibility of perhaps keeping on the maintenance work ourselves. What are your views on that, Duffy?" "I don't know," said Duffy, "but it's worth looking into. We shouldn't need any machinery for that, and I could hand the supervision over to a foreman. You'd save $4,000 a year there, say. You'd only need about one fifth of the men, but you could keep on the oldest. You wouldn't save any space, so I suppose the rent would be the same. I shouldn't think the other expenses would be more than $5,200 a year." "What about materials?" asked Walsh. "We use about 10 percent of the total on maintenance," Duffy replied.

"Well, I've told Packages that I'd let them know my decision within a week," said Walsh. "I'll let you know what I decide to do before I write to them."

Robinson Corporation

Late in 1972, A. J. Robinson decided to introduce a new product to the line of games, toys, and novelties manufactured by his company. In order to do so, he would have to buy a new piece of production equipment because none of his existing machines could be adapted to perform the necessary operations. Mr. Robinson had been intending to add such a machine to fill out the flexibility of his plant, but had delayed until he had the right concept for a new product. Even if the proposed new product failed, Mr. Robinson was confident he could find other products which would keep the new equipment operating profitably.

Sales of the new product were forecast at $100,000 per year, from which a sales commission of 15 percent would be paid to Robinson's sales agents. Direct manufacturing costs were budgeted at $30,000 for materials and $45,000 for labor, leaving a pretax profit of $10,000. The new machine would cost $30,000, delivered and installed, and was expected to have an economic life of ten years, with zero salvage value.

The Robinson Corporation was able to borrow money at 8 percent, although it would not plan to negotiate a loan specifically for the purchase of this equipment.

QUESTIONS

1. Ignoring the effect of income taxes, what is the internal rate of return (IRR) on this investment?

2. Assuming that the machine is depreciated on a straight-line basis over 10 years, and that the income tax rate is 48 percent, what is the IRR on an aftertax basis?

3. If Mr. Robinson stated that he was willing to purchase this machine as long as it yielded a return of 10 percent after taxes, should he make the investment? What is the "present value profit" on the investment?

4. Actually, Mr. Robinson used the sum-of-years'-digits method of depreciation in calculating taxable income. At a 10 percent discount rate, how does that affect the profitability of the investment?

This case was prepared by Professor Richard F. Vancil.

5. Mr. Robinson has found that his investment in working capital (receivables and inventories, less payables) amounts to approximately 15 percent of sales. Will the additional $15,000 investment for this new product decrease the rate of return on investment to less than his 10 percent criterion?

6. Mr. Robinson bought the machine, and the operating results turned out as forecast. In late 1973, he discovered that the manufacturer of the machine had brought out a new model which was more automated. The new machine sold for $50,000 and would permit labor savings of $10,000 per year, thus doubling the operating profit on the product. As a result of the technological advance, Mr. Robinson expected that the one-year old machine could be sold for only $10,000, despite the fact that its book value was $24,545. If Mr. Robinson bought the new machine and depreciated it on sum-of-years'-digits over 10 years, would the investment meet his 10 percent aftertax criterion?

7. If the one-year-old machine had no salvage value at all, would replacing it with the new machine still be desirable?

8. Mr. Robinson was loathe to throw away a nearly new machine, and thought that he might be better off to keep it one more year and then replace it. Would he be better off?

───◄ C A S E   I – 12 ►───

Riverbend Telephone Company

The Riverbend Telephone Company is independently owned and operates in the area between the west bank of the Short River and the state line. The company provides local telephone service to customers in several adjacent communities, and its lines connect with those of other companies to provide long distance telephone service. Operating as a public utility, the Riverbend Telephone Company is subject to regulation by the State Public Service Commission which periodically reviews service and must approve all changes in rates.

In recent years, the population of the area served by the company had grown rapidly as a result of a new bridge which facilitated daily commuting over the Short River to a nearby city. As a result of this growth, company personnel and equipment had been hard pressed to meet all demands for installation of new telephones and maintenance. For a time the company had used an outside contractor to handle overload work, but several poor experiences had caused abandonment of that practice. By late 1969 it was obvious that the company needed at least one new maintenance truck and crew.

The need to obtain a new truck arose at a critical period for the company. Earlier, Riverbend had made heavy commitments to purchase telephone equipment needed to improve service. Recent payments for new equipment had strained the net working-capital position of the firm. Stockholders were unable to provide additional resources and hoped to avoid selling additional shares which would dilute their ownership. Interest rates were quoted at 9 percent on short-term notes and above 10 percent on long-term loans. Since the company had been earning only about 8 percent on net assets, the firm hoped to avoid unnecessary borrowing until interest rates dropped somewhat.

In November 1969, Warren Freeman, general manager of Riverbend, requested bids for the new truck from four truck dealers. The lowest bid received was from the Reliable Motors Company who quoted a cash price of $3,800 including all taxes and delivery charges. As an alternative, Reliable would lease the truck to Riverbend Telephone for five years at an annual rate of $900.

The truck which Riverbend Telephone Company needed was similar to several others which they already owned. At Mr. Freeman's request, the company accountant used records to estimate the cost of operating the new truck. His estimates are shown in Exhibit 1. The truck was expected to last for five years, at which time it could probably be sold for about $300. If the truck were purchased it would be depreciated by the straight-line method because that was the only method allowed by the State Public Service Commission.

EXHIBIT 1
Estimated operating expense of maintenance truck

Type of expenses	Year of operation				
	1	2	3	4	5
Gasoline	$ 450	$ 450	$ 450	$ 450	$ 450
Repairs and maintenance	100	116	131	145	158
Tires..................................	—	95	95	95	95
Insurance.............................	300	300	300	300	300
Registration and taxes................	106	90	75	61	48
Depreciation (straight-line method)*	700	700	700	700	700
Total expenses	$1,656	$1,751	$1,751	$1,751	$1,751

* Assumes original cost of $3,800, life of five years, and salvage value of $300.

If the truck were leased, Riverbend Telephone would have to pay the annual lease charge on or before the first day of each year. In addition, they would be responsible for all costs of operation and maintenance of the truck except for tires which Reliable Motors would supply. The proposed agreement also made Riverbend responsible for all risks to the truck and property damage, collision, personal injury, fire, and theft. Finally, Riverbend would reimburse Reliable for all costs of vehicle registration and taxes.

Mr. Freeman was unsure how he should view the alternatives presented by Reliable Motors. Leasing the truck would reduce the immediate demands on Riverbend Telephone's financial resources. Still, the prospect of paying $4,500 over five years when the truck could be purchased new for $3,800 raised questions about how well he would be serving company stockholders if he leased rather than purchased the truck. On the other hand, the operating expenses and lease payments would be allowable expense duductions in calculating income for tax purposes. Since the company had been paying and expected to continue paying income taxes of 40 percent, an increase in expenses of $900 per year would not really cost that much.

The effect of his choice on Riverbend's rate of return earned on net assets was also important to Mr. Freeman. In 1969 the State Public Service Commission had allowed another telephone company to raise its rates to provide revenues to increase its rate of return to just above 9 percent on net assets. In an attempt to raise Riverbend's return without requesting higher rates,

Mr. Freeman had not approved any new investments that would provide a rate of return on investment below 10 percent unless they were absolutely necessary. Since the truck had to be acquired and the choice was only whether it should be leased or purchased, Mr. Freeman was unsure whether his 10 percent return minimum made any difference in this case.

Mr. Freeman also wanted to consider how the State Public Service Commission might view leased assets in evaluating rates of return earned by utilities. Purchased assets were always included in total investment net of accumulated depreciation, and all operating expenses including depreciation were allowable deductions in determining annual income. While he was not able to ascertain exactly what the Commission might want, he reasoned that Riverbend could probably include all operating expenses and the lease payments among annual expenses in reports to the Commission, but he was unsure whether investment should be increased by the "fair value" of the leased asset before calculating return on net assets.

QUESTIONS

1. Should the company buy or lease the new truck? (Assume that Riverbend Telephone uses the straight-line method of depreciation for tax purposes as well as for reports to shareholders and the State Public Service Commission.)

2. If Riverbend Telephone purchased the truck and chose to depreciate it for income tax purposes only using the double-declining-balance method, would this affect your decision to buy or lease? Assume that the annual depreciation expense would be:

Year	Depreciation
1970	$1,520
1971	912
1972	546
1973	328
1974	194

3. If the truck is leased, how should Mr. Freeman report investment and annual income for the Riverbend Telephone Company to the State Public Service Commission?

——«CASE I–13»——

Majestic Tool Company

————«∞»————

Carlos Sanchez, head of the engineering department of the pipeline parts and equipment division of Majestic Tool Company, shut his office door and walked over to his desk. It was early in February 1978, and he had only 48 hours to come up with a recommendation pertaining to the possible purchase of a numerically controlled milling machine.

The proposed machine, designed to replace a five-year-old general-purpose machine, could be purchased for $125,000, delivered and installed. The older, general-purpose machine would be sold to a neighboring firm.

THE COMPANY

Majestic Tool Company, based in New Orleans, Louisiana, was founded in 1936. For most of its early life, the firm had supplied pipeline parts and equipment to the oil and gas industry located in Louisiana, Texas, and Oklahoma. As time passed, however, the firm had expanded its operations. The initial expansion was geographic, with the Middle East and other foreign oil and gas producing areas, added to the geographic coverage. In the early 1970s, a line of high-technology products was added to the firm's product portfolio.

A series of moves, beginning in the mid 1970s, resulted in Majestic moving more and more toward becoming a regionally based conglomerate. A specialty chemical company was added in late 1975. A chain of home improvement centers was acquired in 1976. In 1977, a regional paint manufacturer and retailer was added.

THE PROPOSED PURCHASE

Majestic's pipeline parts and equipment division had witnessed several very good years as of late. The 1973 oil embargo had spurred the demand for increased drilling and exploration activities. That, in turn, had resulted in discoveries which increased the demand for Majestic's products. (See Exhibit 1.)

This case was written by Professor M. Edgar Barrett. Copyright © 1978 by M. Edgar Barrett.

EXHIBIT 1

MAJESTIC TOOL COMPANY
Pipeline Parts and Equipment Division
Condensed 1977 Income Statement

Net sales	$12,418,200
Cost of goods sold	6,414,300
Gross margin	6,003,900
Operating expenses	3,801,538
Profit before tax	2,202,362
Provision for taxes (at 40 percent effective rate)	880,945
Net income	$ 1,321,417

In late 1977, a machine tool manufacturer had proposed that Majestic acquire a numerically controlled milling machine. The proposed machine had the capacity to handle all of the work now assigned to a five-year-old general-purpose machine. The general-purpose machine was currently run on a two-shift basis. Two operators were needed to operate the machine.

The proposed machine would also be run on a two-shift basis. It, however, would only require one operator per shift. Furthermore, the operators would be able to perform their own maintenance and setup, thus freeing some staff time for other projects.

FINANCIAL CONSIDERATIONS

The economic life of the general-purpose machine originally had been estimated at 10 years. The original cost of $96,000 had been depreciated to date by $45,000. This reflected the fact that the machine's estimated net salvage value at the end of its useful life was $6,000.

The old machine could be sold to a neighboring firm. Carlos had talked to the purchasing agent at that firm and had received a bid of $24,000 net of all removal and transport costs. Any loss on the sale, he realized, would be a deductible expense for income tax purposes.

The new machine's estimated economic life was also 10 years. The scrap value of the machine was more problematical. Carlos thought that it could easily be zero, given the cost of removal and disassembly.

Machine operators of the type involved with either of the two machines earned about $8.50 an hour, including fringe benefits. Additional costs of $7,000 annually probably could be avoided by the purchase of the new machine. Finally, when asked about the financial effects of having the operators do their own maintenance, the plant superintendent estimated that this would allow the company to eliminate about $1,200 in contracted maintenance work.

Carlos knew that the company expected capital expenditures of this type to generate a minimum 15 percent return on a discounted basis. While he had been told that the firm used this rate and ignored the specific financing vehicle used to raise the cash involved when it evaluated projects, he thought that such a policy might not be applicable to this situation. He knew that the firm still owed $12,000, at 10 percent interest, on the old machine. Furthermore, he knew that financing for the new machine could easily be raised at a 12 percent interest rate.

THE DECISION

Carlos sensed that now might be a good time to buy. The price of numerically controlled milling machines had dropped slightly from the prior year. It was not at all unlikely, however, that they would go up again within the next year.

A positive recommendation from him would be taken quite seriously, or so Carlos thought. He, however, wanted to be able to present a convincing case in financial terms for whatever recommendation he finally made.

QUESTION

What should Carlos Sanchez recommend? Why?

⸺≺ CASE I-14 ≻⸺

The Super project

In March 1967 Crosby Sanberg, manager of financial analysis at General Foods Corporation, told a casewriter, "What I learned about incremental analysis at the Business School doesn't always work." He was convinced that under some circumstances "sunk costs" were relevant to capital project evaluations. He was also concerned that financial and accounting systems did not provide an accurate estimate of "incremental costs and revenues" and that this was one of the most difficult problems in measuring the value of capital investment proposals. Mr. Sanberg used the Super project as an example.[1]

Super was a new instant dessert, based on a flavored, water-soluble, agglomerated powder. Although a four-flavor line would be introduced, it was estimated that chocolate would account for 80 percent of total sales.

General Foods was organized along product lines in the United States. Foreign operations were under a separate division. Major U.S. product divisions included Post, Kool-Aid, Maxwell House, Jell-O, and Birds Eye. Financial data for General Foods are given in Exhibits 1, 2, and 3.

The capital investment project request for Super involved $200,000 as follows:

Building modifications	$ 80,000
Machinery and equipment	120,000
	$200,000

Part of the expenditure was required for modifying an existing building, where Jell-O was manufactured. Available capacity of a Jell-O agglomerator would be used in the manufacture of Super, so that no cost for the key machine was included in the project.[2] The $120,000 machinery and equipment item represented packaging machinery.

This case was made possible by the cooperation of General Foods Corporation. It was prepared by Harold E. Wyman, lecturer.

[1] The name and nature of this new product have been disguised to avoid the disclosure of confidential information.

[2] Agglomeration is a process by which the processed powder is passed through a steam bath and then dried. This "fluffs up" the powder particles and increases solubility.

EXHIBIT 1

THE SUPER PROJECT
Consolidated Balance Sheet of General Foods Corporation
Fiscal Year Ended April 1, 1967
($ millions)

Assets

Cash	$ 20
Marketable securities	89
Receivables	180
Inventories	261
Prepaid expenses	14
Current assets	564
Land, buildings, equipment (at cost, less depreciation)	332
Long-term receivables and sundry assets	7
Goodwill	26
Total	$929

Liabilities and Stockholders' Equity

Notes payable	$ 22
Accounts payable	86
Accrued liabilities	73
Accrued income taxes	57
Current liabilities	238
Long-term notes	39
$3\frac{3}{8}\%$ debentures	22
Other noncurrent liabilities	10
Deferred investment tax credit	9
Stockholders' equity	
Common stock issued	164
Retained earnings	449
Common stock held in treasury, at cost	(2)
Stockholders' equity	611
Total	$929

Common stock—shares outstanding at year-end 25,127,007

EXHIBIT 2
**Common stock prices of General Foods Corporation
(1958–1967)**

Year	Price range
1958	$24 $-39\frac{3}{4}$
1959	$37\frac{1}{8}-53\frac{7}{8}$
1960	$49\frac{1}{8}-75\frac{1}{2}$
1961	$68\frac{5}{8}-107\frac{3}{4}$
1962	$57\frac{3}{4}-96$
1963	$77\frac{5}{8}-90\frac{1}{2}$
1964	$78\frac{1}{4}-93\frac{1}{4}$
1965	$77\frac{1}{2}-89\frac{7}{8}$
1966	$62\frac{3}{4}-83$
1967	$65\frac{1}{4}-81\frac{3}{4}$

EXHIBIT 3 Ten-year summary of statistical data of General Foods Corporation, 1958–1967 (all dollar amounts in millions, except assets per employee and figures on a share basis)

	1958	1959	1960	1961	1962	1963	1964	1965	1966	1967
Earnings:										
Sales to customers (net)	$ 1,009	$ 1,053	$ 1,087	$ 1,160	$ 1,189	$ 1,216	$ 1,338	$ 1,478	$ 1,555	$ 1,652
Cost of sales	724	734	725	764	769	769	838	937	965	1,012
Marketing, administrative, and general expenses	181	205	236	261	267	274	322	362	406	449
Earnings before income taxes	105	115	130	138	156	170	179	177	185	193
Taxes on income	57	61	69	71	84	91	95	91	91	94
Net earnings	48	54	61	67	72	79	84	86	94	99
Dividends on common shares	24	28	32	35	40	45	50	50	53	55
Retained earnings—current year	24	26	29	32	32	34	34	36	41	44
Net earnings per common share	1.99	2.21	2.48	2.69	2.90	3.14	3.33	3.44	3.73	3.93
Dividends per common share	1.00	1.15	1.30	1.40	1.60	1.80	2.00	2.00	2.10	2.20
Assets, liabilities, and stockholders' equity:										
Inventories	169	149	157	189	183	205	256	214	261	261
Other current assets	144	180	200	171	204	206	180	230	266	303
Current liabilities	107	107	126	123	142	162	202	173	219	238
Working capital	206	222	230	237	245	249	234	271	308	326
Land, buildings, equipment:										
gross	203	221	247	289	328	375	436	477	517	569
net	125	132	148	173	193	233	264	283	308	332
Long-term debt	49	44	40	37	35	34	23	37	54	61
Stockholders' equity	287	315	347	384	419	454	490	527	569	611
Stockholders' equity per common share	11.78	12.87	14.07	15.46	16.80	18.17	19.53	20.99	22.64	24.32
Capital program:										
Capital additions	28	24	35	40	42	57	70	54	65	59
Depreciation	11	14	15	18	21	24	26	29	32	34
Employment data:										
Wages, salaries, and benefits	128	138	147	162	171	180	195	204	218	237
Number of employees (000)	21	22	22	25	28	28	30	30	30	32
Assets per employee (000)	21	22	23	22	22	23	24	25	29	29

THE MARKET

The total dessert market was defined as including powdered desserts, ice creams, pie fillings, and cake mixes. According to a Nielsen survey, powdered desserts constituted a significant and growing segment of the market; their 1966 market share had increased over the preceding year. Results of the Nielsen survey follow:

Dessert market (August–September 1966 compared with August–September 1965)

	Market share August–September 1966	Percent change from August–September 1965	
		Share	Volume
Jell-O.....................	19.0%	3.6	40.0
Tasty	4.0	4.0	(new)
Total powders	25.3	7.6	62.0
Pie fillings			
and cake mixes...........	32.0	−3.9	(no change)
Ice cream	42.7	−3.4	5.0
Total market	100.0		13.0

On the basis of test market experience, General Foods expected Super to capture a 10 percent share of the total dessert market. Eighty percent of the expected volume of Super would come from a growth in total market share or growth in the total powdered segment, and 20 percent would come from erosion of Jell-O sales.

PRODUCTION FACILITIES

Test market volume was packaged on an existing line, inadequate to handle long-run requirements. Filling and packaging equipment to be purchased had a capacity of 1.9 million units on a two-shift, five-day workweek basis. This represented considerable excess capacity, since 1968 requirements were expected to reach 1.1 million units, and the national potential was regarded as 1.6 million units. However, the extra capacity resulted from purchasing standard equipment, and a more economical alternative did not exist.

CAPITAL BUDGETING PROCEDURE

Capital investment project proposals submitted under procedures covered in *The General Foods Accounting and Financial Manual* were identified as falling into one of the following classifications:

1. Safety and convenience.
2. Quality.
3. Increase profit.
4. Other.

These classifications served as a basis for establishing different procedures and criteria for accepting projects. For example, the Super project fell in the third classification "increase profit." Criteria for evaluating projects are given in Exhibit 4. In discussing these criteria, Mr. Sanberg noted that the payback and return guidelines were not used as "cutoff" measures. Mr. Sanberg added: "Payback and return on investment are rarely the only measure of acceptability. Criteria vary significantly by type of project. A relatively high return might be required for a new product in a new business category. On the other hand, a much lower return might be acceptable for a new product entry which represented a continuing effort to maintain leadership in an existing business by, for example, filling out the product line."

EXHIBIT 4
Criteria for evaluating projects by General Foods Corporation

The basic criteria to be applied in evaluating projects within each of the classifications are set forth in the following schedule:

Purpose of project	*Payback and ROFE criteria*
a. **Safety and convenience:**	
1. Projects required for reasons of safety, sanitation, health, public convenience, or other overriding reason with no reasonable alternatives. Examples: sprinkler systems, elevators, fire escapes, smoke control, waste disposal, treatment of water pollution, etc.	Payback—return on funds projections not required but the request must clearly demonstrate the *immediate* need for the project and the lack or inadequacy of alternative solutions.
2. Additional nonproductive space requirements for which there are no financial criteria. Examples: office space, laboratories, service areas (kitchens, rest rooms, etc.)	Requests for nonproductive facilities, such as warehouses, laboratories, and offices should indicate the advantages of owning rather than leasing, unless no possibility to lease exists. In those cases where the company owns a group of integrated facilities and wherein the introduction of rented or leased properties might complicate the long-range planning or development of the area, owning rather than leasing is recommended. If the project is designed to improve customer service (such as market centered warehouses) this factor is to be noted on the project request.
b. **Quality:** Projects designed primarily to improve quality.	If Payback and ROFE cannot be computed, it must be clearly demonstrated that the improvement is identifiable and desirable.

EXHIBIT 4 (*continued*)

Purpose of project	*Payback and ROFE criteria*
c. Increase profit:	
1. Projects that are justified primarily by reduced costs.	Projects with a Payback period *up to 10 years* and a 10-year return *on* funds *as low as 20 percent* PBT are considered worthy of consideration, provided (1) the end product involved is believed to be a reasonably permanent part of our line or (2) the facilities involved are so flexible that they may be usable for successor products.
2. Projects that are designed primarily to increase production capacity for an existing product.	Projects for a proven product where the risk of mortality is small, such as coffee, Jell-O Gelatin, and cereals, should assure a payback in *no more than 10 years* and a 10-year PBT return on funds of *no less* than 20 percent.
3. Projects designed to provide facilities to manufacture and distribute a new product or product line.	Because of the greater risk involved such projects should show a high potential return *on* funds (not less than a 10-year PBT return of 40 percent) Payback period, however, might be as much as *10 years* because of losses incurred during the market development period.*
d. Other: This category includes projects which by definition are excluded from the three preceding categories. Examples: standby facilities intended to insure uninterrupted production, additional equipment not expected to improve profits or product quality and not required for reasons of safety and convenience, equipment to satisfy marketing requirements, etc.	While standards of return may be difficult to set, some calculation of financial benefits should be made where possible.

* These criteria apply to the United States and Canada only. Profit-increasing capital projects in other areas in categories c1 and c2 should offer at least a 10-year PBT return of 24 percent to compensate for the greater risk involved. Likewise, foreign operation projects in the c3 category should offer a 10-year PBT return of at least 48 percent.

Estimates of payback and return on funds employed were required for each profit-increasing project requiring a total of $50,000 or more of new capital funds and expense before taxes. The payback period was the length of time required for the project to repay the investment from the date the project became operational. In calculating the repayment period, only incremental income and expenses related to the project were used.

Return on funds employed (ROFE) was calculated by dividing 10-year average profit before taxes by the 10-year average funds employed. Funds employed included incremental net fixed assets plus or minus related working capital. Start-up costs and any profits or losses incurred prior to the time when the project became operational were included in the first profit and loss period in the financial evaluation calculation.

CAPITAL BUDGETING ATMOSPHERE

A General Foods accounting executive commented on the atmosphere within which capital projects were reviewed as follows: "Our problem is not one of capital rationing. Our problem is to find enough good solid projects to employ capital at an attractive return on investment. Of course, the rate of capital inputs must be balanced against a steady growth in earnings per share. The short-term impact of capital investments is usually an increase in the capital base without an immediate realization of profit potential. This is particularly true in the case of new products.

"The food industry should show a continuous growth. A cyclical industry can afford to let its profits vary. We want to expand faster than the gross national product. The key to our capital budgeting is to integrate the plans of our eight divisions into a balanced company plan which meets our overall growth objectives. Most new products show a loss in the first two or three years, but our divisions are big enough to introduce new products without showing a loss."

DOCUMENTATION FOR THE SUPER PROJECT

Exhibits 5 and 6 document the financial evaluation of the Super project. Exhibit 5 is the summary appropriation request prepared to justify the project to management and to secure management's authorization to expend funds on a capital project. Exhibit 6 presents the backup detail. Cost of the market test was included as "other" expense in the first period because a new product had to pay for its test market expense, even though this might be a sunk cost at the time capital funds were requested. The "adjustments" item represented erosion of the Jell-O market and was calculated by multiplying the volume of erosion times a variable profit contribution. In the preparation of Exhibit 6, costs of acquiring packaging machinery were included but no cost was attributed to the 50 percent of the capacity of a Jell-O agglomerator to be used for the Super project because the *General Foods Accounting and Financial Manual* requested that capital projects be prepared on an incremental basis as follows:

> The incremental concept requires that project requests, profit projections, and funds-employed statements include only items of income and expense and investment in assets which will be realized, incurred, or made directly as a result of, or are attributed to, the new project.

EXHIBIT 5
Capital project request form of General Foods Corporation

NY 1292-A 12-63
PTD. IN U.S.A.

December 23, 1966
Date

"Super" Facilities   66-42
Project Title & Number

Jell-O Division - St. Louis
Division & Location

New Request [X]   Supplement [ ]

Expansion-New Product [X] A
Purpose   [ ] R

PROJECT DESCRIPTION

To provide facilities for production of Super, chocolate dessert. This project included finishing a packing room in addition to filling and packaging equipment.

· SUMMARY OF INVESTMENT	
NEW CAPITAL FUNDS REQUIRED	$ 200M
EXPENSE BEFORE TAXES	--
LESS: TRADE-IN OR SALVAGE, IF ANY	--
Total This Request	$ 200M
PREVIOUSLY APPROPRIATED	--
Total Project Cost	$ 200M

FINANCIAL JUSTIFICATION*		
ROFE (PBT BASIS) - 10 YR. AVERAGE	62.9	%
PAYBACK PERIOD April, F'68 Feb. F'75 FROM TO	6.83	YRS.
NOT REQUIRED	[ ]	
* BASED ON TOTAL PROJECT COST AND WORKING FUNDS OF	$ 510M	

ESTIMATED EXPENDITURE RATE		
QUARTER ENDING Mar. F19 67	$	160M
QUARTER ENDING June F19 68		40M
QUARTER ENDING F19		
QUARTER ENDING F19		
REMAINDER		

OTHER INFORMATION		
MAJOR [ ] SPECIFIC [ ] ORDINARY BLANKET [ ]		
INCLUDED IN ANNUAL PROGRAM YES [ ] NO [ ]		
PER CENT OF ENGINEERING COMPLETED	80	%
ESTIMATED START-UP COSTS	$	15M
ESTIMATED START-UP DATE		April

LEVEL OF APPROVAL REQUIRED
[ ] BOARD   [ ] CHAIRMAN   [ ] EXEC. V.P.   [ ] GEN. MGR.

SIGNATURES		DATE
DIRECTOR CORP. ENG.		
DIRECTOR B & A		
GENERAL MANAGER		
VICE PRESIDENT		
EXEC. VICE PRESIDENT		
PRESIDENT		
CHAIRMAN		

For Division Use - Signatures	
NAME AND TITLE	DATE

EXHIBIT 5 (*continued*)
Instructions for capital project request form NY 1292–A

The purpose of this form is to secure management's authorization to commit or expend funds on a capital project. Refer to *Accounting and Financial Manual* Statement No. 19 for information regarding projects to which this form applies.

NEW REQUEST—SUPPLEMENT—Check the appropriate box.

PURPOSE—Identify the primary purpose of the project in accordance with the classifications established in Accounting and Financial Statement No. 19, i.e., Sanitation, Health and Public Convenience, Non-Productive Space, Safety, Quality, Reduce Cost, Expansion—Existing Products, Expansion—New Products, Other (specify). Also indicate in the appropriate box whether the equipment represents an addition or a replacement.

PROJECT DESCRIPTION—Comments should be in sufficient detail to enable Corporate Management to appraise the benefits of the project. Where necessary, supplemental data should be attached to provide complete background for project evaluation.

SUMMARY OF INVESTMENT
New capital funds required—Show gross cost of assets to be acquired.
Expense before taxes—Show incremental expense resulting from project.
Trade-in or salvage—Show the amount expected to be realized on trade-in or sale of a replaced asset.
Previously appropriated—When requesting a supplement to an approved project, show the amount previously appropriated even though authorization was given in a prior year.

FINANCIAL JUSTIFICATION
ROFE—Show the return on funds employed (PBT basis) as calculated on Financial Evaluation Form NY 1292–C or 1292–F. The appropriate Financial Evaluation Form is to be attached to this form.
Not required—Where financial benefits are not applicable or required or are not expected, check the box provided. The nonfinancial benefits should be explained in the comments.
In the space provided, show the sum of The Total Project Cost plus Total Working Funds (line 20, Form NY 1292–C or line 5, Form NY 1292–F) in either of the first three periods, whichever is higher.

ESTIMATED EXPENDITURE RATE—Expenditures are to be reported in accordance with accounting treatment of the asset and related expense portion of the project. Insert estimated quarterly expenditures beginning with the quarter in which the first expenditure will be made. The balance of authorized funds unspent after the fourth quarter should be reported in total.

OTHER INFORMATION—Check whether the project is a major, specific ordinary, or blanket, and whether or not the project was included in the Annual Program. Show estimated percentage of engineering completed; this is intended to give management an indication of the degree of reliability of the funds requested. Indicate the estimated start-up costs as shown on line 32 of Financial Evaluation Form NY 1292–C. Insert anticipated start-up date for the project; if start-up is to be staggered, explain in comments.

LEVEL OF APPROVAL REQUIRED—Check the appropriate box.

EXHIBIT 6
Financial evaluation form of General Foods Corporation ($000)

NY.1292-C 10-64
PTD. IN U.S.A.

Division	Jell-O	
Location	St. Louis	
Project Title	The Super Project	
Project No.	67-89	
Date		
Supplement Sr.		

PROJECT REQUEST DETAIL	1ST PER.	2ND PER.	PER.	PER.	PER.	PER.
1. Land	$					
2. Buildings	80					
3. Machinery & Equipment	120					
4. Engineering						
5. Other (Explain)						
6. Expense Portion (Before Tax)	$ 200					
7. Sub-Total						
8. Less: Salvage Value (Old Asset)	$ 200					
9. Total Project Cost*						
10. Less: Taxes on Exp. Portion						
11. Net Project Cost	$ 200					

RETURN ON NEW FUNDS EMPLOYED – 10-YR. AVG.

		PAT (C ÷ A)	PBT (B ÷ A)	
A – New Funds Employed (Line 21)	$ 380		$ 380	
B – Profit Before Taxes (Line 35)			$ 239	
C – Net Profit (Line 37)	$ 115			
D – Calculated Return		30.2 %	62.9 %	

PAYBACK YEARS FROM OPERATIONAL DATE

Part Year Calculation for First Period		- Yrs.
Number of Full Years to Pay Back		6.00 Yrs.
Part Year Calculation for Last Period		0.83 Yrs.
Total Years to Pay Back		6.83 Yrs.

FUNDS EMPLOYED	1ST PER. F 68	2ND PER. F 69	3RD PER. F 70	4TH PER. F 71	5TH PER. F 72	6TH PER. F 73	7TH PER. F 74	8TH PER. F 75	9TH PER. F 76	10TH PER. F 77	11TH PER.	10-YR. AVG.
Same as Project Request												
12. Net Project Cost (Line 11)	$ 200	200	200	200	200	200	200	200	200	200		
13. Deduct Depreciation (Cum.)	19	37	54	70	85	98	110	121	131	140		
14. Capital Funds Employed	$ 181	163	146	130	115	102	90	79	69	60		113
15. Cash	124	134	142	151	160	160	169	169	178	173		157
16. Receivables												
17. Inventories	207	222	237	251	266	266	281	281	296	296		260
18. Prepaid & Deferred Exp.												
19. Less Current Liabilities	(2)	(82)	(108)	(138)	(185)	(184)	(135)	(195)	(207)	(207)		(150)
20. Total Working Funds (15 thru 19)	329	274	271	264	241	242	255	255	207	207		267
21. Total New Funds Employed (14 + 20)	$ 510	437	417	394	356	344	345	334	336	327		380

PROFIT AND LOSS												
22. Unit Volume (in thousands)	1100	1200	1300	1400	1500	1500	1600	1600	1700	1700		1460
23. Gross Sales	€2200	2400	2600	2800	3000	3000	3200	3200	3400	3400		2920
24. Deductions	88	96	104	112	120	120	128	128	136	136		117
25. Net Sales	2112	2304	2496	2688	2880	2880	3072	3072	3264	3264		2803
26. Cost of Goods Sold	1100	1200	1300	1400	1500	1500	1600	1600	1700	1700		1460
27. Gross Profit	1012	1104	1196	1288	1380	1380	1472	1472	1564	1564		1343
28. Gross Profit % Net Sales	%											
29. Selling Expense	1100	1050	1000	900	700	700	730	730	750	750		841
30. Gen. and Admin. Costs												
31. Research Expense												
32. Start-up Costs	15											2
33. Other (Explain) Test Mkt.	360	200										36
34. Adjustments (Explain) Erosion	180	200	210	220	230	230	240	240	250	250		225
35. Profit Before Taxes	$ 643	(146)	(14)	168	450	450	502	502	564	564		239
36. Taxes	(334)	(76)	(7)	87	234	234	261	261	293	293		125
36A. Add: Investment Credit	(1)	(1)	(1)	(1)	(1)	(1)						(1)
37. Net Profit	(308)	(69)	(6)	82	217	217	242	242	271	271		115
38. Cumulative Net Profit	(308)	(377)	(383)	(301)	(84)	133	375	617	888	1159		
39. New Funds to Repay (21 less 38)	$ 818	814	800	695	440	211	(30)	(283)	(552)	(832)		

EXHIBIT 6 (*continued*)
Instructions for preparation of form NY 1292–C (financial evaluation)

This form is to be submitted to Corporate Budget and Analysis with each profit-increasing capital project request requiring $50,000 or more of capital funds and expense before taxes.

Note that the 10-year term has been divided into 11 periods. The first period is to end on the March 31st following the operational date of the project, and the P&L projection may thereby encompass any number of months from 1 to 12, e.g., if the project becomes operational on November 1, 1964, the first period for P&L purposes would be 5 months (November 1, 1964 through March 31, 1965). The next 9 periods would be fiscal years (F'66, F'67, etc.) and the 11th period would be 7 months (April 1, 1974 through October 30, 1974). This has been done primarily to facilitate reporting of projected and actual P&L data by providing for fiscal years. See categorized instructions below for more specific details.

PROJECT REQUEST DETAIL—*Lines 1 through 11* show the breakdown of the Net Project Cost to be used in the financial evaluation. *Line 8* is to show the amount expected to be realized on trade-in or sale of a replaced asset. *Line 9* should be the same as the "Total Project Cost" shown on Form NY 1292–A, Capital Project Request. Space has been provided for capital expenditures related to this project which are projected to take place subsequent to the first period. Indicate in such space the additional costs only; do not accumulate them.

FUNDS EMPLOYED
Capital funds employed—Line 12 will show the net project cost appearing on line 11 as a constant for the first 10 periods except in any period in which additional expenditures are incurred; in that event show the accumulated amounts of line 11 in such period and in all future periods.

Deduct cumulative depreciation on *line 13*. Depreciation is to be computed on an incremental basis, i.e., the net increase in depreciation over present depreciation on assets being replaced. In the first period depreciation will be computed at one half of the first year's annual rate; no depreciation is to be taken in the 11th period. Depreciation rates are to be the same as those used for accounting purposes. *Exception:* When the depreciation rate used for accounting purposes differs materially from the rate for tax purposes, the higher rate should be used. A variation will be considered material when the first full year's depreciation on a book basis varies 20% or more from the first full year's depreciation on a tax basis. The 10-year average of Capital Funds Employed shall be computed by adding line 14 in each of the first 10 periods and dividing the total by 10.

Total working funds—Refer to Financial Policy No. 21 as a guide in computing new working fund requirements. Items which are not on a formula basis and which are normally computed on a five-quarter average shall be handled proportionately in the first period. For example, since the period involved may be less than 12 months, the average would be computed on the number of quarters involved. Generally, the balances should be approximately the same as they would be if the first period were a full year.

Cash, based on a formula which theorizes a two weeks' supply (2/52nds), should follow the same theory. If the first period is for three months, two-thirteenths (2/13ths) should be be used; if it is for five months, two-twenty-firsts (2/21sts) should be used, and so forth.

Current liabilities are to include one half of the tax expense as the tax liability. The 10-year averages of Working Funds shall be computed by adding each line across for the first 10 periods and dividing each total by 10.

PROFIT AND LOSS PROJECTION
P&L categories (*lines 22 through 37*)—Reflect only the incremental amounts which will result from the proposed project; exclude all allocated charges. Include the P&L results expected in the individual periods comprising the first 10 years of the life of the project. Refer to the second paragraph of these instructions regarding the fractional years' calculations during the 1st and 11th periods.

Any loss or gain on the sale of a replaced asset (see line 8) shall be included in line 33.

As indicated in the caption Capital Funds Employed, no depreciation is to be taken in the 11th period.

The 10-year averages of the P&L items shall be computed by adding each line across for the 11 periods (10 full years from the operational date) and dividing the total by 10.

EXHIBIT 6 (*concluded*)

Adjustments (*line 34*)—Show the adjustment necessary, on a before-tax basis, to indicate any adverse or favorable incremental effect the proposed project will have on any other products currently being produced by the corporation.

Investment credit is to be included on line 36–A. The Investment Credit will be spread over 8 years, or fractions thereof, as an addition to PAT.

RETURN ON NEW FUNDS EMPLOYED—Ten-year average returns are to be calculated for PAT (projects requiring Board approval only) and PBT. The PAT return is calculated by dividing average PAT (line 37) by average new funds employed (line 21); the PBT return is derived by dividing average PBT (line 35) by average new funds employed (line 21).

PAYBACK YEARS FROM OPERATIONAL DATE
Part year calculation for first period—Divide number of months in the first period by 12. If five months are involved, the calculation is $\frac{5}{12} = .4$ years.

Number of full years to pay back—Determined by the last period, excluding the first period, in which an amount is shown on line 39.

Part year calculation for last period—Divide amount still to be repaid at the end of the last full period (line 39) by net profit plus the *annual* depreciation in the following year when payback is completed.

Total years to pay back—Sum of full and part years.

Exchange of memos on the Super project

After receiving the paper work on the Super project, Mr. Sanberg studied the situation and wrote a memorandum arguing that the principle of the preceding quotation should not be applied to the Super project. His superior agreed with the memorandum and forwarded it to the corporate controller with the covering note contained in Appendix A. The controller's reply is given in Appendix B.

APPENDIX A

To: J. C. Kresslin, Corporate Controller
From: J. E. Hooting, Director, Corporate Budgets and Analysis

March 2, 1967

SUPER PROJECT

At the time we reviewed the Super project, I indicated to you that the return on investment looked significantly different if an allocation of the agglomerator and building, originally justified as a Jell-O project, were included in the Super investment. The pro rata allocation of these facilities, based on the share of capacity used, triples the initial gross investment in Super facilities from $200,000 to about $672,000.

I am forwarding a memorandum from Crosby Sanberg summarizing the results of three analyses evaluating the project on an:

I.   Incremental basis.
II. Facilities-used basis.
III. Fully allocated facilities and costs basis.

Crosby has calculated a 10-year average ROFE using these techniques. Please read Crosby's memo before continuing with my note.

* * * * *

Crosby concludes that the fully allocated basis, or some variation of it, is necessary to understand the long-range potential of the project.

I agree. We launch a new project because of its potential to increase our sales and earning power for many years into the future. We must be mindful of short-term consequences, as indicated by an incremental analysis, but we must also have a long-range frame of reference if we are to really understand what we are committing ourselves to. This long-range frame of reference is best approximated by looking at fully allocated investment and "accounted" profits, which recognize fully allocated costs because, in fact, over the long run all costs are variable unless some major change occurs in the structure of the business.

Our current GF preoccupation with only the incremental costs and investment causes some real anomalies that confuse our decision making. Super is a good example. On an incremental basis the project looks particularly attractive because by using a share of the excess capacity built on the coat tails of the lucrative Jell-O project, the incremental investment in Super is low. If the excess Jell-O capacity did not exist, would the project be any less attractive? In the short term, perhaps yes because it would entail higher initial risk, but in the long term it is not a better project just because it fits a facility that is temporarily unused.

Looking at this point from a different angle, if the project exceeded our investment hurdle rate on a short-term basis but fell below it on a long-term basis (and Super comes close to doing this), should we reject the project? I say yes because over the long run as "fixed" costs become variable and as we have to commit new capital to support the business, the continuing ROFE will go under water.

In sum, we have to look at new project proposals from both the long-range and the short-term point of view. We plan to refine our techniques of using a fully allocated basis as a long-term point of reference and will hammer out a policy recommendation for your consideration. We would appreciate any comments you may have.

APPENDIX A (*continued*)

To: J. W. Hooting, Director, Corporate Budgets and Analysis
From: C. Sanberg, Manager, Financial Analysis

February 17, 1967

**Super project: A case example of
investment evaluation techniques**

This will review the merits of alternative techniques of evaluating capital investment decisions using the Super project as an example. The purpose of the review is to provide an illustration of the problems and limitations inherent in using incremental ROFE and payback and thereby provide a rationale for adopting new techniques.

ALTERNATIVE TECHNIQUES

The alternative techniques to be reviewed are differentiated by the level of revenue and investment charged to the Super project in figuring a payback and ROFE, starting with incremental revenues and investment. Data related to the alternative techniques outlined below are summarized [at the end of this appendix].

Alternative I: Incremental basis

Method—The Super project as originally evaluated considered only incremental revenue and investment, which could be directly identified with the decision to produce Super. Incremental fixed capital ($200M) basically included packaging equipment.

Result—On this basis the project paid back in 7 years with a ROFE of 63 percent.

Discussion—Although it is General Foods' current policy to evaluate capital projects on an incremental basis, this technique does not apply to the Super project. The reason is that Super extensively utilizes existing facilities, which are readily adaptable to known future alternative uses.

Super should be charged with the "opportunity loss" of agglomerating capacity and building space. Because of Super the opportunity is lost to use a portion of agglomerating capacity for Jell-O and other products that could potentially be agglomerated. In addition, the opportunity is lost to use the building space for existing or new product volume expansion. To the extent there is an opportunity loss of existing facilities, new facilities must be built to accommodate future expansion. In other words, because the business is expanding Super utilizes facilities that are adaptable to predictable alternative uses.

Alternative II: Facilities-used basis

Method—Recognizing that Super will use half of an existing agglomerator and two thirds of an existing building, which were justified earlier in the Jell-O project, we added Super's pro rata share of these facilities ($453,000) to the incremental capital. Overhead costs directly related to these existing facilities were also subtracted from incremental revenue on a shared basis.

Result—ROFE 34 percent.

Discussion—Although the existing facilities utilized by Super are not incremental to this project, they are relevant to the evaluation of the project because potentially they can be put to alternative uses. Despite a high return on an incremental basis, if the ROFE on a project was unattractive after consideration of the shared use of existing facilities, the project would be questionable. Under these circumstances, we might look for a more profitable product for the facilities.

In summary, the facilities-used basis is a useful way of putting various projects on a common ground for purposes of *relative* evaluation. One product using existing capacity should not necessarily be judged to be more attractive than another practically identical product which necessitates an investment in additional facilities.

Alternative III: Fully allocated basis

Method—Further recognizing that individual decisions to expand inevitably add to a higher overhead base, we increased the costs and investment base developed in Alternative II by a provision for overhead expenses and overhead capital. These increases were made in year five of the 10-year evaluation period, on the theory that at this point a number of decisions would result in more fixed costs and facilities. Overhead expenses included manufacturing costs, plus selling and general and administration costs on a per unit basis equivalent to Jell-O. Overhead capital included a share of the distribution system assets ($40M).

Result—ROFE 25 percent.

Discussion—Charging Super with an overhead burden recognizes that overhead costs in the long run increase in proportion to the level of business activity, even though decisions to spend more overhead dollars are made separately from decisions to increase volume and provide the incremental facilities to support the higher volume level. To illustrate, the Division—F1968 Financial Plan budgets about a 75 percent increase in headquarters' overhead spending in F1968 over F1964. A contributing factor was the decision to increase the sales force by 50 percent to meet the demands of a growing and increasingly complex business. To further illustrate, about half the capital projects in the F1968 three-year Financial Plan are in the nonpayback category. This group of projects comprised largely overhead facilities (warehouses, utilities, etc.), which are not directly related to the manufacture of products but are necessary components of the total business. These facilities are made necessary by an increase in total business activity as a result of the cumulative effect of many decisions taken in the past.

The Super project is a significant decision which will most likely add more overhead dollars as illustrated above. Super volume doubles the powdered dessert business category; it increases the Division businesses by 10 percent. Furthermore, Super requires a new production technology: agglomeration and packaging on a high-speed line.

CONCLUSIONS

1. The incremental basis for evaluating a project is an inadequate measure of a project's worth when existing facilities, with a known future use, will be utilized extensively.

2. A fully allocated basis of reviewing major new product proposals recognizes that overheads increase in proportion to the size and complexity of the business and provides the best long-range projection of the financial consequences.

Alternative evaluations of Super project (figures based on 10-year averages; $000)

	I Incremental basis	II Facilities-used basis	III Fully allocated basis
Investment:			
Working capital	$267	$267	$267
Fixed capital			
Gross	200	653	672
Net	113	358	367
Total net investment	380	625	634
Profit before taxes*	239	211	157
Rofe	63%	34%	25%
Jell-O project			
Building	$200 × $\frac{2}{3}$ = $133		
Agglomerator	640 × $\frac{1}{2}$ 320		
	$453		

* Note: Assumes 20 percent of Super volume will replace existing Jell-O business.

APPENDIX B

To:	Mr. J. E. Hooting, Director, Corporate Budgets and Analysis
From:	Mr. J. C. Kresslin, Corporate Controller
Subject:	SUPER PROJECT

March 7, 1967

On March 2 you sent me a note describing Crosby Sanberg's and your thoughts about evaluating the Super project. In this memo you suggest that the project should be appraised on the basis of fully allocated facilities and production costs.

In order to continue the dialogue, I am raising a couple of questions below.

It seems to me that in a situation such as you describe for Super, the real question is a *management decision* as to whether to go ahead with the Super project or not go ahead. Or to put it another way, are we better off in the aggregate if we use half the agglomerator and two thirds of an existing building for Super, or are we not, on the basis of our current knowledge?

It might be assumed that, for example, half of the agglomerator is being used and half is not and that a minimum economical size agglomerator was necessary for Jell-O and, consequently, should be justified by the Jell-O project itself. If we find a way to utilize it sooner by producing Super on it, aren't we better off in the aggregate, and the different ROFE figure for the Super project by itself becomes somewhat irrelevant? A similar point of view might be applied to the portion of the building. Or if we charge the Super project with half an agglomerator and two thirds of an existing building, should we then go back and relieve the Jell-O projects of these costs in evaluating the management's original proposal?

To put it another way, since we are faced with making decisions at a certain time on the basis of what we then know, I see very little value in looking at the Super project all by itself. Better we should look at the total situation before and after to see how we fare.

As to allocated production costs, the point is not so clear. Undoubtedly, over the long haul, the selling prices will need to be determined on the basis of a satisfactory margin over fully allocated costs. Perhaps this should be an additional requirement in the course of evaluating capital projects, since we seem to have been surprised at the low margins for Tasty after allocating all costs to the product.

I look forward to discussing this subject with you and with Crosby at some length.

—◄CASE I–15►—

Texana Petroleum Corporation

Clint Mitchell, director of the Research and Applications Group of Texana Petroleum Corporation, was glaring out the window of his 16th floor office. He had just been informed that his proposal for $22 million in capital expenditure funds had been denied by corporate management.

The denial was a particularly distressing blow to Clint as the project involved had been developed in-house over a three-year period. It had become a symbol to many of his managers of a way for Texana to use its technical expertise to enhance the overall corporate goal of diversifying into different, but related, businesses.

THE COMPANY

Texana Petroleum Corporation was a sizable, partially integrated oil and gas company. While the firm was not in the same league as the largest (or "seven sisters") oil companies, it was sizable in its own right. The firm's consolidated revenues for 1977 had exceeded $3 billion, with net income approaching $160 million.

The firm had a divisionalized organizational and management structure. The three major divisions operated in production and exploration, wholesale and retail marketing, and industrial chemicals. Smaller divisions were operating in surface transportation and in pipeline activities. The Research and Applications Group was also treated as a separate division for purposes of funding and evaluation.

THE RESEARCH AND APPLICATIONS GROUP

Texana's Research and Applications Group (TRAG) was formed in 1970. At its inception, it consisted of the combined research and development departments of the various divisions of the overall corporation. The decision to consolidate these separate activities into one central group was premised

This case was written by Professor M. Edgar Barrett. Copyright © 1978, 1979 by M. Edgar Barrett.

on the dual assumptions that: (1) there were significant economies of scale in the research and development area; and, (2) it was important to provide some organizational buffer between the research scientist and the day-to-day activities of line management.

Several years after TRAG was formed, the corporate charter for the division was significantly broadened. In mid-1972, corporate management decided that TRAG's responsibilities were to be expanded to include having it function in a limited role as an in-house new products group. This decision was taken after a careful analysis of the overall firm's activities had indicated that there were significant missed opportunities in the new product development area.

The analysis in question had found that, compared to some of their major competitors, Texana's new product development activities appeared to have two major weaknesses. First, the largely technical background of their overall management team seemed to create a bias toward the technical aspects of the business and away from the marketing and consumer aspects. Second, those projects that did not fit neatly into one of the five existing line management divisions appeared, in fairly large numbers, to fall by the wayside during the capital expenditure analysis process.

As of mid-1978, TRAG was functioning as both a research and development group and as a new products group. The divisional staff included a large complement of R&D personnel, a market research staff, an administrative complement, and several product departments. Several new products were currently being manufactured and sold by the division.

CORPORATE STRATEGY

Texana's corporate management had said, on several occasions, that corporate policy called for gradual diversification into business segments outside the oil and gas industry. This policy was premised on the belief that the corporation needed to strike a balance between earning maximum returns for its shareholders and building on those technical and other strengths which the firm had developed in the oil and gas industry. For many years, these two goals were not seen as clashing. In recent years, however, corporate management had come to believe that the oil and gas industry was drifting, inevitably, toward a regulated, public utility type of status. It was their opinion that this did not bode well for the future prosperity of the industry.

Texana's diversification strategy called for going into business segments close to, but not in, the petroleum (or oil and gas) industry. The corporate management wished to build on existing strength, in businesses they knew something about, without having to take those risks inherent in ventures totally unrelated to their existing business and technological base. The managerial and technical personnel of TRAG had been encouraged to focus much of their effort toward the development of new or revised products which fit into this desired strategy.

THE NEW FIBER PROPOSAL

The proposal which had just been turned down by corporate management involved the expenditure of funds for the construction of a medium-sized plant. It also included funds for the working capital needed to operate the plant upon completion. The plant in question would cost $18 million to construct, with $4 million needed for working capital at full capacity. Summary financial details for the project are shown in Exhibit 1.

The proposed plant was designed to produce a new fiber tentatively called Texalene. This fiber was to be manufactured by a new process from a raw material which was, in effect, a by-product of the gasoline refining process. The supply of raw material was, therefore, reasonably well assured. The new fiber had been thoroughly tested and patented. The fiber's initial markets would include both textiles and industrial uses, the latter in the form of pipes and fittings.

The new fiber had been discovered four years earlier by one of TRAG's research scientists. The first two years had been consumed by product testing and the acquisition of the appropriate patents needed to protect the firm's interests. Once these two phases were complete, discussions with personnel from Texana's industrial chemicals division and extensive market research efforts occurred.

The management of Texana's industrial chemicals division had been quite supportive of the overall project. They saw Texalene as being capable of opening up a potentially significant new market segment. This, they thought, was consistent with the overall corporate strategy. The potential new market would overlap nicely with areas that they had hoped to expand into over the next few years. This fact, plus the overall depressed nature of the industrial chemicals business, had led them to be quite enthusiastic about Texalene. Both they and the TRAG management felt that Texalene would ultimately be transferred to the industrial chemicals division.

The response from several potential industrial users had also been quite positive. Clint Mitchell, mindful of the fact that the currently depressed industrial chemicals market had led corporate management to be more than a little skeptical of financial projections related to chemicals, had pressed several potential customers to provide written evidence of their reaction to the product. Somewhat to his surprise, he had been able to obtain a written commitment from two of them which meant, in effect, that not less than 50 percent of the plant's production capacity for the first six years was presold. The commitment, under certain conditions, bound Texana to provide up to 70 percent of the plant's production capacity to these two

EXHIBIT 1
Texalene Fiber Plant—Summary financial details ($ millions)

	1979	1980	1981	1982	1983–92	1993
Sales.	$ 8.78	$ 18.29	$ 26.08	$31.62	$31.45	$31.45
Operating costs* (in cash)	10.50	13.74	18.48	19.16	19.18	19.18
Special marketing costs	0.80	1.29	0.50	0	0	0
Additional R&D costs	0.50	0.30	0	0	0	0
Plant start-up costs	0.70	1.30	0	0	0	0
Depreciation	0.15	1.30	1.40	1.40	1.25	1.25
Profit before tax	−3.87	0.36	5.70	11.06	11.02	11.02
Profit after tax†	−0.54	0.42	2.99	5.53	5.51	5.51
Add: depreciation	0.15	1.30	1.40	1.40	1.25	1.25
Cash from operations	−0.39	1.72	4.39	6.93	6.76	6.76
Investment: PP&E	−14.14	−2.36	−1.40	0	0	0
NWC	−1.30	−1.61	−1.10	0	0	0
Return of NWC	0	0	0	0	0	4.0
Net cash flow	−15.83	−2.25	1.89	6.93	6.76	10.76

Note: Data compilation assumes normal production volume achieved in 1982.

* The raw material, a by-product of the gasoline refining process, was costed at the highest of its current alternative uses.

† Includes investment tax credit of $1.4, $.24 and $.14 million in 1979, 1980, and 1981.

customers. The sales price contained a price escalation clause tied to the cost of the principal raw materials.

THE DECISION

Clint did not even pretend to fully understand why the corporate management had rejected TRAG's proposal. The project struck him as fitting particularly well into Texana's corporate strategy. It built on existing knowledge and strengths at the same time that it provided a modest amount of diversification. It tied nicely into the industrial chemical division's strategy for expansion and had the active support of that division's management. Finally, it was the most visible result to date of TRAG's attempts to develop and foster new product lines.

What seemed particularly inconsistent about the denial of funds was that the project promised to be quite profitable. Given the exhortations over the past year or so about the need to improve the firm's overall financial performance, Clint had thought that this particular project would be a "sure bet" for funding.

Summary financial statements for Texana Petroleum are shown in Exhibit 2.

EXHIBIT 2
Five-year summary of financial data ($ millions)

	1973	1974	1975	1976	1977
Operations:					
Total revenues	$1,549	$2,730	$2,648	$2,848	$3,073
Net income	148	222	138	158	156
Return on common equity	15.7%	20.6%	12.1%	13.1%	12.2%
Financial position:					
Working capital	234	265	269	308	248
Net property, plant, and equipment	848	935	967	1,028	1,191
Investments and other assets	107	108	111	99	109
Employed capital	1,189	1,308	1,347	1,435	1,548
Long-term debt	249	228	212	225	265
Shareholders' equity	940	1,080	1,135	1,210	1,283
Number of employees	8,025	8,178	8,080	8,260	8,420

QUESTIONS

1. How attractive, in financial terms, was the proposed Texalene Fiber Plant?

2. Why do you think the project was turned down?

3. What are the implications, if any, of your answer to question 2?

— PART TWO —

Cost accounting systems, planning, and analysis of performance

◄CASE II–1►

Broadside Boat Builders, Inc.

Located in Cornish, New Hampshire, Broadside Boat Builders served the boaters using the New England lake, river, and coastal waters with a small, lightweight fiberglass sailboat capable of being carried on the roof of a Volkswagen. While the firm could hardly be considered as one of the nation's industrial giants, its burgeoning business had required it to institute a formal system of cost control.

Mr. Decatur, Broadside's president, explained that, "Our seasonal demand opposed to a need for regular, level production means that we must keep a good line of credit at the Windsor banks. Modern cost control methods and consistent inventory valuation procedures enhance our credibility with the bankers and more importantly have enabled us to improve our methods and procedures. Our foremen have realized the value of good cost accounting and the main office has, in turn, become much more aware of problems in the barn."

Broadside's manufacturing and warehouse facilities consisted of three historic New England barns converted to make 11-foot Silver Streak sailboats for "fun and adventure." The company's plans for the near-term future included the addition of 15- and 18-foot sailboats to its present line. Longer-term plans called for adding additional sizes and styles in the hope of becoming a major factor in the regional boat market.

The Silver Streak was an open-cockpit day sailer sporting a mainsail and small jib on a 17-foot, telescoping, aluminum mast. It was ideally suited to the many small lakes and ponds of the region and after three years it had become quite popular. It was priced at $450 complete.

Manufacturing consisted basically of three processes; molding, finishing, and assembly. Molding included mixing of all ingredients to make the fiberglass hull, performing the actual molding, and removing the hull from the mold. Finishing included hand additions to the hull for running and standing rigging, reinforcement of the mast and tiller steps, and general sanding of rough spots. Assembly consisted of the attachment of cleats, turnbuckles, drain plugs, tiller, and so forth, and the inspection of the boat with mast, halyards, and sails in place. The assembly department also prepared the boat for storage or shipment.

This case was prepared by William Earner and Assistant Professor M. Edgar Barrett.

All masts, sails, tillers, and hardware were purchased from outside. The molds were good for 250 hulls each and were easily attached to the injection-type equipment used in production.

Mixing and molding fiberglass hulls, while manually simple, required a great deal of expertise, or "eyeball," as it was known in the trade. Addition of too much or too little catalyst, use of too much or too little heat, or failure to allow proper time for curing could each cause a hull to be discarded. Conversely, spending too much time on adjustments to mixing or molding equipment or on personalized supervision of each hull could cause severe underproduction problems. Once a batch of fiberglass was mixed there was no time to waste being overcautious or it was likely to "freeze" in its kettle.

With such a situation, and the company's announced intent of expanding their product line, it became obvious that a standard cost system would be necessary to help control costs and to provide some reference for foreman performance.

Davey Jones, the molding foreman, and Rick Ober, Broadsides' chief accountant, agreed, after lengthy discussion, to the following standard costs:

Materials:	Glass cloth—120 ft² @ $.40	=	$48.00
	Glass mix—40 lbs @ $.75	=	30.00
Direct labor:	Mixing—0.5 hrs @ $4.00	=	2.00
	Molding—1.0 hrs @ $4.00	=	4.00
Indirect costs:	Absorb at $3 per hull*	=	3.00
Total cost to mold hull			= $87.00

* The normal volume of operations for overhead derivation purposes was assumed to be 450 hulls per month. The estimated indirect cost equation was

$$\text{Budget} = \$1.44 \times \text{hulls} + \$702$$

Analysis of operations

After several additional months of operations, Mr. Ober expressed some disappointment about the apparent lack of attention being paid to the standard costs. He observed that although standards existed, they were infrequently met. Molders tended to have a cautious outlook toward mixing too little or "cooking" too long. No one wanted to end up throwing away half of a hull because of too little glass mix.

In reviewing the most recent month's production results, Mr. Ober noted the following actual costs for production of 430 hulls:

Materials:		
Purchased	60,000 ft² glass cloth	@ $.39/ft²
	20,000 lbs glass mix	@ $.76/lb
Used	54,000 ft² glass cloth	
	19,000 lbs glass mix	
Direct labor:	Mixing 210 hrs. at $4.10/hr.	
	Molding 480 hrs. at $4.00/hr.	
Overhead:	Incurred $1,400	

Before proceeding with further analysis, Ober called Jones to arrange a discussion of variances. He also told Decatur, "Maybe we should look into an automated molding operation. Although I haven't finished my analysis, it looks like there will be unfavorable variances again. Jones insists that the standards are reasonable, then never meets them!"

Decatur seemed disturbed and answered, "Well, some variances are inevitable. Why don't you analyze them in some meaningful manner and discuss your ideas with Jones. In molding, he is an expert whose opinion I respect. Then the two of you meet with me to discuss the whole matter!"

QUESTIONS

1. Determine the direct cost and overhead variances. Why do you think they occur?

2. Do you think Broadside's standards are meaningful? How would you improve them?

3. Are the direct cost variances in mixing a significant matter for Decatur's concern? Why?

────<C A S E II – 2>────

Universal Motors Ltd.

It was July 1975, and Frederick Vernon had just joined the accounting staff at Universal Motors Ltd. Mr. Vernon had spent the first several days on the job becoming familiar with the operations of Universal Motors Ltd. and, in particular, with the cost accounting system employed. He had been taken on a complete plant tour prior to being hired and has seen many of the operations again during his first few days on the job. In addition, his new boss, Jim Catlett, controller of Universal Motors Ltd., had spent the better part of one day describing the company's cost accounting system to him.

By combining the information gained from these trips and conversations, with some data he had gathered on his own, Mr. Vernon thought that he would have the basis for drawing some sound conclusions about the overall system. He expected that Mr. Catlett would, in the near future, ask for his opinion of the current cost accounting system.

COMPANY BACKGROUND

Universal Motors Ltd. was a British subsidiary of the American company, Universal Corporation. It was the manufacturer of a range of OEM and replacement market parts, primarily destined for use in automobiles or trucks. Valves and capacitors are examples of the kind of products which were produced. The plant was located in central England.

RECORDKEEPING REQUIREMENTS

The cost system of Universal Motors Ltd. was derived from that of the parent company, Universal Corporation. However, as was true of many aspects of the parent-subsidiary relationships of other firms, the cost system employed was not a carbon copy of that used by the parent.

This case was made possible by a firm which chooses to remain anonymous. In addition, some aspects of the cost accounting system have been altered or simplified in order to focus on the system's essence rather than on its full complexity. The case was prepared by Associate Professor M. Edgar Barrett.

The total cost system employed was comprehensive, complex, and produced multiple and, sometimes, conflicting types of data. This was due in part to the wide range of products produced and in part to the multiple recordkeeping requirements imposed by needs of the corporate and external users of data supplied by the system. For example, the system had to be capable of producing data for each of the following purposes:

a. Determining the expected normal or standard cost of a product.
b. Determining the periodic revenue and expense of the firm according to British accounting standards, which included Fifo inventory assumptions.
c. Determining and documenting the current costs and known, near-term increases in costs for purposes of filings before the price commission.
d. Analyzing the results of current operations for purposes of management control.

Due to the inherent complexity of the overall system, Mr. Vernon had decided to focus his attention on one major volume product. In addition, he decided to initially focus upon the standard cost for this product, how it was derived and how it was used in managerial reporting. The product selected was a valve packed for resale.

THE STANDARD COST SYSTEM

Mr. Catlett had described the company's cost system as being basically a standard cost system. The significance of using such a system, he said, was that it had a variety of uses and advantages. First, it allowed the company to compare its normal production costs over a series of years. Second, it established a standard for use in judging any one period's actual expenditures. Third, it established a standard for use as an input to the pricing decisions of the company. Finally, it allowed the company to avoid recording the actual cost of every item, thereby greatly simplifying the accounting and data processing procedures.

During each month, actual costs for such items as direct labor, direct materials, and the various burden (or overhead) accounts were accumulating. The workers were paid, material was purchased, and bills for items such as electricity, oil, and insurance were received and paid. However, the actual costs of these items were not taken directly into the inventory accounts. Rather, the inventory accounts contained a predetermined standard cost per item for each of the various products involved. If the total actual costs varied from the total standard costs, as was nearly always the case, most of the variations were posted to inventory variance accounts.[1] The variations

---

[1] See later portions of the case and Exhibit 10 for a more complete description and analysis.

were then reported and examined periodically as a means of focusing attention upon deviations from the expected level of production and efficiency. Finally, the balances contained in the inventory variance accounts were transferred to the Cost of Sales account based on a formula derived from the average inventory turnover.

Establishing standard costs

The budget year for Universal Motors Ltd. ran from September to August. The preparation of the standard costs, and of the overall annual budget, began in February.

The first phase in establishing standard costs was to determine a standard direct materials cost for each of the company's products. A bill of materials, with each type of material and its usage—including factors for wastage—was obtained from the industrial engineering department for each of the company's products. At the same time, a complete price list for all the types of materials purchased was obtained from the purchasing department. Both the bill of materials and the price list reflected the actual situation in February. They were then adjusted for known or likely changes between February and the first of September. The modifications made to these documents, to bring them into line with the expected situation in September, were subject to review and challenge by the finance department. Once these two documents were completed, standard direct materials costs for each of the company's products could be obtained by attaching prices to each item on a product's bill of materials.

Direct labor

The next phase in the derivation of the standard costs involved the determination of standard direct labor costs. Two source documents were involved here also. First, the industrial engineering department would provide an estimate of the standard time needed for each of the operations required to produce or assemble parts and products. The *budgeted standards* from the current year, updated to February and identified as *current standards* were used as the starting point (See Exhibit 1). They were then modified for any planned alterations between February and September.

Second, the payroll department would provide a listing of the actual wage rates per department being paid in February. This listing was then modified for any anticipated changes in wage rates between February and September. By combining the estimated standard time listing with the estimated standard

EXHIBIT 1
Standard labor-hours

PLANT 1				PART NUMBER 07967673	RESALE PACK VALVE		AS 13.1.75 SHEET 01	
ST OP	FN OP	DEPT	GRP	OPERATION DESCRIPTION	STAND.[1] HOURS	ADO[2]	TOTAL[3]	BUDGET[4] HOURS
05	20	108	98	ALL OPERATIONS	1.165	0.271	1.436	1.414
80	20	108	98	TRANS FROM 7967667	4.780	1.040	5.820	5.415
		108			5.945	1.311	7.256	6.829

Notes:

[1] Current standard hours for those operations that had been time studied.
[2] Applied Direct Operators: current standard hours for those operations that had not been time studied.
[3] Current standards for labor-hours, reflecting the originally budgeted standards updated for methods changes since the date of preparation of the original budget.
[4] Originally budgeted standard hours, including ADO at originally budgeted amounts.

Source: Company records. All figures have been disguised and the format altered.

wage listing, a standard direct labor cost was obtained for each part and product. This standard direct labor cost, of course, was at the industrial engineering department's level of efficiency.

This standard cost was then presented to the manager of the department involved who would either accept it or submit an efficiency ratio to account for planned inefficiencies. If such an efficiency ratio was submitted, the budgeted standard direct labor cost would be arrived at by negotiations between the department or factory manager on the one hand and the budget review committee on the other. In addition, any planned inefficiencies granted by the budget review committee were subject to review at the senior management level. Any planned inefficiencies granted were included as an upward adjustment of the labor rate per standard hour (see Exhibit 3).

At this point, a computer printout called the product cost accumulation sheet was made available. This printout gave the details on the labor-hours and the material cost per 1,000 products (Exhibit 2).

Manufacturing burden. The third phase in the derivation of the standard costs involved the determination of the manufacturing burden to be applied to each product. The overall determination of the standard manufacturing burden depended, in turn, upon the determination of five other factors or pieces of data. These subphases involved the determination of (*a*) a standard volume and mix of products and product variants for the coming budget year; (*b*) the total standard labor, in sterling, at standard volume for each productive department; (*c*) the total standard burden to be incurred within each productive department; (*d*) the total standard burden to be incurred within each service department; and, finally, (*e*) the method of allocation for allocating the service departments' standard burden to the productive departments.

The determination of the standard volume and mix of products and product variants began when the industrial engineering department provided a "declared capacity," by major product line, for the coming year. This declared capacity included the effects of making allowance for tea breaks, slow starts, and an average number of breakdowns. The declared capacity was then scaled down to 80 percent of the original figure, resulting in a standard volume figure for each major product line.[2] Still undetermined at this point was the mix within each major product line.

Meanwhile, the sales department provided the accounting staff with a detailed estimate of the sales for the coming year. This forecast was known as the budget volume forecast and it was broken down by product and product variant.[3] By exploding this forecast into part numbers for each product

---

[2] Valves and capacitors are examples of major product lines.
[3] A particular type of valve would be an example of a product variant.

EXHIBIT 2
Product cost accumulation sheet

0007967673 A/C 13 PRODUCT OIH

		HOURS PER 1000						MATERIAL VALUE PER 1000[6]					
		DEPT	HRS	DEPT	HRS	DEPT	HRS	CODE	COST	CODE	COST	CODE	COST
***********[1]	1.00	0108	7.256					TLS	1.750	ENG	1.814		
0000001746[2]	0.10							591	2.214				
0000001747[3]								591	1.310				
0003610679[4]	89.00 072							500	0.481				
0007967667[5]	1.00	0101	3.323	0105	6.078	0108	1.388	530	29.403	550	8.717	591	3.402
		0117	0.038										
TOTALS		0101	3.323	0105	6.078	0108	8.644	500	0.481	530	29.403	550	8.717
		0117	0.038					591	6.926	TLS	1.750	ENG	1.814
						LAB	18.083	MAT	45.527	TLS	1.750	ENG	1.814

Notes:

[1] Assembly of components into final product (see Exhibit 1).

[2] Inner carton.

[3] Outer carton, one for each ten valves.

[4] Printed instructions, 89 meters of printed instructions.

[5] Production and assembly of all individual components, in total.

[6] See "Miscellaneous Items" in case for description of tools (TLS) and engineering (ENG) costs.

Source: Company records. All figures have been disguised and the format altered.

variant, a sales forecast by individual part number was available. This disaggregated forecast was then separated into major product lines and the forecasted volume of each product variant was scaled up (or down) to bring the forecast volume of each product line back to the above-mentioned standard volume. The standard volume and mix of products and product variants for the coming year was now available. This standard volume and mix, in conjunction with the already determined standard direct labor cost per part, was then used to determine a total standard volume, standard labor cost by department.

Next, the managers of each productive and service department were asked to budget their planned expenses for nondirect labor, nondirect materials, and other overhead items at standard volume for the coming year. These original budgets were then subject to a budget review prior to being consoli-

EXHIBIT 3

1975 M. Y. COST STANDARDS
LABOUR AND MANUFACTURING BURDEN RATES

ISSUED: 4.9.1974
PAGE: 2 OF 8

PLANT NO.	DEPARTMENT NO.	DEPARTMENT NAME	BUDGETED EFFICIENCY OVERALL[1]	RATE PER STANDARD HOUR £.000[2]	MANUFACTURING BURDENS % VARIABLE	FIXED	TOTAL
1.	101	Multi-Spindle Autos and Cold Forming Shop	94	1.111	259.1	164.2	423.3
	102	Single Spindle Automatic Shop	96	1.111	81.4	53.0	134.4
	105		91	0.996	201.4	106.0	307.4
	107	General Machine Shop	90	1.014	127.8	94.8	222.6
	108	Assembly A	93	1.010	124.7	83.5	208.2
	110	Assembly B	92	0.920	109.0	65.4	174.4
	115	Assembly C	89	0.955	78.3	67.1	145.4
	117	General Press Shop	92	1.017	206.6	141.9	348.5
	118	Assembly D	89	0.943	83.8	64.2	148.0
	120	Assembly E	92	0.951	80.3	64.8	145.1
	121	Assembly F	96	0.972	109.1	61.2	170.3
	123	Assembly G	92	0.920	87.7	75.7	163.4
	124	Service Workshop	99	0.949	77.6	57.0	134.6
1.		PLANT TOTAL:	94	0.972	123.7	82.1	205.8
2.	201	General Machine Shop	89	1.075	163.8	125.7	289.5
	202	General Press Shop	92	1.088	159.9	97.8	257.7
	203	Assembly H	89	1.010	81.7	64.8	146.5
	204	Assembly J	93	0.970	121.3	182.8	304.1
	205	Assembly K	100	0.910	73.0	56.5	129.5
	206	Assembly L	92	1.014	136.7	99.2	235.9
			95	1.000	219.7	125.2	344.9
				0.983	151.8	131.8	283.6
					73.7	57.0	130.7
							157.8

Notes:

[1] The industrial engineering department's level of efficiency was set equal to 100.

[2] Including any planned inefficiencies as upward adjustments.

Source: Company records. Data has been disguised.

dated into the overall plantwide budget. Then various methods were used to allocate the service departments' costs back to the producing departments. For example: utility costs were allocated on the basis of periodic assessments by plant engineering; personnel department costs were allocated on the basis of a head count; and, some items were allocated on the basis of the current year's use by department. Items not easily allocable on a specific identification basis were apportioned according to the ratio of the department's direct labor cost to the company's total direct labor cost at standard volume.

The sum of the allocated and the internal costs gave the total manufacturing burden expected for each productive department at standard volume. These totals were then divided by the standard volume, standard direct labor cost to determine a standard manufacturing burden rate. Finally, this burden rate was split into variable and fixed portions in order to acknowledge that part of the burden did not vary with the level of production (Exhibit 3).

Miscellaneous items. The final phase in the derivation of the standard costs involved setting up standards for five miscellaneous categories which Universal Motors Ltd. had decided to set up separate from the three broad categories of costs already discussed. These five categories were: employee benefits variable (EBENV); employee benefits fixed (EBENF); tools; engineering (ENG); and overtime and shift premiums for all classes of employees (PREMS). The first and last of these were defined as being variable with the level of production and the standard costs for these categories were determined in a manner similar to that used to determine the standard cost of direct labor. The other three categories were treated as fixed expenses and the standard costs for these items were determined in a manner similar to that used to determine the standard cost of manufacturing burden.

The next step in setting up this standard cost system was to apply the standard rates to each of the items manufactured. In substance, this was done by using the standard costs shown on the detailed key part production cost sheet to debit the inventory account for each unit of product completed. An example of this production cost sheet is shown in Exhibit 4. The product described is a valve packed for resale. The standard costs of most parts were calculated on the basis of 1,000 units.

The standard labor costs were shown in the upper left hand corner, by department, in both hours and pound sterling. The related manufacturing burden, subdivided into variable and fixed categories, was then shown for each of the productive departments. Next, the direct materials involved were shown by broad category (e.g., sheet steel, rubber) and by pound sterling. Next, the five miscellaneous categories referred to above were shown in terms of pound sterling. Finally, the total production cost, broken into variable and fixed components was shown at the bottom of the page. A schematic showing the interrelationship of various product cost data feeding into the production cost sheet is shown in Exhibit 5.

EXHIBIT 4

DETAILED KEY PART B/STK PRODUCTION COSTS

PAGE NO. 1

DEPT	TOTAL DIRECT LABOR		****** MANUFACTURING BURDEN ****			GROUP **** MATERIAL *****	
		*	VARIABLE	FIXED	TOTAL	ACCOUNT	VALUE
	HOURS.DEC	££.DEC	££.DEC	££.DEC	££.DEC		££.DEC
0101	3.323	3.692	9.566	6.062	15.628	75008	.481
0105	6.078	6.054	12.193	6.417	18.610	75308	29.403
0108	8.644	8.730	10.886	7.290	18.176	75508	8.717
0117	0.038	0.039	0.081	0.055	0.136	75918	6.926
						TOTAL	45.527

** MISCELLANEOUS ****

EBENV	8.451
EBENF	1.931
TOTAL	10.382
TOOLS	1.750
ENG	1.814
PREMS	4.455

TOTAL	18.083	18.515	32.726	19.824	52.550

TOTAL VARIABLE COST   109.674
TOTAL FIXED COST   25.319
TOTAL PRODUCTION COST   134.993

17 JULY 1975
CHANGE CODE   75 MY
ACCT NO. 13   PRODUCT OIH
PART NO. 0007967673

Source: Company records. Data has been disguised.

EXHIBIT 5
Interrelationship of product cost data

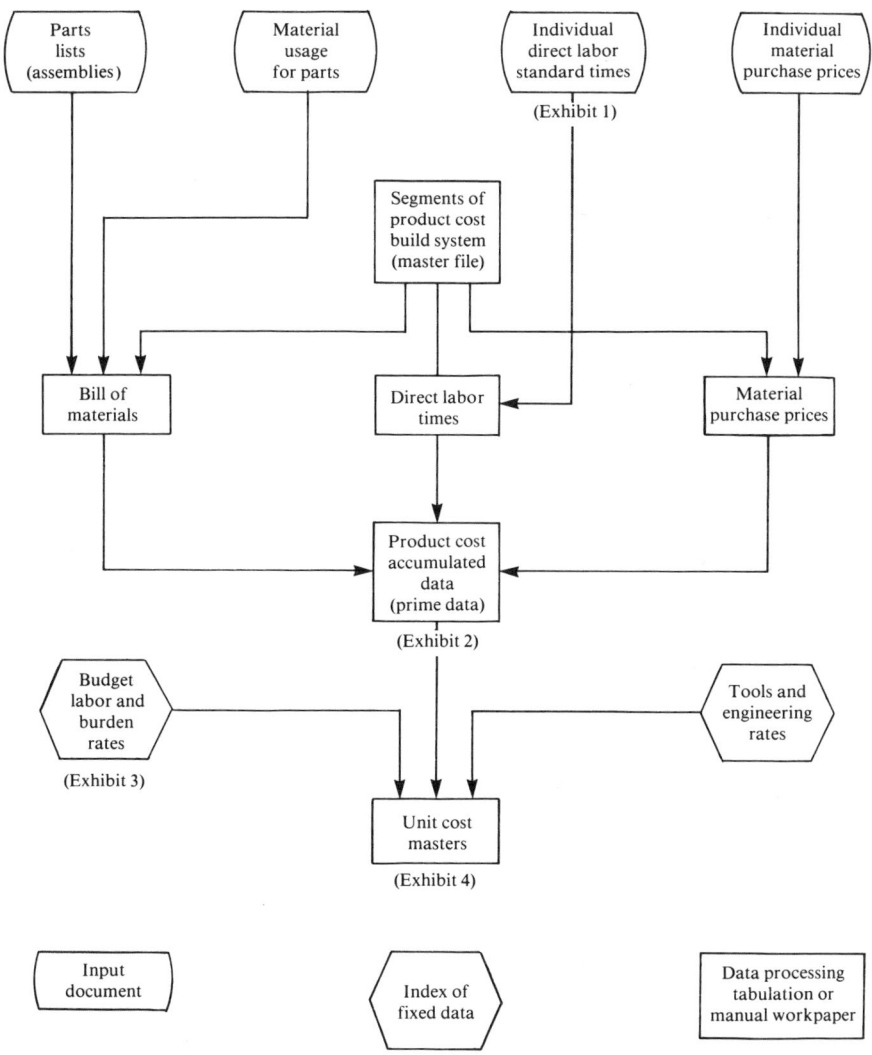

Source: Company records.

Accounting entries

While the substance of the standard cost system could be envisioned by focusing upon the production cost sheet (Exhibit 4), the actual flow of accounting entries made via the Universal Motors Ltd. data processing system was quite complex. As an example of that complexity, a schematic

84

EXHIBIT 6
Interrelationship of labor and manufacturing burden analysis and distribution of data:
Partial flowchart

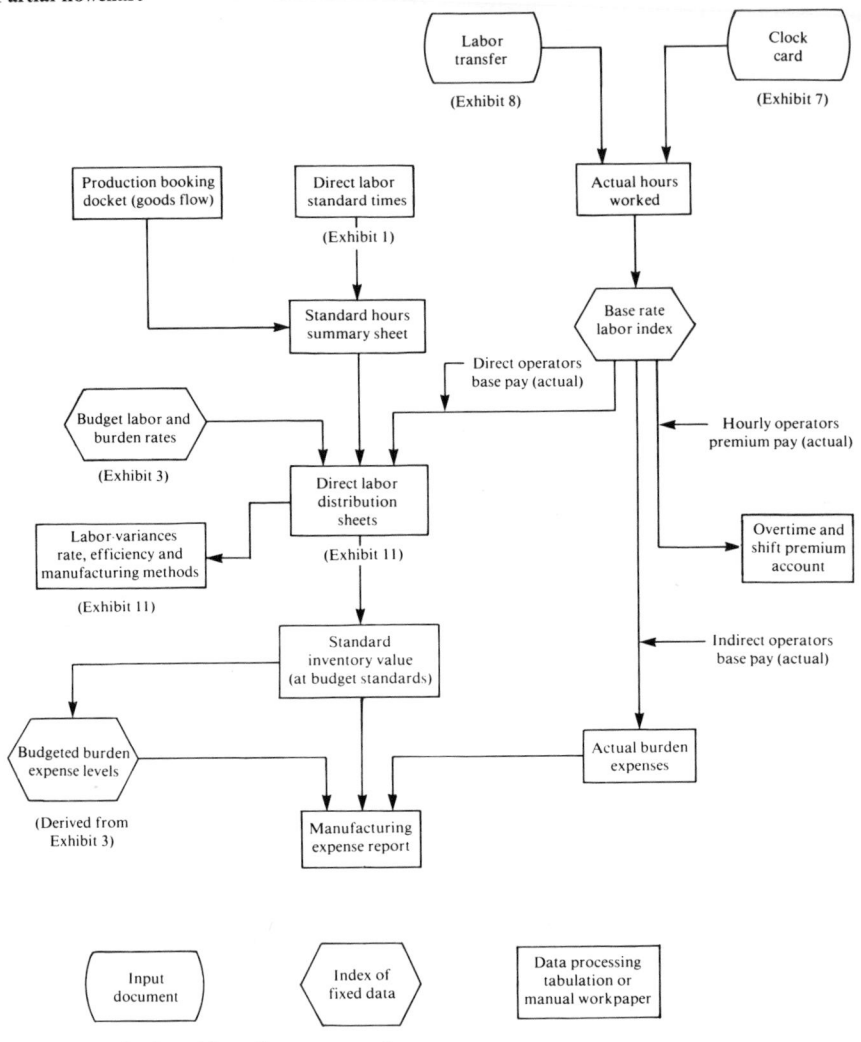

Source: Condensed from Company records.

showing part of the flow of accounting data for direct labor and manufacturing burden is shown in Exhibit 6. An overview of the accounting entries related to the basic, broad categories of expenses and revenues is presented below.

Direct materials.   As soon as any material was purchased, the full purchase price of the item was credited to Accounts Payable and the standard purchase price was debited to the appropriate basic inventory account (e.g., Sheet steel, Rubber). Any resulting difference between the credit and the various debits was posted to a purchase price variance account. As finished products were recorded as entering the finished goods warehouses, a debit was made to Finished Goods Inventory and a credit was made to all basic inventory accounts shown on the production cost sheet.[4]

This latter set of entries, it should be noted, resulted in the finished goods inventory being carried at originally *budgeted standards* rather than at *current standards*. However, it should be noted that a "methods variance" reflecting the difference between current standards and the original budget standards times the materials transferred into finished goods inventory was capable of being shown separately for purposes of analysis.[5]

"Yield checks," which were designed to determine how much material was actually being used to produce a product were conducted periodically. They resulted in the current standard being updated and the estimated monthly usage variance being changed. The estimated monthly usage variance was an amount which was credited monthly to each basic inventory account with the offsetting debit going into an account called Inventory—Materials Variance. Finally, a physical inventory was taken on a periodic basis with any necessary adjustment in the basic inventory accounts being posted to an income statement account titled Inventory Loss or Wastage.

Direct labor. The basic documents for recording both direct and indirect operators labor costs were the clock card (Exhibit 7) and the labor transfer card (Exhibit 8). Each direct and indirect operator was required to use and submit weekly a clock card on which his starting and stopping times for each day were shown. A payroll clerk then entered the proper number of hours into the six possible categories at the bottom of the page and forwarded the card to data processing. The labor transfer cards were used to record the fact that labor time had been used for other than the normal activity of the department in question. They were also forwarded to data processing.

Once data processing had obtained all of the clock cards and labor transfer cards for the period, these were matched with the payroll cost records to obtain the actual labor costs. These costs, in turn, were divided between direct labor (direct operators), indirect labor (indirect operators), and overtime and shift premium. The processing then continued as shown in Exhibit 6. Summaries of the data by department were supplied to the cost office by data processing.

Manufacturing burden. The method of handling manufacturing burden was similar for each productive department. The burden rate determined

---

[4] The materials actually passed through an intermediate inventory account known as Work in Process. However, this is not central to understanding the system.

[5] A flowchart summarizing the accounting entries is shown in Exhibit 10.

EXHIBIT 7
Clock card

Employee no.	Station	Week ending	Pay station
105003		13 6 75	25

Name	D.P. Code	Home Department
E. Johnson	4999	108

	Account	Department	Group
Charge	80001	108	98

		Hours
	Premium holiday	

Monday to Friday 4 hours and less	Vacation mark "V"	Leaver mark "L"

Overtime approved

Supervisor

	Sat.	Sun.	Mon.	Tues.	Wed.	Thurs.	Fri.	
			7.25	7.20	7.20	7.23		
			1.26	1.27	1.27	1.28		
			4.30	4.30	4.30			
								Total
D/S								31.25
E/S								
N/S								
33⅓								
50								
100								
								31.25

Source: Company records.

earlier (Exhibit 3) would be applied to the budgeted standard direct labor-hours for the amount of product produced to determine the amount of burden to be absorbed. The amount so determined would be debited to the Finished Goods Inventory account and credited to various burden accounts such as Indirect Labor, Depreciation, and Insurance. During the period in question, actual manufacturing burden expenses would be accumulating as debits to these burden accounts. The difference between the sum of the actual burden expenses and the absorbed manufacturing burden was divided into two variance accounts. The first, Inventory—Manufacturing Burden Vari-

EXHIBIT 8
Labor transfer card

DATE	DEPT/GP.(1)	ACCOUNT (2)	(3) PLEASE TICK			DEPT/GP. (4)	ACCOUNT (5)	SEQUENCE
11-6-75	108/98	80001	Dayshift	X	1	108	7220	
			Eveningshift		2			
	TRANSFERRED FROM		Nightshift		3	TRANSFERRED TO		
FOREMAN			LABOUR TRANSFER AUTHORISATION					
	HOURS	DEC.	CLOCK NO.			REASON FOR TRANSFER OR CHARGE TO EXPENSE		
	16	-	4999			Re-inspecting + salvaging scrapped valves		
	16	-(6)	TOTAL			(7) Cost Office use only		

Source: Company records.

ance, contained an amount determined by applying the burden rate mentioned above to the difference between the budgeted standard direct labor-hours and actual direct labor-hours incurred in producing the product. The second, Unabsorbed Manufacturing Burden, contained the remainder of the unabsorbed burden expenses.

When the transactions discussed above had been made, all direct material, direct labor, and manufacturing burden were charged into the Finished Goods Inventory account at budgeted standard cost and a series of variance accounts had been debited or credited for the difference between actual and standard.

Cost of sales. Before monthly operating statements could be prepared, an analysis of the sales by product number had to be completed. This resulted in a computerized listing of all sales made during the month, subdivided by product and part number and showing the net sales price. The total net sales price from this listing became a debit to Accounts Receivable and a credit to Sales.

Meanwhile, based on the total volume of each product sold and the standard costs shown on the production cost sheets, a credit was made to the various finished goods inventory accounts with the offsetting debit going to Cost of Sales, an expense account. Next, any amounts shown in either the Inventory Loss or Wastage account or the Unabsorbed Manufacturing Burden account were closed by charging them directly against the income statement. Finally, based on a series of formulas related to average inventory turnover, a portion of the balances of the three inventory variance accounts and the Purchase Price Variance account were transferred to the Cost of Sales account. When this work was done, the controller's office was in a position to create a monthly operating statement (see Exhibit 9) by closing the books.

EXHIBIT 9
Statement of net income, June 1975

Line No.	TITLE OF ACCOUNT	ACCOUNT NO.	TOTAL SUBSIDIARY	COMMODITY		GROUPS VALVES
1	Net Sales - Outside	8010				366.5
2	- Allied	8020				
3	- Intra-Divisional	8030				3.1
4	Total Net Sales					369.6
5	Factory Cost of Sales - Outside	8210				332.1
6	- Allied	8220				
7	- Intra-Divisional	8230				4.3
8	Total Factory Cost of Sales[1]					336.4
9	Net Factory Profit Before Factory Cost Adjustment					33.2
10	Add (Deduct) Factory Cost Adjustments[2]	8400				(4.0)
11	Net Factory Profit After Adjustments					29.2
12	Deduct (Add) Commercial Expense:					
13	Administration Expense	8605				2.0
14	Selling Expense	8610				5.5
15	Sales Promotion Expense	8615				1.9
16	Consumer Influences Expense	8620				
17	Loading and Shipping Expense	8640				
18	Product Warehousing & Delivery Expense	8645				
19	Parts & Accessory Whse. & Distribution Expense	8650				5.0
20	Parts & Accessory Merchandising Expense	8655				0.4
21	Product Service Expense	8660				
22	Resale Expense - Branches & Retail Stores	8690				
23	Bad Debt Expense	8695				
24	State & Local Tax Expense	8697				
25						
26						
27	Total Commercial Expenses					14.8
28	Deduct (Add) Other Deductions	8800				7.1
29						
30	Add (Deduct) Other Income	9000				2.0
31	Add (Deduct) Reversal of Prov. for Depreciation	9160				2.3
32	Operating Profit					12.0
33	Deduct (Add) Special Profit and Loss Items	9200				
34						
35						
36	Income Before Income Taxes					12.0
37	Deduct (Add) Income Taxes	9300				
38	Net Income					

[1] Net of all variances except unabsorbed overhead and inventory loss.
[2] Basically, unabsorbed overhead and inventory loss.
  Source: Company records. All figures have been disguised and the format altered.

A flowchart summarizing the entries described above is given in Exhibit 10.

EXHIBIT 10
Flowchart[1]

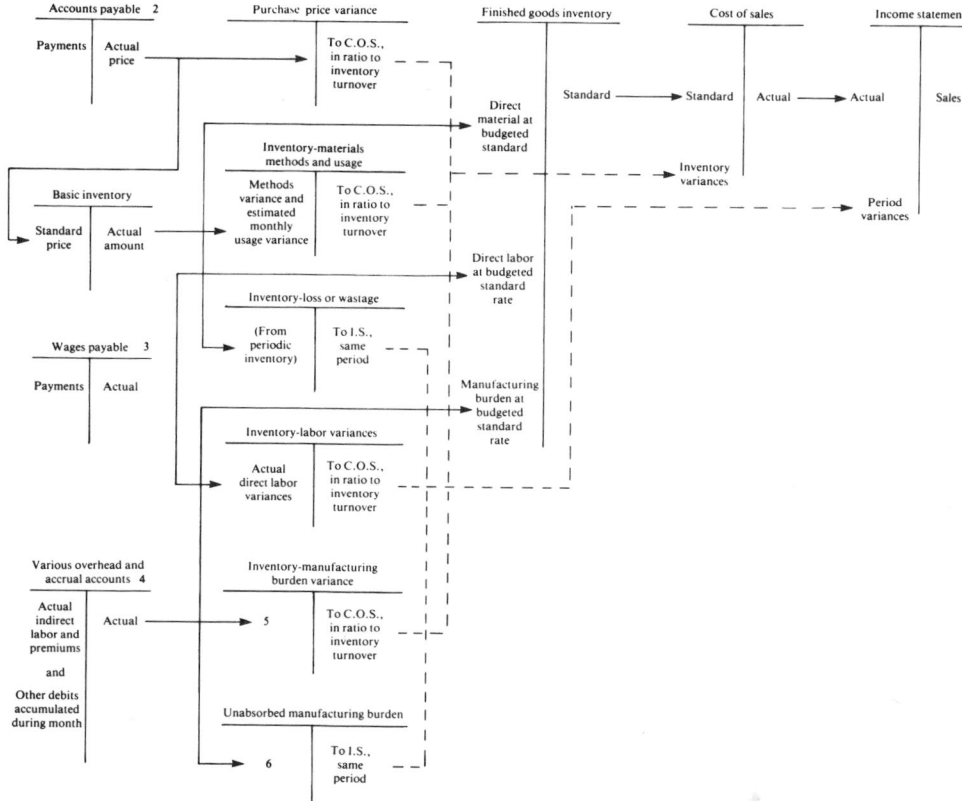

Notes:

[1] For purposes of simplification, neither Work in Process Inventory nor the five miscellaneous categories of costs discussed in the case are separately shown.

[2] For direct materials.

[3] For direct labor.

[4] Depreciation expense would be an example of such an account.

[5] Burden rate (Exhibit 3) multiplied by difference between actual labor-hours at standard rate and budgeted labor-hours at standard rate.

[6] Remaining burden *or* difference between actual manufacturing burden expense and the burden rate (Exhibit 3) times the actual labor-hours at standard rate.

Source: Casewriter's notes.

OTHER REPORTS ISSUED

A variety of reports was issued for purposes of management reporting and control. They normally were focused upon variations between expected results and actual achievements. An example of one of these, a monthly report of direct and applied direct labor, is shown in abridged form as Exhibit 11.

EXHIBIT 11

| | | MONTHLY DIRECT AND APPLIED DIRECT LABOUR DISTRIBUTION | Department | Assembly A - 108 |
| | | | Month of | June 1975 |

LINE	DETAIL	W/E May 30, '75 5 Days Hrs £ P	W/E June 6, '75 5 Days Hrs £ P	W/E June 13, '75 5 Days Hrs £ P	W/E June 20, '75 5 Days Hrs £ P	TOTAL MONTH 20 Days Hrs £ P	ACCRUAL 3 Days Hrs £ P	REVERSAL 2 Days Hrs £ P	ACCTG. MONTH 21 Days Hrs £ P
1	TOTAL D.O. CLK HRS			3051 · 3642 · 14					
2	TOTAL A.D.O. CLK HRS			888 · 1238 · 27					
3	GROSS ACT DIR LAB			3939 · 4880 · 41					
4	LESS: SCRAP			(2 · 68)					
5	NET ACT DIR LAB			4877 · 73					
6	A/RATE (5 ÷ 3)	FORMAT IDENTICAL		£1.238	FORMAT IDENTICAL TO THAT OF				
7		TO THAT OF WEEK			WEEK ENDING JUNE 13, 1975				
8	HRS (L3) AT STD RATE £.939	ENDING JUNE 13		- · 3698 · 33					
9									
10	CUR S/HRS AT S/RATE £1.010			3300 · 3333 · 66					
11	CUR S/HRS AT B/RATE								
12	BUD VARIANCE-HRS			100 · 101 · 02					
13	LESS SCRAP			(2 · 68)					
14	TOTAL S/LAB For Auth			3432 · 00					
	VARIANCE ANALYSIS								
15	RATE (8-3)			(1182 · 08)					
16									
17	EFFICIENCY (10-8)			(364 · 67)					
18	WAGE AWARD (10-11)								
19	BUD VAR HRS (12)			101 · 02					
20	TOTAL VARIANCE (14-5)			(1445 · 73)					
21	NET S/LAB (10-13)			3330 · 98					
22	EXCESS LAB (15-17)			1546 · 75					
23	ACT DIR LAB (5)			4877 · 73					
24					*Illustrative, normally done monthly				

Source: Company records. Data has been disguised.

─── CASE II–3 ───
The Hyatt Hill Health Center

BACKGROUND

The Hyatt Hill Health Center (HHHC) was established in New York City in 1968. It was sponsored by the Follen Hospital, widely considered to be among the leading hospitals in the United States in terms of the quality of its medical care, research, and teaching. The Health Center was established on an experimental basis in order to provide community-centered health care to the residents of the town of Bedford, in which it was located. Bedford is a lower income area which suffers from a heavy incidence of medical, dental, psychiatric, and social problems. For example, before the Health Center was established, it was estimated that over 40 percent of Bedford's adults needed dental plates. Also, a significant proportion of its population consisted of confirmed or incipient alcoholics and drug abusers.

Because there were few physicians residing in Bedford, its residents used the emergency room of the Follen Hospital as a substitute for a family physician. As a result, they received sporadic therapeutic medical care and few of them received any preventive care.

The purpose of the Health Center was to provide adequate preventive as well as therapeutic care and to do so by becoming an accepted force in the Bedford community. This wasn't an easy mission; for Bedford was geographically isolated from the rest of New York City, and its residents (who were largely composed of one closely knit ethnic group) were traditionally suspicious of any "outsiders." Despite the heavy incidence of mental health problems in the area, the residents of Bedford were particularly resistant to receiving the services of social workers and psychiatrists.

HISTORY OF THE HHHC

Many communities in New York City asked the Follen Hospital to locate a health center in their areas. The Bedford community was chosen for location of the Center because it had the relatively highest community-utilization rate of the Follen's outpatient facilities. Additionally, Bedford community leaders expressed enthusiasm for the location of the Center in their midst.

This case, made possible by a firm which chooses to remain anonymous, was prepared by Associate Professor Regina Herzlinger.

And although the mean income in Bedford was not high, it possessed a sufficient diversity in the distribution of income to be commended as a potential site for a health center which included financial self-sufficiency as one of its primary objectives. Finally, very few physicians were working in the Bedford area, and some were near retirement; there was, thus, a strong indication of future need for adequate health facilities in the area.

The HHHC was, in many senses, an experiment in the delivery of medical care. Its services were restricted to the Bedford community, for example, to enable measurement of the impact of the Center on the health of an isolated community. Additionally, it contained many administrative and technical innovations which were consciously experimental and to be studied by the Evaluation Department in the Center.

OBJECTIVES

The experimental nature of the HHHC is readily apparent in the objectives assigned to it by Follen Hospital. These objectives include the following:

1. To be a prevention-oriented, family-centered source of health care, available to all community residents.
2. To deliver less fragmented, more extensive medical services and to utilize clinical information-recording methods that will facilitate the delivery of such services.
3. To test the feasibility and success of providing health services that are usually provided by schools and city health departments.
4. To provide for on-the-job training and employment of resident non-professionals.
5. To determine the impact that a community health center would have on the utilization of the Follen's facilities by residents of the community in which the center is located.
6. To develop a community health center which can, through the various financing mechanisms available to it, become financially self-sufficient.

The financial objectives of the HHHC—self-sufficiency and reduction of costs for the Follen—were as important to its administrators and the Follen Hospital as the medical objectives. This goal, however, was not meant to be attained in the short run; but only after the Center had established itself in the Bedford community.

ORGANIZATION AND PERSONNEL

The Hyatt Hill Health Center is composed of the following departments: pediatrics, internal medicine, nursing, mental health, social service, nutrition, dental, and specialists. Most of its practitioners hold joint appointments at the Follen Hospital. They are considered to be of high professional calibre, and are incurring substantial opportunity costs by working at the Health

Center. They are highly effective practitioners, who have dedicated themselves to demonstrating that a community health center can indeed provide effective therapeutic and preventive medical care and, thus, have a significant impact on its target area.

In addition to its goal of delivering community health care, the HHHC also serves as a training ground for members of the Follen Hospital or NYC Department of Health staff who are interested in community medicine. Training activities are conducted in all of HHHC's departments but are particularly concentrated in the mental health, social service, and nutrition departments.

Funding

The Health Center, which has a yearly operating budget of nearly $1 million is funded from a variety of sources, including the Follen Hospital. The Follen underwrites the cost of some personnel and equipment. In addition, it completely renovated the building in which the HHHC is located from a state of dilapidation into a convenient and comfortable health facility.

In order to gather the data required by Follen Hospital, every practitioner in the Health Center completes the form displayed in Exhibit 1 immediately after every encounter with a patient. The data on the encounter forms are then entered on a computer terminal which is connected to the Follen Hospital's system. The data are processed at the Follen Hospital to provide the information necessary for compliance with the HEW requirements and sent to the HHHC.

Personnel

The central actors in the HHHC are the executive director, Dr. Steven Kyler; the manager of the evaluation unit, Dr. Jack Martin; the chiefs of services; and the assistant executive director for administration, Neil Hershey. Dr. Kyler, in both theory and practice, sets the tone of the HHHC. He is a well-known pediatrician who was head of the Follen's Children's Clinic before assuming his present responsibility. He is particularly known for his work in the training of nurse-practitioners. He was born in the Bedford area and has been involved with the HHHC from its inception and originated many of its novel approaches. The various chiefs of services are distinguished physicians with impeccable academic and professional backgrounds. With them resides considerable power in the determination of the specific form and content of health care delivery. Dr. Martin is a practicing physician whose role is to serve as an internal evaluator of the HHHC and as a catalyst for the development and implementation of innovative ideas for the Center. Mr. Hershey is a CPA and a lawyer. His function is to supervise the work of the accounting, medical records, personnel, and maintenance departments. In addition, he administers the technical services of the HHHC (laboratories

EXHIBIT 1
Encounter forms

2 > Professional no.:	1 > Date:	Encounter Form, Medical Departments
☐ ☐ ☐	☐ ☐ ☐ ☐ ☐ ☐	
	mo. day year	

3 > Visit:

- 1 ○ walk-in
- 2 ○ visit kept
- 3 ○ visit broken

Date of Birth
_____

Visit location:

- 1 ○ HHHC
- 2 ○ Home
- 3 ○ School or Club
- 4 ○ Other

➤ Unit no.: ☐ ☐ ☐ ☐ ☐ ☐

8 > Family no.: ☐A ☐ ☐ ☐ ☐

Name: _____

---

10 > Duration of visit:

☐ ☐ minutes

For shared visit, enter time spent by other professional (MD or nurse)

☐ ☐ minutes

12 > Assessment status:

- 1 ○ not started
- 2 ○ in process
- 3 ○ completed this visit
- 4 ○ complete prior visit

Treatment plan status, at this visit:

- 1 ○ not needed
- 2 ○ short-term, in process
- 3 ○ short-term, completed
- 4 ○ long-term

13 > Check or enter *one* based on primary reason for visit:

- 1 ☐ acute prob. or followup
- 2 ☐ chronic problem
- 3 ☐ treatment or lab only
- 4 ☐ checkup or physical
- 5 ☐ school health physical
- 6 ☐ well child visit
- 7 ☐ prenatal or postnatal
- 8 ☐ health education
- 9 ☐ family counseling
- 10 ☐ family planning

Other activity code: ☐ ☐

Comments or chargeable services (injections, treatments, etc.)

14 > Code only diagnoses related to primary reason for visit and ENTER CODE below

A.

	B. presumptive / confirmed	C. mild / moderate / severe
1.	1. ☐ 2. ☐	1. ☐ 2. ☐ 3. ☐
2.	☐ ☐	☐ ☐ ☐

15 Referrals: Made To:	A in HHHC	B out- side	C Follen	Received From:	D in HHHC	E out- side	F Follen	
1. nursing								
2. dental health								
3. nutrition								
4. ENT								
5. eye								
6. speech, hearing								
7. local physician or dentist								
8. medical and specialties								
9. surgical and specialties								
10. mental health								
11. physical therapy								
12. other agencies								

EXHIBIT 1 (*continued*)

2 > Professional no.:	1 > Date:	Encounter Form,

H ☐☐

mo.　day　year

**Encounter Form,
Social Service, and
Mental Health Departments**

3 > Visit:

1 ◯ walk-in
2 ◯ visit kept
3 ◯ visit broken

Date of Birth
_____

Visit location:

1 ◯ HHHC
2 ◯ Home
3 ◯ School or Club
4 ◯ Other

➤ Unit no.: ☐☐☐ ☐☐ ☐

8 > Family no.: A ☐ ☐☐☐☐

Name: _____

---

10 > Duration of visit:

☐☐ minutes

Modification of charges:

☐ half charge
☐ no charge

---

12 > Assessment status:

1 ◯ not started   3 ◯ completed this visit

2 ◯ in process   4 ◯ complete prior visit

Current status of treatment planned at assessment:

1 ◯ not needed   3 ◯ short-term, completed

2 ◯ short-term, in process   4 ◯ long-term

---

13 > Activity during this contact consisted of: (check one)

60 ☐ patient-interview   63 ☐ group therapy
61 ☐ others in family-interview   64 ☐ psych. testing
62 ☐ patient and family-interview   65 ☐ other

Additional services:

---

14 > Primary problem: (code primary problem and enter *only* code)

A. Enter CODE

P ☐☐☐

B. *presumptive* / *confirmed* 1 ☐ 2 ☐

C. *mild* / *moderate* / *severe* 1 ☐ 2 ☐ 3 ☐

15 Referrals: Made To:	A in HHHC	B out-side	C Follen	Received From:	D in HHHC	E out-side	F Follen	Check, if current involvement:
1. nursing				1.				☐
2. dental health				2.				☐
3. nutrition				3.				☐
8. medical and specialties				8.				☐
10. mental health				10.				☐
13. KPR Center				13.				☐
14. Schools				14.				☐
15. Wheeler State Hospital				15.				☐
16. Police/courts				16.				☐
17. Self/friend				17.				☐
18. VHA/USA				18.				☐
12. Other agencies				12.				☐

EXHIBIT 1 *(concluded)*

2⟩ Professional no.:	1⟩ Date:	Encounter Form, Dental Department

D ▯ ▯

Date: ▯▯ ▯▯ ▯▯
　　　　mo.　day　year

3⟩ Visit:

1 ◯ walk-in
2 ◯ visit kept
3 ◯ visit broken

Date of Birth
_____

Visit location:

1 ◯ HHHC
2 ◯ Home
3 ◯ School or Club
4 ◯ Other

➡ Unit no.: ▯▯▯ ▯▯ ▯▯

8⟩ Family no.: A▯ ▯▯▯▯

Name: _____

10⟩ Duration of visit: ▯▯ minutes

12⟩ Assessment status:

1 ◯ not started　　3 ◯ completed this visit
2 ◯ in process　　4 ◯ complete prior visit

Treatment plan status, at this visit:

1 ◯ not needed　　3 ◯ completed
2 ◯ in process　　4 ◯ needed, but not started

14⟩ CODE services and enter CODES in order of importance:

	permanent	deciduous	service in process	service completed	tooth code	surface	tooth code	surface	no charge	courtesy fee	Bill	Paid	Other
F ▯▯▯▯	1◯ 2◯		1◯ 2◯						□	□	□	□	
▯▯▯▯	1◯ 2◯		1◯ 2◯						□	□	□	□	
F ▯▯▯▯	1◯ 2◯		1◯ 2◯						□	□	□	□	
F ▯▯▯▯	1◯ 2◯		1◯ 2◯						□	□	□	□	
F ▯▯▯▯	1◯ 2◯		1◯ 2◯						□	□	□	□	

Further services and comments:

15　Referrals: Made To:	A in HHHC	B out-side	C Follen	Received From:	D in HHHC	E out-side	F Follen	
1. nursing								
2. dental health								
3. nutrition								
4. ENT								
5. eye								
6. speech, hearing								
7. local physician or dentist								
8. medical and specialties								
9. surgical and specialties								
10. mental health								
11. physical therapy								
12. other agencies								

and neighborhood aides), as well as the in-service training programs for health aides and nurse-practitioners.

THE CONTROL SYSTEM—BACKGROUND

Late in 1969, a researcher who was interested in studying the costs of ambulatory medical care facilities visited the Health Center. At the time, Steven Kyler was becoming increasingly concerned over the potential for the achievement of the HHHC's financial self-sufficiency goal. Although the Center had a good financial accounting system for billing and external reporting, it had no managerial accounting data. Thus, Dr. Kyler didn't know the total costs of his departments, of different kinds of cases, and of his practitioners. Since the only financial data available to him were the costs of the different line-items on his budget, Dr. Kyler couldn't really assess the feasibility of his Center's accomplishing its financial self-sufficiency goals. He thus agreed to the installation of a management control system which would provide him with the data he wanted.

At that time, there was also an uncomfortable feeling among some of the HHHC's administrative and medical personnel that costs were "above average" for this kind of system and that administrative costs in particular were out of control. They attributed this to the costs involved in setting up the Center; to the additional paperwork required from the HHHC due to its multiple funding sources; to the additional costs of training Bedford personnel; and to general inefficiency in the support departments. However, since the sources of these costs were not determined, and since there were no standards that could be used to ascertain whether costs were, in fact, too high, there was no way to prove or disprove the feeling that costs were above average.

In addition, some of the HHHC's medical personnel felt that the nursing staff wasn't being efficiently utilized. There was also some concern that the Bedford population of 16,000 was too small to support a Center of the HHHC's size. Some practitioners estimated that a minimum registrant population of 20,000 to 30,000 was necessary for fulfillment of the self-sufficiency goals of the Center. Given the absence of data relating the cost of providing health care to the volume of health care provided, these estimates couldn't be validated.

THE NEW MANAGEMENT CONTROL SYSTEM

The purpose of the new management control system was to provide those individuals having some control over the costs of providing medical services with information which would reveal the impact that their actions have on the level of these costs.

Given this objective, the researcher's first step in the design of the new MCS was to determine to whom this information should be provided. The

Health Center is composed of two distinct types of departments: mission units, such as internal medicine, which fulfill the Center's primary mission of providing health care; and support units, such as accounting, which exist in order to support the mission units in achieving their goals. Theoretically, each mission and each support department could have been designated as a responsibility center, since each represents a subunit of the Health Center whose director has clearly defined authority and responsibility. However, since the objective of the new MCS was to provide information to individuals who directly deliver health services, only the mission departments were designated as reponsibility centers. In the Health Center, these departments included the pediatrics, internal medicine, community mental health, nursing, dental health, social service, and nutrition departments. Since these departments generate revenue by charging fees to their patients, they were further designated as profit centers.

The method which was used to calculate the cost data which were supplied to the heads of each of the mission departments is indicated in Exhibit 2.

EXHIBIT 2

Symbol	Meaning
$x	Fixed cost of the department
$yj	Salary per minute of physician j
zj	Time, in minutes, that physician j was available
Nij	Number of encounters of type i by physician j
Tij	Time spent on encounters of type i by physician j
Nwj	Number of walk-in patients treated by physician j
Twj	Time spent on walk-in encounters by physician j
Nrj	Number of patients who made appointments treated by physician j
Trj	Time spent on appointment encounters by physician j

1. The total time spent in patient care by physician j:

$$Tj = \sum_i Tij$$

2. The direct labor cost of physician j:

$$\$DLCj = (Tj)(\$yj)$$

3. The total time spent in nonpatient care activities by physician j:

$$Qj = Zj - Tj$$

4. The direct overhead cost of physician j:

$$\$DOHj = (Qj)(\$yj)$$

5. The total time spent in nonpatient care activities by physicians in the department:

$$Q = \sum_j Qj$$

6. The fixed overhead cost of physician j:

$$\$FOHj = \left(\frac{Qj}{Q}\right)(\$x)$$

EXHIBIT 2 (*continued*)

7. The total cost of physician j:

$$\$TCj = \$DLCj + \$DOHj + \$FOHj$$

8. The proportion of the total cost of physician j attributable to encounters of type i:

$$\$TCij = \left(\frac{Tij}{Tj}\right)(\$TCj)$$

9. The average cost of encounters of type i for physician j:

$$\$ACij = \frac{\$TCij}{Nij}$$

10. The average cost per encounter for physician j:

$$\$ACj = \frac{\$TCj}{\sum\limits_{i} Nij}$$

11. The total costs of walk-ins and regular appointments for physician j:

$$\$TCwj = \left(\frac{Twj}{Tj}\right)(\$TCj)$$

$$\$TCrj = \left(\frac{Trj}{Tj}\right)(\$TCj)$$

12. The average cost of walk-ins and regular appointments for physician j:

$$\$ACwj = \frac{\$TCwj}{Nwj}$$

$$\$ACrj = \frac{\$TCrj}{Nrj}$$

13. The average cost for the department of walk-in and regular appointments:

$$\$ACw = \frac{\sum\limits_{j} TCwj}{\sum\limits_{j} Nwj}$$

$$\$ACr = \frac{\sum\limits_{j} TCrj}{\sum\limits_{j} Nrj}$$

14. The average cost for the department of an encounter:

$$\$AC = \frac{\sum\limits_{j} TCwj + \sum\limits_{j} TCrj}{\sum\limits_{j} Nwj + \sum\limits_{j} Nrj}$$

15. The total cost for the department of encounters of type i:

$$\$TCi = \sum\limits_{j} TCij$$

16. The average cost for the department of encounters of type i:

$$\$ACi = \frac{\$TCi}{\sum\limits_{j} Nij}$$

As indicated in that exhibit, two types of information were required in order to perform the necessary calculations. The first type was the fixed cost of running each of the departments (see Exhibit 3). (These costs were fixed in the sense that their level did not depend on the volume nor types of health care rendered by the mission departments.) Through consultation with the Health Center staff, the fixed cost of the Center for a typical month was established. Next, the fixed cost of the Center was allocated among the mission departments. Some components of the Center's fixed cost, such as salaries, could be directly traced to each department. Other components, such as heat and electricity, were shared costs and were allocated to the mission departments on the basis of their utilization of the component. For example, each department's share of the Center's electric bill was determined by its proportion of the Health Center's square footage. Similarly, the costs of operating the support units were allocated to the mission departments by appropriate utilization measures. For instance, the cost of the accounting department was allocated to the mission departments on the basis of their proportionate share of patients' bills. In some instances, *imputed* costs were employed; thus, if a piece of equipment were donated to the Center, its cost was designated as the price at which that equipment could be purchased from its manufacturer.

The second type of required information was data describing each of the practitioners in a department. This descriptive data included the following items for each practitioner:

1. His salary, on a per minute basis.
2. The total number of minutes he was available to render health services.
3. The number of patients he treated, by type of encounter.
4. The time spent on each type of encounter.
5. The number of walk-in patients he treated.
6. The time spent on walk-in encounters.
7. The number of patients who made appointments he treated.
8. The time spent on encounters for which appointments were made.

These data were obtained from the encounter forms contained in Exhibit 1. Using these two types of information, a number of calculations were performed, and Exhibit 3 contains them. These calculations relate the quantities of the various types of medical care rendered to the costs of providing such care. The quality of patient services was controlled by the screening of all professional appointments by the chiefs of the services of the Follen, a continuing peer review by the department chiefs at the Health Center, and the random review of medical records by the utilization review committee at the hospital.

Control of nonpatient care-related activities was achieved through the use of time sheets which measured the time spent in activities like research, teaching, management, and related activities. They were completed, once

EXHIBIT 3

	Salaries						Departmental fixed cost								
	Direct patient care	Direct overhead	Fringe	Furniture and equipment	Supplies	Rent	Heat and power	Evaluation	Medical records and accounting	Administration	Service Reps	HHHC out patient	General	Total	Percent of total
Pediatrics	$ 2,400	$ 1,956	$ 610	$ 16	$ 441	$ 162	$ 20	$1,117	$ 817	$ 490	$ 220	$ 40	$ 330	$ 8,609	11.9
Internal medicine	3,336	1,331	653	23	467	189	33	894	1,170	533	239	43	359	9,270	12.9
Nutrition	537	260	68	4	—	42	7	381	264	189	81	15	127	1,975	2.7
Nursing	4,148	4,371	657	62	320	398	60	394	455	2,313	931	187	1,557	15,853	22.0
Dental	1,140	2,407	493	84	150	162	20	333	0	877	—	71	590	6,327	6.6
Mental health	737	4,814	554	41	—	382	47	331	187	1,246	—	101	838	9,278	12.8
Social services	502	4,906	421	30	—	301	40	458	258	1,720	243	139	1,158	10,176	14.1
Specialists	854	447	—	14	—	—	—	269	413	112	51	9	75	2,244	3.1
Eye clinic	478	172	29	96	—	126	13	165	253	267	—	22	179	1,800	2.5
Laboratory	1,147	645	143	46	275	41	7	—	666	567	243	46	382	4,208	5.8
Radiology	139	392	49	189	272	68	7	—	387	189	80	15	127	1,914	2.7
Therapists	—	—	—	7	—	47	7	39	25	95	40	8	64	332	0.5
Total	$15,418	$21,701	$3,677	$612	$1,925	$1,918	$261	$4,381	$4,895	$8,598	$2,128	$696	$5,786	$71,986	

EXHIBIT 4
Average cost per professional for each visit type (September 1970, medical department)

Visit description	Physician 1	Physician 2	Physician 3	Total department
	Professional code			
Acute problem or followup	$ 9.85	$10.99	$15.47	$10.97
Chronic problem	12.86	15.07	27.51	15.32
Treatment or lab only	2.89	9.97	—	7.11
Checkup or physical exam	24.93	25.93	20.63	24.89
School health physical.............	8.11	—	—	8.11
Prenatal visit....................	9.66	—	—	9.66
Walk-in visit....................	9.45	11.45	19.10	10.73
Appointment visit	16.24	17.63	21.91	17.72
All visits	12.52	13.58	21.21	14.07

every three months, by every Health Center professional. The results were routinely tabulated, translated into full costs, and distributed so that the managers and practitioners could gauge the relative allocation of costs in their nonpatient care related activities.

Exhibit 4 contains the results of the calculations described above for the month of September 1970, for each physician in the medical department and for that department as a whole.

Using the calculated data contained in Exhibit 4, a method for assessing the monthly performance of each physician in the medical department (and, similarly, for physicians in other departments) was devised. This method involved comparing actual performance to "average" performance in a normal month. For each practitioner in each department, the number of encounters of each type and amount spent on each encounter type were determined. Using this information and the salary of the practitioner, his average cost for each type of encounter was calculated for the normal month. In Exhibit 5, this quantity is called the predicted standard cost. If, in a subsequent month, a physician's *actual* average cost for each type of encounter differed from this *predicted* average cost, the difference could have arisen from one or both of two sources. First, he could have become more or less *efficient* by decreasing or increasing the average amount of time he spent on each type of encounter. Second, he could have increased or decreased his capacity utilization by increasing or decreasing the proportion of his available time during which he provided direct patient care. The third and fourth columns of Exhibit 5 explain the differences between predicted and actual average costs in terms of changes in the physician's efficiency and capacity utilization:

$$\begin{array}{c} \text{Average cost} \\ \text{per visit} \end{array} = \begin{array}{c} \text{Predicted} \\ \text{standard cost} \end{array} + \begin{array}{c} \text{Differential} \\ \text{effect of change} \\ \text{in efficiency} \end{array} + \begin{array}{c} \text{Differential effect} \\ \text{of change in capacity} \\ \text{utilization} \end{array}$$

EXHIBIT 5
Sample monthly performance indicators, September 1970, medical department, physician 2

Visit type	Average cost per visit	Predicted standard cost*	Differential effect of change in efficiency	Differential effect of change in utilization of capacity	Total cost	Total revenues	Revenue less cost
Acute problem	$10.99	$12.22	$(−2.53)	$1.30	$1,253	$ 912	$ (−341)
Chronic problem	15.07	16.66	(−2.70)	1.11	1,763	936	(−827)
Treatment or lab only	9.97	6.66	2.28	1.03	60	48	(−12)
Checkup or physical exam	25.93	24.81	(−0.07)	1.19	259	80	(−179)
All visits	13.58	15.91	(−3.55)	1.22	3,335	1,976	(−1,359)

Note: Numbers do not balance precisely because of rounding errors.
* Standard efficiency and utilization capacity as adjusted for actual total costs in the month of September.

THE MANAGEMENT CONTROL PROCESS

During the development of the control system, the researcher continually consulted with the management and practitioners of the Center. This was done to insure that the data to be produced by the management control system were understood and reflected the procedures of the HHHC in an equitable manner.

After the MCS was implemented, the data it produced were distributed periodically to the heads of all mission departments and to the administrative officers of the Center. The implications of the data were discussed at executive and departmental meetings. In addition, meetings were held between the Center director and individual practitioners in all departments, during which allocations of time were reviewed using the MCS data as a focal point. The data were, therefore, routinely and actively used in the managerial process.

Results

Cost trends. After implementation of the new MCS, the average cost per encounter dropped in six of the seven mission departments (see Exhibit 6). The decline in costs was most significant in the social service, mental health, and dental health departments. Smaller drops were recorded for the nutrition, internal medicine, and nursing departments. The only department showing an increase in average cost per encounter was the pediatrics department, which registered a 6 percent increase.

EXHIBIT 6
Average cost, by mission department, per quarter

Department	Average cost				Percent change (loss) third quarter 1970 to second quarter, 1971
	Third quarter 1970	Fourth quarter 1970	First quarter 1971	Second quarter 1971	
Social service	$43.81	$29.95	$27.31	$23.40	(−61)%
Mental health	47.25	31.57	27.77	26.21	(−57)
Dental health	22.69	18.40	15.72	16.22	(−33)
Nutrition	12.65	11.25	10.45	10.54	(−18)
Pediatrics	10.59	11.37	12.16	11.19	6
Internal medicine	16.07	14.09	14.72	15.07	(−6)
Nursing	35.27	35.16	36.20	32.42	(−9)

The sources of these changes in average cost per encounter are indicated in Exhibit 6. The structure of Exhibit 6 is analogous to that of Exhibit 5. The average cost per encounter in each mission department in the first quarter of 1971 was compared with what its average cost in that quarter would have been if its efficiency and capacity utilization had remained as they were in the third quarter of 1970. Thus the difference between the actual cost per encounter and the predicted (or standard) cost per encounter, is due to changes in departmental efficiency and capacity utilization.

EXHIBIT 7
Source of the difference between standard and actual cost per visit (first quarter of 1971)

Department	Standard cost per visit	Actual cost per visit	Difference (variance) between standard and actual cost	Differential effect of change in efficiency	Differential effect of change in utilization of capacity
Social service	$61.10	$27.31	$ 33.79	$ 5.37	$28.42
Mental health........	53.65	27.77	25.88	0.23	25.65
Dental health	32.88	15.72	17.16	0.41	16.75
Nutrition	24.97	10.45	14.52	6.04	8.48
Pediatrics	15.64	12.16	3.48	(−0.57)	4.05
Internal medicine.....	14.72	14.00	0.72	(−0.14)	0.86
Nursing.............	28.34	36.20	(−7.86)	(−11.15)	3.29

For example, if the efficiency and capacity utilization of the mental health department in the first quarter of 1971 had remained unchanged from the third quarter of 1970, the average cost per encounter would have been $53.65. The actual cost in the first quarter of 1971 was $27.77. The difference between these two costs ($25.88) was due to an increase in efficiency, which reduced the average cost by 23 cents, and an increase in capacity utilization, which decreased the average cost by $25.65.

Managerial impact

The reactions to the new MCS among the professional staff at the HHHC were mixed. Mr. Hershey, the assistant executive director for administration, praised the new MCS:

> Before the MCS was implemented, a lot of people were worried about how the Center was to become self-supporting and how each department could become self-supporting. The primary impact of the MCS has been how to get more efficient resource utilization. People in social service and mental health never used to consider the costs of work they did outside the Center in the community. In other departments, people didn't worry about downtime and its cost. The increased cost-consciousness of the staff is shown by the hiring of lower salaried people to perform some tasks that used to be undertaken, unnecessarily, by highly paid professionals.

Dr. Martin, the head of the evaluation unit, agreed with Hershey that the MCS had led to an increased awareness of costs, but was critical of the way in which the MCS was implemented:

> Before the MCS, there was relatively little interest in costs, and there was no idea of how to determine what they were. The MCS made people aware of costs and what they had to do to lower them.
>
> But the MCS wasn't implemented correctly. What the MCS never had was the intensive feedback loop it should have had. The staff didn't participate as much as they should have, and the system is too reprimanding and not sufficiently rewarding.

Dr. Strand, the head of the social service unit, admits that the MCS has made him and his staff more aware of time constraints and the need to set priorities, but is worried about the impact of the system:

> The system tells us that we should be spending more time on direct patient care and less time out in the communities, doing such things as helping to create a community recreation center. We see these community activities as preventive medicine but there's no way to measure the long-term effects of these activities. There's a real conflict—these community activities are beneficial, but the more time we spend on them, the less revenue we can generate for the Center.

Dr. Long, head of the internal medicine department, had two complaints about the MCS.

> The only thing that really happened was a greater focusing on cost issues. The MCS brought about a philosophical change on the part of the Center's administration to increase the volume of direct patient care. I, and many others, think that the system led to a decreased emphasis on the quality of care and on preventive medicine.
>
> Another thing is that administrative costs were never studied. There has not been any perceptible change in administrative costs, nor has any thought been given to altering the physical facilities of the Center.

⎯⎯⎯⎯⎯⎯⎯✕CASE II-4✕⎯⎯⎯⎯⎯⎯⎯

Managing against expectations (A): A note on profit variable analysis

Not surprisingly, a major function of accounting is facilitating accountability—measuring the performance of individuals in terms appropriate to their assigned responsibilities—ROI for "investment center" managers, profits for "profit center" managers, and costs for "cost center" managers. Not all aspects of a manager's performance can be captured in accounting measures. This is particularly true for measures of activity in just one period. Nevertheless, measures of periodic profit, cost, or revenue performance do provide a point of departure from which a more comprehensive performance assessment can begin. It is no accident that the last figure on an earnings statement, net earnings, has provided the basis for the now more ubiquitous phrase "the bottom line."

If a manager is charged with profit responsibility, the measure of how much profit was earned is clearly relevant in evaluating the manager's performance. Nevertheless, the statement, "the profit last month was $3,000," is, by itself, not very informative. There is a need for some criterion by which the $3,000 can be judged to represent good, bad, or indifferent performance.

In almost every case we have some criteria which are used implicitly, if not explicitly—the profit last month, the profit for the same month last year, the profit for a company or department of similar size. An argument can be made that the use of return on investment is an attempt to put profit performance on a more universally comparable basis. The concept of investment is applicable across companies and profit per dollar of investment has meaning in and of itself. Even with the use of ROI, most financial statements prepared for internal use show figures for "this month," "year-to-date," "this month last year," and "year-to-date last year." Financial statements of publicly held companies also show figures for both the current and previous year to provide a base point for evaluation of current performance.

THE BENCHMARK

Although measures of past performance are widely used as benchmarks or as evaluation criteria, they are not the only criteria which can be used, nor

This technical note was prepared by Professors Neil C. Churchill and John K. Shank.

are they always the best basis for evaluating performance. An alternative which requires more sophistication and managerial judgment is to use a measure of *expected performance*. Such a figure could be something as simple as last year's profit, last year's profit plus 10 percent or last year's profit plus $20,000. It could also be, for a cost center, a carefully thought through set of standard costs at each possible level of activity. For a business as a whole, it could be a one-year profit plan—a detailed profit budget.

Whatever the nature of the activity and however sophisticated the analysis, the essence of this approach is to establish a target level of expected results and then to compare actual performance with this expectation. Such a comparison provides a picture not only of what actually happened but also of how actual results differed from what was expected and by how much.

MANAGING AGAINST EXPECTATIONS

The comparison of actual performance against target provides management with a guide as to which areas of activity warrant investigation and which ones seem to be going essentially as planned and thus can probably be safely ignored for the moment. This is a basic application of the technique of *management by exception* which is an essential ingredient of any formal management system for allocating the time of managers to those areas that most need attention.

The efficacy of any system for managing against expectations depends, of course, on the appropriateness of the expectations used as the benchmarks for comparison. The more dependable the benchmarks and the more closely they fit the nature of the activity, the greater the reliance that can be placed on the difference (variance, in the accountant's terminology) between actual and expected results. With highly dependable benchmarks, such as engineered standards for routinely produced components, relatively small variances from standard can be cause for immediate investigation. On the other end of the scale, it would be rather inappropriate to compare the actual profits of a new division or product line with profits planned a year before and conclude that small differences are good and large differences are bad. The causal factors are not well enough understood and the methods for putting them together are not tested enough to allow such dependence on simple comparisons. Rather the detailed assumptions underlying the estimates need to be examined and compared to what really occurred before any conclusions can be drawn. In such cases, analysis of the difference between actual and expected results is but a *starting point* for developing an understanding of what really occurred, determining the implications for the company, and assessing the performance of those in charge.

ANALYZING DIFFERENCES

There is a methodology for analyzing business activities in order to better understand the differences between actual and expected results. This methodology is often referred to as "analysis of variances." It involves nothing more than starting with an overall difference between actual and expected performance and then "peeling the onion," one layer at a time, to obtain more and more detailed explanations for the differences between what happened and what was expected to happen. With relatively imprecise or uncertain information on either what happened or what was expected, the "peeling" might stop early, focusing instead on a more informal approach. When more complete data are available, when expectations are held with more confidence, and when there is greater understanding of the underlying activity, the formal analysis can be more extensive.

Like any technique, analyzing differences must involve considerable judgment. Thus what is needed is:

1. A description, in accounting terms, of what happened and a description in the same terms of what was expected—even if the criteria being used as "expectations" is only what happened last year rather than a carefully thought through concept of what "ought to be."
2. A realization that the process is designed to produce insight. It will not produce *answers* and should be applied with a healthy dose of management judgment.

The methodology of managing against expectations can best be explored through a series of increasingly more detailed examples, each of which involves more detailed accounting information and more analytic rigor. The same sample will be used throughout the exposition, but previously undisclosed detailed data will be added at each succeeding level.

The most crude form of a profit variance analysis is as follows:

Expected profits........	$3,000	
Actual profits..........	3,045	
Profit variance	$ 45	Favorable

The first level of analysis (level 0) identifies the fact that actual profits were $45, or 1.5 percent more than expected. Exploring the situation a bit further, we could expand the analysis as follows:

Level 1

	Expected	Actual	Difference	
Revenues	$10,000	$11,025	$1,025	favorable
Expenses......	7,000	7,980	980	unfavorable
Profit*	$ 3,000	$ 3,045	$ 45	

* We will use the terms *profits* and *earnings* interchangeably.

Here we see a substantial favorable variance in revenues of $1,025 (10.3 percent) which is largely offset by an unfavorable expense variance of $980 (14.0 percent). This illustrates one danger in stopping too soon—what appears to be a small total variance may actually be the result of larger but offsetting differences. We will deem as *level 1* an analysis which compares, on as detailed a basis as desired, actual and expected performance for the various line items in the earnings statement. This is an important first step, but it is only a first step.

Level 2

The next level of variance analysis is to attempt to isolate the effects of changes in the level of business activity from the effects associated with changes in prices, costs, or operating efficiencies. The most useful way to carry this out is to use the concept of a *flexible or variable budget*. This is simply an intermediate evaluation criterion of what our profit expectations would have been if we could have precisely predicted what the actual level of activity would be—as though we had perfect foresight with respect to sales volume and sales mix.

To our example we add the flexible budget column and expand the detail of expenses to separate variable cost of sales from the relatively fixed period costs. This latter step is not essential but simplifies the presentation.

	(1) Original expected performance		(2) Flexible budget (actual volume and actual mix)		(3) Actual results	
Sales........	2,000 units @ $5	$10,000	2,100 units	$10,350*	2,100 units @ $5.25	$11,025
Variable cost of sales....	2,000 units @ $3	6,000	2,100 units @ $3	6,300	2,100 units @ $3.29	6,910
Period costs..		1,000		1,000		1,070
Total costs ..		7,000		7,300		7,980
Profit		$ 3,000		$ 3,050		$ 3,045

* The $10,350 consists of 1,320 units of one product, at standard sale price, and 780 units of a second product, also at standard price. The resulting average price is not quite $5 due to the fact that the actual mix of sales between the two products differs from the planned mix. This is analyzed in level 3 below.

This way of looking at what happened indicates that profits were $50 greater than originally expected because of the higher level of sales activity. This is column (2) versus column (1), where only the volume of units sold varies. Standard costs and standard prices are still used. The fact that actual profits were $5 less than the flexible budget of $3,050 indicates that at the actual activity level, price increases did not offset increases in costs. Prices were $675 above plan ($11,025 − $10,350) while expenses were $680 above plan ($7,980 − $7,300). Of course, price and volume are not independent; it is conceivable that more units could have been sold if prices had been raised less. If this had occurred, the favorable sale price variance would have been reduced and the variance due to sales volume would have increased. Even with this lack of independence, isolating volume effects from other factors is important in understanding and evaluating what has occurred.

To review so far, the level 1 analysis compares what actually happened to some expectation of what should have happened. The level 2 analysis elaborates the comparison, breaking the total difference into two parts by saying "what would my benchmark have been if I had perfect knowledge of what the level of activity would be"—the flexible budget. With this concept, the difference between the original expectation and the flexible budget can only represent sales activity differences since expected prices and expected costs are used in both measures. Differences between the flexible budget and actual results can only be due to cost and price differences since the level of sales activity (volume and mix) is the same in both measures. This separation of sales activity-related variances from cost/price-related variances is both powerful in itself and fundamental to the analysis which follows.

Level 3

The cost/price and sales activity variances can each be analyzed further. For the sales activity variance, this involves a split into the part due to volume changes and the part due to a changed composition or mix of the items sold. For the cost/price variance, level 3 involves splitting out the sales price variance from the cost variances and decomposing the cost variances by cost categories.

   Sales activity differences.   If the company sold only one product in one size, the sales activity variance of $50 calculated above would be due entirely to sales volume changes. If, however, more than one product is sold, the difference can be composed of both overall sales volume changes and change in the *mix* or relative amounts of the different products sold. Consider the following extension of our example.

Expected sales

Product	Units	Price per unit	Revenue
A	1,200 (60%)	$4.00	$ 4,800
B	800 (40%)	6.50	5,200
Total......	2,000		$10,000

Actual sales

Product	Units	Price per unit	Revenue
A	1,320 (63%)	$4.40	$ 5,808
B	780 (37%)	6.688	5,217
Total......	2,100		$11,025

   Using these data, we can decompose the sales activity variance into two parts by introducing a new intermediate column. This column shows expected profits with sales at 2100 units but in the same proportions as originally expected (product A sales = 60% or 1260 units, and product B = 40%, or 840 units). These numbers would lead to expected profits of $3,200. This is shown as follows:

	(1)			(2)		(3)	
	Original expected performance			Revised budget at actual volume with standard mix		Flexible budget (actual volume and actual mix)	
Sales	2,000 units @ $5	$10,000		2,100 units @ $5	$10,500*	2,100 units	$10,350
Variable cost of sales	2,000 units @ $3	6,000		2,100 units @ $3	6,300	2,100 units @ $3	6,300
Period costs ...		1,000			1,000		1,000
Total costs		7,000			7,300		7,300
Profit		$ 3,000			$ 3,200		$ 3,050

*Product	Units	Price per unit	Revenue
A	1,260	$4.00	$ 5,040
B	840	6.50	5,460
	2,100		$10,500

If we compare column (2) with column (3), we get a difference due entirely to product mix that is $150 unfavorable. The variance due solely to sales volume (assuming no variation in mix), is $200 favorable. This is shown in column (1) versus column (2). The net of these two is the $50 F shown at level 2. You should note that expected costs and expected prices are used in all three columns.

Cost/price differences. The sales price variance is just actual sales units × expected prices versus actual sales units × actual prices. This comparison, as shown on page 110, is $10,350 versus $11,025 or $675 favorable.

The expense differences isolated earlier were:

	Expected costs (flexible budget)	Actual costs	Cost differences
Variable costs........	$6,300	$6,910	$610 U
Period costs	1,000	1,070	70 U
Total	$7,300	$7,980	$680 U

Further analysis of the cost differences can be made if additional information is available on the nature of the costs incurred.

Consider the following expected costs for products A and B in our example:[1]

Variable cost per unit:	
Labor: 0.3 hrs. at $5 per hour..................	$ 1.50
Material and supplies: 0.5 units at $2 per unit	1.00
Other variable costs	.50
Total variable costs, per unit.....................	$ 3.00
Other expenses, fixed, per period	$1,000

---

[1] In a typical company, different products would have different expected costs. Thus, the flexible budget for expenses would involve mix considerations as well as volume. For this analysis we will ignore the mix factor, believing it to be sufficiently well illustrated in the revenue section to permit its application to costs. We will consider products A and B as costing the same—but sold in different markets.

With this detail, the flexible budget at 2100 units of activity would be:

```
Labor: 0.3 per hr. per unit × 2,100 units = 630 hrs. @ $5/hr. .....   $3,150
Material: 0.5 units per unit × 2,100 units = 1050 @ $2/unit .....      2,100
Other variable costs: $.50 per unit × 2,100 units ..............      1,050
Period costs .........................................                1,000
         Total flexible budget  ...............................      $7,300
```

Let us further extend the example by assuming that the expenses actually incurred were as follows:

```
Labor:   Labor: 580 hours at $5.50 per hr. .........   $3,190
         Material: 1,120 units at $2.30 per unit .....  2,576
         Other variable costs ...................       1,144
         Period costs ..........................        1,070
                                                       $7,980
```

With this more detailed information, the variance analysis can separate out at level 3 the labor, material, and overhead differences as follows:

	Flexible budget	Actual	Difference
Labor..................	$3,150	$3,190	$ 40 U
Material................	2,100	2,576	476 U
Variable overhead	1,050	1,144	94 U
Period costs............	1,000	1,070	70 U
Total	$7,300	$7,980	$680 U

Level 4

The last level we will examine involves decomposing the sales mix variance by products and evaluating the impact of market position on sales volume changes. For cost/price variance, it involves decomposing the sales price variance by products and the cost variance by efficiency-in-use versus purchase price changes.

Sales mix variance. The overall $150 sales mix variance can be broken down by product as follows:

Product	Flexible budget–units	Actual units	Difference– units	Expected profit contribution/unit	Mix variance
A	1,260 (60%)	1,320 (63%)	60	$1.00	$ 60 F
B.....	840 (40%)	780 (37%)	(−60)	3.50	210 U
Total	2,100 (100%)	2,100 (100%)	0		$150 U

Note that the total difference in units must be zero because we are concerned only with the profit difference due to sales mix fluctuations at the actual sales volume level. As can be seen in the example, the unfavorable performance is the result of selling fewer units of the high margin product (product B) than would be expected at an overall volumn level of 105 percent of plan. When several products are involved, the mix variance results are not as obvious as they are here.

Sales volume variance. In looking closer at the $200 F sales volume variance, let us assume that the company has traditionally had an 8 percent share of the market and expects this to be the case in the current period during which the market was expected to be approximately 25,000 units. This would produce the original expectation of $4,000 of profit contribution (25,000 × 8% × $2 per unit).[2] If the market increased to 28,000 units while the company's sales went up to 2,100 units, the company's market share was actually only 7.5 percent. This interplay between the company's growth and that of the market it serves can be usefully analyzed as follows:

(a) Change in expected profit due to market size change
= (Expected total market − Actual total market) × (Expected market share) × (Expected profit contribution per unit at expected mix)
= (25,000 − 28,000) × 8% × $2
= $480 F[3]

That is, the profit should have gone up by $480 due just to change in the size of the overall market. If the company could have maintained its market share, its expected profit in a 28,000 unit market would have been $4,480. It did not, however, and the effect of the decrease in market share is as follows:

(b) Market share variance
= (Expected market share − Actual market share) × (Actual market volume) × (Expected profit contribution per unit at expected mix)
= (.08 − .075) × (28,000 units) × $2.00 per unit
= $280 U[4]

This is the profit lost because of a decrease in market share. The combined result from volume and share changes ($480 − $280) is the total sales volume variance of $200 F shown at level 3.

Sales price variance. The sales price variance, as calculated at level 3, was $675 favorable. This can be detailed as follows:

Product	Expected price	Actual price	Unit price difference	Actual units	Sales price variance
A	$4.00	$4.40	$.40	1,320	$528 F
B	6.50	6.688	.188	780	147 F
Total.......				2,100	$675 F

---

[2] Sales price of $5 less expected variable cost of $3, at the expected mix.
[3] Representing $1,200 of sales at expected prices, less $720 of expected variable costs.
[4] $700 in sales, at expected prices, less $420 in expected variable costs.

Cost variances. On the cost side the analysis can proceed further by separating out the efficiency-in-use element from the purchase price element for each cost component. This separation is almost universally calculated in the following way:[5]

Purchase price difference = (Expected price − Actual price) ×
× Actual quantity used

$$= (P_E - P_A) \times Q_A$$

Efficiency-in-use difference = (Expected quantity − Actual quantity) ×
× Expected price

$$= (Q_E - Q_A) \times P_E$$

Thus, in our example we would have, by cost element:

Labor price variance	= ($5 − $5.50) × 580	= $290 U
Labor efficiency variance	= (630 − 580) × $5	= 250 F
Total labor variance shown at level 3		= $ 40 U

This is the difference between the flexible budget figure of $3,150 and the actual labor cost of $3,190. Similarly for materials:

Material price variance	= ($2.00 − $2.30) × 1,120	= $336 U
Material efficiency variance	= (1,050 − 1,120) × $2.00	= 140 U
Total material variance shown at level 3		$476 U

We could summarize this analysis differently, by nature of the variance, as follows:

Efficiency variances	
Labor	$250 F
Material	140 U
Subtotal	$110 F
Purchase price variances	
Labor	$290 U
Material	336 U
Subtotal	626 U
Other (variable $94, period $70)	164 U
Total expense difference	$680 U

Which method of looking at the cost variances is "better" depends on what actions caused them. While labor efficiency was very good, the labor

---

[5] This reconciles the total difference, as can be seen by multiplying out the two equations and adding them together:

$$\text{Purchase price variance} = P_E Q_A - P_A Q_A$$
$$+$$
$$\text{Efficiency variance} = P_E Q_E - P_E Q_A$$
$$=$$
$$\text{Total variance} = P_E Q_E - P_A Q_A$$

rate or "price" increase more than offset the benefits. If this was due to substituting more efficient but higher priced labor for that normally used, then showing labor rate and efficiency variances together (or even not separating them at all) could be more useful. If, on the other hand, purchase price increases produced pressure to really use workers and material efficiently, then showing the data by type of variance is useful for it reveals that expenses were $626 more than expected, due to price increases. After adding in the spending variances on other costs ($164) the total was $115 ($790 − $675) more than could be passed on via sales price increases. The methodology is the same; which format is preferable depends upon managerial judgment.

In summary

We started with actual profit performance of $3,045 in a period and found first that it was $45 more than expected. Then we looked a bit deeper and found that profit was $50 better because of increased sales volume but $5 worse because of increased costs of operation that were not passed on in higher sales prices. Pulling out all stops, we finally determined that the situation was much more complex.

The overall market grew by 3,000 units more than planned (28,000 units versus 25,000). This should have yielded a $480 F profit variance in the period However, market share slipped .5 percent which caused a $280 U profit variance. Furthermore, the sales mix included a higher than planned proportion of the low margin product and this led to a $150 U profit variance. Cost performance was also unfavorable. Materials variance was $40 U, labor variance $476 U, other variable costs variance $94 U, and period cost spending variances $70 U. Considering all these negative factors, the overall profit variance was favorable by $45 only because of $675 in sales price increases. A much different picture is thus presented than that suggested by the simple statement that profits were $45 higher than expected.

This multi-level analysis is illustrated in summary form in Exhibit 1. Further levels could, of course, be added if desired. The overall market change could be decomposed into economy-wide factors and industry specific factors. The market share change could be broken down by products. The sales mix variance could be decomposed by geographic region or customer class. Sales price changes could be decomposed into "list price" changes and discount changes (either early payment discounts or quantity discounts). Cost variances could be broken into controllable and noncontrollable segments by responsibility centers. The analysis can stop any time the next level does not produce useful enough management information.

The discussion has focused on a manufacturing firm with two products. The concept is equally applicable in retail, financial or service organizations. The focus is a separation of sales activity-related and cost/price-related

EXHIBIT 1 Explaining profit variations (a sequential analysis approach)

Level 0

Expected profit = $3,000
Actual profit   = 3,045
Variance   = $ 45 F

Level 1

	Expected	Actual	Variance
Sales revenue	$10,000	$11,025	$1,025 F
Costs	7,000	7,980	980 U
Profit	$ 3,000	$ 3,045	$ 45 F

Overall variance = $45 F

Level 2

Variance due to level of sales activity

Original expected performance ... $3,000
Flexible budget ... 3,050
Difference ... $ 50 F

Variance due to cost/price changes

Flexible budget ... $3,050
Actual results ... 3,045
Difference ... $ 5 U

Level 3

Difference due to sales volume

Original expectation ... $3,000
Expected profit at actual volume with standard mix ... 3,200
Difference ... $ 200 F

Difference due to sales mix

Expected profit at actual volume with standard mix ... $3,200
Flexible budget ... 3,050
Difference ... $ 150 U

Product A ... $ 60 F
Product B ... 210 U

Sales price variance

Expected sales at actual volume and mix ... $10,350
Actual sales ... 11,025
Difference ... $ 675 F

Product A ... $528 F
Product B ... 147 F

Cost variances

Labor ... $ 40 U
Materials ... 476 U
Other variable costs ... 94 U
Period costs ... 70 U
Difference ... $680 U

Efficiency variances ... $110 F
Purchase price variances ... 626 U
Overhead variances ... 164 U
Difference ... $680 U

Level 4

Difference due to overall market changes

$480 F

Difference due to market share changes

$280 U

• • •

Level 5

• • •

differences from expectations. Decomposing the profit variance one level at a time is a very powerful management tool. Understanding the specific impact of the various factors is the first step in undertaking appropriate corrective actions.

——∙CASE II-5∙——

Midwest Ice Cream Company

Frank Roberts, marketing vice president of Midwest Ice Cream Company, was pleased when he saw the final earnings statement for the company for 1973 (see Exhibit 1). He knew that it had been a good year for Midwest, but he hadn't expected the results to be quite this good.

Only the year before the company had installed a new financial planning and control system. This was then the first year that figures comparing budgeted and actual results were available. Jim Peterson, president of Midwest, had asked Frank to make a short presentation at the next board of directors meeting commenting on the major reasons for the favorable operating income variance of $71,700. He asked him to draft his presentation in the next few days so that the two of them could go over it before the Board meeting. Mr. Peterson wanted to illustrate to the board how an analysis of the profit variance could highlight those areas needing management attention as well as those deserving of a pat on the back.

The financial planning and control system at Midwest Ice Cream

The following description of the financial planning and control system which was installed at Midwest in 1972 is taken from an internal company operating manual:

THE PLANNING FUNCTION

The beginning point in making a profit plan is separating cost into fixed and variable categories. Some costs are pure variable and as such will require an additional amount with each increase in volume levels. The manager has little control over this type of cost other than to avoid waste. The accountant can

---

This case was prepared by Associate Professor John K. Shank and William J. Rauwerdink, Research Assistant.

EXHIBIT 1

MIDWEST ICE CREAM COMPANY
Earnings Statement
December 31, 1973

Month			Year to date	
Actual	**Budget**		**Actual**	**Budget**
		Sales—net	$9,657,300	$9,645,300
		Manufacturing cost of goods sold		
		Schedule A–2*	6,824,900	6,725,900
		Delivery—Schedule A–3	706,800	760,800
		Advertising—Schedule A–4	607,700	578,700
		Selling—Schedule A–5	362,800	368,800
		Administrative—Schedule A–7	438,000	448,000
		Total expenses	8,940,200	8,882,200
		Income from operations	717,100	763,100
		Other income—Schedule A–8	12,500	12,500
		Other expense—Schedule A–9	6,000	6,000
		Income before taxes	723,600	769,600
		Provision for income taxes	361,800	
		Net earnings	361,800	

Analysis of variance from forecasted operating income

Month			Year to date	
		(1) Actual income from operations	$717,100	
		(2) Budgeted profit at forecasted volume	645,400	
		(3) Budgeted profit at actual volume	763,100	
		Variance due to sales volume— [(3) minus (2)]	117,700 F	
		Variance due to operations— [(1) minus (3)]	46,000 U	
		Total variance—[(1) minus (2)]	$ 71,700 F	

* Schedules A–3 through A–9 have not been included in this case. Schedule A–2 is reproduced as Exhibit 2.

easily determine the variable manufacturing cost per unit for any given product or package by using current prices and yield records. Variable marketing cost per unit is based on the allowable rate, for example 6 cents per gallon for advertising. Costs that are not pure variable are classified as fixed, but they, too, will vary if significant changes in volume occur. There will be varying degrees of sensitivity to volume changes among these costs, ranging from a point just short of pure variable to an extremely fixed type of expense which has no relationship to volume. The reason for differentiating between fixed and variable so emphatically is because a variable type cost requires no decision as to when to add or take off a unit; it is dictated by volume. Fixed costs on the other hand require a management judgment and decision to increase or decrease the cost. Sugar is an example of a pure variable cost. Each change in volume will automatically bring a change in the sugar cost; only the yield can be controlled. Route salesmen's salaries would be an example of a fixed cost that is fairly sensitive to volume, but not pure variable. As volume changes, pressure will be felt to increase or decrease this expense, but management must make the decision; the change in cost level is not automatic. Depreciation charges for plant would be an example of a relatively extreme fixed cost in that large increases in volume can usually be realized before this type of cost is pressured to change. In both cases, the fixed cost requires a decision from management to increase or decrease the cost. It is this dilemma that management is constantly facing; to withstand the pressure to increase or be ready to decrease when the situation demands it. It would be a mistake to set a standard variable cost for items like route salesmen's salaries or depreciation based on past performance, because they must constantly be evaluated for better and more efficient methods of doing the task.

The first step in planning, then, is to develop a unit standard cost for each element of variable cost by product and package size. Examples of four different products and/or packages are shown in Step 1. As already pointed out, the accountant can do this by using current prices and yield records for material costs and current allowance rates for marketing costs. Advertising is the only cost element not fitting the explanation of a variable cost given in the preceding

STEP 1
Establish standards for selling price, variable expenses, and marginal contribution per gallon (vanilla ice cream)

	Regular			Premium
Item	One-gallon paper container	One-gallon plastic container	Two-gallon paper container	One-gallon plastic container
Dairy ingredients	.53	.53	.53	.79
Sugar	.15	.15	.15	.15
Flavor	.10	.10	.105	.12
Production	.10	.16	.125	.16
Warehouse	.06	.08	.07	.08
Transportation	.02	.025	.02	.025
Total manufacturing	.96	1.045	1.00	1.325
Advertising	.06	.06	.06	.06
Delivery	.04	.04	.04	.04
Total marketing	.10	.10	.10	.10
Total	1.06	1.145	1.10	1.425
Selling price	1.50	1.70	1.45	2.40
Marginal contribution/before packaging	.44	.555	.35	.975
Packaging	.10	.25	.085	.25
Marginal contribution/gallon	.34	.305	.265	.725

paragraph. Advertising costs are set by management decision rather than being an automatic cost item like sugar or packaging. In this sense, advertising is just route salesmen's expense. For our company, however, management has decided that the allowance for advertising expense is equal to 6 cents per gallon for the actual number of gallons sold. This management decision, therefore, has transformed advertising into an expense which is treated as variable for profit planning. After the total unit variable cost has been developed, this amount is subtracted from the selling price to arrive at a marginal contribution per unit, by product and package type. At any level of volume, it is easy to determine the contribution that should be generated to cover the fixed costs and provide profits. This will be illustrated in Step 4.

Step 2 is perhaps the most critical of all the phases in making a profit plan, because all plans are built around the anticipated level of sales activity. Much thought should be given in forecasting a realistic sales level and product mix. Consideration should be given to the number of days in a given period, as well as to the number of Fridays and Mondays, as these are two of the heaviest days and will make a difference in the sales forecast.

STEP 2
Vanilla ice cream sales forecast (000 gallons)

	January	February	...	December	Total
One gallon—paper	100	100	...	100	1,200
One gallon—plastic	50	50	...	50	600
Two gallon—paper	225	225	...	225	2,700
One gallon (premium)	120	120	...	120	1,440
Total..............	495	495	...	495	5,940

Other factors that should be considered are:

1. General economic condition of the marketing area.
2. Weather.
3. Anticipated promotions.
4. Competition.

Step 3 involves the setting of fixed cost budgets based on management's judgment as to the need in light of the sales forecast. It is here that good planning makes for a profitable operation. The number of routes needed for both winter and summer volume are planned. The level of manufacturing payroll is set.[1] Insurance and taxes are budgeted, and so on. After Step 4 has been performed, it may be necessary to return to Step 3 and make adjustments to some of the costs that are discretionary in nature.

---

[1] Because this system is based on a one-year time frame, manufacturing labor is considered to be a fixed cost. The level of the manufacturing work force is not really variable until a time frame longer than one year is adopted.

STEP 3
Budget fixed expenses

	January	February	...	December	Total
Manufacturing expense					
Labor.................	$ 7,280	$ 7,280	...	$ 7,920	$ 88,000
Equipment repair.......	3,332	3,332	...	3,348	40,000
Depreciation...........	6,668	6,668	...	6,652	80,000
Taxes.................	3,332	3,332	...	3,348	40,000
Total	20,612	20,612	...	21,268	248,000
Delivery expense					
Salaries—general.......	10,000	10,000	...	10,000	120,000
Salaries—drivers	10,668	10,668	...	10,652	128,000
Helpers	10,668	10,668	...	10,652	128,000
Supplies..............	668	668	...	652	8,000
Total	32,004	32,004	...	31,956	384,000
Administrative expense					
Salaries	5,167	5,167	...	5,163	62,000
Insurance	1,667	1,667	...	1,663	20,000
Taxes................	1,667	1,667	...	1,663	20,000
Depreciation...........	833	833	...	837	10,000
Total	9,334	9,334	...	9,326	112,000
Selling expense					
Repairs	2,667	2,667	...	2,663	32,000
Gasoline	5,000	5,000	...	5,000	60,000
Salaries	5,000	5,000	...	5,000	60,000
Total	12,667	12,667	...	12,663	152,000

Step 4 is the profit plan itself. By combining our marginal contribution developed in Step 1 with our sales forecast, we arrive at a total marginal contribution by month. Subtracting the fixed cost budgeted in Step 3, we have an operating profit by months. As mentioned above, if this profit figure is not sufficient, then a new evaluation should be made of the fixed costs developed in Step 3.

The following four tables illustrate each of the four planning steps for a hypothetical ice cream plant.

THE CONTROL FUNCTION

To illustrate the control system, we will take the month of January and assume the level of sales activity for the month to be 520,000 gallons, as shown in Exhibit A. Looking back to our sales forecast (Step 2) we see that 495,000 gallons had been forecasted. When we apply our marginal contribution per unit for each product and package, we find that the 520,000 gallons have produced $6,125 less standard contribution than the 495,000 gallons would have produced at the forecasted mix. So even though there has been a nice increase in sales volume, the mix has been unfavorable. The $6,125 represents the difference between standard profit contribution at forecasted volume and standard profit contribution at actual volume. It is thus due to differences in volume and to differences

STEP 4
The profit plan

	Marginal contribution (see Step 1)	Gallons sold	January	February	. . .	December	Total
One gallon—paper.	.34	100,000	$ 34,000	$ 34,000	. . .	$ 34,000	$ 408,000
One gallon—plastic.	.305	50,000	15,250	15,250	. . .	15,250	183,000
Two gallon—paper.	.265	225,000	59,625	59,625	. . .	59,625	715,500
One gallon—premium.	.725	120,000	87,000	87,000	. . .	87,000	1,044,000
Total marginal contribution.			195,875	195,875	. . .	195,875	2,350,500
Fixed cost (see Step 3)							
Manufacturing expense.			20,612	20,612	. . .	21,268	248,000
Delivery expense			32,004	32,004	. . .	31,956	384,000
Administrative expense			9,334	9,334	. . .	9,326	112,000
Selling expense			12,667	12,667	. . .	12,663	152,000
Total fixed			74,617	74,617	. . .	75,213	896,000
Operating profit.			121,258	121,258	. . .	120,662	1,454,500
Income tax			60,629	60,629	. . .	60,331	727,250
Net profit			$ 60,629	$ 60,629	. . .	$ 60,331	$ 727,250

EXHIBIT A
January

	Actual gallon sales (000)	Standard contribution per gallon	Total standard contribution
One gallon—paper..........	90	.340	$ 30,600
One gallon—plastic	95	.305	28,975
Two gallon—paper	245	.265	64,925
One gallon—premium........	90	.725	65,250
Total	520		189,750

Forecast (Step 2): 495,000 gallons

Forecasted marginal contribution (at 495,000 gallons) 195,875
Over (under) forecast................................. (6,125)

	Planned	Actual
Gallons	495,000	520,000
Contribution	$195,875	$189,750
Average per gallon	.3957	.3649
Difference		$.0308

Variance due to volume:
25,000 gallons × $.3957 = $9,892 F
Variance due to mix:
$.0308 × 520,000 gallons = 16,017 U
Total variance = 6,125 U

EXHIBIT B
Manufacturing cost of goods sold, January

Month		Item	Year to date	
Actual	Budget		Actual	Budget
$312,744	$299,000	Dairy ingredients		
82,304	78,000	Sugar		
56,290	55,025	Flavorings		
38,770	37,350	Warehouse		
70,300	69,225	Production		
11,514	11,325	Transportation		
571,922	549,925	Subtotal—variable		
7,300	7,280	Labor		
4,065	3,332	Equipment repair		
6,668	6,668	Depreciation		
3,332	3,332	Taxes		
21,365	20,612	Subtotal—fixed		
$593,287	$570,537	Total		

in average mix. The impact of each of these two factors is shown on the bottom of Exhibit A.

Exhibit B shows a typical departmental budget sheet comparing Actual with Budget. A sheet is issued for each department so the person responsible for a particular area of the business can see the items that are in lines and those that need his attention. In our example, there is an unfavorable operating variance of $22,750. You should note that the budget for variable cost items has been adjusted to reflect actual volume, thereby eliminating wide cost variances due strictly to the difference between planned and actual volume.

Since the level of fixed costs is independent of volume anyway, it is not necessary to adjust the budget for these items for volume differences. The original budget for fixed cost items is still appropriate. The totals for each department are carried forward to an earnings statement, Exhibit C. We have assumed all other departments' Actual and Budget are in line, so the only operating variance is the one for manufacturing. This variance added to the sales volume and· mix variance of $6,125 results in an overall variance from the original plan of $28,875, as shown at the bottom of Exhibit C.

EXHIBIT C
Earnings statement, January

Month		Item	Year to date	
Actual	*Budget*		*Actual*	*Budget*
$867,750	$867,750	Total ice cream sales		
593,287	570,537	Manufacturing cost of goods sold		
52,804	52,804	Delivery expense		
31,200	31,200	Advertising expense		
76,075	76,075	Packaging expense		
12,667	12,667	Selling expense		
9,334	9,334	Adminstrative expense		
775,367	752,617	Total expense		
92,383	115,133	Profit or loss		
46,192	—	Provision for income taxes		
$46,191	—	Net profit (loss)		

Actual profit before taxes .... $ 92,383   (1)
Original profit forecast (Step 4)   121,258   (2)
Revised profit forecast based on actual volume   115,133   (3)

$$\begin{array}{cc} (2) & -(3) \end{array}$$
Variance due to volume and mix (unfavorable) ..... $ 121,258 - 115,133 = \$ 6,125 \text{ U}$

$$\begin{array}{cc} (3) & -(1) \end{array}$$
Variance due to operations (unfavorable) .... $ 115,133 - 92,383 = 22,750 \text{ U}$

$$\begin{array}{cc} (2) & (1) \end{array}$$
Total variance .... $(121,258 - 92,383) = \$28,875 \text{ U}$

The illustration here has been on a monthly basis, but there is no need to wait until the end of the month to see what is happening. Each week, sales can be multiplied by the contribution factor to see how much standard contribution has been generated. This can be converted to one fourth of the monthly forecasted contribution to sales if volume and mix are in line with forecast. Neither is it necessary to wait until the end of the month to see if expenses are in line. Weekly reports of such items as production or sugar can be made, comparing Budget with Actual. By combining the variances as shown on weekly reports, and adjusting the forecasted profit figure, an approximate profit figure can be had long before the books are closed and monthly statements issued. More important, action can be taken to correct an undesirable situation much sooner.

THE PROFIT PLAN FOR 1973

Following the four-step approach outlined above, the management group of Midwest Ice Cream prepared a profit plan for 1973. The timetable they followed was as follows:

		October 1972 (weeks) 1 2 3 4	November 1972 (weeks) 1 2 3 4
I	Variable cost standards....................	X	
II–A	Sales forecast	X	
II–B	Approval of sales forecast	X	
III–A	Preliminary payroll budget..................	X	
III–B	Preliminary budget for other operating expenses..........................	X	
III–C	Approval of payroll budget and other expenses budget	X	
IV–A	Preliminary profit plan		X
IV–B	Approval of profit plan.....................		X
IV–C	Board of Directors meeting		X

Based on an anticipated overall ice cream market of about 11,440,000 gallons in their marketing area and a market share of 50 percent, Midwest forecasted overall gallon sales of 5,720,329 for 1973. Actually, this forecast was the same as the latest estimate of 1972 actual gallon sales.[2] Rather than trying to get too sophisticated on the first attempt at budgeting, Mr. Peterson had decided to just go with 1972's volume as 1973's goal or forecast. He felt that there was plenty of time in later years to refine the system by bringing in more formal sales forecasting techniques and concepts.

---

[2] Since the 1973 budget was being done in October 1972, final figures for 1972 were not yet available. The latest revised estimate of actual gallon volume for 1972 was thus used.

This same general approach was also followed for variable product standard costs and for fixed costs. Budgeted costs for 1973 were just expected 1972 results, adjusted for a few items which were clearly out of line in 1972. A summary of the profit plan for 1973 is shown below:

Profit plan for 1973:

	Standard contribution margin per gallon	Forecasted gallon sales	Forecasted contribution margin
Vanilla	$.4329	2,409,854	$1,043,200
Chocolate	.4535	2,009,061	911,100
Walnut	.5713	48,883	28,000
Buttercrunch	.4771	262,185	125,000
Cherry swirl	.5153	204,774	105,500
Strawberry	.4683	628,560	294,400
Pecan Chip	.5359	157,012	84,100
Total	$.4530	5,720,329	$2,591,300

Breakdown of budgeted total expenses:

	Variable	Fixed	Total
Manufacturing	$5,888,100	$ 612,800	$6,500,900
Delivery	187,300	516,300	703,600
Advertising	553,200	—	553,200
Selling	—	368,800	368,800
Administrative	—	448,000	448,000
Total	$6,628,600	$1,945,900	$8,574,500

Recap:	
Sales	$9,219,900
Variable cost of sales	6,628,600
Contribution margin	2,591,300
Fixed costs	1,945,900
Income from operations	$ 645,400

ACTUAL RESULTS FOR 1973

By the spring of 1973 it had become clear that sales volume for 1973 was going to be higher than forecast. In fact, Midwest's actual sales for the year totaled over 5,968,000 gallons, an increase of about 248,000 gallons over budget. Market research data indicated that the total ice cream market in Midwest's marketing area was 12,180,000 gallons for the year as opposed to the budgeted figure of about 11,440,000 gallons.

The revised profit plan for the year at the actual volume level is shown below:

Revised profit plan for 1973 (budgeted profit at actual volume):

	Standard contribution margin per gallon	*Actual gallon sales*	*Forecasted contribution margin*
Vanilla	$.4329	2,458,212	$1,064,200
Chocolate	.4535	2,018,525	915,400
Walnut	.5713	50,124	28,600
Buttercrunch	.4771	268,839	128,300
Cherry swirl	.5153	261,240	134,600
Strawberry	.4683	747,049	349,800
Pecan Chip	.5359	164,377	88,100
Total	$.4539	5,968,366	2,709,000

Breakdown of budgeted total expenses:

	Variable	*Fixed*	*Total*
Manufacturing	$6,113,100	$ 612,800	$6,725,900
Delivery	244,500	516,300	760,800
Advertising	578,700	—	578,700
Selling	—	368,800	368,800
Administrative	—	448,000	448,000
Total	$6,936,300	$1,945,900	$8,882,200

Recap:	
Sales	$9,645,300
Variable costs of sales	6,936,300
Contribution margin	2,709,000
Fixed costs	1,945,900
Income from operations	$ 763,100

The fixed costs in the revised profit plan are the same as before, $1,945,900. The variable costs, however, have been adjusted to reflect a volume level of 5,968,000 gallons instead of 5,720,000 gallons, thereby eliminating wide cost variances due strictly to the difference between planned volume and actual volume. Assume, for example, that cartons are budgeted at 4 cents per gallon. If we forecast volume of 10,000 gallons the budget allowance for cartons is $400. If we actually sell only 8,000 gallons but use $350 worth of cartons, it is misleading to say that there is a avorable variance of $50. The variance is clearly unfavorable by $30. This only shows up if we adjust the budget to the actual volume level.

Carton allowance	$.04 per gallon
Forecast volume	10,000 gallons
Carton budget	$400
Actual volume	8,000 gallons
Actual carton expense	$350.
Variance (based on forecast volume)	$400 − $350 = $50 Favorable
Variance (based on actual volume)	$320 − $350 = $30 Unfavorable

For costs which are highly volume dependent, variances should be based on a budget which reflects the volume of operation actually attained. Since the level of fixed costs is independent of volume anyway, it is not necessary to adjust the budget for these items for volume differences. The original budget for fixed cost items is still appropriate.

Exhibit 1 referred to earlier is the earnings statement for the year. The figures for the month of December have been excluded for purposes of this case. Exhibit 2 is the detailed expense breakdown for the manufacturing

EXHIBIT 2

MIDWEST ICE CREAM COMPANY
Schedule A–2
Manufacturing Cost of Goods Sold
December 31, 1973

Month			Year to date	
Actual	*Budget*		*Actual*	*Budget*
		Variable costs:		
		Dairy ingredients	$3,679,900	$3,648,500
		Milk price variance	57,300	—
		Sugar	599,900	596,800
		Sugar price variance	23,400	—
		Flavoring (including fruits and nuts)	946,800	982,100
		Cartons	567,200	566,900
		Plastic wrap	28,700	29,800
		Additives	235,000	251,000
		Supplies	31,000	35,000
		Miscellaneous	3,000	3,000
		Subtotal	6,172,200	6,113,100
		Fixed costs:		
		Labor—cartonizing and freezing	425,200	390,800
		Labor—other	41,800	46,000
		Repairs	32,200	25,000
		Depreciation	81,000	81,000
		Electricity and water	41,500	40,000
		Miscellaneous	1,500	30,000
		Spoilage	29,500	
		Subtotal	652,700	612,800
		Total	$6,824,900	$6,725,900

department. The detailed expense breakdowns for the other departments have been excluded for purposes of this case.

ANALYSIS OF THE 1973 PROFIT VARIANCE

Three days after Jim Peterson asked Frank Roberts to pull together a presentation for the board of directors analyzing the profit variance for 1973, Frank came into Jim's office to review his first draft. He showed Jim the following schedule:

Favorable variance due to sales:		
Volume...............................	$117,700 F	
Price*	12,000 F	$129,700 F
Unfavorable variance due to operations:		
Manufacturing........................	99,000 U	
Delivery	54,000 F	
Advertising..........................	29,000 U	
Selling..............................	6,000 F	
Administration	10,000 F	58,000 U
Net variance—favorable		$ 71,700 F

* This price variance is the difference between the standard sales value of the gallons actually sold and the actual sales value (9,657,300 − 9,645,300).

Frank said that he planned to give each member of the board of directors a copy of this schedule and then to comment briefly on each of the items. Jim Peterson said he thought the schedule was okay as far as it went, but that it just didn't highlight things in a manner which indicated what corrective actions should be taken in 1974 or which indicated the real causes for the favorable overall variance. He suggested that Frank try to break down the sales volume variance into the part attributable to sales mix, the part attributable to market share shifts, and the part actually attributable to volume changes. He also suggested breaking down the manufacturing variance to indicate what main corrective actions are called for in 1974 to erase the unfavorable variance. How much of the total was due to price differences versus quantity differences, for example. Finally, he suggested that Frank call on John Vance, the company controller, if he needed some help in the mechanics of breaking out these different variances.

As Frank Roberts returned to his office he considered Jim Peterson's suggestion of getting John Vance involved in revising the schedule to be presented to the board. Frank did not want to consult John Vance unless it was absolutely necessary because Vance always went overboard on the technical aspects of any accounting problem. Frank couldn't imagine a quicker way to put the board members to sleep than to throw one of Vance's number-filled, six-page memos at them. Jim Peterson specifically wants a nontechnical presentation for the board, Frank thought to himself, and that rules out John Vance. Besides, he thought, you don't have to be a

CPA to just focus in on the key variance areas from a general management viewpoint.

A telephone call to John Vance asking about any written materials dealing with mix variances and volume variances produced in the following day's mail the two-page excerpt from the company accounting manual which is reproduced as the Appendix. Armed with this excerpt and his common sense Frank Roberts dug in again to the task of preparing a nontechnical breakdown of the profit variance for the year.

APPENDIX

Step 1: Compute planned profit contribution

	Planned sales in units	Standard profit contribution per unit	Planned profit contribution
Product A	16,000	1.0152	$16,243
Product B	8,000	.9514	7,611
Product C	20,000	.8529	17,058
Product D	20,000	.7921	15,842
Product E	8,000	.7504	6,003
Product F	8,000	.9365	7,492
Total......	80,000		

Standard profit contribution at planned volume $70,249

Step 2: Compute standard profit contribution at actual volume

	Actual sales in units	Standard profit contribution per unit	Standard profit contribution
Product A	5,000	1.0152	$ 5,076
Product B........	5,000	.9514	4,757
Product C........	5,000	.8529	4,265
Product D	36,000	.7921	28,516
Product E........	28,000	.7504	21,011
Product F........	5,000	.9365	4,683
Total......	84,000		

Standard profit contribution at actual volume $68,308

Step 3: Compare planned standard contribution with actual standard contribution

From Step 1 ..... $70,249
From Step 2   68,308
Difference....... $ 1,941 Unfavorable

	Planned	Actual
Units	80,000	84,000
Standard Contribution	$70,249	$68,308
Average per unit	.879	.814
Difference..........	$ .065	Unfavorable

Step 4: Compute the volume and mix variances

Variance due to volume:

$$4,000 \text{ units} \times \$.879 = 3,512 \text{ F}$$

Variance due to mix:

$$\$.065 \times 84,000 \text{ units} = \frac{5,453 \text{ U}}{1,941 \text{ U}}$$

Total variance = 1,941 U = Mix variance + Volume variance

QUESTIONS

1. What changes, if any, would you make in the variance analysis schedule proposed by Frank Roberts?

2. Can the suggestions offered by Jim Peterson be incorporated without making the schedule "too technical" for the Board of Directors?

3. Indicate the corrective actions you would take for 1974, based on this profit variance analysis, if you were Jim Peterson. Also indicate those areas which deserve commendation for 1973 performance.

――――《CASE II-6》――――

Hanson Industries (A)

Alden B. (Denny) Hanson, president, reviewed the fiscal year (FY) 1978 results, and reflected on the dynamic growth of Hanson Industries since its founding in 1970.[1] A unique and successful concept of ski boot design had facilitated Hanson's successful entry into this competitive market place. With $9.8 million in revenues for FY 1978, Hanson management estimated that they had captured more than 25 percent of the domestic market in Hanson's price range.

However, Denny realized that having entered the skiing equipment business, Hanson Industries faced special challenges due to the seasonality of their sales, and their dependence on the weather. Denny believed that Hanson had developed strategies to minimize the problems which might occur in these areas. But even having achieved $9.8 million in revenues, Hanson was considered a small company, which was privately held by relatively few shareholders. Denny was aware that small companies faced special challenges which required creativity on the part of their managers.

THE INDUSTRY

The skiing industry is part of the high-growth leisure industry in the United States.

> A study by the Economic Unit of *U.S. News and World Report* shows that the total spent on leisure far exceeds annual outlays for national defense, or for home building.
>
> If past trends are a guide, leisure time expenditures can be expected to double every eight or nine years, the study predicts.[2]

Within this leisure market, snowskiing was ranked 18th in a list of "25 sports with the most participants"; it had 11 million individual participants in 1976.[3] Snowskiing was the second fastest growing sport from 1973 to 1976, showing a 42 percent increase (see Exhibit 1).

This case was prepared by Julie H. Hertenstein, research assistant, under the supervision of Professor William J. Bruns, Jr.

[1] Fiscal Year 1978 began April 1, 1977 and ended March 31, 1978.

[2] "People Are Shelling Out More Than Ever for a Good Time," *U.S. News and World Report*, February 21, 1977, p. 40.

[3] "The Boom in Leisure Where Americans Spend $160 Billion," *U.S. News and World Report*, May 23, 1977, p. 40.

EXHIBIT 1
Fastest growing participant sports in the United States, 1973-1976

Sport	Percent increase
Tennis	45
Snowskiing	42
Jogging	31
Snowmobiling	19
Basketball	17
Bowling	16
Bicycling	14
Pool/Billiards	9
Boating	8
Camping	7

Source: Data from "The Boom in Leisure, where Americans spend $160 Billion," *U.S. News and World Report*, May 23, 1977, p. 63.

Hanson management believed that their potential market was somewhat smaller, being comprised of those more dedicated skiers who were likely to purchase their own equipment. This market consisted of 4 to 4.5 million skiers in the United States, and a total of 10 million skiers worldwide. Hanson management believed that this market was growing at 10 to 15 percent per year.

The skiing industry, by its very nature, was a seasonal industry. Retail equipment dealers did nearly all of their business in the months preceeding and during the snow season. In the Northern Hemisphere where most skiing was done, this meant the months of August through March.

The seasonality and the length of the season were factors taken into account by manufacturers. The manufacturer of skiing equipment was faced with retailers who were trying to keep their inventories low until just prior to the start of the season when they wanted to be well stocked. By the time any trends could be discerned during the retail selling season, time was so short that there could be little reaction on the part of the manufacturer that would have any impact on profitability.

Not only was the skiing business seasonal, but the success of a season was highly dependent upon the weather. A "poor" snow year was one that had too little snow. In the ski season of 1976-77 a poor snow year in the western United States had several effects on Hanson. First, it slowed the collection of accounts receivable, since the dealers (retailers) did not have cash coming in to pay Hanson. Second, it reduced the orders received late in the season (these are called "reorders"; see "Order Cycle" below), resulting in a slight reduction of Hanson's sales for that year. In addition a poor snow year caused orders for the following year to be below normal levels, because the poor sales meant that the dealer began the following year with above normal inventory levels. Successive years with poor snow conditions could cause major changes in markets and dealer structure.

The state of the economy was not of as much concern to Hanson management as was the weather. Indeed, management believed that during a recession, their sales actually went up, because layoffs and reduced working hours provided people more leisure time to pursue such activities as skiing. This phenomenon was noticed in other leisure time activities as well:

> The recession of the past two years put no visible dent in total spending for leisure. Outlays for everything from tennis balls and snowmobiles to speed boats and foreign vacations soared to 146 billion dollars in 1976.[4]

HANSON'S MARKETING STRATEGY

The ski boot market was a well-established and competitive marketplace. In 1978, there were 38 manufacturers, and Hanson was the only new firm to successfully enter the market in seven years, while six other boot manufacturers had abandoned the ski boot market. The majority of manufacturers were Italian firms, although a few manufacturers existed in each of the following countries: Austria, Germany, Japan, Switzerland, and the United States. The largest manufacturer worldwide was the Italian firm, Nordica. Hanson management believed that the majority of their competition came from firms outside the United States.

Hanson Industries chose to position themselves at the top of the ski boot market. Their policy was to limit themselves to the high-priced segment of this market, and they believed the high-priced segment to be sizeable. The Ski Retailers Council tallies about 4.5 million skiers who spend at least $400 each on their outfits, which include skis, boots, bindings, gloves, and apparel.[5]

Hanson management believed that the individuals who purchased Hanson boots were experienced skiers. These customers had planned their purchase in the prior season, and they were likely to purchase their Hanson boots prior to the beginning of the ski season. Customer characteristics isolated Hanson somewhat from the effects of a poor snow season because the customer was a dedicated skier, because the purchase was made before the quality of the snow season was known, and because many Hanson customers were willing to travel wherever snow conditions were best.

One of the keys to Hanson's successful penetration of this tough market was the unique design of their ski boots. The patented rear entry concept, designed by Chris Hanson, was considered revolutionary. Chris's design balanced the objectives of comfort and skiing performance (see Exhibit 2). One piece of evidence of the significance of the design was the use of the Hanson Avanti for competition purposes by Champion Skier Hank Kashiwa when he won the World Pro Skiing Championship in 1975. Another piece

---

[4] "People Are Shelling Out More Than Ever for a Good Time," *U.S. News and World Report*, February 21, 1977, p. 40.

[5] Ibid.

EXHIBIT 2
The Hanson design

The Hanson ski boot represents a significant departure from traditional design approaches. The dilemma of conventional ski boot design has been the conflict between comfort and performance. Ski boot design originally evolved from the hiking boot, therefore, the design always utilized front entry. This front entry design made a resolution of the comfort versus performance conflict very difficult.

The problem revolved around the fact that each designer accepted the premises of his predecessors. Chris Hanson did not. He refused to accept the problem of comfort versus performance as an inevitable factor in ski boot design. He realized that conventional boots with their ponderous hardware, tongues and ridges were an inadequate answer. Consequently, he completely redesigned. His answer: to provide entry through the back of the boot. The result: a new direction in ski boot technology. This leadership in design was recognized by Fortune magazine when they recently selected the Hanson boot as one of the twenty-five best designed factory made products in America today.

of evidence was the selection of the Hanson Avanti by *Fortune* magazine in May 1977 as one of the 25 best-designed factory-made products available in America. In announcing the selections, Walter McQuade of the board of editors of *Fortune* wrote:

> On these and the following pages *Fortune* presents the twenty-five best-designed factory-made products available in America today. Selected with the assistance of an eminently qualified jury, the products make up a group of those rare mass-produced items that can generate not only covetous admiration but sometimes affection. A man may cherish his Porsche 911 almost as much as his dog.
>
> It was eighteen years ago that *Fortune* published a similar attempt to define the apogee of product design. . . .[6]

Specifically, *Fortune* described the design of the Hanson Avanti as follows:

> Hanson Avanti ski boots, designed by Chris A. Hanson and manufactured in Boulder, Colorado, look as though they were meant for the moon. The rigid outer shell of glossy polyurethane elastomer gives the skier support where he needs it. If the purchaser so chooses, the fit can be molded to the contours of his foot by filling "bladders" between the liner and the shell. . . . $198.[7]

By FY 1978, Hanson was marketing four models of adult boots—Citation, Exhibition, Avanti, and Esprit (see Exhibit 3). New models of boots were continually being added, and older models dropped. The expected model life was three years, although some models had been in existence for more than three years.

Dealer selection was an important part of Hanson's marketing strategy. Because of Hanson's high price position, it was important to select the appropriate dealer to convey that image and insure customer satisfaction. Additionally, the Hanson boot, with its unique design and fitting methods

---

[6] *Fortune*, May 1977, pp. 270–77.
[7] Ibid.

required the dealer to have sufficient expertise to market the boot. Finally, the target customer was a dedicated skier, which required the dealer to have a detailed understanding of the technical aspects of skiing. These factors made dealer selection a critical aspect of Hanson's strategy, requiring careful identification of appropriate dealers for Hanson boots. The majority of Hanson's dealers were either ski shops which specialized in skiing equipment and attire, or sporting goods shops which specialized in equipment and clothing for a variety of sports. Most of these dealers were considered small businesses (over two thirds had less than $1 million sales annually).

A final element of Hanson's marketing strategy was the development of international markets. They opened their first foreign subsidiary in

EXHIBIT 3
Advertising

HANSON'S ESPRIT

FINALLY A GREAT SKI BOOT FOR WOMEN

When you consider how many superb women skiers there are, you'd think that manufacturers would be spending a lot more time creating products specifically for your needs. Unfortunately all too often women get stuck with cheapened, unresponsive versions of men's boots.

So when Hanson set out to build a women's boot, they determined that there would be no compromise in excellence or performance.

They began by creating a new lower back and a special seamless liner to fit the contours of a woman's leg. They softened the shell slightly for a bit more supple flex. And for comfort they added their Flolite™ fitting system.

They styled it in either white or sand and they called it the Esprit. For the spirit in you.

HANSON'S CITATION.

THE PERFECT LINK BETWEEN FOOT AND SKI

Hanson created the Citation for skiers who push the limits. Who stretch the boundaries of their capabilities. Skiers who can accept nothing less than the best.

Our boot fitting experts can show you how the Citation is designed to match the dynamics of your foot—to transmit your commands accurately and precisely to your ski. The shell is sculptured to fit closely to the contours of your foot—providing an uncanny feel for the snow while eliminating unnecessary bulk. (They weigh a mere 7 pounds per pair.)

Your feet will love the Citation's Flolite™ fitting system—snugly and gently enveloping your foot—ensuring a precise and accurate fit.

So if you are deserving of the very best—come in and visit our boot experts. We'll help you reward yourself with a new Citation.

138

EXHIBIT 3 (*continued*)

HANSONS CAN HELP YOU BE A BETTER SKIER

We don't think the idea is at all far-fetched.

In fact, it is the considered opinion of most boot experts that how well a ski boot matches the dynamics of your body—how well it provides information to your foot and transmits action to the ski—determines how well you will ski.

Our boot experts can show you how Hansons are designed to work with you. not against you. Rather than force your ankle into an unnatural, uncomfortable bent position, the sole bed of a Hanson is engineered to achieve just the precise amount of forward lean—putting you in the perfect natural position to initiate turns with an absolute minimum of effort.

We'll show you how Hanson's elastomeric shell is ergonomically designed to approximate the dynamics of the human ankle by permitting a wide range of movement while giving you the proper support.

And what's more, all of this is done without encasing your foot in a medieval torture chamber. So let our boot experts slip your foot into Hanson's seamless wrinkle-free liner. You'll like the way Hanson has removed all those cumbersome and painful buckles, seams, and straps from the sensitive front of the foot. And your feet can relax under the snug gentle touch of Hanson's Flolite™ fitting system.

Make sense?

Then stop in and visit with our boot experts. We'll prove to you that feet that feel good ski better than feet that don't.

Switzerland in 1974. By 1978 Hanson also had subsidiaries in Germany and Austria and distributors throughout the world. International revenues represented 28 percent of total revenues and were growing faster than domestic revenues. Besides expanding Hanson's potential market, international expansion also helped to isolate Hanson from the effects of a poor snow season in any major ski region.

HANSON'S HISTORY

Hanson Industries was founded in 1970, and the first year of operations, FY 1971, was a developmental year dedicated to boot design and preparation for production. In FY 1972 Hanson shipped 2,300 pairs of boots to retailers. By FY 1978 this had grown to 85,000 pairs, and revenues reached $9.8 million (see Exhibit 4 for financial statements).

Revenues had grown fairly consistently during Hanson's history, but earnings were more erratic. During the first three years of its existence Hanson recorded significant losses. Although Hanson made a small profit in FY 1974, a large loss was reported in FY 1975 which had not been anticipated by management. There was no single reason for this loss, but a number of factors contributed to it. One factor was the move into a new facility which caused several problems. Unexpected expenses occurred in conjunction with the move, and savings which were forecast to occur due to consolidation of operations in a single location failed to materialize.

A second factor was an overly optimistic sales forecast. When Hanson failed to reach expected order levels by the end of June, Hanson continued to operate at the forecast level, believing they could "make up" the extra

EXHIBIT 4
Income statements ($000)

	FY 1976	FY 1977	FY 1978
Net sales	$5,753	$7,671	$9,776
Cost of goods sold	3,040	4,140	5,177
Gross margin	2,713	3,531	4,599
Selling, general and administrative, product development costs	1,737	2,298	2,779
Operating earnings	976	1,233	1,820
Interest	436	428	507
Income before tax and extraordinary item	540	805	1,313
Tax provision	314	468	400
Earnings before extraordinary item	226	337	913
Extraordinary item—income tax benefit attributable to utilization of net operating loss carry forwards	314	468	251
Net earnings	$ 540	$ 805	$1,164

HANSON INDUSTRIES (A)
Consolidated Balance Sheet
($000)

	3/31/76	3/31/77	3/31/78
Current assets			
Cash	$ 163	$ 81	$ 156
Receivables, net	692	1,378	1,556
Inventories	1,352	2,104	1,729
Prepaid expenses	99	124	262
Total current assets	2,306	3,687	3,703
Net fixed assets	861	1,122	2,138
Patents and other	171	191	207
Other assets	$3,338	$5,001	$6,048
Current liabilities			
Accounts payable	475	956	944
Advance payment on sales orders	61	12	—
Notes payable—banks	1,100	2,082	1,547
Income taxes payable	—	—	16
Current Installment long-term debt	109	35	1,010
Total current liabilities	1,745	3,084	3517
Deferred income tax	—	—	133
Long-term debt	1,929	1,407	642
Stockholders' equity			
Common stock	1,126	1,166	1,249
Additional paid-in capital	105	105	105
Retained earnings (deficit)	(1,567)	(763)	402
Total stockholders' equity	(336)	509	1756
Total liabilities	$3,338	$5,001	$6,048

volume through additional advertising and promotion rather than recognizing that it was a sluggish selling year.

A third factor was a lack of sufficiently tight planning and control systems within Hanson Industries, so that management was not fully aware of the degree of the problem until FY 1975 had ended.

Partly as a result of FY 1975, Hanson implemented procedures for a tight annual planning and budgeting process, described in detail in Hanson Industries (B). Although Hanson's executives had an overview of where the company would be 2 to 5 years in the future, the efforts of the operating

EXHIBIT 5

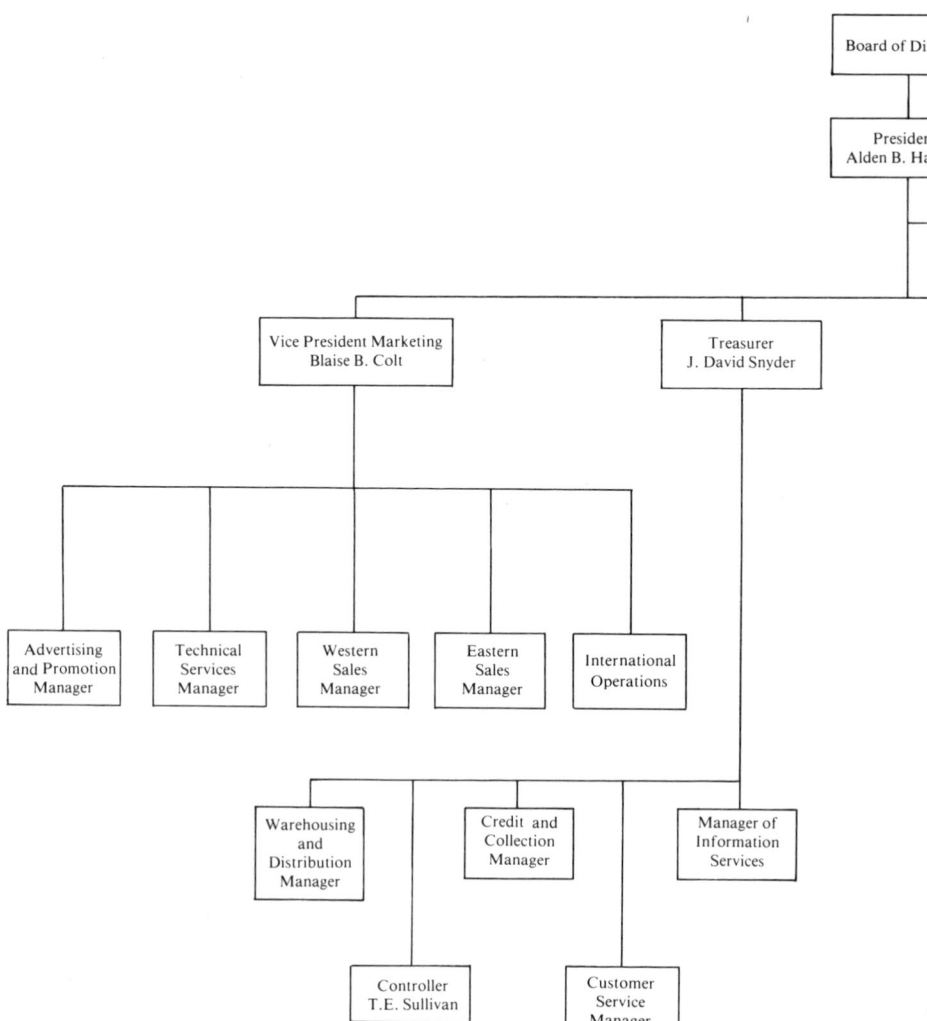

managers were focused on this annual plan and budget (see Exhibit 5 for current organization chart). Hanson's management developed procedures which enabled them to react to changes in the order level from that forecast, thus reducing the possibility of another loss year like 1975.

After implementing these procedures, the earnings situation improved in FY 1976, with before tax net income of $540,000. Earnings continued to increase through FY 1978.

In FY 1979, Hanson management expected revenues to continue to grow. Early in the planning process this rate was forecast to be around 20 percent

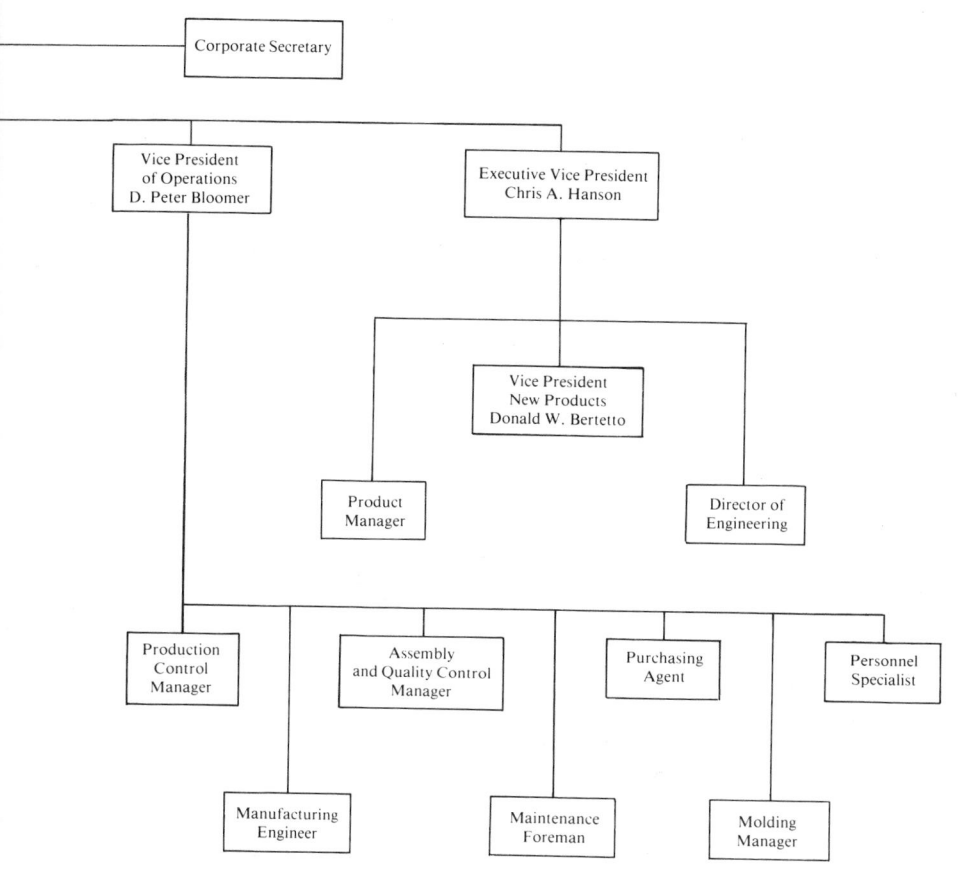

but was later revised upward to exceed 30 percent. By FY 1984 Hanson predicted revenues from ski boots would exceed $26 million. After 1984 they expected the unit volume of their sales to increase proportional to growth in the market.

In 1978, Hanson management was considering the possibility of diversification. Diversification alternatives which had been considered were either new products which could be developed by Hanson, or firms which could be acquired by Hanson. As of August 1978, no action had been taken to diversify Hanson Industries.

ORDER CYCLE

Hanson's order season was divided into two parts: the stocking order season, and the reorder season. The stocking order season began in March and ran through June. It was, as the name implies, a period when the dealers were placing orders to "stock up" their ski inventory for the following ski season. The stocking order season was characterized by heavy marketing, promotion, and high discounts (up to 10 percent above discounts on reorders) by manufacturers. In addition, extended terms for payment were offered to dealers during the stocking order season. This was an attempt to get the dealers to order early, so that the manufacturers could adjust their production to actual demand. Boots ordered during the stocking order season were not shipped until after July, which conformed to the dealer's desire to keep inventories low.

The stocking order season began with the March Ski Show, sponsored by Ski Industries of America, a trade association (see "Ski Show" below). The Ski Show was order intensive and normally 25 percent to 30 percent of Hanson's total orders for the year were taken during the six-day show.

Following the Ski Show, Hanson sales representatives conducted a thorough campaign to cover their entire territory before the end of the stocking order season. During this campaign, a key objective was to cover all Hanson dealers who either did not attend the Ski Show, or who attended but did not place an order. Mid-June marked the end of the stocking order season. At this time, Hanson had received 85 percent of the total orders for the year. Denny Hanson reflected on the importance of gearing operations to reflect the fact that the June 15 order level represented 85 percent of the years total activity.

> One time, in 1975, we failed to gear operations to reflect this fact. That year, orders were running less than the forecast. At the end of June orders were only 70 percent of the original forecast, but we felt we could make up the remaining 30 percent with extra marketing and promotional effort. However, the dealers were very conservative after a couple bad snow years. The additional orders did not reach 30 percent and this was one factor which contributed to the loss year in 1975.

The reorder season lasted from the first of July to the end of February. Although normally a few small dealers placed initial orders during this season, most dealers were placing mid-season orders to replenish low stocks of popular items. In a normal year, the reorder season accounted for 15 percent of Hanson's orders. However, a poor snow season caused reorders to fall short of the normal 15 percent.

THE SKI SHOW

The March Ski Show, sponsored by Ski Industries of America, was the main event kicking off the stocking order season. This six-day event was held annually in a huge Las Vegas convention center where manufacturers displayed everything having to do with skiing—skis, bindings, ski poles, ski boots, ski clothing, and even snow making equipment. Attendance at the Ski Show was limited to representatives of manufacturers and retailers, and it drew more than 20,000 people representing approximately 6,000 retail organizations and 200–300 manufacturers. In addition to providing the dealers the opportunity to see new products and place orders, the Ski Show also provided the dealers the opportunity to speak with more senior individuals in the manufacturer's organization than those whom they would normally see.

Annually, Hanson's marketing organization made intensive preparation for the Ski Show. A sales representative visited each dealer to determine the prior year's sales, and the dealers' current inventory of Hanson boots. The sales representative then prepared an estimate of the dealers' expected sales for the following year.

The marketing staff prepared a computer data base for the IBM 3741 minicomputer they would take to the Ski Show. The purpose of taking this computerized data to the Ski Show was twofold. First, it was a tool to help the sales representative make the sale and, second, it provided Hanson management frequent feedback on order results at the Show. The data base included the actual orders for each dealer the prior year, the estimated order for each dealer for the following year, and a breakdown of Hanson's expected total sales for the Ski Show. In addition to this data base, Hanson had a program with the capability of creating a "typical" order of any size. This enabled a dealer to suggest an order size, and the minicomputer would output an order showing "typical" mix of models, sizes, and colors determined by Hanson's historical data.

Normally on the first day of the Ski Show, few orders were placed. The dealers visited manufacturers' exhibits, examined products, and made appointments to see their sales representatives. By the end of the first day, Hanson sales representatives normally expected to have their appointment books filled for the entire show.

During the sales appointment, the dealer and the sales representative sat down in a private office and discussed the information the sales representative had gathered on the dealer's prior years' sales and current inventory levels. Since the Ski Show occurred immediately following the end of the ski season, the dealers were very much aware of what did and did not sell. They then discussed orders for the following year based on the estimate prepared by the sales representative. If the dealer wanted to see a sample order of a particular size, they went to the IBM 3741 and requested it. If the dealer desired, this sample order could be modified to fit the dealer's knowledge of his particular market, or they could start from scratch and enter a completely different order into the IBM 3741.

If the dealer decided to place the order, this fact was keyed into the IBM 3741, and the order was entered into the permanent order file. If the dealer decided not to place the order at this time, he could choose to take away a "hard copy" (e.g., computer printout) version of the order they had discussed for further consideration.

Each morning, Hanson management received a computer printed sales report of the previous day's activities. This showed each order placed, and compared it with the previous year's order and this year's expected order for that dealer. The computer also produced summary reports detailing the mix of orders received by model, size, and color, and compared this to the mix of orders Hanson had expected to receive at the trade show.

Hanson management believed that the Ski Show was important not only from the standpoint of taking the actual orders, but it provided very important information on the changing mood of the dealers. For example, in one year the dealers might be reacting to a very successful selling season and be very optimistic in anticipation of another good selling season; they would be willing to stock up to a high inventory level. Another year, the dealers might be more conservative as is the case frequently after a bad snow season. They would want to run their inventories down low, preferring to stock out if the snow season was good than to have high inventories if the snow season was poor. Hanson management believed that this understanding was useful in Hanson's planning.

MANUFACTURING

The Hanson ski boot had three major components—the outer shell, the foam liner, and the flo pac—plus assorted hardware such as rivets, screws, buckles and cables.

The outer shell was hard plastic with a smooth finish (see Exhibit 6 for details). The outer shell was produced by an injection molding process in which small particles of the plastic raw material were poured into the molding equipment where heat and pressure were used to convert the particles to a liquid. This liquid was injected into the boot mold under high pressure, then cooled to produce the molded plastic shell. The molds were expensive, costing $40,000 to $50,000 each, and each required approximately six months to

EXHIBIT 6
Components of the boot: Outer shell

Components of the Boot

Shell

There are two basic shell designs in the adult models. The Avanti, Exhibition, and Esprit are one type of design, and the Citation represents the other.

The Avanti type of shell is composed of two halves which are riveted, screwed, and glued together. Four rivets are inserted in the beam on the top of the boot. The rivet heads point toward the outside of the boot with the exception of the rivet at the front of the left boot which is inserted with the rivet head to the inside. A tongue and groove arrangement runs through the front of the beam, down the toe of the boot, through the length of the sole, and up the heel. This arrangement prohibits the entry of water into the boot and unites the shell halves into a rigid bond. Four screws and a silicone sealant join the sole

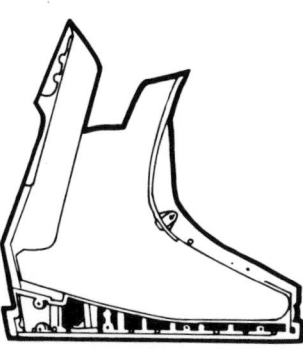

Avanti

together. The shell halves are composed of an injection molded polyurethane elastomer with a high gloss finish.

The floating front cuff is joined to the shell with an el clip which hangs from the upper rivet on the front beam. The front tab on the Exhibition and Esprit rises 13 millimeters above the shell. The Avanti front tab rises 50 millimeters above the shell and the Citation rises 70 millimeters.

The shell flexes naturally using the resiliency of the plastic for resistance. This approach is much smoother than a hinged system in which the materials of the upper and lower shell are forced to bind against one another as the upper rocks forward.

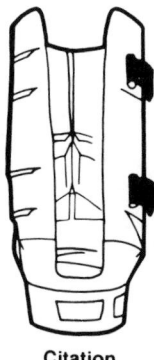

Citation

The Citation shell is constructed of a one piece injection molded polyurethane elastomer. Because of the one piece molding, the need for rivets, screws, and glue is eliminated. The result is a very light weight shell which is extremely durable yet flexible. The shell is molded so the upper is a thinner gauge than the lower. The material is 8 millimeters thick on the bottom of the shell tapering to 3 millimeters at the top. The shell is therefore stiffer below the ankle and softer above it. The purpose of this design is to provide for natural ankle movements, easing shock absorption and better carving. The beam along the top of the boot is hollow. As the boot is flexed, pressures are dispersed by the "V" shape of the beam preventing pressure directly on the instep. Over the toes is a cavity for a Flolite™ reservoir.

EXHIBIT 7
Components of the boot: Foam liner

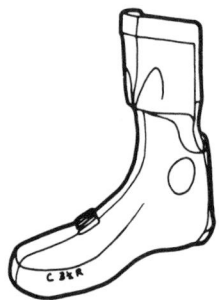

Liners

Surrounding the skier's foot is a seamless, micro-cellular polyurethane elastomer liner. The smooth molded surfaces ensure that there are no wrinkles or seams to cause pressure points. The liner provides consistent padding which is uniform in density and thickness while being extremely durable. These liners are also very easy to modify. The Exhibition and Esprit will have a separate instep pad which fits over the front of the liner. Imprinted on the toe area are markings indicating the type, the size and whether it is a left or a right liner.

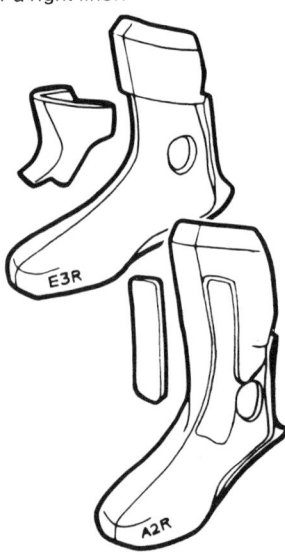

EXHIBIT 8
Components of the boot: Flo pac

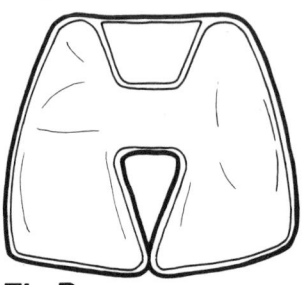

Flo Pacs

The Hanson Flolite™ is unique because of its light weight materials and hydraulic pressure equalizing properties. The patented flo material is composed of micro-beads and a hydrocarbon matrix. The beads are hollow spheres which measure 3/1000ths of an inch in diameter. Each of these micro-beads traps a dead air space which adds to the insulating properties of the boot. The fluid hydrocarbon matrix provides for a constantly conforming pressure distribution around the foot while, at the same time, resisting quick foot movements well enough to translate those movements without distortion to the skis. The Flolite™ is packaged in a polyurethane envelope which fits in a cavity around the liner. In other flow type boots, the flow is packed directly into the liner. The purpose of a flow fitting material is to disburse pressures around the foot. The purpose of a liner is to provide padding and comfort. In putting the two functions into one package, other boot companies always have to make a trade off between padding and pressure distribution. By separating the flo pac and the liner, the Hanson boot eliminates this trade off. The result is a better performing, more comfortable boot.

make. A separate mold was required for each size of each model of boot, but work on several sizes could be done concurrently. A full set of molds required 12 months to complete.

The foam liner was produced by a liquid injection molding process where two liquids were injected into the mold. The chemical reaction between the liquids caused the foam to expand to fill the mold, and solidify (see Exhibit 7 for details). After the foam liners were removed from the molding machine, they went through a hand trimming process before final assembly.

The third component was the flo pac. The flo pac consisted of a semisolid material enclosed in a plastic envelope (see Exhibit 8 for details). This envelope surrounded the foot in the completed boot, and the semisolid material conformed to the shape of the foot.

After the production of the three major components, and production or acquisition of the hardware, the boot was assembled and put into inventory (see Exhibit 9).

When Hanson began manufacturing the boots under their current production methods in FY 1973, they contracted many of the manufacturing operations to outside manufacturers. The operations performed in-house were production of the foam liners, and final assembly. As the firm grew, manufacturing operations previously contracted were brought in-house. The operation which most recently came in-house was the manufacture of flo pacs. Few operations remained outside in 1978. In June of 1978, 123 of Hanson's 182 total employees were involved in manufacturing operations. Nearly half of these were considered by Hanson management to be skilled workers.

EXHIBIT 9
Manufacturing flowchart

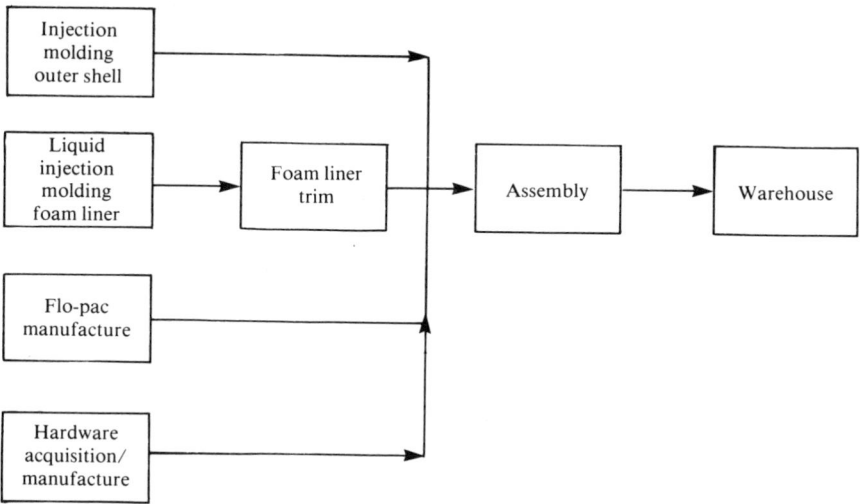

148

EXHIBIT 10

Hanson followed a level production strategy. As can be seen from Exhibit 10, by January the product line policy was set and market forecasts were developed. Budgets had been developed to support the level of activity required to meet the market forecast (see Hanson Industries (B)). Beginning in January, Hanson's vice president of operations had approval to manufacture up to 60 percent of the budgeted level for any product. Since Hanson would get no orders from dealers until the March Ski Show, they preferred to be somewhat conservative with this early manufacturing. But management had confidence in manufacturing to the 60 percent level, which kept operations at full production at least until April. Because they were manufacturing to forecast, this early production was characterized by long production runs. After the March Ski Show was over, the early stocking orders indicated any adjustments needed in the forecast level of production or mix of boot models and colors. By mid-September, the character of the production strategy had changed from a "to forecast" strategy to a "to order" strategy characterized by much shorter production runs.

Although international shipments were made from April through June, domestic shipments, which represented the bulk of Hanson's business, began in July, peaked in August, and remained at a high level until December when they dwindled down.

SUMMARY

In 1971, Hanson Industries entered the fast growing ski business through the manufacture of ski boots. The boots' unique design and excellent skiing performance enabled Hanson to enter a market with many established competitors, and gain significant market share. Their marketing strategy aimed at the dedicated skier allowed them to minimize the effects of poor snow seasons, and they developed a budgeting system which enabled them to react to changes from the anticipated level of sales. By 1978, revenues and earnings had been strong for three years, and Hanson management continued to consider whether or not they should diversify.

——◄CASE II-7►——
Hanson Industries (B)

In early July 1978, Alden B. (Denny) Hanson was reviewing the fiscal year (FY) 1979 Final Budget Revision which had just been completed. As he thought back over the planning and budgeting processes which had begun nearly a year earlier, he wondered whether the current budgeting processes were the most appropriate for Hanson Industries. More specifically, he considered whether Hanson should arrive at their final budget earlier than June 30, the end of the third month of their fiscal year.[1]

PRODUCT LINE PLANNING

The first steps in the processes of budgeting involved discussions of growth objectives, product line planning, and pricing strategies. Budgeting, to a large degree, was a function of the anticipated volume of sales and mix of products. The ability of Hanson Industries to establish a reasonable, useful budget was dependent upon management's ability to understand their markets and to plan their product line and sales forecasts accordingly.

Planning the product line was a key strategic process largely controlled by Hanson's executives: Denny Hanson, president, Chris Hanson, executive vice president, Don Bertetto, vice president new products, and Dave Snyder, treasurer. In April 1977, these executives received inputs from the marketing group suggesting a model line-up for FY 1979 (see Exhibit 1). Between April and October strategies for FY 1979 were developed. Many informal discussions by the above executives and the vice president marketing and Pete Bloomer, vice president operations took place. Sales and marketing in FY 1978, and the current market strengths of the dealer organizations

---

This case was prepared by Julie H. Hertenstein, research assistant, under the supervision of Professor William J. Bruns, Jr.

[1] Fiscal year 1979 at Hanson Industries began on April 1, 1978 and ended on March 31, 1979.

EXHIBIT 1

MEMORANDUM

TO: Alden B. Hanson, Chris A. Hanson, J. David Snyder, Don Bertetto
FROM: Carl S. Rapp (V.P. Marketing until December 31, 1977)
DATE: April 5, 1977
SUBJECT: Possible model line-up
Fiscal 79

First suggested possible model line-up is outlined as follows:

	Men's line			*Women's line*	
Price	*Model*	*Size*	*Price*	*Model*	*Size*
$138	New 1-piece	$1\frac{1}{2}$–$4\frac{1}{2}$	$120	Women's version	$\frac{1}{2}$, $1\frac{1}{2}$, $2\frac{1}{2}$
168	Avanti	1–5	148	Esprit	1–3
198	Citation	$2\frac{1}{2}$, $3\frac{1}{2}$, $4\frac{1}{2}$	170	Citation (ladies')	$\frac{1}{2}$, $1\frac{1}{2}$
220	Citation	$2\frac{1}{2}$–$4\frac{1}{2}$			

---

were reviewed. Dave Snyder and Denny Hanson had also reviewed the company's financial situation and the possible capital expenditures and future growth, and determined what they felt a sustainable rate of growth would be.

PLANNING MEETING

In October, the first formal meeting was held by the operating managers to begin planning the budget for FY 1979. Included in this group were Denny Hanson, president; Chris Hanson, executive vice president; Don Bertetto, vice president new products; Pete Bloomer, vice president operations; Blaise Colt, then general manager of international operations, vice president marketing; and Dave Snyder, treasurer. The meeting was held in a hotel conference room away from Hanson headquarters, so that the operating managers could devote full attention to the planning effort. At this meeting, the operating managers began to formalize plans for FY 1979. Three key decisions had to result from this meeting. The first concerned the models and sizes of boots which Hanson would produce for FY 1979. The second concerned the prices for these models. And third, volume objectives had to be established. The review and the informal discussions which had taken place prior to the meeting were important to making these decisions. For example, the relationship between the price of a pair of boots and volume of sales meant that prices of each model in the product line had to be set such that Hanson met its growth objectives at the same time a sustainable rate of growth was not exceeded.

The operating managers first reviewed the model lineup which had earlier been proposed by marketing (Exhibit 1). This model lineup had included a new model of boot for FY 1979. A review of the various lead times required indicated that there was neither sufficient time to produce promotional models for the March Ski Show, nor would there be enough time for ski testing before the boot was put into production. Based on these considerations the committee proceeded to reject the proposal for a new boot model in FY 1979. However, the remaining models were approved for FY 1979.

The operating managers then discussed the pricing structure for the approved model lineup. The managers wanted Hanson to grow, but they also wanted to make sure that Hanson had the manufacturing capacity and organizational ability to handle the growth. They used price and volume projections prepared by the sales staff to set prices which would result in a manageable and sustainable rate of growth.

PRELIMINARY JANUARY BUDGET

The models, prices and resulting volumes agreed upon by the operating managers became the basic planning parameters for preparing the FY 1979 budget. Dave Snyder issued a memo documenting these planning parameters (see Exhibit 2). This memo also served to notify the operating managers to

EXHIBIT 2

MEMORANDUM

TO: Executive staff
FROM: J. David Snyder
DATE: 21 October 1977
SUBJECT: Planning parameters—Fiscal 1979

During the meetings at the Harvest House, we arrived at the following product line and volumes.

Product line—fiscal 1979

Model	Colors	Sizes	Retail price	Percent of line
Esprit	Sand	1, 2	$150	20
	Light grey	N, M, W		
Avanti	Red	1, 2, 3, N, M, W	160	16
		4, 5, M, W		
Citation	White	$\frac{1}{2}$, $1\frac{1}{2}$, $2\frac{1}{2}$	180	18
(ladies')	Blue	N, M, W		
Citation	Midnight	$2\frac{1}{2}$, $3\frac{1}{2}$, $4\frac{1}{2}$	200	26
(recreation)	Light Grey	M, W		
Citation	White	$2\frac{1}{2}$, $3\frac{1}{2}$, $4\frac{1}{2}$	220	20
	Flame	M, W		100
Promo/rental	Black	1, 2, 3, N, M, W	120	
		3, 4, M, W		

EXHIBIT 2 (*continued*)

Memorandum
Page two
21 October 1977

<table>
<tr><td></td><td colspan="4">Volumes for fiscal 1979</td></tr>
<tr><td>***Domestic***</td><td></td><td></td><td></td><td></td></tr>
<tr><td>1st quality.........</td><td>64,800</td><td>Esprit</td><td>(20%)</td><td>12,960</td></tr>
<tr><td></td><td></td><td>Avanti</td><td>(16%)</td><td>11,368</td></tr>
<tr><td></td><td></td><td>Citation (L)</td><td>(18%)</td><td>11,664</td></tr>
<tr><td></td><td></td><td>Citation (R)</td><td>(26%)</td><td>16,848</td></tr>
<tr><td></td><td></td><td>Citation</td><td>(20%)</td><td>12,960</td></tr>
<tr><td></td><td></td><td></td><td></td><td>64,800</td></tr>
<tr><td>Promo/rental ......</td><td>12,000</td><td></td><td></td><td></td></tr>
<tr><td>Total domestic.....</td><td>76,800</td><td></td><td></td><td></td></tr>
<tr><td>***Export***</td><td></td><td></td><td></td><td></td></tr>
<tr><td>Subsidiaries ....</td><td>15,000</td><td></td><td></td><td></td></tr>
<tr><td>Distributors ....</td><td>11,800</td><td></td><td></td><td></td></tr>
<tr><td>Total export.......</td><td>26,800</td><td></td><td></td><td></td></tr>
<tr><td>Total volume ......</td><td>103,600</td><td></td><td></td><td></td></tr>
</table>

Line for Canada would be as for domestic. Other international markets would receive 1978 product line with perhaps different colors.

If any of the above differs from your notes, please let me know.

We can discuss any necessary changes at any time.

J. David Snyder
Treasurer

---

begin preparing their budgets. They had until the last week of November to provide Dave Synder with their preliminary budgets. Using the specified planning parameters, the operating managers focused independently on each of their areas of responsibility to determine what resources were required to meet the level of activity.

Denny Hanson explained that one thing which specifically is not provided to the operating managers with the materials to be used during budget preparation was last year's budgeted amounts or actual results.

> We want the managers to think through each item they are budgeting, and not simply to use last year's figure, or a projection based on last year's figure. Of course, last year's budgeted and actual amounts are available to the manager.

But by not including them with the budget planning information, the manager must consider whether this is an appropriate source for the data, or whether another means of estimating is better.

A description of the types of evaluations performed and decisions made will be undertaken by looking at the operations department which, because it included all manufacturing, comprised the largest element of Hanson's budget.

Pete Bloomer's immediate concern was whether Hanson had sufficient manufacturing capacity in the various production areas to produce the forecast number of pairs of boots. This required that the total annual volume first be broken down into a production forecast (see Exhibit 3), and that these monthly forecasts be compared with the capacity of each production area. In those areas where capacity was insufficient, Pete had two alternatives, he could either propose the addition of capacity, or he could purchase parts

EXHIBIT 3

HANSON INDUSTRIES (B)
Budget Narrative
Production Schedule
Fiscal 1979

There are 222 working days between January 1, 1978, and the anticipated completion date of November 17, 1978. During this time, we would produce at the rate of 467 pair per day or 2,333 pair per week (actual quotas would be 2,400 pair per week, which would get the job completed six days early—November 9, 1978).

The rate beginning December 4, 1978, will be 1,600 pair per week or 370 pair per day. We would have an inventory of model year 1979–80 boots equaling 28,900 pair or more by March 31, 1979 (minimum).

			Boots serialized	
Month	*Number of working days*	*Current month*	*Cumulative to date (model year)*	*Cumulative to date (fiscal year)*
January 78	19	8,866	8,866	
February 78	19	8,866	17,732	
March 78	24	11,200	28,932	
April 78	20	9,333	38,265	9,333
May 78	24	11,200	49,465	20,533
June 78	20	9,333	58,798	29,866
July 78	19	8,866	67,664	38,732
August 78	25	11,666	79,330	50,398
September 78	19	7,934	87,264	58,332
October 78	20	9,333	96,597	67,665
November 78	15	7,000	103,597*	78,398
	8	3,733		
December 78	15	4,785		83,183
January 79	24	7,656		90,839
February 79	19	6,061		96,900
March 79	21	6,699		103,599

* November 17, 1978.

externally. A number of factors entered into his decisions: Hanson was pursuing a goal of becoming self-sufficient in manufacturing; lead times required for adding capacity varied by production area; and finally, he could not ignore current financial constraints. Each of these issues had to be resolved before the budget was prepared, since they affected the nature and timing of expenses.

Pete also held meetings with managers of the various areas reporting to him to discuss the future requirements they saw which might have an impact on the budget. Frequently, suggestions for improving operations originated in these discussions, such as an idea to newly automate a manufacturing operation. Pete evaluated the feasibility of such project, and where the evaluation indicated, included the project in his budget.

When issues such as capacity expansion or changes in manufacturing process had been resolved, preparation of the actual manufacturing FY 1979 budget began. Pete had some manufacturing costs which were not variable, such as leased equipment. Forecasting these costs for FY 1979 was straightforward. For the costs which vary directly with production, such as materials, direct labor, and indirect labor, Hanson had developed standard costs for each of the manufacturing operations. Therefore, once the production forecast was complete, monthly budgeted amounts for these expenses could be computed directly from the standards.

Other expenses, such as those related to the size of manufacturing staff, were more difficult to forecast. A significant increase in production would clearly require additional staff. However, since staffing would not vary directly with production, Pete Bloomer used his best judgment to determine the size of manufacturing staff and related expenses which would be required.

The preparation of the operations budget illustrates why the forecasted level of activity was a determining factor. For operations, the relevant "level of activity" was the number of pairs of boots to be produced. For the other operating managers preparing their budgets concurrently with Pete Bloomer, the relevant level of activity might be somewhat different. In the new product area, the relevant level of activity might be the number of new products or product changes to be worked on. In the marketing area, the number of pairs of boots might be relevant to the advertising budget, but the forecast number of dealers would be relevant for estimating the size of sales force required.

In late November, after budgets had been prepared for each department, they were sent to Dave Snyder, who began to consolidate the results. Because individual managers prepared their budgets without consulting each other directly and with few guidelines other than the sales volume and product mix parameters, Dave did not expect to produce a final budget on the initial consolidation. He considered this to be a tentative look at the proposed budget, which would allow Hanson management to evaluate the three key areas of cash flow, capital expenditures, and revenue and profitability. Necessary adjustments would then be made in each of these three areas. Action considered during the budgeting process will be discussed below.

Cash flow, capital expenditures, and revenues and profits

Cash flow was always an item of concern to Hanson. The company followed a level production strategy, yet their sales were extremely seasonal (see Hanson Industries (A)). This resulted in cash disbursements which were nearly level during the year, with a concentration of cash receipts in the months October through February. (See Exhibit 4.) Hanson normally relied

EXHIBIT 4
Seasonality of Hanson's cash receipts and cash disbursements

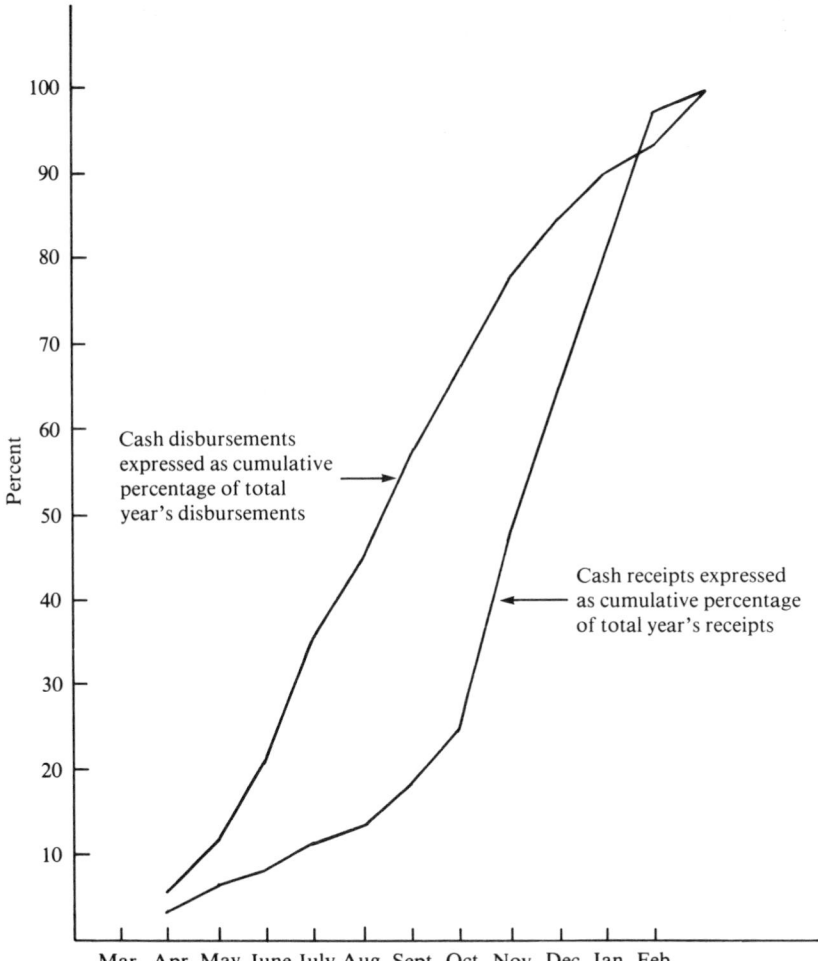

on short-term borrowing under a line of credit to meet cash needs during March through September (see Hanson Industries (C) for a detailed description of Hanson's financing). This line of credit was secured primarily by inventory and receivables as collateral. As a result, during the budgeting process, Dave Snyder matched cash disbursements against cash available from receipts and through borrowing capacity. Frequently this preliminary consolidation showed cash requirements in a given month in excess of cash available from all sources. In such cases there was discussion and negotiation between the managers to develop understanding of what adjustments could be made. For example, the manufacturing schedule might be adjusted, the dealer prepayment program could be stressed, or capital expenditures might be delayed to a time in which the cash requirements were not as tight.

The capital expenditures were reviewed from the standpoint of Hanson's overall manufacturing strategy and capacity as well as from the financing aspect. One objective of Hanson's management was to move toward self-sufficiency in manufacturing with the exception of simple hardware such as screws. (See Hanson Industries (A) for the history of manufacturing operations.) In evaluating capital expenditures, Hanson management always considered the impact of a particular expenditure on this objective. They also gave consideration to how to finance the capital expenditures, whether through cash, new debt, sale of stock, or capital leases. Any limitation on their access to capital necessarily limited their capital expenditure program.

The third area of concern was revenues and profitability. Denny Hanson sets targets for revenue and profit growth. If, upon review, revenue and profits were not consistent with targets, Denny Hanson or Dave Snyder would negotiate with individual managers considering such actions as increasing sales targets or hiring an engineer to reduce manufacturing costs.

COMPLETING THE JANUARY BUDGET

The process just described was an iterative one. Dave Snyder consolidated the budget figures, and he, Denny, and Chris reviewed the key areas. Where adjustments needed to be made, they reviewed alternative courses of action, and negotiated with individual operating managers. The agreements reached with these managers resulted in revisions to the operating manager's budget, which required a new consolidation. The consolidation was again reviewed to see if the changes produced the desired results. If not, negotiations began again with the managers. The process was repeated until a budget was produced which was acceptable to Hanson management (see Exhibit 5).

The deadline for completion of the iterations was January 16, 1978. The deadline was two weeks prior to the board of directors meeting scheduled for January 30, 1978. At that meeting, the board reviewed management's operating plan for FY 1979, and approved the FY 1979 preliminary budget.

EXHIBIT 5

HANSON INDUSTRIES (B)
Fiscal Year 1979 Budget
Prepared January 25, 1978 ($000)
Income Statement

	Apr	May	Jun	Jul	Aug	Sep	Oct	Nov	Dec	Jan	Feb	Mar	Total
Revenues:													
Gross sales: Boots, accessories, parts	$113	$130	$243	$757	$2,083	$2,117	$1,855	$1,862	$1,643	$626	$325	$106	$11,860
Less: Discounts:													
U.S. anticipation				20	50	40	40	14					164
Stocking				50	125	113	88	84	20				480
Reorder				1	3	2	2	10	18	11	3		50
International						16	15	12	10	1	1		60
Return	30	50	20	5	5	5	10	10	20	20	20	20	200
Allowances	5	5	5		5	5	5	5	5	5	5	5	50
Freight: International	5	5	5	5	5	4	4	5	4	5	4		40
Domestic					4	4	4	4	4	4	2		30
Royalties	1	1	2	5	12	12	11	10	9	4	2	1	70
Total deductions	41	61	32	83	204	197	175	154	86	50	35	26	1,144
Net revenues	72	69	211	674	1,879	1,920	1,680	1,708	1,557	576	290	80	10,716
Net cost of goods sold:													
Boots, accessories, parts	62	61	123	309	858	882	800	848	757	280	150	66	5,196
Gross margin	10	8	88	365	1,021	1,038	880	860	800	296	140	14	5,520
Total operating expenses	321	268	254	312	356	375	389	395	375	353	313	356	3,967
Operating income	(311)	(260)	(166)	53	665	663	491	465	405	(57)	(173)	(242)	1,553
Tax allowance				9	118	118	90	85	80				500
Net income	$(311)	$(260)	$(166)	$44	$547	$545	$401	$380	$345	$(57)	$(173)	$(242)	$1,053

EXHIBIT 5 (*continued*)

Fiscal 1979 Budget Prepared January 25, 1978
Capital Expenditures

	Apr	May	Jun	Jul	Aug	Sep	Oct	Nov	Dec	Jan	Feb	Mar	Total
Capital expenditures:													
Capitalized R&D	$ 9	$ 10	$ 9	$ 9	$ 10	$ 9	$ 9	$ 10	$ 9	$ 9	$ 10	$ 9	$112
Shop equipment	6	12	2	3		1			1				25
Citation—R	16	14	14	14									58
Citation	17	17	17	17									68
Kids boots			6	6	6	6							24
New model				15	15	30	30			15	15	15	135
Miscellaneous								12	12	12	12	10	58
Total new products	48	53	48	64	31	46	39	22	22	36	37	34	480
Manufacturing	25	26	25	25	26	25	25	26	25	25	26	25	304
Marketing	1	1	1	1						1		1	6
Administration					1	1	1	1	1		1		6
Remodel	20	20	20	20									80
Total including new products	94	100	94	110	58	72	65	49	48	62	64	60	876
Adjustment	(20)	(20)	(20)	(20)	(20)	(20)	(20)	(20)	(20)	(20)			(200)
Principal on contract purchases:													
Old	6	7	6	6	7	6	6	7	6	6	7	6	76
New	2	3	2	2	3	2	2	3	2	2	3	2	28
Total capital expenditures	$ 82	$ 90	$ 82	$ 98	$ 48	$ 60	$ 53	$ 39	$ 36	$ 50	$ 74	$ 68	$780

THE PRELIMINARY BUDGET

The preliminary budget as approved by the board served as the basis for Hanson's operations January through June. Two activities, in particular, were dependent upon approval of this budget. The first was the annual negotiations with the bank to provide short-term financing. Hanson's goal was to have the short-term financing arrangements for FY 1979 completed by the end of February 1978. The second activity dependent on the completion of the budget was manufacturing. Since the first orders for FY 1979 would not be received until late March, the production which took place early in the year had to be based upon forecast. Hanson's policy was that the vice president of operations was authorized to manufacture up to 60 percent of the forecast FY 1979 production based on the January forecasts.

As described in Hanson Industries (A), the first sales for the FY 1979 selling year were made at the March 1978 Ski Show in Las Vegas. In March 1978, orders ran 10 percent above Hanson's forecast, even though the forecast was 20 percent higher than the previous year. Still, orders from the Ski Show, which usually represented 25 percent to 30 percent of Hanson's total orders for the year, were not considered by management to be a sufficient basis on which to revise the entire budget. It was, however, considered to be a significant trend to be followed closely, and in April management began to consider what operational changes would be required if this level of demand were to hold for the entire selling season.

THE FINAL BUDGET REVISION

In June, Hanson began to prepare the final budget revision. Usually, Hanson had 85 percent of their total orders for the year in-house by June 15, and they assumed that the winter of 1978–79 would be a normal snow season. Based on the 85 percent orders received, Dave Snyder calculated the year's total orders assuming that reorders would account for an additional 15 percent. He then discounted this total by 5 percent, allowing for order cancellation and returns, and this became the full budget level. (See Exhibit 6.) Management's objectives for the final budget were:

1. At the June 15 (85 percent) order level, Hanson should make a small profit, even if no additional orders were received.
2. At the full budget level, Hanson would make a good return on its shareholders investment.
3. Any sales beyond the full budget level would further improve the earnings picture.

Orders for FY 1979 were greater than Hanson had projected in November 1977, and the new projection indicated that revenues would be 11 percent

EXHIBIT 6
Orders, Shipments, and Revenues, June 30, 1978

	Orders 6/16	Projected orders/.85	Ship 95 percent	Wholesale price	Percent	$000
First quality:						
Esprit: White	9,326	10,972	10,423	$ 84	14.3	$ 876
Sand	2,521	2,966	2,811	84	3.9	236
Avanti: Flame	7,198	8,468	8,045	96	11.0	772
Midnight	8,164	9,605	9,125	96	12.5	876
Citation R: Blue	6,928	8,151	7,743	114	10.6	883
Midnight	13,287	15,632	14,850	114	20.4	1,693
Citation I: Flame	5,461	6,425	6,104	132	8.4	806
White	9,811	11,542	10,965	132	15.1	1,447
Slalom	2,485	2,924	2,778	144	3.8	400
Total first quality	65,181	76,685	72,844		100.0	7,992
Black promo	$682,000		12,313	62.50		770
Accessories		758*	750			750
Parts						100
Total domestic revenue		85,157				$9,612

* Projected orders/.90.

higher than in the preliminary January budget. Therefore, in preparing the final budget, Hanson management was primarily concerned with how to meet this increased demand in the most cost effective way.

Denny Hanson explained how any difference between the June order level and the October forecast would result in an adjustment to the final budget.

Let's assume that we had forecast that we would sell 95,000 pairs of boots. This means we anticipated 100,000 orders, allowing 5 percent for returns and cancellations. By the end of June, then, we expected to have orders for 85,000 pairs. Suppose we only had orders for 75,000 pairs of boots. The 75,000 is considered to be 85 percent of the orders we will receive and becomes the basis for our revised projection, and revised budget, as follows:

Orders received June 15 = 75,000

Estimated total orders for FY = 75,000/.85 = 88,235

Total sales (total orders × .95) = 88,235 × .95 = 83,823

Based on our actual sales and revised budget, we will take actions to make sure that a profit will be made at the sales level represented by the 75,000 orders, as stated in the first objective. We might cut expenses, or delay capital expenditures, or both. Because of our growth, we have frequently been able to "reduce" projected expenses by slowing growth rather than by cutting back. If we had planned to add 10 people in manufacturing staff and now we only add 2, that reduces the projected manufacturing expense. I feel it is unlikely that we would have to lay people off to meet our objectives.

On June 5, 1978 Dave Snyder issued a memorandum to operating managers requesting their inputs for the final budget revision. This memorandum also contained additional instructions on this final step in the preparation of final operating budgets (see Exhibit 7). The final budget revision process resembled the earlier processes in that it was iterative and involved negotiations with managers. However, the major issues remained the same; cash flow, capital expenditures, and revenue and profitability.

By the end of the first week in July, Dave Snyder had compiled the fiscal year 1979 final budget revision (see Exhibit 8). This final revision, like the earlier budget which had been prepared in January, was reviewed by the board of directors and then reviewed with the bank. After these reviews and approvals, the processes of producing the FY 1979 budget were considered to be complete.

In its final revised form, the budget became the basis for evaluating managerial performance. Actual results were compared to budgeted amounts each month and cumulatively through the fiscal year, and variances from the budget were thoroughly investigated, discussed, and explained by the managers involved. But even during preparation the budget and budgeting processes had affected all operations of the Company. Because the budget was much more than a set of targets or objectives, it affected all levels of management. By seeking to build on realistic projections, which gave the

EXHIBIT 7

MEMORANDUM

TO: A.B. Hanson, C.A. Hanson, D.W. Bertetto, B.B. Colt,
     R.D. Bloomer, T. E. Sullivan
FROM: J. David Snyder
SUBJECT: Fiscal 1979 planning parameters
DATE: 5 June 1978

The final fiscal 1979 budget is due by June 23. In order for me to meet this date, I need your operating and capital budgets by Monday, June 19. These need to be by expense account line item by month.

Please have your operating area's expenses on the following table which represents shipping plans from Boulder.

	Domestic		
	First quality	*Black promo*	*International*
April 1978			1,000
May			1,262
June		6,500	8,000
July	12,800	6,088	10,000
August	16,565		6,000
September	12,800		
October	12,800		1,000
November	9,035		
December	9,035		1,438
January 1979	2,259		
February			
March			
Total	75,294	12,588	28,700

Also assume an accessories sales budget of $700,000 with a shipping pattern similar to the First Quality Domestic pattern above.

For those expenses which vary by time frame, the following shows how many weeks are in each month: April 4, May 5, June 4, July 4, August 5, September 4, October 4, November 5, December 4, January 5, February 4, March 4. This has particular effect for hourly personnel. Salaried personnel are paid by the month so their salary expense does not vary by months of different lengths.

Do not budget FICA, Group Insurance, Unemployment, Rent, Lease Equipment, Telephone, or Depreciation. I will add these.

Be sure to include your own salaries in this round of budgeting.

PLEASE HAVE YOUR COMPLETE PACKAGE TO ME BY JUNE 19. Ted and I are ready to answer any questions you may have.

J. David Snyder
Treasurer

EXHIBIT 8

HANSON INDUSTRIES (B)
Fiscal Year 1979 Final Budget Revision
Prepared June 15, 1978 ($000)
Income Statement

	Apr–May	Jun	Jul	Aug	Sep	Oct	Nov	Dec	Jan	Feb	Mar	Total
Revenues												
Gross sales: Boots, accessories, parts	$247	$225	$1,726	$2,486	$2,259	$1,984	$1,600	$1,610	$557	$241	$160	$13,095
Less: Discounts:												
U.S. anticipation			20	35	34	35	14					138
Stocking			100	150	100	100	70	23				543
Reorder	(26)		2	4	6	10	15	20	5	2	2	40
International					10	10	10	10	10			50
Returns	55	30	5	5	5	5	10	10	25	25	25	200
Allowances	17					2	3	3	5	10	10	50
Freight: International and domestic	3		18	24	17	17	13	13	3			108
Royalties	2		13	17	13	13	10	9	2	1	1	81
Total deductions	51	30	158	235	185	192	145	88	50	38	38	1,210
Net revenues	196	195	1,568	2,251	2,074	1,792	1,455	1,522	507	203	122	11,885
Net cost of goods sold:												
Boots, accessories, parts	209	135	706	996	928	790	665	721	255	141	95	5,641
Gross margin	(13)	60	862	1,255	1,146	1,002	790	801	252	62	27	6,244
Total operating expenses	505	274	369	409	428	448	420	388	344	349	233	4,165
Operating income	(518)	(214)	495	846	718	554	370	413	(92)	(287)	(206)	2,079
Tax allowance			111	183	138	107	72	82				693
Net income	(518)	(214)	384	663	580	447	298	331	(92)	(287)	(206)	1,386

EXHIBIT 8 (*continued*)

Fiscal 1979 Final Budget Revision
Prepared June 15, 1978
Capital Expenditures ($000)

	Apr–May	Jun	Jul	Aug	Sep	Oct	Nov	Dec	Jan	Feb	Mar	Total
Research & development:												
Capitalize labor	$15	$8	$8	$10	$7	$9	$12	$8	$12	$8	$11	$108
Capitalize supplies		2	2	2	2	2	12	2	2	2	2	20
Mold making equipment–Phase 1			60	50	80	8						198
Mold making equipment–Phase 2								30	30	16		76
Injection molds	58											58
New location investment			5	10	5		4					24
Pantographs	46											46
Metal for molds			10	10	4	5	5	5	5	5	5	54
Total research and development	119	10	85	82	98	24	23	45	49	31	18	584
Operations:												
Assembly			3									3
Flo	1					12						13
Foam	17		10	10	10	9	5			3		64
Injection molding		16	2	10	10	9		5				52
Material handling				14				6				20
Operations services	1	2	2	2	2	2	2	2	2	2		19
General	5	4	4	4	10				6			33
Total operations	24	22	21	40	32	32	7	13	8	5		204
Warehouse		4	4	4	4	4	3	2				25
Service center		2	2	2	2							8
Administration	13		1			1	10		1		1	27
Marketing	1			5	6		1			1		14
Total capital commitment	157	38	113	133	142	61	44	60	58	37	19	862
Back out leased equipment	(46)		(60)	(50)	(80)	(8)		(30)	(30)	(16)		(320)
Add lease payments	16	12	12	12	16	16	18	18	18	18	18	174
Dollar flow for capital equipment	127	50	65	95	78	69	62	48	46	39	37	716

budget high credibility both inside the Company and with the bank and investors, the budget had far reaching effects both during preparation and as finally revised.

Denny Hanson was comfortable with, and confident about, budget processes at Hanson. The January budget was based on careful thought by key managers and provided a basis for planning and controlling operations until the final revised budget was complete. He felt certain that all managers knew what was expected of them, and he knew that even a poor snow season in a major ski region was unlikely to lead to disastrous results. Even though a great deal of time and effort was needed to produce the budget, at the same time managers were being forced to think about their tasks of manufacturing and selling ski boots and securing needed financing during the year. After all, those were still the major tasks to be accomplished in profiting from Chris Hanson's designs around which the Company had grown.

◄ CASE II–8 ►

Hanson Industries (C)

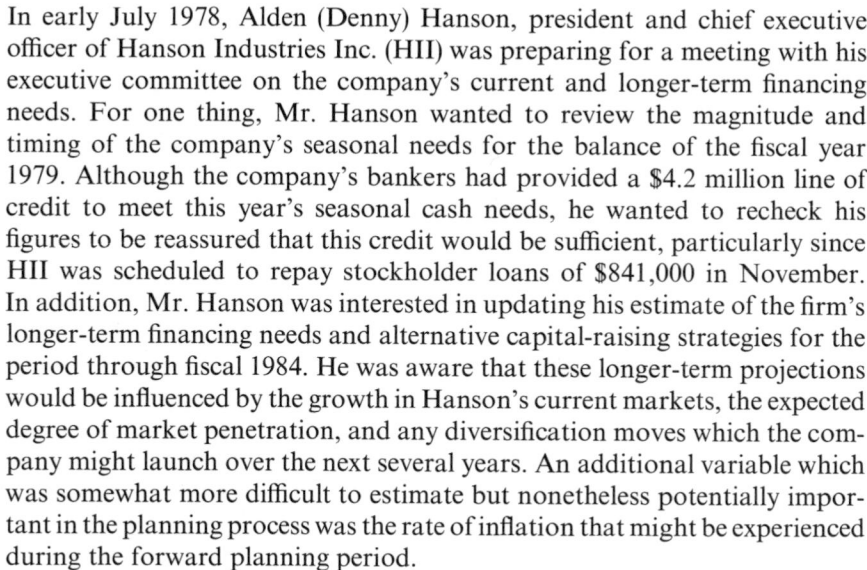

In early July 1978, Alden (Denny) Hanson, president and chief executive officer of Hanson Industries Inc. (HII) was preparing for a meeting with his executive committee on the company's current and longer-term financing needs. For one thing, Mr. Hanson wanted to review the magnitude and timing of the company's seasonal needs for the balance of the fiscal year 1979. Although the company's bankers had provided a $4.2 million line of credit to meet this year's seasonal cash needs, he wanted to recheck his figures to be reassured that this credit would be sufficient, particularly since HII was scheduled to repay stockholder loans of $841,000 in November. In addition, Mr. Hanson was interested in updating his estimate of the firm's longer-term financing needs and alternative capital-raising strategies for the period through fiscal 1984. He was aware that these longer-term projections would be influenced by the growth in Hanson's current markets, the expected degree of market penetration, and any diversification moves which the company might launch over the next several years. An additional variable which was somewhat more difficult to estimate but nonetheless potentially important in the planning process was the rate of inflation that might be experienced during the forward planning period.

COMPANY BACKGROUND

Hanson Industries Inc. was a leading manufacturer of high-quality ski boots. Although it was a relatively new entrant to the market, by 1977 the company's revenues ranked it among the top 10 ski boot manufacturers worldwide.[1] HII commanded a 25 percent share of the U.S. market for high-quality ski boots, which was growing at an estimated 10–15 percent per year. While the bulk of its operations was geared toward U.S. skiers, the international portion of the company's business was growing faster than the domestic portion. The company expected that in FY 1979, its international revenues would represent about 28 percent of total sales.

One of the keys to Hanson's successful penetration of this tough market was the unique design of its ski boots. The revolutionary patented rear-entry concept, designed by Chris Hanson, balanced the objectives of comfort and skiing performance sought by the experienced skier. In May 1977, *Fortune Magazine* named the specially engineered boot in a worldwide competition "one of the 25 best-designed products available in America." By FY 1978, Hanson was marketing four models of adult boots and newer models were continually being added as older models were dropped.

Past-operating performance

Hanson Industries was founded in 1970. The first year of operations, FY 1971, was devoted to development of boot design and preparation for production. In FY 1972, Hanson shipped 2,300 pairs of boots to retailers. By FY 1978 this had grown to 85,000 pairs, and revenues had reached $9.8 million.

While sales had shown continued growth during Hanson's relatively brief history, earnings were more erratic. During the first three years of its existence, Hanson recorded significant losses. Although the company made a small profit in FY 1974, a large loss was reported in FY 1975 which had not been anticipated by management. A number of factors were identified as contributing to the loss, including overly optimistic sales projections, high expense levels, loose budgeting procedures, and the cost of moving the firm into a new plant facility. As the result of corrective measures taken by management, earnings improved in FY 1976, with before tax net income of $540,000. Earnings continued to increase through FY 1978 (see Exhibit 1).

Hanson management expected net revenues to continue to grow at an impressive rate during FY 1979. Sales projections made early in the planning process had later been revised upward so that it was now expected that net

---

[1] The majority of Hanson's competitors were based outside the United States. See Hanson (A) for a more detailed description of markets and competition.

EXHIBIT 1

HANSON INDUSTRIES (C)
Income Statements
($000)

	1976	1977	1978
Net sales	$5,753	$7,671	$9,776
Cost of goods sold	3,040	4,140	5,177
Gross margin	2,713	3,531	4,599
Selling, general and administrative	1,585	2,109	2,519
Product development	152	189	260
Operating earnings	976	1,233	1,820
Interest expense	436	428	507
Income before tax and extraordinary item	540	805	1,313
Tax provision	314	468	400
Earnings before extraordinary item	226	337	913
Extraordinary item tax benefit from utilization of operating loss carry forwards	314	468	251
Net earnings	$ 540	$ 805	$1,164
Earnings per common share Earnings before extraordinary item	$ 0.39	$ 0.57	$ 1.50
Extraordinary item	0.53	0.79	0.41
Net earnings	0.92	1.36	1.91
Weighted average number of common shares outstanding	585,889	590,566	607,761

Notes: (a) Depreciation and amortization for 1976, 1977, and 1978 was $341, $396, and $561, respectively. (b) Tax differentials between domestic and foreign earnings accounted for much of the premium taxes paid in 1976 and 1977.

sales would reach $12 million for the year. By FY 1984, Hanson predicted revenues from ski boots would approximate $26 million; beyond that point it was expected that unit volume of sales would only increase proportionate to overall growth in the market.

THE ORDER CYCLE

HII's ski boot business was extremely seasonal and could be broken down into the ordering, shipment, and collection phases. The ordering phase was comprised of two parts: the stocking order period and the reorder period. During the stocking order period from March through June, Hanson's sales representatives conducted an intensive marketing campaign, commencing with the equipment dealers' annual Ski Show held in Las Vegas in March. The timing of this show was important in that it was held just after the end of the previous ski season when both manufacturers and equipment dealers were aware of past equipment sales performance and retail inventory levels. Hanson usually received 25–30 percent of its total orders at this Ski Show and another 55–60 percent of the orders between April and June when the sales representatives contacted all the dealers who had not attended the show. Discounts were offered to customers, ranging from 4 percent to 12 percent, and accounts were typically payable on the 10th day of the second or third month following shipment, depending upon the date of their requested shipment. These terms were similar to—and slightly tighter than—the terms offered by HII's competitors.

The reorder period accounted for the remaining 15 percent of Hanson's sales and started in July, when dealers reordered to replenish their supplies. A 2 percent discount was available to these customers for payment by the 10th of the month following shipment.

Sparse snow years affected the order phase in two fiscal years. The first effect was felt almost immediately in the year the snow did not fall, and manifested itself as a reduction in the reorders received. The second, and more pronounced, effect was felt during the stocking order period in the following spring. At that time, dealers' inventories were higher than their normal levels and dealers were wary of placing large initial stocking orders, for fear of experiencing two consecutive poor snow years and the consequent falloff in demand.

Shipments began in July, peaked in August, and remained at a high level until December, when they trailed off. The largest part of Hanson's collections on accounts receivable began in December following the shipment phase. In a normal business year, the collection period was about 75 days. However, a poor snow year, such as fiscal 1977, had the effect of significantly stretching the collection period. In 1977 operations had followed budgeted levels quite closely until mid-December, when it became obvious that the country was experiencing a poor snow year. This had two important impacts on Hanson. First, $450,000 worth of reorders that were expected between mid-December and mid-January failed to materialize and the company was forced to lower January production levels by that amount. Second, the dealers lacked the cash to completely fulfill their December and January payment obligations to Hanson, leading to a $550,000 slowdown in receivables collections. In consequence, a total of $550,000 in receivables went past due by mid-January and were no longer eligible as collateral to support seasonal bank borrowings. The combination of the newly disqualified receivables and the $450,000 reduction in finished goods inventory generated by the curtailed January production schedule eliminated approximately $1 million of assets which had been counted on as collateral for bank borrowings during the fourth quarter of 1977. Payment on the receivables did eventually trickle in during the late spring and summer and inventory was worked down during the following fiscal year.

THE PRODUCTION AND FINANCING CYCLE

Manufacturing commenced in January and production schedules were subsequently modified and adjusted as the shape and size of the order pattern became clearer. A level production policy was adopted for three reasons. HII did not want to lay off skilled workers (50 percent of their 123-person production force) who were key to the manufacture of the ski boots. In addition, the company did not have sufficient physical capacity to turn out an entire year's production after March when the first orders were received. Finally, management had sufficient confidence in their sales forecasts to manufacture up to 60 percent of such projections in advance of firm orders.

Hanson's seasonal marketing efforts and level manufacturing operations created a substantial liquidity management challenge. Although by June the company had produced approximately 60 percent of the year's expected volume of finished boots, it wasn't until November that most of the year's finished goods inventory was converted to accounts receivable; it was December before the bulk of receivables collections began flowing in (see Exhibits 2 and 3).

David Snyder, HII's treasurer, typically developed a preliminary cash budget in January, before the start of the fiscal year, and on the basis of that projection made appropriate arrangements for funding the coming season's cash needs. Based on the results of sales efforts and orders received during the spring, the budget was reviewed at the end of June and revisions were made as necessary.

As one means of generating cash during the early season, Hanson offered some of its largest and most valued customers a prepayment program in exchange for substantial discounts. In fiscal 1978 customer prepayments totaled $1 million, thus reducing the firm's cash shortfall while at the same time providing an attractive profit motive for customers to buy Hanson products.

Hanson's management also practised very tight internal cash management control. In fact, Mr. Snyder believed that the optimum target for the firm's cash balances was zero, since Hanson was highly leveraged financially and would have had to pay interest to support any cash balances maintained at the bank.

Despite these efforts to conserve or stretch cash within the firm, Hanson had still found it necessary to arrange substantial short-term loans from banks and finance companies and longer-term financing from principal stockholders. Although current seasonal financing was being handled exclusively with a group of commercial banks, HII had made use of some commercial financing in the past. Commercial financing companies made more frequent audits of the borrower's operations and finances than was typical for the banks and usually levied a higher interest charge (oftentimes 4 to 5 percent over prime). Because of its frequent monitoring and higher interest rate, the

EXHIBIT 2
Fiscal 1979 cash budget ($000)

| | April–May | 1978 | | | | | | | 1979 | | |
		June	July	Aug.	Sept.	Oct.	Nov.	Dec.	Jan.	Feb.	Mar.
Cash receipts	$1,463	$ 500	$ 250	$ 450	$ 588	$1,000	$1,054	$2,518	$2,300	$1,000	$ 500
Cash outflow											
Material purchases	375	251	330	433	208	208	431	252	241	201	201
Out-of-pocket expenses	802	500	621	714	661	622	634	551	476	514	389
Interest	43	24	29	36	45	54	56	58	43	24	19
Capital expenditure	127	50	65	95	78	69	62	48	46	39	37
Pay back stockholder loans	—	—	—	—	—	—	841	—	—	—	—
Collateral base											
Receivables		310	1,176	2,564	3,206	3,794	3,862	2,730	1,321	817	626
Inventory		1,058	927	844	656	529	554	477	700	905	1,119
Raw materials and fixed assets		670	670	670	670	670	670	670	670	670	670

EXHIBIT 3

HANSON INDUSTRIES (C)
Quarterly Balance Sheets
($000)

	3/31/77	7/31/77	9/30/77	12/31/77	3/31/78
Cash	$ 101	$ 117	$ 100	$ 117	$ 156
Accounts receivable	1,359	2,342	3,488	3,456	1,556
Inventories:					
Raw materials	538	671	709	596	600
Work in process	162	237	204	269	226
Finished products	1,404	1,583	1,470	798	903
Total	2,104	2,491	2,383	1,663	1,729
Prepaid expenses	179	283	261	172	262
Total current assets	3,743	5,233	6,232	4,408	3,703
Gross fixed assets	1,958	2,225	2,533	2,903	3,393
Depreciation	(836)	(946)	(999)	(1,082)	(1,255)
Net fixed assets	1,122	1,279	1,534	1,821	2,138
Patents and other	136	151	151	145	207
Total assets	$5,001	$ 6,663	$7,917	$ 7,374	$ 6,048
Accounts payable	$ 956	$ 1,241	$1,021	$ 815	$ 944
Advance payments on sales orders	12	622	107	20	—
Notes payable–banks	2,082	3,124	3,824	2,804	1,547
Notes payable– stockholders	—	—	—	200	1,010
Total current liabilities	3,050	4,987	4,952	3,839	3,517
Deferred income tax	—	—	—	—	133
Contracts payable	161	163	526	339	642
Notes payable– stockholders	1,281	1,246	1,246	1,046	—
Capital stock	1,272	1,283	1,284	1,284	1,354
Retained earnings:					
Prior	(763)	(763)	(763)	(763)	(763)
Fiscal 1978		(253)	672	1,629	1,164
Total	(763)	(1,016)	(91)	866	402
Total stockholders' equity	509	267	1,193	2,150	1,756
Total liabilities and stockholders' equity	$5,001	$ 6,663	$7,917	$ 7,374	$ 6,048

finance company felt comfortable in extending a larger amount of funds against inventory and accounts receivable collateral than would normally be true for a commercial bank. Commercial financing had been particularly helpful to HII during periods of extraordinary funds needs (such as sparse snow years) when available bank credit was inadequate.

It was the company's goal, however, to move toward exclusive reliance on commercial bank funding, primarily because of the potentially lower cost of such borrowings to Hanson and secondarily because of the higher quality corporate image it portrayed. In February 1978, Hanson had obtained approval of a $4.2 million revolving line of credit for fiscal 1979 at 3.75 percent over prime with a group of three banks led by the United Bank of Denver, which was in a good geographical position to maintain day-to-day contact with Hanson.[2] HII could draw against this line of credit to the extent of 70 percent of the cost of finished goods inventory and 80 percent of current accounts receivable. The fact that the banks had reduced the interest rate charge in FY 1979 was seen by Mr. Hanson as an indication of the company's improved credit standing in the eyes of these lenders (see Exhibit 4). That conviction was further strengthened when the banks informed HII that the personal guarantees of the major stockholders would not be required as a condition of the 1979 credit line.

Denny Hanson recognized the value of longer-term financial planning as a supplement to season cash budgeting and he therefore determined to make tentative projections of financial needs and resources for the five years following fiscal 1979. For the purposes of these projections, he assumed that the company's sales growth would approximate 20 percent for fiscal 1980 and that subsequent increases would bring net sales to $26 million (in constant dollars) by the end of fiscal 1984, at which point annual increases would be limited to the rate of overall growth in the high-priced ski boot market. He expected that accounts receivables would, at worst, be proportional to revenues and would under these circumstances approximate 15.5 percent of net sales at fiscal year end. Though there were no plans for a major change in credit policies, it was possible that the company's strengthening market position would permit the credit manager to shorten modestly the credit terms extended to customers. Inventory, which had been inordinately depleted at year-end 1978 by higher-than-anticipated sales, was expected to be rebuilt to a level of approximately 20 percent of sales. Accounts payable at the end of FY 1979 were expected to remain at approximately the same dollar amount as at year-end 1978 but would rise proportionately with sales thereafter.

Mr. Hanson expected annual capital expenditures to approximate $500,000 in each of the next five years to maintain the company's position in the markets they were now serving and to meet the five year, $26 million revenue target. (This would be roughly equal to the depreciation generated during these years.) No significant replacement of equipment now in use was anticipated during the next five years and it was assumed that HII's plant facilities would continue to be leased. Barring significant changes in the federal tax laws, the company's tax rate was expected to be an effective 40 percent of operating profit for the years 1979–84, taking into consideration investment tax credits and other incentives to invest in new capital equipment.

---

[2] In July 1978 the prime rate was 9 percent. The credit line for fiscal 1978 had also been $4.2 million and had carried an interest rate of 4 percent over prime.

EXHIBIT 4

HANSON INDUSTRIES (C)
Consolidated Balance Sheets
($000)

	3/31/76		3/31/77	3/31/78
Current assets				
Cash		$ 163	$ 81	$ 156
Receivables, net		692	1,378	1,556
Inventories				
Raw materials and purchases	$350		$ 538	$600
Work in process	164		162	226
Finished products	838		1,404	903
Total		1,352	2,104	1,729
Prepaid expenses		99	124	262
Total current assets		2,306	3,687	3,703
Fixed assets				
Machinery and equipment		1,223	1,720	2,502
Leasehold improvements		110	126	220
Office furniture and equipment		97	112	143
Leased property under capital leases		—	—	528
Less accumulated depreciation and amortization		569	836	1,255
Total net fixed assets		861	1,122	2,138
Patents and other		171	191	207
Total assets		$3,338	$5,001	$6,048
Total liabilities				
Accounts payable		$ 475	$ 956	$ 944
Advance payment on sales orders		61	12	—
Notes payable–banks		1,100	2,082	1,547 (a)
Income taxes payable		—	—	16 (b)
Current installments– long-term debt		109	35	1,010 (c)
Total current liabilities		1,745	3,084	3,517
Deferred income tax		—	—	133 (d)
Long-term debt		1,396	1,281	—
Notes payable to banks		506	—	—
Capital leases and other		27	126	642 (e)
Total		1,929	1,407	642
Stockholders' equity				
Common stock		1,126	1,166	1,249
Additional paid-in capital		105	105	105
Retained earnings (deficit)		(1,567)	(763)	402
Total stockholders' equity		(336)	509	1,756
Total liabilities		$3,338	$5,001	$6,048

Notes:

(a) Borrowings under the revolving line of credit were personally guaranteed by the major stockholders, and were secured by all of the accounts receivables, inventories, machinery and equipment, furniture, trademarks, and patent rights.

(b) Income taxes were payable in quarterly installments in July, September, December, and March, based on the previous year's tax payments. Year-end balances were the difference between actual and estimated tax liabilities for the current year.

(c) Current installments on long-term debt: 3/31/78

Officers and stockholders	841,000
Installment purchases	80,000
Capital leases	89,000
	1,010,000

(d) This item arose from an alternative treatment of profits on international sales and was expected to grow by 50–100 percent in each of the next several years.

(e) The present value of future commitments were discounted at 10.5 percent per year. Installment contracts totaled $239,000 and capitalized leases were $403,000. Approximately 18 percent of the remaining year-end present value would be amortized in each of the years 1979–83.

Hanson's management had devoted considerable time and thought to possible diversification options available to the company. One logical move would be into the manufacture of custom molds for other than their own needs. Beyond that, a variety of opportunities in the general recreation market had been considered and one or two acquisition possibilities (calling for between $500,000 and $1,500,000 of HII investment) had been examined each year since 1973. Management sought to sustain HII's growth over the long term rather than allow the company to plateau as the saturation point in ski boot sales approached in the early 1980s. However, the shape and timing of the company's future diversification moves would obviously be constrained by HII's projected financial resources. Thus, management wondered what rate of future growth could reasonably be sustained with the financial resources likely to be available to it.

As part of Hanson's forward planning process, Denny Hanson sought an appropriate capital structure strategy to support the company's future growth and diversification. Once the shareholder loans had been eliminated, there was always the possibility that additional long-term capital could be raised from both conventional debt and equity suppliers to supplement any excess funds which might be generated internally.

A public offering of common stock was one such possibility. In the past, HII had compensated some of its employees with shares of the company's equity stock. That practice might be attractive in the future if HII could assure some degree of liquidity for the stock, either by committing sufficient excess cash to repurchase the stock according to some earnings or book value formula or by establishing a public market for the shares. However, in July 1978, investment bankers were characterizing the U.S. equity market as "soft" and the future outlook for new issues was uncertain. Many market observers attributed this at least in part to the uncertain outlook for inflation and the consequent effect on the economy. The consumer price index had risen nearly 10 percent on an annualized basis thus far during 1978 and economic forecasts were divided on the direction it would take in the year ahead.

Additional debt capital was another possible source of future financing, although its cost and availability would also be effected by the future inflationary trend. Management had not yet determined an appropriate mix of debt and equity funds for HII, but they believed that their stockholders, whose investment objectives stressed capital appreciation, might prefer to avoid the earnings dilution involved in equity financing if possible. They might be attracted to a financing plan which continued to emphasize the use of borrowed funds, even if that implied a capital structure more heavily weighted with debt than might be typical for this kind of company.

Crans–Mon S.A.

INTRODUCTION

Hans van der Rein advanced to the presidency of Crans–Mon S.A. from the position of vice president of manufacturing. During his first review of company-wide budgetary procedures, he expressed dissatisfaction with existing practices in the planning and control of selling and distribution costs. He expressed his concerns to the controller and requested him to develop an improved system.

Crans–Mon produced a complete line of household and industrial cleaning compounds in three manufacturing facilities located within the European Economic Community. These plants supplied five sales divisions, organized along national boundaries, which sold the C–M brand lines to wholesalers, retailers, and large industrial customers. Organizationally, the sales divisions were structured along market, rather than product lines. In addition to the wholesale, retail, and industrial departments each division had a warehouse and an administrative services department. The latter included such activities as advertising and promotion, accounting, personnel, and public relations. Department heads reported to the sales division manager, who was responsible to the corporate vice president of marketing. Sales divisions were essentially autonomous except for their dependence on the manufacturing plants for product supply and upon corporate headquarters for centralized computer processing of operating and accounting data.

EXISTING BUDGETING PROCESS

Sales forecast

Dag Farley, vice president of marketing, initiated the annual budgetary process by transmitting to the sales divisions a general statement of expectations as to economic trends which would impact on the market and price of C–M Products. Sales division managers modified and expanded on these guidelines to reflect (*a*) conditions in their respective markets and (*b*) the

This case was prepared by Professor Earl D. Bennett. Copyright © 1976 by l'Institut pour l'Etude des Methodes de Direction de l'Entreprise (IMEDE), Lausanne, Switzerland. Reproduced by permission.

planned levels of advertising and promotional efforts. Based on this information, historical sales records, and personal knowledge of his market, each department head prepared a forecast of sales by product line and by month for the first six months of the budget year. Forecasts for the remaining six months were in total by product line. Quarterly, these sales forecasts were rolled forward with explanations of any significant deviations from prior forecasts.

After review and reconciliation of differences at the division level, a consolidated forecast was submitted to the vice president of marketing for review, approval, and corporate consolidation. This consolidated forecast formed the basis for production planning. In his former capacity as vice president of manufacturing, Hans found this process quite satisfactory for production scheduling in the three plants. However, he was not fully aware of the sales expense budgeting process until he became president.

Sales expense budget

Concurrent with the transmittal of corporate marketing guidelines, the controller provided each sales division with a detailed printout of actual expenses by the marketing department for the preceding year and current year to date. In addition, a year-to-date comparison of actual monthly expenses to budget was prepared for the sales departments, warehouse, and service departments. The monthly budget equaled $\frac{1}{12}$ of the annual budget.

Guided by these records and plans for achieving his sales forecasts, the department head prepared an annual budget by natural expense classification. After review and approval at division level, sales department budgets were combined to form a sales-function expense budget and forwarded to headquarters with expense budgets for the warehouses and service departments. At headquarters, Dag Farley performed similar review, reconciliation, and consolidation procedures with the controller serving as coordinator in the preparation of company-wide operating budgets for presidential review and approval.

The president expressed the belief that the sales expense budget suffered from two basic weaknesses.

1. It was impossible for any one to ascertain, with any feeling of certainty, the reasonableness of the estimates made by the various department heads. Clearly, the expenses of the preceding year did not constitute adequate standards against which these expense estimates could be judged, since selling conditions were never the same in two different years. One obvious cause of variation in selling expenses was the variation in the "job to be done," as defined in the sales forecast.
2. Selling conditions often changed substantially after the budget was adopted, but there was no provision for reflecting corresponding changes in the selling expense budget. Neither was there a logical basis for relating

selling expenses to the actual sales volume obtained or to any other measure of sales effort. The chief executive believed that it was reasonable to expect that sales expenses would increase, though not proportionately, if actual sales volume were greater than the forecasted volume; but that with the existing method of control it was impossible to determine how large the increase in expenses should be.

As a means of overcoming these weaknesses, the president suggested the possibility of setting selling expense standards on a fixed and variable basis, a method similar to the techniques used in the control of manufacturing expenses. He also suggested consideration of this approach in budgeting for warehouse operations, but requested the controller to proceed, first, with the study of sales expenses.

The controller approached the vice president of marketing to obtain the cooperation of the sales divisions. Dag reacted: "What the hell! Selling isn't like producing a batch of compounds. Anyone in the selling game knows that sometimes customers fall all over each other in their hurry to buy, and other times, no matter what we do, they won't even nibble. It's a waste of time to make fancy formulas for selling expense budgets under conditions like that." In response, the controller explained that the president had requested the study. "Well," Dag commented, "Hans may have to learn the hard way. Contact the Holland division. They're the most cooperative and you'll need all the help you can get. But, I still think it's a waste of their time and yours."

ALTERNATIVE APPROACH

Before contacting Konrad Kramer, Holland division manager, the controller conducted a general review of the sales volume and expense trends of the Holland Division during the past five years. He also examined data from prior special studies of selling costs which had been used in allocating costs to products, customers, functions, and territories, and in the determination of minimum order quantities. Based on this review, the controller approached Konrad with the suggestion that in considering the relevant range of volume, the lower limit be set at the minimum sales volume which the Holland division was most likely to experience in the foreseeable future.

After being briefed on the project, Mr. Kramer assigned a staff assistant the task of studying the past sales records of the company over several business cycles, the long-term outlook for sales, and sales trends in other companies in the industry. From the report prepared by his assistant, Mr. Kramer concluded that sales volume would not drop below 45 percent of the current level of the division. Mr. Kramer then attempted to determine the selling expenses which would be incurred at the minimum volume by developing a hypothetical selling organization which in his opinion would be required to sell merchandise equivalent to 45 percent of current capacity, complete as to the number of persons needed to staff the three selling departments. He also included the advertising function, although performed within the service department. Based on this hypothetical organization, the staff assistant estimated total salaries and expenses by line item for operation at the minimum sales volume. After review and revision, Mr. Kramer forwarded the report to the controller.

The controller decided that the variable portion of the selling expense standard should be expressed as a specified amount per sales dollar. He realized that the sales dollar, as a measuring stick, had certain disadvantages in that it would not reflect such important influences on costs as the size of the order, the selling difficulty of certain territories, changes in buyer psychology, and so forth. The sales dollar, however, was the measuring stick most convenient to use, the only figure readily available from the records then being kept, and a figure which all the individuals concerned clearly understood. The controller believed that a budget which varied with sales would certainly be better than a budget which did not vary at all. He planned to

EXHIBIT 1
Holland division budget for "miscellaneous expense" (guilders)

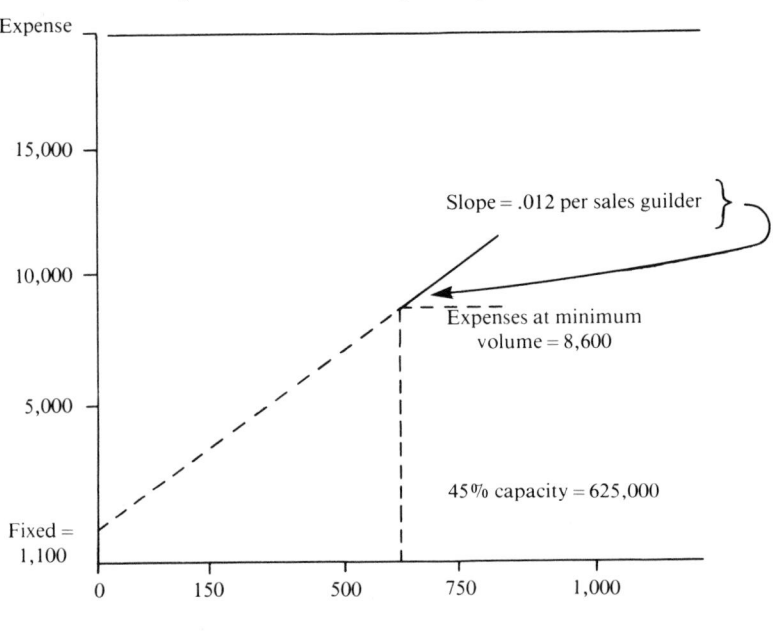

Sales volume (000)

devise a more accurate measure of causes of variation in selling expenses after studying the nature of these factors over a longer period of time.

As a basis for setting the initial expense standards, the controller prepared a series of charts on which the actual annual expenditures for the principal groups of expense items were correlated with sales volumes. Using these charts, which showed to what extent the principal expense items had fluctuated with sales volume in the past, and modifying them in accordance with his own judgment, the controller determined a rate of variation for the variable portion of each item of selling expense. The controller thought that after the new system had been tested in practice, it would be possible to refine these rates, perhaps by the use of a technique analogous to the time-study technique which was employed to determine certain expense standards in the factory.

At this point the controller had both a rate of variation and one point (i.e., at 45 percent capacity) on the selling expense curve for each expense item. He was therefore able to construct a formula for each item by extending a line through the known point at the slope represented by the rate of variation. He determined the height of this line at zero volume and called this amount the fixed portion of the selling expense formula. The diagram in Exhibit 1 illustrates the procedure, although the actual computations were mathematical rather than graphic. He then prepared Exhibit 2 which showed the fixed portion (column 1) and the variable rate (column 2) by expense item.

EXHIBIT 2
Holland division sales function budget comparisons (guilders)

	Budget components at 45 percent capacity		Old budget at $\frac{1}{12}$ of annual	New budget at formula rates	Actual expenses	Over (Under)	
	Fixed (1)	Variable rate (2)	(3)	(4)	(5)	Old budget (6)	New budget (7)
Sales-net of tax on value added (TVA)	625,000		1 Million	800,000	800,000		
Administrative salaries	10,000	—	10,000	10,000	10,000	—	—
Sales commissions		.070	70,000	56,000	56,000	14,000	—
Advertising and promotion	900	.020	20,000	16,900	18,900	1,100	(2,000)
Travel	2,850	.015	18,250	14,850	16,750	1,500	(1,900)
Office salaries	600	.006	6,000	5,400	6,000	—	(600)
Office supplies	1,650	.004	6,500	4,850	4,000	2,500	850
Employee benefits	450	.002	2,000	2,050	2,000	—	50
Space rental	4,750	—	4,750	4,750	4,750	—	—
Depreciation	3,900	—	3,900	3,900	4,900	(1,000)	1,000
Utilities	800	.001	1,500	1,600	2,000	(500)	400
Miscellaneous	1,100	.012	12,750	10,700	9,850	2,900	850
Total	27,000	.130	155,650	131,000	135,150	20,500	(4,150)

To contrast the old system and the proposed change he entered the old budget for a recent month in column 3, the budget determined under the formula approach (column 4) and then the actual expenses for the month (column 5). The over–under columns (6 and 7) resulted from comparison of actual expenses with the two budgets.

The controller planned to discuss with Mr. Kramer the test results of this new approach before drafting his report and recommendations for the vice-president of marketing. Unless he encountered serious objections from Kramer and Farley, he intended to recommend adoption of the approach on a test basis. After a test period of several months, he anticipated incorporation of some refinements. He was convinced that the concept could be applied with greater precision to warehouse operations, whereas, improvements in the planning and control of service departments expense would necessitate a different approach.

⎯⎯◄CASE II – 10 ►⎯⎯

Larsen–Walker, Ltd.

In early April 1976, Miles Foster, general manager—finance of Larsen–Walker, Ltd. was reviewing his notes in preparation for an upcoming management committee meeting. It was at this meeting that he intended to propose that the company shift their budgeting process to what he chose to refer to as an adjustable budget.

The system of budgeting and reporting currently employed by Larsen–Walker had evolved over a period of some 20 years. For many years, it had served as an effective management control device. In the last few years, however, its effectiveness had been put increasingly into question as the result of a series of changes in the firm's business environment. Most specifically, a continuing series of negative variances had caused many of the firm's operating managers to simply disregard the entire system.

Company background

Larsen–Walker, Ltd., headquartered in Hurlingham, England, manufactured steering and general components for trucks, construction equipment,

This case was written by Charles T. Sharpless, MBA candidate, and Professor M. Edgar Barrett. Copyright © 1979 by M. Edgar Barrett.

farm machinery, and other off-road vehicles. These components were sold worldwide to original equipment manufacturers. They were also sold to distributors and retailers for sale in the replacement parts market.

A partial list of the company's major products included manual and power steering gears, steering columns, steering linkages, pistons, valves, valve train components, and water pumps. The company's manufacturing facilities were largely assembly plants, dependent upon independent suppliers for parts and materials. These parts and materials were sourced from suppliers located in a number of different countries.

While the company had developed a worldwide reputation with original equipment manufacturers, most of the firm's marketing operations were concentrated in Western Europe and the British Isles. Its manufacturing operations were primarily located in Great Britain. There were, however, two foreign plants, one in Canada and one in South America. Encouraged originally by the prospect of the postwar markets in Western Europe, the company had concentrated on expanding its British Isles marketing network over onto the continent.

Contemporary environmental issues

At present, the demand for steering gears, steering linkages and certain other general components far outstripped Larsen–Walker's ability to assemble and supply them. Several of the firm's plants were operating at their current, practical capacity. Despite this, the company had still been forced to ration some of the more scarce components.

Despite the inability to satisfy the demand for some key products, few of the firm's present problems related directly to (theoretical) plant capacity. Rather, they involved such things as foreign exchange, unreliable supply schedules, labor unrest and an unsettled political situation.

The firm's steering gear and steering linkage assembly operations, for example, had experienced a number of recent problems. These operations, based in Devon, England, sourced a number of components from suppliers located in foreign countries. The largest such supplier was located in West Germany. Larsen–Walker's contracts with this supplier were generally denominated in deutsche marks. Thus, the recent fall of pound sterling had resulted in the firm's incoming costs showing a significant increase. The German supplier, however, had been most reliable in meeting both delivery schedules and quality standards.

The firm's Italian suppliers, on the other hand, had become increasingly unreliable, particularly in terms of meeting the delivery schedules on large orders. The incoming pound sterling costs of their components, however, had held quite steady over the last year or so.

Even within the British Isles, the dependability of the firm's suppliers was no longer what the firm would have hoped for. The recently witnessed inflation rates, which were well above postwar standards and expectations, had taken their toll in several ways. First, the year-to-year increase in both labor and component costs had been well above the company's expectations—even after consideration of the initiation of "cost tolerances" (see later discussion). Second, a few of the firm's suppliers had begun to demand semiannual contract price changes, rather than the more normal annual arrangements. Finally, the firm had not found it easy to pass on price and cost increases to their customers.

The local inflation problem was compounded by the recent upsurge in labor strife. A marked deterioration in labor relations appeared to have occurred in the 1973/1974 period. Since that time, Larsen–Walker had rarely gone more than 90 days without some form of labor unrest upsetting their own production schedules. To make matters worse, many of their British-based suppliers had also suffered from labor problems. This had resulted in their often being unable to deliver components on schedule or in the desired quantities.

Finally, the political situation—both within Great Britain and in the rest of Western Europe—was not as supportive as it once had been. The West German government had recently raised the effective income tax rate on foreign subsidiaries by nearly 10 percent. Larsen–Walker's sales subsidiary in that country would inevitably be affected by that ruling. Early next month, a government bill calling for the nationalization of the British aircraft and shipbuilding industries was to be voted on in both houses of Parliament. If Great Britain's recent trend toward nationalization were to continue, the vehicle components business would be a likely candidate.

Organizational structure

Larsen–Walker's line management structure was initially divided into five distinct operating divisions: engine components; steering components; general components; OEM sales; and aftermarket operations. (see Exhibit 1.) The engine components division had manufacturing facilities in Hurlingham and Argentina. Steering components were manufactured solely at Devon. The general components division, the largest manufacturing division, had plants in both Wales and Canada.

The marketing operations were organized to serve two related, but distinguishable, markets. The OEM sales division was responsible for sales and marketing efforts directed toward original equipment manufacturers. This division was organized into four separate sales territories. Larsen–Walker enjoyed healthy market share positions in both the British Isles and Western Europe. The other two sales territories were less healthy, but were felt to hold good long-term potential. The aftermarket sales division was responsible for the sale of replacement parts on a worldwide basis.

EXHIBIT 1 Organization chart

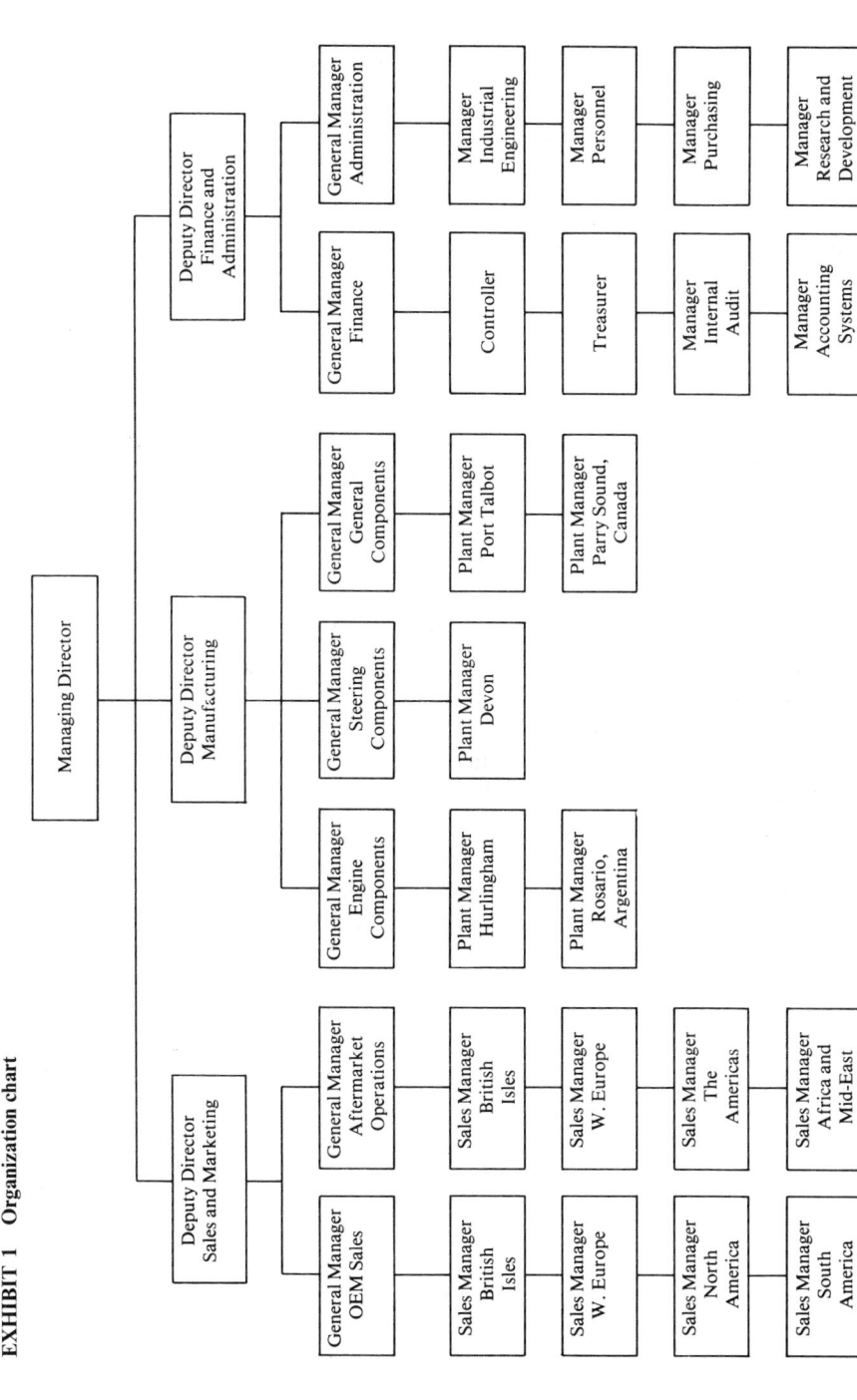

The staff portion of Larsen–Walker's management structure was headed by a deputy director. Two general managers, including Miles Foster, reported directly to this person.

Products manufactured or assembled by any of the three manufacturing divisions were transferred to the responsibility of one of the two marketing divisions prior to sale to the firm's customers. Thus, the ultimate measurement of product profitability occurred in the marketing arena.

THE MANAGEMENT CONTROL SYSTEM

A variety of responsibility centers, budgeting techniques, reports, and meetings were employed by Larsen–Walker, Ltd., to plan, monitor, and control the operations of the overall firm. For example, the firm's senior management had divided the firm into profit centers, standard cost centers, and discretionary expense centers. The three manufacturing divisions, as well as the individual plants of which they were comprised, were all treated as standard cost centers. The two sales and marketing divisions, as well as the four individual sales territories contained within each, were all treated as profit centers. Thus, the marketing managers were viewed as having profit responsibility. The various components of the finance and administration area were all viewed as discretionary expense centers.

Annual budgets were prepared for each of the five divisions, their component parts, and each major staff function. This budgeting process took place during the July-to-November period of the year preceding the budget year in question. Once set, budgets were rarely, if ever, changed during the course of the year. A flexible budget was used for those portions of the business where costs were expected to vary with production or sales levels.

Quarterly meetings were scheduled with all plant, sales territory, major staff function, and divisional general managers in order to review the results of the most recent three month period. As of late, these had not been as productive as senior management might have hoped. The problem centered around the fact that the operating managers had a tendency to blame the continual negative variances on factors said to be beyond their control.

The derivation and budgeting of standard manufacturing costs

Larsen–Walker employed a standard direct-costing system whereby all variable costs of production and assembly were assigned to a specific product line. Fixed costs, or those that were not viewed as varying with the level of production were also given standard (or budgeted) cost levels. These costs, however, were charged against the manufacturing plant as a whole rather than against any one specific product line or model.

Standard costs for each year were ultimately subject to approval by the firm's budget committee, which consisted of the controller, the general manager—finance and the three general managers from the manufacturing division.[1] The original budgets and, hence, the standard costs included within them, however, were arrived at by a process of negotiation between the appropriate plant or department manager, that manager's immediate superior, and a representative from the controller's office.

The primary sources of outside counsel used by the controllers department were the purchasing department and the industrial engineering department. These departments were responsible for gathering accurate data and updating the departmental records each year. The purchasing department provided data on the cost of raw materials and preassembled parts. Much of this was gathered from suppliers' invoices and trade association and governmental statistics.

The industrial engineering department provided data about standard labor times and appropriate material usage rates and waste factors. The labor time rates were derived by the use of a time catalogue known as *Methods Time Measurement.* All production workers' jobs were broken down into constituent parts, by product line or model, and a standard time assigned. The material usage rates and waste factors were derived from in-plant studies.

Both production-line labor and most material and/or subassembly costs were viewed by the firm as varying with the level of production. Hence, the standard direct-labor costs and standard direct-material costs were both assigned to specific product lines or models.

Standard direct-labor costs were determined by multiplying the appropriate standard labor times by standard wage rates. The standard wage rates were estimated from current union contracts and from estimated cost-of-living index changes projected into the budget year.

Standard direct-material costs were determined by multiplying the usage rates by cost data provided by the purchasing department and amended for expected price increases during the budget year.

Those overhead costs which varied directly with the volume of production were also assigned to specific product lines and models. Such costs were budgeted via the use of standard variable overhead costs. A factor, applied to a product line's or model's standard direct-labor cost, was used to arrive at this budgeted amount. The standard variable-overhead cost for steering linkages, for example, was currently set at 125 percent of standard direct-labor cost. The standard variable-overhead factor was periodically examined and reinterpreted.

All other costs, i.e., those not included as part of the standard direct costing system, were considered to be fixed costs and were budgeted on a

---

[1] In the case of the budgets for the marketing divisions or the staff functions, appropriate managers from these areas were substituted for the three manufacturing division general managers.

category-by-category, plant-wide basis. The standards used for each of the categories were arrived at by process of negotiation.

Cost tolerances

Several years ago, in response to what seemed to be a constant flow of complaints about the tightness of the standards used in the budgeting process, the budget committee authorized the use of "cost tolerances" in standard cost center budgets and reports. Cost tolerances were deemed to be acceptable levels of negative variations from the already determined standard cost figures. They were used only in the case of standard direct costs.

Cost tolerances were budgeted as a per unit adjustment to the standard direct cost of each product line within the manufacturing division. Despite the fact that they were budgeted on a per unit basis, they were designed to provide some measure of protection against negative variances emanating from any of five possible sources. These possible sources included unexpected material or preassembled component part price increases (including foreign exchange related changes), unexpected material wastage, unforeseen wage inflation, direct labor efficiency items called nonstandard labor costs,[2] and abnormal increases in variable overhead costs.

Cost tolerances were set for each plant and product line as the result of negotiations between the plant manager, that manager's immediate supervisor, and a representative from the controller's office. As little consensus existed as to what, *a priori*, was an appropriate level of cost tolerances, the amount of such cost tolerances differed substantially within the manufacturing divisions and, occasionally, within production plants as well.

The reporting system for standard cost centers

Each of the three manufacturing divisions, the five manufacturing plants, and the major product-line departments within each plant were responsible for submitting monthly operating reports to headquarters in Hurlingham (Exhibit 2). These reports contained records of monthly performance as well as year-to-date figures. These "actual" figures were compared with the standard direct cost figures on a flexible budget basis and variances were computed. These variances, net of the already approved cost tolerances, were shown next to the actual monthly and year-to-date figures.

The monthly operating reports also contained a revised annual forecast. This forecast was designed to represent the operating manager's best projection as to what the remainder of the operating year would look like. This

---

[2] *Nonstandard labor costs* was a term adopted to include any sort of unproductive use of direct labor. As such, they might be caused by machine down time, undercapacity plant utilization, or inefficient scheduling.

Monthly operating report

Plant: Port Talbot

Amounts in £000 — Negative variances in (brackets)

	Month of March		Year thru March		Variable cost items	Balance of year		Revised annual		Monthly change
	Actual	Variance	Actual	Variance		Forecast	Variance	Forecast	Variance	
Direct labor	123.9	(17.8)	371.8	(56.4)		1,075.1	(138.9)	1,446.9	(195.3)	(10.8)
Direct labor premiums[1]	22.2	(2.9)	63.5	(9.6)		193.4	(22.5)	256.9	(32.1)	(3.3)
Indirect labor	31.8	(4.6)	95.4	(13.6)		294.2	(18.8)	389.6	(32.4)	(2.5)
Indirect labor premiums[1]	5.9	(0.8)	16.9	(2.3)		49.7	(5.1)	66.6	(7.4)	(2.2)
Materials	427.8	(38.0)	1,353.9	(140.1)		3,775.9	(376.6)	5,129.8	(516.7)	(27.9)
Components	273.7	(31.8)	825.3	(107.9)		2,400.3	(253.8)	3,225.6	(361.7)	(28.8)
Fringe benefits	76.2	(10.9)	227.4	(33.6)		687.9	(53.6)	915.3	(87.2)	(6.1)
Other variable overhead	146.4	(13.8)	464.8	(70.3)		1,249.0	(79.7)	1,713.8	(150.0)	(14.1)
Cost tolerances	n.a.	[22.3]²	n.a.	[75.6]		n.a.	[149.8]	n.a.	[225.4]	n.a.
Total variable	1,107.9	(120.6)	3,419.0	(433.8)		9,725.5	(949.0)	13,144.5	(1,382.8)	(95.7)
					Fixed cost items					
Administrative, nonlabor	31.1	(1.0)	92.3	(2.2)		276.9	(6.8)	369.2	(9.0)	(2.5)
Depreciation	293.8	(6.2)	884.2	(20.8)		2,682.1	(70.1)	3,566.3	(90.9)	(7.6)
Utilities, etc.	32.6	(1.2)	85.3	(3.1)		257.1	(10.4)	342.4	(13.5)	(1.2)
Staff salaries	70.5	(2.0)	211.6	(5.9)		646.9	(6.1)	858.5	(12.0)	(2.0)
Staff premiums[1]	15.6	(0.8)	45.6	(4.2)		148.1	(11.8)	193.7	(16.0)	(1.5)
Fringe benefits	27.2	(1.2)	82.4	(2.6)		253.2	(5.7)	335.6	(8.3)	(1.3)
Other fixed costs	8.4	—	20.9	(0.5)		69.0	(3.8)	89.9	(4.3)	(0.1)
Total fixed costs	479.2	(12.4)	1,422.3	(39.3)		4,333.3	(114.7)	5,755.6	(154.0)	(16.2)
Total costs	1,587.1	(133.0)	4,841.3	(473.1)		14,058.8	(1,063.7)	18,900.1	(1,536.8)	(111.9)

n.a. = Not available.
[1] Premiums represent overtime and shift differential payments.
[2] The variance shown in the "cost tolerances" row reflects the amount of allowed variance. It is not included in the subtotals or totals.

forecast was revised monthly and, when combined with the actual year-to-date data, led to the creation of an annual forecast. This annual forecast, by definition, was a combination of actual and forecasted data in every monthly report except that issued for the month of December.

The monthly operating reports for the standard cost centers were also divided into variable and fixed cost sections. The variable cost section was included in all such reports. The fixed cost section was shown only in the case of plants and divisions.

The derivation and budgeting of profit center standards

The two sales and marketing divisions, as well as the four individual sales territories contained within each of them, were all treated as profit centers. The products manufactured or assembled by each of the three manufacturing divisions were transferred to the responsibility of one of the eight sales territories shortly after their final assembly and testing.[3] The transfer price employed by Larsen–Walker consisted of the standard direct cost for the product, including cost tolerances. Thus, the sales territory managers were charged with earning a large enough gross profit to cover their own fixed costs, the fixed costs of manufacturing, and the costs incurred by the staff portion (finance and administration) of Larsen–Walker's management structure.

The budgeted profit figure for each profit center was derived in a four step process. The first step was to estimate the sales price, in pound sterling, of each product sold by the profit center. This was done by taking the current sales price and revising it to take into consideration expected increases (or decreases) in sales price during the coming year. For those products sold outside the British Isles and for which the selling price was quoted in local currency, an estimated exchange rate was also used.[4]

Having estimated the sales price, attention was directed toward an estimate of the sales volume. The volume was initially estimated by the territorial sales manager. His estimate was challenged by the divisional sales manager and by a representative of the controller's office.

Next, the variable costs associated with the various products were estimated. The cost of goods sold, comprised of the abovementioned transfer price, was not under the influence of the territory manager. Thus, only such things as transportation, sales discounts, and duties and tariffs needed to be estimated.

---

[3] While fiscal responsibility for the products was transferred at this point, the physical movement of the goods to the sales territory's warehouse might not occur immediately.

[4] About half the sales volume of products sold outside the British Isles was quoted in local currency. The sales territory manager was held responsible for results in British currency, i.e., pounds sterling.

Finally, the fixed costs of the individual sales territory (or sales division) were estimated. When combined with the data in the first three steps, this data allowed the formation of a budgeted profit for the profit center in question. This budgeted profit figure was then presented to the firm's budget committee for approval. About 40 percent of the initial budgets were referred back for revision.

The final step in the budgeting process for both the profit centers and the standard cost centers was a review by a committee consisting of the managing director and the three deputy directors. This committee approved most of the budgets which reached them. They had, however, on about one occasion out of five, sent the budgets back for further revision.

The reporting system for profit centers

Both of the sales and marketing divisions, as well as each of the eight sales territories, were responsible for submitting monthly profit summaries to Hurlingham (see Exhibit 3). These summaries, which were similar in format to those used by the manufacturing operations, contained records of monthly performance, year-to-date performance, forecasts for the balance of the year, new annual forecasts, and changes in the annual forecast since the last monthly profit summary.

The report also contained a summary of variances from the budgeted profit figures (see Exhibit 4). This summary broke down the variances into five categories: price (price changes); exchange rate (effects of actual exchange rates not being at budgeted level); other variable costs (price and/or use variances); volume and mix (standard contribution at standard exchange rate, multiplied by differences between standard and actual mix or volume); and, fixed costs (price and/or use variances). While the sales managers had often argued that neither exchange rate changes nor volume and mix changes were entirely under their control, the managing director took the position that it was up to them to offset negative variances through either improved volume, improved mix, or price increases.

The quarterly operating reviews[5]

While the operating reports, profit summaries, and variance summaries were reviewed by both local and corporate management on a monthly basis, the in-depth and face-to-face reviews were held only on a quarterly basis. These quarterly operating reviews, as they were formally called, were held by the managing director and at least one of the three deputy directors with all plant, sales territory, major staff function, and divisional general managers.

---

[5] The derivation and measurement of staff performance is omitted for the sake of brevity. The process was similar to that employed for fixed costs in the standard cost centers.

EXHIBIT 3
Monthly profit summary

	Amounts in £000				Monthly profit summary	Negative variances in (brackets)				
	Month of March		Year thru March		Area: A–O, Western Europe	Balance of year		Revised annual		
	Actual	Variance	Actual	Variance		Forecast	Variance	Forecast	Variance	Monthly change
	4,235	(19)	11,489	(489)	Sales revenue	34,840	(1,351)	46,329	(1,840)	(261)
	1,694	24	4,382	160	Cost of goods sold	14,046	462	18,428	622	24
	523	(12)	1,495	(65)	Other variable costs	4,623	(360)	6,118	(425)	(66)
	2,018	(7)	5,612	(394)	Contribution	16,171	(1,249)	21,783	(1,643)	(303)
	46	(1)	125	(7)	Administrative, nonlabor	393	(13)	518	(20)	(3)
	103	(5)	315	(25)	Depreciation and facilities	820	(15)	1,135	(40)	(6)
	28	(1)	79	(3)	Utilities, etc.	236	(13)	315	(16)	(2)
	147	(4)	411	(15)	Advertising and sales	1,204	(106)	1,615	(121)	(16)
	123	(10)	336	(20)	Distributor costs	959	(81)	1,295	(101)	(13)
	88	(3)	256	(15)	Travel and entertainment	699	(42)	955	(57)	(7)
	163	(8)	445	(23)	Sales salaries	1,201	(30)	1,646	(53)	(6)
	35	(1)	119	(6)	Sales premium	292	(7)	411	(13)	(1)
	78	(3)	213	(12)	Staff salaries	611	(16)	824	(28)	(2)
	19	(1)	36	(2)	Staff premium	169	(4)	205	(6)	(1)
	85	(2)	239	(6)	Fringe benefits	675	(14)	914	(20)	(2)
	53	(3)	151	(7)	Other	449	(6)	600	(13)	(2)
	1,050	(49)	2,887	(535)	Territorial profit	8,463	(1,596)	11,350	(2,131)	(364)

EXHIBIT 4
Monthly variance summary

| | Amount in £000 | | | | Negative variances in (brackets) | | | | | |
| | Month of March | | Year through March | | Balance of year | | Revised annual | | Monthly change | |
Source of variance	Sales	Territory profit	Sales	Territory profit	Sales	Territory profit	Sales	Territory profit	Sales	Territory profit
Price[1]	135	135	516	516	1,512	1,512	2,028	2,028	215	215
Exchange rate[2]	43	21	235	117	242	119	477	236	108	53
Other variable costs[3]	n.a.	(8)	n.a.	(42)	n.a.	(228)	n.a.	(270)	n.a.	(16)
Volume and mix[4]	(197)	(171)	(1,051)	(1,025)	(3,294)	(2,772)	(4,345)	(3,802)	(584)	(492)
Fixed costs[5]	n.a.	(26)	n.a.	(101)	n.a.	(222)	n.a.	(323)	n.a.	(28)
Total variance	(19)	(49)	(489)	(535)	(1,351)	(1,596)	(1,840)	(2,131)	(261)	(268)

Area: A–O Western Europe

n.a. = Not available.
[1] Variances resulting from changes in prices, given standard exchange rates.
[2] Variances resulting from differences between actual and budgeted exchange rates.
[3] Price and/or use variances, given standard exchange rates.
[4] Variances resulting from standard contribution at standard exchange rates multiplied by differences between standard and actual volume and mix.
[5] Price and/or use variances.

The stated purpose of these meetings was to allow an in-depth look at each major business unit on a quarterly basis. The unit manager was supposed to present an analysis of the unit's performance over the past three months, to forecast the results for the remainder of the year (including an explanation of corrective steps designed to reduce negative year-to-date variations), and to offer in-depth explanations of how and why any significantly negative variances had occurred.

In recent meetings, however, a good deal of time had been spent discussing the validity of the originally budgeted figures. Many of the managers expressed the view that predetermined standards and budgets were of questionable value in times of inflation, foreign exchange turbulence, labor unrest and plant capacity problems. Instead, they asserted, the firm should be focusing its effort on an attempt to insure that the forecasts for upcoming periods were accurate. This, they thought, was crucial to the survival and eventual prosperity of a United Kingdom based firm.

Miles Foster had become increasingly concerned about the view that it was the forecasts which really counted. He knew, however, that the deputy director for sales and marketing and the two general managers reporting to him had been placing most of their recent emphasis upon the changes from month to month in the forecast for the balance of the year. This mentality seemed to be showing up as late in the manufacturing area as well. This casual treatment of the monthly and year-to-date figures troubled Mr. Foster.

THE PROPOSAL: AN ADJUSTABLE BUDGET

The adjustable budget foreseen by Miles Foster represented a reasonably sharp departure from Larsen–Walker's current budgeting system. His proposed new system called for automatic adjustments to the operating budget whenever any of several prespecified events occurred. Any such changes to the budget would be applicable only for the part of the year still remaining when the adjustment occurred.

Essentially, the idea was that a set of specified external variables would be assigned bases, or threshold values. If the variance between the threshold value and the actual current situation exceeded a predetermined amount, those budgets affected by the variable in question would be adjusted.

In the case of manufacturing operations, Mr. Foster felt that there were three variables which should be monitored during the budget year. These variables were:

Exchange rates between supplier's country and the U.K.

Specific price levels of major externally sourced components.

Production downtime attributable to problems with suppliers.

A budget change triggered by the first variable would result in the budgeted figure for materials and/or components being altered. The same would be true in the case of the second variable. A change caused by the last variable would result in the budgeted figures for direct labor, direct labor premiums and, possibly, indirect labor and indirect labor premiums being altered. These latter changes would be designed to offset the effects of downtime caused by not having key components available for production. Adoption of these three "trigger variables" would, in Mr. Foster's opinion, eliminate the need for the budget category titled cost tolerances.

Mr. Foster felt that only two variables needed to be monitored in the case of the sales and marketing divisions. These two variables were:

Exchange rates between the U.K. and those countries where sales were booked in local currency

Volume changes attributable to product shortages

A budget change triggered by the former variable would result in the budgeted sales and, hence, contribution and profit figures being adjusted. A change triggered by the latter would affect the same budgeted figures.[6]

Foster felt that his adjustable budget system would be a significant improvement over the current state of affairs. In particular, he thought, it should reverse the trend toward focusing more and more attention on the forecast figures, with the resultant downplaying of the monthly and year-to-date variances.

---

[6] No "trigger variables" were proposed for those budgets dealing with the finance and administration staff departments.

◄ CASE II-11 ►

The Quaker Oats Company

Harry T. Ambrose had recently been appointed The Quaker Oats Company's director of long-range planning. An MBA with nine years of managerial experience (but no previous exposure to the management of formal planning systems), in early 1971 Mr. Ambrose had the task of guiding the company through what was essentially the initiation of formal, long-range planning.

THE COMPANY

During the five-year period ended June 1970, Quaker Oats' per share earnings grew at an average annual rate of 11 percent. That performance was in striking contrast to the company's record in the five previous years, when earnings were almost on a plateau, and represented one of the best records achieved in the packaged-food industry in the second half of the 1960s. Exhibit 1 presents a five-year review of Quaker Oats' financial performance.

A highly successful product-development program was the principal contributor to the improved earnings record of the company. Out of fiscal 1970's revenues of $598 million, the company spent $7.4 million on research and development, 21 percent higher than in fiscal 1969 and almost twice the amount spent five years earlier. Management felt that those expenditures were fully justified by the success achieved in the introduction of such new products as Aunt Jemima Complete Pancake Mix, Aunt Jemima Frozen French Toast, Quaker Instant Oats, King Vitamin (a nutritional cereal for children), and Ken-L Ration Burgers.

Also contributing to the company's improved earnings record was management's decision to minimize commodity operations and emphasize consumer-product areas in order to take greater advantage of the company's marketing capabilities. The decision to reduce commodity operations resulted in the divestiture of a line of country elevators in 1967 and a sizable feed operation early in 1969 and the acquisition of Fisher-Price Toys, a manufacturer of toys for preschool children, later that year. In addition, Quaker made several acquisitions outside the United States, including pet-food companies in England and Canada and a leading manufacturer of chocolate in Mexico.

This case was prepared by Ronald M. Hall, research assistant, under the supervision of Professor Richard F. Vancil.

EXHIBIT 1

THE QUAKER OATS COMPANY AND SUBSIDIARIES
Statement of Consolidated Income and Reinvested Earnings ($000)
Year Ended June 30

	1970	1969	1968	1967	1966
Revenues:					
Net sales	$597,652	$553,879	$547,194	$555,133	$498,358
Other income–net	2,745	2,738	956	881	432
	600,397	556,617	548,150	556,014	498,790
Cost and expenses:					
Cost of goods sold	399,426	375,661	382,419	403,010	358,178
Selling, general and administrative expenses	142,572	129,675	122,693	115,132	103,750
Interest expense	4,433	2,083	2,315	2,417	1,950
	546,431	507,419	507,427	520,559	463,878
Income before federal and foreign income taxes	53,966	49,198	40,723	35,455	34,912
Federal and foreign income taxes	25,823	23,492	19,400	16,673	17,340
Income before extraordinary items	28,143	25,706	21,323	18,782	17,572
Extraordinary (charges) credits (net of income taxes)	—	(1,092)	—	898	—
Net income	28,143	24,614	21,323	19,680	17,572
Reinvested earnings:					
Dividends: Preferred stock	490	495	507	528	568
Common stock	11,737	10,704	9,710	8,868	8,864
Earnings reinvested during the year	15,916	13,415	11,106	10,284	8,140
Balance at beginning of year	139,567	129.996	118,890	108,606	100,466
Transfer to common stock re stock split	(3,731)	—	—	—	—
Excess of cost over par value of treasury preferred stock retired (95,489 shares)	—	(3,844)	—	—	—
Balance at end of year	$151,752	$139,567	$129,996	$118,890	$108,606
Per common share:*					
Income before extraordinary items	$ 2.21	$ 2.04	$ 1.72	$ 1.51	$ 1.41
Extraordinary (charges) credits	—	(.09)	—	(.07)	—
Net income	2.21	1.95	1.72	1.58	1.41
Dividends declared	$ .94	$ .87	$ .80	$ .73	$ .73

* Adjusted for stock splits.

In recognition of the change in the company's product line and the broadening scope of its operations, Robert D. Stuart, Jr., the president and chief architect of Quaker Oats' growth since 1962, announced in September 1970 a reorganization of the company's management structure. The reorganization decentralized all operations into four major profit centers

196

called groups: grocery products (United States and Canada), international grocery products, industrial and institutional products, and toys and recreational products. Mr. Stuart stated that the toy and recreational group would be expanded considerably by means of internal growth and acquisitions. The decentralized corporate structure was expected to facilitate the implementation of top management's plans to continue to expand and diversify the enterprise. Exhibit 2 presents Quaker Oats' management structure prior to, and after, the 1970 reorganization.

EXHIBIT 2A
Executive reporting relationships, April 1, 1968

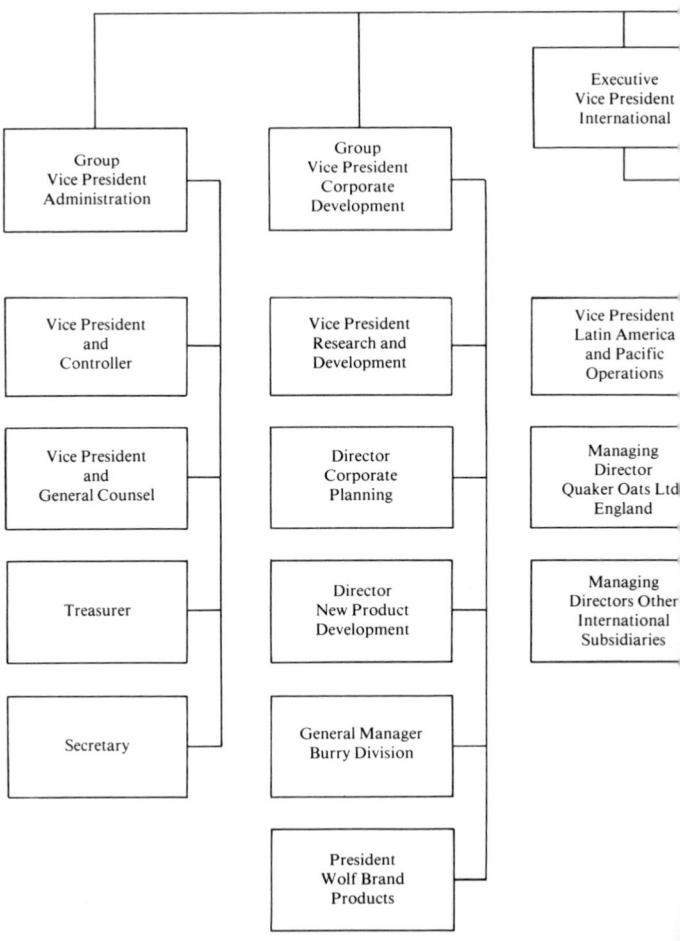

Note: This organization chart shows official lines of authority and responsib does not limit channels of contact in any way. Location of positions on the page or in to each other is not significant.

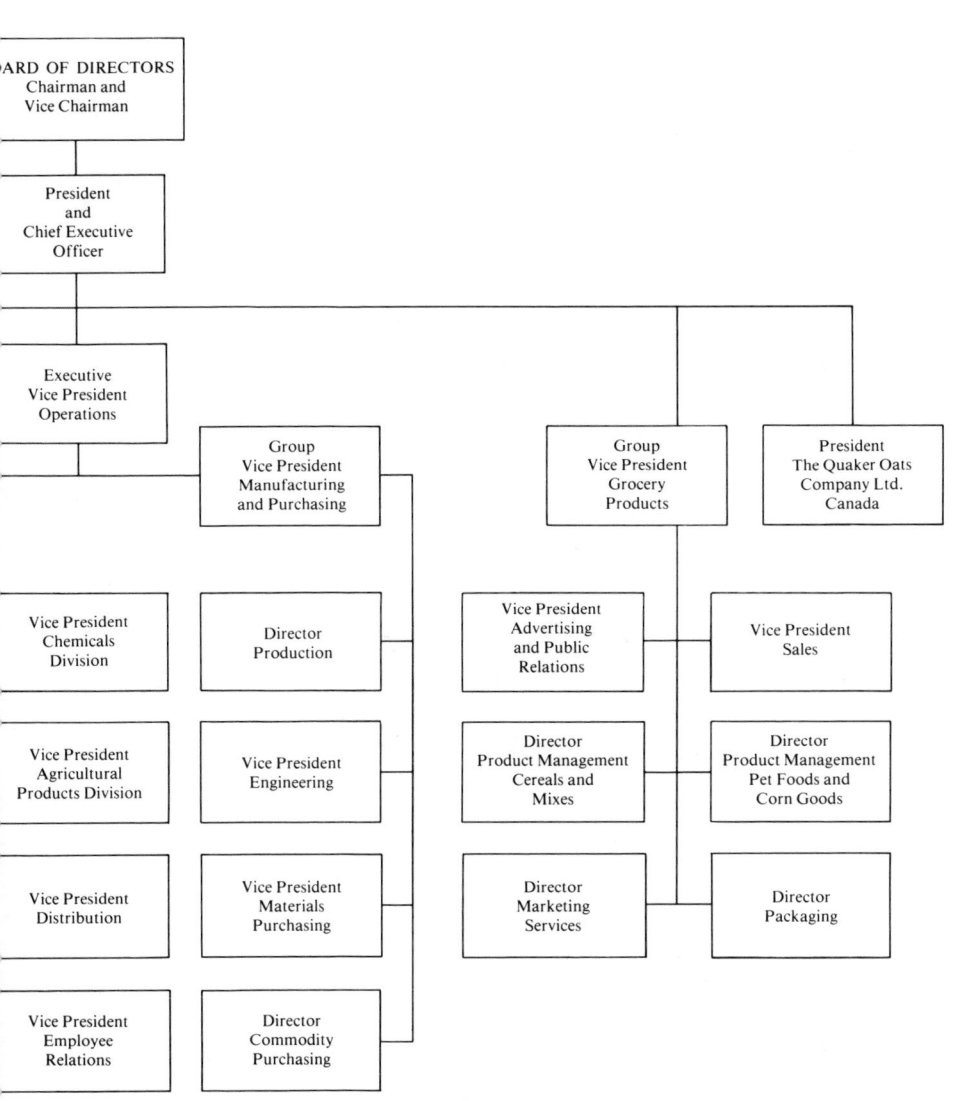

198

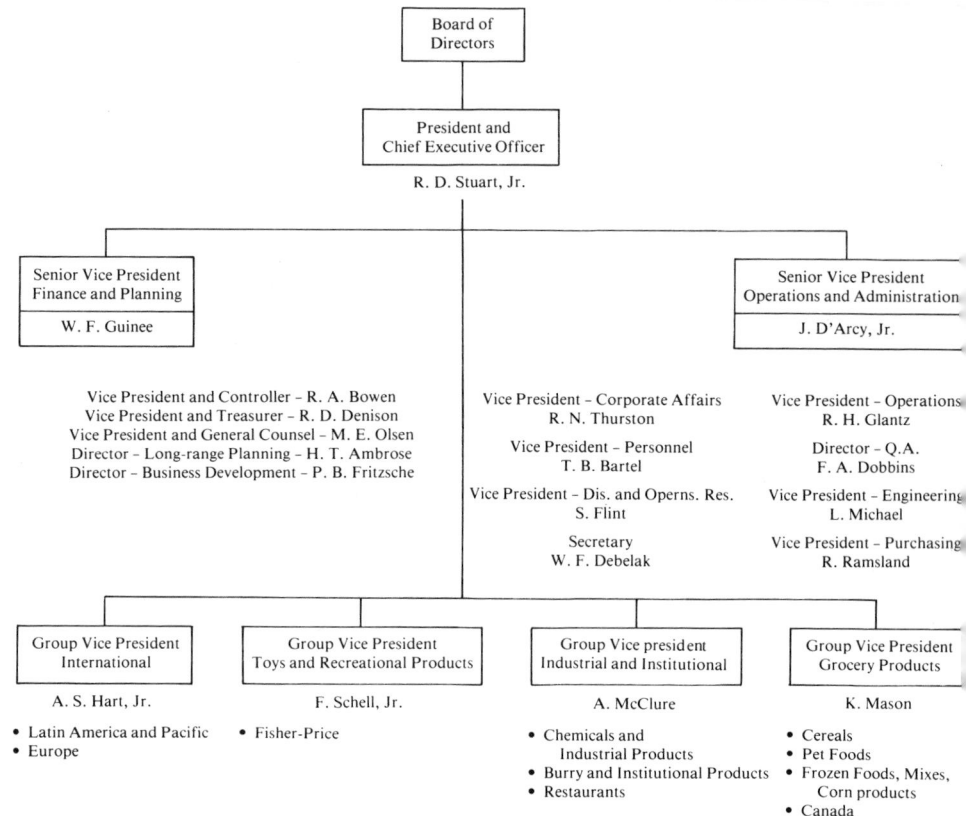

PLANNING HISTORY

Quaker began long-range planning in fiscal 1965. The plans created that year, and annually thereafter, were primarily numbers-oriented estimates of income and requirements of capital. Emphasis was placed on the first year of the annual, three-year plans; the last two years were more or less extrapolations of the first year. Concentration was on existing businesses, which were treated in great financial detail.

Initially, responsibility for supervision of both long- and short-range plans reposed with a director of corporate planning. However, the corporate planner's heavy involvement in acquisition studies and negotiations coupled with his limited staff capability forced him to rely upon the controller's office for staff support in supervising, reviewing, and consolidating the company's plans. By mid-1968 responsibility for short-range planning (annual two-year plans) had been shifted to the corporate controller's office, which created a department entitled profit planning and analysis (PP&A) to handle the task. Responsibilities for long-range planning and acquisitions were split. When the director of long-range planning left the company in early 1969, the long-range planning position was left vacant.

Robert A. Bowen, vice president and controller since the mid-1960s, stated that while he had been in a position to directly influence the company's planning he had endeavored to gain a more explicit grasp of what made the business tick. He had collected, through the planning process, detailed quantitative indicators of product group performance over the previous three to four years. The *back data*, as he termed this information, included historical comparisons of product expenses and asset utilization. In addition, Mr. Bowen had accumulated comparative information on 10 of Quaker Oats' chief competitors. He had distributed relevant portions of the back data to Quaker's managers annually as a part of the planning process. Mr. Bowen intended to continue this practice which he believed aided operating managers in formulating realistic operating plans.

However, in 1969 overall responsibility for Quaker's long-range planning processes was assumed by W. Fenton Guinee. Previously the vice president of marketing services, Mr. Guinee had recently been appointed to the position of group vice president of corporate development. (In September 1970 his title was again changed to senior vice president finance and planning.) After, in his words, "taking awhile to figure out what long-range planning was . . . through reading and discussion with the president and business school contacts," Mr. Guinee decided that Quaker needed more strategic thinking and fewer numbers in its plans. He characterized the company as evolving from a rather homogeneous business to a montage of partial profit centers and functional organizations in substantially different businesses and having different needs. Mr. Guinee thought that the information flows represented by plans should be altered to fit the changing management structure. In particular, plans should reflect the rationale behind operating management's decisions and performance.

HARRY AMBROSE'S JOB

Following extensive discussions with the president, in September 1970 Mr. Guinee appointed Harry T. Ambrose to the position of director of long-range planning. Mr. Ambrose was to aid Mr. Guinee in designing and overseeing a formal planning system which recognized the changing management needs of the company. Ambrose was instructed to work closely with the head of the profit planning and analysis department in coordinating a formal planning system which accounted for both short-term and long-term planning needs.

To guide Mr. Ambrose in his work, Mr. Guinee gave him copies of memorandums exchanged by Stuart and Guinee which laid out their expectations regarding the formal planning system. Following is a summary of their position:

A. The purpose of long-range planning was to be:
   1. Develop agreement among divisional, group, and corporate management on written goals and strategies based on projections of long-term needs.
   2. Identify future resource needs of skills, personnel, organization, finances and new businesses to allow for their development in an orderly manner.

B. No substantive changes in the concept, content, and administration of the two-year planning effort were to be contemplated.

C. The long-range plan was to cover five fiscal years beginning after the current fiscal year. (Quaker's fiscal year ran from July 1 to June 30.) The content of the long-range plan was to include:
   1. Description of current state of the business and of each of its major functional areas.
   2. Assumptions about future economy, social and political environment, technological developments, and competition.
   3. Recommended objectives.
   4. Recommended strategies.
   5. Identification of risks.

   The plans were to include statements describing a selected strategy supported by numbers defining the magnitude of growth, investments, and risks. The alternative strategies considered were to be described along with the reason for the one recommended. Compared to the two-year plan, in the five-year plan relatively greater emphasis was to be placed on the written statements and recommendations with numbers being used to provide reasonably quantified approximations of the direction chosen rather than as an instrument for controlling or for measuring managerial performance.

D. Responsibility for development of divisional plans was to rest with divisional vice presidents and/or general managers; for group plans, with group vice presidents; and for corporate plans with the planning committee (identified as the president plus the two senior vice presidents).

E. Divisional management was to be responsible for securing approval of their plans from group management, who in turn was to be responsible for securing approval of group plans from the planning committee. The latter was to review group plans in detail, direct appropriate modifications and the development of a consolidated corporate plan for presentation to the executive committee of the board of directors.

F. Responsibility for the format and administration of both two-year and long-range plans was to be that of the senior vice president finance

EXHIBIT 3
Delineation of responsibilities in planning

	Two year		Five year	
	*PP&A**	*L-R P*†	*PP&A*	*L-R P*†
Develop manual	Primary	Collaborative	Collaborative	Primary
Develop financial format	Primary	None	Primary	Collaborative
Develop format for statement and recommendations	Primary	None	Collaborative	Primary
Provide financial back data	Primary	None	Primary	None
Coordinate planning	Primary	None	None	Primary
Consolidate into corporate figures.	Primary	None	Primary	None
Critique plans	Primary	Collaborative	Collaborative	Primary
Identify deviations from plan	Primary	None	None	Primary

* PP&A—Profit Planning and Analysis under direction of vice president controller.
† L-R P—Long-Range Planning.

and planning. Responsibilities of individual departments in finance and planning were to be as indicated in Exhibit 3.

G. For the first annual planning process, both the two-year and long-range planning efforts were to proceed concurrently, commencing in January 1971 and concluding in June of that year. Timing of future planning was to be reviewed after the completion of 1971's planning.

H. Review of the five-year plans was to be focused upon the quality of current and previous analyses and conclusions rather than the accuracy of numerical projections. Whereas responsibility for achievement of two-year plan goals was to rest primarily with the person responsible for operating a particular area, responsiblity for the strategies selected in the five-year plan was to be shared between the person recommending the plan and the person approving it.

Remarks by Fenton Guinee

What we are trying to accomplish with our planning system must be considered in light of the corporate situation. Our determination to achieve profitable diversification as a basis for future growth has spurred some notable changes in the way the company is managed.

Operational responsibilities were restructured last September so that many of our managers now have overall responsibility for all four functions (marketing, finance, production, and personnel) instead of only one. We have found that this is a very difficult reorientation for some managers to make.

Even if we had not reorganized in 1970, we probably would reintroduce long-range planning now. Quaker needs to be looking beyond its immediate future and next year's profits to the issues which will determine its long-term viability.

But, also, we expect the introduction of a planning system at a time when the managers' tasks are changing to help them to define their new tasks. Sure, the work load is going to be enormous, but we are forcing them to look beyond their own previous functional expertise immediately. Therefore, they are going to develop as general managers much quicker.

Harry's task is to work out a working balance between the amount and quality of effort that managers put into short-term versus long-term planning. Right now we don't know what this balance should be. We do know, however, that each type of planning is important in its own right.

Short-term planning is well established at Quaker. We have fine budgeting and control systems. The managers use them and seem to believe in them. But the quality of the decisions made through these systems may begin to deteriorate if the decision makers lose pace with corporate objectives and strategies. Long-range planning should function to maintain this pace through the introduction of new information, analysis, and properly disseminated decisions.

Harry Ambrose's comments

I suppose that I was selected for this job because my background was in line management (not staff) and because I am on good terms with most of the division managers. I was formerly director of materials purchasing under the old functional corporate setup and I got to know most of the present division managers pretty well because my job took me all over the company.

Mr. Stuart and Mr. Guinee have pretty well thought out what they want planning to do and how Quaker ought to go about doing it. Nevertheless, there always remain a number of practical problems to be ironed out. This much I know from my own experience as a manager and from my investigations into how other companies plan.

I don't expect that we are going to leap right into an ideal planning system immediately. With the uncertainty arising from the new corporate structure and the two-year planning going on at the same time as long-range planning, I expect that long-range planning is not going to get as much attention as I would like.

Therefore, I think that I should try to achieve some limited objectives in planning this year. First, I would like to establish in the managers' minds that long-range planning is here to stay and is an important part of their jobs. Second, I would like to educate them in the rationale of long-range planning. In particular, I need to break them away from thinking that long-range planning is the extrapolation of short-term quantitative relationships. Quaker's managers must come to realize that different kinds of factors are at work in the long term and that because many of these factors are very intangible their handling requires the use of a disciplined, logical technique.

There are a lot of factors which will determine the utimate success or failure of the planning program. Certainly one of these factors will be the kind and quality of cooperation that I get from PP&A. It appears to me that the delineation of responsibilities in planning between PP&A and the long-range planning department was based primarily upon existing staff capabilities. In essence, any of the planning which dealt with financial statements was assigned to PP&A.

Financial analysis is their specialty and they have a staff of about 12 skilled people. The long-range planning department consists of myself plus an assistant and a secretary.

Fortunately, I have a good working relationship with the head of PP&A. We have managed to resolve amicably differences of opinion relating to the format and content of the long-range plans. In general, he tends to see more of a need in the plans for detailed, precise information than I do. For example, one of our arguments revolved around whether to round off all financial data in the plans to the nearest thousand dollars or the nearest million dollars. I finally managed to persuade him that the larger figure was adequate to indicate the direction and magnitude of financial results—which was all that was necessary for the long-range plans.

The head of PP&A also would like to see (as would I) the long-range plans precede the short-range plans so that the former could be used to provide direction for the latter. However, we differ on the question of how tight the linkage between long-range plans and short-range plans should be. His opinion (which is shared by Mr. Guinee) is that the forecast performance in the first two years of the five-year plan should be required to match precisely the forecast performance in the short-range plan. I believe that he feels this requirement is necessary to gain commitment to, and inject reality in, the long-range plans. I feel that it would be more useful at this time to concentrate more upon developing the managers' ability to create alternative strategies than to tie them to a rigid planning program.

⸺CASE II–12⸺

Bultman Automobiles, Inc.

William Bultman, the part owner and manager of an automobile dealership felt the problems associated with the rapid growth of his business were becoming too great for him to handle alone. (See Exhibit 1 for current financial statements.) The reputation he had established in the community led him to believe that the recent growth in his business would continue. His long-standing policy of emphasizing new car sales as the principal business of the dealership had paid off, in Mr. Bultman's opinion. This, combined with close attention to customer relations so that a substantial amount of repeat business was available, had increased the company's sales to a new high level. Therefore, he wanted to make organizational changes to cope with the new situation. Mr. Bultman's three "silent partners" agreed to this decision.

Accordingly, Mr. Bultman divided up the business into three departments: a new car sales department, a used-car sales department, and the service department. He then appointed three of his most trusted employees managers of the new departments: John Ward was named manager of new car sales, Marty Ziegel was appointed manager of used car sales, and Charlie Lassen placed in charge of the service department. All these men had been with the dealership for several years.

Each of the managers was told to run his department as if it were an independent business. In order to give the new managers an incentive, their remuneration was calculated as a straight percentage of their department's gross profit.

Soon after taking over as the manager of the new car sales department, John Ward had to settle upon the amount to offer a particular customer who wanted to trade his old car as part of the purchase price of a new one with a list price of $7,200. Before closing the sale, Mr. Ward had to decide the amount of discount from list he would offer the customer and the trade-in value of the old car. He knew he could deduct 15 percent from the list price of the new car without seriously hurting his profit margin. However, he also wanted to make sure that he did not lose out on the trade-in.

During his conversations with the customer, it had become apparent that the customer had an inflated view of the worth of his old car, a far from uncommon event. In this case, it probably meant that Mr. Ward had to be prepared to make some sacrifices to close the sale. The new car had been

EXHIBIT 1

BULTMAN AUTOMOBILES, INC.
Income Statement
For the Year Ended December 31, 1978

Sales of new cars			$2,293,125
Cost of new sales	$1,893,843		
Sales remuneration	97,422		
			1,991,265
			301,860
Allowances on trade*			69,669
			232,191
Sales of used cars.....................		1,437,414	
Appraised value of used cars	$1,144,365		
Sales remuneration	54,936		
		1,199,301	
		238,113	
Allowances on trade*		36,669	
			201,444
			433,635
Service sales to customers...............		208,506	
Cost of work		154,191	
		54,315	
Service work on reconditioning			
Charge............................	141,948		
Cost..............................	146,586	(4,638)	
			49,677
			483,312
General and administrative expenses			295,026
Profit before taxes			$ 188,286

* Allowances on trade represents the excess of amounts allowed on cars taken in trade over their appraised value.

in stock for some time, and the model was not selling very well, so he was rather anxious to make the sale if this could be done profitably.

In order to establish the trade-in value of the car, the manager of the used car department, Mr. Ziegel, accompanied Mr. Ward and the customer out to the parking lot to examine the car. In the course of his appraisal, Mr. Ziegel estimated the car would require reconditioning work costing about $400, after which the car would retail for about $2,100. On a wholesale basis, he could either buy or sell such a car, after reconditioning, for about $1,800. The wholesale price of a car was subject to much greater fluctuation than the retail price, depending on color, trim, model, and so forth. Fortunately, the car being traded in was a very popular shade. The retail automobile dealers handbook of used car prices, the *Blue Book* gave a cash buying price range of $1,550 to $1,650 for the trade-in model in good condition. This range represented the distribution of cash prices paid by automobile dealers for that model of car in the area in the past week. Mr. Ziegel estimated that he could get about $1,250 for the car "as is," (that is, without any work being done to it) at next week's auction.

The new car department manager had the right to buy any trade-in at any price he thought appropriate, but then it was his responsibility to dispose of the car. He had the alternative of either trying to persuade the used car manager to take over the car and accepting the used car manager's appraisal price, or he himself could sell the car through wholesale channels. Whatever course Mr. Ward adopted, it was his primary responsibility to make a profit for the dealership on the new cars he sold, without affecting his performance through excessive allowances on trade-ins. This primary goal, Mr. Ward said, had to be "balanced against the need to satisfy the customers and move the new cars out of inventory—and there was only a narrow line between allowing enough on the used car and allowing too much."

After weighing all these factors, with particular emphasis on the personality of the customer, Mr. Ward decided he would allow $2,400 for the used car, provided the customer agreed to pay the list price for the new car. After a certain amount of haggling, during which the customer came down from a higher figure and Ward came up from a lower one, the $2,400 allowance was agreed upon. The necessary papers were signed, and the customer drove off.

Mr. Ward returned to the office and explained the situation to Ronald Bradley, who had recently joined the dealership as accountant. After listening with interest to Mr. Ward's explanation of the sale, Mr. Bradley set about recording the sale in the accounting records of the business. As soon as he saw the new car had been purchased from the manufacturer for $5,000 he was uncertain as to the value he should place on the trade-in vehicle. Since the new car's list price was $7,200 and it had cost $5,000, Mr. Bradley reasoned the gross margin on the new car sale was $2,200. Yet Mr. Ward had allowed $2,400 for the old car, which needed $400 repairs and could be sold retail for $2,100 or wholesale for $1,800. Did this mean that the new car sale involved a loss? Mr. Bradley was not at all sure he knew the answer to this question. Also, he was uncertain about the value he should place on the used car for inventory valuation purposes.

Bradley decided that he would put down a valuation of $2,400, and then await instructions from his superiors.

When Marty Ziegel, manager of the used car department, found out what Bradley had done, he went to the office and stated forcefully that he would not accept $2,400 as the valuation of the used car. His comment went as follows:

"My used car department has to get rid of that used car, unless John (new car department manager) agrees to take it over himself. I would certainly never have allowed the customer $2,400 for that old tub. I would never have given any more than $1,400 which is the wholesale price less the cost of repairs. My department has to make a profit too, you know. My own income is dependent on the gross profit I show on the sale of used cars, and I will not stand for having my income hurt because John is too generous towards his customers."

Mr. Bradley replied that he had not meant to cause trouble, but had simply recorded the car at what seemed to be its cost of acquisition, because he had been taught that this was the best practice. Whatever response Ziegel was about to make to this comment was cut off by the arrival of William Bultman, the general manager, and Charlie Lassen, the service department manager. Mr. Bultman picked up the phone and called John Ward, the new car sales manager, asking him to come over right away.

"All right, Charlie," said Bultman, "now that we are all here, would you tell them what you just told me."

Mr. Lassen, who was obviously very worried, said: "Thanks Bill; the trouble is with this trade-in. John and Marty were right in thinking that the repairs they thought necessary would cost about $400. Unfortunately, they failed to notice that the rear axle is cracked, which will have to be replaced before we can sell the car. This will use up parts and labor costing about $300.

"Besides this," Lassen continued, "there is another thing which is bothering me a good deal more. Under the accounting system we've been using, my labor cost for internal jobs is calculated by taking the standard blue book price for the labor required for a job and deducting 25 percent.[1] Normally, the blue book price is about equal to the estimated time required to do the work, multiplied by twice the mechanic's hourly rate. On parts, an outside customer pays list price, which has about a 40 percent gross margin, but on internal work the parts are charged at cost plus 20 percent, which is less than half the margin. As you can see from my department statement, calculating the cost of parts and labor for internal work this way didn't even cover a pro rata share of my department's overhead and supplies. I lost 4,600 bucks on internal work last year.

"So," Lassen went on, "on a reconditioning job like this which costs out at $700, I don't even break even. If I did work costing $700 for an outside customer, I would be able to charge him about $950 for the job. The blue book gives a range of $920 to $980 for the work this car needs, and I have always aimed for the middle of the blue book range. That would give my department a gross profit of $250, and my own income is based on that gross profit. Since it looks as if a high proportion of the work of my department is going to be the reconditioning of trade-ins for resale, I figure that I should

---

[1] In addition to the blue book for used car prices, there is a blue book which gives the range of charges for various classes of repair work. Like the used car book, it is a weekly, and is based on the actual charges made and reported by motor repair shops in the area.

be able to make the same charge for repairing a trade-in as I would get for an outside repair job. In this case, the charge would be $950."

Ziegel and Ward both started to talk at once at this point. Mr. Ziegel, the more forceful of the two, managed to edge Mr. Ward out: "This axle business is unfortunate, all right, but it is very hard to spot a cracked axle. Charlie is likely to be just as lucky the other way next time. He has to take the rough with the smooth. It is up to him to get the cars ready for me to sell."

Mr. Ward, after agreeing that the failure to spot the axle was unfortunate added: "This error is hardly my fault, however. Anyway, it is ridiculous that the service department should make a profit out of jobs it does for the rest of the dealership. The company can't make money when its left hand sells to its right."

William Bultman, the general manager, was getting a little confused about the situation. He thought there was a little truth in everything that had been said, but he was not sure how much. It was evident to him that some action was called for, both to sort out the present problem and to prevent its recurrence. He instructed Bradley, the accountant, to "work out how much we are really going to make on this whole deal," and then retired to his office to consider how best to get his managers to make a profit for the company.

A week after the events described above, William Bultman was still far from sure what action to take to motivate his managers to make a profit for the business. During the week, Charlie Lassen, the service manager, had reported to him that the repairs to the used car had cost $774, of which $360 represented the cost of those repairs which had been spotted at the time of purchase, and the remaining $414 was the cost of supplying and fitting a replacement for the cracked axle. To support his own case for a

EXHIBIT 2
Analysis of service department expenses for the year ended December 31, 1978

	Customer jobs	Reconditioning jobs	Total
Number of jobs	183	165	348
Direct labor	$ 64,158	$ 49,292	$123,450
Supplies	22,236	19,653	41,889
Department overhead (fixed)	18,936	15,639	34,575
	105,330	94,584	199,914
Parts	48,861	52,002	100,863
	154,191	146,586	300,777
Charges made for jobs to customers or other departments	208,506	141,948	350,454
Profit (loss)	54,315	(4,638)	49,677
General overhead proportion			34,248
Departmental profit for the year			$ 15,429

higher allowance on reconditioning jobs, Lassen had looked up the duplicate invoices over the last few months, and had found other examples of the same work that had been done on the trade-in car. The amount of these invoices totalled $906, which the customers had paid without question, and the time and materials that had gone into the jobs had been costed at $670. As described by Lassen earlier, the cost figures mentioned above included an allocation of departmental overhead, but no allowance for general overhead or profit. In addition, Lassen had obtained from Mr. Bradley, the accountant, the cost analysis shown in Exhibit 2. Lassen told Bultman that this was a fairly typical distribution of the service department expense.

─── CASE II-13 ───

Laitier S.A.

"It is terribly frustrating to be evaluated as a profit center when I do not have complete control over revenues," said Henri Goudal, managing director of Laitier S.A. "The Export Division is responsible for over 75 percent of our total sales. They determine the price, the destination and the quantity of most of the milk we sell. We have no direct authority over that department, yet we are held responsible when sales are poor. If they do not perform up to expectations, then we cannot meet the budgeted profit target for which we are held responsible by headquarters."

COMPANY BACKGROUND

Laitier S.A. was a Belgian-based subsidiary of Universal Brands, a widely diversified U.S. food manufacturer. Of Laitier's fiscal 1975 sales of 2,300 million Belgian francs, 2,140 million (93 percent) were milk products, 90 million (4 percent) were metal cans, and 70 million (3 percent) were pet food products. Laitier had two milk-processing plants in Belgium, one making evaporated milk and the other condensed (sweetened) milk. These plants supplied products for export to more than 80 countries spread throughout

This case, made possible by a firm which chooses to remain anonymous, was prepared by William A. Sahlman, research assistant, and Associate Professor M. Edgar Barrett.

210

Eastern Europe, Africa, the Pacific Basin, and Central and South America. No milk products were sold within Belgium.

Laitier also had a can manufacturing plant in Belgium. Half of the output of that plant was used internally, and half was sold to outside customers, including Universal's German subsidiary. Finally, Laitier was in the process of introducing a line of Denmark-manufactured pet food products into the Belgium market.

Approximately 76 percent of Laitier's total milk production in terms of volume (72 percent of milk product revenues) was evaporated milk. The remaining 24 percent (28 percent) was condensed milk. Both products were sold to two different categories of outlets. The first category was foreign governments who purchased large quantities of milk for distribution to the poor. The second category for Laitier was the more traditional retail-oriented distribution network. That is, Laitier's products were sold to local distributing agents in each country who would in turn sell the milk to retail outlets.

Sales destined for retail distribution were handled by Universal's Export Division, a separate company from Laitier. Both companies were located in Brussels, Belgium. The Export Division was headed by a general manager who reported directly to the vice president of marketing at Universal Headquarters in Chicago. The general manager of the Export Division had no formal reporting relationship with the managing director of Laitier, though it was necessary to coordinate the activities of the two groups. Well over 75 percent of Laitier's unit production (and of milk product revenues) was

EXHIBIT 1

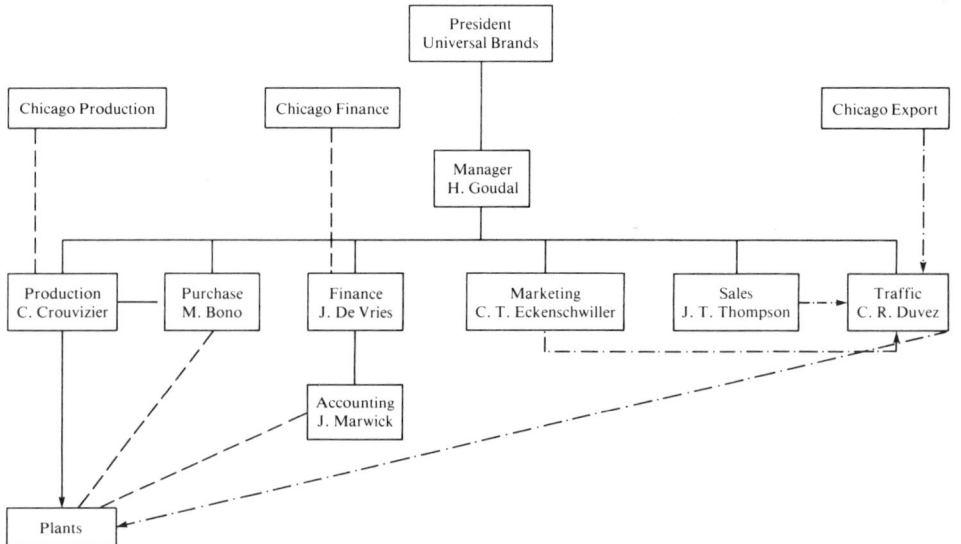

channeled through the Export Division. The Export Division also handled export sales for other European Universal subsidiaries.[1]

The remainder of Laitier's milk production was sold by an internal marketing group (see Exhibit 1). Generally, these sales were made directly to foreign governments which distributed the milk to the poor. This business was done on a bid basis, with Laitier submitting a bid directly to the foreign government, usually on a large quantity of milk. Laitier was also directly in charge of one or two markets in which the milk was intended for retail distribution. However, sales to these markets were small in relation to total sales.

THE PRODUCTION PROCESS

The production process at Laitier was relatively simple. Laitier did not own any dairy farms. The company purchased milk from farmers in the area around the processing plant. There were no formal contracts between Laitier and the farmers, though the company had established a very strong, long-term relationship with its milk suppliers. As a result, Laitier felt that it had a moral if not a legal commitment to purchase all the milk produced by these farmers.

The raw milk was processed by Laitier at one of its two plants, one for evaporated milk and the other for condensed milk.[2] Within these two broad product categories, several variations were possible. Laitier had three standard levels of fat content milk, which it could produce according to market needs. Laitier could also produce several different standard sugar content levels in its condensed milk.

The processed milk was put into a number of standard containers. Laitier used six different sizes of tin cans and three different sizes of paper cartons. Beginning in 1972, Laitier produced its own cans, supplying approximately one half its can needs from this source. Cartons were purchased from outside sources.

Because Laitier's products were sold in a very large number of countries, labeling created some difficulties. Laitier purchased labels from a local printer who could react quickly to their needs. Labels were printed directly on the cartons by the carton manufacturer, who also could provide the necessary flexibility to Laitier.

---

[1] As a separate company, the Export Division was not actually required to handle the milk products of Laitier. They could handle the milk from whichever Universal subsidiary had the lowest overall cost and wished to sell through them.

[2] Laitier always had the option of turning the raw milk it purchased into a less processed product such as butter. Laitier might make this kind of intermediate conversion if it believed it had an excess supply of milk or could make a larger profit in butter than on evaporated or condensed milk.

Once packaged, the milk was prepared for shipping by Laitier. Depending upon the final destination, the milk had different packaging requirements. Laitier was responsible for arranging for all transportation of its products, including those sold through the Export Division, to the port of final destination.

RAW MILK: INTERVENTION PRICES AND RESTITUTIONS

Because raw milk was such an important cost component for Laitier, the process by which milk prices were set was of crucial importance. The price Laitier paid for raw milk was determined during periodic negotiations between all the milk users and the farmers in the region around each plant. The Belgian Government did not directly control raw milk prices. However, the European Economic Community did influence the level of prices through a system of EEC "intervention prices" for intermediate milk products (e.g., butter or powdered milk). Essentially, the EEC Agricultural Committee set a price for powdered milk, for example, which gave the farmer the option of selling his milk in unprocessed form or converting his raw milk to powdered milk and selling it directly to the EEC at the intervention price.[3,4] Because the farmer always had the option to sell to the EEC, he would not accept too low a price for his milk from processors like Laitier.

The system of intervention prices designed by the EEC was intended to maintain income stability for the farmers. However, the resulting raw milk prices were higher than those in New Zealand or in the United States, both of which were larger exporters of processed milk. In order to make EEC produced milk products competitive in the world market, the EEC had to subsidize exports through a system of restitutions. A restitution was a rebate given to processors like Laitier when they delivered their products outside the EEC. The level of restitutions was set by the EEC Agricultural Committee in Brussels and could amount to as much as one third of the raw milk cost (see Exhibit 2). Even after restitutions, raw milk could represent as much as 50 percent of Laitier's manufacturing cost. When the intervention price levels were changed, the restitutions generally were also changed. However, there was always considerable uncertainty about the extent to which higher raw milk costs would be offset by increased restitutions.

Because the levels of intervention prices and restitutions were sensitive political issues within the EEC, planning at companies like Laitier was very difficult. To facilitate planning for milk processors, the EEC allowed exporters to "pre-fix" a restitution for the next six months. To illustrate, Laitier could tell the EEC it intended to export a certain amount of evaporated milk

---

[3] Laitier also had the option of converting some of its raw milk supply into powdered milk, for example, if it believed this was a more profitable alternative than processing the milk.

[4] In the last few years, the EEC had accumulated a surplus supply of powdered milk amounting to 1 million tons. This milk was to be distributed as development aid.

EXHIBIT 2

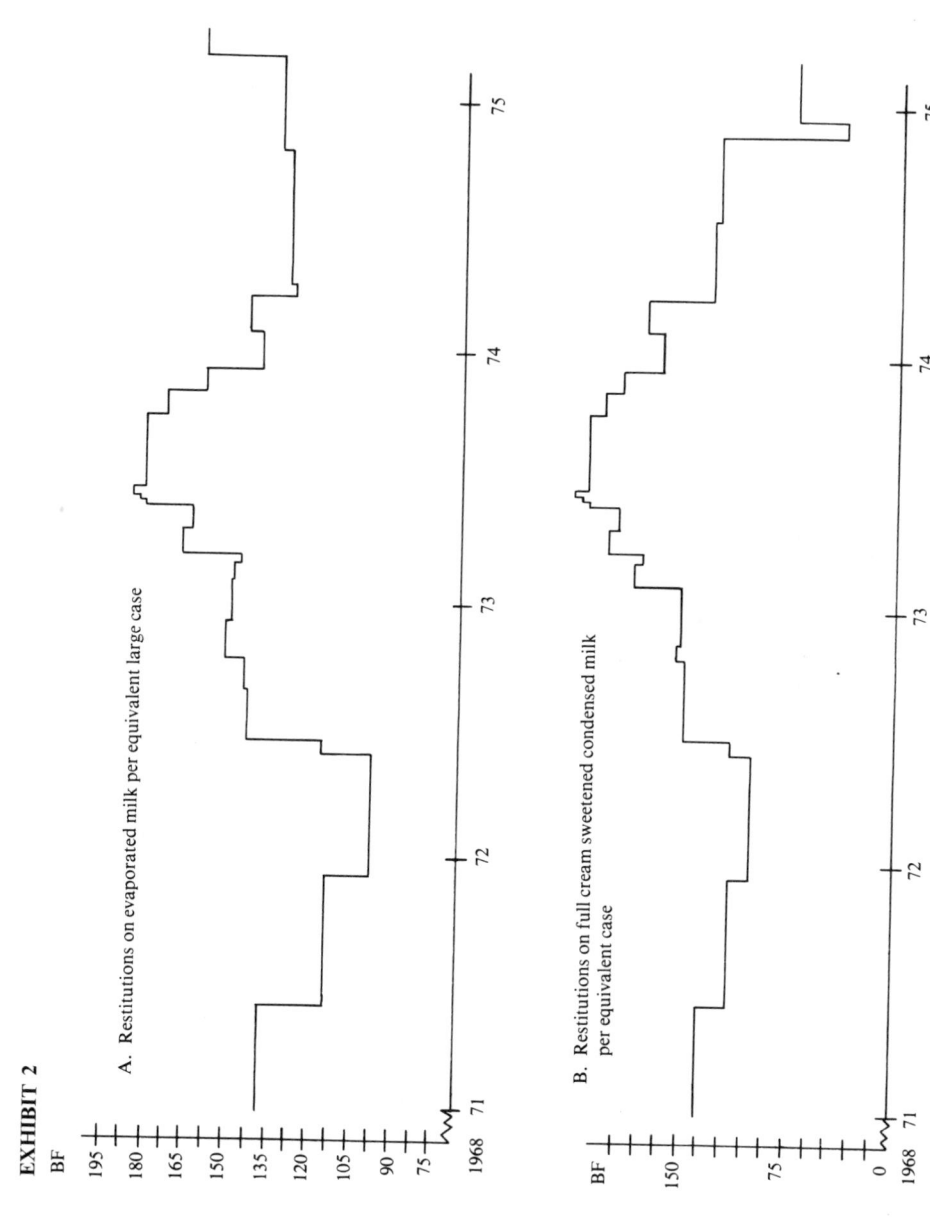

A. Restitutions on evaporated milk per equivalent large case

B. Restitutions on full cream sweetened condensed milk per equivalent case

in the next six months. The EEC would then guarantee a restitution for that period for that quantity of exports. Unfortunately, if the intervention price increased during the six months, then Laitier was faced with higher milk costs with no relief from an increased subsidy. Also, if Laitier did not export the quantity of milk products it originally estimated with the EEC, then it was penalized, and actually had to pay a fine to the EEC. Laitier, of course, always had the option of not pre-fixing the restitution if it believed that the intervention price would increase in the near future. The hope was that the restitution would also increase, thus protecting Laitier from the higher milk costs.

In order for Laitier to determine its restitution policy and its milk and other raw materials needs, it was very important to obtain accurate forecasts of milk product sales. As noted previously, Laitier depended on the Export Division for the sales of over 75 percent of its milk production. Thus, Laitier had to rely on sales estimates from the Export Division to do its planning.

The process by which sales estimates were made at Laitier involved two iterative steps. First, Laitier provided unit manufacturing cost estimates to the Export Division. A distinction was made between fixed and variable costs in order to allow the marketing people to base their pricing decisions on the contribution margin of each product (see Exhibit 3). The traffic department within Laitier also provided estimates of shipping costs to each of

EXHIBIT 3

LAITIER S.A.—Belgium
Monthly Export Cost Estimates in Belgian Francs
August 10, 1975

	Evaporated milk— 9 percent butter fat		Condensed (sweetened) milk	
	Large cases	Small cases	8 percent butter fat	Skim
Line				
1. Cases available August September October November				
2. Milk cost	427.50	354.82	364.52	213.14
2a. Sugar.....................	—	—	146.61	144.45
3. Packaging material	107.80	115.81	96.71	93.02
4. Total material cost	535.30	470.63	607.84	450.61
5. Miscellaneous*	27.41	24.95	36.65	30.65
6. Restitution	148.76	123.05	123.35	26.95
7. Total out-of-pocket cost......	413.95	372.53	521.14	454.31

Note: All figures have been disguised. At time of case, one U.S. dollar was equal to approximately 39 Belgian Francs.
* Fuel, power, freight, and interest expense, among others.

the export markets.[5] The Export Division then provided sales price and volume estimates by product line for each market to Laitier. The process involved a certain degree of negotiation between the Export Division and Laitier, though it was difficult for Laitier to question the accuracy of the Export Division's forecasts.

The internal marketing group at Laitier also had to estimate sales of milk products generated internally. These estimates—when combined with those generated by the Export Division—formed the basis for production, purchasing, and restitution policy at Laitier.

BUDGETING AND PERFORMANCE EVALUATION

The process of forecasting revenues, costs, and therefore profits was formalized in Laitier's budgeting system. In August of each year, Laitier submitted to corporate headquarters a complete budget package for the next two fiscal years as well as a profit estimate for the third year.[6] The top management of Laitier made an oral presentation of Laitier's budget to Universal's management.[7] The final budget was arrived at through a process of negotiation between Laitier, the Export Division and the Universal management.

In addition to the initial budget, every month Laitier prepared a revised forecast of the current fiscal year. Every three months, a new budget for the current fiscal year was prepared. Finally, in February of each year, Laitier also submitted a revised budget for the next fiscal year (in addition to the revised budget for the rest of the current fiscal year).

These budgets formed the basis for performance evaluation of Laitier during the year. Universal required two different types of reports from Laitier. First, every month Laitier had to submit a brief (5–6 page) summary of its operations. Second, each quarter Laitier had to submit a series of reporting forms. The first group of forms showed the most recent budget (a complete income statement) for the next fiscal year, the revised forecast and the original budget for the current fiscal year, and the actual results for the previous fiscal year. These reports were also broken out by major product group. That is, detailed sales, costs, and operating profit before tax estimates for such product groups as evaporated milk, condensed milk, pet food, and cans would be shown (see Exhibit 4).

A second series of forms showed the marketing expenses in aggregate and for each major product line. Marketing expenses included advertising, promotion, selling, distribution, commissions, and market research expenses. A third series of forms was devoted to nonoperating income and expenses

---

[5] Transportation costs could be as high as 30 percent of the cost of the finished product.

[6] Laitier operated on an October 1 to September 30 fiscal year.

[7] Beginning in 1975, the Export Division manager was scheduled to be present at the budget presentation to Universal management.

EXHIBIT 4
Statement of profit and loss

		Fiscal 1976		Revised fiscal 1975		Actual fiscal 1974	
			Per unit		Per unit		Per unit
Product—evaporated (export*)							
1	Net sales in cases	2,422,000		2,262,060		2,006,973	
2	Gross sales less returns	1,666,505	688.07	1,453,312	642.49	1,170,161	583.04
3	Distribution expenses	260,728	107.65	212,153	93.79	137,239	68.38
4	Trade payments	7,823	3.23	6,628	2.93	9,272	4.62
5	Taxes and duties						
6	Net sales	1,397,954	577.19	1,234,531	545.77	1,023,650	510.04
7	Cost of sales	1,258,471	519.60	1,084,742	479.55	971,158	453.99
8	Gross profit	139,483	57.59	149,790	66.22	112,492	56.06
9	Selling expenses	48,852	20.17	40,264	17.80	30,286	15.09
10	General expenses	24,995	10.32	18,616	8.23	16,076	8.01
11	Operating profit	65,636	27.10	90,910	40.19	66,130	32.96
Product—condensed (export*)							
12	Net sales in cases	452,300		511,792		482,804	
13	Gross sales less returns	380,340	841.46	381,701	745.51	328,025	679.14
14	Distribution expenses	32,924	72.84	25,231	49.28	17,180	35.57
15	payments	556	1.23	394	0.77	816	1.69
16	Taxes and duties						
17	Net sales	346,860	767.39	356,076	695.46	310,029	641.88
18	Cost of sales	324,441	717.79	331,791	648.03	278,338	576.27
19	Gross profit	22,419	49.60	24,285	47.43	31,691	65.61
20	Selling expenses	9,257	20.48	6,164	12.04	5,356	11.09
21	General expenses	6,197	13.71	6,103	11.92	4,907	10.16
22	Operating profit	6,965	15.41	12,018	24.49	21,428	44.36

Product—evaporated (own trade)[†]

		Per unit		Per unit		Per unit
1 Net sales in cases	427,000	630.94	374,040	597.67	196,781	501.58
2 Gross sales less returns	269,411	63.14	223,529	62.22	98,811	22.33
3 Distribution expenses	26,961	8.16	23,270	10.31	4,399	12.63
4 Trade payments	3,484		3,856		2,488	
5 Taxes and duties						
6 Net sales	238,966	559.64	196,403	525.14	91,924	466.62
7 Cost of sales	225,486	528.07	181,715	485.87	91,711	465.54
8 Gross profit	13,480	31.57	14,688	39.27	213	1.08
9 Selling expenses	2,434	5.70	1,952	5.22	1,062	5.39
10 General expenses	4,274	10.01	3,403	9.10	1,426	7.24
11 Operating profit	6,772	15.86	9,332	24.95	(2,275)	(11.55)

Product—condensed (own trade)[†]

		Per unit		Per unit		Per unit
12 Net sales in cases	320,000	874.72	320,256	751.52	361,453	708.71
13 Gross sales less returns	279,910	60.83	240,486	40.81	255,844	24.79
14 Distribution expenses	19,466	4.16	13,059	7.99	8,949	6.01
15 Trade payments	1,331		2,557		2,170	
16 Taxes and duties						
17 Net sales	259,113	809.73	224,870	702.72	244,725	677.91
18 Cost of sales	230,877	721.49	210,678	658.37	213,647	591.82
19 Gross profit	28,236	88.24	14,192	44.35	31,078	86.09
20 Selling expenses	1,872	5.85	2,266	7.08	2,058	5.70
21 General expenses	4,483	14.01	3,648	11.40	3,892	10.78
22 Operating profit	21,881	68.38	8,278	25.87	25,128	69.61

Note: All figures in this exhibit have been disguised.

* "Export" sales were those handled directly by the Export Division.

† "Own Trade" sales were those handled by Laitier's marketing group.

EXHIBIT 5
Detailed profit and loss commentary: Fiscal 1976 versus revised fiscal 1975*

Evaporated (exports)
Line

1   Fiscal 1976 shows a sales volume increase of 159,940 cases. Most significant changes:
  Decrease: Jamica 117,000, Chad 34,000, Botswana 63,500.
  Increase: Nigeria 257,000, Turkey 46,440, Okinawa 26,000, Angola 20,390,
      Rhodesia 24,610.
2   Total *gross sales* per unit for fiscal 1976 is BFr.45.58 higher, viz.
  Gross sales—Excl. restitutions (a result of increased selling prices) 67.38
  Export restitutions (reduced) (21.80)
    The calculations included the last known restitution rates and are those effective
  as from March 26, 1975.
3   *Distribution expenses* per unit for fiscal 1976 is BFr.13.86 higher.
  This can be attributed to the ever increasing freight rates since October 1974.

Condensed (exports)
12   Fiscal 1976 sales volume is 59,492 cases lower.
  Increase: Taiwan 68,241
  Decrease: Trinidad 98,133, Botswana 29,600.
13   Total *gross sales* per unit for fiscal 1976 is BFr.95.95 higher, viz.
  Gross sales (excl. restitutions)
  The calculations included the last known restitution rates and are those effective as
  from March 26, 1975.

  The apparently high increase of gross sales per unit in fiscal 1976 is mainly due to
  the impact of the Bangladesh tender (100,000) in fiscal 1975 at the low selling price
  $8.04 = BFr.313.56.

  When omitting such Bangladesh sales the increase per unit mainly caused by the
  fact that in fiscal 1975 the restitutions on the above mentioned Bangladesh sales
  were "pre-fixed" at a high rate of BFr.199.60.
14   *Distribution expenses* per unit for fiscal 1976 is BFr.23.56 higher.
  When omitting the Bangladesh business (f.o.b. deliveries) the increase per unit for
  fiscal 1976 will only amount to BFr.1.47.
  Such relatively minor increase in 1976 can be attributed to a higher incidence of
  f.o.b. shipments.
20   *Selling expenses* per unit for fiscal 1976 is BFr.8.44 higher.
  The apparently lower expense per unit for fiscal 1975 is mainly caused by the impact
  of the Bangladesh sales at a low BFr.1.85 commission per unit on 100,000 cases.

  When omitting the impact of the Bangladesh commissions the increase in selling
  expenses would be some BFr.2.77 only and this can be explained by commissions
  on the higher average gross selling price per unit in fiscal 1976.

Evaporated (own trade)
1   Sales volume in fiscal 1976 increased by 52,960 cases mainly due to:
  Increase: Bulgaria 10,760, Venezuela 69,000.
  Decrease: Tunisia 26,800.
2   Total *gross sales* per unit in fiscal 1976 is BFr.33.27 higher, due to an increase in selling
  prices per unit of BFr.42.39 and a reduction in restitution rates of BFr.9.12.
  The calculations include the last known restitution rates and are those in effect from
  March 26, 1975.

Condensed (own trade)
12   *Sales volume* in fiscal 1976 decreased by 256 cases mainly due to increased sales to
  Venezuela of 13,100 cases and reduced sales to Bulgaria of 11,000 cases and to Angola
  of 1,744 cases.
13   Total *gross sales* per unit for fiscal 1976 is BFr.123.20 higher due to increased unit
  selling prices by BFr.141.99 and to reduced restitution rates by BFr.18.79.
14   *Distribution expenses* increases by BFr.20.02 per case in 1976 due to increased freight
  rates.

  Note: All of the locations and figures in this exhibit have been disguised.
  * Similar forms were also used to compare Revised 1975 with Actual 1974 and Revised 1975 with Original
Budget 1975.

and to such miscellaneous items as tax computation, foreign exchange transactions, and inventories.

A fourth series of forms was devoted to a detailed explanation of each item in the total company and individual product line profit and loss budgets. Laitier was required to make and analyze three comparisons. First, the most recent budget for the next fiscal year was compared to the revised budget for the current fiscal year. Each significant change from one year to the next had to be explained (see Exhibit 5). The second required comparison was between the most recent revised budget for the current fiscal year and the original budget for the same year. Finally the most recent revised current year budget was compared with the actual prior year results.

A final series of reports was devoted to presenting and analyzing the most recent detailed manufacturing and packing cost budget for each product sold within each major product line. As with the profit and loss budgets, Laitier was required to make a series of comparisons of each significant cost item with prior budgets and with actual results from the previous year.

In summary, Laitier was responsible for preparing the initial budget and subsequent revisions thereof. The Export Division supplied volume and price estimates for each market they controlled, and Laitier did the same for its own markets. In addition, Laitier supplied all the transportation and production cost forecasts. Laitier was also responsible for preparing the reporting forms for submission to Universal. The comparative analysis required on those forms was done by Laitier. The Export Division was asked by Laitier to explain any significant volume or price variations from budget, and their explanations were included in Laitier's reporting forms.

Laitier was evaluated by Universal as a profit center, just as were each of Universal's other foreign subsidiaries. The Export Division was also treated by Universal as a profit center. Henri Goudal, managing director of Laitier was evaluated by Universal on his performance relative to the budgets negotiated by Universal and Laitier. These budgets (and Laitier's reported results) covered the entire Laitier operation. Thus, the full financial impact of the sales handled for Laitier by the Export Division were included. The Export Division also received credit for these sales and their resultant contribution to profit.

The informal discussion

In early September 1975, Henri Goudal and the finance manager of Laitier, Jan de Vries, discussed Universal's performance evaluation of Laitier with the casewriters. The conversation began when a casewriter asked Mr. Goudal for his opinion about the treatment of Laitier as a profit center. The following is a paraphrased summary of that discussion.

Goudal: Conceptually, I believe treating a subsidiary as a profit center is a very useful way to motivate managers. The problem arises, however, that, as presently organized, Laitier is not completely in control of its profits. This makes it difficult to view us as one might view some other subsidiary. For example, the other Universal subsidiaries in Europe do the bulk of their business in their domestic markets. They only export what they cannot use domestically.

Unfortunately, Laitier has not been able to operate in the Belgian market, primarily because it is incredibly price competitive. We cannot make an adequate return on our investment by selling milk products domestically. As a result, we are very much dependent on the Export Division for our sales.

However, as I said before, I have no direct authority over that department. They are responsible only to the vice president of marketing back in Chicago.

De Vries: I agree with Henri. In the processed milk business, the revenues are the crucial determinants of profitability. Many of our costs are either fixed or extremely difficult to control. For example, our labor costs are only controllable in the long run. We cannot fire people as one can in the United States. We can only decrease our labor force through attrition, and even that is sometimes difficult. Also, because the union we deal with bargains at the national level with all milk processors, we have very little impact on the cost of labor.

Similarly, the cost of milk, which represents a very large proportion of our total manufacturing cost, cannot really be controlled by Laitier.

The EEC basically determines our cost both by setting the intervention price and by fixing restitutions. All we can try to do is to predict EEC policy. We certainly cannot control it.

The point is that revenues are the primary factor in the profitability of our milk business. If revenues are bad, then so are our profits.

Casewriter: How does your relationship with the Export Division affect the budgeting process?

De Vries: We supply the Export Division with an estimate of our production and shipping costs. They, in turn, give us their volume and price forecasts. The problem is that it is very difficult for us to assess the reasonableness of their predictions. In the past, we have discovered that they have almost always been too optimistic. Our response to that problem has been to put reserves into our profit and loss forecast. If we didn't put in reserves, we would not be able to meet our profit target.

Goudal: One response on our part to the overall problem of not fully controlling our own destiny has been to try to exercise more control over our profits. Introducing the pet food line is an example. We wanted both to diversify away from milk products and to be solely responsible for one business venture. Our can plant provides the same diversification benefits and gives us a lower packaging cost in our milk business. We also make a very respectable profit on our external sales of cans. We have hired an extra marketing fellow here at Laitier to investigate other diversification possibilities.

CASE II-14

Birch Paper Company

"If I were to price these boxes any lower than $480 a thousand," said James Brunner, manager of Birch Paper Company's Thompson division, "I'd be countermanding my order of last month for our salesmen to stop shaving their bids and to bid full cost quotations. I've been trying for weeks to improve the quality of our business, and if I turn around now and accept this job at $430 or $450 or something less than $480, I'll be tearing down this program I've been working so hard to build up. The division can't very well show a profit by putting in bids which don't even cover a fair share of overhead costs, let alone give us a profit."

Birch Paper Company was a medium-sized, partly integrated paper company, producing white and kraft papers and paperboard. A portion of its paperboard output was converted into corrugated boxes by the Thompson division, which also printed and colored the outside surface of the boxes. Including Thompson, the company had four producing divisions and a timberland division, which supplied part of the company's pulp requirements.

For several years each division had been judged independently on the basis of its profit and return on investment. Top management had been working to gain effective results from a policy of decentralizing responsibility and authority for all decisions but those relating to overall company policy. The company's top officials believed that in the past few years the concept of decentralization had been successfully applied and that the company's profits and competitive position had definitely improved.

Early in 1957 the Northern division designed a special display box for one of its papers in conjunction with the Thompson division, which was equipped to make the box. Thompson's staff for package design and development spent several months perfecting the design, production methods, and materials that were to be used; because of the unusual color and shape, these were far from standard. According to an agreement between the two divisions, the Thompson division was reimbursed by the Northern division for the cost of its design and development work.

When the specifications were all prepared, the Northern division asked for bids on the box from the Thompson division and from two outside companies. Each division manager was normally free to buy from whatever supplier he wished; and even on sales within the company, divisions were expected to meet the going market price if they wanted the business.

221

In 1957, the profit margins of converters such as the Thompson division were being squeezed. Thompson, as did many other similar converters, bought its paperboard and its function was to print, cut, and shape it into boxes. Though it bought most of its materials from other Birch divisions, most of Thompson's sales were made to outside customers. If Thompson got the order from Northern, it probably would buy its linerboard and corrugating medium from the Southern division of Birch. The walls of a corrugated box consist of outside and inside sheets of linerboard sandwiching the fluted corrugating medium. About 70 percent of Thompson's out-of-pocket cost of $400 for the order represented the cost of linerboard and corrugating medium. Though Southern had been running below capacity and had excess inventory, it quoted the market price, which had not noticeably weakened as a result of the oversupply. Its out-of-pocket costs on both liner and corrugating medium were about 60 percent of its selling price.

The Northern division received bids on the boxes of $480 a thousand from the Thompson division, $430 a thousand from West Paper Company, and $432 a thousand from Eire Papers, Ltd. Eire Papers offered to buy from Birch the outside linerboard with the special printing already on it, but would supply its own inside liner and corrugating medium. The outside liner would be supplied by the Southern division at a price equivalent of $90 a thousand boxes, and would be printed for $30 a thousand by the Thompson division. Of the $30, about $25 would be out-of-pocket costs.

Since this situation appeared to be a little unusual, William Kenton, manager of the Northern division, discussed the wide discrepancy of bids with Birch's commercial vice president. He told the vice president, "We sell in a very competitive market, where higher costs cannot be passed on. How can we be expected to show a decent profit and return on investment if we have to buy our supplies at more than 10 percent over the going market?"

Knowing that Mr. Brunner had on occasion in the past few months been unable to operate the Thompson division at capacity, it seemed odd to the vice president that Brunner would add the full 20 percent overhead and profit charge to his out-of-pocket costs. When asked about this, Brunner's answer was the statement that appears at the beginning of the case. He went on to say that having done the developmental work on the box, and having received no profit on that, he felt entitled to a good mark-up on the production of the box itself.

The vice president explored further the cost structures of the various divisions. He remembered a comment the controller had made at a meeting the week before to the effect that costs which were variable for one division, could be largely fixed for the company as a whole. He knew that in the absence of specific orders from top management, Mr. Kenton would accept the lowest bid, which was that of the West Paper Company for $430. However, it would be possible for top management to order the acceptance of another bid if the situation warranted such action. And though the volume represented by the transactions in question was less than 5 percent of the volume of any of the divisions involved, other transactions could conceivably raise similar problems later.

⸺◄ CASE II – 15 ►⸺

Del Norte Paper Company (A)

⸺◄∞►⸺

"If I had purchased the kraft linerboard for the African box sale from one of our mills, I would have paid $360 per ton, $140 per ton higher than the price I actually paid by purchasing the linerboard in the spot market," said Frank Duffy, managing director of Del Norte Paper's Italian subsidiary (DNP–Italia). "I can't possibly make a profit for Del Norte if I have to pay so much for my principal raw material."

Del Norte Paper Company was a large, fully integrated paper manufacturer. Sales for 1974 were about $2.8 billion, making Del Norte Paper one of the 75 largest industrial companies in the United States. The company's product line ranged from raw pulp to a large variety of converted paper products, including corrugated boxes.

DNP–Italia purchased kraft linerboard from outside suppliers and converted it into corrugated boxes. These boxes were sold primarily within Italy, though occasional sales were made outside of Italy. DNP–Italia had six plants, each of which represented a separate profit center.

THE AFRICAN BID

In mid-1975, an African firm asked a number of paper companies to submit bids on a large quantity of corrugated boxes. In total, 22 companies submitted bids, including DNP–Italia and another Del Norte subsidiary, DNP–Deutschland. The bids were said to have ranged from approximately $340 per ton to over $550 per ton, with most of them within 5 percent of $400 per ton. Del Norte–Italia won the contract by submitting the lowest bid from a

---

This case was prepared with the cooperation of a firm which chooses to remain anonymous. All numbers and names have been disguised and certain other aspects have been altered. The case was written by William Sahlman, research assistant, under the supervision of Associate Professor M. Edgar Barrett.

firm viewed as being capable of meeting the customer's desired delivery and quality standards.

The price quoted by DNP–Italia had been substantially below that quoted by DNP–Deutschland. The primary difference between the two bids was the raw material (kraft linerboard) cost calculation embedded in each. DNP–Deutschland had formed its estimate using a per ton price for kraft linerboard of $360 while DNP–Italia had used $220. The $360 per ton figure was the price (inclusive of freight) quoted for export by a Del Norte Paper Mill located in the Eastern United States. The $220 figure was the price for kraft linerboard of comparable quality in the European "spot" market.

There were basically two reasons why the Del Norte Paper mill price was so much higher than the European spot price. First, Del Norte Paper was a member of the Kraft Export Association (KEA), a group of kraft linerboard manufacturers which was responsible for setting and stabilizing linerboard prices for the export market. The Del Norte Paper Company mill could not, as a member of the KEA, offer a lower price to its own converting plant than to any other external customer.

The second reason for the large price differential was the extremely weak economic conditions present in mid-1975. The paper and container industries were suffering from a worldwide slump. As a result of this slump, many non–KEA producers of kraft linerboard were selling their product at very low prices. This was the exact opposite situation as had existed in 1973, a year in which there was a worldwide paper and container economic boom, when the spot price for kraft linerboard had actually exceeded by a small amount the KEA set price.

DEL NORTE'S TRANSFER PRICING SYSTEM

Prices on domestic (U.S.) intracompany sales of linerboard at Del Norte Paper were set at the "market" level. That is, the transfer price was the price at which the linerboard could be bought or sold in the market place. However, on international intracompany sales, the product price was set at a level determined by the Kraft Export Association. The KEA price could vary according to market conditions, but tended to fluctuate less than the so-called spot price. Officials of Del Norte Paper in San Francisco estimated that even if all foreign subsidiary managers agreed to take all of the KEA-priced Del Norte Paper linerboard available, some 60 to 65 percent of their linerboard would have to come from other sources.[1]

When a Del Norte Paper converting plant located in the United States purchased its linerboard from a company mill, the profit made by the mill

---

[1] This 60 to 65 percent was basically in grade lines not produced by DNP mills in the United States. In addition, it generally consisted of lower quality material than was normally found in the American market.

on the transaction was included as part of one of the reported profit figures of the converting plant. The method employed for allocating the profit was rather complex. At the time of preparing the annual budget, the converting plant made a commitment to purchase a specific amount of kraft linerboard from a specific mill. The income statement of the converting plant was then credited with the actual mill profit resulting from delivery of actual orders placed against the commitment.

The figure used for the "mill profit" was determined by taking the mill profit applicable to the specific shipment after a full allocation of both fixed and variable costs and amending it for two specific items. First, any manufacturing variances were added to, or subtracted from, the mill profit. Second, in the event that the converting plant did not take as much of the mill's production as expected, the proportional cost of the resulting mill downtime was charged to the converting plant.

In Del Norte's international operations, the profit allocation process was similar. The foreign converting plant entered into a commitment for its U.S. produced requirements. The "mill profit," as defined above, was credited to the converting plant and its manager. However, in contrast to domestic operations, the set of financial statements in which this amount was credited were not made freely available to the foreign subsidiary's managing director and other management personnel. The reason for this was to maintain a legal, arms'-length business relationship. Such statements of "integrated profit" were, however, available upon request to the managing director of each foreign subsidiary.

THE AFRICAN SALE

The bid submitted by DNP–Italia to the African customer was $400 per ton of corrugated boxes. DNP–Italia's direct costs (variable costs) were approximately $325 per ton of which 72 percent or $235 represented the cost of kraft linerboard.[2]

The bid submitted by DNP–Deutschland was $550 per ton of corrugated boxes. DNP–Deutschland's direct costs on the transaction were approximately $460 of which $385 represented the cost of kraft linerboard.

The average Del Norte Paper mill had a direct cost per ton of linerboard of $190.[3] Thus, the contribution per ton at the mill was approximately $170, given the KEA selling prices of $360 per ton. The $170 contribution figure

---

[2] Editor's note: This figure represents the linerboard cost per ton of corrugated box sold. The actual cost per ton of linerboard used was $220.

[3] The direct cost figure of $190 per ton at the linerboard mill included the cost of raw wood going into the mill. Approximately 30 percent to 40 percent of the raw wood used by the mill was purchased from the Del Norte Paper Company Woodlands division at a market determined transfer price.

minus the actual freight costs from the United States to Germany (approximately $45 per ton) and the allocated overhead at the mill level would have been credited to the DNP–Deutschland converting mill had Germany won the contract.

An informal discussion

Late one afternoon in July 1975, Frank Duffy, managing director of DNP–Italia held a discussion with John Powell, general manager of international operations of Del Norte Paper's container division. The specific topic of the discussion was the African container sale, but the conversation also touched on the transfer pricing system used by Del Norte Paper.

Duffy: John, you know I would prefer to buy all my linerboard from a Del Norte Paper mill, but I just cannot compete if I have to pay $360 per ton. The price competition in the box market has been absolutely fierce this year. If I paid that much for linerboard, I would have to price my corrugated boxes below cost in order to win any contracts. If I am supposed to be a profit center, you can't expect me to report a loss on every sale I make—which is exactly what I would do using $360 per ton of linerboard.

Powell: But you would get credited with the mill profit in the transaction—you wouldn't have to report a loss.

Duffy: Maybe on your books I wouldn't show a loss, but on my books I sure would. We never see that profit here in Italy. The transaction is noted in some secret little book back in San Francisco. How am I supposed to convince my plant managers and sales people they are being credited with the mill profit when they never see it?

Furthermore, from a financial point of view, the transfer pricing system doesn't make sense. Even if the mill profit were put directly into our profit and loss statement, our cash flow would not benefit. As you know, John, this is a completely self-financed operation in Italy. If I have to borrow more money than I need to, then I incur extra interest costs. There is no offsetting credit for these expenses.

Powell: I sympathize with you, Frank, but we also have a responsibility to keep our mills operating. Further, by not purchasing Del Norte Paper linerboard when times are bad, you run the risk of not being able to buy linerboard from our United States mills when there is a shortage like there was two years ago. As you know, we're moving increasingly toward long-term commitments for delivery by our kraft linerboard mills. You also don't help maintain the pricing stability we've been working so hard to establish through the KEA.

Duffy: I appreciate the problem, but I also have the responsibility to keep my plants running. Unlike the United States, I can't fire any of my laborers in Italy—the unions just won't allow it. Any orders I can get to keep those laborers busy is pure contribution to me.

Powell: I still think you're making a mistake by not purchasing Del Norte Paper linerboard. However, we're not going to resolve the issue today. If it were not for this damn recession, the problem probably wouldn't even exist. If it's OK with you, Frank, I'd like to have a chance to give the problem some more thought.

———CASE II-16———

Enager Industries, Inc.

"I don't get it. I've got a nifty new product proposal that can't help but make money, and top management turns thumbs down. No matter how we price this new item, we expect to make $130,000 on it pretax. That would contribute over 10 cents per share to our earnings after taxes, which is more than the 9 cent earnings-per-share increase in 1978 that the president made such a big thing about in the shareholders' annual report. It just doesn't make sense for the president to be touting EPS while his subordinates are rejecting profitable projects like this one."

The frustrated speaker was Sarah McNeil, product development manager of the consumer products division of Enager Industries, Inc. Enager was a relatively young company, which had grown rapidly to its 1978 sales level of over $74 million. (See Exhibits 1–4 for financial data for 1977 and 1978.)

EXHIBIT 1

ENAGER INDUSTRIES, INC.
Income statements for 1977 and 1978
($000, except earnings per share figures)

| | Year ended December 31 | |
	1977	1978
Sales	$70,731	$74,225
Cost of goods sold	54,109	56,257
Gross margin	16,622	17,968
Other expenses:		
Development	4,032	4,008
Selling and general	6,507	6,846
Interest	594	976
Total	11,133	11,830
Income before taxes	5,489	6,138
Income tax expense	2,854	3,192
Net income	$ 2,635	$ 2,946
Earnings per share (500,000 and 550,000 shares outstanding in 1977 and 1978 respectively)	$5.27	$5.36

This case was prepared by Professor James S. Reece.

EXHIBIT 2

ENAGER INDUSTRIES, INC.
Balance Sheets for 1977 and 1978
($000)

	As of December 31	
	1977	1978
Assets		
Cash and temporary investments	$ 1,404	$ 1,469
Accounts receivable	13,688	15,607
Inventories	22,162	25,467
Total current assets	37,254	42,543
Plant and equipment:		
Original cost	37,326	45,736
Accumulated depreciation	12,691	15,979
Net	24,635	29,757
Investments and other assets	2,143	3,119
Total assets	$64,032	$75,419
Liabilities and Owners' Equity		
Accounts payable	$ 9,720	$12,286
Taxes payable	1,210	1,045
Current portion of long-term debt	—	1,634
Total current liabilities	10,930	14,965
Deferred income taxes	559	985
Long-term debt	12,622	15,448
Total liabilities	24,111	31,398
Common stock	17,368	19,512
Retained earnings	22,553	24,509
Total owners' equity	39,921	44,021
Total liabilities and owners' equity	$64,032	$75,419

Enager had three divisions, consumer products, industrial products, and professional services, each of which accounted for about one third of Enager's total sales. Consumer products, the oldest of the three divisions, designed, manufactured, and marketed a line of houseware items, primarily for use in the kitchen. The industrial products division built one-of-a-kind machine tools to customer specifications; i.e., it was a large "job shop," with the typical job taking several months to complete. The Professional Services division, the newest of the three, had been added to Enager by acquiring a large firm which provided land planning, landscape architecture, structural architecture, and consulting engineering services. This division had grown rapidly, in part because of its capability to perform "environmental impact" studies, as required by law on many new land development projects.

Because of the differing nature of their activities, each division was treated as an essentially independent company. There were only a few corporate-level managers and staff people, whose job was to coordinate the

EXHIBIT 3

ENAGER INDUSTRIES, INC.
Statements of changes in financial position for 1977 and 1978
(cash basis; $000)

	Year ended December 31	
	1977	*1978*
Sources of funds:		
Provided by operations	$ 5,748	$ 6,660
Increase in long-term debt (net)	724	2,826
Issurance of common stock	—	2,144
Increased current liabilities		
Accounts payable	634	2,566
Taxes payable	130	(165)
Current portion of long-term debt	—	1,634
Total sources	$ 7,236	$15,665
Uses of funds:		
Plant and equipment	$ 5,239	$ 8,410
Increase in investments and other assets	18	976
Dividends	900	990
Increased current assets:		
Cash and temporary investments	154	65
Accounts receivable	257	1,919
Inventories	668	3,305
Total uses	$ 7,236	$15,665

EXHIBIT 4
Ratio analysis for 1977 and 1978

	1977	*1978*
Net income ÷ Sales	3.7%	4.0%
Gross margin ÷ Sales	23.5%	24.2%
Development expenses ÷ Sales	5.7%	5.4%
Selling and general ÷ Sales	9.2%	9.2%
Interest ÷ Sales	0.8%	1.3%
Asset turnover[1]	1.10x	0.98x
Current ratio	3.41	2.84
Quick ratio	1.38	1.14
Days' cash[1]	8.1	7.9
Days' receivables[1]	70.6	76.7
Day's inventories[1]	149.5	165.2
EBIT ÷ Assets[1]	9.5%	9.4%
Return on invested capital[1,2,3]	5.6%	5.6%
Return on owner's equity[1]	6.6%	6.7%
Net income ÷ Assets[1,4]	4.1%	3.9%
Debt/capitalization[1]	24.0%	28.0%

[1] Ratio based on year-end balance sheet amount, not annual average amount.
[2] Invested capital includes current portion of long-term debt.
[3] Adjusted for interest expense add-back.
[4] Not adjusted for add-back of interest; if adjusted, 1977 and 1978 ROA are 4.6 percent and 4.5 percent.

activities of the three divisions. One aspect of this coordination was that all new project proposals requiring investment in excess of $500,000 had to be reviewed by the corporate vice president of finance, Henry Hubbard. It was Hubbard who had recently rejected McNeil's new product proposal, the essentials of which are shown in Exhibit 5.

EXHIBIT 5
Financial data from new product proposal

1. Projected asset investment[1]

Cash	$ 50,000
Accounts receivable	150,000
Inventories	300,000
Plant and equipment[2]	500,000
Total	1,000,000

2. Cost data:

Variable cost per unit	3.00
Differential fixed costs (per year)[3]	170,000

3. Price/Market estimates (per year):

Unit price	Unit sales (000)	Break-even volume (units)
$6	100	56,667
7	75	42,500
8	60	34,000

[1] Assumes 100,000 units' sales.
[2] Annual capacity of 120,000 units.
[3] Includes straight-line depreciation on new plant and equipment.

PERFORMANCE EVALUATION

Prior to 1977, each of the three Enager divisions had been treated as a profit center, with annual division profit budgets negotiated between the president and the respective division general managers. In 1976 Enager's president, Carl Randall, had become concerned about high interest rates, and their impact on the company's profitability. At the urging of Henry Hubbard, Randall had decided to begin treating each division as an investment center, so as to be able to relate each division's profit to the assets the division used to generate its profits.

Starting in 1977, each division was measured based on its return on assets, which was defined to be the division's net income divided by its assets. Net income for a division was calculated by taking the division's "direct income before taxes," and then subtracting the division's share of corporate administrative expenses (allocated on the basis of divisional revenues) and its share of income tax expense (the tax rate applied to the division's "direct income before taxes" after subtraction of the allocated corporate administrative expenses). Although Hubbard realized there were other ways to define a division's income, he and the president preferred this method since "it made the sum of the [divisional] parts equal to the [corporate] whole."

Similarly, Enager's total assets were subdivided among three divisions. Since each division operated in physically separate facilities, it was easy to attribute most assets, including receivables, to specific divisions. The corporate-office assets, including the centrally controlled cash account, were allocated to the divisions on the basis of divisional revenues. All fixed assets were recorded at their balance sheet values, i.e., original cost less accumulated straight-line depreciation. Thus the sum of the divisional assets was equal to the amount shown on the corporate balance sheet ($75,419,000 as of December 31, 1978).

In 1976, Enager had as its return on year-end assets (net income divided by total assets) a rate of 3.8 percent. According to Hubbard, this corresponded to a "gross return" in 1976 of 9.3 percent; he defined gross return as equal to earnings *before* interest *and* taxes (EBIT) divided by assets. Hubbard felt that a company like Enager should have a gross (EBIT) return on assets of at least 12 percent, especially given the interest rates the corporation had had to pay on its recent borrowings. He therefore instructed each division manager that the division was to try to earn a gross return of 12 percent in 1977 and 1978. In order to help pull the return up to this level, Hubbard decided that new investment proposals would have to show a return of at least 15 percent in order to be approved.

1977-1978 RESULTS

Hubbard and Randall were moderately pleased with 1977's results. The year was a particularly difficult one for some of Enager's competitors, yet Enager had managed to increase its return on assets from 3.8 percent to 4.1 percent, and its gross return from 9.3 percent to 9.5 percent. The professional services division easily exceeded the 12 percent gross return target; consumer products' gross return on assets was 8 percent; but industrial products' return was only 5.5 percent.

At the end of 1977, the president put pressure on the general manager of the industrial products division to improve its return on investment, suggesting that this division was not "carrying its share of the load." The division manager had bristled at this comment, saying the division could get a higher return "if we had a lot of old machines the way consumer products does." The president had responded that he did not understand the relevance of the division manager's remark, adding, "I don't see why the return on an old asset should be higher than that on a new asset, just because the old one cost less."

The 1978 results both disappointed and puzzled Carl Randall. Return on assets fell from 4.1 percent to 3.9 percent, and gross return dropped from 9.5 percent to 9.4 percent. At the same time, return on sales (net income divided by sales) rose from 3.7 percent to 4.0 percent, and return on owners' equity also increased, from 6.6 percent to 6.7 percent. These results prompted Randall to say the following to Hubbard:

> You know, Henry, I've been a marketer most of my career; but, until recently, I thought I understood the notion of return on investment. Now I see in 1978 our profit margin was up and our earnings per share were up; yet two of your return on investment figures were down, one—return on invested capital—held constant, and return on owners' equity went up. I just don't understand these discrepancies.
>
> Moreover, there seems to be a lot more tension among our managers the last two years. The general manager of the professional services division seems to be doing a good job, and she's happy as a lark about the praise I've given her. But the general manager of industrial products looks daggers at me every time we meet. And last week, when I was eating lunch with the division manager at consumer products, the product development manager came over to our table and really burned my ears over a new product proposal of hers you rejected the other day.
>
> I'm wondering if I should follow up on the idea that Karen Kraus in personnel brought back from that two-day organization development workshop she attended over at the university. She thinks we ought to have a one-day off-site "retreat" of all the corporate and divisional managers to talk over this entire return-on-investment matter.

QUESTIONS

1. Why was McNeil's new product proposal rejected? Should it have been? Explain.

2. Evaluate the manner in which Randall and Hubbard have implemented their investment center concept. What pitfalls did they apparently not anticipate?

3. What, if anything, should Randall do now with regard to his investment center approach?

──── CASE II–17 ────

Del Norte Paper Company (C)

In early July 1975, Frank Duffy, managing director of the Italian subsidiary of the container division of Del Norte Paper Company (DNP–Italia), was sitting in his Torino office thinking about a recent informal discussion held between himself, two casewriters, and certain members of his staff. The topic of the discussion had been the problems of applying the corporate capital budgeting system to a foreign subsidiary such as DNP–Italia.

At approximately the same time, Hans Lowenstein, managing director of the German subsidiary of the container division (DNP–Deutschland), was sitting in his Frankfurt office thinking about a very similar meeting in which he had recently participated. Once again, the discussion had been focused on Del Norte Paper Company's capital budgeting system and its impact on a foreign subsidiary.

Duffy and Lowenstein had held their respective meetings in order to prepare themselves for an August meeting on the same topic with John Powell, general manager international operations of the container division. Both Duffy and Lowenstein believed that Del Norte's capital budgeting system had had an adverse impact on their ability to manage. Both were currently wondering how to convey in an effective manner the reservations that their respective management teams had about the corporate capital budgeting system.

ORGANIZATION STRUCTURE

Del Norte Paper had a product line management structure. The company was divided into seven broad product lines called strategic product groups, each headed by a corporate vice president. The strategic product group was further divided into more narrowly defined product divisions, each headed by a division vice president. For example, the container division was structurally part of the container–containerboard strategic product group (see Exhibit 1).

The product divisions were comprised of several geographical regions, each headed by a regional manager. In the container division, a distinction

---

This case was prepared with the cooperation of a firm which chooses to remain anonymous. All numbers and names have been disguised and certain other aspects have been altered. The case was written by William A. Sahlman, research assistant, and Associate Professor M. Edgar Barrett.

234

EXHIBIT 1
Del Norte Paper Company organization chart

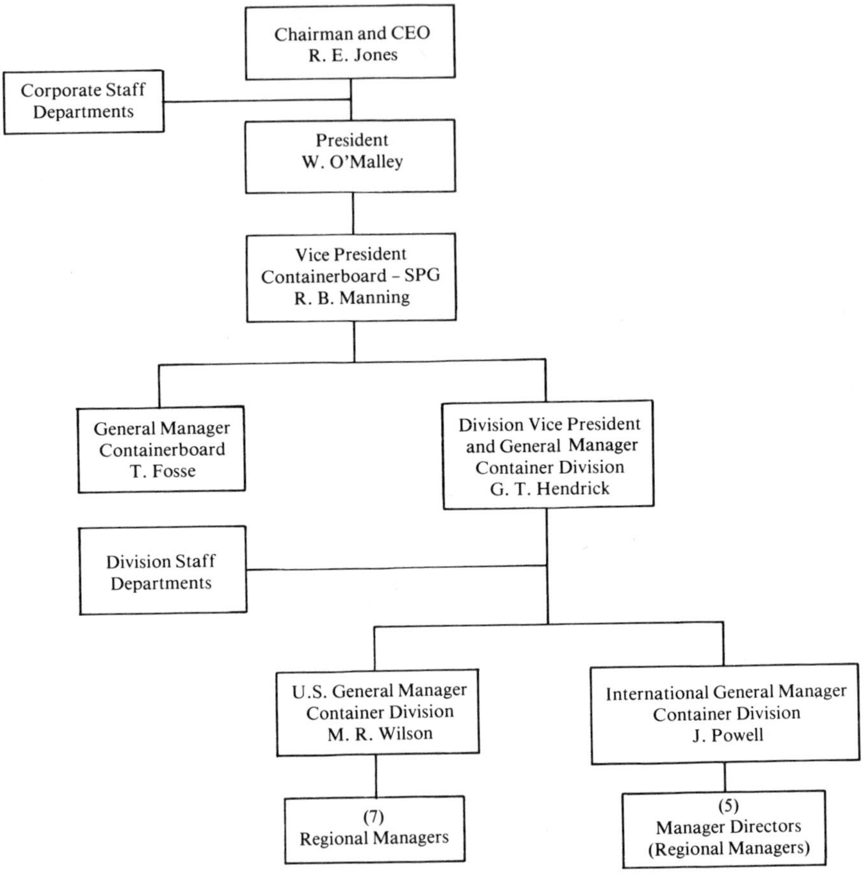

```
                          ┌─────────────────────┐
                          │   Chairman and CEO  │
                          │     R. E. Jones     │
     ┌──────────────┐     └─────────────────────┘
     │Corporate Staff│────────────┤
     │ Departments  │     ┌─────────────────────┐
     └──────────────┘     │      President      │
                          │     W. O'Malley     │
                          └─────────────────────┘

                          ┌─────────────────────┐
                          │   Vice President    │
                          │ Containerboard – SPG│
                          │    R. B. Manning    │
                          └─────────────────────┘

     ┌──────────────────┐        ┌──────────────────────────┐
     │ General Manager  │        │  Division Vice President  │
     │  Containerboard  │        │  and General Manager      │
     │    T. Fosse      │        │    Container Division     │
     └──────────────────┘        │      G. T. Hendrick       │
                                 └──────────────────────────┘
     ┌──────────────────┐
     │  Division Staff  │────────────┤
     │   Departments    │
     └──────────────────┘

     ┌──────────────────────┐        ┌────────────────────────────┐
     │ U.S. General Manager │        │ International General Manager│
     │  Container Division  │        │     Container Division      │
     │     M. R. Wilson     │        │         J. Powell           │
     └──────────────────────┘        └────────────────────────────┘

     ┌──────────────────┐            ┌──────────────────────┐
     │       (7)        │            │         (5)          │
     │Regional Managers │            │  Manager Directors   │
     └──────────────────┘            │ (Regional Managers)  │
                                     └──────────────────────┘
```

was also made between the international and the domestic operations. The former was headed by John Powell, general manager international operations, who reported directly to the vice president of the Container division.

The international segment of the Container division was divided into 5 regions, each headed by a managing director. Each region in turn was comprised of several plants serving different sales territories. Each plant was responsible for both production and marketing. The plants were headed by plant managers. Each strategic product group, each product division, each regional subsidiary, and each plant was evaluated by Del Norte Paper as a profit center. Return on investment was also an important evaluation factor.

DNP–Italia and DNP–Deutschland

DNP–Italia, with headquarters in Torino, had six container plants. Sales for 1974 were approximately $56 million while net income after an adjustment reflecting a switch to Lifo accounting was around $2.9 million. In contrast to the performance in 1974, 1975 sales were expected to decline due to the economic recession, and an operating loss was probable.

The Italian box market was very competitive. At least in part, this was due to the fact that there were no less than 100 significant producers of boxes in Italy. Most of these companies were family-owned and quite small. While Del Norte Paper believed it was the third largest company in the market, it supplied well under 10 percent of the country's box needs.

DNP–Deutschland, with headquarters in Frankfurt, had four container plants. Sales for 1974 were approximately $63 million and net income after an adjustment reflecting a switch to Lifo accounting was about $5.0 million. The recession was having a less drastic impact on DNP–Deutschland than on DNP–Italia. Thus, 1975 sales were expected to increase slighly and net income was expected to decline only a small amount from record 1974 levels.

Competition also existed in the German market. However, the major competition consisted less of small, family-owned companies and more of large multinational, integrated paper companies. DNP–Deutschland's most important competitors were Bowater, International Paper, Mead Corporation, Unilever, and Union Camp.

THE FORMAL CAPITAL BUDGETING SYSTEM

The capital budgeting system used by DNP–Italia and DNP–Deutschland was essentially the same as that used by all Del Norte Paper subsidiaries, domestic and foreign. Corporate headquarters had instituted a formalized process for submitting capital investment requests. These procedures were outlined in considerable detail in a 250-page *Capital Investment Manual*[1] which was distributed to the financial personnel of each major division and subsidiary.

The *Capital Investment Manual* contained an explicit set of guidelines as to the amount of money that any one manager could spend without approval from a higher authority. A regional managing director such as Frank Duffy or Hans Lowenstein was not authorized to spend greater than $500 on capital projects without first getting approval from a higher authority. Any repair or maintenance projects over $10,000 also had to be approved by higher authority. However, he was authorized to spend the smaller of 10 percent or $10,000 on changes in the scope or on an overrun on an already approved project. Items falling within these limits were funded from Division Capital Fund–General. The overall size of this fund was negotiated each year as part of the overall capital budgeting review process.

The *Capital Investment Manual* also contained an explicit categorization of capital expenditure requests (Exhibit 2). The classification included such things as Cost Reduction (Code C) and Budgeted Repairs (Code E). Finally,

---

[1] This manual was written in English, and had not been translated into any foreign language.

EXHIBIT 2
Categorization of capital expenditure requests

Code	Title	Description
A	Maintenance	To maintain properties, products and services. This category also includes a separate item called Division Capital Fund—General. The purpose of this fund is to provide fixed capital for individual projects that do not exceed the division manager's approval authority level for individual projects. The money can be allocated to new unbudgeted projects which arise during the year or to "scope changes."*
B	Investments	To improve properties, products, and services to meet future requirements for product quality and customer services.
C	Cost reductions	To reduce costs (labor, materials, utilities, freight, etc.)
D	Expansion	To increase capacity.
E	Budgeted repairs	Major maintenance projects which are not associated with a capital project. There is also a provision for the establishment of a Division Repair Fund to provide for new unbudgeted capital projects, and repair expense requirements for overruns or changes in the scope of approved projects. Once again, approval authority levels remain in effect.
F	Automobile and trucks	

Note: Capital budget items Codes A, B, C and D were classified as either a Major Capital Investment (MCI) or a regular capital budget item. All Code E and F items were regular capital budget items. Basically, projects were MCIs if they involved a relatively large investment (more than $300,000) and/or resulted in a significant change in the product line of the subsidiary (e.g., launching a new product or an acquisition). All MCIs had to be approved by the Del Norte Paper Company board of directors. All other Code A, B, C, D, E and F investment projects were regular capital budget items. These smaller projects could be approved at lower levels of authority depending on the amount of money involved.
* A scope change is either a cost overrun or a minor change in the nature of the investment.

there was a distinction drawn between Major Capital Investments (MCIs) and regular capital budget items. All MCIs had to be approved by the Del Norte Paper Company board of directors.

The capital budgeting cycle

The capital budgeting cycle began in February of the year preceding the year in which the funds would be used. The regional managing director and several other members of his management team would attend meetings with the engineers, production managers, marketing managers, and plant general managers of each of the plants in order to determine expected equipment needs for the following year. The regional office explained any changes in the budget forms and schedule and provided estimated economic trends for the following year in order to facilitate planning.

Between February and April, initial "want lists" for the capital and repair budgets were prepared by the plant managers. These want lists were subject to review by both regional management and John Powell during mid- and late April. After these reviews, the plant managers prepared budgets containing documents for each specific project within the final want lists. Regular capital budget items for all but budgeted repairs and motor vehicles were supported by three pages of quantitative and qualitative analysis (Exhibit 3)[2].

Requests for budgeted repairs and motor vehicles were supported by less comprehensive, two-page documents. Major capital investments, or MCIs, required considerably more detailed documentation. Instead of listing a single annual savings or income figure, precise estimates for each year of the project were needed. Projections for 12 years were usually required for MCIs. The amount of additional supporting analysis was also commensurably larger.

The completed working packages, with supporting documentation, were submitted to regional management in mid-May. Regional management reviewed the completed budgets and forwarded seven copies of each plant's Capital and Repair budget to San Francisco by late May. John Powell then reviewed the projects with the respective regional managements and indicated which projects he considered to be acceptable in light of the overall International Operation's needs and priorities. The list of acceptable projects with possible further revisions from the foreign subsidiary was then submitted to container division headquarters in early July. This revised list also included a priority ranking of projects by the regional management team.

Between early July and early August final revisions to the Capital and Repair budget were made by Container division in consultation with the subsidiary management. During the first week of August, this revised budget was reviewed with Del Norte Paper corporate personnel from the corporate budget and measurements department. The purpose of this review was to insure that analysis and presentations conformed to standard Del Norte Paper Company procedures. Next, in the middle of August, the budget was presented to the container–containerboard strategic product group vice president. After his review, the consolidated container division capital and repair budget was sent to the printers. Shortly thereafter, it was distributed to authorized personnel within the container–containerboard strategic product group.

The formal submission of all capital expenditure requests to the Del Norte Paper Company board of directors by each strategic product group and each division occurred in early December. After these individual budgets had been approved by the board of directors (sometime in January), then funds were released by the board to the responsible managers. That is, for example,

---

[2] The figures for the DCF return on investment were calculated in San Francisco and added to the documentation after submission of the forms by the regional subsidiary.

EXHIBIT 3

1975 CAPITAL AND REPAIR BUDGET

REGULAR CAPITAL BUDGET ITEM ANALYSIS—CODES A-D

DIVISION/SUBSIDIARY: Container/Italy
MILL/PLANT: Fondi

Item Name —Floor Conveyors	*Annual Savings:*		*Key Indicators:*
Code —C	Gross Savings:		
Item Number—5	Additional Profit	$	Months To Complete — 8
	Cost Reduction Savings & Additional Costs:		Quantities:
	Labor	38,800	M Units Per Year — —
	Materials	—	No. Of Employees — 4
Investment:	Utilities	—	
Capital:	Freight	—	% Return On Investment:
Fixed $45,000	Other	—	Regular — 39
Working $ —	Total Gross Savings	38,000	DCF — 47
Total Capital $45,000	Depreciation (8.33%)	(3,700)	
Contingent Expense $ —	Other Noncash Charges	—	Payback Period (Years) — 2
Memo-Leased Assets $ —	Income Taxes (50%)	(17,500)	
	Annual Net Savings	$ 17,600	

Description, justification, and assumptions:

In the 1974 capital budget, we proposed that the layout of the Fondi plant be changed to include a complete line of conveyors as well as an automatic strapping unit. The Fondi plant obtained the single-head strapper and now requires the final conveyor installation. The plant now must have one forklift driver per shift to move the pallets from the palletizing area to the strapper. Two men are also required to load nonunitized bundles into trucks by hand. This proposal includes complete conveyorization from the palletizing area to the finished goods department. This and the unitizing of bundles, will enable us to eliminate the two forklift drivers as well as two truck loaders.

Exchange rate: Lire 637 = $1 US

CS-11 (1/73)   Date: 9/20/74   Code: C   Item No.: 5   Page 1

Editor's Note: The form is standard and all the numbers except the DCF return are filled in by DNP–Italia. The DCF figures are provided by container division in San Francisco.

EXHIBIT 3 (*continued*)

1975 CAPITAL AND REPAIR BUDGET

DIVISION/SUBSIDIARY: Container/Italy

REGULAR CAPITAL BUDGET ITEM ANALYSIS—CODES A–D   MILL/PLANT: Fondi

ITEM NAME: Floor conveyors   CODE: C   ITEM NUMBER: 5

Investment:	
Fixed Capital:	
Powered Conveyor	$37,000
Installation & Freight	8,000
Subtotal—Fixed Capital	45,000
Working Capital:	
Subtotal—Working Capital	—
Total Capital	45,000
Contingent Expense:	
Total Contingent Expense	—
Total Capital & Contingent Expense	$45,000
Memo-Leased Assets:	
Must Lease	—
Purchase Price	—
Total Leased Assets	$ —
Exchange rate: Lire 637 = $1 US	

Annual Gross Savings:

Direct Labor Savings

1. Wage rates:
   Forklift driver = $5.54/hour
   Truck loader = $5.10/hour

   1975 forecasted rates of which 48% is fringe benefits

2. Savings:
   2 forklift drivers × $5.54 × 1,821 hrs/year
   $$= \$20,200 = \$20,200$$

   2 truck loaders × $5.10 × 1.821 hrs/year
   $$= \$18,600 = \$18,600$$

   Total Annual Gross Savings = $38,800 $38,800

CB-11 (1/73)   Date: 9/20/74   Code: C   Item No.: 5   Page 2

EXHIBIT 3 (*concluded*)

\	\	\	\	\	\	\	\	\	\	\

1975 CAPITAL AND REPAIR BUDGET

ENDORSEMENTS AND RECOMMENDATIONS

DIVISION/SUBSIDIARY: Container/Italy
MILL/PLANT: Fondi

[X] ANNUAL CAPITAL AND REPAIR BUDGET   [ ] INDIVIDUAL PROJECT

Item Name: Floor Conveyor
Code: C   Item Number: 5

Description	Capital			Contingent Expense	Annual Net Savings	% Return on Investment		Payback Period (years)	Quantities	
	Fixed	Working	Total			Reg.	DCF		M Units Per Year	No. Empl.
Capital	$45,000	$---	$45,000	$---	$17,600	39	47	2	-	4
Repair				$---						
Memo - Leased Assets			$---							

Exchange Rate: Lire 637 = $1 US

SIGNATURE OF MANAGERS:

FUNCTION	Facility/Region Signature Title Date	Division Signature Title Date	Product Group Signature Title Date	Corporate Signature Title Date
Marketing		TP Black 10/6/74		
Engineering	D Crleure 9/20/74			
Manufacturing		DF C.L..... 10/2/1		
Woodlands				
Others (Specify)				
Finance	X Ciyle 9/20/74	RA Slor 10-4		
Executive	H Ma... 9-20-74	Rendl 10/2/74		
	F Nify 9-20-74	M Allacore w/i		

Date: 9/20/74   Page: A

the board released the funds to the container–containerboard strategic product group vice president who released the funds to the container division vice president. He in turn allocated money to the general manager of international operations who released the funds to the international subsidiaries. It was at this point that subsidiaries such as DNP–Deutschland could order the equipment approved for purchase.

The time delay between the ordering of the equipment and the actual delivery depended on the nature of the item and on the individual supplier. When, as in 1974, the paper industry was experiencing a worldwide economic boom, equipment lead times were very long. As much as one year could transpire after placement of an order before the piece of equipment was operating in the plant.

Once a capital expenditure budget was approved, formal submission of a set of documents for tracking the progress of each project on a monthly basis was required from each plant. Capital and repair budget status reports (Exhibit 4) were used for this purpose. An explanation had to be included on these forms for any significant variations from budget. It should also be noted that the foreign subsidiary management was held responsible for

CONTAINER DIVISION (INTERNATIONAL)
Capital Budget ☒
Repair Budget ☐

CAPITAL AND REPAIR BUDGET STATUS REPORT

Plant: Hamburg
Manager: Kurt Studmann
Period Ended: June 1975

Item Name	Budg. Exch. Rate	Budget Yr. Code Item No.	Approvals			Debits		Estimated Balance To Complete	(Over) Under Budget			Completion Date
			Amount	Additions (Deletions)	Total	Current Year	Total To-Date		Exchange Rate Var.	Controllable Var. $	Controllable Var. %	
1973 Capital Budget												
Building	3.18	73 D-202	247.000	220.000	467.000	77.681	709.119	28.553	(51.552)	(219.120)	(46.9)	SEP. 75
Machinery & Equipment	3.18	73 D-202	283.000	(60.000)	223.000	99.131	229.097	—	(3.807)	(2.290)	(1,0)	AUG. 75
Total 1973 Capital Budget	3.18	73 D-202	530.000	160.000	690.000	176.812	938.216	28.553	(55.359)	(221.410)	(32.1)	
1974 Capital Budget												
Transformer	2.89	74-C-4	26.000	—	26.000	8.495	10.030	26.422	(1.312)	(9.140)	(35.0)	SEP. 75
Wasto Cyclone	2.89	74-A-3B	7.000	—	7.000	603	9.980	1.636	(589)	(4.027)	(57.5)	AUG. 75
Flexo Folder and Automatic Stitcher	2.89	74-D-5	—	676.000	676.000	225.262	225.262	478.211	(18.795)	(8.678)	(1.3)	NOV. 75
Automatic Die Cutter	2.89	74-D-6	—	551.000	551.000	34.568	34.568	538.816	(2.350)	(20.034)	(3.6)	MAR. 76
Total 1974 Capital Budget			33.000	1.227.000	1.260.000	268.928	279.840	1.045.085	(23.046)	(41.879)	(3.3)	
1975 Capital Budget												
Lathe	2.66	75-A-3A	10.000	—	10.000	—	—	10.406	—	(406)	(4,1)	FEB. 75
Maintenance Shop	2.66	75-A-3B	9.000	—	9.000	—	—	9.366	—	(366)	(4,1)	JAN. 75
Capacitors	2.66	75-A-3C	5.000	—	5.000	—	—	5.203	(51)	(203)	(4,1)	OCT. 75
Fuel Oil Tanks	2.66	75-A-4	23.000	—	23.000	1.307	1.307	22.628	—	(884)	(3,8)	SEP. 75
Forklift Truck	2.66	75-A-5	18.000	—	18.000	15.375	15.375	3.356	(600)	(131)	(0,7)	OCT. 75
Automatic Sheet Length Control	2.66	75-C-6	32.000	—	32.000	745	745	32.555	(29)	(1.271)	(4,0)	SEP. 75
Total 1975 Capital Budget			97.000	—	97.000	17.427	17.427	83.514	(680)	(3.261)	(3,4)	
GRAND TOTAL			660.000	1.387.000	2.047.000	463.167	1.235.483	1.157.152	(79.005)	(266.550)	(13.0)	

EXHIBIT 4 (*continued*)

CONTAINER DIVISION (INTERNATIONAL)
Capital Budget □
Repair Budget ☒

Plant: Hamburg
Manager: Kurt Stoudmann
Period Ended: JUNE 1975

Item Name	Budg. Exch. Rate	Budget Yr. Code Item No.	Approvals			Debits		Estimated Balance To Complete	(Over) Under Budget			Completion Date
			Amount	Additions (Deletions)	Total	Current Year	Total To-Date		Exchange Rate Var.	Controllable Var. $	%	
1974 Repair Budget												
Repair Corrugator Steam System	2.89	74-E-2	18.000	—	18.000	12.442	23.538	—	(872)	(4.666)	(25, 9)	COMPLET.
B Flute Corrugator Rolls	2.89	74-E-4	—	47.000	47.000	74	74	48.836	(3)	(1.907)	(4, 1)	AUG. 75
C Flute Corrugator Rolls	2.89	74-E-5	—	47.000	47.000	74	74	48.836	(3)	(1.907)	(4, 1)	AUG. 75
Corrugators Belt	2.89	74-E-6	—	12.000	12.000	9.665	9.665	2.822	(377)	(110)	(0, 9)	OCT. 75
Corrugators Electrical Repair	2.89	74-G-7	—	17.000	17.000	6.653	6.653	11.038	(260)	(431)	(2, 5)	NOV. 75
Flexo Folder and Automatic Stitcher	2.89	74-D-5	—	6.000	6.000	290	290	5.957	(12)	(235)	(3, 9)	NOV. 75
Automatic Die Cutter	2.89	74-D-6	—	8.000	8.000	—	—	8.323	—	(323)	4, —	MARCH 76
Total 1974 Repair Budget			18.000	137.000	155.000	29.198	40.294	125.812	(1.527)	(9.579)	(6, 2)	
1975 Repair Budget				—Six line items were shown in this space (editor)								
Total 1975 Repair Budget			93.000	—	93.000	2.405	2.405	94.382	(94)	(3.693)	(4, —)	
GRAND TOTAL			111.000	137.000	248.000	31.603	42.699	220.194	(1.621)	(13.272)	(5, 4)	

expenditures in U.S. dollars. This necessitated the inclusion of a figure for exchange rate variance. These variances were often substantial, due to the volatility of exchange rates under a floating rate world monetary system.

Other aspects

There were two other significant aspects of the system. These two aspects dealt with obtaining "approval in principle" and with the control system for dealing with cost overruns or changes in the scope of an already approved project.

There was a provision in the Del Norte Paper *Capital Investment Manual* for submitting projects for approval in principle. These projects required the same kind of documentation as normal projects. If one of the projects was approved, then funds would be allocated by the board of directors or by the appropriate corporate division manager to the project. However, the funds were not released for spending during the year unless a formal request for their release was made by the manager who had submitted the original request for the project.

Subject to an overall limitation on the annual total, the regional managing director could spend up to $10,000 on changes in the scope of an overrun of an already approved project, with the additional limitation that such an expenditure could not exceed 10 percent of the original budget for the project. Scope changes or cost overruns beyond this limitation had to be approved by a higher level of authority. Approval for such an item was sought by submitting a two-page request. Such requests could be submitted at any time, but the response time could vary from one to three months.

The informal discussion at DNP–Italia

Late on July 4th, 1975, several members of the management team at the Torino office of DNP–Italia gathered for a discussion of the corporate capital budgeting system and its effects on DNP–Italia's operations. Present throughout the meeting were: B. Rizzo, director of operations; R. Angelo, director of business systems; L. Guppi, controller; D. Corleone, engineering manufacturing service manager; G. Pruitt, a marketing executive from Del Norte's Seattle office who was just in the process of being transferred to Torino, and the two casewriters. Frank Duffy, due to a previous engagement, did not join the meeting until 5:30 P.M.

The discussion was begun by a casewriter asking Dr. Rizzo for his view of the capital budgeting system. The following paragraphs consist of paraphrased excerpts from the meeting:

Rizzo: I think that the capital budgeting system is, theoretically, very good. A big company like DNP needs a standard system to help with planning and to help people communicate with each other.

However, the system can also be used to frustrate people . . . to block them from doing what they want to do. I often think that San Francisco has used the system to prevent investments from being made in Italy. There's such a misguided way of measuring manpower reductions. And, then there's the matter of that standard format.

Casewriter: I'm not sure that I understand.

Rizzo: Well, I think the basic problem is that American logic just doesn't fit well in Italy. The market moves faster here. We have over 100 major and minor competitors, and most of them are small, family-owned companies. If you counted every small producer, then the number of competitors is something over 1,000. If, in order to maintain or gain a new customer, new equipment is required, our competitors will have the machine installed before we get approval to spend any money.

Corleone: When we want to buy a machine, it takes an absolute minimum of six months and maybe as much as a year to get approval from San Francisco. That could mean 18 months or more from the time of the original request to the time we have a machine in operation. It's very difficult to compete when you can't react quickly to changing customer needs.

Rizzo: The problem goes beyond the time lag. Every project we submit to San Francisco for approval has to be described on standard forms. If we want to buy a machine in order to be able to attract the kind of orders I just mentioned, San Francisco requires us to identify the actual customer for the product and the probable marginal sales volume.

Also, there are a number of investments we should make for long-run strategic reasons, but which are difficult to get approved in San Francisco because they show a relatively low rate of return. Other considerations such as not antagonizing customers, keeping market share, not allowing a major competitor to enter one of our markets, etc., are more important than strictly quantitative aspects. Sometimes, a 20 percent return is better than a 30 percent return, but this is a very difficult concept to put on the standard forms.

Casewriter: The problem with the standard format, is that partially a problem of differences in terms between Italian and English?

Guppi: Well that's clearly a problem, but more so because of the overall need to translate from Italian to English to Italian as we move from the plants to San Francisco and then back to the plants.

However, there are some serious problems with these standard forms. For example, the Italian government has a policy of providing tax breaks *and* low interest rate loans to induce companies to invest in Southern Italy.[3]

We've been trying for several years to buy some more machinery for one of our plants in that area. However, we weren't allowed to include the tax and interest savings in the calculations submitted with the proposal. Interest savings aren't allowed to be shown and a flat tax rate of 50 percent is required. As a result, we've been consistently turned down.

As another example of the problem of using standard U.S. forms for all our capital expenditure requests, we are required to use the U.S. tax rate of 50 percent

---

[3] Essentially, a grant of 30 percent to be returned to the company three years after installation of the machine (editor).

to calculate our net cash flow. This doesn't make any sense in Italy where the tax rate is less than 50 percent.

Casewriter: Benito, you also mentioned some problems in the measurement of manpower reductions.

Rizzo: Yes, one of my major frustrations with the system is in trying to justify labor-saving investments to San Francisco. Our labor situation today in Italy is very much different from that in the United States.[4] We have serious problems with high absenteeism, strikes, low productivity, and inflating wage rates. In spite of this, it is almost impossible to fire one of our laborers and we can't force people to resign simply because we have obtained some labor-saving equipment. One of our primary management goals is to replace labor with machines as rapidly as possible. Sometimes it is extremely difficult for us to assign the proper quantitative value to our labor-saving proposals.

Casewriter: Why is that? What kinds of problems do you encounter?

Rizzo: Well, let me give you an example. We often have to keep six men on the payroll to man a machine that only requires four operators. If we come up with a proposal of an automatic machine, we can only show a saving based on the reduction of the four people and not based on the six we have to maintain on the payroll.

As I mentioned before, the acquisition of new equipment would not necessarily reduce the number of operators—particularly by the full six. However, it would reduce the amount of worker fatigue and it would simplify the functions of the operators.

Due to the existing labor situation in Italy, there is a resulting slowdown in production whenever worker fatigue is involved. Absenteeism is higher, standard manning is not maintained, rotation of personnel becomes the rule, rest breaks are difficult to control, and there are often conflicts with plant unions. The net result is that in order to insure four-man production, we have to keep six men on the payroll. Yet, we are not allowed to assign a monetary value to the other benefits of replacing labor with machines.

To make matters worse, we're required to use only those labor rates that are already contractually obligated.

Well, that may be all right for a plant with an annual wage increase of 5 or 10 percent. But it's ridiculous when you are looking at an increase of 30 or 40 percent on an annual basis.

Corleone: Another problem is San Francisco's definition of manpower reduction. If we propose the purchase of a machine which results in a labor use reduction of four man-hours per day, we are not allowed to include this savings in our financial calculations. It's true, at least in the short run, that our payroll costs are not reduced (because we can't just fire the fellow for one-half day per day). But, by replacing this worker with a machine—even if for only four man-hours per day—DNP–Italia will be better off in the long run. San Francisco doesn't appreciate this concept.

Because we can't use estimates of future wage rates or estimates of the other benefits of buying labor-saving devices, the return on investment figures we submit to San Francisco are lower than they should be. Sometimes, very good projects have been turned down because the discounted cash flow return was too low.

---

[4] Rizzo handled labor negotiations for DNP–Italia.

At this point, Frank Duffy joined the meeting. A brief summary of the discussion to date was provided by one of the casewriters and the conversation with Rizzo continued.

Rizzo: I'd like to return to this issue of how long it takes to get investments approved in San Francisco. I've worked for this company ever since they acquired my previous employer, in 1961. The plant they bought then was widely acknowledged in the industry as the most efficient and profitable container plant in Italy. Neither that plant, nor the rest of DNP–Italia has that reputation today.

Why? I'll tell you why. San Francisco didn't approve one request for machinery purchase between 1964 and 1972. All of our major competitors had acquired Flexo's[5] between the mid-1960s and 1972. In 1972, we still didn't have any. Finally, we said: "Look, we don't have one and everybody else does!" The ROI was no better that year, but we got approval for a machine. This is why I said that the system has been used to block investments in Italy.

Casewriter: Frank, how did things look to you when you arrived in 1973?

Duffy: Well, there certainly was a morale problem when I arrived here. No one was sure whether DNP intended to remain in Italy or not. In fact, I rather suspect that some of them viewed me as having been sent in to preside over a dissolution.

This comment brought nods of agreement from several members of the management.

Duffy: In fairness, I think that DNP's senior management had had some doubts during the late 1960s about the wisdom of remaining in Italy. However, they have basically been committed to Italy right along. Unfortunately, the management personnel here weren't convinced of that.

The Flexo investments have been a significant morale booster, mainly because they were seen as a tangible sign of DNP's commitment to Italy. Unhappily, the economy is in rotten shape and our Flexo investments don't look very good at this particular moment. I think that this is a short-run phenomenon, though. The Flexo's should provide a very adequate long run return.

Casewriter: Do you still see some problems with the system?

Duffy: Yes. I really do think that it takes too long to get a project approved. This is true whether the proposal goes through the formal budgeting cycle or goes outside that cycle. For example, in October 1974 a large consumer goods company in Italy approached us about making a certain kind of box for them. The investment required would be about $200,000. One major advantage of the project would be that it would allow us to diversify the product mix of the plant involved. We looked at the project for about three months before submitting a special proposal to San Francisco. That was at least four months ago, and we have still not received a definitive response. I have a huge stack of telexes on my desk about this matter. If the economy had not caused our customer's business to turn sour, I am sure we would have lost the deal to a competitor.

Another problem with the capital budgeting system is that it decreases our managerial flexibility. We received approval last December for a corrugated stacker

---

[5] A high-speed machine for folding and shaping containerboard into boxes (editor).

at one of our plants. However, I no longer want the machine in that plant because of the difficulty we're having getting people off of that plant's payroll. I asked San Francisco in February if it would be acceptable to put the machine in another plant where we need it and where attrition would allow us to save some labor. It's now July, and I still don't have approval. I've already started building the foundation for the machine in the other plant so that the machine can be put in place during the annual August shutdown. Otherwise, I'd have to wait another full year.

Rizzo: One frustration I think we all feel with the system is that capital spending is so cyclical. When profits are up, money is easy. But we should really be making our investments when profits are down. We could gain market share then, especially from our smaller competitors who couldn't afford to make the investment.

Guppi: This capital spending cyclicality is especially disturbing because this subsidiary is self-financing. The money is normally borrowed locally. It doesn't even come from corporate funds.

Angelo: I believe the major source of our difficulties is poor communications between Italy and San Francisco. However, I think this is continually improving.

Duffy: That's absolutely true, Bob. Even in the two and one-half years I've been here, there has been a dramatic improvement. However, I still maintain that more flexibility needs to be built into the system. Why, I just discovered the other day that, technically, I can't switch a forklift truck from one plant to another without approval from San Francisco.

The informal discussion at DNP-Deutschland

Late on July 8th, 1975, several members of the management team of DNP–Deutschland gathered in the Frankfurt office of the managing director, Hans Lowenstein, for a discussion of the Del Norte Paper corporate capital budgeting system and its effects on DNP–Deutschland's operations. Present through the meeting were: Hans Lowenstein, managing director; Alex Stuart, regional controller and director of administration; and Thomas Buskey, planning manager.

The discussion began when one of the casewriters asked Mr. Lowenstein for his opinion about the capital budgeting system. The following is a paraphrased summary of that discussion:

Lowenstein: In my opinion, the worst problem with the capital budgeting system at Del Norte is that it is too tight. I have practically no spending authority within the system—I have to get the head office to approve *everything* I buy that costs over $500. With the inflation we've experienced in the last few years, it's almost impossible to buy anything that costs *less* than $500.

Also, because the system is so tight, there are tremendous delays between the time we see a need to purchase some equipment and the time we actually get approval from San Francisco to spend the money. There have been projects we have submitted to San Francisco which have taken well over six months to get approved. It would be one thing if the project were a new $10 million plant. I would understand the delay then. But I'm talking about $10,000 forklifts and other small items.

Just to give you an illustration of the time delay problems, we submitted an emergency request a few months ago to build a $13,000 first aid room in one of our plants. The government had ordered us to put in the aid room or pay a stiff fine. It took *two months* and a pile of telexes to get San Francisco to act. The government might have shut the whole plant down if we hadn't decided to start putting in the room before we got San Francisco's approval. I hate to be placed in a position where I have to go outside the system in order to operate this business.

Stuart: The effect of these time delays is devastating. First, you have to remember that even after we get approval to spend the money, it can take another six months to get the equipment in the plant and working. Over the intervening period, the cost of the equipment will have gone up because of inflation. We try to build in an inflation estimate in our expenditure requests, but it's been almost impossible to make accurate forecasts for the last few years. Also, if you build in too large a reserve for inflation, your reported return begins to go down.

By the time we have received approval and ordered the equipment, there is already a budget overrun. If the overrun is greater than 10 percent of the original request, then we have to submit a new request for the extra funds. That can be delayed in San Francisco for another three months. The whole process can start again if the exchange rate changes over the intervening time period.

Lowenstein: It doesn't make sense to take up valuable top management time with overrun requests caused by inflation. This business adapts to inflation: if our costs go up, generally our prices keep pace. All our projections should be in constant dollars, and all inflation-caused overrun requests should be approved by the regional manager—*not* by San Francisco.

Stuart: Just to give you another example of how long the process can take, we purchased a box plant in Stuttgart a couple of years ago. We decided to expand the plant shortly after we bought it. We submitted our request for $1 million, but did not get final approval for one full year. By that time, the exchange rate had changed and actual inflation had exceeded our forecast. Even before the expansion was started, we had to submit a new request. That took another six months to get approved!

Lowenstein: I might be able to understand this initial approval delay—the plant expansion was a major project for us. But, for it to take six months to get the overrun request approved is just ridiculous!

Casewriter: What other problems do you see with the capital budgeting system?

Stuart: One of my major complaints is that our expenditure requests have to be standardized before they are submitted to San Francisco. We have to fill in our capital budget forms exactly as prescribed in the *Capital Expenditure Manual*. But, some of their requirements just don't make good sense.

Lowenstein: We have also encountered another problem with labor saving-related investments. If we buy a machine now in order to avoid hiring two men next year when we know our volume will be higher, San Francisco won't allow us to include the wage savings for those two men in our profit calculations. Their view is that we must spend the money before we can save it. Once again, this makes the ROI we report to the head office lower than it really is.

Casewriter: What acceptance criteria does San Francisco use for capital investment proposals?

Lowenstein: I wish I knew. Frankly, we get very conflicting signals on that subject. Sometimes projects are turned down even though the ROI is very high, while others get turned down because the ROI is too low.

Just the other day, we submitted a proposal to San Francisco for putting in strapping facilities at our Hamburg plant. Essentially, all our competitors have begun to offer free palletizing of cartons for their customers. Our customers came to us and asked for the same service. A number of them threatened to change suppliers if we didn't offer the service. We sent in an emergency request for the project, noting that we ran a very considerable risk of losing a substantial number of customers if we didn't offer the palletizing service.

Two months after the initial request, we received a telex from head office saying that the project was unacceptable because the investment showed no return. However, if we do not make the investment, we might lose up to 60 percent of our business. The problem was that we couldn't include on the standard forms the true relevant costs in our return calculations. We have to make this investment![6]

EXHIBIT 5

July 14, 1975
Telex from John Powell (San Francisco) to DNP–Deutschland

please review the hamburg request for strapping unit. as it now reads, must reject.

need positive—not negative—reason to invest dlrs 168,000 to lose dlrs 145,000/year.

every prior installation—worldwide—has resulted in annual labor savings.

July 15, 1975
Telex from Alex Stuart (DNP–Deutschland) to John Powell

this machine* is absolutely necessary to run the business. john, i have personally read letters from customers requesting that their orders be delivered in palletized loads. these customers represent 20,074 short tons or 67% of our actual sales volume. our competitors are offering palletized loads at no extra cost. that is why this item was coded a 'to maintain properties, products and services' 'they do not require a return but are one by definition.' to maintain our facilities competitive.

the reason that, contrary to other worldwide installations, ours does not produce labor savings is because, as we explained in our request, we use the truck drivers to help us load the trucks and not our own people, nonetheless, i would appreciate it if you could telex me examples of prior installations of this type to see how labor savings were computed and whether the same computations could be applicable to us. in summary, john, this item is a must for us to remain competitive, particularly in a tight-market situation like the one we are living in.

---

* The strapping unit (editor).

---

[6] See Exhibit 5 for a sampling of the telexes exchanged between San Francisco and DNP–Deutschland on this matter.

The whole matter is especially aggravating because we wouldn't even be using Del Norte Paper corporate funds. This subsidiary is completely self-financed.

Casewriter: How does San Francisco view emergency requests for capital?

Lowenstein: There are several problems with submitting projects for approval outside the normal capital budgeting cycle. First, we are not allowed to submit any project over $100,000. Second, the time required for approval can be exceedingly long—up to six months. This time delay is unnecessary and defeats the purpose of submitting emergency requests in the first place. Finally, there is the risk that one will be penalized for submitting too many emergency requests, even if each project is very good.

Casewriter: Are there any other problems you can see with the capital budgeting system?

Buskey: Yes. Recently, we have had some battles with the treasurer's department at corporate headquarters about equipment purchase decisions. We had received approval to buy a Swiss carton-folding machine. The treasurer called us up and said we should purchase an English machine instead, because the exchange rate was so favorable.

In the first place, the English machine isn't nearly as reliable as the Swiss machine. Also, because the machine won't be delivered for six months, we bear the exchange risk if the Treasury Department's forecasts turn out to be wrong. As a profit center, DNP–Deutschland has to bear full responsibility for decisions made by the treasurer's office.

Lowenstein: There's also another problem I should mention. DNP–Deutschland is organizationally part of the container division. As such, our energies are focused on producing cartons and making investments in the carbon business. A problem arises, however, when we are presented with noncontainer investment opportunities. For example, last year, I heard of an opportunity for us to buy a very profitable little paper mill.

I submitted the investment proposal to the container division. Because it was not strictly in the container business, they turned it down. I talked to some of our people in the mill side of operations, but it was difficult to make them enthusiastic about the project. As a result, one of our competitors bought the mill and is making a very handsome profit. Del Norte can't afford to miss these opportunities.

────< C A S E I I – 1 8 >────

MRC, Inc. (consolidated)

In mid-1966, Archibald Brinton, president, and others of the top management of MRC, Inc. were considering a $25-million capital-budget proposal which would carry one of the company's divisions into the production of polyester fiber. Through its ARI division, the company was already heavily involved in the production of rayon fiber for tire cord; however, this market was rapidly shrinking because of the competitive inroads of nylon and polyester. An entry into polyester fiber might allow MRC to preserve its market position in tire cord and also move the company into the production of polyester fiber for other end uses.

Background, MRC, Inc.

Between 1961 and 1965, MRC had nearly tripled sales and earnings by implementing an active program of diversification by acquisition (Exhibit 1). During this period, acquisitions had been concluded at an average rate of one new company per year. Five of these transactions had been major. Ross Engineering had increased MRC sales in 1957 by $27 million. The purchase of Surface Combustion in 1959 had added about $38 million to annual sales. In 1961, American Rayon had boosted the company's growing sales volume by about $55 million. And the acquisition of Steel City Electric and National Castings in 1963 and 1965 had added about $16 million and $73 million, respectively, to annual sales.

   In 1966, annual sales of MRC's 13 divisions were more than $340 million. No single division accounted for as much as 20 percent of total sales, but the largest five divisions contributed 70 percent of the total. The most important product lines in terms of sales were (1) industrial furnaces and heat-treating equipment; (2) parts used in the manufacture of railroad rolling stock and other foundry products; (3) rayon fiber for automobile tire cord and apparel fabrics; (4) auto, truck, and bus frames; and (5) power brake systems for autos, trucks, and buses.

   All marketing, purchasing, manufacturing, R&D, personnel, and accounting were handled at the division level. Each division had its own general manager who reported directly to Brinton and was responsible for the growth and profitability of his division. Depending on the earnings and

EXHIBIT 1
Six-year summary of financial data ($ millions except per share data)

	1961	1962	1963	1964	1965	1966
Operations						
Sales						
Automotive and transportation	$ 57.8	$ 73.2	$ 80.9	$ 82.5	$ 94.2	$102.6
Capital goods	42.7	48.2	47.3	65.1	94.8	125.7
Buildings and construction	12.4	18.3	31.2	33.4	34.5	33.5
Railroad	—	—	—	—	39.6	42.7
Consumer goods	16.5	15.0	14.9	16.2	18.7	18.0
Aerospace and defense	8.3	11.6	15.7	13.9	14.3	21.6
Total	137.6	166.3	190.1	211.1	296.1	344.1
Net income	5.5	5.9	7.6	8.7	14.1	17.6
Earned on total capital	5.3%	6.3%	7.8%	9.1%	10.4%	12.1%
Earned on common equity	5.3	6.5	8.2	9.7	12.6	13.7
Common stock						
Net income per share	$ 0.84	$ 0.97	$ 1.47	$ 1.82	$ 2.66	$ 3.33
Dividends per share	0.75	0.75	0.75	0.85	0.95	1.22
Market price	13–11	14–10	16–12	19–15	26–18	30–22
Dividend payout ratio	49%	45%	33%	31%	28%	31%
Average annual price-earnings ratio	15.1	11.3	10.5	10.3	8.2	7.9
Average annual dividend yield	5.8%	6.0%	4.9%	4.6%	4.4%	4.7%
Number of shareholders	13,125	12,165	11,750	12,725	12,750	15,150
Financial position						
Working capital	$ 58.6	$ 47.4	$ 50.1	$ 49.3	$ 69.4	$ 70.2
Net property, plant, and equipment	42.4	43.8	44.6	49.3	66.6	72.4
Long-term debt	—	—	—	13.5	9.0	7.9
Preferred and common shareholders' equity	105.6	96.5	100.6	91.9	134.2	142.3
Additions to property, plant, and equipment	1.4	2.5	3.2	9.9	9.1	14.4
Number of employees	8,000	8,500	9,000	9,300	14,000	14,600

growth of his division, a division manager could get stock options and earn an annual bonus of up to 60 percent of his base salary. Divisional sales and earnings goals were formalized in an annual budget and in a rolling five-year plan; these were formulated by each general manager and submitted each November for review by Brinton and the corporate staff.

The corporate staff provided legal, administrative, and financial support to the divisions and handled external affairs, financing, and acquisitions as well. The staff, including corporate officers, numbered less than 60, of whom about half were secretarial and clerical.

Brinton felt that he exercised adequate control over the decentralized organization through his power to hire and fire at the division-manager level and, more important, through control of the elaborate capital-budgeting system (Appendix).

Background, American Rayon, Inc.

In the spring of 1961, MRC had merged with ARI by an exchange of MRC common stock valued at $38.6 million. Almost all of ARI's sales consisted of rayon fiber; more than 60 percent of these sales consisted of rayon cord for use in the production of automobile tires. At the time of the merger, ARI was the third largest U.S. producer of rayon, had over $22 million of cash and marketable securities, was free of debt, and operated a modern central manufacturing facility (Exhibit 2). Furthermore, while the longer-term outlook for the rayon industry was grim, the near-term picture was appealing. It was estimated that ARI would be able to maintain current volume, prices, and margins through 1964, followed thereafter by annual sales declines of 10–15 percent. Capital spending needs under a gradual liquidation strategy would average no more than $300,000 annually. In view of MRC's need for finance to sustain its acquisition program, purchase of ARI by an exchange of shares had seemed attractive.

EXHIBIT 2

MRC, INC. (consolidated)
Balance Sheet and Cash Flow Forecasts for American Rayon, Inc. ($million)
At December 31, 1960

Assets		*Liabilities and Net Worth*	
Cash	$ 2.6	Accounts payable	$ 2.9
U.S. government		Accrued items	1.1
securities	20.0		
Accounts receivable	11.9		
Inventories	10.5		
Net plant	23.9		
Other	.3	Net worth	65.2
Total	$69.2	Total	$69.2

Pro forma cash flow forecasts						
	1961	*1962*	*1963*	*1964*	*1965*	*1966*	*1967*
---	---	---	---	---	---	---	---
Sales	$ 55	$ 55	$ 55	$ 52	$ 49	$ 43	$ 40
Net earnings	2.5	2.8	2.8	1.9	1.4	1.0	.4
Depreciation	3.0	3.0	3.0	3.0	3.0	3.0	3.0
Cash flow from operations	5.5	5.8	5.8	4.9	4.4	4.0	3.4

Efforts to diversify ARI

From 1961 to 1966, ARI performed profitably, although the declining 1963–66 trend was unsatisfactory:

Year	Sales index of ARI fibers division	Pretax profit as 2 percent of sales
1961	100	6%
1962	100	8
1963	112	10
1964	115	9
1965	118	7
1966	124	4

The aggregate use of rayon in tire cord continued to decline during this period, and efforts were undertaken to reduce the division's dependence on the tire-cord market. In 1964, after the retirement of the original division manager, MRC invested $8 million in a facility to produce high-wet modulus rayon staple fiber, which was used principally in wearing apparel.[1] At the time this project was proposed by the new division manager, the selling price of the fiber was between 44 cents and 45 cents a pound. ARI management had felt that the price would decline to about 36 cents a pound within five years and stabilize there. At this reduced price level, the plant addition promised a five-year payback and a healthy DCF-ROI.

According to Archibald Brinton:

> ARI had process problems during the first year after the facility opened. These problems cut heavily into the division's profits. We also had some problem in getting the textile manufacturers to switch to our fiber. The textile people won't switch to the fiber of a new manufacturer until it's been thoroughly tested and evaluated. This testing is a costly and time-consuming process.
>
> By the beginning of the second year after the plant was completed, the selling price of high-wet modulus rayon was down to 26 cents a pound.
>
> Man-made fiber manufacture is a continuous process production operation. You run the plants 24 hours a day, seven days a week. The production costs are such that you have to run at close to capacity to make any profit. If you cut back production very far, you might as well shut down entirely. We had a choice. If you cut production, your unit costs skyrocket; if you keep producing, your inventories skyrocket. With us it was a question of whether we might be better off shutting the plant down completely until prices firmed. We finally decided to keep it running and made staple fiber until it was coming out of our ears. Prices are firming now, but although we've had three price rises in the last nine months, they are still not up to 36 cents a pound.

In 1966, ARI was still heavily dependent on rayon tire cord. During 1965, total industry production of rayon tire cord had amounted to 210-million pounds. This production was split among ARI (25 percent), American Viscose Corporation Division of FMC (30 percent), Beaunit Corporation (23 percent), and American Enka Corporation (23 percent).

---

[1] Staple fiber is short-length fiber (approximately 1 to $1\frac{1}{2}$ inches) such as is found in cotton bolls.

Threats to the tire-cord market

By 1966, the only real market remaining for rayon tire cord was the original-equipment tire market.[2] Of the 210 million pounds of rayon tire cord used for all classes of tires in 1965, about 150 million pounds went into the 50 million passenger-car tires required by the original-equipment manufacturers (OEMs). The OEMs had purchased rayon-cord tires almost exclusively through 1965, but nylon started to break into this market when Chevrolet division of General Motors Corporation indicated in 1966 that it would provide tires with nylon cord on the 1968 models. "The use of . . . nylon for Chevrolet production for this first year could mean a market of approximately 10 million tires. . . ."[3]

If rayon cord were ultimately displaced from OEM passenger-car tires, the rayon industry stood to lose approximately 150 million pounds of its market. As this last market started to change, rayon producers would find it increasingly difficult to remain price-competitive with nylon.

> The nylon producers may be in position . . . to further reduce the price of their material. However, the rayon producers most probably will not be in a position to do the same because of the decrease . . . in usage of their materials.[4]

> Du Pont recently pointed to acetate yarn as an example of a fiber having passed the low point in raw material price and already having capitalized fully on the lower cost attainable through very large scale of production. . . . This may also be the case for rayon staple fiber.[5]

The rise of polyester

While nylon was rapidly replacing rayon as the principal fiber in tire cord, a new fiber, polyester, was becoming important. Five million pounds of this fiber had been used in 1963 by tire manufacturers, 19 million pounds was the estimated use in 1966, and a Goodyear spokesman predicted that 100 million pounds would be used in tire cord by 1970.

Polyester was considered by some to be the "third generation" man-made fiber after rayon and nylon. The fiber had shown very rapid growth in recent years (Exhibit 3). After Du Pont's polyester patent had expired in July 1961, competition had rapidly appeared, prices had declined, and new markets had opened up to the fiber. Much of polyester's success up

---

[2] Original-equipment tires are purchased from tire manufacturers and placed on new cars by auto manufacturers.

[3] C. A. Litzler, "The Fluid Tire Cord Situation," *Modern Textiles Magazine*, September 1966, p. 22.

[4] Ibid.

[5] National Advisory Commission on Food and Fiber, *Cotton and Other Fiber Problems and Policies in the United States*, Technical Papers, vol. 2 (Washington, D.C., 1967), p. 43.

EXHIBIT 3
U.S. fiber consumption (millions of pounds) and prices (dollars per pound)

	Natural fibers				Man-made fibers					
	Cotton		Wool		Rayon		Nylon		Polyester	
Year	Pounds	Staple price	Pounds	Staple price	Pounds	Staple price	Pounds	Staple price	Pounds	Staple price
1910.....	n.a.	$	n.a.	$	*	$		$		$
1930.....	2,617		263		119	.40				
1935.....	2,755		418		200	.31				
1940.....	3,959		408		300	.25	*			
1945.....	4.516	.39	645		420	.25	25			
1950.....	4,683	.57	635	1.41	650	.36	75	1.65	*	
1955.....	4,382	.39	414	1.08	966	.34	231	1.48	13	1.60
1956.....		.33		1.08	870	.32	246	1.30	20	1.35
1957.....		.36		1.22	836	.31	293	1.30	38	1.41
1958.....		.33		.90	750	.31	293	1.20	44	1.41
1959.....		.30		1.02	848	.33	356	1.06	79	1.36
1960.....	4,191	.31	411	1.07	716	.28	376	.92	110	1.36
1961.....		.31		1.03	797	.28	455	.92	112	1.24
1962.....	4,188	.30	429	1.09	884	.28	551	.92	162	1.14
1963.....	4,040	.29	412	1.18	960	.28	625	.92	223	1.14
1964.....	4,244	.29	357	1.28	975	.28	745	.92	274	.98
1965.....	4,477	.29	387	1.19	1,046	.28	861	.82	416	.84
1966.....	4,633est.		370est.		1,026est.		978est.		545est.	

Fibers compete for shares of the total fiber market principally on the basis of relative prices and relative quality characteristics. Relative prices appear to have been an important consideration in the substitution of rayon for cotton in certain uses. The noncellulose fibers offer serious price competition for apparel wool. However, price advantage has not accounted for the rapid increase in share of the fiber market gain by noncellulose fibers, although sharply reduced prices in recent years have undoubtedly expanded their use.

Synthetic fibers yield a greater amount of fabric from a pound of fiber than does cotton, thus reducing the price of synthetic fiber per unit of product output. The equivalent net weight pounds of cotton staple for each pound of man-made fiber is (a) rayon staple fiber, 1.10, (b) nylon and polyester staple fiber, 1.37.

n.a. = not available.
* Date of fiber introduction.
Sources: *Statistical Abstract of the United States—1967*, pp. 642, 760, 761; *Textile Organon*, December 1966, p. 199 and February 1967, pp. 28, 29; *Modern Textiles Magazine*, December 1965; and National Advisory Commission on Food and Fiber, *Cotton and Other Fiber Problems and Policies in the United States*, Technical Papers, vol. 2 (Washington, D.C.: the Commission, 1967), pp. 24, 33, 36, 39.

to 1966 was due to the enthusiasm that greeted the introduction of stay-press fabric in wearing apparel. In 1956, the total production of polyester fiber for all uses had been about 20 million pounds. By 1965, polyester output reached over 400 million pounds. Du Pont, the major producer of polyester fiber, accounted for well over half of U.S. production.[6]

---

[6] *Oil, Paint and Drug Reporter*, November 21, 1966, pp. 4 and 52.

Alternatives in the face of change

In mid-1966, the management of MRC was considering alternative courses of action with regard to the ARI division. The profits of this division were unsatisfactory in relation to the amount of capital required to support its operations. The market for ARI's major product line faced even greater near-term difficulty than in the past (owing to the Chevrolet decision); thus, MRC had to (1) continue realizing progressively less-satisfactory returns on the assets employed by ARI or (2) commit a substantial amount of new capital to production facilities for new fibers or (3) abandon certain areas of the rayon business.

Leaving the market. Abandoning the rayon business entirely or in part presented a problem, since the physical plant of ARI was on the books of the company at a net book value of about $20 million. If this was sold substantially below book value, MRC would have to absorb a substantial nonrecurring loss on the sale, which would probably reduce the company's 1966 earnings per share below the level achieved in 1965. This loss would be nonrecurring; nonetheless, MRC management felt that investors might confuse it with a downturn in earnings from normal operations. The company was in the middle of its fifth consecutive year of earnings progress in 1966. Its stock price had moved up steadily since 1961 in response to these earnings gains, and management was reluctant to risk this share-price progress through investor misunderstanding.

Investing in new fibers. Selling the ARI division was not a particularly attractive alternative; however, investing in facilities to produce newer fibers also raised some difficult problems. First, since nylon seemed to have already neared a peak in tire-cord use, an investment in a facility to produce this fiber would be practically obsolete by the time it was completed. On the other hand, polyester had not reached the level of acceptance in tire production which would justify the construction of a large new plant just to serve this segment of the polyester market. New fiber plants had to be large to be economically competitive (Exhibit 4). Economies of scale are clearly evident here, as they are in most chemical production processes.[7] Similar production economies could be expected in polyester-fiber production. For this reason, if MRC went into the production of polyester tire cord, it would be necessary to produce polyester fiber for other uses as well. This would put the company into the textile-fiber business against firms such as Du Pont. Except for the venture into high-wet modulus rayon staple fiber in 1964, the company had had little contact with textile mills

---

[7] S. C. Schuman, "How Plant Size Affects Unit Costs," *Chemical Engineering,* May 1965, pp. 173–76.

258

EXHIBIT 4
Variation in unit cost of production with size of plant

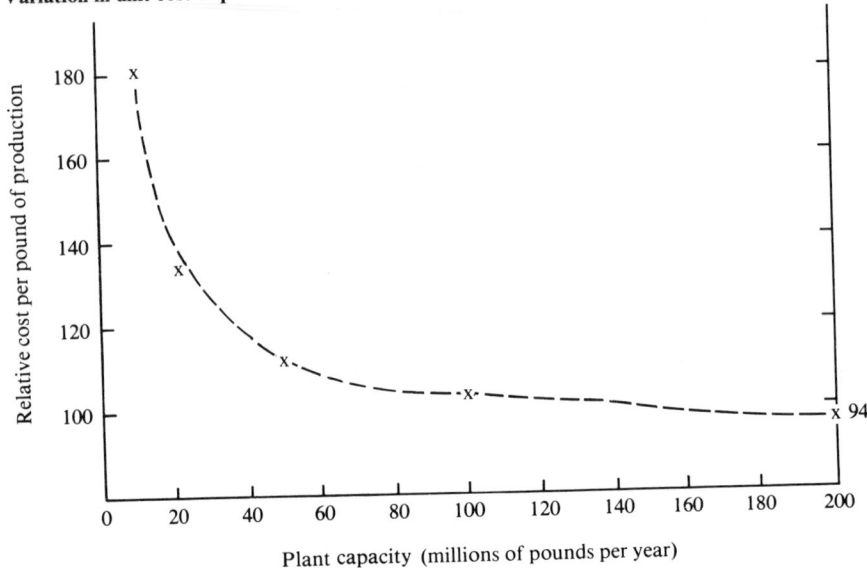

Plant capacity (millions of pounds per year)

Source: Based on a chart in Jesse W. Markham, *Competition in the Rayon Industry* (Cambridge: Harvard University Press, 1952), p. 150.

and had competed directly with large apparel fiber manufacturers such as Du Pont only to a limited extent.

The polyester proposal

In mid-1966, the top management of MRC was considering a specific proposal that would carry the corporation into large-scale production of polyester fiber for tire cord and apparel fabrics. This proposal had been initiated by the ARI division general manager, John Wentworth, an experienced and highly regarded young executive who had been lured away from Monsanto Company after MRC's experience with high-wet modulus rayon staple fiber.

From 1966 through 1971, the project would require an investment of $25.2 million. About $20.2 million of this amount would be used to construct a new plant for the production of polyester fiber; $5 million would be added to working capital to support the increased level of sales.

By 1969, the new facility would have given ARI the capacity to produce up to 50 million pounds a year of polyester fiber and resin. Ten million pounds would go into tire cord, 30 million pounds would be marketed as staple fiber in competition with firms such as Du Pont, and 10 million pounds of resin chips would be sold to other polyester fabricators (Exhibit 5).

EXHIBIT 5
Earnings and cash flow forecasts for polyester project ($ millions)

	1967	1968	1969	1970	1971–80	1981
Sales	6.37	21.72	32.90	32.82	32.60	32.60
Cash costs (Note A)	6.23	14.44	20.80	20.80	20.80	20.80
Plant start-up costs	0.75	1.50	0	0	0	0
Special marketing costs	0	1.80	0	0	0	0
Depreciation expense	0.1	1.3	1.7	1.7	1.4	1.40
Profit before tax	−0.70	2.68	10.40	10.32	10.40	10.40
Profit after tax (Note B)	0.55	1.74	5.30	5.16	5.20	5.20
Cash flow from operations	0.65	3.04	7.00	6.86	6.60	6.60
Investment (plant, equipment, working capital)	−14.90	−7.50	−2.00	−0.80	0	0
Return of working capital	0	0	0	0	0	5.00
Net cash flow	−14.25	−4.46	5.0	6.06	6.60	11.60
Internal rate of return = 26% —— Payback period = Year 6.						

Notes:
A.   Equals (38¢ × staple poundage + 43¢ × tire poundage + 21¢ × resin poundage + $3 million).
B.   Includes investment-tax credit of $0.9, $0.4, and $0.1 million in 1967, 1968 and 1969.

	Assumed volume (million pounds)					Assumed price (cents per pound)				
	1967	1968	1969	1970	1971–1980	1967	1968	1969	1970	1971–1980
Staple	0	18.8	30	30	30	78.5	72.5	70.5	70.5	70.5
Tire	7.5	10.0	10	10	10	85	80.9	79.5	79.5	79.5
Resin	0	0	10	10	10	38	38	38	37.2	35

The competitive environment

During the months while MRC management was evaluating the new fiber project, the competitive situation in polyester was in considerable turmoil. In late March 1966, Du Pont announced that it would build a new polyester facility capable of producing 200 million pounds a year by the end of 1968. The plant was to be twice the size of Du Pont's two other polyester plants. This facility, plus other announced additions at Du Pont's other polyester plants, would raise the company's capacity in polyester fiber from 240 million pounds a year in February 1966 (versus 456 million pounds for the industry at that date) to over 600 million pounds a year by the end of 1968 (Exhibit 6).

In April 1966, *Chemical Week* mentioned a number of other important competitive factors in the polyester situation:

> Polyester sales in '65 increased 50 percent over '64 and '66 growth is projected for at least 35 percent to 500 million pounds. Demand got out of hand last year because a 14-cent per pound price decrease was coupled with an unexpectedly enthusiastic acceptance of polyester blends in durable-press apparel. . . .
>
> If all announced new capacity is built as scheduled, by the end of '68 U.S. production capability would be nearly 1.25 billion pounds per year. . . .

EXHIBIT 6
Current and planned capacity of polyester fiber competitors

	Polyester capacity February 1966 (million pounds)	Announced expansion by end of 1968 (million pounds)	Number of plants end of 1968	Other[‡] fibers manufactured	Total sales volume of company in 1965 ($ millions)	Average return on total capital (1961–65)
Allied Chemical	0	?	?	N	$1,121	10%
American Enka	0	?	?	N, R	193	11
American Viscose (division FMC)	0	?	?	A, R		
Beaunit Fibers (division Beaunit Corp.)	0	?	?	R		
Chemstrand (division Monsanto)	20	40	1	N	1,468	9
Du Pont	240	360	3	A, N	3,020	19
Fiber Industries*	95	155	2	A, N, R	862	8
Firestone Tire & Rubber	0	?	?	N	1,610	9
Goodyear Tire & Rubber	60	40	1		2,226	10
Hercules	0	30	1		532	13
ARI Fiber (division of MRC)	0	?	?	R		
Phoenix Works, Inc. (subsidiary Bates Mfg. Co.)	0	25	1			
Tennessee Eastman Co. (division Eastman Kodak)	50	100	2	A		
U.S. Rubber Company	0	?	?			
Vectra Co.[†] (division National Plastic Products)	0	?	?	N		
	465	750	11			

* Owned 62.5% by Celanese Corp. of America.
† Jointly owned by Enjay Chemical Co. & J. P. Stevens & Co.
‡ A = Acetate; N = Nylon; R = Rayon.

With the Du Pont capacity disclosure, other polyester fiber producers theorize that marginal producers may scale down expansion plans and potential producers may think twice before entering the market. Intense competition in other fibers is in store as well.[8]

The point of decision

It was in this environment that the management of MRC had to make its decision on the polyester-fiber proposal.

APPENDIX: CAPITAL BUDGETING PROCEDURES OF MRC, INC.

The formal capital budgeting procedures of MRC were outlined in a 49-page manual written for use at the divisional level and entitled *Expenditure Control Procedures*. This document outlined (1) the classification scheme for types of funds requests, (2) the minimum levels of expenditure for which formal requests were required, (3) the maximum expenditure which could be authorized on the signature of corporate officers at various levels, (4) the format of the financial analysis required in a request for funds to carry out a project, and finally (5) the format of the report which followed the completion of the project and evaluated its success in terms of the original financial analysis outlined in (4).

Classification scheme for funds requests

The manual defined two basic classes of projects: profit improvement and necessity. Profit improvement projects included:

a. Cost reduction projects.
b. Capacity expansion projects in existing product lines.
c. New product line introductions.

Necessity projects included:

All projects where profit improvement was not the basic purpose of the project, such as those for service facilities, plant security, improved working conditions, employee relations and welfare, pollution and contamination prevention, extensive repairs and replacements, profit maintenance, and services of outside research and consultant agencies. Expense projects of an unusual or extraordinary character included in this class were those expenses which did not lend themselves to inclusion in the operating budget and could normally be expected to occur less than once per year.

---

[8] *Chemical Week*, April 2, 1966, p. 21.

Minimum amounts subject to formal request

Not all divisional requests for funds required formal and specific economic justification. Obviously, normal operating expenditures for items such as raw materials and wages were managed completely at the level of the divisions. Capital expenditures and certain nonrecurring operating expenditures were subject to formal requests and specific economic justification if they exceeded certain minimum amount levels specified below.

Project Appropriation Requests shall be issued as follows:

1. Capital. Projects with a unit cost equal to or more than the unit cost in the following schedule shall be covered by a Project Appropriation Request: items with lesser unit costs shall be expensed.

Land improvements and buildings	$1,000
Machinery and equipment	500
Tools, patterns, dies, and jigs	250
Office furniture and office machines	100

2. Expense. Expenses of an unusual or extraordinary character which do not lend themselves to inclusion in the operating budget and could normally be expected to occur less than once per year shall be covered by a Project Appropriation Request.

The minimum amount at which a Project Appropriation Request for expense is required is $10,000.

Approval limits of corporate officers

Officers at various management levels within MRC had the authority to approve a division's formal request for funds to carry out a project subject to the maximum limitations shown below.

Approvals. Requests shall be processed from a lower approval level to a higher approval level in accordance with the chart below to secure the approving authorities' initials (and date approved) signifying approval. Lower approvals shall be completed in advance of submission to a higher level.

	Highest approval level required
Expense projects:	
Minimum up to $10,000	Division manager
$10,000 up to $50,000	Corporate president
$50,000 and over	Board of directors
Capital projects:	
Minimum up to $5,000	Division manager
$5,000 up to $50,000	Corporate president
$50,000 and over	Board of directors

Expense and capital combinations:
Required approvals shall be the higher approval level required for either the capital or expense section in accordance with the above limits.

Project appropriation request

The formal financial analysis required in a request for funds was called a project appropriation request (PAR). . . . The key output factors in the analysis (which included the amount of the total appropriation, the discounted cash flow rate of return on the investment, and the payback period) are summarized on the opening page . . . for easy reference.

The PAR originated at the divisional level and circulated to the officers whose signatures were necessary to authorize the expenditure. If the project was large enough to require the approval of an officer higher than the division manager, then five other men in the corporate financial group also reviewed the proposal. This group included the controller, the tax manager, the director of financial planning, the treasurer, and the vice president of finance. These men did not review very small projects, however, since capital items under $5,000 never reached the corporate office. Division managers could authorize these small projects on their own signature.

Project evaluation report

On each PAR, the corporate controller had the option of indicating whether or not he desired a project evaluation report (PER). When requested, the division manager submitted this report one year after the approved project was completed. The report indicated how well the project was performing in relation to its original cost, return on investment (ROI), and payback estimates.

Scrutinizing a PAR at the presidential level

In discussing capital budgeting at MRC, Brinton stated that the largest projects, involving more than $1 million, were almost always discussed informally between the president and the division manager at least a year before a formal PAR was submitted. He said:

> Let's look at a project involving a facilities expansion. The need for a new plant addition in most of our business areas doesn't sneak up on you. It can be foreseen at least a couple of years in advance. An enormous amount of work is involved in submitting a detailed economic proposal for something like a new plant. Architects have to draft plans, proposed sites have to be outlined, and construction lead times need to be established. No division manager would submit a complete request for a new facilities addition without first getting an informal green light that such a proposal could receive favorable attention. By the time a formal PAR is completed on a large plant addition, most of us are pretty well sold on the project.

In response to the question, what are the most significant items that you look at when a new PAR lands on your desk? Brinton replied:

The size of the project is probably the first thing that I look at. Obviously, I won't spend much time on a $15,000 request for a new forklift truck from a division manager with an annual sales volume of $50 million.

I'd next look at the type of project we're dealing with to get a feel for the degree of certainty in the rate of return calculation. I feel a whole lot more comfortable with a cost reduction project promising a 20 percent return than I would with a volume expansion project which promises the same rate of return. Cost reduction is usually an engineering problem. You know exactly how much a new machine will cost and you can be fairly certain about how many man-hours will be saved. On a volume expansion you're betting on a marketing estimate and maybe the date for getting a plant on stream. These are fairly uncertain variables.

On a new product appropriation, things get even worse. Here you're betting on both price and volume estimates, and supporting data can get awfully thin. Over all, I think our cost reduction projects have probably yielded higher returns and have been less risky than either plant expansion or new product proposals. They don't, of course, eat up anything like the amount of capital that the other two types of projects can require.

The third and perhaps most important item that I look for is the name of the division manager who sent the project up. We've got men at the top and at the bottom of the class just like any organization. If I get a project from a man who has been with the company for a few years, who has turned a division around, or shown that he has a better command of his business than anyone else in his industry, then I'll usually go with his judgment. If his business is going to pot, however, I may take a long hard look, challenge a lot of the assumptions, and ask for more justification.

Fourth, I look at the ROI figure. If the project is a large one, I have the finance people massage the numbers to see what happens to the ROI if some of the critical variables like volume, prices, and costs are varied. This is an area where knowing your division manager is enormously important. Some men, particularly those with a sales background, may be very optimistic on volume projections. In this kind of situation you feel more comfortable if you can knock the volume down 25 percent and still see a reasonable return.

I haven't established formal and inviolable hurdle rates which each and every project must clear. I want to avoid giving the division people an incentive to stretch their estimates on marginal projects or, alternatively, to build in fat cushions—insurance policies—on great projects. Still, I generally look for a minimum DCF-ROI of about 12 percent on cost reduction proposals, 15–16 percent on large volume-expansion projects and 18–20 percent or even more on new-product introductions. But these aren't magic numbers. Projects showing lower yields are sometimes accepted.

◄CASE II-19►

The Galvor Company (R–3)

CONTROL SYSTEM

When M. Barsac replaced M. Chambertin as Galvor's controller in April 1964, at the age of 31, he became the first of a new group of senior managers resulting from the acquisition by Universal Electric. It was an accepted fact that in the large and sprawling Universal organization, the controller's department represented a key function. M. Barsac, who was a skilled accountant, had had 10 years' experience in a large French subsidiary of Universal.

He recalled his early days with Galvor vividly and admitted they were, to say the least, hectic:

> I arrived at Galvor in early April 1964, a few days after M. Chambertin had left.[1] I was the first Universal man here in Bordeaux and I became quickly immersed in all the problems surrounding the change of ownership. For example, there were no really workable financial statements for the previous two years. This made preparation of the Business Plan, which Mr. Hennessy and I began in June, extremely difficult. This plan covers every aspect of the business, but the great secrecy which had always been maintained at Galvor about the company's financial affairs made it almost impossible for anyone to help us."

Barsac's duties could be roughly divided into two major areas: first, the preparation of numerous reports required by Universal, and, second, supervision of Galvor's internal accounting function. While these two areas were closely related, it is useful to separate them in describing the accounting and control function as it developed after Universal's acquisition of Galvor.

To control its operating units, Universal relied primarily on an extensive system of financial reporting. Universal attributed much of its success in recent years to this system. The system was viewed by Universal's European controller, M. Boudry, as much more than a device to "check up" on the operating units:

> In addition to measuring our progress in the conventional sense of sales, earnings, and return on investment, we believe the reporting system causes our

---

Copyright © 1967 by l'Institut pour l'Etude des Méthodes de Direction de l'Entreprise (IMEDE) Lausanne, Switzerland. Reproduced by permission.
[1] M. Chambertin remained on the payroll as a part-time consultant for legal problems.

operating people to focus their attention on critical areas which might not otherwise receive their major attention. An example would be the level of investment in inventory. The system also forces people to think about the future and to commit themselves to specific future goals. Most operating people are understandably involved in today's problems. We believe some device is required to force them to look beyond the problems at hand and to consider longer range objectives and strategy. You could say we view the reporting system as an effective training and educational device.

BACKGROUND[2]

The Galvor Company had been founded in 1936 by M. Georges Latour, who continued as its owner and president until 1964. Throughout its history, the company had acted as a fabricator, buying parts and assembling them into high-quality, moderate-cost electric and electronic measuring and test equipment. In its own sector of the electronics industry—measuring instruments—Galvor was one of the major French firms; however, there were many electronics firms in the more sophisticated sectors of the industry which were vastly larger than Galvor.

Galvor's period of greatest growth began around 1950. Between 1950 and 1961 sales grew from 2.2 million 1961-new francs to 12 million, and aftertax profits from 120,000 1961-new francs to 1,062,000. Assets as of December 31, 1961 totalled 8.8 million new francs. (One 1961-new franc = 20 cents.) The firm's prosperity resulted in a number of offers to purchase equity in the firm, but M. Latour had remained steadfast in his belief that only if he had complete ownership of Galvor could he direct its affairs with a free hand. As owner/president, Latour had continued over the years to be personally involved in every detail of the firm's operations.

In 1962, M. Latour explained to a casewriter how he controlled Galvor:

> At the month's end, M. Chambertin sends me the following figures for the month: net sales, total purchases, direct and indirect labor, R&D expenses, manufacturing overhead, inventory levels, gross profits, commissions, sales taxes, my personal account, and net profit. I check these figures against previous levels in order to determine whether we are up to standard or should take some corrective measures. Finally, I check our balance sheet, total overhead as a percent of sales, and our sales to each country. Of all these figures, I am most interested in the net profit figure. Since I sign all our important checks, this gives me another way of keeping an eye on our purchasing.

As of early 1962, M. Latour was concerned about the development of adequate successor management for Galvor. In January 1962, Latour hired a technical director as his special assistant, but this person resigned in November 1963. Following the 1963 unionization of Galvor's workforce,

---

[2] This section has been summarized from earlier cases in the Galvor series.

which Latour had opposed, Latour (then 54 years old) began to entertain seriously the idea of selling the firm and devoting himself to family, philanthropic, and general social interests. On April 1, 1964 Galvor was sold to Universal Electric Company for $4.5 million worth of UE's stock. M. Latour became chairman of the board of Galvor, and David Hennessy was appointed as Galvor's managing director. Hennessy at that time was 38 years old and had been with UE for nine years.

THE BUSINESS PLAN

The heart of Universal's reporting and control system was an extremely comprehensive document—the Business Plan—which was prepared annually by each of the operating units. The Business Plan was the primary standard for evaluating the performance of unit managers and everything possible was done by Universal's top management to give authority to the plan.

Each January, the Geneva headquarters of Universal set tentative objectives for the following two years for each of its European operating units. This was a "first look"—an attempt to provide a broad statement of objectives which would permit the operating units to develop their detailed business plans. For operating units which produced more than a single product line, objectives were established for both the unit as a whole and for each product line. Primary responsibility for establishing these tentative objectives rested with eight product-line managers located in Geneva, each of whom was responsible for a group of product lines. On the basis of his knowledge of the product lines and his best judgment of their market potential, each product-line manager set the tentative objectives for his lines.

For reporting purposes, Universal considered that Galvor represented a single product line, even though Galvor's own executives viewed the company's products as falling into three distinct lines—multimeters, panelmeters and electronic instruments.

For each of over 300 Universal product lines in Europe, objectives were established for five key measures:

Sales.

Net income.

Total assets.

Total employees.

Capital expenditures.

From January to April, these tentative objectives were negotiated between Geneva headquarters and the operating managements. Formal meetings were held in Geneva to resolve differences between the operating unit managers and product-line managers or other headquarters personnel.

Negotiations also took place at the same time on products to be discontinued. Mr. Hennessy described this process as a "sophisticated exercise which includes a careful analysis of the effect on overhead costs of discontinuing a product and also recognizes the cost of holding an item in stock. It is a good analysis and one method Universal uses to keep the squeeze on us."

During May, the negotiated objectives were reviewed and approved by Universal's European headquarters in Geneva and by corporate headquarters in the United States. These final reviews focused primarily on the five key measures noted above. In 1966, the objectives for total capital expenditures and for the total number of employees received particularly close surveillance. The approved objectives provided the foundation for preparation of business plans.

In June and July, Galvor prepared its Business Plan. The plan, containing up to 100 pages, described in detail how Galvor intended to achieve its objectives for the following two years. The plan also contained a forecast, in less detail, for the fifth year hence—for example, for 1971 in the case of the plan prepared in 1966.

Summary reports

The broad scope of the Business Plan can best be understood by a description of the type of information it contained. It began with a brief one-page financial and operating summary containing comparative data for:

Preceding year (actual data).
Current year (budget).
Next year (forecast).
Two years hence (forecast).
Five years hence (forecast).

This one-page summary contained condensed data dealing with the following measures for each of the five years:

Net income.
Sales.

Total assets
Total capital employed (sum of long-term debt and net worth).

Receivables.
Inventories.
Plant, property, and equipment.
Capital expenditures.
Provision for depreciation.

Percent return on sales.
Percent return on total assets.
Percent return on total capital employed.
Percent total assets to sales.
Percent receivables to sales.
Percent inventories to sales.

Orders received.
Orders on hand.

Average number of full-time employees.
Total cost of employee compensation.
Sales per employee.
Net income per employee.
Sales per $1,000 of employee compensation.
Net income per $1,000 of employee compensation.

Sales per thousand square feet of floor space.
Net income per thousand square feet of floor space.

Anticipated changes in net income for the current year and for each of the next two years were summarized according to their cause, as follows:

Volume of sales
Product mix
Sales prices
Raw material purchase prices
Cost reduction programmes
Accounting changes and all other causes

This analysis of the causes of changes in net income forced operating managements to appraise carefully the profit implications of all management actions affecting prices, costs, volume or product mix.

Financial statements

These condensed summary reports were followed by a complete set of projected financial statements—income statement, balance sheet, and a statement of cash flow—for the current year and for each of the next two years. Each major item on these financial statements was then analysed in detail in separate reports which covered such matters as transactions with headquarters, proposed outside financing, investment in receivables and inventory, number of employees and employee compensation, capital expenditures, and nonrecurring write-offs of assets.

Management actions

The Business Plan contained a description of the major management actions planned for the next two years with an estimate of the favorable or unfavorable effect each action would have on total sales, net income and total assets. Among some of the major management actions described in Galvor's 1966 Business Plan (prepared in mid-1965) were the following:

1. Implement standard cost system.
2. Revise prices.
3. Cut oldest low-margin items from line.
4. Standardize and simplify product design.
5. Create forward research and development plan.
6. Install punch-card inventory system.
7. Implement product planning.

Separate plans were presented for each of the functional areas—marketing, manufacturing, research and development, financial control, and personnel and employee relations. These functional plans began with a statement of the function's mission, an analysis of its present problems and opportunities, and a statement of the specific actions it intended to take in the next two years.

Among the objectives set for the control area in the 1966 Business Plan, M. Barsac stated that he hoped to:

1. Better distribute tasks.
2. Make more intensive use of IBM equipment.
3. Replace nonqualified employees with better trained and more dynamic people.

The Business Plan closed with a series of comparative financial statements which depicted the estimated item-by-item effect if sales fell to 60 percent or to 80 percent of forecast or increased to 120 percent of forecast. For each of these levels of possible sales, costs were divided into three categories: fixed costs, unavoidable variable costs, and management discretionary costs. Management described the specific actions it would take to control employment, total assets, and capital expenditures in case of a reduction in sales and when these actions would be put into effect. In its 1966 Business Plan, Galvor indicated that its program for contraction would be put into effect if incoming orders dropped below 60 percent of budget for two weeks, 75 percent for four weeks or 85 percent for eight weeks. It noted that assets would be cut only to 80 percent in a 60 percent year and to 90 percent in an 80 percent year "because remodernization of our business is too essential for survival to slow down much more."

APPROVAL OF PLAN

By mid-summer the completed Business Plan was submitted to Universal headquarters, and beginning in the early fall meetings were held in Geneva to review each company's Business Plan. Each plan had to be justified and defended at these meetings, which were attended by senior executives from both Universal's European and American headquarters and by the general managers and functional managers of many of the operating units. Universal viewed these meetings as an important element in its constant effort to encourage operating managements to share their experiences in resolving common problems.

Before final approval of a company's Business Plan at the Geneva review meeting, changes were often proposed by Universal's top management. For example, in September 1966, the 1967 forecasts of sales and net income in Galvor's Business Plan were accepted, but the year-end forecasts of total employees and total assets were reduced about 9 percent and 1 percent respectively. Galvor's proposed capital expenditures for the year were cut 34 percent, a reduction primarily attributable to limitations imposed by Universal on all operating units throughout the corporation.

The approved Business Plan became the foundation of the budget for the following year, which was due in Geneva by mid-November. The general design of the budget resembled that of the Business Plan except that the various dollar amounts, which were presented in the Business Plan on an annual basis, were broken down by months. Minor changes between the overall key results forecast in the Business Plan and those reflected in greater detail in the budget were not permitted. Requests for major changes had to be submitted to Geneva no later than mid-October.

REPORTING TO UNIVERSAL

Every Universal unit in Europe had to submit periodic reports to Geneva according to a fixed schedule of dates. All units in Universal, whether based in the United States or elsewhere, adhered to essentially the same reporting system. Identical forms and account numbers were used throughout the Universal organization. Since the reporting system made no distinction between units of different size, Galvor submitted the same reports as a unit with many times its sales. Computer processing of these reports facilitated combining the results of Universal's European operations for prompt review in Geneva and transmission to corporate headquarters in the United States.

The main focus in most of the reports submitted to Universal was on the variance between actual and budgeted results. Sales and expense data were presented for both the latest month and for the year to date. Differences between the current year and the prior year were also reported because these were the figures submitted quarterly to Universal's shareholders and to newspapers and other financial reporting services.

Description of reports

Thirteen different reports were submitted by the controller on a monthly basis, ranging from a statement of preliminary net income which was due during the first week following the close of each month, to a report on the status of capital projects due on the last day of each month. The monthly reports included:

1. Statement of preliminary net income.
2. Statement of income.
3. Balance sheet.
4. Statement of changes in retained earnings.
5. Statement of cash flow.
6. Employment statistics.
7. Status of orders received, cancelled and outstanding.
8. Statement of intercompany transactions.
9. Statement of transactions with headquarters.
10. Analysis of inventories.
11. Analysis of receivables.
12. Status of capital projects.
13. Controller's monthly operating and financial review.

The final item, the controller's monthly operating and financial review, often ran to 20 pages or more. It contained an explanation of the significant variances from budget as well as a general commentary on the financial affairs of the unit.

In addition to the reports submitted on a monthly basis, approximately 12 other reports were required less often, either quarterly, semiannually, or annually.

COST OF THE SYSTEM

The control and reporting system, including preparation of the annual Business Plan, imposed a heavy burden in both time and money on the management of an operating unit. M. Barsac commented on this aspect of the system in the section of Galvor's 1966 Business Plan dealing with the control functional area.

> Galvor's previous administrative manager (controller), who was a tax specialist above all, had to prepare a balance sheet and statement of income once a year. Cost accounting, perpetual inventory valuation, inventory control, production control, customer accounts receivable control, budgeting, etc. did not exist. No information was given to other department heads concerning sales

results, costs and expenses. The change to a formal monthly reporting system has been very difficult to realize. Due to the low level of employee training, many tasks such as consolidation, monthly and quarterly reports, budgets, the Business Plan, implementation of the new cost system, various analyses, restatement of prior year's accounts, etc. must be fully performed by the controller and chief accountant, thus spending 80 percent of their full time in spite of working 55–60 hours per week. The number of employees in the controller's department in subsequent years will not depend on Galvor's volume of activity, but rather on Universal's requirements.

Implementation of the complete Universal Cost and Production Control System in a company where nothing existed before is an enormous task, which involves establishing 8,000 machining and 3,000 assembly standard times and codifying 15,000 piece parts.

When interviewed early in 1967, M. Barsac stated:

Getting the data to Universal on time continues to be a problem. We simply don't have the necessary people who understand the reporting system and its purpose. The reports are all in English and few of my people are conversant in English. Also, American accounting methods are different from procedures used in France. Another less serious problem concerns the need to convert all of our internal records, which are kept in francs, to dollars when reporting to Universal.

I am especially concerned that few of the reports we prepare for Universal are useful to our operating people here in Bordeaux. Mr. Hennessy, of course, uses the reports as do one or two others. I am doing all that I can to encourage greater use of these reports. My job is not only to provide facts, but to help the managers understand and utilize the figures available. We have recently started issuing monthly cost and expense reports for each department showing the variances from budget. These have been well received.

Mr. Hennessy also commented on meeting the demands imposed by Universal's reporting system:

Without the need to report to Universal, we would do some things in a less formal way or at different times. Universal decides that the entire organization must move to a certain basis by a specified date. There are extra costs involved in meeting these deadlines. An example was applying the punch-card cost system to our piece-parts manufacturing operation before we were really ready to tackle the job. It should be noted, also, that demands made on the controller's department are passed on to other areas such as marketing, engineering and production.

M. Boundry, Universal's European controller, acknowledged that the cost of the planning and reporting system was high, especially for smaller units:

The system is designed for a large business. We think that the absolute minimum sales volume for an individual unit to support the system is about $5 million; however, we would prefer at least $10 million. By this standard, Galvor is barely acceptable. We really don't know if the cost of the system is unnecessarily burdensome in the sense that it requires information which is not

274

worth its cost. A reasonable estimate might be that about 50 percent of the information would be required in any smartly managed independent business of comparable size, another 25 percent is required for Universal's particular needs, and 25 percent is probably "dead underbrush" which should be cleaned out. Ideally, every five years we should throw the system out the window and start again with the essentials.

EXHIBIT 1
Organization of controller's department (January 1967)

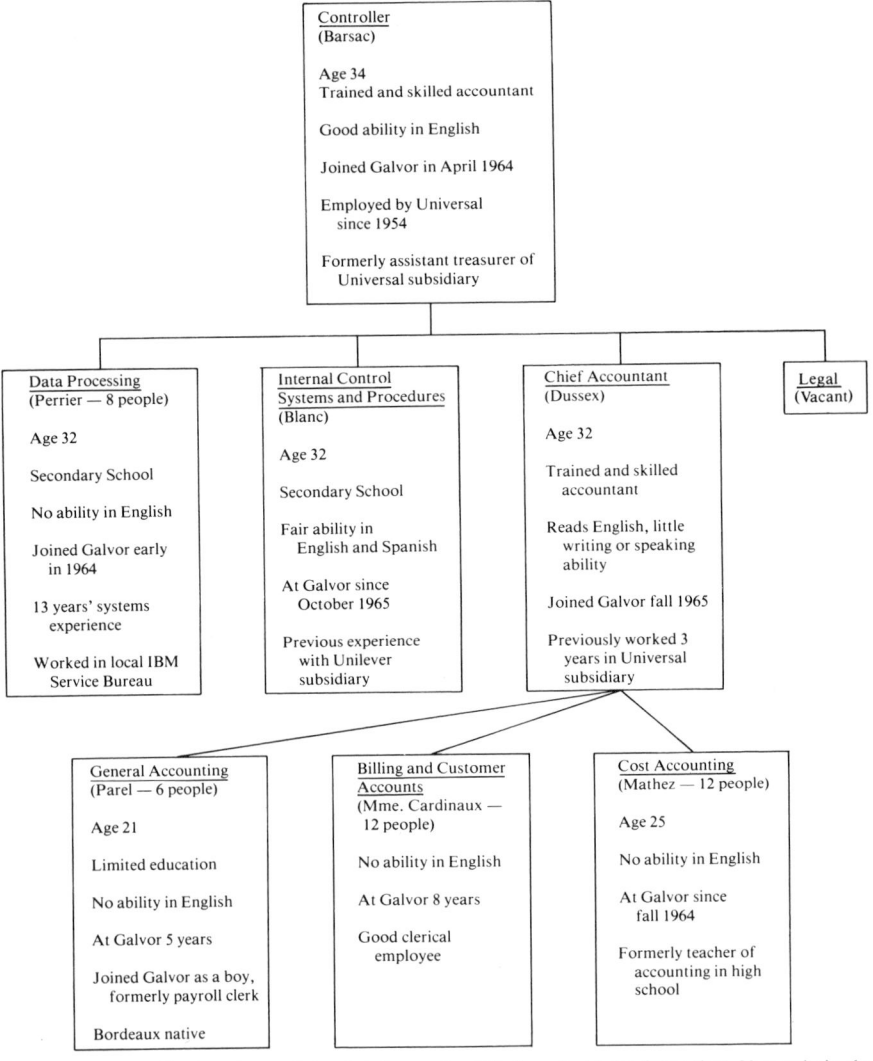

Note: Immediately prior to Galvor's takeover by UE, there had been fewer than 20 people in the controller's department.

As an indication of some of his department's routine activity, M. Barsac noted that at the end of 1966 Galvor was preparing about 10,000 punch cards and 200 invoices each working day. At that time the company had approximately 12,000 active customers.

Early in 1967, 42 people were employed in the controller's department, about 6 percent of Galvor's total employees. The organization of the department is described in Exhibit 1.

HEADQUARTERS PERFORMANCE REVIEW

Galvor's periodic financial reports were forwarded to M. Boudry in Geneva. The reports were first reviewed by an assistant to M. Boudry, one of four financial analysts who together reviewed all reports received from Universal's operating units in Europe.

In early 1967, Boudry described the purpose of these reviews:

> The reviews focus on a comparison of performance against budget for the key measures—sales, net income, total assets, total employees, and capital expenditures. These are stated as unambiguous numbers. We try to detect any trouble spots or trends which seem to be developing. Of course, the written portions of the reports are also carefully reviewed, particularly the explanations of variances from budget. If everything is moving as planned, we do nothing.

> The reports may contain a month-by-month revision of forecasts to year-end, but if the planned objectives for the year are not to be met we consider the situation as serious.

> If a unit manager has a problem and calls for help, then it becomes a matter of common concern. He can probably expect a bad day in explaining how it happened, but he can expect help too. Depending on the nature of the problem, either Mr. Forrester, Galvor's product-line manager, or one of our staff specialists would go down to Bordeaux. In addition to the financial analysts, one of whom closely follows Galvor's reports, we have specialists on cost systems and analysis, inventory control, credit, and industrial engineering.

> We have not given Galvor the help it needs and deserves in data processing, but we have a limited staff here in Geneva and we cannot meet all needs. We hope to increase this staff during 1967.

With reference to Galvor's recent performance, M. Boudry stated:

> Galvor is small and we don't give it much time or help unless its variances appear to be off. This happened in the second half of 1966 when we became increasingly concerned about the level of Galvor's inventories. A series of telexes on this matter between Mr. Hennessy and M. Poulet, our director of manufacturing here in Geneva, illustrate how the reports are used. [See Exhibits 2 through 5.]

> We feel the situation is under control and the outlook for Galvor is okay despite the flat performance between 1963–65 and the downturn in 1966. The Company has been turned about and 1967 looks promising.

EXHIBIT 2
Telex from Poulet to Hennessy concerning level of inventory

TO: HENNESSY—GALVOR
FROM: POULET—UE
DATE: SEPT. 26, 1966

FOLLOWING ARE THE JULY AND AUGUST INVENTORY AND SALES FIGURES
WITH THEIR RESPECTIVE VARIANCES FROM BUDGET.

THOUSANDS OF DOLLARS

| | *JULY* | | | | *AUGUST* | |
	ACTUAL	*BUDGET*	*VARIANCE*	*ACTUAL*	*BUDGET*	*VARIANCE*
INVENTORY	2,010	1,580	(430)	2,060	1,600	(460)
SALES TO DATE	3,850	3,900	(50)	4,090	4,150	(60)

LATEST AUGUST SALES FORECAST REFLECTS DECREASE IN YEAR-END SALES
OF 227 VS INCREASE OF 168 IN YEAR-END INVENTORIES OVER BUDGET.

REQUEST TELEX LATEST MONTH-BY-MONTH INVENTORY AND SALES FORECAST
FROM SEPTEMBER TO DECEMBER, EXPLANATION OF VARIANCE IN INVENTORY
FROM BUDGET AND CORRECTIVE ACTION YOU PLAN IN ORDER TO ACHIEVE
YEAR-END GOAL. INCLUDE PERSONNEL REDUCTIONS, PURCHASE MATERIAL
CANCELLATIONS, ETC.

POULET

EXHIBIT 3
Telex from Hennessy to Poulet concerning level of inventory

TO: POULET—UE
FROM: HENNESSY—GALVOR
DATE: SEPT. 27, 1966

YOUR 26.9.66
MONTHLY INVENTORY FORECAST SEPTEMBER TO DECEMBER BY
CATEGORY FOLLOWS:

THOUSANDS OF DOLLARS	*SEPT. 30*	*OCT. 31*	*NOV. 30*	*DEC. 31*
RAW MATERIALS	53	51	50	50
PURCHASED PARTS	180	185	190	195
MANUFACTURED PARTS	95	93	93	91
WORK IN PROCESS	838	725	709	599
FINISHED GOODS	632	694	683	705
OTHER INVENTORIES	84	84	82	80
ENGINEERING IN PROCESS	55	58	48	44
RESERVE	(14)	(14)	(14)	(20)
INDICA[1]	50	52	55	55
TOTAL	1,973	1,928	1,896	1,799

[1] Indica S.A. was a wholly owned Parisian subsidiary of Galvor, which made dials and faces for measuring instruments. Only 10 percent of Indica's sales were to its parent.

EXHIBIT 3 (*continued*)

THE MAIN EXPLANATIONS OF PRESENT VARIANCE ARE THREE POLICIES ADOPTED END 1965 AND DISCUSSED IN MONTHLY LETTERS BUT WHICH LEFT DECEMBER 1966 BUDGET OPTIMISTICALLY LOW. FIRST WAS TO HAVE REASONABLE AMOUNTS OF SELLING MODELS IN STOCK WITHOUT WHICH WE COULD NOT HAVE ACHIEVED 19% INCREASE IN SALES WE ARE MAKING WITH OUTMODED PRODUCT.

SECOND POLICY WAS TO MANUFACTURE LONGER SERIES OF EACH MODEL BY DOUBLE WHEREVER SALES WOULD ABSORB IT, OTHERWISE MANY OF OUR COST REDUCTIONS WERE NEARLY ZERO. THIS MEANS OUR MANUFACTURING PROGRAM ANY MONTH MAY CONTAIN FIVE MONTHS WORTH OF 15 MODELS INSTEAD OF 10 WEEKS WORTH OF 30 MODELS (OUT OF SEVENTY).

THIRD WAS NEW POLICY OF REDUCING NUMBER OF PURCHASE ORDERS BY MAINTAINING A MINIMUM STOCK OF MANY THOUSANDS OF LOW VALUE ITEMS WHICH YOU AGREED WOULD AND DID INCREASE STOCK UPON FIRST PROCUREMENT BUT WE ARE ALREADY GETTING SLIGHT REDUCTION

CORRECTIVE ACTIONS NUMEROUS INCLUDING RUNNING 55 PEOPLE UNDER BUDGET AND ABOUT 63 BY YEAR END PLUS REVIEWING ALL PURCHASE ORDERS MYSELF PLUS SLIDING A FEW SERIES OF MODELS WHICH WOULD HAVE GIVEN SMALL BILLING IN 1966 INTO 1967 PLUS THOSE POSTPONED BY CUSTOMERS. THIS WILL NOT HAVE DRAMATIC EFFECT AS NEARLY ALL THESE SERIES ARE PROCURED AND HAVE TO BE MADE FOR RELATIVELY SURE MARKETS BUT SOME CAN BE HELD IN PIECEPARTS UNTIL JANUARY. WE ARE WATCHING CAREFULLY STOCK OF SLOW MOVING MODELS AND HAVE MUCH CLEANER FINISHED STOCK THAN END 1965.

FINAL AND GRAVE CONCERN IS ACCURACY OF PARTS, WORK IN PROCESS, AND FINISHED GOODS VALUATION SINCE WE BEGAN STANDARD COST SYSTEM. INTERIM INVENTORY COUNT PLUS VARIANCES VALUED ON PUNCH CARDS STILL DOESNT CHECK WITH MONTHLY BALANCE USING CONSERVATIVE GROSS MARGINS BUT NEARLY ALL GAPS OCCURRED FIRST FOUR MONTHS OF SYSTEM WHEN ERRORS NUMEROUS AND LAST 4 MONTHS NEARLY CHECK AS WE CONTINUE REFINING. EXTENSIVE RECHECKS UNDERWAY IN PARTS, WORK IN PROCESS, AND FINISHED GOODS AND CORRECTIONS BEING FOUND DAILY.

YOUR INVENTORY STAFF SPECIALISTS ARE AWARE OF PROBLEM AND PROMISED HELP WHEN OTHER PRIORITIES PERMIT. WILL KEEP THEM INFORMED OF EXPOSURE WHICH STARTED WITH RECODING ALL PARTS AND BEGINNING NEW BALANCES WITH NEW STANDARDS AND APPEARS CLOSELY RELATED TO ERRORS IN THESE OPERATIONS. WE CAN ONLY PURGE PROGRESSIVELY WITHOUT HIRING SUBSTANTIAL INDIRECT WORKERS.

                                                              HENNESSY

EXHIBIT 4
Telex from Poulet to Hennessy concerning level of inventory

TO: HENNESSY—GALVOR
FROM: POULET—UE
DATE: NOV. 10, 1966

SEPTEMBER INVENTORY INCREASED AGAIN BY 64,000 COMPARED TO
AUGUST WHILE SEPTEMBER SALES WERE 145,000 UNDER BUDGET
REFERRING TO YOUR LATEST TELEX OF SEPTEMBER 27 IN WHICH YOU
GAVE A BREAKDOWN OF THE SEPTEMBER FORECAST. REQUEST
DETAILED EXPLANATION FOR NOT MEETING THIS FORECAST IN SPITE
OF YOUR CURRENT CORRECTIVE ACTIONS.

SEPTEMBER	YOUR FORECAST	ACTUAL	VARIANCE
RAW MATERIALS	53	96	(43)
PURCHASED PARTS	180	155	25
MANUFACTURED PARTS	95	108	(13)
WORK IN PROCESS	838	917	(79)
FINISHED GOODS	632	723	(91)
OTHER INVENTORIES	84	87	(3)
ENGINEERING IN PROCESS	55	52	3
RESERVE	(14)	(14)	(14)
INDICA	50	51	(1)
TOTAL NET	1,973	2,175	(202)

IN ORDER TO MEET YOUR DECEMBER FORECAST OF 1,799 YOUR WORK
IN PROCESS HAS TO BE REDUCED BY 318. THIS MEANS A REDUCTION
OF ABOUT 100 PER MONTH FROM SEPTEMBER 30 TO DECEMBER 31.
THEREFORE, I ALSO WOULD LIKE ACTUAL ACHIEVEMENTS AND
FURTHER REDUCTION PLANS DURING OCTOBER, NOVEMBER, AND
DECEMBER CONCERNING THE POINTS MENTIONED IN YOUR SAME
TELEX OF SEPTEMBER 27. CONSIDER AGGRESSIVE ACTIONS IN THE
FOLLOWING SPECIFIC AREAS:

1. REALISTIC MASTER PRODUCTION SCHEDULES.
2. SHORT TERM PHYSICAL SHORTAGE CONTROL TO INSURE
    SHIPMENTS.
3. WORK-IN-PROCESS ANALYSIS OF ALL ORDERS TO ACHIEVE
    MAXIMUM SALEABLE OUTPUT.
4. MANPOWER REDUCTION.
5. ELIMINATION OF ALL UNSCHEDULED VENDOR RECEIPTS.
    HAVE YOU ADVISED OTHER UNIVERSAL HOUSES NOT TO SHIP IN
    ADVANCE OF YOUR SCHEDULE UNLESS AUTHORIZED?
6. ADVISE FULL DETAILS ON ALL CURRENT SHORTAGES FROM OTHER
    UNIVERSAL HOUSES WHICH ARE RESPONSIBLE FOR INVENTORY
    BUILD-UP.

                                                    POULET

EXHIBIT 5
Telex from Hennessy to Poulet concerning level of inventory

TO: POULET—UE
FROM: HENNESSY—GALVOR
DATE: NOV. 15, 1966

YOUR 10.11.66

WE NOW HAVE OCTOBER 31 FIGURES. OUR ACTUAL ACHIEVEMENTS FOLLOW: RAW MATERIALS 54 VARIANCE PLUS 3, PURCHASED PARTS 173 VARIANCE MINUS 12, MANUFACTURED PARTS 110 VARIANCE PLUS 17, WORK IN PROCESS 949 VARIANCE PLUS 224, FINISHED GOODS 712 VARIANCE PLUS 18, OTHER 82 VARIANCE MINUS 2, ENGINEERING 54 VARIANCE MINUS 4, RESERVE MINUS 14 VARIANCE NIL, INDICA 55 VARIANCE PLUS 3, TOTAL 2,175 VARIANCE PLUS 247. EACH ITEM BEING CONTROLLED AND THE ONLY SIGNIFICANT VARIANCES 224 WORK IN PROCESS AND 18 FINISHED GOODS ARE MY DECISION UPON SALES DECLINE OF SEPTEMBER AND OCTOBER OF 311 TO DELAY COMPLETION OF SEVERAL SERIES IN MANUFACTURE IN FAVOR OF ANOTHER GROUP OF SERIES, MOSTLY GOVERNMENT, WHICH ARE LARGELY BILLABLE IN 1966 IN ORDER TO PARTLY REGAIN SALES. LAST EIGHT DAYS ORDERS AND THEREFORE SALES ARE SHARPLY UP AND NONE OF THIS WORK IN PROCESS WILL BE ON HAND MORE THAN 3 TO 6 WEEKS LONGER THAN WE PLANNED.

NEVERTHELESS YOU SHOULD BE AWARE WE MANUFACTURE 4 TO 8 MONTHS WORTH OF MANY LOW VOLUME MODELS AND EXAMPLE OF HOW WE DETERMINE ECONOMIC SERIES WAS FURNISHED YOUR STAFF SPECIALIST THIS WEEK. WE CANNOT OTHERWISE MAKE SIGNIFICANT COST REDUCTIONS IN A BUSINESS WHERE AT LEAST 70 OF 200 MODELS HAVE TO BE ON SHELF TO SELL AND TYPICAL MODEL SELLS 15 UNITS MONTHLY. REGARDING YOUR 5 SUGGESTIONS AND TWO QUESTIONS WE ARE CARRYING OUT ALL 5 POINTS AGGRESSIVELY AND HAVE NO INTERHOUSE SHORTAGES OR OVERSHIPMENTS.

HENNESSY

Although the comprehensive reporting and control system made it appear that Universal was a highly centralized organization, the managements of of the various operating units had considerable autonomy. For example, Hennessy, who was judged only on Galvor's performance, was free to purchase components from other Universal units or from outside sources. There were no preferred "in-house" prices. A slight incentive was offered by Universal to encourage such transactions by not levying certain headquarters fees, amounting to about 2 percent of sales, against the selling unit.

Similarly, Universal made no attempt to shift its taxable income to low-tax countries. Each unit was viewed as though it were an independent company subject to local taxation and regulation. Universal believed that this goal of maximizing profits for the individual units would in turn maximize

Universal's profits. Forcing every unit to maximize its profits precluded the use of arbitrary transfer prices for "in-house" transactions.

RECENT DEVELOPMENTS AT GALVOR

A standard cost system, which included development and tooling costs as well as manufacturing and assembly, had been in effect since March 1966. Accordingly to Mr. Hennessy:

> We had hoped to start in January, but we were delayed. On the basis of our experience in 1966, all standards were reviewed and, where necessary, they were revised in December. We now have a history of development and tooling experience which we have been accumulating since 1965. This has proved extremely useful in setting cost standards. Simultaneously we have integrated market and sales forecasts more effectively into our pricing decisions.

Before Universal acquired Galvor, a single company-wide rate was used to allocate factory overhead to the costs of products. For many years this rate was 310 percent of direct labor. In a discussion of his pricing policies in 1962, M. Latour said, "I have been using this 310 percent for many years and it seems to work out pretty well, so I see no reason to change it."

Chambertin had long argued that the less complex products were being unfairly burdened by the use of a single overhead rate, while electronic products should bear more.

Latour's response to this argument was:

> I have suspected that our electric products are too high priced, and our electronic products are too low priced. So what does this mean? Why should we lower our prices for multimeters and galvanos? At our current prices we can easily sell our entire production of electric products.

Chambertin remained convinced that eventually Galvor would be forced by competitive pressures to allocate its costs more realistically.

In 1966, as part of the new standard cost system, Galvor did indeed refine the procedure for allocating overhead costs to products. Fifteen different cost centers were established, each with a separate burden rate. These rates, which combined direct labor cost and overhead, ranged from 13.19 francs to 38.62 francs per direct labor hour.

Concluding his comments about recent developments, Mr. Hennessy said:

> A formal inventory control system went into effect in January 1967. This, together with the standard cost system, allows us for the first time to really determine the relative profitability of various products, and to place a proper valuation on our inventory.
>
> We are installing a new IBM 6400 in February which we will use initially for customer billing and for marketing analysis. We hope this will reduce the number of people required in our customer billing and accounts-receivable operations from 12 to 6, or 7.

───◄CASE II–20 ►───

Texas Instruments Incorporated

────···◄∞►···────

MANAGEMENT SYSTEMS

Since the end of World War II, sales of Texas Instruments Incorporated (TI) had grown at an average compound rate of 25 percent per year, reaching $764 million in 1971. Over the same period, profits had grown at a rate of 24 percent. This growth had been internally generated, with the exception of one acquistion in 1959 which amounted to about 25 percent of TI sales in that year. Exhibit 1 presents a 10-year review of the company's growth which indicates that it was accompanied by conservative financial policies. Publicly traded shares of TI stock had historically sold at a higher-than-average multiple of earnings.

This case describes the management systems that were developed within TI to assist its executives in achieving a sustained rate of internally generated growth. The particular focus of this case is on the company's formal system for strategic long-range planning, a system which TI called its Objectives, Strategies, and Tactics system (OST). The case also discusses TI's organization systems and reporting systems.

Corporate structure

In 1972, TI was a technologically oriented company with diversified interests in industrial, government/military (about one third of sales) and consumer markets. Operations were organized into four groups. These groups were not based on such typical organizing categories as product lines or types of customers served. Instead, each of the four groups reflected a different perspective as to how TI products and services could be related to a customer's processes and systems. The *materials group* dealt with products that would be raw materials for a customer's production process. The *components group* was concerned with products that would be subassemblies in the customer's process or replaceable parts in his equipment. The *equipment group* produced machines that would perform sensing or processing operations in the customer's system. The *services group* provided systems support and services for a customer's operations.

This case was prepared by R. F. Vancil with the assistance of Texas Instruments Incorporated.

EXHIBIT 1

TEXAS INSTRUMENTS INCORPORATED AND SUBSIDIARIES
Ten-Year Review
Years Ended December 31
($000)

	1971	1970	1969	1968	1967	1966	1965	1964	1963	1962
Operations:										
Net sales	$764,258	$827,641	$831,822	$671,230	$568,507	$580,314	$436,369	$327,579	$276,477	$240,693
Income before provision for income taxes	59,478	52,043	60,301	50,362	41,098	63,722	46,273	34,857	25,087	16,381
Provision for income taxes	25,755	22,182	26,790	24,038	18,243	29,768	21,434	16,816	12,948	7,824
Net income	33,723	29,861	33,511	26,324	22,855	33,954	24,839	18,041	12,139	8,557
Earned per common share (average outstanding during year)*	3.05	2.71	3.06	2.41	2.11	3.30†	2.46	1.80	1.22	.85
Cash dividends paid per common share*	.80	.80	.80	.80	.75	.55	.50	.40	.32	.24

Financial condition:									
Total current assets	$414,706	$349,642	$336,924	$277,393	$242,915	$253,705	$186,721	$123,500	$105,967	$ 90,263
Total current liabilities	153,308	138,685	147,653	120,235	97,520	112,142	89,072	65,627	50,985	37,216
Working capital	261,398	210,957	189,271	157,158	145,395	141,563	97,649	57,873	54,982	53,047
Property, plant, and equipment (net)	154,954	171,436	182,377	145,835	138,883	123,752	81,215	56,354	47,852	42,634
Long-term debt, less current portion	94,778	86,801	94,595	52,927	54,265	51,935	48,708	3,937	5,700	7,463
Shareowners' equity	328,702	303,236	281,548	253,462	234,134	217,320	132,618	111,293	97,761	88,651
Common shares (average outstanding during year)*	11,042,736	11,036,115	10,959,489	10,909,686	10,845,663	10,291,973	10,091,248	10,011,217	9,894,919	9,866,837
Employees at year-end	47,259	44,752	58,974	46,747	38,736	38,686	34,519	24,551	21,616	18,166
Shareowners at year-end	16,210	17,738	17,808	18,649	20,065	19,903	16,566	15,867	15,827	17,031

* Adjusted for stock split in 1966 and for stock distribution in 1963. Except for 1966, there would have been no significant difference if earnings per share had been computed on basis of shares outstanding at year-end. In 1966, earnings per common share outstanding at year-end were $3.14.

EXHIBIT 2

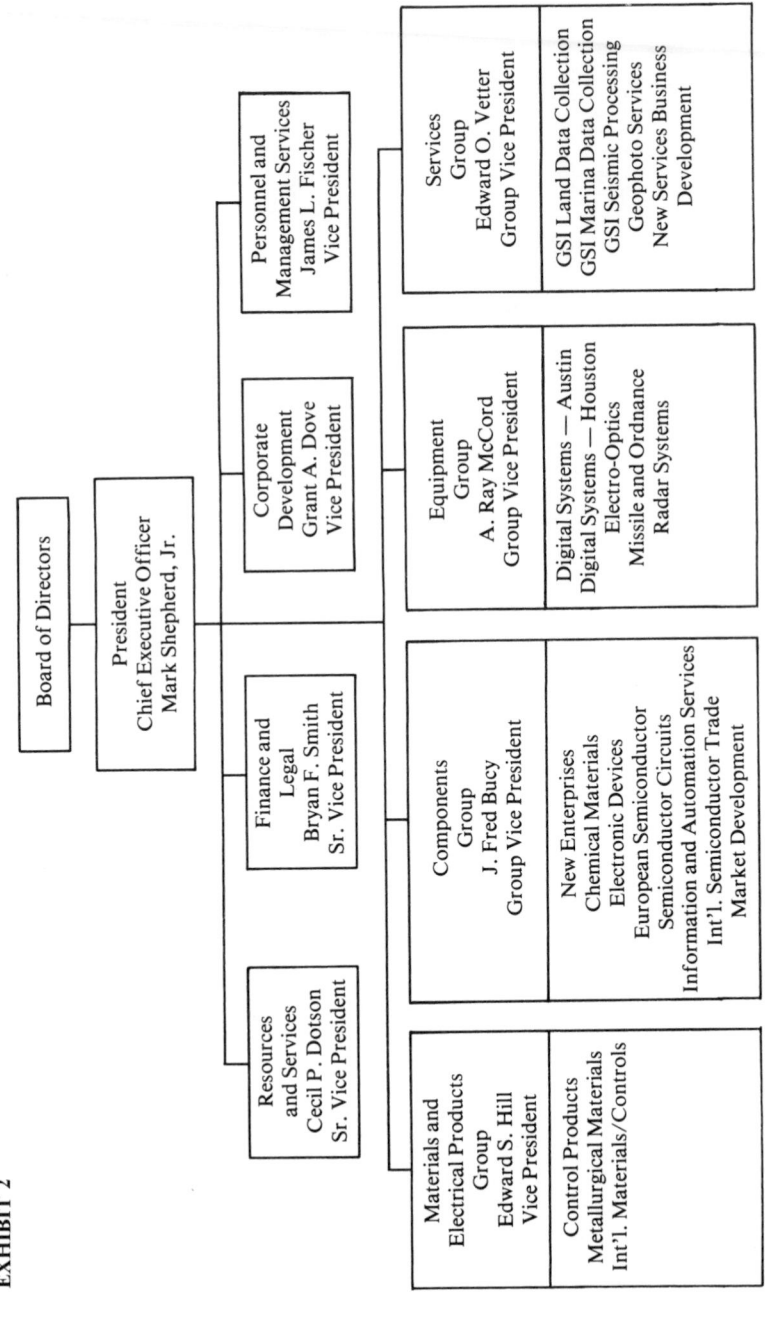

Board of Directors

President
Chief Executive Officer
Mark Shepherd, Jr.

Resources
and Services
Cecil P. Dotson
Sr. Vice President

Finance and
Legal
Bryan F. Smith
Sr. Vice President

Corporate
Development
Grant A. Dove
Vice President

Personnel and
Management Services
James L. Fischer
Vice President

Materials and
Electrical Products
Group
Edward S. Hill
Vice President

Control Products
Metallurgical Materials
Int'l. Materials/Controls

Components
Group
J. Fred Bucy
Group Vice President

New Enterprises
Chemical Materials
Electronic Devices
European Semiconductor
Semiconductor Circuits
Information and Automation Services
Int'l. Semiconductor Trade
Market Development

Equipment
Group
A. Ray McCord
Group Vice President

Digital Systems — Austin
Digital Systems — Houston
Electro-Optics
Missile and Ordnance
Radar Systems

Services
Group
Edward O. Vetter
Group Vice President

GSI Land Data Collection
GSI Marina Data Collection
GSI Seismic Processing
Geophoto Services
New Services Business
Development

Given this operational structure depicted in Exhibit 2, the various groups within TI were all natural customers for each other. Moreover, the development of any new product or service to be marketed by TI was likely to require the coordinated, cooperative effort of most, if not all, of the four groups.

The four operating groups were broken down further into divisions and then again into 77 product customer centers (PCCs) which operated like complete small business organizations with their own short-term profit responsibility. Texas Instruments credited the PCC with contributing much toward developing a spirit of customer responsiveness and innovation in management and also toward developing entrepreneurial managers.

OBJECTIVES, STRATEGIES, AND TACTICS

The primary reason that TI had developed its OST system was to facilitate the management of innovation. The need for such a system was expressed by S. T. Harris, officer of the board, as follows:

> As the organization grows, it gets more complex. Hundreds and then thousands of people are involved, often in multiple locations. The number of customers grows. Operations extend into many states and often into many countries. Governments all over add complexities of reporting and of regulation—some of them necessary, some of them not. To exploit an invention or innovation fully and to get broad distribution, the price must come down. The margin between price and costs gets narrower. At a relatively early stage in the development, so far as this invention or innovation is concerned, it becomes far more important that the principal managers be good administrators than good innovators. The administration in a technologically based business may often require good, or even deep technical skill, but at this stage what counts is the aid that kind of knowledge brings to administration, not to innovation.
>
> To handle the growth and increasing complexity, the organization decentralizes into groups, divisions, departments, and branches. The total job is divided up and cut into the size pieces that a good administrative manager can get his arms around. This is logical and good management practice. But unless the general managers understand their jobs thoroughly, the company is in danger of becoming no more than the sum total of the decentralized parts, loosely governed at the corporate level, primarily from a financial point of view.
>
> Consequently, though the organization as a whole may have far more of the tools, the opportunity, and the skilled people needed for innovation, the exposure of any one manager is restricted. He simply fails to see the larger opportunities to solve problems of the right scale for the whole corporation.
>
> Another undesirable pattern which too often develops is the gravitation of resources toward short-term problems with a consequent neglect of long-term, major impact programs. As a result, the organization can be misled into believing that it is making sound investments for the future, when, in truth, the resources may be largely consumed in responding to current crises.[1]

---

[1] These remarks by Mr. Harris are excerpted from a speech he delivered at the London Graduate School of Business Studies on May 22, 1970.

The system which TI developed to improve its management of innovation was based on a formal structure of hierarchical goals. This structure was described by Grant A. Dove, vice president for corporate development, in the following terms:

> The OST system amounts to a statement of goals and the plans for achieving these goals at the appropriate level in the organization. The goals expressed in OST form a structure, or hierarchy, beginning with the corporate objective and extending downward to business objectives and strategies, and finally, tactics. [Figure 1.]
>
> Our corporate objective states the economic purposes, the reasons for existence of the organization. It also states in broad terms our product, market, and technical goals. It defines our responsibilities to our employees, our shareowners, our community, and society as a whole. And, it establishes the financial goals by which we measure our contribution to the economic development of society.
>
> The corporate objective is supported by a set of business objectives. Each of these is expressed in terms of (1) a business charter which establishes the boundaries of the business, (2) an appraisal of the potential opportunities we perceive in this business, (3) a study of the technical and market trends, and (4) the overall competitive structure of industry serving this business.
>
> Performance measures are established which include specific goals for financial factors, such as sales, profit, return on assets, and served available market penetration for 5 and 10 years ahead.
>
> In addition, we attempt to project the market and the product mix, to establish technical goals, and to identify obstacles or boundaries limiting the business.
>
> Finally, we attempt to look at ourselves in a mirror and critique the overall objective. We carefully evaluate the competition, the threats and contingencies we might have to meet, market shifts we might anticipate, and attempt to evaluate what we must make happen in order to achieve success of the objective. The ranking of these key factors, then provides a priority list for future management attention.

FIGURE 1
A hierarchy of goals

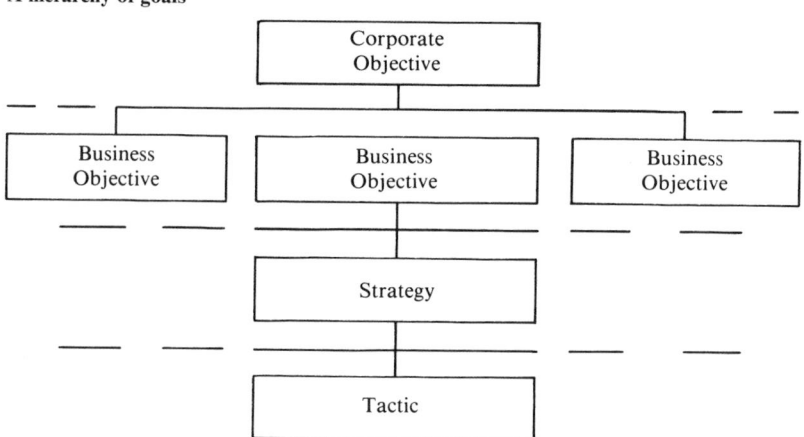

We expect the objective to be challenging enough, even shocking enough, to force a radical rethinking of the strategies and tactics. For example, any time we have enough well-defined strategies to give us a high confidence level in exceeding the goals stated in a business objective, then that business objective probably is not ambitious enough, and the probability of truly innovative strategic thinking is likely to be low.

At the next level in the goal structure is the strategy statement. The strategy describes in detail the environment of the business opportunity to be pursued in support of the objective. Normally, there will be several strategies supporting each objective. Altogether, we had more than 50 strategies operating in 1969. For example, if we had an objective to achieve certain goals in the automobile market, we might have one strategy involving automobile electronics, one involving material applications, and perhaps another for safety systems. The strategy looks ahead over a number of years, normally from 5 to 10, and intermediate check points are defined along the way providing milestones against which to judge progress. Progress measurement is an element of a strategy not included at the objective level. Finally, the contribution of the strategy to the overall objective is defined in quantitative measures and a critique is formulated which assigns a success probability to the strategy.

Next in the goal hierarchy is the tactical action program, or TAP. [Examples are given in Exhibit 3.] A TAP is a detailed action plan of the steps necessary to reach the major long-range check points defined by the strategies. It normally is short term, covering 6 to 18 months of effort. For each planned tactic, a

EXHIBIT 3
Examples of tactical action programs

TI's management selected three examples to illustrate three different types of TAPs: (1) a technology–product development program with long-time horizon and relatively large investment, (2) a marketing-oriented program with rather specific short-term goals and relatively small-scale investment, and (3) an internal capability development program of moderate scale and time horizon, oriented neither to products nor markets but to the generalized manufacturing process.

1. Under our overall strategy in the Radar Systems Business, we have a TAP to accomplish certain specific business objectives in *air traffic control*, which has a well-developed milestone structure out for three years, and less frequent milestones on out to six or seven years. Funding of the TAP is accomplished on an annual basis using the OST decision packages. This TAP is technologically oriented, and aimed at developing the next generation radar, display, and information management systems required for future air-traffic-control problems.

2. Another TAP is designed to impact our long-established line of products for thermal overload protection of electric motors. Basically this is a marketing-oriented program, with only secondary impact on product design activities. It contains specific actions relating to certain markets and certain accounts, with goals of specified increases in market penetration during the planned year. This program has a much shorter time horizon than (1) above, and tends to be a one-year program typically, subject to revaluation of its continuing need at year end.

3. Another example is selected from a nonproduct type strategy. We have an overall strategy for development and implementation of advanced manufacturing techniques containing a TAP to integrate directly the mechanical design process into the manufacturing process. This involves using automation and software skills to put the designer into the manufacturing loop.

---

responsible individual is designated, a start and finish schedule is established, and the required resources are defined.

As we progress downward through the OST system, plans are formulated at an increasing level in detail. We have major goals at the objective level, major milestones at the strategy level, and individual responsibility with resource allocation at the tactic level. Below the tactic level, each TAP is broken down into individual work packages which we manage by means of standard program management techniques. The detailed planning at this level provides the basis for planning and control of resources through the OST structure.[2]

ORGANIZATION SYSTEMS

Mr. Dove described how the OST system operated within the context of the corporation's formal organization structure, as follows:

What we have with OST is a system that gives us a method of planning, review, and control which cuts across the operating structure of groups, divisions, and PCCs. It provides a mechanism for assembling capabilities and challenging efforts to achieve results that could not be achieved by any one organizational element.

The two-hat concept

One way to visualize this overlay is to use a matrix with the traditional organizational units across the top and the OST structure at the left margin. [Figure 2.] Typically, the matrix organization concept has been used to illustrate the overlapping of a project organization with a functional technology organization. Here, the matrix is showing something entirely different. It is showing

FIGURE 2
Organization matrix OST/operating

			GROUP 2						GROUP 1	
			Division A			Division B				
O	S	T	PCC	PCC	PCC	PCC	PCC	PCC	PCC	
		1	X							
		2	X							
	A	3			X					
		4					X			
1		5							X	
		1			X					
	B	2			X					
		3	X							

---

[2] These remarks, and other quotations attributed to Mr. Dove in this case, are excerpted from his speech at the London School of Business Studies on May 22, 1970.

the relation between a strategic mode and an operating mode within the same organization.

One of the roles of a strategy manager, as indicated here, is to identify the TAPs required, represented by Xs in the matrix, and to pull them together from across the company into a coordinated strategic plan. Many times the strategy manager also is the manager of a product-customer center, especially if there is one PCC able to take a dominant role in the strategy. Nearly always, the strategy or tactic manager also will have an operating role to play. Only in rare cases does the strategy manager or tactic manager have that job as his full-time assignment.

Frequently, an objective manager also will be a division manager, though this is not always the case. When it is the case, we simply have a single manager wearing two hats with clearly designated goals for both growth and profitability. This now gives us a way to tie our long-range strategic plans to our short-term operational planning and control activities.

Through the OST overlay, we have a goal structure for strategic activities as well as operating activities. Not only can we measure profit and loss performance operationally, but we also can allocate resources through the OST structure and measure our progress toward these strategic goals. Now, your new idea has a home. It can be given resources for further development and, if the progress warrants, heavier support later. A number of outcomes are possible. Your idea might develop as a tactic. Or, it might even be the catalyst which would lead to a new major corporate goal at the objective level. Whatever the case, your idea would be clearly a part of the OST structure and would be recognized and supported by deliberate choice. It won't have to be bootlegged, or dropped completely through the crack.

Thus, at Texas Instruments, our managers are given a dual responsibility for both strategies and operations. In recent years, we have deliberately tried to create an environment in which it becomes natural for managers to distinguish between their operating and strategic modes. Lest I mislead you, let me reemphasize that we are talking about two modes within the same organization, and not about two distinct organizational structures. In fact, in the majority of cases—say about 75 percent—the execution of both modes is through a single manager.

There are a number of reasons why we have chosen to develop the second, or strategic, mode, within the organization. First, the strategic mode gives us a mechanism for large-scale opportunities, or those requiring combinations of resources not found in a single unit. Second, it gives us a mechanism for planning and controlling our investments for the future, and for making sure that we do achieve the desired balance of priorities between short-term and long-term activities.

To achieve this balance, it was necessary to structure the system so that each manager, in his strategic role, would have roughly the same influence and stature as in his operating role. [This structuring involved two distinct steps.] The first involved the simple decision to allocate strategic resources through the strategy managers. In the case of a single manager serving both the operating and strategic role, this amounted to a separation of strategic investments from operating activities in a manager's profit and loss statement. In other words, he and his managers were given visibility to plan and control both the strategic and operating components of his business. In the exceptional case where we would have full-time strategy managers, this created a mechanism for the allocation of a strategic budget apart from the operating profit and loss statement. In either case, the strategic budget represents funds that the strategy manager can choose to spend anywhere in the organization to get the skills and resources which he needs.

Incentive compensation systems

The second step was the development of a compensation structure, which measured performance as well as operating performance. An important part of this structure is what we refer to as key personnel analysis (KPA). KPA is a system of annual comparative assessment of individual TIers. The procedure involves classification of TIers into five comparative rating groups, and eventually a paired comparison based upon contributions during the current year, for individuals in the top group.

Starting with the immediate supervisor, individuals are rank-ordered on the basis of their relative performance and contribution, and an adjustment to base salary is recommended. The ranks are combined at successive levels of the organization until the department level is reached. The department manager identified "bench mark" people among those in his department. Bench marks are those people judged as having made equal contributions, even though they are in different functions and job grades. This procedure permits merging of the rankings reaching the department level into a single department ranking. Each person then is placed in one of five comparative rating groups of 20 percent each. The top 20 percent is paired-compared—that is, each person is paired with every other person, and one of each pair is selected against the contribution criterion. From this, a new rank ordering is achieved. The process is repeated at division and group levels, bench-marking each time to produce merged rankings. Several crosscuts are made on job grade and job function, including a separate ranking by the president of all strategy and objective managers. Incentive bonus award recommendations based on the rankings are made up for up to 20 percent of the salaried population. The KPA approach has provided an effective way to reward strategic performance.

During a series of interviews in the spring of 1972, several TI executives acknowledged that one effect of the KPA system was to create a competitive environment within the company. These executives thought the system was constructive, nevertheless, because peer rivalry encouraged better performance. "As a practical matter," one manager said, "KPA is not as much of a zero-sum game as it sounds like. The system does force us to examine performance at the very lowest levels in the organization and attempt to identify people who have done a superlative job. As the ranking process moves up the hierarchy, however, only a very few people from the lower levels manage to survive the screening. The informal test that each of us uses in identifying our key personnel is, who is contributing most to the success of the business? The net effect of the process is that almost all of the managers in the higher ranks participate in the bonus pool. It would be a rare event, for example, for a PCC manager not to receive a bonus."

Another aspect of TI's incentive compensation systems was a stock-option plan. One participant in this program commented, "It's really a very unusual plan. Most stock-option plans involve an award of so many shares to an individual, and the only restriction on his right to exercise the options is that he must stay with the company for several years; the options vest at, say, 20 percent of the shares each year. In our plan, an award is made for a certain number of shares, but vesting is conditional upon the company meeting a specified earnings per share target each year. The fact that all executive options are tied to the same EPS target thus establishes a common goal for the management team. To some extent, this group goal tends to mitigate the individual competition that is inherent in our KPA system."

Committee structure

TI's top management had formed two important operating committees, the OST committee and the management committee. Commenting on the composition and role of these committees, Mr. Gene Helms, TI's manager of Advanced Corporate Planning, spoke as follows:

> In 1969, TI created an OST Committee to make strategic resource allocations, and review strategic activities. The OST committee has 13 permanent members including the president, the four group vice presidents, and other officers including the vice president of corporate development (to whom I report). The committee meets about 18 times a year for a full day. The agenda for each meeting normally is settled beforehand and includes a rigorous reexamination of at least one business objective or consideration of a major new business opportunity. Topics discussed are: (1) the appropriateness of the objective in light of current information; (2) progress in the strategic development of the objective; (3) any actions which should be taken at the corporate level to accelerate or otherwise modify the strategic programs for that objective. Besides this, managers of key strategies and tactis frequently meet with the OST committee for progress reviews, or when initiation of new programs is under consideration.
>
> Since each of the eight business objectives is reviewed at least once a year, and because most TI managers have some tasks to perform for at least one and often several objectives, there is now more of a tendency on the part of our managers to look upon OST as a living and important system. Also, the OST meetings provide a forum for the consideration of new objectives in light of our changing corporate situation.
>
> Another important feature of the OST committee's function is the impact that it has had upon strategic conflict resolutions. All of our objective managers now report (in the strategic mode) to the OST committee. In the operational mode they report to their group vice presidents who sit on both the OST and management committees. (The latter committee has nearly the same composition as the OST committee, but at separate meetings it treats operational issues and the overall allocation of resources between the operating and strategic modes.) In the OST committee meetings, members are expected to adopt a corporate perspective. The fact that no member is associated exclusively with any single objective, but

that all members are responsible for the management of the objectives, facilitates unbiased consideration of the objectives.

THE RESOURCE ALLOCATION PROCESS

Continuous review

Mr. Dove described the review process of the OST committee in the following terms:

> The objectives and strategies contain all the essential elements of our long-range plan. In fact, the OST documentation is our long-range plan. In the operational mode, we budget and control to an annual plan, which is just a snapshot of one year of the long-range plan.
>
> Figure 3 is a schematic representation of our planning cycle. Throughout the year we are concentrating on our objectives and strategies, revising the basic premises and checkpoints. This gives us the environment and guidelines we need for the more detailed annual planning to follow. Then, in the fall and winter, with the economic and market outlook in mind, we set our annual goals and the split of funds between the strategic and operating modes. Tactics are revised and new ones generated. We normally have many more defined tactics than we can afford to undertake at any one time.
>
> The tactics are then grouped into logical, stand-alone decision packages which are rank-ordered by the strategy managers. Based upon the guidelines for strategic funding of business objectives and individual strategies a cutoff line is drawn, and packages above the line are given a tentative approval. Those falling below the line are not discarded, but remain in what we call our "creative backlog" and have an opportunity to move up for approval at a later time when resources become available. This process is repeated at the objective level, where adjustments in the allocation between strategies may be made, and decision packages

FIGURE 3
Planning cycle

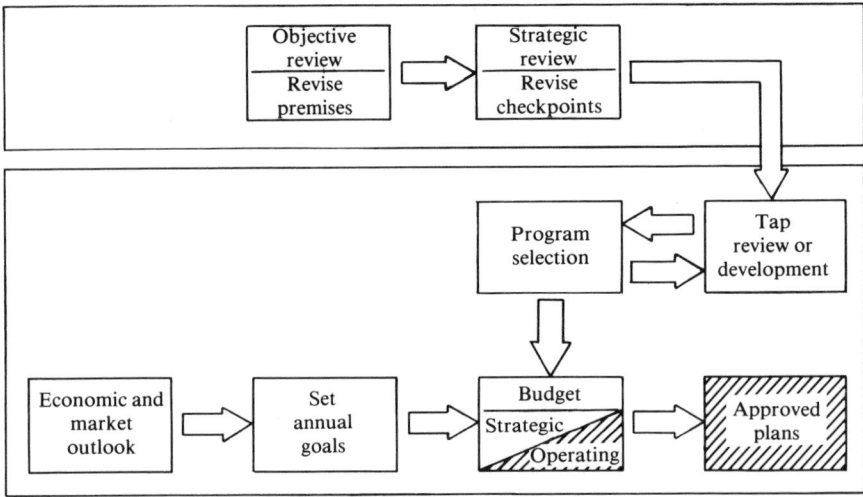

falling below the cutoff line at the strategy level have another opportunity for approval. Finally, we allocate a segment of the strategic funding directly from the corporate level to certain decision packages. This provides an opportunity to fine-tune the resource allocation between objectives and to consider appeals on selected packages falling below the cutoff line at the strategy and objective level. But mostly, this gives us a mechanism for starting new ventures which for the various reasons could not normally be undertaken by one of the operating units.

What I want to emphasize here is that the objectives and strategies give us a living and dynamic long-range plan, tying the activities together from top to bottom. We are attempting to space our objective reviews throughout the year so that top management can devote time for an in-depth study of each objective, and yet never be more than 12 months away from the most recent objective review.

Elaborating on Mr. Dove's comments, Mr. Helms said, "One of the reasons that this continuous updating process works as well as it does is because of our computer-assisted planning model. We call it modplan, for 'model planning,' but it's really nothing more than a very simple computer program which takes much of the arithmetic out of revising any long-range plan, or shorter-term forecast. An objective manager can specify 10 key variables for his business over the next 10 years and have these converted

EXHIBIT 4

Long-Range Objective Model
Dollars ($millions) □ □ Indices ($K / $MNSB)

Objective_____   Manager_____

		1971	1972	1973	1974	1975	1976		1981
	Served Available Market								
	Net Sales Billed								
	GPM								
	Operating D + A								
	Operating Profit								
	OST D + A								
	Total D + A								
	Div Oth Inc/(Exp)								
	Organization Profit								
	Total People (000's)								
	Net Space Avail (t^{2}000's)								
	Current Assets								
	Net Fixed Assets								
	Total Assets								
	Capital Expenditures								
	Depreciation								
	Organization Pft ROA%								

by the computer into condensed, conventional financial statements and related statistics. Having such a tool thus permits the OST committee to focus on the specific actions that the manager must take in order to make his assumptions come true."

"The net effect of this planning flexibility," Mr. Helms continued, "is that at any particular point in time we *do* have a long-range plan, represented by the sum of the modplans that have currently been approved for each of our objective managers. On the other hand, changes in these plans are so frequent that we really don't take the trouble to prepare a nice thick volume called 'The Plan' the way many companies do. The only real plan, therefore, is the set of TAPs that will be undertaken during the next year or two, and the specific funding of those takes place as a part of the annual budgeting process."

Budgeting and forecasting

"We really have two budgets for the year," Helms continued, "one for OST funds and the other for operating expenses. The key point is that expenditures associated with each category appear as separate and distinct line items on the P/L statement for each unit. We begin with P/L models for the coming year consolidated from each unit to give a first approximation to our scale of operations and expected profitability. At this point, all OST funds are considered discretionary, and in effect, are accrued in one big pot for allocation purposes. Zero-based budgeting is applied to the operating segment of expenses. The OST package is allocated among objectives, and then to strategies and TAPs using the OST decision package approach."

"The balance between the OST expenses package and the operating expense package is a top-level, long-term/short-term type tradeoff. The key principle is that operating profit (as measured before OST expenditures) must meet certain standards for each business, and the zero-based budgeting approach gives visibility to help at the operating profit level. The size of the OST pot, of course, is influenced strongly by the total operating profit, and the pressure naturally is to beat down operating expenses so that we can invest more in OST programs.

"The preceding remarks primarily apply to the setting of targets for key P/L indexes (operating expense, operating profit, OST expense, etc.) at the corporate level. In succeeding phases of the planning cycle, new information appears as both operating and OST decision packages which are matched to the available budgets. The iterative loop is closed by providing for appeals upward which can result in adjusting the original targets.

"We simply are dividing a total expense package into two segments so that we can look at each segment from a different viewpoint. The operating segment is examined from the viewpoint of operating efficiency and maximizing year-ahead profits. The strategic segment is considered on a company-wide basis as though it were completely discretionary and is the element in our resource allocation process which permits decisions to change the business mix, product emphasis, or overall direction of the company.

"The entire OST pool is not necessarily allocated to the objective managers at the beginning of the year. We retain approximately 10 percent of it as a contingency for subsequent use by the OST committee for new opportunities that may arise. The use of OST funds can be modified during the year by managers at any of the three levels. A TAP manager is permitted to change the nature of his activity on his own discretion, as long as it doesn't change the tactical goal which he is committed to achieve. Similarly, changes and re-allocation of funds may be made at the strategy manager or objective manager level as long as there is no change in the goal which has been approved by higher authority.

"We had a recession in 1970, as you will recall, and that spring, as it became apparent that we were going to have trouble meeting our earnings' commitment, we did begin to cut back on OST funding. By early summer, however, it was apparent that the downturn was hitting us rather severely. The choice that top management had to make was whether or not to continue to reduce the spending on OST projects. Mark Shepherd finally drew a line, saying that he would not cut OST funds below a certain level. There is no way of knowing what the right answer is in such a situation, of course, but he believed strongly that we should not mortgage our future simply for the sake of current year profitability. Subsequently, we held OST funding at about the same level in 1971 until we were sure we were out of the woods. Our funding for 1972 now exceeds the amount we were spending in 1969.

"Once our OST and operating expense budgets are set for the coming year, our detailed budgeting then proceeds. We only budget future performance by quarter. Actually, we prepare our quarterly budget as much as 10 quarters in advance. Right now, each of our PCCs has a quarterly budget running through the balance of this year and for all of 1973. This summer they'll extend that budget, again by quarters, through 1974. This is not as much work as it sounds like, because the level of detail is still not very great; the quarterly budget is also prepared with computer assistance and uses somewhat more input assumptions than the objective models. In effect, preparing a quarterly budget is simply the task of providing more detailed assumptions for the modplan that has been approved by the OST Committee.

"As the year progresses, each manager prepares a rolling forecast four to six months in advance. In December, for example, the manager will submit a revised monthly forecast for the next three months and will, for the first time, provide a monthly forecast for the three months of the second quarter of the coming year. In January, the forecast for the five months February through June is revised. The forecast is revised again in February for the remaining four months, and in March the cycle starts over again with a revision of the forecast for April through June and a presentation of the first monthly forecast for July through September. These forecasts are at the level of detail sufficient for analysis of actual performance. We think it's the right away to do planning and budgeting; we start with annual gross data 10 years out in modplan, convert that to quarterly budget data for up to 10 quarters out, and then convert that to monthly forecasts for up to six months. Another advantage of this approach is that it eliminates any problem of interface between the long-range planning activity and budgeting. All budgeting and forecasting are coordinated by the corporate operation's controller; he starts to track expected corporate performance more than two years ahead of the event. Starting at that point, it's easy to get consistency between the first quarterly budget and the then current modplan. Any subsequent revisions in the budget that may be necessary are then coordinated through the controller's department."

Planning methodology

"As you've gathered by now," Helms continued, "we're not very enthusiastic around here for elaborate methodological approaches to planning. Speaking philosophically, it seems to me there's a major problem of injecting methodology into a human organization. The literature abounds with elegant solutions to well-formulated problems. However, very few well-formulated problems appear in strategic business management. Even fewer businessmen are prepared to accept someone else's strategic model as a guide to their own behavior. Too often, we've tried to extend into the strategic planning area the same points of view which have proved successful operating planning approaches. Because they have been applied to more routine tasks, these approaches have not been required to interact strongly with variations in management style. In strategy, style is everything, and planning approaches must deal with style variations effectively, or fail.

"At TI, we have proceeded on the premise that long-range planning can be imbedded successfully within the primary operating organization. Our commitment to accomplish this has placed first priority on matters of organization development and culture, rather than on matters of pure planning methodology. This has been implemented by creating the OST structure of goals, and superimposing it upon our traditional organization structure. By doing so, we are building in a consciousness of the future. We are creating a distinct orientation toward two different time frames. When successful, this creates two management modes within the same organization: a strategic mode and an operating mode.

"Consistent with this philosophy," Mr. Helms continued, "we do formalize the results of our planning activities with an annual planning conference. It's held in early December each year, lasts for three days, and about 500 of our managers attend some part of that conference. Each operating group is allocated a part of the agenda, and in the course of three days each division manager, each PCC manager, each objective manager, and each strategy manager will speak briefly to the group; that's about 90 men in all. About 150 of the highest ranking managers attend the entire three-day conference, and other managers come in to listen to the part that is relevant to their sphere of activities. The purpose of such a conference, of course, is primarily communication; it helps to keep the corporation knit together. Another advantage, however, is that each manager makes a public commitment of what he proposes to achieve during the coming year, and we think that helps to ensure that he really will try to deliver on his commitment."

REPORTING SYSTEMS

"Our reporting systems are not all that unique," Helms explained, "but obviously they're very important in allowing us to ensure that our plans are being executed as intended. Because of our dual-mode approach to management, our reporting systems focus on both the PCC Manager and the TAP Manager."

Mr. Dove described the effects of dual responsibilities on a profit-center on a PCC manager in the following terms:

Suppose we have a common situation where you happen to be a strategy manager and a PCC manager, both at the same time. You are responsible both for current operating results and for a long-range strategy. How will you reconcile the two roles, and how will you avoid the temptation to delay and cut back strategic efforts every time an operating crisis comes along?

Let's look at a simplified profit and loss statement for the PCC [Figure 4]. As a typical PCC manager, you will be expected to wear two hats, the first as an

FIGURE 4

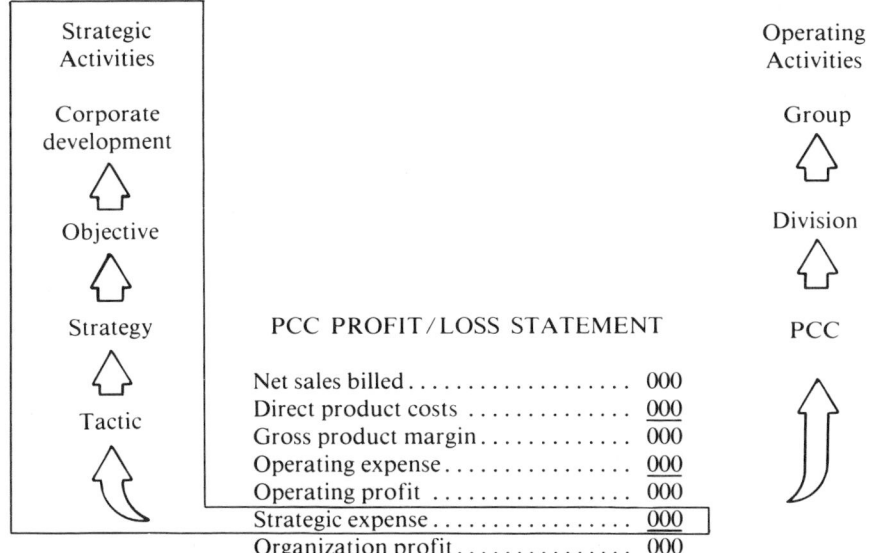

Strategic Activities		Operating Activities
Corporate development		Group
Objective		Division
Strategy	PCC PROFIT/LOSS STATEMENT	PCC
Tactic	Net sales billed 000	
	Direct product costs 000	
	Gross product margin 000	
	Operating expense 000	
	Operating profit 000	
	Strategic expense 000	
	Organization profit 000	

operating manager concerned with today's operating results, and the second as a manager of strategic activity for longer range results. For today's operations, you will be measured relative to your planned operating profit. Within limits, you are free to make adjustments in the operating expense budget in order to bring about maximum operating profit. But remember that you also have a strategic hat to wear. This means that you also are going to be measured by how effectively you utilize the strategic expense. In other words, how well are you achieving the milestones and checkpoints established at the time the strategic expenditures were approved?

Once the plans are made and resources allocated, objective, strategy and TAP managers are given decentralized authority to obligate the expense, capital, and people resources, make adjustments as necessary to meet the goals, and resolve conflict as it occurs. The results and progress on strategic activities will be reviewed first by the TAP manager, and then successively at the strategy manager level, the objective manager level, and by the corporate development function. Through this path, the strategic resources are allocated and controlled. Accountability for operating profit, on the other hand, is through the product-customer center to the division and group levels. As we shall see, the responsibilities for strategic and operating activities tend to converge closer and closer to single individuals as we move up higher in the organization. As a result, group and division managers are wearing both hats and have responsibilities for both operating profit and strategic expense. This, in turn, means that they are accountable for the bottom line on the P/L statement—the organization profit.

"In fact, of course," Helms said, "our reporting system is much more detailed than the simplified example Mr. Dove displayed. Here (Exhibit 5) is a copy of one page from the actual report for one PCC manager for one month. As you can see, we make the usual comparisons of actual against budget and forecast. In addition, on other pages in the report, we get an opportunity to see how good a forecaster the manager is because we can track actual against several previous months' forecasts."

"One of the problems in getting a system like OST started is in framing the definitions of just what expenses fall into the OST pool. We started out by asking each group manager to present his own proposal for the expenses which he viewed as discretionary. We then tried to resolve the differences in perspective among the group managers, but even today we have slightly different definitions of what types of expenses constitute OST activities. More important than a rigid definition that is applicable to all groups is the consistency of the definition within any given operating unit. Here it's very important for top management to take a hard-nosed approach in order to make sure that OST activities are not being funded sub rosa out of operating expenses.

"When each TAP is funded, it's given a project order number, and all costs on that TAP are charged against that account number. About 80 percent of the total OST expenditure is for personnel costs—primarily engineering. Fortunately, because of our early history in government contracting, our engineers were used to keeping records of their time. Accumulating TAP

EXHIBIT 5

MONTHLY COMPARISON

MARCH

OPERATING UNIT   RESPONSIBILITY

	YEAR TO DATE			PCT. OF PLAN	DESCRIPTION	CURRENT MONTH COMPARISON				
	ACTUAL	PLAN	LAST YEAR			MONTH ACTUAL	MONTH FORECAST	QTR ACT/FCST	QTR PLAN	QTR VARIANCE
1	10473	6960	6069	150	NSE $	4085	2600	10473	6960	3513
2	12003	10546	11339	114	BACKLOG TOTAL	12003	11908	12003	10546	1457
3	1747		1071		BACKLOG DELINQ	1747	1600	1747		-1747
4	62908	54200	49439	116	NUB	22418	19200	62908	54200	8708
5	7744	6680	7268	116	NSB - TOTAL	2798	2400	7744	6680	1064
6	563	550	372	102	DIRECT LABOR	215	195	563	550	-13
7	3124	3125	3534	100	DIRECT MATL	1218	1038	3124	3125	1
8	881	880	755	100	MFG OVERHEAD	307	310	881	880	-1
9	356	365	276	98	OTHER OVERHEAD	126	124	356	365	9
10	136	130	120	105	COST ADJ - NET	48	48	136	130	-6
11					OTHER MFG COST					
12	638	-160	189	-399	INV REDUCTION	125		638	-160	-798
13	2046	1790	2022	114	GPM	759	685	2046	1790	256
14	26.4	26.8	27.8	99	GPM % NSB	27.1	28.5	26.4	26.8	-.4
15	175		187		OPER D+D EXP	61	59	175		-175
16	56		55		CST D+D EXP	18	18	56		-56
17	1815	1790	1780	101	DIV PROFIT	680	608	1815	1790	25
18	23.4	26.8	24.5	87	DIV PF % NSB	24.3	25.3	23.4	26.8	-3.4
19	917	915	993	100	OPERATING D+A	310	308	917	915	-2
20	11.8	13.7	13.7	86	OPER D+A % NSB	11.1	12.8	11.8	13.7	1.9
21	44.8	51.1	49.1	88	OPER D+A % GPM	40.8	45.0	44.8	51.1	6.3
22	-292	-278	-209	105	DIV OTH INC/EXP	-103	-100	-292	-278	-14
23	837	597	820	140	OPER PROFIT	346	277	837	597	240
24	10.8	8.9	11.3	121	OPER PF % NSB	12.4	11.5	10.8	8.9	1.9
25	75	75	55	100	OST D+A EXP	25	25	75	75	
26	992	990	1048	100	TOTAL D+A EXP	335	333	992	990	-2
27	12.8	14.8	14.4	86	TOT D+A % NSB	12.0	13.9	12.8	14.8	2.0
28	48.5	55.3	51.8	88	TOT D+A % GPM	44.1	48.6	48.5	55.3	6.9
29	762	522	765	146	ORGAN PROFIT	321	252	762	522	240
30	9.8	7.8	10.5	126	ORGAN PF % NSB	11.5	10.5	9.8	7.8	2.0
31	19.5	13.6	20.6	143	ORGAN PRF ROA	25.0	19.1	19.5	13.6	5.9
32	870	668	1080	130	TOTAL OTH ASSET	870	810	870	668	-202
33	4524	4612	4121	98	RECEIVABLES	4524	4750	4524	4612	88
34	146	173	142	84	REC/MIL NSB	146	162	146	173	27
35	3196	3395	2905	94	INV - NET	3196	3425	3196	3395	199
36	103	127	100	81	INV/MIL NSB	103	117	103	127	24
37					UNLIQ PROG PAY					
38					UPP/MIL NSB					
39	2022	2485	2415	81	NFA-MFG EQ OWN	2022	2362	2022	2485	463
40	6167	6632	7038	93	NFA - TOTAL	6167	6512	6167	6632	465
41	199	248	242	80	NFA/MIL NSB	199	222	199	248	49
42	14757	15307	15144	96	EOM ASSETS	14757	15497	14757	15307	550
43	476	573	521	83	ASSETS/MIL NSB	476	527	476	573	97
44	1168	486	265	240	ORGAN CASH FLO	1507	729	1168	486	682
45	205	400	73	51	TOTAL CAP EXP	-114	80	205	400	195
46	325	335	320	97	TOTAL DEP EXP	112	21	325	335	10
47	219	308	113	71	TOTAL CAP AUTH	81	78	219	308	89
48	737	700	655	105	DIRECT PEOPLE	737	740	737	700	-37
49	161	162	183	99	INDIR EX PEO	161	162	161	162	1
50	1165	1116	1124	104	TOTAL PEOPLE	1165	1164	1165	1116	-49
51	26.6	23.9	25.9	111	NSB/PERSON	26.6	23.2	26.6	23.9	2.7
52	2.6	1.9	2.7	137	ORGAN PRF/PER	2.6	2.4	2.6	1.9	.7
53	1316		1105		TOTAL PAYROLL	468		1316		-1316
54	91	95	96	96	NET SO FT AVAL	91	101	91	95	4
55	2938	3555	3302	83	SO AVL/MIL NSB	2938	3437	2938	3555	617

costs by project greatly facilitates separating out OST expenses from the operating expenses in any given PCC.

"Then, of course, we track the performance on each TAP with a monthly status report such as that shown in Figure 5.

FIGURE 5
Program status review

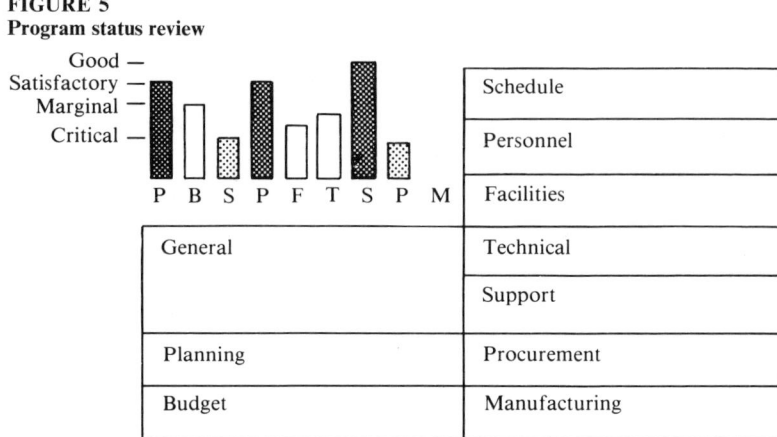

"For management review, the status of each TAP is reported monthly in a simplified format which enables us to tell at a glance how the TAP stands on a number of critical factors. Yellow and red bars indicate that higher level management action is needed to solve a problem. Monthly reports covering detailed financial data and manpower resources also are distributed to TAP, strategy, and objective managers."

EFFECTIVENESS OF MANAGEMENT SYSTEMS

At lunch, midway through the interviews in the spring of 1972, several TI executives chatted with the casewriter about the effectiveness of TI's planning system. One of the executives described the operation of the system in the following items: "The sum total of our efforts to change the future of TI can probably be divided into three pieces: (1) efforts which should be managed as a part of the system but which escape the system and occur as sub rosa activities, (2) efforts which are managed as a part of the system but are not affected by it—that is, activities that would be undertaken whether we had such a system or not, and (3) efforts which are affected because of the system by which proposals are reviewed and approved."

In the ensuing discussion, there was general agreement among the TI executives at that lunch that perhaps 15 percent of the total discretionary efforts of the corporation were in category 1, perhaps 30 percent in category 2, but that more than 50 percent of the company's innovative, future-oriented activities were being better managed because of the OST system.

PART THREE

Management issues in the
financial reporting process

Goldfinger Incorporated

ALTERNATIVE REALIZATION CRITERIA

Early in 1970, Goldfinger Incorporated was formed to acquire and operate a Nevada mining property using newly developed extraction methods capable of processing profitably low-grade ores containing small quantities of gold.

Operations began promptly in 1970. Engineers' reports based upon extensive geological surveys indicated that 1.6 million ounces of gold would be recovered over the life of the mining properties. The mining properties were located in an arid mountainous area and would have no residual value after the gold deposits were exhausted. The existing equipment and property improvements were expected to be used during the period of production and would be abandoned thereafter. All production and operating expenses were paid during the year. Goldfinger's cash receipts and disbursements for the year are summarized in Exhibit 1.

The Gold Reserve Act of January 1934 defined the U.S. dollar as 15 and $\frac{5}{21}$ grains of gold $\frac{9}{10}$ fine. Since there are 480 grains of pure gold to the ounce, the mint price for $\frac{9}{10}$ fine gold became $35. Since the adoption of the

EXHIBIT 1
Schedule of cash receipts and disbursements for the year 1970

Cash receipts:		
Sales of capital stock at par value		$10,000,000
Collections from sales (30,000 ounces at $35 per ounce)		1,050,000
		11,050,000
Cash disbursements:		
Cost of mining properties (including all mineral rights,		
engineers' surveys, roads, mine shafts, and equipment).......	$8,000,000	
Production costs	2,250,000	
Delivery expenses	25,000	
Administrative expenses	150,000	
Total disbursements		10,425,000
Cash on hand—Balance at December 31, 1970		$ 625,000

This case was prepared by F. Robert Madera, research assistant, under the direction of David F. Hawkins, assistant professor of Business Administration.

gold bullion standard and through the date of this case it was illegal for the ordinary citizen to have in his possession more than a nominal amount of gold. The U.S. Treasury stood ready to buy gold from miners or importers at the $35 mint price, and to sell to industrial users, dentists, foreign governments or central banks at the same price. Thus, gold was readily marketable at the fixed price of $35 and this price was subject to change only by the federal government.

Goldfinger's production records for 1970 showed the following information:

Sold, delivered, and proceeds collected............	30,000 ounces ($\frac{9}{10}$ fine)
Sold and delivered but proceeds not collected.....	20,000
Produced but not sold or delivered..............	40,000
Total production	90,000 ounces ($\frac{9}{10}$ fine)

QUESTIONS

1. Prepare a balance sheet at December 31, 1970 and an income statement for the year based on each of the following:
   a. Revenues are recognized upon the receipt of cash.
   b. Revenues are recognized at time of sale and delivery.
   c. Revenues are recognized upon the basis of production.
   (Ignore any income tax considerations.)

2. Evaluate the three sets of statements which you prepared in terms of the criteria of:
   a. Usefulness.
   b. Feasibility.
   c. Conformity to accepted definitions of income.

——◄CASE III–2 ►·——

Metolius Acres

————··◄◯◯►··————

It was early January 1979, and Ernest Gmur was trying to sort out his notes in respect to a Central Oregon farm property called Metolius Acres. Herr Gmur hoped to be able to construct several sets of pro forma financial statements for the farm prior to continuing his discussions with a local realtor.

While his interest in the farm was primarily focused upon potential capital gains, he did want to have some idea of how well it might do as an operating farm. He knew that the investors he represented, through the Lucerne Investors Group of Zug, Switzerland, would expect a thorough analysis on his part.

BACKGROUND

Herr Gmur had settled upon Metolius Acres as his prime purchase prospect after a three-day tour of farm property in Central Oregon. He had been aided in his search by Ken Morrow, a local realtor. Gmur and Morrow had driven by a score of properties, actually visiting four or five of them in person. Metolius Acres, a 1,500-acre wheat farm with river frontage and a view of the Cascade Mountains, struck him as being the most attractive prospect.

Unfortunately, the data that Mr. Morrow had been able to put together about the farm was neither complete nor well organized. Gmur understood that this was due to the fact that the farm in question was not actively on the market. Morrow, being a reasonably resourceful realtor had gathered all of his data from sources external to the farm. A friend of his who managed the adjoining farm, an extension agent for the state university, and an employee of the local grain elevator had all supplied useful data.

Earlier that morning, Morrow had dropped by at Gmur's rented condominium with the following data:

> **Land value.** Farms of similar size and condition are currently selling for $2,000 per acre. This would imply a value of $3 million.

This case was prepared by Professor M. Edgar Barrett. Copyright © 1979 by M. Edgar Barrett.

Residential buildings. The residential portion of the buildings appear to be worth about $70,000.

Farm buildings and equipment. Based on data from an adjoining farmer, the farm buildings and equipment appear to be worth about $100,000 and $140,000, respectively.

Inventory. Metolius Acres held title to 28,000 bushels of wheat at the local grain elevator as of December 31, 1978. This was in contrast to the fact that there had been none held there by the farm on January 1, 1978.

Sales. The farm sold 140,000 bushels of wheat to the elevator operator during 1978. It appeared that this was their only sales outlet.

Prices. The elevator operator had paid, on average, $2.95 per bushel for its 1978 purchases. The closing bid, on December 31, had been $3.40.

Operating expenses. The local agricultural extension agent had provided the following pro forma estimates for a wheat farm of about this size:

Seed, fertilizer, and chemicals...............	$ .395
Machinery rentals, with operator............	.106
Other costs	.084
Variable cost per bushel	$ .585
Salaries and wages	$ 54,000
Property taxes..........................	26,000
Other expenses, including transient labor	28,000
Total annual costs	$108,000

Upon some questioning, Morrow opined that farm buildings and residential buildings should probably be depreciated over a 25-year life. Farm equipment he thought, should be viewed as having a five-year life. Further, he thought, the farm's inventory—computed on a direct cost basis—could easily be financed by short-term debt. A cash balance of $10,000 should easily cover any routine cash needs.

As he started out the door, he added: "I assume, of course, that you're aware that most farms around here prepare income statements based on the assumption that revenue should be recognized when the wheat is harvested. Thus, you'll need to include the last 28,000 bushels in your sales computations."

Gmur told Morrow that this made no sense to him. "Besides," he said, "How could you bookkeep such a thing?"

Morrow, much to Gmur's surprise, responded to that aspect of the question quite quickly. "That's no problem. You can either revalue the inventory, or set up an unbilled accounts-receivable account, whichever you prefer. Either way you'd reflect some profit on this winter wheat."

QUESTIONS

1. Prepare two pro forma income statements for 1978. The first should be based on normal accrual accounting, while the second should follow Morrow's advice.

2. Prepare two pro forma balance sheets for Metolius Acres as of December 31, 1978 based on the same assumptions as above.

3. Prepare two pro forma funds flow statements for 1978 based on similar assumptions.

4. Based on the case data, what should Gmur be prepared to pay for Metolius Acres?

Note: For purposes of the above three questions, you may assume that the following estimates of value, as of January 1, 1978 had been made available to you:

a.	Land value	$ 1,750 per acre
b.	Residential buildings	40,000
c.	Farm buildings	85,000
d.	Farm equipment	160,000

You may also assume that there were no capitalized expenditures during 1978 in respect to the above four items. Finally, you may prepare the pro forma financial statements on the assumption that the farm had been purchased—at market value—On January 1, 1978.

⸻CASE III-3⸻

Charles Crowne Company

At a meeting on January 16, 1974 of the three officers of the Charles Crowne Company, a general construction firm located in a large midwestern city, John Crowne, vice president and treasurer, raised a question concerning the method the company was using in recording profits on its construction contracts. He remarked that during a recent conversation he had been told by the treasurer and office manager of a building supply firm that a construction company could report its profits either on a percentage of completion or on a completed-contract basis and that the choice of method could have a material effect on a company's net income and financial statements. John Crowne's statement puzzled the other two officers who asked for a detailed explanation of the alternatives. In reply, Crowne stated that he could not explain the percentage method or its significance since time pressure had prevented him from questioning his friend about the methods. He added that he was certain that the company was presently following the job-completion method of recording profit or loss on contracts only at the completion of the contracts.

John noted that the company's financial statements were furnished to architects and bonding companies who used them as a means of appraising a contractor's ability to perform a contract he was bidding on. In view of the way in which the statements were used, all officers agreed they should be aware of the available alternatives since the use of a different method might influence the company's success in obtaining contracts from architects and gaining coverage from bonding companies.

Another factor mentioned was the future prosperity of the Charles Crowne Company and the construction industry in general. Although over the long run the officers expected to expand the volume of company business, the prospects for 1974 did not appear too favorable. As a final consideration, John Crowne noted that the company would soon have to furnish financial statements with its request to the Second National Bank for financial assistance for a proposed office and storage building that would be constructed in the spring of 1974. John wondered whether the company's bank credit standing would be influenced by a change in accounting methods.

At the conclusion of the meeting, John Crowne agreed to question his friend about the available alternatives in detail, to review their application to the Charles Crowne Company, and then to submit his recommendation to the other two officers.

COMPANY BACKGROUND

In 1936, Charles Crowne founded his own masonry contracting firm as a single proprietorship employing a crew of five men. Although the firm grew slowly up to 1961, Mr. Crowne had restricted the company's operations to the masonry business. In 1961 Mr. Crowne's son, John, joined the firm after obtaining a degree in architectural engineering. Shortly thereafter, the company started a gradual move into the general construction field. By 1966, the firm was engaged almost entirely as a general contractor, devoting its major effort to institutional projects such as garages, churches, and fire stations.

In bidding on projects as a general contractor, the Charles Crowne Company usually compiled estimates of the cost to construct a project, adding to these costs a percentage for overhead and profit. A large part of the estimates would be based on the bids of subcontractors for special portions of a job. The general contractor would then compile the total estimate for the project and submit a bid. If the contract was obtained, the contractor would then award subcontracts to those subcontractors who had submitted the lowest bid for portions of the project. The contracts received were almost always of a fixed-price nature.

On January 1, 1973 the company was incorporated with Charles Crowne, president, holding 60 percent of the common stock, John Crowne, vice president and treasurer, holding 30 percent, and Larry Shane, who was not related to the Crownes, owning 10 percent and holding the position of secretary and office manager.

Although the company acted as general contractor on all projects in which it was engaged, it continued to perform all masonry work on its contracts. In addition, the company employed a force of carpenters on company jobs to handle all rough carpentry work and also to assist in supervision of company-employed laborers and the subcontractors. Most work on company projects was performed by subcontractors.

Charles Crowne frequently acted as the general superintendent on the most important company jobs while John Crowne traveled between all other job sites carrying out general supervision and checking on work progress and performance. Mr. Shane handled all office work including the compilation of estimates and proposals for new contracts. Each evening the officers met to discuss the status of jobs and future plans of the company.

RESULTS OF 1973

Because of the high volume of institutional construction activity, 1973 was a record year for the Charles Crowne Company. Sales value of contracts completed in 1973 according to preliminary figures was $1,143,303.06, as compared with the previous high in 1969 of $819,348.76. Net profit before taxes and officers' compensation in 1973 was estimated at $106,113.74 whereas $62,809.12 had been earned in 1972 (see Exhibits 1, 2, 3, 4).

EXHIBIT 1

CHARLES CROWNE COMPANY
Income Statement
For Year Ended December 31, 1973

Sales value of completed contracts		$1,143,303.06
Cost of contracts completed		1,026,112.10
Gross income from contracts.............................		117,190.96
Add: Discounts earned		10,832.66
		128,023.62
Less:		
General and administrative expense	$21,909.88	
Officers' compensation	69,140.00	91,049.88
Net income before tax		36,973.74
Federal taxes		13,893.22
Net income..		$ 23,080.52

EXHIBIT 2
Sales and income, 1967–1972

	Sales value of contracts completed	Gross income from contracts (including discounts earned)	Profit before officers compensation and tax*
1972	$661,384.74	$87,565.50	$62,809.12
1971	340,381.42	38,199.54	24,589.42
1970	581,220.50	49,487.42	32,562.96†
1969	819,348.76	77,423.84	59,475.38
1968	548,424.04	77,799.12	61,713.66
1967	481,302.00	63,071.82	52,816.34

* During the years 1967–72 the company was operated as a partnership.
† In 1970, the company suffered a loss of $6,921.26 on a contract having a value of $63,628. This was the largest loss incurred in recent years.

EXHIBIT 3
Contracts completed in 1973

Contracts	Costs	Profit
$ 9,061.10	$ 7,390.38	$ 1,670.72
6,970.00	6,566.60	403.40
82,493.66	72,055.38	10,438.28
23,652.00	24,136.52	(484.52)
6,114.00	4,838.70	1,275.30
23,569.00	22,141.30	1,427.70
147,164.00	141,677.58	5,486.42
45,823.84	41,250.24	4,573.60
58,011.66	53,530.28	4,481.38
362,522.40	320,875.78	41,646.62
33,600.00	32,705.52	894.48
43,702.00	37,265.74	6,436.26
27,731.08	25,872.30	1,858.78
3,801.30	3,110.62	690.68
90,199.76	78,103.42	12,096.34
55,314.00	47,195.98	8,118.02
14,070.00	13,556.50	513.50
37,598.00	29,630.64	7,967.36
30,206.06	28,995.40	1,210.66
41,699.20	35,213.22	6,485.98
$1,143,303.06	$1,026,112.10	$117,190.96

EXHIBIT 4

CHARLES CROWNE COMPANY
Balance Sheet
As of December 31, 1973

Assets

Current assets:

Cash in bank	$ 74,317.34	
Cash on hand	100.00	
Accounts receivable—contracts	84,559.22	
Accounts receivable—other	12,342.18	
Raw materials inventory	49,372.86	
Work in process	(7,183.48)	
Deposit accounts	2,341.86	
Notes receivable	11,918.78	
		227,768.76

Property assets:

Trucks, tools, and equipment office furniture	$12,922.98	
Less: Accumulated depreciation	2,090.66	
		10,832.32
		$238,601.08

Total assets $238,601.08

Liabilities

Current liabilities:

Accounts payable—trade	$ 75,426.66	
Accounts payable—miscellaneous	3,503.24	
Accrued taxes	12,531.66	
Accrued insurance	2,079.00	
Accrued management compensation	21,980.00	
		115,520.56

Stockholders:

Stock	$100,000.00	
Retained income	23,080.52	
		123,080.52

Total liabilities and equity $238,601.08

EXHIBIT 5
Status report of contracts

Project	Amount of contract	Gross billing 12/31/73	Retainage 10 percent	Net billings rendered 12/31/73	Net billings collected 12/31/73	Costs to 12/31/73	Cost estimated to complete
220 Fire station	$232,294.00	$116,970.00	$11,697.00	$105,273.00	$ 65,446.66	$102,751.50	$106,230
221 Municipal garage	110,220.00	90,780.00	9,078.00	81,702.00	47,602.00	76,578.18	9,040
224 Fire station	121,950.00	12,250.00	1,250.00	11,025.00	392.12	11,486.84	100,250
	$464,464.00	$220,000.00	$22,000.00	$198,000.00	$113,440.78	$190,816.52	$215,520

The status report of contracts in process (see Exhibit 5) as of December 31, 1973 showed that three contracts having a total value of $464,464 were in various stages of completion. A total cost of $190,816.52 had been incurred to date on these contracts. Of the three contracts the company had in process at the close of the calendar year, two were for fire stations and one for a municipal garage. All contracts had been started after August 1973 and were estimated to be completed in the spring or early summer of 1974. No revenue or costs on these contracts had been recorded in the income statement for 1973.

OUTLOOK FOR 1974

The officers of the company felt that the construction outlook for their area was not too bright. Overall construction activity seemed likely to be high, but the officers believed that profit margins would fall. Increasing competition in the field of institutional construction was expected because a downturn in residential building was forcing residential contractors into the institutional field. As a result, the company had lowered its provision for general overhead and profit in recent bids for new contracts to approximately 10 percent of the contract sales value. In the past, it had been company practice to include a profit of 10 percent, plus a provision for general and administrative overhead of 5 percent in its proposals. Although the officers realized that it was possible that the company might register losses on one or more contracts as a result of bidding at a lower figure than normal, they felt that the losses, if incurred, would be small, and hoped that, in the aggregate, volume would tend to wash out any individual loss and give the company a fair profit. Company records showed that where losses had been incurred on contracts in the past, they had never exceeded 11 percent of the contract value.

Company officers expected to submit bids in 1974 on projects that were similar in nature to projects in progress or recently completed. As of January 8, 1974, the company had no backlog of contracts on which it had not started work. Activity in the granting of contracts was usually low in January and February but customarily picked up in March.

It was not the present intention of company officers to try to obtain contracts for projects having an individual value in excess of $400,000. There were several reasons for this policy. First was the fact that officers desired to spread the risk between a number of contracts. Second was a consideration of keeping the company name before the architects in the area. Architects generally acted as agents for project owners and were usually responsible for examining the reliability of contractors who were bidding on a project. Contractors who were unknown or not considered reliable usually had their bids eliminated from further consideration. The officers of the company recalled that it had taken several years to acquaint architects in their area with the company name and its ability to perform a job. If they committed the company to one or two large long-term contracts, the officers believed they would effectively remove the name of the company from the sight of architects for a considerable period of time. They were unwilling to do this since they felt that they would have difficulty in reestablishing the company with architects when the long-term contracts were completed.

A third reason for not seeking contracts over $400,000 concerned the very important role of the bonding companies. Charles Crowne Company, like every contractor, was usually required to post certain bonds with the architect (or the project owner) which guaranteed that the company would complete the contract according to specifications. Frequently, a clause was included in contracts which specified that the contractor would pay a penalty if the project was not completed by a given date. Nonfulfillment of the stated provisions could result in the forfeiture of the bond and a consequent payment by the bonding company in the stipulated amount of the coverage to the architect and project owner. In order to prevent contractors from overextending themselves, the bonding companies imposed a maximum limit on the contracts that any contractor could have outstanding at any one time. The bonding companies would not provide a bond on a contract if as a result of taking on this contract the total sales value of outstanding contracts exceeded 10 times the contractor's net worth. Thus, with the Charles Crowne Company's net worth as of December 31, 1973 of $123,080.52, total contracts of $1,230,800 could be handled at the present time. Therefore, by taking on contracts having a value over $400,000, the officers believed the company would be restricted in satisfying the first and second considerations outlined above. Even if the ratio should be suddenly increased, thereby allowing the company to expand its work, there would be further problems of obtaining a capable work force and acquiring the necessary equipment.

ACCOUNTING PROCESS

Recording of costs

The company's accounting system was not complex and was capable of being handled on a part-time basis by an outside accountant. This accountant worked two nights a week at the company offices updating the cost and general ledgers, the general journal, and handling other necessary accounting work. The accountant's main job was to keep accurate records of the costs incurred for each job or contract. Separate subledgers for each contract were kept to facilitate this work.

As job costs were incurred by the company, they were posted or charged to the appropriate job or contract ledger after being recorded in the general journal. A voucher was also made out recording the supplier's or subcontractor's name and address along with the amount payable and filed as a liability. Charges for company-employed labor were recorded at the job site and forwarded back to the office. The recording specified for each man, the hours worked, his rate, and the nature of the work performed. These records along with being posted to the appropriate jobs, were also used as the basis for computing payrolls. The total of the balances in the job ledger accounts was the company's "work in process."

The job cost accounts tended to be similar for each job. Separate sub-accounts were maintained for each subcontract. For instance, on Job 220, a fire station under construction, there were over 20 subcontracts for various portions of the total job.

Separate job subaccounts were also established for major categories of direct costs incurred by the company. For example, separate job accounts were kept for company masonry labor and carpentry labor and for company-purchased masonry and carpeting materials. Separate project accounts were also provided when unusual portions of a contract were to be completed by the company. For instance, in completing Job 220 the company was to install the slide poles to be used in the fire station, and also erect a flagpole. Costs incurred for these purposes would be charged to special slide pole and flag-pole accounts. In addition, job accounts were established for the supervisory costs of each job and for the cost of performance bond insurance.

Finally, a separate account called General Conditions was also established for each job. It was used for all job costs not charged to other accounts. The account contained such items as the cost of the construction shack, telephone and other utilities, general office supplies, wages of timekeeper and watchman (if necessary), and the wages of laborers that could not be easily separated into other accounts. This account did not include any of the company's general and administrative expenses which were not allocated to the jobs.

Billing

On contracts in process the Charles Crowne Company usually submitted a monthly "application for payment" to the architect who represented the project owner. Exhibit 6 shows the detail provided on the application. The items with an asterisk beside them are for company portions of the job while remainder are for subcontracted sections of the job.

Several steps were involved in determining the amount billed by the contractor. First, an officer of the company estimated the physical percentage of completion of each major portion of the contract. Thus, in the case of the masonry item on Exhibit 6, it was estimated that masonry work was 90 per-cent complete at the end of the month. Since masonry had been estimated at 78 percent of completion at the close of the prior month, then 12 percent of the $51,200 value attached to masonry, or $6,120, was deemed to be the gross amount that should be billed for the current month. Noteworthy is the fact that costs incurred to date as a percentage of total estimated costs did not determine the percentage of completion. Thus, the gross billing of $6,120 for

316

EXHIBIT 6

APPLICATION FOR PAYMENT

AIA FORM 702

FIELD COPY

CONTRACTOR'S APPLICATION NO. **Four (4)**

ARCHITECT'S JOB No. ___56133___ PERIOD FROM **Dec. 1** TO **Dec. 31**

TO ___City of Burriston___ OWNER, APPLICATION IS MADE FOR

PAYMENT, AS SHOWN BELOW, IN CONNECTION WITH THE ___Architectural___ WORK

FOR YOUR ___Fire Station___ PROJECT

DESCRIPTION OF WORK	CONTRACT AMOUNT	THIS APPLICATION		COMPLETED		BALANCE TO FINISH
		LABOR	MATERIALS	%	TO DATE	
* Performance Bond	2,400				2,400	-
Site Work	3,500				3,150	350
* Masonry	51,200	6,120		90	46,080	5,120
Concrete Work	16,140				8,910	7,230
Precast Concrete Panels	25,520	18,520		72.5	18,520	7,000
Aluminum Sash	8,030					8,030
Sash Erection	1,700					1,700
Structural Steel	24,580				19,600	4,980
Glass & Glazing	5,240					5,240
* Carpentry	8,974					8,974
Finish Hardware	3,080					3,080
Modern Fold Door	740					740
Roofing & Sheet Metal	6,600					6,600
Overhead Doors	21,560					21,560
Hollow Metal Work	6,640				2,000	4,640
Resilient Floor & Base	3,390					3,390
Hard Tile	1,540					1,540
Acoustical Work	3,300					3,300
* Chalkboard & Tackboards	500					500
* Caulking & Weatherstrips	1,020					1,020
* Aluminum Sign Allowance	600					600
* Plaque Allowance	400					400
* Exterior Louvers	730				730	-
* Slide Poles	9,020		8,020	89	8,020	
Asphalt Paving	5,620				2,810	2,810
* Flag Pole	1,020		750	73.5	750	270
Plastering	4,710					4,710
Painting	3,190					3,190
Toilet Partitions	620					620
* General Conditions	6,400	1,000		62.5	4,000	2,400
Curtain Wall Panels	4,330					4,330
TOTAL	232,294	25,640	8,770	50	116,970	115,324

THIS IS TO CERTIFY THAT THE WORK AS LISTED ABOVE HAS BEEN COMPLETED IN ACCORDANCE WITH THE CONTRACT DOCUMENTS, THAT ALL LAWFUL CHARGES FOR LABOR, MATERIALS, ETC., COVERED BY PREVIOUS CERTIFICATES FOR PAYMENT HAVE BEEN PAID AND THAT A PAYMENT IS NOW DUE IN THE AMOUNT OF

___Thirty Four Thousand, Four Hundred, and 10 100/00___ DOLLARS ($ ___34,410.00___)

FROM WHICH RETAINAGE OF ___10___ % AS SET OUT IN THE CONTRACT DOCUMENTS SHALL BE DEDUCTED $ 3,441.00

Net Billing $ 30,969.00

___Charles Crowne Company___ CONTRACTOR

DATE ___1/3___ 19 _74_   PER ___Larry Shane___

(COPYRIGHT 1953 THE AMERICAN INSTITUTE OF ARCHITECTS)

the current month could be either equal to, less than, or greater than the actual costs incurred in the month plus the allowances for profit and overhead that were predicated in bidding the job.

As in the case of masonry, a similar estimating procedure was followed on the other items of the job. The items were then summed to obtain the gross billing for the current month. From this total gross billing an amount called retainage, agreed to in the contract as 10 percent of the gross billing, was deducted to obtain the net billing due the contractor. The application was then forwarded to the architect who had the job of verifying the percentage of physical completion claimed by the contractor. If the architect considered the percentage billed as valid, he certified the application and requested on a separate form that the project owner forward the net billing to the contractor. The contractor usually received his progress payment within 15 days after the date of billing.

Recording of income

As mentioned above, the company used the completed contract method in recording income from contracts. Under this system the profit or loss on a contract was not booked until the contract was completed and accepted by the project owner.

The company recorded the billings, net of retainage, with an entry such as the following one for Job 220 in December:

	Debit	Credit
Accounts Receivable—Contracts (Job 220)	30,969.00	
Work in Process (Job 220)		30,969.00

Using this method the work in process account for Job 220 had a credit balance in it as of December 31, 1973 which represented billings (net of retainage) in excess of costs.

At the final billing of a contract, the company billed the owner for all retainage using the same entry as above, and thus crediting the retainage to the Work in Process account. When the contract was complete, the credit balance in the Work in Process account was the profit on the contract. This amount was then closed out to a profit and loss account.

QUESTIONS

1. Determine the effect on net income for 1973 of the three incomplete projects (Exhibit 5) if the percentage-of-completion method of revenue recognition is adopted by Charles Crowne Company for financial statement (but not income tax) purposes. Consider each of the following methods of estimating degree of completion:
   a. Percentage of cost incurred to total estimated cost.
   b. Independent estimate of degree of completion as used by Charles Crowne Company for billing purposes. (It may be assumed that billings have been brought up to date as of December 31, 1973.

2. How would the adoption of a percentage-of-completion method be reflected on the Charles Crowne Company balance sheet as of December 31, 1973?

3. Assume that during January 1974, additional costs of $17,248.50 were incurred on Job 220. Difficulties were encountered during the month, and on January 31, 1974,

it is estimated that the cost to complete the project will amount to $100,000. As of January 31, 1974, gross billings on Job 220 total $125,000. Using the two percentage-of-completion methods, determine the effect of Job 220 on net income for January.

4. What should John Crowne's recommendations be?

⸻⸺◄CASE III–4►⸺⸻
Metroplex Developers, Inc.

Jeff Deerfield, president of Metroplex Developers, Inc., was sitting in his Dallas office thinking about a recent conversation between himself, the firm's vice presidents of finance and marketing, and the firm's corporate controller. It had been a particularly eventful year for Metroplex. The disagreements that had arisen during this recent conversation seemed somehow to highlight this fact in Jeff's mind.

The conversation, and the resulting disagreement, had focused upon the operating statement for one aspect of Metroplex's activities during the past year. The particular aspect in question was the commercial center portion of the fledgling firm's North *Royal* development project. As this was the firm's first major project, it seemed to Jeff that he should be particularly sensitive to how this particular disagreement was resolved.

COMPANY BACKGROUND

Metroplex Developers, Inc., was a joint venture formed and financed by Sierra Industries, Inc., and the Lucerne Investors Group. The former was a significant factor in the North American pulp, paper, and lumber industry. It was based in a medium-sized city in the Pacific Northwest region of the United States. The latter was an investment firm with administrative offices located in Zug, Switzerland. It represented a small but influential group of European investors. Both firms were privately held.

Metroplex Developers, Inc., had been formed in mid-1976. It was the final result of a series of discussions and negotiations between the two parent firms that had begun in late 1974. Both of the parents were committed, for somewhat different reasons, to the idea of building a significant market position in the land development and real estate investment business in the state of Texas.

This case was prepared by Professor M. Edgar Barrett, with the assistance of Leslie Cox and Charles T. Sharpless, research assistants. Copyright © 1978 by M. Edgar Barrett.

Officers of both of the parent firms had agreed that no funds would be withdrawn from the joint venture during the first five years of its life. Any cash flow resulting from Metroplex's activities was to be reinvested in the business. Also, the parent firms had agreed, in principle, to provide possible further infusions of capital. These further infusions might, under certain conditions, amount to as much as $5 million each during this initial five-year period.

This commitment of financial resources on the part of the parent firms followed from their expressed intent of seeing that Metroplex Developers, Inc., was capable of capitalizing upon any attractive investment or development opportunities that might develop over the next few years. They both desired that Metroplex become a significant factor in the fast-growing metropolitan area encompassing the cities of Dallas and Fort Worth, Texas. A later move into the Houston and San Antonio markets had also been discussed.

THE NORTH ROYAL PROJECT

The first project attempted by the Metroplex Developers' management team involved a 140-acre parcel of land located adjacent to a major expressway running north out of downtown Dallas. The land, located some 15 miles north of the city center, was purchased in September 1976, at a price of $4,313,000.

The site was bounded on the north by a major east-west thoroughfare. A recent bond election had resulted in the approval of funds necessary to widen this thoroughfare to six lanes. The road improvement project was tentatively scheduled for completion in late 1979.

The site was seen as particularly attractive due to its proximity to several large employers and to the fast-growing North Dallas residential area. Several major electronics firms were located within a five-mile radius of the property. Two major industrial parks were located within the same distance. Much of the recent residential growth in Dallas County had occurred in the same general area.

After gaining approval from the local zoning authorities, the parcel of land was divided into three major components and the entire project was dubbed *North Royal*. The three major sections of the project were identifiable primarily by their intended end use. The first section, destined to contain retail stores, small shops, and several small office buildings, involved the 30 acres of the property located closest to the expressway. It was this piece of land that was at the center of the current disagreement.

The second section of land covered approximately 50 acres and was destined to be occupied by a multifamily unit subdivision. The third section, located farthest from the expressway, was to be developed into a single family unit subdivision.

Metroplex began to develop the original farm land into plots suitable for development purposes in early 1977. The land was first surveyed, with corner markers installed. The plat plan—inasmuch as it related to public streets—was then filed with, and approved by, the city. The firm then focused most of its energy upon preparing the commercial center portion of the project.

The land was first cleared of buildings and vegetation. Several portions of the property were filled or graded to remove excessive depressions or elevations. Storm drains, sewer pipes, and water mains were then installed. Large mains were also installed at this point to carry the yet-to-be-installed underground utilities (e.g., electricity, telephone, and natural gas). Finally, permanent access roads were built and dedicated to the city.

By the end of 1977, well over half of the total land development work expected to be done on the commercial center aspects of the project was complete. Over $700,000 was expended during 1977 on this aspect of the overall North Royal project. Exhibit 2 provides a summary of these costs by category. It also provides an estimate of the remaining expenditures needed to bring the commercial center to a final, salable form.

Three parcels of commercial land were sold during 1977. One was sold to a national motor inn company for use as the site of a 120-unit motor inn. A second was sold to a chain of restaurants and coffee shops for use as a 24-hour coffee shop and restaurant. The third was sold to a regional insurance company. It was to be the site for a seven-storey office building.

Negotiations were also in process in respect to two more parcels. The first, on which a letter of intent had been received, would be occupied by a major local restaurant. The second parcel, on which negotiations had just begun, was destined to be used as the site for a four-storey medical and allied arts building.

Allocation of initial land cost

The most perplexing aspect of the initial accounting for the North Royal project was the allocation of land costs among the three major sections of the overall project. The land destined for use as the commercial center was clearly more valuable than either of the other two sections. Similarly, the land destined for use as apartment sites was felt to be more valuable than that to be used as the location of single family homes. The problem, however, was to determine how much more valuable.

The issue was further clouded by the fact that the entire 140-acre parcel had been zoned as farm land at the time of its purchase by Metroplex. Most of the latter part of 1976 had been spent gaining approval from the local authorities for the three new zoning classifications. Finally, some members of the Metroplex management team had noted that the values of the three sections of the project were most probably interrelated. An attractive and successful commercial center, for example, should enhance the attractiveness of the nearby multifamily unit property.

Clint Eversole, Metroplex's corporate controller, had finally decided to allocate the land cost on the basis of early 1977 fair market values. He received an informal appraisal from a local realty firm and used it as the primary basis for allocation. $1,950,000 was allocated to the commercial center on the basis of a $65,000 per acre appraised value. The multifamily unit section of the property was appraised at $25,300 per acre, which resulted in $1,265,000 of land cost being allocated to this section. The remaining portion of the cost, $1,098,000, was then assigned to the single family unit subdivision.

Discussion of 1977 operating statements

The recent discussion about Metroplex's operating statements had been initiated by Mr. Deerfield. Early in January 1978, he had asked Clint Eversole to prepare a preliminary operating statement summarizing the results of 1977 as they related to the commercial center portion of the North Royal project. Clint prepared the statement shown in Exhibit 1. It was this statement which provoked most of the discussion referred to earlier.

EXHIBIT 1

NORTH ROYAL DEVELOPMENT PROJECT
Commercial Center Portion
Operating Statement
For the Year Ending December 31, 1977

Sales revenue			
Plot number 5		$ 400,100	
Plot number 4		329,350	
Plot number 6		396,396	
Total revenue			$ 1,125,846
Cost of sales			
Allocated land cost		1,950,000	
Development cost incurred to date			
(See Exhibit 2)		707,354	
Total cost of sales			2,657,354
Gross profit			(1,531,508)
Operating Expenses			
Advertising and public relations		9,750	
Commissions to outside brokers		43,767	
Inspection fees		1,480	
Legal and accounting		17,525	
Recording and filing		2,816	
Photo and renderings		3,391	
Salaries: Salespeople	$35,670		
Office	24,366		
Engineering	25,490	85,526	
Property taxes		8,394	
Miscellaneous		2,595	
Total operating expenses			$ 175,244
Net contribution to corporate level			$(1,706,752)

Excerpts from the late January meeting of the four company officers are reproduced below.

Jeff Deerfield (president): You've all had a chance by now to glance over Clint's report. Clint prepared this, at my request, so we would have a chance to review the 1977 results on our North Royal commercial center. It contains, as you can see, the actual cash basis revenues and expenses incurred to date as well as some limited accruals and deferrals.

I must say that I'm concerned about the picture portrayed by this statement. We'll be asked, sooner or later, for a similar set of statements by either Sierra or Lucerne, or both. While neither of them are particularly concerned about short-term earnings, I'm not convinced that this statement gives an honest and accurate portrayal of what we accomplished during 1977.

Christine Crouzier (vice president finance): Clint's report appears to simply ignore the fact that we have an inventory of partially developed lots on hand. Why can't we just total up all of the costs—actual and expected—allocate them across all of the lots and set up an inventory account? Then, we could recognize the revenue we've actually received, along with the matched cost of the lots sold. This would allow us . . .

Pat Reynolds (vice president sales): Hold on a minute, Chris! You're talking about setting this up like a manufacturing company. We're not a manufacturer with a nice regular flow of product.

For example, how would you handle the costs that you deferred and parked in the inventory account if sales happen to slow down or taper off? Real estate is basically a cash flow business, as we all know. Your ideas would result in our ignoring some major out-of-pocket costs.

Christine Crouzier: I understand your concern, Pat. We are in a cash flow business, particularly over the long run. We are also in the capital gains business, however. Our corporate strategy calls for a negative cash flow for most of the next four or five years. That's no justification for showing negative profits as well.

Clint Eversole (corporate controller): We used to use something called the percentage-of-completion method at the construction company where I worked several years ago. Perhaps we could adapt it to fit our needs.

The general idea would be that we recognize our revenues and expenses in proportion to the amount of the project that we have actually completed to date. For example, we've spent about 68 percent of what we expect to spend on the commercial center (Exhibit 2). We could recognize the same proportion of the expected sales revenues. This would certainly come closer to showing the real economics of the project.

Pat Reynolds: I don't buy your idea either! You'd be assuming that we have definite offers at fixed prices for the remaining lots in the commercial center. Besides, how would you handle the lot that we intend to build our own spec[1] building on? Are we to consider it to be sold, as well?

Jeff Deerfield: Clint's idea may not be as bad as it sounds. We're not talking about either tax reporting or reports to the public. Our concern has to be one of how we can best portray the results of our ongoing operation.

---

[1] Speculative [editor].

EXHIBIT 2

NORTH ROYAL DEVELOPMENT PROJECT
Commercial Center Portion
Summary of Actual and Expected Development Costs

Account title	Expenditures during 1977 Materials and subcontract	Labor	Estimated remaining expenditures Materials and subcontract	Labor	Estimated total
100 Lot improvement					
02 Soil and drainage analyses	$ 6,580	—	—	—	$ 6,580
04 Preliminary lot clearing	40,677	$ 10,825	—	—	51,502
06 Stump grinding	8,526	6,472	—	—	14,998
08 Blasting	14,016	—	—	—	14,016
10 General excavation	13,060	12,104	—	—	25,164
12 Landscaping	8,764	—	—	—	8,764
14 Lot grading	23,430	6,204	—	—	29,634
Total	115,053	53,605			150,658
120 Road construction					
21 Surveying	7,438	—	$ 3,567	—	11,005
22 Preliminary clearing	10,311	12,605	—	—	22,916
23 General excavation	14,765	11,231	—	—	25,996
24 Grading	28,450	5,486	15,436	$ 3,689	53,061
25 Gravel and paving	25,630	—	14,325	—	39,955
26 Concrete curbing	8,442	2,014	4,260	2,403	17,119
27 Landscaping	9,450	—	3,211	1,894	14,555
28 Maintenance	4,328	3,114	5,666	4,442	17,550
Total	108,814	34,450	46,465	12,428	202,157
130 Electrical work					
32 Conduits	5,678	—	5,783	—	11,461
34 Copper wiring	15,430	4,251	12,430	3,866	35,977
36 Auxiliary station	35,677	11,856	21,083	9,785	78,401
38 General wiring	10,325	4,332	9,427	4,677	28,761
Total	67,110	20,439	48,723	18,328	154,600
140 Sewage system					
41 6″ sewer	14,327	4,873	10,312	2,649	32,161
43 12″ sewer	35,666	6,547	30,425	5,684	78,322
45 16″ sewer	8,760	4,568	2,427	2,435	18,190
46 Cast iron manholes	9,450	453	7,568	371	17,842
47 Grading	14,323	4,321	10,734	2,877	32,255
49 Maintenance	6,951	2,564	4,992	1,957	16,464
Total	89,477	23,326	66,458	15,973	195,234
150 Drainage system					
52 12″ reinforced concrete piping	12,643	2,541	4,521	1,078	20,783
53 18″ reinforced concrete piping	14,432	4,228	7,964	2,776	29,400
54 24″ reinforced concrete piping	16,367	5,664	7,634	4,422	34,087
56 30″ reinforced concrete piping	9,435	3,510	6,217	1,597	20,759
58 Cast iron manholes	10,667	487	5,321	240	16,715
59 Drainage basins	6,452	400	3,436	212	10,500
Total	69,996	16,830	35,093	10,325	132,244
160 Water mains					
62 6″ copper piping	10,645	2,584	8,430	2,287	23,946
63 10″ copper piping	46,767	7,640	35,429	6,655	96,491
64 12″ copper piping	2,340	1,151	2,421	1,310	7,222
67 Water hydrants	5,380	295	4,237	273	10,185
Total	65,132	11,670	50,517	10,525	137,844
500 Temporary accounts					
12 Temporary lighting	1,540	2,435	—	—	3,975
14 Temporary roads	2,535	5,290	—	—	7,825
16 Temporary drainage	2,420	5,347	—	—	7,767
18 Security	11,425	—	—	—	11,425
Total	17,920	13,072	—	—	30,992
Miscellaneous costs	12,450	6,010	12,773	5,265	36,498
Grand totals	$545,952	$161,402	$260,029	$72,844	$1,040,227

You're right, Pat, that we don't have definite offers for any of our remaining lots. That's why we've got you out pounding the streets. My limited experience in this city, however, is that the price of developed land only goes one way—up! Thus, we'll probably gain by not having all of our lots sold.

Pat Reynolds: I'm not convinced. You people may well be on the way to creating a monster. Our operations are really quite complex.

EXHIBIT 3
North Royal development project: Plot plan for entire project

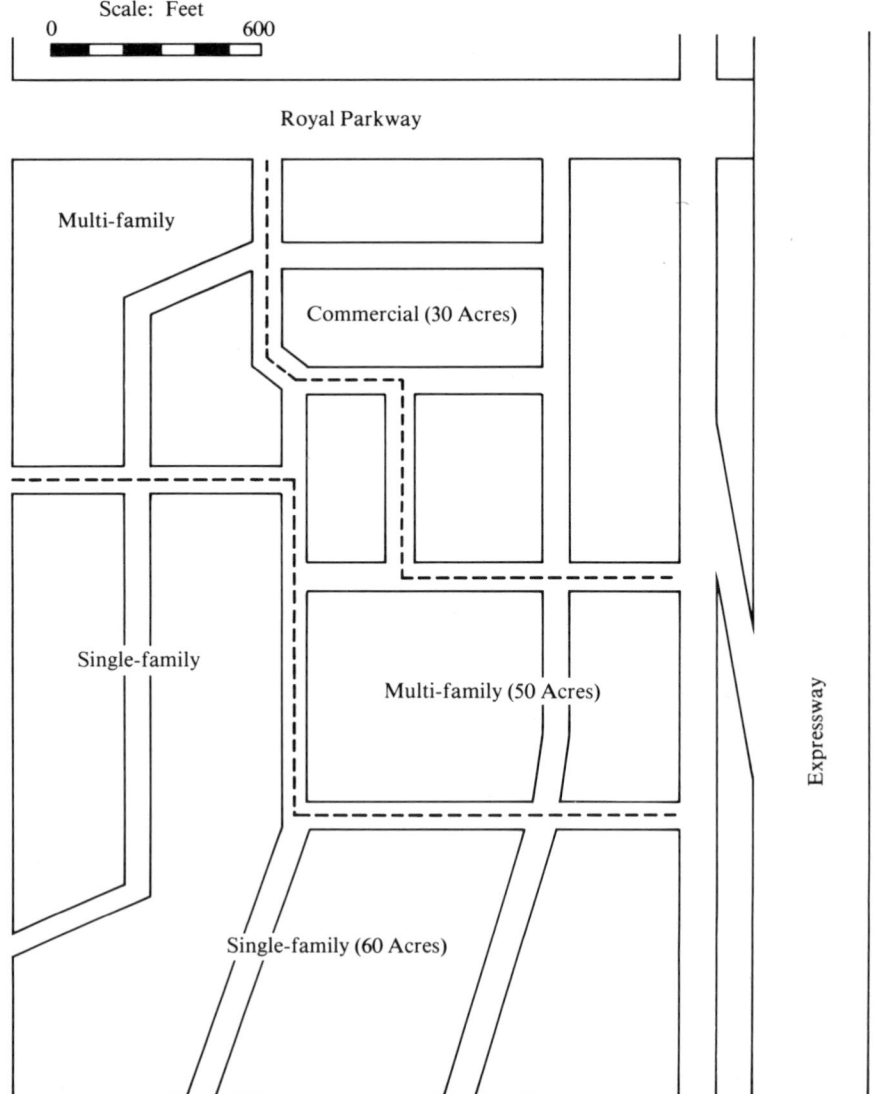

For example, we knowingly gave La Hacienda a 20 percent discount on our asking price in order to get them in early. We did the same thing with our sale to Golden Plates Enterprises. Do these plots represent less profitable sales, an investment in the future, or both?

In addition, we don't really know whether the letter of intent on the restaurant plot will ever be exercised.

Christine Crouzier: We know our business is complex, Pat. You ignore a few other issues, however. For example, there is the problem that Clint's current reporting method is going to result in a very low reported cost for the lot that we intend to develop by ourselves.

Pat Reynolds: That's fine with me. We'd at least be conservative in our measurement.

Jeff Deerfield: It seems to me that we better get our act cleaned up on this matter. It's only a matter of a month or so before our backers come down for their annual visit. We'd be smart if we had this issue resolved well before then.

Clint, why don't you work with Pat and Chris individually and come up with two or three pro forma operating statements? We'll then get back together to resolve the issue.

EXHIBIT 4
North Royal development project: Commercial center portion

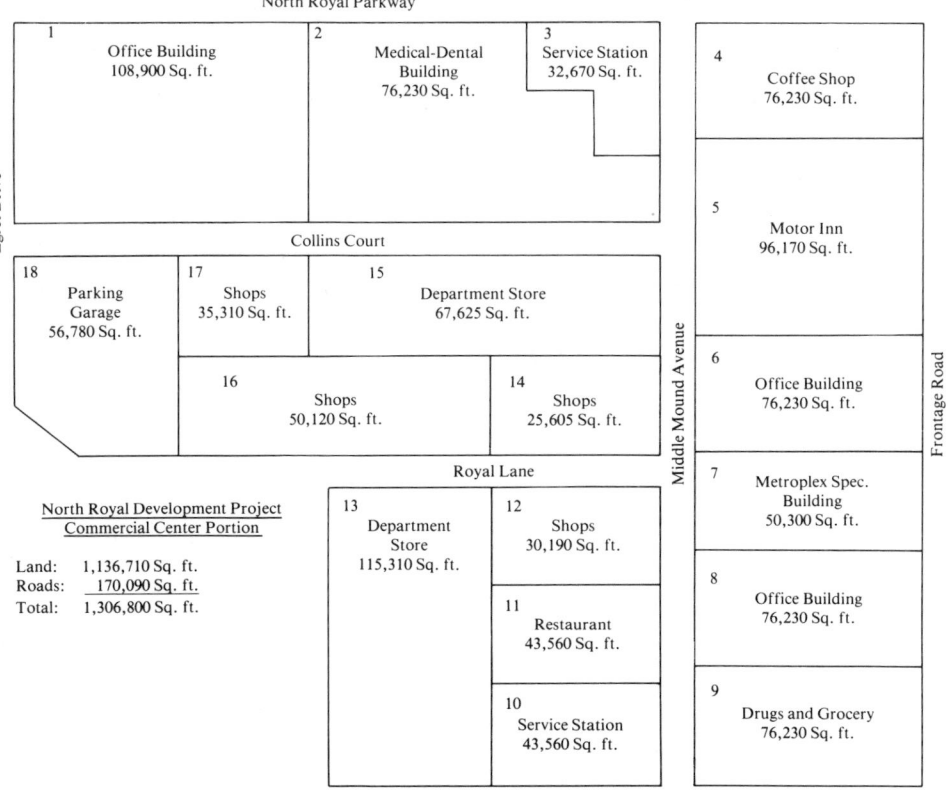

EXHIBIT 5
North Royal development project: Commercial center sales summary

| | Basic data | | | | | Supplementary data | | | | |
Plat number	Date of sale	Actual selling price	Budgeted price	Variance from budget	Planned occupant or buyer	Square feet	Footage percent	Frontage feet	Price per foot	Comments
1	—	—	$ 555,390	—	Office building	108,900	8.3	1,126	$5.10	—
2	Discussion stage	—	388,773	—	Medical Leasing, Inc.	76,230	5.8	709	5.10	Currently negotiating
3	—	—	169,884	—	Service station	32,670	2.5	416	5.20	—
4	June 1977	$329,350	411,642	$(82,292)	Golden Plate Enterprises	76,230	5.8	761	5.40	Restaurant to open 2/1/78
5	July 1977	400,100	500,084	(99,984)	La Hacienda Motor Inns	96,170	7.4	514	5.20	Inn under construction
6	Nov. 1977	396,396	396,396	0	Sun Belt Insurance Group	76,230	5.8	416	5.20	Groundbreaking due 3/1/78
7	—	—	261,560	—	Metroplex spec building	50,300	3.8	318	5.20	—
8	—	—	396,396	—	Office building	76,230	5.8	416	5.20	—
9	—	—	396,396	—	Drugs and grocery	76,230	5.8	761	5.20	—
10	—	—	209,088	—	Service station	43,560	3.3	416	4.80	—
11	Pending	—	209,088	—	Turf 'N' Surf, Inc.	43,560	3.3	208	4.80	Letter of intent received
12	—	—	144,912	—	Shops	30,190	3.3	367	4.80	—
13	—	—	518,895	—	Department store	115,310	8.8	991	4.50	—
14	—	—	120,312	—	Shops	25,065	2.0	324	4.80	—
15	—	—	324,600	—	Department store	67,625	5.3	566	4.80	—
16	—	—	225,540	—	Shops	50,120	3.8	416	4.50	—
17	—	—	169,488	—	Shops	35,310	2.8	208	4.80	—
18	—	—	255,510	—	Parking garage	56,780	4.3	732	4.50	—
Roads	—	—	—	—	—	170,090	13.0	—	—	—
Totals			$5,603,954			1,306,800	100.0	9,665	—	

──CASE III-5──

Stirling Homex (A)

During the late 1960s a number of companies, spurred by the Department of Housing and Urban Development's (HUD) $67 million "Operation Breakthrough," attempted to revolutionize the technology of the housing industry. One of these companies, Stirling Homex, pioneered the concept of "modular" housing which used many of the techniques of automobile assembly to mass produce, transport, and install large numbers of completed housing units in clusters. The substantial savings in labor costs due to mass production and the ability to construct entire housing projects on site in a matter of days were especially attractive to federal, state and local housing authorities searching for ways to improve housing, particularly for lower income groups.

Stirling Homex was started in 1967 by William and David Stirling, Jr., brothers who ran a small homebuilding company in Avon, New York. The company obtained risk capital from Harper Sibley, Jr., a Western Union heir who was an experienced construction investor, in order to begin mass production. Homex estimated it could build a modular home, exclusive of land, for between $16,000 and $25,000. From the beginning, the company attracted considerable national publicity through its technological innovations and its close identification with HUD. Several HUD bureaucrats joined the Homex management and HUD secretary George W. Romney was flown by Homex to Avon to see the company's facilities. Homex used some of its first modular units for a suburban Rochester housing project with 275 dwelling units; on-site construction was completed in 36 hours. In 1969, the company developed a system of jacks to raise modules so other units could be slipped under them without the use of a crane. The next year Homex sent a 2,000-feet-long train of modules to Corinth, Mississippi to supply emergency housing after a hurricane destroyed hundreds of homes. Homex was the first to transport modular units by train.

Between 1969 and 1970 when Homex went public, the company sold most of its units in the Rochester area, more than half, according to some sources, to companies in which the Homex management had investments. The offering prospectus showed earnings of $1 million on sales of $10 million for fiscal 1969. The public issue of stock came out in February 1970 at

---

This case was prepared by Assistant Professor M. Edgar Barrett with the assistance of Jonathan Brown, research assistant.

$16.50 a share and doubled within 24 hours. By the middle of March Homex stock was selling for $51.75.

In 1970, Homex won a HUD contract to construct a 13-storey apartment house in Memphis. The company also said it had a "tentative understanding" with the Greater Gulfport (Mississippi) Housing Development Corporation to build $100 million worth of modular housing. To produce for what the company saw as a lucrative market in the South, Homex planned to lease a 350,000-square-feet plant in Gulfport. The plant would be financed by county industrial revenue bonds to be approved by local voters.

The 1971 annual report revealed Homex's intention to market its products to a broader consumer spectrum. In addition to public housing projects and high rise apartments, the company was offering modular units for town-houses, rivate residences, college housing, efficiency apartments, hotels, and motels. During the year the company doubled its manufacturing facilities at Avon and created the U.S. Shelter Corporation, a wholly owned subsidiary, to provide construction and permanent financing for its customers. Earnings per share were 24 cents in fiscal 1970 and 37 cents in 1971. Management anticipated increased sales and revenues for fiscal 1972.

REVENUE RECOGNITION

Stirling Homex recognized the sale of a modular unit when it was produced if the unit was assigned to a specific contract and if there was an identified site plan and a financially capable purchaser. Homex did not require progress payments from its buyers nor did the company demand that the housing site itself be approved by the purchaser. Some of the contracts were in the form of letters of intention to buy from reputable institutions such as public housing authorities whose final decisions were often delayed by red tape, changing budgets or the necessity of seeking voter approval through public referenda.

According to people familiar with the company, Homex's profit margin came essentially from the production of modular units; revenues from installation operations, recognized on a percentage of completion basis, were allocated on an estimated break even point. Neither the February 1970 offering prospectus nor the July 1970 annual report broke down revenues and costs between production and installation. The 1970 annual report stated that "contracts generally provided for payment upon completion and receipt of all approvals necessary for occupancy, or for payment upon completion of each respective phase." Because of the quality of its receivables, due in the most part from public housing authorities, no provision for doubtful accounts was considered necessary.

Exhibit 1 contains a complete set of Homex's audited financial statements for the fiscal year ended July 31, 1971.

EXHIBIT 1

STIRLING HOMEX CORPORATION AND CONSOLIDATED SUBSIDIARIES
Consolidated Balance Sheets July 31, 1971
With Comparative Figures for 1970

Assets

	1971	1970
Current assets:		
Cash (Note 11)	$ 3,196,457	$ 2,778,077
Preferred stock proceeds receivable (Note 2)	19,000,000	—
Receivables (Notes 1 and 3)	37,845,572	15,486,119
Inventories (Note 5):		
Raw materials, work in process and salable merchandise at lower of cost (first-in, first-out) or replacement market	2,614,200	2,167,603
Land held for development or sale, at cost	1,878,343	1,583,621
Prepaid expenses and other current assets	226,530	124,765
Total current assets	64,761,102	22,140,185
Investment in unconsolidated subsidiary (Note 1)	1,134,579	—
Long-term receivables (Note 4)	4,225,349	541,124
Property, plant, and equipment at cost, less accumulated depreciation and amortization: 1971—$733, 705; 1970—$230,921 (Notes 6 and 8)	9,426,941	5,245,745
Deferred charges, less accumulated amortization: 1971—$586,011; 1970—$153,894 (Note 7)	2,558,792	944,109
	$82,106,763	$28,871,163

Liabilities and Stockholders' Equity

	1971	1970
Current liabilities:		
Current portion of long-term debt (Note 8)	$ 295,630	$ 333,036
Notes payable to banks–unsecured (1971—6 to 6½%; 1970—8 to 8½%) (Note 11)	37,700,000	11,700,000
Accounts payable	4,025,254	2,480,834
Due to unconsolidated subsidiary (Note 1)	76,894	—
Accrued expenses and other liabilities	577,377	232,819
Current and deferred income taxes (Note 9)	3,528,125	1,387,338
Total current liabilities	46,203,280	16,134,027
Long-term debt (Note 8)	236,588	496,489
Deferred income taxes (Note 9)	2,098,767	587,265
Option deposit on land contract (Note 5)	235,000	—
Stockholders' equity:		
$2.40 cumulative convertible preferred stock (Note 2):		
Authorized 500,000 shares, $1.00 par value; shares subscribed: 1971—500,000 (aggregate involuntary liquidation value—$20,000,000); 1970—none	500,000	—
Common stock (Notes 2 and 10):		
Authorized 15,000,000 shares, $.01 par value; shares issued: 1971—8,909,200; 1970—8,897,400	89,092	88,974
Additional paid-in capital (Note 2)	26,554,453	8,446,738
Retained earnings	6,370,333	3,117,670
	33,513,878	11,653,382
Less treasury stock at cost (60,000 shares)	180,750	—
Total stockholders' equity	33,333,128	11,653,382
Commitments and contingencies (Note 11)		
	$82,106,763	$28,871,163

See accompanying Notes to Consolidated Financial Statements

EXHIBIT 1 (*continued*)
STIRLING HOMEX CORPORATION AND CONSOLIDATED SUBSIDIARIES
Consolidated Statement of Income
Year Ended July 31, 1971 with Comparative Figures for 1970

	1971	*1970*
Revenues:		
Manufacturing division—trade (Note 3)	$29,482,271	$16,492,770
Installation division (Note 3):		
Trade	7,230,878	5,601,357
Affiliate	—	459,941
Equity in undistributed net income of subsidiary (Note 1)	134,579	—
Total revenues	36,847,728	22,554,068
Costs and expenses:		
Cost of sales:		
Manufacturing division	17,729,078	9,919,327
Installation division	6,601,413	5,240,388
Administrative and selling expenses	4,048,113	2,390,604
Interest expense	1,838,461	648,181
Total costs and expenses	30,217,065	18,198,500
Income before federal and state income taxes	6,630,663	4,355,568
Federal and state income taxes (Note 9):		
Current	368,000	1,965,982
Deferred	3,010,000	354,397
	3,378,000	2,320,379
Net income	$ 3,252,663	$ 2,035,189
Average common shares outstanding (Note 12)	8,881,938	8,649,483
Earnings per common share (Note 12)	$ .37	$ .24

See accompanying Notes to Consolidated Financial Statements

STIRLING HOMEX CORPORATION AND CONSOLIDATED SUBSIDIARIES
Consolidated Statement of Changes in Financial Position
Year Ended July 31, 1971 with Comparative Figures for 1970

	1971	*1970*
Source of working capital:		
Net income	$ 3,252,663	$2,035,189
Expenses not requiring outlay of working capital:		
Depreciation and amortization	529,116	220,227
Amortization of deferred charges	432,117	133,288
Deferred income taxes (noncurrent)	1,511,502	184,776
Undistributed net income of finance subsidiary	(134,579)	—
Working capital provided from operations	5,590,819	2,573,480
Net proceeds from sales of stock:		
Public offering of common stock	—	5,985,715
Private sale of common stock	—	516,500
Common stock issued under qualified stock option plan	37,200	—
Public offering of preferred stock	18,570,633	—
Long-term borrowings	51,402	124,677
Decrease in long-term receivables	10,000	43,421
Option deposit received on land contract	235,000	—
Total source of working capital	24,495,054	9,243,793

EXHIBIT 1 (*continued*)

	1971	1970
Application of working capital:		
Purchase of treasury stock...............................	180,750	—
Additions to property, plant and equipment	4,710,312	4,422,506
Additions to deferred charges..........................	2,046,800	735,093
Reduction in long-term debt.............................	311,303	3,052,140
Increase in noncurrent portion of long-term receivables........	3,694,225	—
Investment in unconsolidated subsidiary....................	1,000,000	—
Total application of working capital	11,943,390	8,209,739
Increase in working capital	$12,551,664	$1,034,054
Changes in working capital:		
Increase in current assets:		
Cash	$ 418,380	$ 1,357,917
Preferred stock proceeds receivable	19,000,000	—
Receivables	22,359,453	12,286,631
Inventories..	741,319	1,236,215
Prepaid expenses and other current assets..................	101,765	34,973
	42,620,917	14,915,736
Increase in current liabilities:		
Current portion of long-term debt and notes payable to banks...	25,962,594	10,721,700
Accounts payable and accrued expenses	1,888,978	2,155,635
Due to unconsolidated subsidiary	76,894	—
Current and deferred income taxes	2,140,787	1,004,347
	30,069,253	13,881,682
Increase in working capital	$12,551,664	$1,034,054

During the year ended July 31, 1971, the Company assigned $4,650,000 of its accounts receivable, without recourse, to an unconsolidated subsidiary for which that subsidiary paid $4,650,000 to the Company. See Note 1.

STIRLING HOMEX CORPORATION AND CONSOLIDATED SUBSIDIARIES
Consolidated Statements of Additional Paid-In Capital and Retained Earnings
Year Ended July 31, 1971 with Comparative Figures for 1970

	1971	1970
Additional paid-in capital:		
Balance at beginning of period	$ 8,446,738	$1,949,813
Excess of proceeds over par value of 400,000 shares of common stock issued in public offering (less expenses of $118,285)	—	5,981,715
Excess of proceeds over par value of 129,000 shares of common stock issued in private sales (less applicable expenses)	—	515,210
Excess of proceeds over par value of 500,000 shares of preferred stock issued in public offering (less expenses of $429,367) (Note 2)	18,070,633	—
Excess of proceeds over par value of 11,800 common shares issued under stock options (Note 10)	37,082	—
Balance at end of period	$26,554,453	$8,446,738

See accompanying Notes to Consolidated Financial Statements

EXHIBIT 1 (*continued*)

	1971	1970
Retained earnings:		
Balance at beginning of period	$ 3,117,670	1,082,481
Net income	3,252,663	2,035,189
Balance at end of period	$ 6,370,333	$3,117,670

Notes to consolidated financial statements July 31, 1971

(1) Principles of Consolidation

The consolidated financial statements include the accounts of the Company and its subsidiaries except for U.S. Shelter Corporation, its financing subsidiary (all of which are wholly-owned). The Company carries its investment in all subsidiaries at equity in the underlying net assets. On consolidation, all significant accounts and transactions with consolidated subsidiaries have been eliminated.

The following are condensed financial statements of the unconsolidated financing subsidiary:

Balance Sheet
July 31, 1971

Assets

Cash	$ 5,171
Accounts receivable—unbilled (Note a)	4,950,000
Other assets	24,593
Due from parent company	76,894
	$5,056,658

Liabilities and Stockholder's Equity

Notes payable—bank (7%) (Note b)	$3,750,000
Payables, accruals and other liabilities	172,079
Stockholder's equity	1,134,579
	$5,056,658

Statement of Income
From Date of Incorporation
(September 25, 1970) to July 31, 1971

Finance income	$544,946
General and administrative expenses	
(including interest expense of $54,917)	263,367
	281,579
Federal and state income taxes—current	147,000
Net income.......................	$134,579

Notes:

(a) Accounts receivable includes $4,650,000 relating to accounts assigned to U.S. Shelter by the Company for which U.S. Shelter remitted cash.

(b) The subsidiary has obtained an unsecured $15,000,000 line of credit from a bank. These funds are being used in financing transactions involving customers of the Company. The Company has not guaranteed this line of credit.

(2) Preferred Stock Offering

On July 29, 1971, the Company, through its underwriters, offered 500,000 shares of $2.40 cumulative convertible preferred stock to the public at $40 per share. Net proceeds of $19,000,000, after deducting an underwriting discount, were received by the Company on August 5, 1971. Additional paid-in capital has been credited with the net proceeds received less the par value of the stock issued ($500,000) and expenses related to the offering ($429,367).

The preferred stock is nonvoting except for certain defined events which would significantly affect the preferred stockholders' equity interests. The preferred shares are convertible into

EXHIBIT 1 (*continued*)

1,379,310 common shares subject to adjustment in certain events, including stock split-ups and stock dividends. At its option, the Company may redeem the preferred stock at an initial price of $50 per share, as of August 1, 1971, ranging downward annually to $40 per share as of August 1, 1981 and thereafter.

(3) Receivables

The Company enters into various modular housing sales contracts which contain an allocation of the sales price between modules (based upon published price lists) and installation work. Sales of modules (Manufacturing Division) are recognized when units are manufactured and assigned to specific contracts. Installation work (Installation Division) is recorded on the percentage of completion method. The contracts generally provide for payment upon completion and receipt of all approvals necessary for occupancy, or for payment upon completion of each respective phase. "Unbilled" receivables represent recorded sales on contracts in process for which billings will be rendered in the future in accordance with the contracts.

Receivables consist of:

	July 31, 1971	July 31, 1970
Contract receivables:		
Billed	$10,382,626	$10,559,145
Unbilled	24,633,799	4,626,370
Total	35,016,425	15,185,515
Income tax refund receivable (Note 9)	2,498,672	—
Current portion of long-term receivables (Note 4)	12,500	17,500
Other receivables	317,975	283,104
	$37,845,572	$15,486,119

Substantially all sales are to local housing authorities and sponsors who qualify for financial assistance from federal agencies of the U.S. Government or who have made arrangements for long-term financing. In light of this, no provision for doubtful accounts is considered necessary.

See the condensed financial statements of U.S. Shelter Corporation in Note 1 for information with respect to receivables assigned by the Company to U.S. Shelter Corporation.

(4) Long-Term Receivables

Long-term receivables consist of:

	July 31, 1971	July 31, 1970
Mortgages receivable:		
Mortgage due June 1, 1974— payments of $2,500 due quarterly with interest at the prime commercial rate in effect on the interest payment date	$ 241,624	$256,624
Mortgage due June 30, 1975— payments of $25,000 due June 30, 1973 and June 30, 1974 and the balance due June 30, 1975. Interest payable annually at the prime commercial rate in effect on the interest payment date	302,000	302,000
	543,624	558,624
Less installments due within one year (Note 3)	12,500	17,500
	531,124	541,124
Long-term portion of contract receivables—unbilled	3,694,225	—
	$4,225,349	$541,124

The mortgage notes are secured by mortgages on the property sold.

334

EXHIBIT 1 (*continued*)

(5) Inventories

Inventories of the Company consist of the following:

	July 31, 1971	*July 31, 1970*
Raw material............	$1,439,960	$ 963,664
Work in process	1,001,632	139,531
Salable merchandise	172,608	1,064,408
	$2,614,200	$2,167,603

Land held for development or sale is recorded at cost plus real estate taxes, mortgage interest, and other related carrying costs. The Company has entered into a contract to sell a parcel of the land with costs of $673,017 for a sale price of $2,100,000. The Company has received nonrefundable payments of $235,000 which have been accounted for as an option deposit.

(6) Property, Plant, and Equipment

Property, plant, and equipment consist of the following:

	Useful life	*July 31, 1971*	*July 31, 1970*
Land and land improvements	20	$ 1,136,499	$1,002,067
Buildings	10 & 45	4,822,055	1,702,924
Machinery, equipment, and tools	2–10	1,735,396	1,071,515
Furniture, fixtures, and office equipment	5–10	942,131	500,951
Other	1–15	135,952	27,998
Construction in progress		1,388,613	1,171,211
		10,160,646	5,476,666
Less accumulated depreciation and amortization		733,705	230,921
		$ 9,426,941	$5,245,745

The straight-line method of depreciation is used for all depreciable assets. Depreciation expense for the years ended July 31, 1971 and 1970 is $529,116 and $220,227; respectively.

(7) Deferred Charges

The unamortized balance of deferred charges consist of:

	Amortization period	*Unamortized balance*	
		July 31, 1971	*July 31, 1970*
Patents pending and trademarks	Legal Life	$ 171,680	$ 88,660
Training and professional development....................	3 years	491,641	148,636
Research and development	5 years	671,897	84,496
Project and production start-up costs	2 to 5 years	844,028	503,539
Property acquisition costs	(a)	379,546	118,778
		$2,558,792	$944,109

(a) Expenditures in connection with property acquisition will be added to the cost of property subsequently acquired.

In the event of project abandonment or other circumstances causing a loss of value to deferred items, the related unamortized costs are charged to current operations.

EXHIBIT 1 (*continued*)

(8) Long-Term Debt

Long-term debt consists of the following:

	July 31, 1971	*July 31, 1970*
Mortgages maturing at various dates through December 31, 1976 and bearing interest at rates ranging from $4\frac{3}{4}\%$ to 6%...........................	$443,176	$704,615
Installment contracts and lease purchase agreements maturing at various dates through August, 1974.........	89,042	124,910
	532,218	829,525
Less payments due within one year.....................	295,630	333,036
	$236,588	$496,489

Land, buildings, and equipment with a net book value of $2,223,803 and $2,232,091 as of July 31, 1971 and July 31, 1970, respectively, are encumbered under the above agreements.

(9) Income Taxes

Deferred taxes relate principally to manufacturing division and installation division sales, depreciation, deferred costs, and capitalized costs. None of the Company's tax returns have been examined by the Internal Revenue Service. The tax refund included in Note 3 relates to refundable advance tax payments and the planned amendment of the prior year's tax returns.

(10) Stock Options

The Company has a qualified stock option plan in effect whereby options to purchase shares of common stock may be granted to officers and key employees at not less than the fair market value on the date of grant. During February, 1971, authorized shares under the plan were increased from 400,000 to 900,000 shares. Options expire five years after the date of grant and are exercisable in cumulative installments of 20% after one year. A summary of activity for the year ended July 31, 1971 follows:

	Option price per share		
	From	*To*	*Shares*
Options outstanding at July 31, 1970................	$ 3.00	$16.50	399,300
New options granted	15.13	22.00	275,500
Less: Options exercised	3.00	12.00	(11,800)
Cancellations...............................	3.00	19.25	(61,900)
Options outstanding at July 31, 1971................	3.00	22.00	601,100
Options outstanding at July 31, 1971 which are currently exercisable...........................	3.00	16.50	58,360

No entries are recorded with respect to options until exercised at which time the excess of the option price over the par value of common stock issued is credited to additional paid-in capital.

(11) Commitments and Contingencies

An action has been brought to enjoin the use of the word "Homex" by the Company. In the opinion of legal counsel, the plaintiff will be unsuccessful in obtaining the relief which it seeks.

A former shareholder of restricted shares of Company common stock has brought an action against the Company and another party, a broker. It is claimed that the Company refused, in concert with the other defendant, to permit the transfer of plaintiff's stock except at a price substantially below its alleged market price. Compensatory damages in the amount of $1,575,000 and treble damages are alleged. In the opinion of management, the suit can be successfully defended. In the opinion of counsel, the claim for treble damages is without merit.

The Company is engaged in other disputes involving claims which, in the aggregate, are insignificant compared to the Company's net worth.

EXHIBIT 1 (*concluded*)

Construction of a manufacturing plant in Mississippi is expected to be commenced in the latter part of 1971 at an approximate cost of $4,900,000. In a contract with the Company, Harrison County (where the plant site is located) has agreed to take the steps necessary to authorize the issuance and sale of tax exempt industrial revenue bonds in an amount necessary to meet the cost of constructing and equipping the plant. The contract also provides for a 30-year lease to the Company of the completed facility and the related land. Semiannual payments in respect of the bonds will be based on principal and interest requirements; an additional $36,325 is due annually for the land. Options to purchase the plant and the land are provided for during and at the end of the lease term. If the bond offering is not consummated, the Company will arrange to finance the cost of the facility itself.

At July 31, 1971, the Company had leases on various equipment and office facilities with terms ranging from two to six years. Minimum annual rentals under such leases amount to approximately $404,000.

Notes payable consist of 90-day unsecured notes to 11 banks bearing interest at a rate $\frac{1}{2}\%$ above the respective bank's best rate on the date of issue. The Company is required to maintain average annual compensating cash balances at each of these banks equal to approximately 15% to 20% of the outstanding indebtedness to such bank.

(12) Earnings Per Share
Earnings per common share are based upon the weighted average number of common shares outstanding during the periods presented after giving retroactive effect to the four for one stock split effected in February 1970. The preferred stock is not considered a common stock equivalent in accordance with Opinion 15 of the Accounting Principles Board of the American Institute of Certified Public Accountants. In addition, the effect of the preferred stock offering, for the fiscal year ended July 31, 1971 on a fully diluted earnings per share calculation is insignificant. Stock options outstanding have not been included in these computations since the effect of their inclusion would be insignificant.

Accountants' report
The Board of Directors and Stockholders
Stirling Homex Corporation:

We have examined the consolidated balance sheet of Stirling Homex Corporation and consolidated subsidiaries as of July 31, 1971 and the related statements of income, additional paid-in capital and retained earnings and changes in financial position for the year then ended. Our examination was made in accordance with generally accepted auditing standards, and accordingly included such tests of the accounting records and such other auditing procedures as we considered necessary in the circumstances. The financial statements for the year ended July 31, 1970, included for comparative purposes, were examined by other accountants.

In our opinion, such financial statements present fairly the consolidated financial position of Stirling Homex Corporation and consolidated subsidiaries at July 31, 1971, and the results of their operations and changes in their financial position for the year then ended, in conformity with generally accepted accounting principles applied on a basis consistent with that of the preceding year.

Rochester, New York
September 15, 1971

PEAT, MARWICK, MITCHELL & CO.

QUESTION

Does the method which Homex used to recognize revenue adhere in your opinion to generally accepted accounting principles, specifically in relation to:

a. The timing of revenue recognition.
b. The allocation of profit.
c. Capitalizing expenses.

Accounting for liabilities: Three questions

————···◄◆►···————

1. What is a liability?

Najeeb E. Halaby was employed as chairman and chief executive officer of Pan American World Airways, Inc., until March 22, 1972 when he was forced to resign by the board of directors. Prior to his resignation, Pan American reported losses as follows:

1969	$30 million
1970	48 million
1971	46 million

In accordance with his employment contract Mr. Halaby continued to receive his base salary of $100,000 per year after his forced resignation. If we assume that his contract expired on 12/31/75, Mr. Halaby is entitled to, and will receive, subsequent to his resignation the following amounts:

1972	$ 75,000 (9 months)
1973	100,000
1974	100,000
1975	100,000

Consider now the accounting question of recording Mr. Halaby's compensation. Three possibilities come to mind:

1. Pan American has incurred a liability and an expense as of March 22, 1972 for Mr. Halaby's future compensation of $375,000.
2. Pan American has incurred a liability and created an asset as of March 22, 1972 for Mr. Halaby's future compensation of $375,000.
3. Pan American has neither incurred a liability, nor an expense, nor created an asset as of March 22, 1972. Instead they will have an expense in each of the future periods for the amount paid to Mr. Halaby.

Define for financial accounting purposes the term *liability*. Operationally this should mean that those items meeting your definition appear on the right hand side of balance sheets and those that do not meet your definition do not. Does Pan American have a liability on March 22, 1975? Why or why not?

———

This case was prepared by Dennis P. Frolin.

2. For a liability with a *known cost*, how is interest accounted for?

A company on January 1, 1975 places through an investment counselor a three year $1 million term note with a private investor. The note has an annual interest rate of 8 percent of the face value, pays interest semiannually on July 1 and January 1 and matures January 1, 1978. The investor paid the counselor $1 million who paid the company $950,000 in cash after deducting the agreed upon $50,000 "finder's fee."

Calculate the interest expense for each of the three years and the amount of the liability on the balance sheet at the end of each of the three years.

3. For a liability with an *unknown cost*, how is interest accounted for?

A company issues on January 1, 1975 a $1,000 five-year 20 percent bond at par receiving cash of $1,000. Each December 31 the outcome of a coin flip determines whether any interest is paid. If the outcome is heads, $200 is paid; if tails, no interest is paid. The face amount of $1,000 is payable on January 1, 1980.

Calculate the interest expense for 1975 assuming the flip shows heads. What if it shows tails?

⸻⋘CASE III–7⋙⸻

Standard Utilities, Inc.

It was late December 1976. Samuel Wilson, treasurer of Standard Utilities was sitting in his oak-paneled office pondering the implications of a proposition put forth earlier that afternoon by one of his assistant treasurers. The proposal called for refunding an existing issue of 7 percent Subordinated debentures.

The assistant treasurer had suggested replacing the existing debentures with a series of 10-year, 7 percent, first mortgage bonds having a maturity value of $10 million. He felt that the underwriting costs associated with any such issue would be minor; probably around $100,000. The proposed issue of bonds would require, as did the existing one, semiannual interest payments on June 30 and December 31. The current market yield on corporate bonds rated similarly to the proposed issue was 8 percent. The firm's financial advisors did not expect interest rates to fall within the next 12 to 18 months.

Among Mr. Wilson's primary concerns was the way in which the proposed refunding would affect the actual cash flow and the reported earnings of Standard Utilities, Inc.

THE ORIGINAL BOND ISSUE

Standard Utilities, Inc., was a mid-size corporation that specialized in the exploration and recovery of natural gas. The high costs of research, development, and exploration dictated that Standard finance new ventures by dipping into the capital markets. On January 1, 1972 the firm issued a series of 10-year, 7 percent, subordinated debentures having a value at maturity of $10 million. The bonds originally sold at a premium since the stated interest rate was above the current market yield—at that time around 6 percent. The debentures were callable at 101.5 subsequent to January 1, 1976.

The debentures, dated January 1, 1972, required semiannual interest payments. There had been virtually no issuance costs as the bonds had been sold directly to the public by Standard Utilities. The annual report to shareholders dated December 31, 1976 disclosed the value of the debentures plus the unamortized bond premium to be $10,426,614.

This case was prepared by Charles T. Sharpless, research assistant, and Professor M. Edgar Barrett. Copyright © 1977 by M. Edgar Barrett.

EXHIBIT 1
Excerpt from *Accounting Principles Board Opinion No. 12*

Questions have been raised as to the appropriateness of the 'interest' method of periodic amortization of discount and expense or premium on debt . . . over its term. The objective of the interest method is to arrive at a periodic interest cost (including amortization) which will represent a level effective rate on the sum of the face amount of the debt and, . . . the unamortized premium or discount and expense at the beginning of each period. The difference between the periodic interest cost so calculated and the nominal interest on the outstanding amount of the debt is the amount of periodic amortization.

In the Board's opinion, the interest method of amortization is theoretically sound and an acceptable method.

Source: Financial Accounting Standards Board, *Financial Accounting Standards* (Chicago: Commerce Clearing House, Inc., 1976), p. 206. (*APB Opinion No. 12* was originally issued in December 1967.)

FINANCIAL REPORTING ISSUES

During the last six years, a number of opinions issued by the Accounting Principles Board had affected the methods used in calculating and reporting bond discounts and premiums. In 1967, *Accounting Principles Board Opinion No. 12* laid the groundwork for the acceptance of the interest method for amortization of bond discounts and premiums. Previous to the issuance of this opinion, corporations had been given the choice of using the interest method or straight line amortization (See Exhibit 1). In 1971, *Accounting Principles Board Opinion No. 21* was issued. It stipulated that the interest method should be used unless another method yielding similar results was employed. That same opinion further stated that discounts and premiums attached to bond issues should be disclosed in the equity section of the balance sheet as adjustments to the face amount of the related bonds. In addition, the opinion claimed that debt issued for cash had a present value measurable by the proceeds received at issuance. This opinion eliminated the earlier practice of reporting bond discounts as prepaid items in the asset portion of the balance sheet (See Exhibit 2). Wilson, accustomed to earlier reporting procedures, had made an extra effort to see that the 1972 debenture issue was reported according to the new generally accepted accounting principles.

APB Opinion No. 26, issued in 1972, stated that differences between the reacquisition price of corporate bonds and their carrying value had to be reported in the profit and loss statement for the current operating year. Previously, firms had the additional choices of amortizing such differences over the remaining life of the original bond issue or over the total life of the new bond issue (See Exhibit 3). In 1976, *Statement No. 4* of the Financial Accounting Standards Board supported the earlier opinions and added that gains and losses on refunding, if material, were to be included in the current period's income statement as extraordinary items (See Exhibit 4).

EXHIBIT 2
Excerpt from *Accounting Principles Board Opinion No. 21*

A note issued solely for cash equal to its face amount is presumed to earn the stated rate of interest. However, in some cases the parties may also exchange unstated (or stated) rights or privileges, which are given accounting recognition by establishing a note discount or premium account. In such instances, the effective interest rate differs from the stated rate.

When a note is received or issued solely for cash, . . . it is presumed to have a present value at issuance measured by the cash proceeds exchanged.

The difference between the present value and the face amount should be treated as discount or premium and amortized as interest expense or income over the life of the note in such a way as to result in a constant rate of interest when applied to the amount outstanding at the beginning of any given period.

The discount or premium . . . is not an asset or liability separable from the note which gives rise to it. . . . The discount or premium should be reported in the balance sheet as a direct deduction or addition to the face amount of the note.

Source: Financial Accounting Standards Board, *Financial Accounting Standards* (Chicago: Commerce Clearing House, Inc., 1976), pp. 304–6. (*APB Opinion No. 21* was originally issued in October 1971.)

EXHIBIT 3
Excerpt from *Accounting Principles Board Opinion No. 26*

The Board concludes that all extinguishments of debt before scheduled maturities are fundamentally alike. The accounting for such transactions should be the same regardless of the means used to achieve the extinguishment.

A difference between the reacquisition price and the net carrying amount of the extinguished debt should be recognized currently in income of the period of extinguishment as losses or gains identified as a separate item.

Source: Financial Accounting Standards Board, *Financial Accounting Standards* (Chicago: Commerce Clearing House, Inc., 1976), pp. 340–42. (*APB Opinion No. 26* was originally issued in October 1972.)

EXHIBIT 4
Excerpt from *Statement of Financial Accounting Standards No. 4*

Gains and losses from extinguishment of debt that are included in the determination of net income shall be aggregated and, if material, classified as an extraordinary item, net of related income tax effect.

Gains and losses from extinguishment of debt that are classified as extraordinary items should be described sufficiently to enable users of financial statements to evaluate their significance. Accordingly, the following information . . . shall be disclosed in a single note to the financial statements:

(a) A description of the extinguishment transactions, including the sources of any funds used to extinguish debt if it is practicable to identify the sources.
(b) The income tax effect in the period of extinguishment.
(c) The per share amount of the aggregate gain or loss net of related income tax effect.

Source: Financial Accounting Standards Board, *Financial Accounting Standards* (Chicago: Commerce Clearing House, Inc., 1976), p. 729. (*FASB Statement No. 4* was originally issued in March 1976.)

THE DECISION

On January 1, 1977, the treasurer's office was faced with the decision about whether or not to refund the 1972 debentures. Mr. Wilson knew that whatever decision he made about the proposed refunding would be carefully reviewed by the firm's executive committee. He also knew that his decision should be made shortly as the assistant treasurer had put a considerable amount of effort into his proposal.

Before proceeding with the overall analysis, however, he decided to review the proposed refunding from the perspective of its likely impact on the firm's financial statements. He knew that the firm's president accorded a high priority to issues surrounding the firm's reported results.

EXHIBIT 5
Present value of $1

Periods	3%	3.5%	4%	5%	6%	7%	8%	9%
1	0.9709	0.9662	0.9615	0.9524	0.9434	0.9346	0.9259	0.9174
5	0.8626	0.8420	0.8219	0.7835	0.7473	0.7130	0.6806	0.6499
10	0.7441	0.7089	0.6756	0.6139	0.5584	0.5083	0.4632	0.4224
20	0.5537	0.5026	0.4564	0.3769	0.3118	0.2584	0.2145	0.1784

EXHIBIT 6
Present value of an annuity

Periods	3%	3.5%	4%	5%	6%	7%	8%	9%
1	0.9709	0.9662	0.9615	0.9524	0.9434	0.9346	0.9259	0.9174
2	1.9135	1.8997	1.8861	1.8594	1.8334	1.8080	1.7833	1.7591
3	2.8286	2.8016	2.7751	2.7232	2.6730	2.6243	2.5771	2.5313
4	3.7171	3.6731	3.6299	3.5460	3.4651	3.3872	3.3121	3.2397
5	4.5797	4.5151	4.4518	4.3295	4.2124	4.1002	3.9927	3.8897
6	5.4172	5.3286	5.2421	5.0757	4.9173	4.7665	4.6229	4.4859
7	6.2303	6.1145	6.0021	5.7864	5.5824	5.3893	5.2064	5.0330
8	7.0197	6.8740	6.7327	6.4632	6.2098	5.9713	5.7466	5.5348
9	7.7861	7.6077	7.4353	7.1078	6.8017	6.5152	6.2469	5.9952
10	8.5302	8.3166	8.1109	7.7217	7.3601	7.0236	6.7101	6.4177
11	9.2526	9.0016	8.7604	8.3064	7.8868	7.4987	7.1389	6.8052
12	9.9539	9.6633	9.3850	8.8632	8.3838	7.9427	7.5361	7.1607
13	10.6349	10.3027	9.9856	9.3935	9.8527	8.3576	7.9038	7.4869
14	11.2960	10.9205	10.5631	9.8986	9.2950	8.7454	8.2442	7.7861
15	11.9379	11.5174	11.1183	10.3796	9.7122	9.1079	8.5595	8.0607
16	12.5610	12.0941	11.6522	10.8377	10.1059	9.4466	8.8514	8.3125
17	13.1660	12.6513	12.1656	11.2740	10.4772	9.7632	9.1216	8.5436
18	13.7534	13.1897	12.6592	11.6895	10.8276	10.0591	9.3719	8.7556
19	14.3237	13.7098	13.1339	12.0853	11.1581	10.3356	9.6036	8.9501
20	14.8774	14.2124	13.5903	12.4622	11.4699	10.5940	9.8181	9.1285

QUESTIONS

1. What is a liability? How should one be measured?

2. Determine the amount of the proceeds from the issuance of the original debentures.

3. Show how the combined book value of the debentures and the unamortized bond premium were determined as of December 31, 1976.

4. *Accounting Principles Board Opinion No. 21* stipulates that bond discounts and premiums should be shown as adjustments to liabilities. Is this a sensible practice? What other alternative treatments might have been selected by the Accounting Principles Board?

5. What important effects would the proposed refunding have on the following:
   a. The balance sheet as of the date of the refunding?
   b. The income statement for the first quarter of 1977?

⸺◄ CASE III-8 ►⸺

Ramada Inns, Inc.

⸺⸺◄∞►⸺⸺

In December 1974, the Financial Accounting Standards Board exposed for comment a proposed statement dealing with the translation of foreign currency transactions and foreign currency financial statements. The Exposure Draft proposed the use of the temporal method for translation, which uses exchange rates approximating those in effect at the time transactions occur. The temporal method is similar in application and effect to the monetary–nonmonetary method which was already being used by a number of United States corporations. The FASB also proposed that translation gains and losses be included in reported net income in the accounting period when they arise.

In response to the Exposure Draft, Carl D. Long, group vice president and chief financial officer, wrote to the Financial Accounting Standards Board on April 25, 1975. His letter is reproduced below.

MR. LONG'S LETTER

April 26, 1975

Financial Accounting Standards
  Board
High Ridge Park
Stamford, Connecticut   06905

Dear Sirs:

    Following is our response to the Exposure Draft "Accounting for the Translation of Foreign Currency Transactions and Foreign Currency Financial Statements." Specifically our response discusses and illustrates what we consider to be a mis-matching of revenue and expenses which can occur through the application of current rates to long-term debt, in conjunction with the use of historical rates for fixed assets.

I.   Effect of Exposure Draft policies on Ramada's reported profits

The effect is shown in the following paragraphs using Ramada's European operations (Ramada Europe) as an example. Ramada translates its foreign currency financial statements into U.S. dollars using the current–noncurrent method and any resulting translation gains or losses are included in current net income. As of February 28, 1975, Ramada Europe's consolidated balance sheet and its balance sheet exposure (stated in equivalent U.S. dollars and based on the current–noncurrent translation method) was as follows:

_____

This case was prepared from public documents of the Financial Accounting Standards Board.

	Balance sheet (at 2-28-75)	Exposure Unexposed	Exposure Exposed
Cash, receivables	$ 2,777	$	$2,777
Inventory, prepaids	317		317
Net fixed assets	35,434	35,434	
Deferred and other	1,490	1,490	
	$40,018	$36,924	$3,094
Short-term payables	$ 3,091		$3,091
Long-term debt			
Swedish kronor	5,465		
German DM	16,090		
French Francs	2,751		
Belgian Francs	5,026		
	29,332	$29,332	
Equity and dollar debt	7,595	7,595	
	$40,018	$36,927	$3,091
Net exposure (long)			$ 3

Several points are apparent from the above balance sheet and exposure report:

1. Ramada Europe is very capital intensive (essentially all fixed assets represent the cost of hotels which are 100 percent owned by Ramada Europe).
2. Ramada Europe has financed its hotels largely with foreign currency debt (most debt is 15–25-year mortgage debt).
3. Ramada's exposure to translation gains and losses under the current–non-current method is negligible.

Ramada's European exposure changes drastically under the translation methods proposed in the FASB draft, as shown below: (Hereafter in this response, we will refer to the translation method proposed in the FASB draft as the monetary–nonmonetary method).

	Balance sheet (at 2-28-75)	Exposure Unexposed	Exposure Exposed
Cash, receivables	$ 2,777	$	$ 2,777
Inventory, prepaids	301	301	
Net fixed assets	35,434	35,434	
Deferred and other	1,490	1,490	
	$40,002	$37,225	$ 2,777
Short-term payables	$ 3,091		$ 3,091
Long-term debt			
Swedish kronor	5,875		
German DM	17,606		
French Francs	3,121		
Belgian Francs	5,375		
	31,977		31,977
Equity and dollar debt	4,934	$ 4,934	
	$40,002	$ 4,934	$35,068
Net exposure (short)			($32,291)

To determine the effect which the monetary–nonmonetary translation method would have on Ramada's earnings, we have prepared balance sheets for Ramada Europe for each quarter beginning with the first quarter of 1973, and have computed translation gains or losses for each quarter using the monetary–non-monetary method. The balance sheets and the basis for their preparation are shown and described in the Attachment. To summarize this attachment we present below the translation gains or losses which would have been reported for each quarter. Also, to illustrate the magnitude of these gains and losses, we have presented Ramada's reported Consolidated net income (for all domestic and foreign operations) for the same quarters.

Quarter		Reported consolidated net income	Translation gain (loss)
1973	Second	$4,047,000	$(1,647,000)
	Third..........	5,485,000	(1,284,000)
	Fourth	2,025,000	1,611,000
1974	First	1,955,000	836,000
	Second	3,220,000	(1,631,000)
	Third..........	3,455,000	1,118,000
	Fourth	23,000	(1,800,000)
1975	First	1,042,000	(2,714,000)
	Second		1,173,000*
	Total		$(4,338,000)†

* Through April 21, 1975.
† Gross losses are $9,076,000 and Gross gains $4,738,000 for a net of $4,338,000.

The large gains and losses shown above illustrate the magnitude of profit fluctuations which Ramada can expect in the future if it must apply the monetary–nonmonetary translation method to its European operations.

In connection with the above comparison we would like to point out the following additional facts.

1. Ramada's primary business activity is the operation of its company owned hotels. In 1975 this activity will account for about 75 percent of consolidated sales and almost 100 percent of foreign sales. The cost of Ramada Europe's hotels represents slightly more than 10 percent of Consolidated fixed assets, and its foreign currency long-term debt also represents slightly more than 10 percent of Consolidated long-term debt.

2. In addition to the European exposure of approximately $32 million (under the monetary–nonmonetary method) Ramada has a further exposure of about $13 million in Canadian dollars. The Canadian currency has not been nearly as volatile as European currencies, but quarterly U.S./Canadian dollar fluctuations of 2 percent to 3 percent are not uncommon and fluc-tuactions of this magnitude would produce additional gains or losses of $260,000 to $390,000 per quarter.

3. The translation gains and losses might be reduced somewhat through the recording of deferred taxes. However, we presently believe that deferred taxes would apply to only about 50 percent of the gross translation gains or

losses. (Hence, net translation gains and losses would be about 75 percent of the amounts shown below).

II. Ramada's view of its exposure from European operations

We feel that the monetary–nonmonetary translation method is not appropriate for Ramada and that this translation method violates the accounting principle of matching revenue and expenses when applied to Ramada.

In our opinion the proper translation method for a company such as Ramada is the current-rate method. Our reasoning for this opinion can first be illustrated by reference to the following flowchart, which describes our approach in building, financing, and operating a foreign hotel.

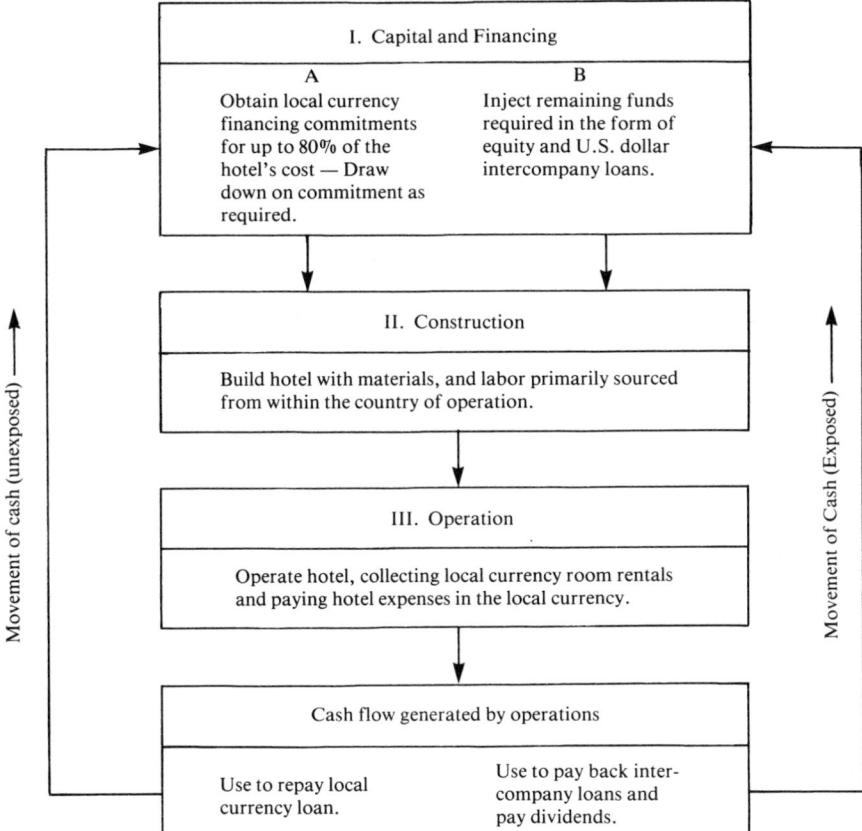

From the flowchart it is apparent to us that only our equity and U.S. dollar loans are exposed. These are exposed because foreign currency earnings and cash flow are used to pay dividends and repay U.S. dollar loans. Following this reasoning, the current rate method is the appropriate method for Ramada since under this method our translation gains and losses would be equal to our total dollar loans and equity, times the percentage by which the U.S. dollar changes in value, relative to the local currency in each country of operation.

Under the current-rate method our net balance sheet exposure would be "long" by about $7.6 million. It should be noted that exposure under the current rate method is the opposite of monetary–nonmonetary exposure. For example under the current rate method we would realize a translation gain when the dollar devalued, whereas a loss would result under the monetary–nonmonetary method.

We have not adopted the current-rate method because it is not permissible under present accounting rules. We therefore have adopted the current–noncurrent method which is permitted and which provides much more realistic results for Ramada than the monetary–nonmonetary method.

III. General discussion

Our argument against the monetary–nonmonetary method is made on the basis of "compatibility" or Objective E of the Exposure Draft. That is, we feel that the monetary–nonmonetary method when applied to Ramada, produces results which are not compatible with expected economic effects.

Objective E was rejected by the FASB. One reason given was "The proposed objective is impractical because foresight would be required to identify the future economic effects of a rate change at the time it occurs." We disagree that the objective is impractical because it is clear to us that a decline in the value of the dollar will increase Ramada's earnings and cash flow in terms of U.S. dollars, while an increase in the value of the U.S. dollar will decrease our earnings and flow in terms of U.S. dollars.

Other arguments against compatibility which were contained in the draft opinion related to areas such as imports and exports, commitments for purchases or sales in another foreign currency and so forth. These arguments do not apply to a company such as Ramada which is almost entirely dependent on the local economy.

The Exposure Draft also mentioned the opposing views that (a) historical costs should be measured in terms of dollars; versus (b) historical costs should be measured in terms of the foreign currency. The Board adopted view (a) and rejected view (b). However the Board's main reason for adoption of view (a) seemed to be that it is mathematically possible to determine the dollar equivalent of the cost of an asset on the date of acquisition. We agree that the use of dollar historical costs for fixed assets is mathematically possible, but we feel that it should not be the only acceptable method and in fact feel that it is not the proper method for us to use.

IV. Conclusions, recommendation

The monetary–nonmonetary method as proposed in the draft would essentially force us to finance all future foreign hotels with U.S. dollars in order to minimize translation losses. This would be unfortunate because (a) it would be against the U.S. public interest as it would cause an outflow of U.S. dollars; (b) it would hamper our expansion if the U.S. government should again impose controls such as the former OFDI regulations; (c) financing in U.S. dollars runs counter to what we should do from an economic standpoint.

We could reduce or eliminate our present exposure under the monetary–nonmonetary method by entering into forward foreign exchange transactions. However, this is not an argument for the monetary–nonmonetary method because

ATTACHMENT
Ramada-Europe balance sheets

	As reported using Ramada's current–Non-current method	As reported but using translation method proposed in FASB draft and exchange rates on dates shown									
		4/21/75	2/28/75	11/30/74	8/31/74	5/31/74	2/28/74	11/30/73	8/31/73	5/31/73	2/28/73
Cash receivables	$ 2,777	$ 2,666	$ 2,777	$ 2,555	$ 2,388	$ 2,472	$ 2,333	$ 2,416	$ 2,555	$ 2,444	$ 2,305
Inventories, prepaids	317	301	301	301	301	301	301	301	301	301	301
Net fixed assets	35,434	35,434	35,434	35,434	35,434	35,434	35,434	35,434	35,434	35,434	35,434
Deferred and other	1,490	1,490	1,490	1,490	1,490	1,490	1,490	1,490	1,490	1,490	1,490
Total	$40,018	$39,891	$40,002	$39,780	$39,613	$39,697	$39,558	$39,641	$39,780	$39,669	$39,530
Short-term payables	$ 3,091	$ 2,967	$ 3,091	$ 2,844	$ 2,658	$ 2,751	$ 2,596	$ 2,689	$ 2,844	$ 2,702	$ 2,566
Long-term debt in local currency	29,332	30,817	31,977	29,238	$27,507	28,616	27,001	27,827	29,422	28,169	26,519
Equity and debt in U.S. dollars	7,595	7,595	7,595	7,595	7,595	7,595	7,595	7,595	7,595	7,595	7,595
Translation gain (loss)		(1,488)	(2,661)	53	1,853	735	2,366	1,530	(81)	1,203	2,850
Total	$40,018	$39,891	$40,002	$39,780	$39,613	$39,697	$39,558	$39,641	$39,780	$39,669	$39,530
Translation gain (loss) for quarter		$ 1,173	$(2,714)	$(1,800)	$ 1,118	$(1,631)	$ 836	$ 1,611	$(1,284)	$(1,647)	

Ramada Inns, Inc. reports earnings on a calendar quarter basis, however, foreign earnings are cut off one month early. That is, Ramada earnings for the quarter ended March 31, 1975 include foreign earnings for the quarter ended February 28, 1975.

such transactions can be costly; and like U.S. dollar financing, they don't make sense from an economic standpoint.

In our opinion the monetary–nonmonetary translation method is not appropriate for Ramada or other capital intensive companies which have similar operations. We believe that the current rate method is clearly the most appropriate for Ramada, and that the Board should permit the use of this method—at least for certain types of companies such as Ramada.

However if the Board does not wish to permit the use of the current rate method at this time we recommend the following alternatives.

A.   Use of the current–noncurrent method.

or

B.   Use of the monetary–nonmonetary method along with deferral of gains and losses that relate to long-term debt used to finance fixed assets.

We are anxious to meet with members of the Financial Accounting Standards Board to further discuss the figures, arguments and comments in this response at any time, and in this connection ask that you contact the undersigned or Donald W. Hair, our director of international accounting.

Notes to Attachment

Foreign exchange markets have been very volatile since 1971 and all indications point to continued volatility for the foreseeable future. In this response we are attempting to demonstrate the effects of this volatility on Ramada, assuming use of the monetary–nonmonetary translation method.

We have done this by starting with actual Ramada–Europe figures as of February 28, 1975 and then restating these figures as though the assets which existed at that time were in existence each quarter for the past two years. Actual foreign exchange rates were used for each quarter to restate local currency debt, current assets, and current liabilities.

Attachment does not consider depreciation or repayment of long-term debt. However, this is not significant because (a) depreciation has no effect on translation gains or losses; and (b) repayment of long-term debt for the two-year period would be under $1 million or 3 percent of total debt.

Figures used in the extreme left column are actual reported figures as of February 28, 1975 with one exception: on April 15, 1975 our Swedish subsidiary received SK 8 million (about U.S. $2 million), being the proceeds of a long-term mortgage. We attempted to draw down this commitment before February 28 but certain technical matters prevented this.

The February 28 balance sheet has been restated as though this commitment had been drawn down by February 28.

QUESTIONS

1.   Does the method of financing foreign operations which Ramada has adopted make good economic sense?

2.   Ramada says it has not adopted the current rate method because it was not permissible (yet it is the most widely used method in many countries). Can you, however, verify that the balance-sheet exposure would be "long" by $7 million under that method?

3.   If the average of all foreign currencies in which Ramada-Europe has borrowed devalued 10 percent versus the dollar in 1976, approximate the translations gain or loss which Ramada-Europe would report in 1975 under the monetary–nonmonetary method? the current-rate method? the current–noncurrent method?

4. Consider the "gains and losses" shown on page 346. If you were part of Ramada's management, how would you explain these "gains and losses" in your reports to shareholders and lenders?

5. With the adoption of *FASB Statement No. 8*, what actions *should* Ramada take? What actions do you think they *will* take?

────◄ CASE III-9 ►──────

Replacement value accounting (A): The Philips N.V. System

In early 1978, N.V. Philips' Gloeilampenfabrieken (Philips Lamp Works) was one of the world's largest manufacturers of electronic equipment. Based in Eindhoven, the Netherlands, the company had operations in approximately 65 countries and employed 384,000 people. Philips reported a 1977 consolidated profit of (U.S.) $278 million on worldwide sales of $13.6 billion. Philips' worldwide sales were most heavily drawn from within member countries of the European Economic Community. Some 52 percent of the company's 1977 sales were made in Europe. North American sales, with about 18 percent of the total, represented the next largest segment.

The accounting procedures of firms based outside of the United States are often very similar to those of American-based firms. They need not be, however, and they are often not. Philips N.V. was one firm whose accounting procedures differed fairly significantly from those of firms based in the United States. This firm employed what they referred to as replacement value accounting, rather than the more widely accepted historic cost accounting. As a result, their financial statements differed in several important respects from those commonly used by most other large, multinational companies.

This case and its sequel, Replacement Value Accounting (B): The Philips N.V. System (Case III-10), focus upon five major aspects of these differences. A brief history of Philips Lamp Works follows. Subsequent to that there is a discussion of inflation-adjusted accounts. This is followed by a listing of the five major aspects with which this case series is concerned, a series of

This case was prepared from published material by Professor M. Edgar Barrett and Katherine B. Penn. It is based, in part, on the same material used to develop an ICCH case called Philips N.V. (A): An Application of Replacement Value Accounting (9-172-078). Copyright © 1978 by M. Edgar Barrett.

quotes and/or paraphrases from a 1960 article by the chief internal auditor of Philips N.V., and a set of exhibits from Philips' 1977 annual report.

COMPANY HISTORY

Philips N.V. was founded in 1891 as a family company. It originally produced incandescent lamps. In 1912, it was incorporated as N.V. Philips Gloei-lampenfabrieken in Eindhoven, the Netherlands. Eight years later, N.V. Gemeenschappelijk Bezit Von Aandeelen Philips' Gloeilampenfabrieken (Philips Lamp Holding Company) was formed. The twin purposes of the holding company were to buy and sell shares of Philips Lamp Works and to ensure that control of the company remained in the Netherlands. In 1977, the Philips Lamp Holding Company (also known as Philips N.V.) owned 99.9 percent of the shares of the Philips Lamp Works.

Philips N.V. was divided into six product divisions. Each of these had broad geographical coverage and authority. In terms of sales, the largest of these was the Home Electronics for Sound and Vision division. The products of this division included television and radio receivers, audio and video recorders, and magnetic tape. One of the smallest divisions was the Lighting and Batteries division. This division accounted for about 10 percent of the firm's 1977 worldwide sales. Philips' products also included large and small household appliances, professional telecommunications equipment, phar-maceuticals, and plastic and metal products.

INFLATION-ADJUSTED ACCOUNTS

For years, the most common basis for preparing financial statements to be used for purposes either internal or external to the firm in question has been what is normally called historic cost accounting. Financial statements prepared on this basis are expressed in terms of one monetary unit, such as the U.S. dollar, and are *not* adjusted in any manner designed to reflect the impact of inflation on the firm's financial position.

Over the last decade or two, however, many firms have begun to issue financial statements which include inflation-adjusted data. Many such statements include the inflation-adjusted data as supplementary information. Some such statements provide inflation-adjusted data as the primary financial information.

Many British-based firms now supply two sets of financial statements: one based on the principles of historic cost accounting, and one adjusted in some manner to reflect the impact of inflation. Since 1976, the U.S. Securities and Exchange Commission (commonly referred to as the SEC) has required that firms subject to its regulatory authority provide replacement cost data on inventories and fixed assets in addition to a complete, audited set of historic cost-based financial statements. Finally, in some South American countries, most notably Brazil, financial statements have been routinely adjusted for the effects of inflation for several years by use of a series of price-level indexes.

Possible adjustments.   Historic cost financial statements may be adjusted for the effects of inflation by either of two types of price-level indexes, or by a combination of the two. A so-called general price-level index provides data about the movement of prices in general, or the average movement of prices over the whole economy. The consumer price index in the United States is an example of such an index. A specific price-level index, on the other hand, is an index which shows the price movement of a specific item, commodity, or group of similar items or commodities. For example, a specific price-level index might provide data about the price movement in wheat or copper pipe over a period of time.

General and specific price-level indexes do not necessarily fluctuate in similar patterns. In a period of inflation, a general price-level index will rise, while the price of *any specific commodity* may fall.

General price-level adjustments.   Some observers have recommended that adjustments to historic cost financial statements be made for general price-level changes only. The result of such an adjustment would be to restate the company's financial position to take the effects of inflation, *in general*, into account. Monetary assets, such as cash and most accounts receivables, decrease in purchasing power during inflationary periods. Therefore, the company loses purchasing power as a function of the amount of inflation and the amount of monetary assets held. Monetary liabilities, such as accounts payable and bank loans are also traditionally fixed in dollar amounts. They will also decrease in purchasing power during periods of inflation. However, the decrease in purchasing power of liabilities is clearly to the company's advantage. The company will be required to pay back less, *in purchasing power*, than it borrowed. Therefore, the company will gain purchasing power if liabilities are greater than monetary assets and will lose purchasing power if liabilities are less than monetary assets. Some observers feel that such gains and losses should be calculated and shown in a firm's financial statements. These gains or losses might be posted to the income statement, or, as some observers recommend, directly to retained earnings.

Nonmonetary items, such as inventory or plant, property, and equipment, are not fixed in dollar amount. The proponents of general price-level adjustment would require that nonmonetary items be adjusted to reflect the historical cost of the item expressed in current dollars. Each asset's historical cost would be multiplied by a correction factor, which would restate the cost of the item in current dollars. The adjusted dollar amount would represent the amount of purchasing power, in today's terms, that was surrendered to acquire the asset. The correction factor would be a ratio of the current general price-level index to the general price-level index that existed at the time the asset was originally acquired. In times of general inflation nonmonetary assets would be revalued upward, as more current dollars would be needed to represent the same amount of purchasing power as was spent in originally acquiring the assets. The increases on the asset side of the balance sheet would be offset by an equity account. The account, which would be shown near or among the owners' equity accounts, would grow in times of inflation and shrink during periods of deflation.

Specific price-level adjustments. Proponents of this approach suggest that historic cost-based financial statements be adjusted only for the changes in the dollar cost of specific items. These changes in cost would be measured by a specific price-level index. Monetary assets and liabilities, by definition, would fluctuate with the general price-level index. The general price-level index is designed to reflect changes in prices over an entire economy. Therefore, it could be used as an index of the purchasing power of the dollar. Most proponents of specific price-level adjustments would argue that gains or losses on monetary assets should be calculated by the use of general price-level indexes. There is not general agreement as to whether such gains or losses should constitute an integral part of the firm's price-level adjusted income statement.

Nonmonetary assets, such as inventories and fixed assets, would be adjusted according to specific price-level changes. For example, an inventory of lumber would be adjusted by multiplying the historic cost of the lumber by a correction factor. Under this method, the correction factor would be the ratio of the current price level of lumber to the price level of lumber at the time the inventory was purchased. Any adjustments that resulted from this process (commonly known as holding gains and losses) could then be considered either as part of income, or as an adjustment to be posted directly to an equity account.

Full price-level accounting. Some observers maintain that financial statements should be adjusted for both general and specific price-level changes. Moreover, according to this viewpoint, the overall change in dollar value of assets should be divided, as nearly as possible, into categories of general or specific price-level changes.

Under this method, the gain or loss from monetary assets and liabilities would again be calculated using a general price-level adjustment. For nonmonetary assets, however, an attempt would be made to separate "nominal gains" and "real gains." Nominal gains are those increases in dollar value of an asset which are due to economy-wide inflation, as measured by the general price-level index. Real gains are defined as the difference between the gain on an asset as measured by specific price-level indexes and the nominal gain on the item. For example suppose the historical cost of the inventory of lumber bought at the beginning of the period is $1,000. At the beginning of the period both the general index and the specific index for lumber might be set to equal 100. At the end of the period, the general price-level index might have risen to 105 while the specific price-level index has risen to 112. The nominal gain would then be $50[(105/100 times $1,000), less $1,000]. The real gain would be $70 [([112/100 times $1,000] less $1,000) − $50].

ACCOUNTING PRINCIPLES USED BY PHILIPS N.V.

The accounting procedures used by Philips N.V. in the preparation of the financial statements differ significantly from those most often seen in other large, multinational enterprises. Five major areas of difference will be addressed in this case and in its sequel, Replacement Value Accounting (B): The Philips N.V. System. The five major areas of difference are as follows:

1. Philips values property, plant, and equipment (fixed assets) at replacement cost. This valuation is also used to determine the periodic amounts of depreciation expense.
2. The company values inventories at the lower of replacement cost or estimated realizable value. This valuation is also used to determine the cost of goods sold.
3. The company recognizes losses on net monetary assets when inflation reduces their purchasing power.
4. When preparing consolidated statements, Philips adjusts the subsidiaries' financial statements as far as is practicably possible to reflect the parent company's accounting procedures. When feasible, the subsidiaries' books are maintained on a basis consistent with that used by the parent company.
5. Philips translates foreign-currency-denominated financial statements at exchange rates designed to reflect actual relationships in the relative purchasing power of each currency involved. This normally means that offical exchange rates are used. It can, however, mean that "purchasing power" rates developed and revised within the economics department of Philips are employed.

This case will deal with the first two of these accounting policies. The remaining three will be discussed in the (B) case.

REPLACEMENT VALUE ACCOUNTING

Professor A. Goudeket, chief internal auditor of Philips Industries, wrote an article explaining Philips' application of replacement value accounting. The article was published by *The Journal of Accountancy* in July 1960. Much of the following text is either quoted or paraphrased from that article.[1] (Paraphrases are enclosed in brackets.)

---

[1] "An Application of Replacement Value Theory," *The Journal of Accountancy*, July 1960, pp. 37–47. Copyright 1960 by the American Institute of CPAs. Reproduced with permission.

356

In the Netherlands, "sound business practice" is the basis from which both economic and accounting principles and conventions have evolved. While in the United States an "accounting principle" reflects a generally accepted practice, in the Netherlands the yardstick is the concept of sound business practice. . . .

General aspects of the theory

The management of a business enterprise, its shareholders, and the public require information on the operation of the enterprise, both as a picture of past performance and as an indication of future possibilities. Thus we are confronted with problems of internal and external presentation of information having both retrospective and prospective objectives. . . .

This implies that the method of calculation of the income and capital must be the same for both [internal and external] purposes. [T]he reports for both purposes may vary only as to the details of information and frequency of issuance. There is therefore no reason to make any further distinction between internal and external requirements.

[. . . T]he operating income of an enterprise, during a certain period, is properly reflected in the income statement only if it shows the revenue of the period[, less] the cost which has been incurred to produce it. The replacement value theory contends that, in order to assure the continuity of the enterprise, all costs incurred must be included in the income statement at their replacement values, and not at the prices which actually may have been paid. It is irrelevant whether or not replacement is actually taking place at the moment the cost is incurred. The replacement value particularly plays a part in establishing the amounts of cost incurred when absorbing raw materials and fixed assets in the product and also in establishing the cost of finished products in sales. It should be noted that the replacement value theory is applicable not only to the cost of fixed assets (depreciation) and materials but also to wages and all other elements of cost.

Background

The principles of Philips' accounting system may be described as follows:

1. [The object of the accounting system is to provide the management of each section of Philips with information it requires to operate. In addition it should provide top management with the information required for central control.]
2. The accounting system . . . is organized . . . with[in a] system of budgetary control, which implies the existence of norms and standards.
3. The accounting system is decentralized[. E]ach section . . . has its own accounting department which prepares a balance sheet and an income statement each month for that particular section[. All statements are prepared] in accordance with principles followed uniformly through[out] the enterprise.
4. [. . . T]he responsible managers of all levels must know periodically the income and the capital employed, both in total and in detail. [All of the figures are calculated using . . .] replacement value [accounting.] In other words, the application of the replacement value theory is not merely a calculation technique used in preparing the annual statements of the concern. It is integrated in the accounting system of all sections of the concern at every

stage. In this way, it is ensured that all information for management is compiled in accordance with this principle[. T]hus the replacement value automatically enters into all management considerations and decisions. . . .

Application

At Philips we hold to the view that there can be no recognition of income for a period unless the capital employed in the business at the beginning of the period has been maintained[. T]hat is to say, . . . it [must be] established that the purchasing power of that capital at the end of the period is equal to that at the beginning of the period [before income can be recognized].

[The following two sections explain how replacement value is determined in the case of fixed assets and inventory accounts.]

Fixed assets

The replacement value [for fixed assets] is determined on the basis of the trend of the specific price levels and not of the general price level[. Therefore] . . . the trend of prices is followed separately for buildings, dwelling houses, machinery, and so on. Each group of assets is regularly revalued by means of index numbers. For instance, for a factory building, revaluation is on the basis of the index numbers for the cost of that type of building; . . . .

[The following accounts are kept in connection with the application of replacement value:]

1. Accounts of fixed assets at replacement value.
2. Accounts of the depreciation of fixed assets at replacement value.
3. Revaluation-surplus for fixed assets.
4. Cost of depreciation of fixed assets.

The accounts under (1) and (2) belong to the group of fixed asset accounts; account (3) is a capital account; account (4) is an income account. By entering every revaluation into the accounts, account (4) will automatically be charged for the depreciation on the basis of replacement value, since the depreciation is a function of the value of the assets and their lives.

If a price increase occurs, the accounts under (1) are increased to the current price level with the account (3) as a contra account. The accounts under (2) are . . .[also increased.] [. . . The increase in the accumulated depreciation account (2) demonstrates that] depreciation provided in previous years has been too low. Therefore, this must be increased in order to provide for complete depreciation of the fixed assets on the basis of the present price level at the end of their useful life, and to insure that adequate funds for replacement will be available. This revaluation of past depreciation should therefore be charged to the income account. In the Philips Company this is not done for two reasons, namely:

1. Due to the size of the concern, the composition of total fixed assets as far as lives are concerned approximates an average. As a result, yearly replacements for all practical purposes are equal to the yearly depreciation.
2. [The income account is adjusted to provide for the maintenance of capital invested in monetary assets. Monetary assets are assets other than inventories, fixed assets, investments, and intangibles. Examples of monetary assets are cash and notes receivable.]

In case of a decline in price levels, the procedure followed is the opposite of what is done in the case of an increase. In the case of a decrease, it must first of all be firmly established that the decrease is the result of a changed price level. If the decrease results from other economic or technical reasons, the decrease must be charged to the profit and loss account. Should the revaluation account be completely exhausted as a result of charges on account of price decreases, then the adjustment of the replacement value will be charged to the income account, since it is a rule that the revaluation reserve may never show a debit balance.

Inventories

[Philips uses a budgetary system with standard costs for all the company's operations. Standard costs are used for all groups of inventories, including goods purchased, semifinished products, and finished goods. Standard costs for a product are calculated by adding the cost of all the constituent parts (including labor and overhead) of that product. The replacement value of an inventory item can then be calculated by adding the costs of the same constituent parts at current replacement prices.] Whenever the fluctuation in [cost] levels is material enough to cause an inventory adjustment, the standard [costs] are adjusted to replacement value by means of index numbers. Individual adjustments of standard [costs] take place periodically, yearly, or at longer intervals, if there is no reason for an adjustment at the end of a particular year. In view of the volume of work involved, the decision for an individual adjustment of [standard costs] is taken with care, having in mind the large degree of integration which exists in Philips.

* * * * *

In the accounting system the following accounts are kept: (1) inventory accounts; (2) adjustment accounts to reflect changes in index numbers; (3) price difference accounts;[2] and (4) revaluation-surplus for inventories. The accounts (1) and (2) are accounts for current assets, (3) is an income account, while (4) is a capital account.

Inventory accounts are kept at standard [costs]. If an interim revaluation takes place, account (2) is debited and account (4) is credited. After revaluation, the inventory movements are valued at standard [cost] times the index and the relative entries are posted to accounts (1) and (2). This means that on a purchase, both accounts are debited, and that account (3), which formerly was debited or credited for the difference between purchase price and standard [cost], is now used for the difference between purchase price and standard [cost] plus the index adjustment. In respect of goods consumed, accounts (1) and (2) are credited; in respect of production both accounts are debited.

Index adjustments accounts

Every division with an individual balance sheet and income account keeps separate accounts for the index adjustment on raw materials, work in process, and finished products.

---

[2] In the United States, such accounts are commonly referred to as purchase price variance accounts [editor].

* * * * *

If the standard [costs] are changed, then the difference is posted to the contra of the revaluation surplus.[3] The balance of the entries on account (2) which so far have been made on that account is reversed to the debit of account (4).[4] If large differences occur between the two entries, an analysis is made of them. . . .

The procedure in the case of a decrease in price level has been indicated under *Fixed Assets.*

* * * * *

In conclusion, a few words should be said about Lifo. It is true that the Lifo method may be looked upon as an approximation of the replacement value principle as far as the income statement is concerned. The Lifo system, however, is a reasonably acceptable solution only if there is high rate of turnover of inventories and if inventories do not decrease in volume. The major disadvantage of the Lifo method is that no standard prices based on current price levels are used, as a result of which the information for management must be inadequate in several respects. Examples of such inadequacies are that in the income statement efficiency variances and price differences are mixed up, and that in the balance sheet the real capital employed is not presented.

Conclusion

* * * * *

We have often noted that financial analysts, when dealing with the annual reports of Philips, did not look upon the revaluation surplus as a capital account but deducted the amounts from the assets concerned. After the foregoing explanations it will be obvious that we believe this to be basically incorrect. But even if one feels the need for comparison pruposes to classify Philips' annual report figures according to a traditional method, one must realize that a very large part of the revaluation has been absorbed in the profit and loss account by way of depreciation of fixed assets and goods consumption, as a result of which that portion of the revaluation surplus must be regarded as earned surplus.

QUESTIONS

1. Do those accounting procedures used by Philips and described in this case fit, mechancially, within the standard double-entry accounting framework?

2. Given Philips' application of the replacement value policies, are there any instances of bias or inconsistency in a conceptual sense?

3. Do the accounting procedures used by Philips in respect to fixed assets and inventories result in "better" information for either management or shareholders than would be produced by a typical historic cost accounting system?

---

[3] That is, in a situation of increased standard cost, they would apparently debit account (1) and credit account (4) [editor].

[4] Likewise, at the time that the standard costs are revised, they would debit account (4) and credit account (2) [editor].

EXHIBIT 1

REPLACEMENT VALUE ACCOUNTING (A):
THE PHILIPS N.V. SYSTEM
Combined Statement of Financial Position
In Millions of Guilders

Assets

	1977		1976	
Property, plant, and equipment:				
Replacement value	22,124.9		20,733.7	
Depreciation	−11,328.2	10,796.7	−10,347.7	10,386.0
Intangible assets		—		—
Investments in nonconsolidated				
associated companies		670.3		587.8
Sundry noncurrent assets		485.6		626.3
Stocks:				
Factory stocks	4,938.8		4,697.6	
Commercial stocks	4,999.0		4,819.5	
	9,937.8		9,517.1	
Advance payments by customers	−711.6	9,226.2	−697.4	8,819.7
Accounts receivable:				
Trade debtors	7,771.1		7,152.7	
Discounted bills	−562.5		−466.6	
	7,208.6		6,686.1	
Other accounts receivable	829.7		754.3	
Prepaid expenses	427.1	8,465.4	506.2	7,946.6
Liquid assets:				
Marketable securities	196.3		225.0	
Cash at bank and in hand	1,267.7	1,464.0	1,502.2	1,727.2
		31,108.2		30,093.6

Capital and Liabilities

	1977		1976	
Shareholders' equity interest:				
Ordinary share capital	1,705.8		1,704.6	
Share premium account	233.2		230.9	
Retained profit	5,548.1		5,254.8	
Revaluation surplus	3,206.1	10,693.2	2,989.2	10,179.5
Minority interests		1,166.9		1,151.2
Sundry provisions:				
Long-term provisions	4,350.1		4,032.7	
Short-term provisions	1,289.0	5,639.1	1,462.6	5,495.3
Long-term liabilities:				
Convertible debenture loans	525.2		519.0	
Other debenture loans	2,007.4		2,071.0	
Other long-term liabilities	1,968.5	4,501.1	2,115.1	4,705.1
Current liabilities:				
Banks	2,223.1		1,920.1	
Accounts payable	4,385.7		4,240.0	
Tax on profit	498.2		617.5	
Accrued expenses	1,762.9	8,869.9	1,568.5	8,346.1
Profit available for distribution	340.3		318.7	
Interim dividend made payable				
in December	−102.3	238.0	−102.3	216.4
		31,108.2		30,093.6

Source: Philips 1977 annual report, pp. 38 ff.

EXHIBIT 2

REPLACEMENT VALUE ACCOUNTING (A):
THE PHILIPS N.V. SYSTEM
Combined Statement of Results
In Millions of Guilders

	1977		*1976*	
Sales		31,164.3		30,435.2
Costs and expenses:				
Cost of sales	− 22,542.8		− 21,948.4	
Selling and general expenses................	− 6,409.6	− 28,952.4	− 6,265.4	− 28,213.8
Trading profit		2,211.9		2,221.4
Other income and charges:				
Interest paid	− 802.2		− 774.6	
Interest received	172.9		154.1	
	− 629.3		− 620.5	
Miscellaneous income	72.1		70.0	
Miscellaneous charges	− 468.8	− 1,026.0	− 388.9	− 939.4
Profit before tax		1,185.9		1,282.0
Tax on profit................		− 490.6		− 610.4
Profit after tax		695.3		671.6
Share in net result of nonconsolidated companies		41.8		0.6
Group profit		737.1		672.2
Minority interests		− 103.5		− 109.7
Net profit		633.6		562.5

Source: Philips 1977 annual report, pp. 37 ff.

Notes to the Combined Statements

These statements relate to the total activities of "Philips" in the world. "Philips"—in the sense in which the term is used in this annual report—consists of two parts:
N.V. Philips' Gloeilampenfabrieken (N.V. Philips) and its subsidiaries.
The United States Philips Trust (the Trust) and its subsidiaries.

N.V. Philips

N.V. Philips is both an operating company in the Netherlands and a holding company of shares in subsidiaries and other associated companies in the Netherlands and many other countries.
The shares of N.V. Philips are almost wholly in the possession of N.V. Gemeenschappelijk Bezit van Aandeelen Philips' Gloeilampenfabrieken (N.V. Gemeenschappelijk Bezit), which is the holding company solely for these shares. The shares in N.V. Gemeenschappelijk Bezit are held by shareholders all over the word.

The Trust

The Trust holds shares in various companies in the U.S.A., principal among which is the North American Philips Corporation (N.A.P.C.). This corporation is both an operating company and a holding company of shares in a number of other companies in the United States.
The Trustee of the Trust is the Hartford National Bank and Trust Company, Hartford, Connecticut, U.S.A. The assets of the Trust are managed by the Trustee in accordance with the directives of the Governing Committee of the Trust.

EXHIBIT 2 (*continued*)

Due to the fact that the holders of shares in N.V. Gemeenschappelijk Bezit are as such also beneficiaries of the Trust, the consolidated figures of N.V. Philips and of the Trust are combined in this annual report. In this way shareholders of N.V. Gemeenschappelijk Bezit receive insight into their total interest in "Philips" as a whole. The holders of the few shares in N.V. Philips that are not in the possession of N.V. Gemeenschappelijk Bezit are likewise beneficiaries of the Trust.

Principles of valuation

Property, plant and equipment

These assets and their depreciation are valued at replacement value or at their value to the business, whichever is the lower. Changes in the replacement value are directly credited or charged to Revaluation surplus.

Intangible assets

Intangible assets are shown in the balance sheet at no value.

Investments in nonconsolidated associated companies

These investments are valued at their net tangible asset value, determined in accordance with the principles adopted in these annual accounts.

Sundry noncurrent assets

These assets are valued at purchase price or at estimated realizable value, whichever is the lower.

Stocks

Stocks, including work in progress, are valued at replacement value or at estimated realizable value, whichever is the lower.

Changes in replacement value are directly credited or charged to Revaluation surplus. The provision for the risk of obsolescence is deducted from the total figure for stocks. Profits arising from transactions within the Philips organization are eliminated.

Accounts receivable

Accounts receivable are shown at nominal value, less the provision for the risk of bad debts.

Liquid assets

Securities are valued at purchase price or at their listed stock exchange price at the end of the financial year, whichever is the lower; however, the shares in N.V. Gemeenschappelijk Bezit van Aandeelen Philips' Gloeilampenfabrieken and debentures of N.V. Philips' Gloeilampenfabrieken and of their subsidiaries are included at a valuation no higher than their par value. Cash at bank and in hand is shown at nominal value.

Minority interests

Minority interests in consolidated companies are valued on the basis of net tangible asset value, determined in accordance with the principles adopted in these annual accounts.

Sundry provisions

These provisions do not relate to specific assets; they are created to meet commitments and risks connected with the course of business.

The provision for pensions is based on actuarial calculations and relates to those pension liabilities that are not funded with separate pension funds or with third parties. Past service liabilities are in general covered over periods not extending beyond the retirement dates of the relevant employees. Together with the provisions of the individual pension funds, the provision created is equal to at least the present value of pension liabilities in respect of the total number of past years of service.

Long-term and current liabilities

These liabilities are taken up at nominal value.

EXHIBIT 2 (*concluded*)

Replacement value

The replacement value is determined, taking technological developments into account, on the basis of the current prices of specific assets, making use inter alia of indices. Transfers to Revaluation surplus pursuant to changes in the replacement value are made after deduction of deferred taxation.

Foreign currencies

In the Combined Statement of Financial Position amounts in foreign currency are converted into guilders at the official exchange rates ruling on the balance sheet date, unless circumstances, as, for instance, the trend of the purchasing power of the currency concerned, call for the adoption of a lower rate.

Exchange differences due to the conversion into guilders of property, plant and equipment and stocks are offset against revaluation surplus for the relevant country; in so far as such revaluation surplus is insufficient for this purpose, the deficiency is included as a miscellaneous charge in the the profit and loss account.

Exchange differences due to the conversion into guilders of nominal assets and liabilities are likewise included as miscellaneous income/charges in the profit and loss account.

In the Combined Statement of Results, sales and results in foreign currencies are converted at the rates applicable in the relevant periods.

The balances of the relevant profit and loss accounts are converted at the end of the year at the rates applied in the Combined Statement of Financial Position. The resultant difference is included under miscellaneous income/charges in the profit and loss account.

Principles of calculating profit

- The sales figure represents the net proceeds from goods and services supplied to third parties.
- Depreciation of property, plant, and equipment is calculated using fixed percentages of the replacement value on the basis of the expected life per category of asset. Write-downs to the value to the business are included under Depreciation.
- Consumption of raw materials and other elements in the cost of sales are also calculated on the basis of replacement value. Write-downs of stocks to a lower realizable value are charged to the cost of sales.
- Provisions for risks inherent in operations are built up in proportion to the volume of business.
- Expenditure on research, development, patents, licenses, copyrights, and concessions is charged in the current year to profit and loss account.
- Net amounts paid in excess of the net tangible asset value for the acquisition of participations in any year are included in the current year as a miscellaneous charge in the profit and loss account.
- For taxes on profit provisions are made on the basis of the profit figure determined in accordance with our principles of valuation, which implies that deferred taxation is taken into account. In so far as the cost of sales differs from historical cost owing to the use of the replacement value, the tax payable on that difference is charged to the provision made for deferred taxation at the time of revaluation.

Criteria for consolidation

The Combined Statements included the financial data of N.V. Philips' Gloeilampenfabrieken, of the United States Philips Trust and of their subsidiaries.

Subsidiaries are defined as companies more than half of whose issued or voting capital is held by
- N.V. Philips or the Trust directly, or by one of them jointly with one or more of its subsidiaries, or
- by one subsidiary or by two or more subsidiaries jointly.

The financial data of these companies are included in full in the consolidation; the minority interests of third parties are shown separately.

A few companies in which the holding, similarly determined, is 50% of the issued or voting capital (joint ventures) are also consolidated; the financial data of these companies are included in the proportion of 50%.

EXHIBIT 3
Calculation of net profit based on accounting principles
customary in the United States of America*

In the United States of America net profit attributable to ordinary shares is customarily determined by reducing net profit-sharing with Supervisory Board, Management and Officers, and with employees, pursuant to the Articles of Association on the subject of Profit Appropriation.

Moreover the accounting principles applied by N.V. Philips' Gloeilampenfabrieken in calculating profit differ in some respects from principles customarily followed in the United States.

An attempt is made below to estimate what adjustment to net profit would be required if those accounting principles customarily followed in the United States were applied that differ substantially from those of N.V. Philips' Gloeilampenfabrieken, viz.

- Depreciation on property, plant, and equipment based on the cost of the assets concerned.
- Cost of sales determined by applying the first-in, first-out method, except to a minor extent, as in the Combined Statements, the last-in, first-out method.
- A write-off period of five years for the amounts paid for the acquisition of participations in so far as the total of such payments in any year exceeds the total net tangible asset value acquired.

The tax effect of the foregoing principles has been taken into account.

	In millions of guilders	*In millions of U.S. $†*
The adjustment is as follows:		
Net profit 1977, shown in the Combined Statement of Results	633.6	277.9
Deduct: Profit-sharing with Supervisory Board, Management and Officers, and employees	− 50.3	− 22.1
Increase of net profit when applying the aforementioned accounting principles customarily followed in the United States	139.2	61.1
Adjusted net profit	722.5	316.9
(including f 3.3 m loss on operations to be discontinued)		
Number of ordinary shares of f 10 of N.V. Philips' Gloeilampenfabrieken outstanding at 31 December 1977	170,581,714	
Per ordinary share of f 10 of N.V. Philips' Gloeilampenfabrieken:		
Adjusted net profit	f 4.24	$1.86
Adjusted net profit, excluding a loss of f 3.3 m for operations to be discontinued	f 4.25	$1.87
Dividend	f 1.70	$0.75

Assuming conversion of all outstanding convertible debentures, the adjusted net profit per ordinary share would be f 3.97 ($1.74).

If the method of historical cost had been applied in the past it is estimated that the item Revaluation Surplus as shown in the Combined Statement of Financial Position as at 31 December 1977, would have appeared as follows:

	In millions of guilders	*In millions of U.S. $†*
Addition to retained profit	1,912.1	838.6
Deduction from property, plant and equipment, stocks, and provision for deferred taxation (net)	1,294.0	567.6
	3,206.1	1,406.2

* Information for American shareholders
† Converted at the rate of f 2.28 per U.S.$
Source: Philips 1977 annual report, p. 50.

⸻◄CASE III-10►⸻

Replacement value accounting (B): The Philips N.V. System

⸻⸺◄∞►⸺⸻

The Philips group of companies is a worldwide manufacturer of electronic equipment. (See Replacement Value Accounting (A): The Philips N.V. System.) The group consists of two major parts: N.V. Philip Gloeillampenfabricken (N.V. Philips) and its subsidiaries; and the United States Philips Trust. N.V. Philips, also known as Philips Industries is both an operating company in the Netherlands and a holding company of subsidiaries throughout the world. Almost all of the shares of N.V. Philips are owned by a holding company, N.V. Gemeenschappelijk Bezit. The U.S. Philips Trust holds shares in several U.S. companies, the most important of which is the North American Philips Corporation. Beneficiaries of the Trust are the shareholders of N.V. Gemeenschappelijk Bezit.

FINANCIAL ACCOUNTING PRACTICES OF PHILIPS

Philips' accounting practices differ from those generally accepted in the United States in several ways. Five of those differences are as follows:

1. Philips values property, plant, and equipment (fixed assets) at replacement cost. This valuation is also used to determine the periodic amounts of depreciation expense.
2. The company values inventories at the lower of replacement cost of estimated realizable value. This valuation is also used to determine the cost of goods sold.
3. The company recognizes losses on net monetary assets when inflation reduces their purchasing power.
4. When preparing consolidated statements, Philips adjusts the subsidiaries' financial statements as far as is practicably possible to reflect the parent company's accounting procedures. When feasible, the subsidiaries' books are maintained on a basis consistent with that used by the parent company.

This case was prepared from published materials by Professor M. Edgar Barrett and Katherine B. Penn. It is based, in part, on the same material used to develop an ICCH case called Philips N.V. (B): An application of Replacement Value Accounting (9-172-079). Copyright © 1978 by M. Edgar Barrett.

366

5. Philips translates foreign currency-denominated financial statements at exchange rates designed to reflect actual relationships in the relative purchasing power of each currency involved. This normally means that official exchange rates are used. It can mean, however, that "purchasing power" rates, developed and revised within the economics department of Philips, are used.

The first two differences were discussed in the (A) case. This case will deal with the last three differences.

OFFICIAL EXPLANATION OF PHILIPS' ACCOUNTING PRACTICES

In his article in the June 1960 issue of the *Journal of Accountancy*, Professor Goudeket also discussed the following issues. Portions paraphrased from the article appear in brackets.[1]

Investments

With regard to investments, the explanation can be brief. As far as consolidated subsidiaries are concerned, the principles of the parent company are also followed by subsidiaries. For the other investments we recommend that the companies keep the accounts along similar lines, since the principles, as already explained, are also appropriate for internal management policy. . . .

Nominal assets financed with stockholders' equity

As already mentioned, we in Philips believe that there can only be a profit if, after the application of the replacement value theory, the purchasing power of stockholders' equity has been maintained. The details of the procedure are given below on the basis of a classification of the balance sheet directed at this problem.

Balance Sheet
As at the Beginning of the Period

Inventories, fixed and intangible assets, and investments	a	Stockholders' equity	c
"Monetary" assets (as previously defined) (all remaining assets)	b	Liabilities	d
	x		x

Inventories, fixed and intangible assets, and investments are revalued according to the procedure set forth above. Since part of the stockholders' equity is invested in other (monetary) assets, the purchasing power of that part will diminish in case of a decrease in value of currency of the country. For this reason we calculate on the basis of the cost-of-living index, how many currency units represent the same purchasing power as the part of capital which at the beginning of the period was invested in monetary assets. In the example given above, this amount equals $b - d$. This balance, multiplied by the inflation factor based on the cost-of-living index, leads to the entry:

---

[1] "An Application of Replacement Value Theory," the *Journal of Accountancy*, July 1960, pp. 37–47. Copyright 1960 by the American Institute of CPAs. Reproduced with permission.

Dr.   Cost of inflation   (income account)
Cr.   Reserve for diminishing purchasing
      power of capital invested in monetary assets   (capital account)

Thus the income statement shows a result after the purchasing power of stock-holders' equity has been maintained.

When making monthly balance sheets and income statements, the necessary information is always available at short notice. The intervals at which the calculations are made are determined by the pace at which the currency of the country is decreasing in value; the faster the pace, the shorter the interval will be.

The foregoing should logically imply that in the case of an increase in the purchasing power of money, a profit should be recorded. With regard to this aspect, the company follows this rule; profits may be recognized to the extent that past losses of this nature have been shown. The profit to be taken is therefore limited to the maximum of the balance of the [balance sheet] account for diminishing purchasing power in monetary assets. . . .

Foreign currencies

With an international concern such as Philips, rates of exchange of foreign currencies are of such importance that, although only indirectly connected with revaluation, they must be discussed. In general we at Philips follow the principle that assets and liabilities in foreign currencies should be converted at the rates of exchange at the balance sheet date. Each unit within the company does this in its own accounts. Exchange differences are charged or credited to the income accounts.

In connection with revaluation, the problem which requires special attention is the establishment of the rates of exchange of currencies. [These rates are used] for computation of the value of foreign investments in the annual financial statements of the parent company and in the consolidated statements. The economic research department works on this problem. The maximum rate of exchange used for conversion purposes is the official quotation. Foreign exchange rates are under continuous investigation in order to determine, country by country, whether each country's internal economic situation, the international positions of its currency, or other considerations, such as restrictions of transfers, might indicate the desirability of using conversion rates other than official rates. In these cases, rates are established in which the trend of the relationship between the purchasing power of the currency of the country concerned and of the Netherlands is carefully considered. At Philips, rates of exchange calculated in this way are called "purchasing power rates."

Since in general there is a relationship between the trend of the price level in a country and the fluctuations in the rate of exchange of its currency, the balance sheet of the foreign subsidiary is converted at the established rate of the country concerned. [At times, this] rate is lower than the one at the previous balance sheet date, [and, as a] result, . . . the (current) net worth of the affiliate, calculated in the currency of the parent company, is lower than the intrinsic value of the investment according to the (parent's) books[.T]his difference—being an unfavorable exchange difference—is set off as far as possible against the amounts which the affiliate in the course of the financial year has credited to the revaluation surplus and to the account for the diminishing purchasing power of capital invested in monetary assets. The remaining balance of the exchange difference account is transferred to the income account.

[Net monetary liabilities of foreign subsidiaries]

Occasionally the balance sheet of a subsidiary, after elimination in intercompany balances, shows a credit balance for capital invested in monetary assets; that is to say, it has more debts owing to third parties than accounts receivable and liquid resources. In such a case, conversion of the foreign currency at a lower rate than the official quotation would not be economically correct. Although from a legal point of view the parent company is not required to provide for a possible shortage of liquid assets, since this will be the case economically, a provision is made for the difference between the purchasing power rate and the official quotation, calculated on the credit balance concerned.[2]

It is generally acknowledged that the currency problem is a very complicated one. We believe that by the procedure adopted we have succeeded in showing the losses due to inflation and finding a solution which is as simple as possible and which serves the determination of income and capital.

In addition to the differences in accounting practices, Professor Goudeket also discussed the effects of the replacement value theory in the areas of tax, dividend policy, and employment of invested capital.[3]

Tax considerations

I think it is clear that tax considerations play an important part in the thinking of many persons who are opposed to the replacement value theory; in my opinion this is not justified.

It is true that in many countries taxes are calculated on the basis of historical cost. In some countries certain provisions in the tax statutes and regulations exist, the use of which reduce the effects of changing prices (e.g., the Lifo inventory

---

[2] The net effect of this policy is that Philips is more likely to recognize a loss than a gain. This is all that you need to understand for purposes of case analysis. However, if you are curious about the mechanics, consider the following example:

Imagine a subsidiary located in country X. At the beginning of the accounting period, both the official exchange rate and Philips' "purchasing power rate" reflect a ratio (country X currency to Dutch guilders) of 2.0:1.0. The foreign currency falls in value, relative to the Dutch guilder, during the accounting period. At the end of the accounting period, the official exchange rate is 3.0:1.0, while the "purchasing power rate" is 4.0:1.0.

Now, consider that the foreign subsidiary maintains a net monetary liability position throughout the accounting period, of 1,000, in country X currency. The issue at hand would be one of determining the amount of the consolidated firm's gain, in either Dutch guilders or country X currency.

As seen in country X currency and via the purchasing power rate, the consolidated firm's gain would be 1,000 [4/2 times 1,000, less 1,000]. Philips, however, would only recognize a gain of 500 [3/2 times 1,000, less 1,000].

On the other hand, if all conditions were identical except that the subsidiary maintained a net monetary asset position of 1,000, a loss of 1,000 would be recognized. Thus, gains are calculated by using whichever exchange rate gives the smallest gain. The rate chosen to calculate a loss, however, is whichever rate produces the largest loss.

[3] "An Application of Replacement Value Theory," *The Journal of Accounting*, July 1960, pp. 37–47. Copyright 1960 by the American Institute of CPAs. Reproduced with permission.

method). This does not imply, however, that accounting followed for tax purposes should also be employed for management purposes or for financial reporting purposes. It is not unusual for major differences to exist between a company's tax returns and its published financial statements. If the replacement value theory is accepted, then it must be conceded that to use tax principles in the accounts is to knowingly disclose an incorrect picture of income and capital which might lead to wrong impressions and decisions. If it is thought appropriate, the variation in taxation resulting from a difference in economic and taxable profits can be shown separately in the annual financial statements.

There is still another reason why advocates of the replacement value theory in particular should not employ tax principles in the accounts. It would, of course, be desirable if the tax authorities too would accept the replacement value theory. However, one cannot expect the tax authorities to do so, or rather to convince them that they should do so, if one follows tax principles for management purposes and for the information of the public.

It seems to me that one demonstrates the great importance of an economically correct presentation by applying it both in the accounting system and in the published annual statements; and by so doing one may hope to succeed in changing the views of the tax authorities.

Dividend policy

The replacement value theory is also important in relation to a company's dividend policy. When profits are computed on the basis of historical cost, there is a risk of distributing dividends which represent not only profits but also part of the funds required for replacements, and consequently for the continuity of the enterprise. If all the historical profits were distributed to shareholders, it might result in the enterprise eventually having to go into the capital market for funds with which to maintain the same volume of business. Some of my American colleagues contend that a well-managed enterprise will of course retain a part of its profits for replacements and that the ultimate position in both cases is the same. The difference, however, is that in the one case only that amount is shown as a profit which can be distributed without danger to the continuity of the enterprise, whereas in the other case a larger amount is disclosed as a profit which, if completely distributed, might endanger the continuity of the enterprise. Even if the distribution of the profits were to be the same in both cases, the historical basis would show a larger profit and a larger profit retention than the replacement value basis. In my view, this would create an entirely wrong impression. . . .

The replacement value theory also plays a role in a company's selling-price policy to the extent that costs are a basis for the determination of the selling prices. Selling prices are also determined by competition, but until competition makes itself felt, selling prices are based in part on costs. The replacement value theory, therefore, may have a direct bearing on the gross income of the enterprise.

Employment of invested capital

The replacement theory is also important in measuring the effective employment of invested capital. If the information on profits is not measured against the real capital employed, then the information is inadequate. The ratio of profits to capital is an important indicator both for the management of the enterprise and for the investor. However, if the capital is not calculated on the basis of replacement value, then the profits are measured against a capital which has little economic meaning. If capital is not adjusted to reflect replacement value, it is nothing but an arithmetical balance on which no opinion of the earning capacity can be based.

Much attention is given to the distinction between earned and capital surplus. Therefore, it is all the more obvious that the increase in capital due to the rise in price levels should not be shown in the balance sheet as part of earned surplus.[4] The use of replacement value theory will automatically achieve this desired result.

---

[4] The term *earned surplus* has been replaced, in American financial statements, by the term *retained earnings* [editor].

····CASE III-11·····

Drago Chemical

In October 1974, Ralph Reeves, managing director of Drago Chemical, was reviewing his financial director's proposal for changes in the company's management control system. The proposed changes, prepared at Mr. Reeves' request, made explicit provision for inflation accounting.

Drago Chemical's manufacturing was centered in Southern England. The company's major products included PVC, plasticizers, polyethylenes, surfactants, and herbicides. The heads of the five manufacturing divisions and the several staff departments reported to the managing director. Over 30 percent of the company's sales were outside the United Kingdom (although mostly within the EEC).

The capital investments of each division were carefully reviewed at the corporate level; in most respects, however, each division manager was free to pursue his business objectives. For control purposes, a division was organized as an investment center. Each was expected to steadily improve current performance while pursuing long-term viability. In August 1974, all divisions had a positive ROI. Nevertheless, there were wide variances in their returns; the two least profitable divisions had ROIs of 2 percent and 4 percent.

In mid-1974, although pleased with Drago's current financial performance (Exhibit 1), Ralph Reeves had become concerned about the impact of in-

---

This case was prepared by Professor F. Warren McFarlan.

flation on the firm's profitability (Exhibit 2). Accordingly, he had asked his financial director to study the internal impact of inflation. He knew the subject of external reporting was under active study in the UK. (Exhibit 3). However, he felt that Drago's approach to this issue for management control and for performance appraisal should be independent of statutory requirements for external reporting and for the Inland Revenue Service.

Mr. Reeves was impressed by the simplicity and comprehensive approach of the financial director's report (Appendix). Nonetheless, he wondered if the proposed procedures would adequately reflect what happened to his stocks of raw materials, works in process, and finished goods. During the last 12 months, this stock had dropped about 2 percent in tonnage, although the mix of products had remained almost the same. In the same 12 months, however, the rapid rise in the prices of raw materials had inflated the value of his stock from slightly over £6.6 million to £11.6 million. (As was common in the UK stock was valued on a first-in, first-out basis.)

Reeves was also mindful of a recent chance conversation with the head of Drago's most important union. The union head had been complimentary

EXHIBIT 1

DRAGO CHEMICAL
Profit and Loss Statement
(£000)

	Half year August 31, 1974	Full year February 28, 1974
Turnover	40,080	48,002
Trading profit		
Before following deductions	3,806	4,604
Depreciation	492	980
Interest charges	354	810
Profit before tax	2,960	2,814
Tax	1,598	1,458
Profit after tax	1,362	1,356

EXHIBIT 2
Inflation in the UK, 1963–1973

Year	Consumer price index	Annual inflation	Cumulative inflation
1963	100	—	—
1964	103	3%	3%
1965	108	5	8
1966	112	4	12
1967	115	3	15
1968	121	5	21
1969	127	5	27
1970	135	6	35
1971	148	10	48
1972	158	7	58
1973	173	10	73

EXHIBIT 3
The state of inflation accounting in the UK—October 1974*

In London, the Sandilands Committee on Inflation Accounting is hard at work in an attempt to produce its recommendations by early 1975. Last May, the Institute of Chartered Accountants published its provisional *Statement of Standard Accounting Practice No. 7 (SSAP 7)*. This contains proposals for adapting conventional historic cost accounts to conditions of inflation. The *Statement* supports the current purchasing power or general price-level method of adjustment. The accountants point out that management must be able to appreciate the effects of inflation on costs, profits, distribution policies, dividend cover, borrowing power, return on investment, and cash requirements.

Although the Institute opinion supports the current purchasing power method, the Sandilands Committee is still analyzing the advantages and disadvantages of the replacement cost method. The replacement cost method has many supporters in industry who argue that it is better to use a more complex system in an effort to approach the truth than to use a rigid, easy-to-apply formula which will always be inaccurate.

The ease of applying the current purchasing power system for the company and the ease of auditing it for the accountant make the system an attractive one. Although the Sandilands Committee has made no disclosures on which way it is leaning, many feel that they will attempt a synthesis of the two methods. There is currently a loophole in *SSAP 7* allowing companies to revalue assets as well as to apply a rigid index to their original purchase cost. If the Sandilands Committee decides to support this decision, the controversy over the two systems may become irrelevant.

* *Financial Times*, October 3, 1974.

about the company's recent results (Exhibit 1), which he had just seen. Then he had expressed the hope that all who had helped to achieve those results could share amicably in the obviously ample rewards.

Of equal concern to Mr. Reeves was a recent letter that Drago's chairman had sent to the stockholders. The chairman had hailed the firm's record performance in sales and earnings; he added that he intended to pay an increased dividend for the year, "up to the maximum" then permitted. Mr. Reeves was partly reassured, since Drago's pretax profit of £2,960,000 came only after deduction of a special one-time contribution of £900,000 to the corporate pension fund. (This was to recognize the fund's increased liabilities, "an inevitable consequence of inflationary pressures upon remuneration.") For that reason, Mr. Reeves felt that the company's real earnings were somewhat higher than the announced figure.

Mr. Reeves had a further bit of relevant information: in the last six months, Drago had incurred a tax liability of £1,598,000 as a result of operations. However, the company had acquired considerable new equipment during the same period. Since the associated tax credits were large enough to balance the liability, no tax would have to be paid.

QUESTIONS

1. How much inflation-adjusted profit do you believe Drago earned during the last six months?

2. Should this inflation-adjusted profit figure be the basis for calculating the firm's return on investment?

APPENDIX: DRAGO CHEMICAL

To: Mr. Ralph Reeves, Managing Director
From: Mr. John Thompson
Date: October 7, 1974

Pursuant to our discussion of last month, I have investigated the feasibility of incorporating an inflation accounting approach into our ongoing Management Control System. It is my opinion that while many aspects of an inflation accounting approach are counter-balancing insofar as their ultimate impact on the firm's profit, the overall impact on profits could be sufficiently significant that we should move to an inflation accounting approach for internal purposes, effective January 1. The rest of this memorandum details the approach I believe we should follow and Exhibit A shows how these procedures would have impacted our stated earnings for the last six months.

Debtors, Creditors, Stock, and Fixed Assets are all subject to inflation adjustments, which will affect the company's real profitability. Accordingly I plan to process these items each quarter to take into account the impact of inflation during the quarter. *The Economist* Intelligence Unit's index (EIU) will be used on an annual basis to revalue our Fixed Assets.* The Retail Price Index (RPI) will be used on other assets and liabilities.

EXHIBIT A
Impact of inflation on company accounts (£000)

	Year ending February 28, 1974	Half year ending August 31, 1974
Profits before tax per conventional accounts	2,822	2,960
Less taxes	1,524	1,599
Profit after tax conventional accounts...............	1,298	1,361
Adjustments		
1. Stocks (restatement of stocks at beginning and end of year)	(370)	(668)
2. Depreciation (additional depreciation due to adjusting fixed asset values)	(524)	(304)
3. Monetary items (gain due to excess of monetary liabilities over monetary assets)	570	278
Net adjustments	(324)	(694)
Profit before tax expressed in £s of current purchasing power at the end of the period	2,498	2,266
Less taxes	1,524	1,599
Profit after tax in £ current purchasing power	974	667

---

* EIU Index is an industry replacement value index created by the Economist Intelligence Unit of *The Economist* magazine. The EIU produces 16 indexes for various industries. An industry index is established by selecting a number of different types of standard equipment

APPENDIX (*continued*)

EXHIBIT B
Calculation of change in profits of a division moving from historical cost accounting to inflation adjusted accounting (March 1, 1975-May 31, 1975)

1. *Historical accounting*
   a. Capital employed

	March 1, 1975	May 31, 1975
Accounts receivable (debtors)	1,000	1,000
Accounts payable (creditors)	400	450
Net monetary assets	600	550
Stock	1,000	900
Net book value, fixed assets	300	289
Total capital employed	1,900	1,739

   b. Profit

Profit before tax and depreciation.............	276
Depreciation (on historically valued assets)	11
Profit before tax.............................	265

2. *Retail price index*

December 31	201
January 31	202
February 28.................................	203
March 31	206
April 30	208
May 31......................................	209

3. *Fixed assets adjusted by EIU index (£000)*

March 1, 1975	400
June 30, 1975...............................	385

4. *Calculations of impact of inflation on profits*

		Gain/(loss)
Net monetary assets	$\left[\dfrac{600 \times 209}{203}\right] - 600 =$	(18)
Opening stock	$\left[\dfrac{1{,}000 \times 209}{(201 + 203) \times \frac{1}{2}}\right] - 1{,}000 =$	(35)
Closing stock	$\left[\dfrac{900 \times 209}{(206 + 209) \times \frac{1}{2}}\right] - 900 =$	7
Depreciation	$\left[\dfrac{400 \times 11}{300} \times \dfrac{209}{203}\right] - 11 =$	(4)
		(51)

representative of the industry. The number of deliveries of a piece of equipment determines its relative importance. The change in the manufacturer's sale price over a certain period of time is then considered and weighted according to the relative importance of each piece of equipment to determine the EIU. The weighting of the various pieces of equipment is revised as the items become obsolete.

APPENDIX (*concluded*)

Quarterly, all Assets and Liabilities will be adjusted for inflation using only the Retail Price Index (the base value of Fixed Assets being the calculated EIU values as of March 1 each year). If anything, we are understating the specific effect of inflation on the company since chemical industry raw material prices have soared in the past 12 months. The table gives a brief feel for the magnitude of the changes in our plant values as a result of using the EIU index.

Net book value (£000)

	Historical	*Current purchasing power*
Plant A	1,538	2,392
Plant B	452	820
Plant C	360	604
⋮		

The specific procedure for calculating the effect of inflation is as follows, and the impact worked out in detail for a hypothetical Division A in Exhibit B:

A. Net monetary assets (i.e., debtors less creditors)

The closing Retail Price Index is divided by the opening Retail Price Index. The percentage uplift multiplied by the value of the opening net monetary assets is the loss (profit if net monetary liability) to be offset against the historically recorded profits.

B. Stock

The index to be used for the opening stock must be back-dated to allow for the period over which that stock was purchased (if 2 month's stock in hand, then the opening index is the average index of those 2 months). This index is divided into the closing index, etc., as above.

The closing stock, on a similar basis, would yield a CPP profit in the period, i.e.;

$$\frac{\text{RPI @ closing date}}{\text{RPI @ Average of last 2 months}} \times \text{Value of closing stock}$$

$$- \text{Value of closing stock} = \text{Profit in period}$$

C. Fixed assets

The depreciation charge is to be uplifted by the proportion the historical costs is to the current value.

───CASE III-12───

Alcan Aluminium Limited (A)

At the Annual General Meeting of Shareholders on March 13, 1975, John H. Hale, executive vice president, finance, of Alcan Aluminium Limited presented the first public set of inflation-adjusted financial statements for Alcan Aluminium Limited. Although Alcan was not required to prepare or disclose such information, management felt that there were environmental factors which made disclosure of the effects of inflation necessary and desirable.

Alcan Aluminium Limited is engaged, through its subsidiaries and affiliates in 33 countries, in all phases of the aluminium business from bauxite mining to finished aluminium and products. Eighty percent of total company assets are in Canada, the United States, Britain, and Europe. Revenues for 1974 of $2.4 billion made Alcan one of the largest companies in the aluminum industry.

INFLATION AND ITS IMPACT

The economic environment in 1974 was affected by significant inflation. Inflation did not begin in the 1970s. However, prior to 1970 inflation in most developed industrialized countries had been fairly steady, with the exception of postwar periods. This continuing inflation had affected the information presented in the financial statements. Managements and the accounting profession were aware that inflation led to some distortions in reports; adding dollars spent on plant and equipment this year to dollars spent on plant and equipment five years ago was rather like adding apples and oranges, or, if you prefer, British pounds and Japanese yen. *Dollars* of one time period simply were not comparable as measures of purchasing power to dollars in another time period. However, since inflation was fairly steady and its effects were thought to be known, little attention was given to them and no action was taken to change accounting standards or reporting practices.

By 1973–74, this situation had changed. Rates of inflation had increased dramatically in many countries, as shown by the data in Exhibit 1. At Alcan,

---

This case was prepared by Julie H. Hertenstein, research assistant, under the supervision of Professor William J. Bruns, Jr.

EXHIBIT 1
Annual rates of inflation shown by price indexes in various countries

	1967–1971 (Average)	1973	1974	1975	1976
Canada	4%	8%	10%	11%	6%
United States*	4	6	11	9	5
United Kingdom	6	9	16	25	15
Germany.............	3	7	7	6	4

Note: All of the above figures are based on the consumer price index or nearest equivalent in the countries concerned and are stated to the nearest whole number.
* The annual rate of inflation in the United States was 7 percent in 1977.
Source: From "World-Wide Developments in Inflation Accounting," Coopers and Lybrand, 1977.

a sense of urgency developed as management came to feel their financial reports were not presenting an accurate picture of the results of operations. Record profits were reported at the same time management realized that the funds generated by operations were insufficient to replace the assets they were using up. Other managements and companies were experiencing the same problems, and the business periodicals frequently began to mention the problems caused by inflation. (Appendix A).

Harold Carstairs, chief accounting officer at Alcan, explained their perception of the situation in this manner:

Everyone knew intuitively that inflation was occurring and that historical costs were not right. You simply can't add the cost of older assets to the cost of new assets and come up with a figure that's meaningful for anyone. The double digit inflation of 1973–74 brought this issue to the forefront. I think that the escalation of oil prices provided a shock which brought everything into focus. Looking at the cost of oil turned attention to what was happening to the costs of inventory and fixed assets.

In their 1974 report to shareholders, Alcan management discussed the effect of this inflation on the company:

Earnings for Alcan . . . surpassed all previous levels. Excluding a $27.4 million gain on the sale of one-half of Alcan's interest in [a] Norwegian company, net income was $141.8 million or $4.11 per share compared with $82.6 million and $2.42 in 1973. . . .

The strong inflationary forces which intensified as the year progressed contributed to increased profits. . . . [These profits] contain an *inventory profit*, estimated at $112 million at the gross profit level, reflecting the fact that in times of rising costs and under the company's general accounting policy of using the *average cost* method to value inventories, the cost charged to cost of sales is less than the current production cost, owing to delay in inventory until the product is sold. The Lifo (last-in, first-out) method of inventory accounting, which is approved for income tax purposes in the United States, was adopted by the company's U.S. subsidiary during the fourth quarter, retroactive to 1 January

1974, and reduced the company's previously reported earnings for the first 9 months by $11.5 million, and for the full year by $13.6 million. . . . The uncertainty of continuing *inventory profits* and the decline in the real value of the dollar should be taken into account in evaluating the level of earnings.

The unprecedent inflationary environment created cost pressures, cash requirements, and other events of a magnitude far greater than anticipated. . . . The large increase in operating working capital absorbed more than 80 percent of the company's total cash generation for the year. . . . Despite an increase in cash generation to a record $275 million, Alcan needed to borrow $193 million on medium and long term, and to increase its short-term borrowings by $88 million, in order to maintain its capital investment program in the face of unprecedented requirements for working capital funds. By year-end, total investment in operating working capital (defined for this purpose as the total of receivables and inventories) reduced by payables and current tax liabilities, had risen by $226 million. This was not only attributable to a growth in physical inventories but also, to a very considerable extent, to the added cost of replacing old inventory with new at higher costs, and of financing sales at higher prices.

Most of the countries in which Alcan operates do not allow income tax relief on *inventory profits*, but the United Kingdom has recently introduced such a measure, and the United States achieves the same result by permitting Lifo accounting. In a continuing business, the whole of the inventory profit is required to finance the growing value of inventory and therefore the imposition of current income taxes on such profits represents an added and unreasonable strain on a company's liquidity. . . .

Expenditures on plant and equipment and investments in 1974 amounted to $268 million, a figure more than double the 1973 total, but one in which a substantial proportion of the increase was accounted for by inflation.

. . . . While Alcan ended 1974 in a relatively strong financial position with no material change in its debt equity structure, the future capital required to maintain and modernize existing facilities and to expand appears out of proportion to the likely availability of funds. . . . The impact of inflation which has already occurred poses major financial problems for Alcan and probably for all others in a capital intensive industry. If traditional standards remain unchanged such as the historical valuation of assets and allowable depreciation thereon, taxation of inventory profits, present norms for debt ratios and present thinking related to *normal* profitability, the ability to finance and sustain modern plant, and to undertake even modest expansion is thrown into serious doubt. . . . In the absence of higher profits than those that have been earned, present procedures effectively erode the capital base of industries such as ours.

Harold Carstairs expanded:

The biggest practical aspect of inflation is in pricing your product. For labor, materials and assets, you need current costs. Fixed assets must constantly be replaced. Therefore, you must earn a return by pricing your products such that you can replace your fixed assets. In the aluminum ingot business, you are dealing with a basic product which is an international commodity and the price of aluminium ingot is mainly determined by supply and demand. No single ingot producer can set the price; therefore we must be aware of our current costs and keep them down, in order to earn an adequate return. In contrast, the fabricated aluminium products are more specialized and sales are primarily local. In this market, Alcan is sometimes able to raise prices in order to pass along increased costs.

ACCOUNTING FOR INFLATION

Although the problems that inflation was creating in financial statements were fairly clear, a solution to those problems was not obvious. The accounting professions in many countries were studying possible solutions, and groups in several countries were drafting proposals for changing financial reporting standards to account for some of the effects of inflation. In 1974, it appeared that similar methods for accounting for inflation would be adopted in the United States and the UK. In February 1974, the Financial Accounting Standards Board (FASB) issued a discussion memorandum on reporting the effects of changes in general purchasing power (GPP) in financial statements. Many observers expected a recommended procedure to be issued by year-end. The Accounting Standards Steering Committee (ASSC) of the Institute of Chartered Accountants in the UK had issued, in January 1973, *Exposure Draft 8*, "Accounting for Changes in the Purchasing Power of Money." This was followed by a provisional *Standard Accounting Practice* in May 1974, urging companies to publish current purchasing power (CPP) information. Both GPP and CPP accounting are concerned with removing the effects that changes in the general purchasing power of money have had on accounts. They measure assets and liabilities in terms of the current balance sheet data using an index to adjust all historical dollar measurements to reflect the current purchasing power used in transactions.

1974 . . . the first step

Noting the attention being given to the problems of accounting for inflation and their possible solutions, managers at Alcan felt it was likely that some version of CPP would soon be adopted in the United States and the UK. Alcan supported the use of this method for shareholder reporting purposes. Management felt that the use of CPP accounting would provide shareholders more useful information than historic statements had because they were expressed in units of purchasing power.

Another factor made it easier for Alcan to prepare inflation-adjusted financial statements. Alcan, with subsidiaries in dozens of foreign nations, was constantly faced with the task of converting from one foreign currency to another, especially converting from various currencies to U.S. dollars for the purposes of financial reporting. Alcan saw very little difference between converting from the German deutsche mark to the U.S. dollar with their differences in purchasing power, and in converting from 1960 dollars to 1974 dollars given their differences in purchasing power. Conceptually, using CPP accounting was an easy transition for them to make.

There were, then, four primary reasons which led to Alcan's decision to begin publicly reporting inflation-adjusted figures. First, inflation was high, and it was having a significant impact upon Alcan's financial statements. Second, it appeared that new accounting standards would soon require this type of inflation reporting, and Alcan wanted to provide useful guidance in the development of inflation accounting standards. Third, Alcan management felt that the CPP method of inflation reporting was appropriate for shareholders purposes. Fourth, they were familiar with the process of foreign currency translation.

Once Alcan decided to implement this public reporting of inflation adjusted financial statements, management had to choose the exact process by which this would be accomplished within the company. This was a complex decision, because Alcan operates in many countries which have different currencies and different rate of inflation. When Alcan management investigated the process, they considered two major alternatives:

1. The first alternative was labeled the "Restate and Translate" method. Under this method each local company would restate its financial position for the change in purchasing power of its currency, and then translate the results into U.S. dollars for consolidation purposes.
2. The second method was labeled the "Translate and Restate" method. This method would involve translation of financial information to U.S. dollars at the exchange rates appropriate at the time of the transaction, and then indexing the consolidated dollar amounts forward using the U.S. implicit price deflator.

Alcan chose the latter method. Since they had translated local statements to U.S. dollars since 1971 (Alcan reported in Canadian dollars prior to 1971), existing records on assets were already expressed in common terms, U.S. or Canadian dollars. Therefore, to restate would require only one inflation index. To "Restate and Translate" would have required an inflation index for every country where the company had operations. Since all necessary data in U.S. dollars was already available at headquarters, restatement could be performed by the headquarters accounting staff without involving staff at other locations.

The next decision which faced Alcan was whether to present statements showing the effects of inflation in the annual report or at the shareholders meeting. Alcan decided to present the information at the annual meeting of shareholders which provided John Hale an opportunity to personally explain Alcan's reasons for preparing this information and to interpret the results as shown in the restated financial statements. John Hale's address to the shareholders and the restated financial statements are included in Exhibit 2. Alcan received little reaction to their disclosure of inflation-adjusted financial

EXHIBIT 2
Accounting for the impact of inflation on Alcan

Each year we publish an Annual Report, which contains the consolidated financial statements of the company and its subsidiaries, to provide shareholders and others who have invested in Alcan with the means to judge the economic performance of the company. Those consolidated financial statements are prepared in accordance with generally accepted accounting principles in North America, which have been developed over a long period in a relatively stable economic environment. Fundamentally, those conventional statements show where money has come from and how it has been used, but in so doing they represent a composite of transactions measured in units of differing purchasing power over many years.

The purchasing power of the dollar has been declining over the years with the rate of inflation increasing significantly during the last few years. For example, $1,000 in 1950 was the equivalent of about $1,500 in 1965 and $2,200 in 1974. Financial statements prepared on the conventional basis, therefore, do not reflect the impact of inflation on the results of operations and the financial position of companies. The fixed assets figure, for example, is an addition of the original cost of assets in the dollars of the year of acquisition—but each year the dollar had a different value—so they are not really directly additive. We have therefore prepared for your information supplementary financial statements in units of current purchasing power—that is, in 1974 dollars.

Various methods have been proposed to recognize the effects of inflation on financial reporting. At first sight, revaluing the assets on a basis of market value or replacement cost might seem to be more satisfactory than simply taking the historic cost and converting it into current dollars. However, both market value and replacement cost require the exercise of expert judgement—and three different experts would probably come up with widely differing figures. On the other hand, producing current dollar accounts is a mathematical exercise such as converting the accounts of a German company, for example, from deutsche marks to dollars. The figures are precise, not based on personal judgment, and can be audited. Consequently, professional accounting bodies in Canada, U.S.A., and UK have selected the current purchasing power method whereby accounts are restated by use of a general index, measuring the rate of inflation from the dates of original transactions to the balance sheet date, and have issued provisional guidelines on the procedures to be used. We have provided you with condensed consolidated financial statements of Alcan for 1974 and 1973, prepared in comparative form showing the conventional and current dollar amounts, with notes explaining the latter, and a reconciliation of the difference between net income in the conventional accounts with that in the current dollar accounts.

Decreases in the purchasing power of the dollar affect individual businesses differently, depending on the amount of the change, and the age and composition of the company's assets and liabilities in a period of inflation. For example, monetary assets (principally cash and accounts receivables) obviously suffer a loss when the purchasing power of the dollar declines, while monetary liabilities, such as long-term debt, result in a gain because the liabilities are repaid in dollars with a lesser value. In capital-intensive companies, such as Alcan, the increase in the depreciation charge for plant and equipment and the reduced obligation for long-term debt, when restated on a current dollar basis, are very significant. Of course the gain on long-term debt represents a loss to the lender, of which all lenders are aware, and they compensate for it by charging a rate of interest high enough to give a margin over expected inflation.

Examination of the accompanying statements shows several significant differences between the historic and current dollar accounts, some of which are obvious and others less so. On balance, Alcan is shown as having withstood the pressures of inflation reasonably well. In periods of double-digit inflation, Alcan's debt structure gives rise to large gains on its monetary liabilities, which offset the increased charges for depreciation and the corrected inventory cost in the current dollar accounts. However, in periods of more modest inflation, such monetary gains will be less, but the higher charge for depreciation will continue. Under current dollar accounting Alcan's debt/equity ratio improves, but the return on shareholders' equity is lower. In that connection one might comment that although the return is lower it does represent a more realistic measure of the return. It is sometimes said that interest on long-term bonds represents

Source: Remarks by John H. Hale, executive vice president, finance of Alcan Aluminium Limited at the Annual General Meeting of Shareholders, March 13, 1975.

EXHIBIT 2 (*continued*)

a "real" interest of about 4 percent plus expected inflation. If that is true, and if we accept that a real interest rate should be about 4 percent, then perhaps a current dollar equity return of 7 percent or 8 percent might be considered normal. Incidentally, you may notice that the inventory profit, which is eliminated in the current dollar accounts, differs from the *inventory profits* reported under the conventional accounting concept. The reason for this is that Alcan's actual costs increased at a rate which differed from the increase in the general price level index used for purposes of the current dollar accounts. And finally, the net book value of shareholders' equity at 31 December 1974 was $45.55 per share in the current dollar accounts, compared to $31.41 per share in the historic accounts.

The company's auditors, Price Waterhouse & Co., have reviewed these supplementary financial statements, and have agreed with the principles and procedures applied in their preparation.

In conclusion, I would like to emphasize that the main purpose of these supplementary financial statements is to demonstrate on a comparative basis Alcan's results of operations and financial position in terms of a common denominator—the current purchasing power of the dollar. I believe such presentations do provide a more realistic picture than the historic accounts, and for that reason they will be adopted more and more widely in the future. In due course one might hope that governments also will accept this view and tax on this basis.

Supplementary comparative consolidated financial statements

	Current dollar purchasing power (*in 1974 dollars*)		Conventional (*as reported*)	
	1974	1973	1974	1973
		(*in millions of U.S. dollars*)		
Results of operations for the year:				
Revenues	$ 2,548.2	$ 2,160.0	$ 2,426.8	$ 1,891.1
Costs, expenses and other items	2,323.1	2,051.5	2,199.9	1,773.7
Income before income taxes	225.1	108.5	226.9	117.4
Income taxes	89.3	39.9	85.1	34.8
Income before extraordinary gain	135.8	68.6	141.8	82.6
Gain on sale of investment	13.2	—	27.4	—
Net income	$ 149.0	$ 68.6	$ 169.2	$ 82.6
		(*in U.S. dollars*)		
Income per common share:				
Before extraordinary item	$ 3.93	$ 2.00	$ 4.11	$ 2.42
Extraordinary item	.38	—	.79	—
Net income	$ 4.31	$ 2.00	$ 4.90	$ 2.42
		(*in millions of U.S. dollars*)		
Balance sheet:				
Current assets	$ 1,376.4	$ 1,091.2	$ 1,343.3	$ 961.3
Deferred receivables and charges	73.4	78.7	73.4	70.8
Investment in companies owned 50% or less	284.0	283.2	211.5	199.3
Property, plant and equipment	4,354.1	4,170.1	2,749.7	2,547.8
Less: Accumulated depreciation and depletion	(2,547.7)	(2,417.4)	(1,420.2)	(1,330.3)
	$ 3,540.2	$ 3,205.8	$ 2,957.7	$ 2,448.9

EXHIBIT 2 (*concluded*)

	Current dollar purchasing power (in 1974 dollars)		Conventional (as reported)	
	1974	1973	1974	1973
	(in millions of U.S. dollars)			
Balance sheet (cont.):				
Current liabilities	$ 701.8	$ 576.6	$ 701.8	$ 519.6
Long-term debt	886.0	825.4	886.0	743.6
Deferred income taxes	160.9	136.3	160.9	122.8
Minority interests	206.1	195.8	116.2	106.3
Shareholders' equity:				
Preferred shares	4.3	6.0	2.6	3.5
Common shares	487.2	477.2	275.7	266.2
Retained earnings	1,093.9	988.5	814.5	686.9
	1,585.4	1,471.7	1,092.8	956.6
	$ 3,540.2	$ 3,205.8	$ 2,957.7	$ 2,448.9
Debt/equity ratio	37/63	38/62	46/54	46/54
Return on shareholders' equity (excluding extraordinary gain)	8.9%	4.7%	13.8%	8.9%

Notes on current dollar purchasing power statement

1. **Index used**

   As Alcan publishes its financial statements in U.S. dollars, the U.S. Gross National Product Implicit Price Deflator was used to convert historic dollars to current dollars. This index is considered sufficiently comprehensive to measure fluctuations in the general purchasing power of the dollar. Based on the latest available statistics, a rate of inflation of 11.3 percent was used for 1974.

2. **Nonmonetary items**

   These include inventories, investments, and fixed assets and related reserves. Inventories at the beginning and the end of the year were restated by (*a*) substituting current dollar depreciation for the historical depreciation element and (*b*) revaluing the remaining costs to current dollars by an appropriate application of the index. Investments and fixed assets were restated to current dollars from historic cost by applying the change in the index between the year of acquisition and the end of 1974. Depreciation of fixed assets was recalculated on the current dollar amount.

3. **Monetary items**

   These comprise cash, receivables, deferred charges, payables, long-term debt, deferred income taxes, and redeemable preferred shares of subsidiaries. The 31 December 1974 balances classified as "monetary" remain unchanged since they are stated in terms of current dollars. Monetary items at 31 December 1973 were converted to 1974 current dollars by applying the change in the index between December 1973 and December 1974.

statements. Only a few inquiries were elicited by the disclosure, with more than half coming from the academic community.

At the same time Alcan published their restated statements, the previously mentioned FASB discussion memorandum and the ASSC provisional standard began to come under serious debate. Members of the accounting profession pointed out both theoretical and practical problems with this method of inflation accounting. (See Appendix B.) It soon became apparent to Alcan that the requirements which earlier in the year had seemed so likely to be adopted would be delayed if not changed greatly in substance.

1975 . . . wait and see

When the time came to prepare the 1975 annual report, Alcan reviewed the situation with regard to inflation-adjusted financial statements. The accounting profession was in a turmoil over the subject and many were arguing that CPP information was not of value. Therefore, Alcan decided not to publish adjusted statements for 1975, but they did continue to prepare such statements for internal management information purposes. However, Alcan management still felt that there was a need for providing inflation-adjusted information to shareholders and they devoted an entire page of the 1975 Annual Report to discussion of this need. (See Exhibit 3.)

EXHIBIT 3
Alcan's views on accounting changes

Inflation accounting

Accounting bodies, companies and regulatory agencies around the world are still considering which method of inflation accounting would most accurately reflect the effect of inflation on a company's financial results. The two most favored methods are the "current cost or replacement value" method and the "current purchasing power" method. In March of 1975, Alcan published financial statements based on current purchasing power. This method in our view is simple, more precise, and not subject to a wide degree of management or professional interpretation. While the use of a single index may not accurately adjust the value of each individual asset to current levels, at least it does reflect the historical costs in terms of a constant currency unit as opposed to a declining one. However, it may be some time before a clear decision is reached by the different accounting and regulatory bodies and, in view of the conflicting state of opinions, we do not plan to publish adjusted statements for the present.

Inventory profit

Nevertheless, there are two areas of accounting adjustments which do require comment. In a period of rising costs, and due to the time taken to pass through inventory, the costs charged to "cost of sales" are no longer current. The profit recorded, while a genuine profit, is only recurring if prices continue to rise ahead of costs. With some products, prices are determined in relation to costs, but in the case of most commodities such as aluminum, the price obtainable depends much more on market factors than on cost, so the relationship is not assured. In addition to its nonrecurring nature, the "inventory profit" is needed in a business to finance the corresponding increase in working capital which results from the cost increases. Consequently it should not be taxed, as it is in Canada (though not in the U.S. or the UK), and can only be distributed to shareholders if it is refinanced in some other way.

In Alcan's case, the inventory profit before tax amounted to $15 million in 1975, as against a figure of $106 million (restated) in 1974.

EXHIBIT 3 (*continued*)

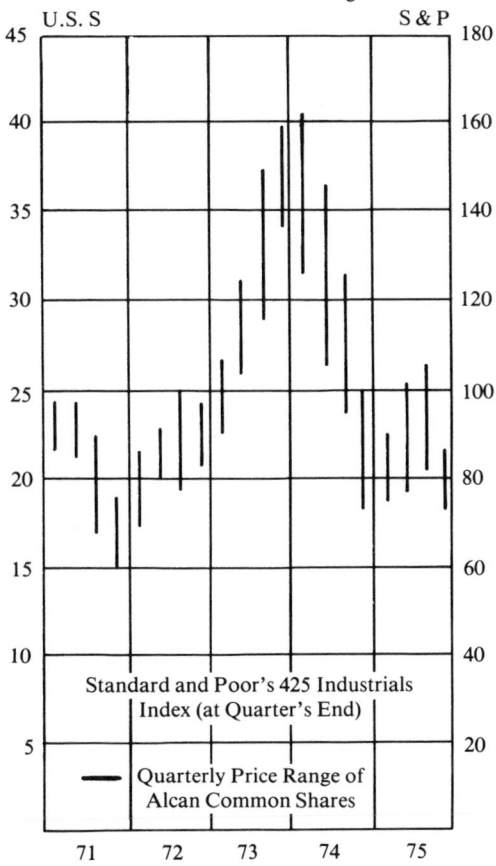

Alcan Aluminum Limited
Price Range of Common Shares
New York Stock Exchange

Debt and foreign exchange

Another controversial topic is the question of revaluing debt for changes in exchange rates. The Financial Accounting Standards Board in the United States has recently published a statement requiring such revaluation, with the resulting profit or loss taken into current income. However, for a company such as Alcan, with its assets and debts widely dispersed in various foreign currencies, and with floating exchange rates, the resulting fluctuations can distort the pattern of earnings. The actual quarterly effect is shown in Note 1 to the Financial Statements [not included—editor]. It will be seen that if we had reported earnings in accordance with the FASB ruling as American companies are now doing, our earnings in 1975 would have been increased by $40 million, although this would be a noncash unrealized profit.

There has not been an equivalent ruling by the Accounting Institute in Canada, and so Alcan has continued to use the generally accepted accounting practice of converting long-term debt at the exchange rate prevailing at the time the debt was incurred, which is the same as the general practice in regard to translating the values of fixed assets recorded in foreign currencies. In this connection, it is perhaps worth noting that in the UK it is proposed that long-term debt should be translated at the current rate of exchange, except to the extent it is covered by fixed assets in the same currency, in which case the unrealized exchange profit or loss is not taken into income but rather into a reserve account. This alternative would eliminate the greater part of the wild fluctuations which Alcan would otherwise experience.

This whole subject is highly controversial at present. We hope that during 1976 we shall be able to decide upon an accounting presentation which is acceptable to the various national accounting and regulatory authorities, but will not cause short-term distortions in our financial results.

1976 . . . the change to replacement costs

In late 1975 and early 1976 the accounting profession seemed to move away from the concept of general price level adjusted financial statements which would be required if GPP or CPP proposals were adopted. In the UK and Australia there were proposals for current cost accounting (CCA), although the exact procedures differed in each country.[1] Then, on March 23, 1976, the U.S. Securities and Exchange Commission announced that they would require large corporations to disclose replacement cost information for inventories, cost of sales, productive capacity, and depreciation expense.[2] (Shortly thereafter, in June 1976, the Financial Accounting Standards Board announced that it was deferring further consideration at this time of Financial Reporting in Units of General Purchasing Power.) Instead of the previously discussed adjustments for changes in the general price level, these new proposals called for the revaluation of specific assets in terms of their "value to the business" (UK), or their "replacement cost" (U.S.).

In accordance with the SEC requirement, Alcan prepared replacement cost information and management included it in their 1976 annual report. (See Exhibit 4.) Developing this information was an extensive exercise for Alcan, requiring more than five person-years of effort. Since the information required was not available at Alcan headquarters, work had to be done at most company locations. Preparing the estimates required the efforts of not only accountants and engineers but also involved management whose opinions were need to determine what and how assets might be replaced. In their presentation, Alcan went beyond the SEC requirement to disclose the information in footnotes and they formulated an income statement and balance sheet incorporating the replacement costs which followed the footnotes to their audited financial statements in the annual report. Alcan felt that this was the format in which the information would be most meaningful to the readers of the financial statements. The conclusions which Alcan drew from their replacement cost statements and a summary of their views of the limitations of these statements are also included in Exhibit 4.

As seen in Exhibit 4, the current replacement value of Alcan's assets was far higher than the historical cost restated to current purchasing power. When discussing this point, John Hale pointed to the similarity of this conclusion to a problem frequently encountered when adjusting for exchange rates between countries. Since countries regulate exchange rates, currencies do not always have equivalent purchasing power. However, the use of historical

---

[1] U.K.: *Exposure Draft 18* issued in November, 1976 by the Accounting Standards Committee. Australia: *Provisional Accounting Standard* issued in October 1976 by the Australian Accounting Standards Committee.

[2] *Accounting Series Release No. 190*, Securities and Exchange Commission, issued March, 1976.

EXHIBIT 4
Alcan's statement on inflation accounting from the 1976 Annual Report

International developments

Inflation, although diminishing, continues to trouble most parts of the world, but no wholly satisfactory method of accounting and reporting the effects of inflation on the financial results of a business has yet been developed. However, in 1975, recognizing the need to provide its shareholders and investors with some appreciation of the impact of past inflation on its business, Alcan published a supplementary set of financial statements for 1974, using the current purchasing power method (CPP) of inflation accounting. This was being advocated at that time in several countries, and gave historical costs restated in current dollars by use of a consumer price index. Subsequently, it became apparent that in a number of countries this method was not considered adequate to meet the problem, and Alcan decided not to publish any supplementary statements last year. However, during 1976 the search for an appropriate method of accounting under inflationary conditions continued, and there have been significant developments in the United Kingdom, Australia and the United States.

In the United Kingdom, the government-appointed Sandilands Committee proposed in September 1975 an inflation-accounting method described as *current cost accounting* (CCA), and this was further refined by the Morpeth Committee in December 1976. The recommended effective date for the larger UK companies to adopt CCA is for periods commencing on or after 1 July 1978.

In Australia, a provisional standard issued in October 1976 by the accounting profession suggested that companies adopt *current cost accounting* (CCA), a procedure carrying the same name but differing somewhat from the method proposed in the UK, for periods starting on or after 1 July 1977. These statements would supplement the conventional historical cost statements. By July 1978, a formal standard is expected which would make CCA mandatory for financial reporting purposes.

In the United States, the Securities and Exchange Commission (SEC) announced in March 1976, in its *Accounting Series Release No. 190*, a requirement for the larger listed companies to provide the estimated "current replacement cost" of productive capacity and inventories with depreciation expense and cost of sales based on those amounts, effective for the year 1976. Unlike the UK and Australian versions of CCA, which will call for audited financial statements, the SEC calls for supplementary information which need not be audited.

Replacement cost data

In accordance with SEC requirements. Alcan's estimated replacement cost data are shown on the opposite page, but within the framework of a consolidated balance sheet and income statement. The latter has only been taken to the "Income before income tax" stage since no appropriate method of accounting for tax under these circumstances has been agreed.

Asset values and operating costs

Alcan's major operating subsidiaries made detailed reviews of their assets, and calculated the replacement cost mainly by valuing specific assets or operating capacities. Valuations of the other assets and those of the remaining smaller subsidiaries were based on appropriate indices.

Generally, replacement costs for the major alumina, power, and aluminum smelter facilities have been developed through engineering estimates of cost per unit of capacity, including appropriate technological improvements, and multiplied by existing capacity to arrive at the estimated total replacement cost.

No attempt has been made to reengineer the entire productive capacity. Nor do the estimates take into account the manifold problems of relocation and consolidation of existing productive facilities, including availability of labour, sources of raw materials and proximity to customers, all of which would necessarily have to be considered in depth before undertaking actual replacement. These studies might significantly alter the cost and manner of replacement.

Furthermore, replacement would also alter the current level of operating costs, due to the greater efficiency in the use of labor and materials in new production facilities of more modern design. However, these cost changes cannot be quantified with any precision. Nevertheless, Alcan believes that they would significantly offset the additional depreciation on a replacement-cost basis.

EXHIBIT 4 (*continued*)

Accumulated depreciation is estimated by the relationship of expired lives to total lives of the existing facilities, applied to the estimated replacement cost of the productive capacity. At this point no attempt has been made to reestimate the useful lives of the assets for the replacement-cost depreciation calculations.

The annual depreciation charge based on replacement values is calculated on the straight-line method, using the historical-cost depreciation rates for existing facilities, applied to the average of the estimated replacement cost of productive capacity as at the beginning and at the end of the year.

Replacement cost of sales is estimated by adjusting historical costs for the inflation occuring during the period between production and sale.

Amounts on the replacement basis related to locations outside the United States have been compiled initially in local currencies and then translated into U.S. dollars at year-end exchange rates for productive capacity and inventories, and at average rates during the year for cost of sales and depreciation expense.

Consolidated balance sheet (31 December 1976) (*in millions of U.S. dollars*)

	Estimated replacement cost basis	Historical cost basis
Current assets:		
Inventories..	$ 923	$ 817
Other	552	552
Property, plant, and equipment (a).........................	7,133	2,997
Less: Accumulated depreciation and depletion	(4,233)	(1,596)
Other assets (b)	320	320
	$4,695	$3,090
Current liabilities	$ 595	$ 595
Debt not maturing within one year	837	837
Deferred income taxes and credits	225	225
Minority interests	207	163
Shareholder's equity:		
Share capital	429	429
Retained earnings	841	841
Replacement reserve...................................	1,561	
	$4,695	$3,090

(a) Land, water rights, and mineral properties have not been revalued and are included in the estimated replacement cost at their historical cost of $83 million. Accumulated amortization and depletion relating to these assets of $8 million also have not been revalued and are included in the replacement data without change.

(b) Includes investments, in companies owned 50% or less, of $207 million which have not been revalued and are included in the estimated replacement cost at the same amount.

Consolidated statement of income (year ending 31 December 1976) (*in millions of U.S. dollars*)

	Estimated replacement cost basis	Historical cost basis
Revenues	$2,671	$2,671
Costs and expenses:		
Cost of sales and operating expenses	2,198	2,155
Depreciation and depletion	278	116
Other	304	304
Income before income taxes	$ (109)	$ 96

EXHIBIT 4 (*concluded*)

Conclusions

Some conclusions may be drawn. In particular:

1. The figures indicate that replacement of existing production capacity would not be justified by the 1976 price structure, even after allowing for the problems stated above (such as the greater efficiency that replaced assets would provide) and the fact that 1976 was a poor year for earnings because of work stoppages. This illustrates a fact that has been frequently stated. Of course, replacement might be justified by the price structure which would be in effect when any particular replacement could be completed.

2. Government treatment of capital-intensive business is not satisfactory where current-cost depreciation—although a measure of the current usage of assets—is not allowed as a cost for income tax purposes, and where in Canada and some other countries (although not the U.S. or the UK) inventory profits are taxed currently. Furthermore, in most countries exercising price controls, the basis of costing is average costing and not current costing, even though the price controls may thus be giving a negative real return.

3. The current replacement value of Alcan's assets is far higher than the historical cost in current dollars, showing that the inflation in machinery and construction costs has far exceeded the consumer price index. In a capital-intensive industry this leads to a very high current-cost depreciation charge, and a corresponding impact on current-cost earnings. However, cash flow is not affected.

4. Under the recommended guidelines, credit is not taken in the replacement-cost net income statement for gains experienced from having debt, or losses resulting from holding monetary assets, such as cash and receivables, in times of inflation. However, this omission seems questionable in a capital-intensive industry where leverage is of great importance to the capital structure. As Alcan has debt and other net monetary liabilities of about one billion dollars, an average inflation rate of 10 percent in the countries where it operates would give an annual gain of about $100 million, greatly improving the current cost picture.

5. The replacement-cost method does not correct for the change in value of currency during the year. Also, it does not call for the restatement of previous years' accounts in current dollars. It, therefore, will not permit a direct comparison of the replacement value accounts of one year with those of prior years.

Summary of Alcan's view

Because of the lack of established standards, the considerable degree of continuing experimentation, and the many subjective judgments required in the compilation of the data, we consider that the figures provided cannot give more than a general impression of the values involved, and that specific comparisons with other reported data are unlikely to be valid.

Furthermore it is our view that an attempt to present a valuation of assets which might replace the existing assets is not sufficiently factual for a satisfactory accounting presentation. We would prefer to see a method which revalues in current dollars the assets which the company actually owns.

The whole problem of inflation accounting is still far from resolved. However, it is likely that considerable progress will be made in 1977 and, when a method is finally agreed, it will mark the most significant development in accounting practice in this century.

---

transaction dates and exchange rates in currency translation is the accepted method for financial reporting purposes. John Hale felt these similarities between problems in the use of exchange rates and inflation adjustment indexes do not mean the methods should not be used. The use of general indexes may mean that reports are not 100 percent "accurate," but the advantages of adjusted data outweigh the disadvantages.

1977 . . . further amplification

In 1977, Alcan again prepared replacement cost data as required by the SEC. They again chose to report this information in their annual report in balance sheet and income statement format (Exhibit 5). Comparative statements for 1976 were also included. However, the 1977 statements included information not disclosed in 1976.

EXHIBIT 5
Inflation accounting

The controversy surrounding inflation accounting has continued during 1977, but still remains unresolved. Caution has prevailed over speed in Canada, the United Kingdom, and Australia. Proposed current cost accounting systems in the latter two countries have been set aside pending further investigation.

In the United States, the Securities and Exchange Commission requires from larger companies the estimated current replacement cost of productive capacity and inventories with depreciation and cost of sales based upon those amounts. Also, the Financial Accounting Standards Board is studying the broader aspects of inflation accounting.

Alcan believes it is helpful to provide the replacement cost information in the form of a consolidated balance sheet and income statement. The latter is only carried to the stage of "income before income tax" because no method of accounting for tax is agreed under these circumstances.

A credit is taken in the net income statement for the gain on net monetary liabilities which arises from the decline in value of the currencies. Since current interest rates reflect inflation (i.e., the "real" interest rates would be much lower) and are charged against operations, it seems correct to credit the offsetting gain arising from the reduced real value of the liability.

Alcan's major subsidiaries have reviewed their assets in detail and computed the replacement cost for the most part by valuing specific assets or operating capacities. Suitable indexes were used to value the other assets and those of the remaining smaller subsidiaries.

In general the replacement costs for the major alumina, power, and aluminum smelter facilities have been developed through engineering estimates of cost per unit of capacity, incorporating appropriate technological improvements, and multiplied by the existing capacity to arrive at the estimated total replacement cost.

There has been no attempt to reengineer the entire productive capacity nor to consider the many and varied problems of relocation and consolidation of existing facilities, such as sources of raw materials, labor supply and nearness to customers. The cost and manner of replacement might be significantly changed by such considerations.

The present level of operating costs would be changed through greater efficiencies in the use of labor and materials afforded by productive capacity of more modern design. These changes cannot be determined with any precision. However, Alcan believes they would significantly offset the additional depreciation on the replacement cost basis.

The accumulated depreciation estimate is based upon the relationship of expired lives to total lives of the existing facilities, applied to the estimated replacement cost of the productive capacity. There has been no attempt to reestimate the useful lives of the fixed assets for purposes of calculating annual depreciation and accumulated depreciation reserve.

The annual depreciation charge based on replacement values is calculated on the straight-line method, using the historical-cost depreciation rates for existing facilities, applied to the average of the estimated replacement cost of productive capacity as at the beginning and at the end of the year.

The replacement cost of sales is determined by adjusting historical costs for the inflation occurring during the period between production and sale.

Replacement values for locations outside the United States have been compiled initially in local currencies and translated into U.S. dollars at year-end exchange rates for productive capacity and inventories, and at average rates during the year for cost of sales and depreciation expense.

The 1976 replacement cost figures have been adjusted from those reported last year to recognize more detailed engineering studies of the replacement cost of some facilities. However,

EXHIBIT 5 (*continued*)

it should be noted that the replacement cost method does not call for restatement of the 1976 amounts in terms of 1977 dollars and therefore does not permit a direct comparison.

Because of the many subjective judgments, lack of established standards and continuing experimentation, Alcan feels that the replacement cost figures provide only a general indication of the values involved and that comparisons with other reported data are unlikely to be valid. Alcan would prefer to see a method which revalues in current dollars the assets which the Company actually owns.

The search for the most appropriate inflation accounting system continues both within the Company and in outside bodies in many countries.

Consolidated balance sheet, 31 December (in millions of U.S. dollars)

	1977		1976	
	Estimated replacement cost basis	*Historical cost basis*	*Estimated replacement cost basis (b)*	*Historical cost basis*
Current assets:				
Inventories	$1,074	$ 956	$ 923	$ 817
Other........................	632	632	552	552
Property, plant, and equipment (a)	8,303	3,150	7,860	2,997
Less: Accumulated depreciation and depletion	(4,877)	(1,690)	(4,697)	(1,596)
Other assets	355	355	320	320
Total assets.................	$5,487	$3,403	$4,958	$3,090
Current liabilities..................	$ 679	$ 679	$ 595	$ 595
Debt not maturing within one year	749	749	837	837
Deferred income taxes and credits	305	305	225	225
Minority interests	287	244	207	163
Shareholders' equity:				
Share capital	429	429	429	429
Retained earnings	997	997	841	841
Replacement reserve	2,041		1,824	
Total liabilities and shareholders' equity	$5,487	$3,403	$4,958	$3,090

Consolidated statement of income, year ending 31 December (in millions of U.S. dollars)

	1977		1976	
	Estimated replacement cost basis	*Historical cost basis*	*Estimated replacement cost basis (b)*	*Historical cost basis*
Revenues........................	$3,058	$3,058	$2,671	$2,671
Costs and expenses:				
Cost of sales and operating expenses	2,314	2,276	2,198	2,155
Depreciation and depletion	304	126	299	116
Other........................	319	319	304	304
	$ 121	$ 337	$(130)	$ 96
Gain from holding net monetary liabilities	60	—	54	—
Income before income taxes..........	$ 181	$ 337	$ (76)	$ 96

(a) Land. water rights, and mineral properties have not been revalued and are included in the estimated replacement cost at their historical cost of $84 million ($83 million in 1976). Accumulated amortization and and depletion relating to these assets of $10 million ($8 million in 1976) also have not been revalued.

(b) Adjusted to recognize more detailed engineering studies of some facilities.

During a period of inflation, a corporation with more monetary liabilities than monetary assets "gains" because such liabilities can be repaid with monetary assets which have less purchasing power than assets obtained when the debts were incurred. In effect, the corporation "benefits" from inflation. In 1976, Alcan had mentioned the need to consider the gain from their net monetary liabilities as well as the impact of the replacement cost of its assets. In 1977, they measured this *gain* and added it to the adjusted financial statements.

The gain on net monetary liabilities is the same as would be measured if a GPP or CPP method were used to report the effects of inflation, and its disclosure reveals Alcan management's preference for such a method. CPP statements are prepared and used for management information purposes in preference to replacement cost statements. Because they feel that CPP is a more meaningful method of reporting the effects of inflation, it is doubtful that the company will continue to estimate and report replacement costs if the SEC should no longer require their disclosure. But their record of concern about the effects of inflation leaves little doubt about that Alcan will continue to develop and use inflation-adjusted information.

APPENDIX A

"Wall Street—Financial Statements Gone Awry"
Business Week, September 14, 1974

Inflation has twisted corporate financial statements into unintelligible pretzels. Because of the widening gap between dollars and purchasing power, the replacement value of assets is understated, and depreciation for most companies has become inadequate. In most cases, earnings are exaggerated.

But by how much? Present accounting techniques describe corporations in terms of dollars. Accountants now want to adopt a system that describes companies in terms of purchasing power, an additional set of numbers to give investors another view of how companies are faring. One such system, called "price-level accounting" adjusts balance sheets and income statements by a price-level index. That gives short shrift to the replacement cost or market value of assets, but it's the system most likely to be adopted by accountants and to be required eventually by the SEC. . . .

"A Controversial Method of Allowing for Inflation"
Business Week, September 14, 1974

"With our revenues expressed in today's dollars and our investment cost expressed in yesterday's dollars," muses U. J. LeGrange, deputy controller of Exxon Corporation, "we are leading people to think our profits are better than they are." Says Robert T. Sprouse, member of the Financial Accounting Standards Board (FASB): "There's a serious question whether you get a meaningful measure of income by deducting 1940 dollars from 1974 dollars."

These days financial executives and accountants are conceding what Wall Street already seems to have figured out for itself: Earnings of most U.S. corporations are far overstated because of the disrupting 1970's brand of double-digit inflation. The problem is that accounting based on historical costs values the assets and materials used by business in terms of old dollars that were spent months or years ago. And that is misleading when it will take a considerably greater number of today's dollars to replace those assets.

"Profits Aren't as Good as They Look"
Henry C. Wallich and Mable I. Wallich
Fortune, March 1974

The ballooning of inventory profits is not the only way in which rapid inflation produces gross exaggeration of corporate returns. Inflation also makes depreciation allowances more and more inadequate. There has been a great deal of talk in recent years about how business is benefiting from fast write-offs, and it may seem hard to believe that these write-offs are nevertheless inadequate. Yet precisely this has been the consequence of the rapid rise in replacement costs.

Accounting tradition and tax law cling to original-cost depreciation. Accountants say that without it they would lose their footing—and certainly the Treasury would lose a lot of revenue. Economists, however, find it less difficult to admit that a company has not really made a profit if its gross income was insufficient to replace the assets used up in generating that income. When inflation is merely creeping, accountants and tax collectors are sure to prevail. But their case collapses when inflation accelerates. Original-cost depreciation at Latin-American inflation rates will rapidly erode business capital unless compensated by exorbitant profit margins.

In the United States a substantial amount of erosion is now going on, despite the liberalizing of depreciation allowances in 1954, 1962, and again in 1971. Using Department of Commerce data, and accepting accelerated depreciation as the appropriate norm, economist George Terborgh of the Machinery and Allied Products Institute finds that in 1973 American nonfinancial corporations were underdepreciating their plant and equipment by more than $7 billion.

APPENDIX B

"Price-Level Restatement: Solution or Problem?"
Alfred M. King
Management Accounting, November 1976

Adoption of price-level restatements, using the approach originally proposed by the FASB, could eventually destroy the fundamental financial strategies businessmen use today. The FASB proposal included the concept of "general purchasing power gain or loss" from holding monetary assets and liabilities. Under this concept, corporate managers would not be fulfilling their responsibilities unless they tried to maximize income under the defined ground rules. Let's assume that current rates of inflation will

394

continue. If we further assume that business executives will desire to maximize reported income, they would feel a very strong incentive to increase debt, relative to equity, and simultaneously try to reduce receivables relative to payables. This financial strategy would have the quickest impact in increasing the "general price level gain" and hence "net income."

Working as he is in a profit-motivated economy, a manager of a public company would be derelict in his duty if he did not try to maximize reported net income. He is also expected to try to maximize cash flow. But when the two concepts collide, reported net income usually wins.

It is difficult to believe that the FASB would reward higher debt ratios, and penalize conservatively financed companies. There is likely to be greater risk of financial insolvency if management—solely because of a change in financial reporting standards—is given a positive incentive to increase debt. And attempts by individual corporations to change their receivable/payable ratios can only end in a redistribution of trade credit between stronger and weaker companies.

"Accounting that Allows for Inflation—Ideas and Trends"
John C. Burton, chief accountant, SEC
Business Week, November 30, 1974

Some have suggested that an accounting measurement system based on the mechanical adjustment of costs by the use of a broad-based general price-level index will achieve many of the benefits of a replacement cost system and will have the advantage of being easy to apply, since there would be no need to determine the replacement cost of the specific assets of a business. While the ease in application cannot be denied, there are serious doubts as to whether any significant benefits will be achieved from such a system. In fact, strong arguments can be made that the data produced by a general price-level adjustment system may be affirmatively misleading rather than helpful to the users.

In essence, financial statements adjusted for general price-level change represent a measurement system based on historical costs expressed in terms of a purchasing power unit instead of historical monetary unit. In the interest of easy communication, this may be called PuPu accounting. There is no reason to think that PuPu accounting will produce any better measure of earning power than will accounting based on historical monetary units. Since the impact of inflation falls differently on various sectors of the economy and various parts of companies, the relationship of historical PuPus to current cash outflows is tenuous at best.

To take one example, suppose that petroleum companies had been using PuPu accounting in the first half of 1974 as the cost of crude oil was being multiplied by three. Under this system, to the extent that costs were passing through inventory, they would be increased by the change in the general price level (perhaps 6 percent) before being matched against revenues. This would have had an insignificant effect on profits. Yet the impact of this dramatically increasing cost on the profits of oil companies that used any inventory system other than Lifo was huge, since the cost of old inventories acquired at less than half of current costs was being matched against revenues, which reflected the economic impact of cost increases.

Not only will PuPu accounting suffer all the disabilities of any historical cost system, but it will have an additional significant potential for misleading investors because it will appear to be an improvement when it is, in fact, not. This danger is particularly acute if the PuPu system is anointed by the Financial Accounting Standards Board as constituting significant and valuable new information.

Additional costs. While the benefits of PuPu accounting are difficult to perceive, the costs of adopting such a system on either a primary or supplemental basis are substantial. In the first place, there are out-of-pocket costs of a considerable magnitude in the mechanical accumulation of data in this format. Computers must be programmed, the dates of asset acquisitions determined, and indexes recorded over time for various countries.

There will also be the cost of educating people to understand what such data mean and what they do not mean. These costs are difficult to measure, but they are likely to be far greater than those of the out-of-pocket variety.

Most users of financial data today have a general familiarity with standard financial statements. They are relatively comfortable with data presented in this fashion. If a new set of data is mandated, a massive educational effort will be required to teach users what they have and how it might be used. It is a safe bet that most users will think they have current value data when in fact they will still have historical cost data expressed in general purchasing power units.

PART FOUR

Comprehensive cases

—◄CASE IV–1►◄—

Wayside Inns, Inc.

————◄∞►◄—

It was May 11, 1977 and Kevin Gray was conducting a routine quarterly inspection of the Memphis Airport Wayside Inn. The property was one of those that fell under his jurisdiction as regional general manager for Wayside Inns, Inc. During his inspection tour Gray was called aside by the Inn's manager, Layne Rembert, who indicated some concern about a proposed expansion of his motel.

"I'm a little worried, Kevin, about that plan to bring 40 more rooms on stream by the end of the next fiscal year."

"Why all the concern, Layne? You're turning away a significant number of customers and, by all indications, the market will be growing considerably."

"Well, I've just spoken with Ed Keider. He's certain that the 80-room expansion at the central Toledo property has lowered his return on investment. I'd really like to chat with you about what effects the planned expansion will have on my incentive compensation and how my income for the year would be affected."

THE COMPANY

Wayside Inns, Inc., located in Kansas City, Missouri, was formed in 1965 as the successor corporation to United Motel Enterprises, a company that operated several franchised motels under licensing agreements from two national motel chains. Due to the complicated and restrictive contract covenants, United was unable to expand the scope of either of their two motel operations through geographical dispersion.

The successor corporation was formed to own, operate, and license a chain of motels under the name Wayside Inns, as well as to continue to operate the present franchises held by United. Management felt that the strategy of developing their own motel chain would afford them greater flexibility and would allow them to more easily attain the long-term growth strategies. Another major reason for the move was that the new corporate

This case was prepared by Charles T. Sharpless, research assistant, under the supervision of Professor M. Edgar Barrett. Copyright © 1978 by M. Edgar Barrett.

strategy would allow management to pursue the implementation of a comprehensive marketing plan which they had been slowly developing over the last seven years.

The company's fundamental strategy was to cater to those business travelers who were generally not interested in elaborate settings. There were no common areas such as lobbies, convention rooms, bars, or restaurants. The chain emphasized instead clean rooms, dependable service, and rates that generally were 15 to 20 percent lower than other national motel chains. A free-standing restaurant was always located on the motel's property—in some cases it was operated by Wayside. In general, however, concessionary leases were granted to regional restaurant chains.

Wayside's management made it a point to locate their properties near interstate highways or major arteries convenient to commercial districts, airports, and industrial or shopping facilities. In a given city, one would often find Wayside Inns at various strategic locations. This strategy was founded on the belief that it was preferable to have a total of 600 rooms in five or six locations within one city rather than have one large hotel with 600 rooms. This strategy resulted in the clustering of hotels in those cities that could support the market. Once several hotels had been built in a particular city, management would seek new properties in regions commercially linked to that city.

Wayside was well aware that their aggressive strategy was successful only to the extent that unit managers followed corporate policies to the letter. In order to insure an aggressive spirit among the unit managers a multifaceted compensation plan was developed. The plan was composed of four elements, but was basically tied to profitability. A base salary was calculated which was loosely tied to years of service, dollar volume of sales, and adherence to corporate goals. An incentive bonus was calculated on sales volume increases. An additional incentive bonus was calculated using the Inn's return on investment. Fringe benefits were the final element and were a significant factor in the package. (See Exhibit 1.) Generally, base salaries ranged from $11,000 to $14,000 and total compensation was in the neighborhood of $16,000 to $20,000. The unit manager always lived on the premises and his wife usually played a role in managing the Inn. As a result, the average couple were in their late 40s or beyond. Many did not have previous motel experience.

The firm had grown substantially since its inception and the prospects for future growth were favorable. The company's expansion strategy had evolved into a three-tiered attack. Most importantly, management actively pursued the construction of new motels seeking an ever-widening geographical distribution. Second, 76 and 116 room properties were expanded if analysis demonstrated that they were operating near or at full capacity. Third, old properties that became a financial burden or did not contribute

EXHIBIT 1
Unit managers' compensation package

___

Base salary

Base salary ranges are calculated on the basis of years of service and relative sales volume for a particular inn. Salaries are subject to annual review and the amount of adjustment will largely depend upon the recommendation of the regional general manager. Every attempt will be made to keep salary levels consistent with competitive chains.

Sales volume incentive

Every unit manager, having earned a profit before taxes, will receive a bonus equal to 1 percent of any revenue increase over the previous year's level. In the event of a revenue decrease, there will be no bonus and the following year's bonus will be calculated using the revenue of the year preceding the decline as a base figure.

Return on investment bonus

Investment will be defined as current assets, fixed assets, other assets, and any deferred expenses. Return is defined as profit before interest expense and taxes.

The formula for the bonus calculation will be:

$$ROI \times PF = ROI \text{ bonus}$$

where:

$$ROI = \frac{EBIT}{Investment} \text{ and } PF = \text{Performance factor}$$

The performance factor is used to differentiate between the larger and smaller investments and to offset the inherent complexities of managing the larger properties.

Size of investment ($)	Value of performance factor ($)*
0–500,000	10,000
500,000–1,000,000	18,000
1,000,000–1,500,000	25,000
1,500,000–2,000,000	31,000
2,000,000–up	35,000

* The regional general manager has the discretion to reduce or increase the value of the performance factor for a particular property upon central headquarter's approval.

Fringe benefits

Each unit manager shall receive an apartment (2 bedrooms, full kitchen, and den) on the premises, a company car for sales calls, laundry service, and local phone service at no expense.

the required rate of return were sold. Wayside Inns were usually constructed in one of three sizes—76 rooms, 116 rooms, or 156 rooms.

Wayside Inns was a public corporation listed on the American Stock Exchange. It had 1,542,850 shares outstanding, with an average float of 400,000 shares. The common stock price had appreciated considerably and analysts felt that investor interest was due to a number of factors but was primarily linked to their innovative marketing strategy. Wayside's average occupancy rate on established properties was 10 to 20 percent higher than competitive motels. Their specifically targeted market segment (the business traveler) was generally unaffected by seasonal or environmental factors. Additional company strengths, considered significant by service industry analysts, were an aggressive management, reduction of construction costs and completion times due to standardization, and efficient quality control of present properties.

THE MEMPHIS AIRPORT WAYSIDE INN

The Wayside Inn at Memphis Airport was one of the mid-sized units in the chain—one of the original 116 room properties. It was located at the intersection of Brooks Road and Airways Road, approximately five miles from the center of the city. The motel opened on February 9, 1969 and had developed a very good following in the succeeding years. While the occupancy rate had averaged near 43 percent for the first year, it had increased steadily over the years. By 1976, it operated at near full capacity for five nights a week. The Inn depended on salesmen and commercial travelers for approximately 80 percent of its revenue.

The property had been originally purchased in 1967 for $150,450. Construction costs for the motel had amounted to approximately $615,345 and furnishings, hardware, software, and office equipment had been purchased for $175,775.

Wayside Inns had contributed an initial equity capitalization of $50,000. The parent had also loaned $175,000 to the subsidiary which was secured by promissory notes. A national insurance company granted a mortgage of $631,550 on the land and physical plant. Finally, $275,795 had been received from Memphis Interstate Bank to finance equipment and supply purchases and to provide the necessary working capital. (See Exhibits 2 and 3 for operating data and Exhibits 4 and 5 for financial statements).

There were approximately 10 competitive motels, which were franchises of the major national chains, within a two-mile radius of the Memphis Airport Inn. There also existed a number of independent motels within the area. However, they were generally of the budget type and did not offer the quality on which Wayside based their reputation. Recent surveys conducted by the Memphis Chamber of Commerce indicated that average occupancy rates hovered near 72 percent and that the average room sold for $17.25.

Expansion plans by the major chains were expected to account for an additional 800 rooms across the whole city in the following 18 months.

The proposed expansion

Wayside's Project Development staff had arrived at a projected schedule of costs that would be associated with the completion of a 40-room expansion. Cost adjustments would be necessary depending on the particular city and conditions. However, variances were not expected to be significant.

Engineering and legal fees were expected to be somewhere in the neighborhood of $12,250. Environmental Impact Studies to comply with federal regulations and the local building permits were estimated to cost $8,500. Construction costs for the expansion and adjoining parking facility were expected to be near $730,000. Such an expansion was expected to generate additional annual, nondirect operating costs of $31,300 (largely for personnel, utilities, and maintenance). Direct room expenses were expected to remain at an average of 23 percent of room revenue. Management and reservation fees paid to the parent were based on a formula of 5 percent of room revenue plus $24 per room per year.

EXHIBIT 2
Selected operating statistics (for the periods January 1 to December 31)

	1976	1975	1974	1973	1972
Occupancy report					
Room nights available	41,975	41,975	41,975	41,975	41,975
Occupied room nights	36,634	35,595	33,454	32,613	31,522
Occupancy rate (%)	87.3	84.8	79.7	77.7	75.1
Room revenue ($)	613,619	560,621	510,173	472,888	446,036
Average room rate ($)	16.75	15.75	15.25	14.50	14.15
Weekly occupancy (%)					
Monday	99	99	95	94	92
Tuesday	99	99	94	92	91
Wednesday	99	98	96	94	89
Thursday	99	97	92	87	86
Friday	91	87	72	70	65
Saturday	61	55	51	50	48
Sunday	63	59	58	57	55
*Turnaway tally**					
Monday	26.1	22.8	15.1	10.1	11.5
Tuesday	27.7	21.0	19.3	16.0	12.1
Wednesday	38.2	33.2	26.9	19.5	13.3
Thursday	43.9	36.3	31.4	20.4	16.6
Friday	22.6	15.8	10.9	5.2	2.4
Saturday	9.6	5.7	2.8	0.2	0.6
Sunday	8.5	6.4	3.0	1.3	0.5

* A turnaway is considered a customer who either calls the motel, requests a room in person, or calls central reservation service and is told there are no vacancies. See Exhibit 3 for further data.

EXHIBIT 3
Daily "turnaway" statistics for 1976

Week	Sun.	Mon.	Tues.	Wed.	Thurs.	Fri.	Sat.
1	0	25	26	36	45	0	0
2	0	23	21	24	25	0	0
3	0	10	11	17	23	3	0
4	0	20	21	16	46	5	0
5	0	16	17	25	38	0	0
6	0	20	15	38	43	7	0
7	0	25	32	45	25	0	0
8	0	10	12	42	46	10	0
9	0	21	14	40	71	12	0
10	0	23	28	39	23	15	0
11	0	19	25	41	45	16	0
12	0	25	30	43	39	20	0
13	0	46	42	24	45	21	0
14	0	28	25	58	40	30	0
15	0	35	14	61	63	32	0
16	0	24	22	25	45	43	4
17	0	13	46	26	49	15	11
18	0	25	29	13	45	12	2
19	0	43	40	61	71	10	15
20	0	22	55	62	68	45	23
21	20	42	36	67	55	46	36
22	22	39	35	50	47	39	33
23	23	22	33	38	35	38	32
24	24	28	25	25	41	17	0
25	10	29	24	15	41	25	10
26	0	24	20	39	35	18	6
27	0	30	18	25	24	42	38
28	25	29	15	35	35	45	27
29	29	26	66	41	82	11	12
30	15	25	50	62	65	18	9
31	13	42	43	47	48	16	5
32	17	31	25	35	50	17	15
33	18	32	16	28	32	18	12
34	12	15	22	23	28	20	14
35	10	14	25	27	26	21	23
36	6	17	24	61	67	15	12
37	19	56	27	43	40	15	16
38	18	55	71	39	42	20	18
39	14	16	35	46	41	23	17
40	5	12	20	48	47	27	6
41	16	23	15	45	53	29	5
42	7	25	18	42	43	31	4
43	0	18	20	41	39	43	4
44	0	19	21	48	53	46	11
45	0	29	23	19	47	47	4
46	0	31	24	25	29	41	16
47	0	20	26	31	33	52	12
48	10	22	16	49	52	26	10
49	15	24	18	40	38	20	8
50	16	21	19	31	41	10	4
51	43	37	45	47	37	15	2
52	35	31	40	38	42	6	20
Total	442	1,357	1,440	1,986	2,283	1,175	498

EXHIBIT 4

MEMPHIS AIRPORT WAYSIDE INN
Income Statement
For the Years Ended December 31

	1975	*1976*
Revenues:		
Room revenue	$560.621	$613,619
Restaurant rental	19,432	21,536
Other	10,532	12,765
Total revenues	590,585	647,920
Operating costs and expenses:		
Room	126,476	144,875
Selling and administrative	136,511	144,691
Depreciation and amortization	37,642	46,752
Utilities	23,610	25,473
Maintenance and repairs	32,672	30,498
Management and reservations fees	30,815	33,464
Operating income:	202,859	222,167
Interest Expense	106,513	95,278
Profit before taxes:	96,346	126,889
Federal taxes	32,746	47,406
Net earnings	$ 63,600	$ 79,483

EXHIBIT 5

MEMPHIS AIRPORT WAYSIDE INN
Balance Sheet

	1975	*1976*
Assets		
Current assets:		
Cash	$ 16,059	$ 15,545
Trade receivables	54,721	63,820
Merchandise	15,617	17,821
Prepaid expenses:		
Insurance	3,098	2,778
Mortgage interest	5,673	5,242
Linens	1,550	1,675
Total current assets	96,718	106,881
Fixed assets:		
Land	150,450	150,450
Building, equipment, furniture, and fixtures	925,160	961,215
Less: Accumulated depreciation	(183,375)	(229,127)
Total fixed assets	892,235	882,538
Other assets:		
Franchise	8,000	7,000
Supplies	19,671	19,826
Total other assets	27,671	26,826
Total assets	$1,016,624	$1,016,245

EXHIBIT 5 (*continued*)

	1975	*1976*
Liabilities		
Current liabilities:		
Accounts payable...................................	$ 45,671	$ 47,583
Taxes payable	15,629	21,472
Accrued expenses	38,978	38,611
Total current liabilities	100,278	107,666
Long-term liabilities:		
Mortgage payable	454,716	429,454
Notes payable......................................	206,000	169,000
Notes payable to parent	90,000	65,000
Total long-term liabilities	750,716	663,454
Net worth:		
Capital stock.......................................	50,000	50,000
Retained earnings..................................	115,630	195,125
Total net worth..............................	165,630	245,125
Total liabilities	$1,016,624	$1,016,245

PERFORMANCE EVALUATION

After dinner that evening, Kevin Gray decided to review his file on Layne Rembert's compensation package and on his related performance evaluation. He checked his records to determine what the Rembert's total compensation had been for 1976. He then performed a rough calculation of what it would be for 1977 if the additional 40 rooms were to have been available during all of this time period (See Exhibit 6).

Over the past few years, Gray had also developed a 20-point performance evaluation report which he used to base his decisions on salary increases (See Exhibit 7). This system was derived from one he had witnessed when he had been previously employed by a national food service organization. While the report had been developed primarily for his own use in helping

EXHIBIT 6
Effect of proposed expansion on Rembert's income

Total compensation for 1976		Projected compensation after expansion	
Base salary......................	$12,500	Base salary......................	$12,500
Sales volume incentive		Sales volume incentive	
$(647,920 - 590,585) \times .01$		$(834,079 - 647,920) \times .01$	
$57,335 \times .01 = $.....	573	$186,159 \times .01 = $.....	1,862
Return on investment bonus		Return on investment bonus	
$\dfrac{222,167}{1,016,245} \times 25,000$		$\dfrac{311,039}{1,785,245} \times 32,000$	
$.2186 \times 25,000 = $...........	5,465	$.1742 \times 32,000 = $..........	5,574
Total compensation	$18,538	Total compensation	$19.936

EXHIBIT 6 (*continued*)
Projected income statement (as calculated by Gray)

Revenue:

Room revenue	$790,332
Restaurant rental	27,047
Other	16,700
Total revenues	834,079

Operating costs and expenses:

Room	181,776
Operating expenses	231,888
Depreciation and amortization	66,115
Management and reservation fees	43,261
Operating income	$311,039

Remarks: Room revenue projected as 47,184 occupied room nights at an average price of $16.75. This figure is attributed slightly to annual growth but largely to turnaways accommodated.

Investment is figured loosely and may vary in actuality, but variance will not significantly affect ROI.

EXHIBIT 7

PERFORMANCE EVALUATION REPORT

	(1) *Poor*	*(2)* *Average*	*(3)* *Good*	*(4)* *Superior*	
Motel environment					
Exterior appearance	_____	_____	_____	_____	× .2 = _____
Interior appearance	_____	_____	_____	_____	× .5 = _____
Maintenance work	_____	_____	_____	_____	× .3 = _____
Room spot check	_____	_____	_____	_____	× .5 = _____
Personnel attitude	_____	_____	_____	_____	× .3 = _____
Managerial factors					
Accurate reports	_____	_____	_____	_____	× .3 = _____
Reservation control	_____	_____	_____	_____	× .2 = _____
Accounts receivable	_____	_____	_____	_____	× .2 = _____
Payroll	_____	_____	_____	_____	× .3 = _____
Controllable costs	_____	_____	_____	_____	× .5 = _____
Occupancy rate	_____	_____	_____	_____	× .5 = _____
Other factors					
Cooperation with RGM	_____	_____	_____	_____	× .3 = _____
Sales calls	_____	_____	_____	_____	× .3 = _____
Personnel turnover	_____	_____	_____	_____	× .3 = _____
Complaints	_____	_____	_____	_____	× .3 = _____
Total	_____	_____	_____	_____	

RANKING

20.0–17.8	Excellent
17.7–15.0	Good
14.9–11.0	Must improve
10.0–5.0	Very poor

to determine who should receive merit increases in salary, Gray placed a great deal of weight on his report. In fact, he was entertaining the notion of recommending that it be instituted companywide. He made no bones about letting unit managers know that he looked for other things than pure return on investment. He felt that there were a number of variables that could seriously affect profitability over which the unit manager had no control. In addition, he believed an efficient operation was to a large extent contingent on customer satisfaction.

◄CASE IV–2►

Pechiney Ugine Kuhlmann–Cebal: A capital investment project

In the fall of 1974, the management of Cebal, one of the two packaging materials manufacturing subsidiaries of the French aluminum giant, Pechiney Ugine Kuhlmann, was studying a proposal to invest FF97.9 million to build a two-piece aluminum can manufacturing plant in northern Italy.[1] The factory would begin production in 1977 and would be jointly owned with the Wilson Division of the Brown Company. The Brown Company was a U.S. manufacturer of packaging materials with 1974 sales of $340 million. The Wilson Division, with 1974 revenues of $112 milion, specialized in the manufacture of two-piece cans (both aluminum and tin) for carbonated drinks and beer.

The managements of Brown and Cebal had already arranged to sell the output of the new plant to the Italian Division of Byron, Ltd., the well-known English beer and beverage producer, under a 5-year contract. Byron, Ltd. had agreed to buy the cans at a price, which would be set initially at 80 lire per can and which would be indexed to the principal cost components of manufacturing. Thus, the Brown/Cebal venture was effectively protected against inflation.

This case was prepared with the cooperation of Pechiney Ugine Kuhlmann, its Cebal Division, and Jean de Menton, a member of Pechiney's executive education staff. The case was written by William A. Sahlman, research assistant, based in part on background materials translated into English by Jacqueline Bugnion of Neuchâtel, Switzerland. The figures and some of the facts relating to the investment proposal have been disguised.

[1] Most cans are three piece—a bottom, a top, and the middle. Two-piece cans are a relatively new phenomenon in Europe.

EXHIBIT 1
Financial review (FF millions)

	1971	1972	1973	1974
Balance sheet:				
Current assets	8,115	9,625	10,608	13,545
Net fixed assets	7,951	8,128	8,386	8,726
Other fixed assets	2,532	2,220	2,345	2,567
Total assets	18,597	19,973	21,340	24,838
Current liabilities	5,041	6,253	7,203	9,713
Medium and long-term debt	5,168	5,181	5,294	5,281
Deferred taxes	1,059	1,145	1,227	1,461
Minority interest	1,286	1,279	1,341	1,626
Shareholders' equity, reserves, and profits for the year	6,043	6,116	6,275	6,759
Income statement:				
Net revenues	13,581	13,425	16,027	22,221
Net income	308	273	365	744
Earnings per share (FF)	12.25	10.85	14.50	29.55
Dividends per share (FF)	12.00	12.00	13.20	13.50
Ratios:				
Current assets to current liabilities	1.61	1.54	1.47	1.39
Debt to total capitalization (equity* plus debt)	.42	.42	.41	.39
Sales to total assets	.73	.67	.75	.89
Net income to sales (%)	2.27	2.03	2.28	3.35
Total assets to shareholders' equity*	2.62	2.75	2.84	3.02
Net income to shareholders' equity* (%)	4.34	3.74	4.86	9.00
Stock price (FF per share):				
High	n.a.	172	167	144
Low	n.a.	130	118	99
Last	n.a.	133	127	118

* Equals shareholders' equity plus minority interests.

PECHINEY UGINE KUHLMANN (P.U.K.)

P.U.K. was the largest French industrial concern, with 1974 revenues of FF22.2 billion. (See Exhibit 1 for selected financial information about P.U.K.) The company had been formed in 1971 with the merger of the Pechiney group, the Ugine–Kuhlmann group, and was divided into five major branches as follows:

	1974 turnover (FF billion)	Percent of 1974 turnover
Aluminum	7.3	33%
Chemicals	4.9	22
Steel and electrometallurgy	3.3	15
Copper mining and nuclear energy	4.9	22
Special products	1.8	8
	22.2	100%

EXHIBIT 2
Organization chart showing position of Cebal

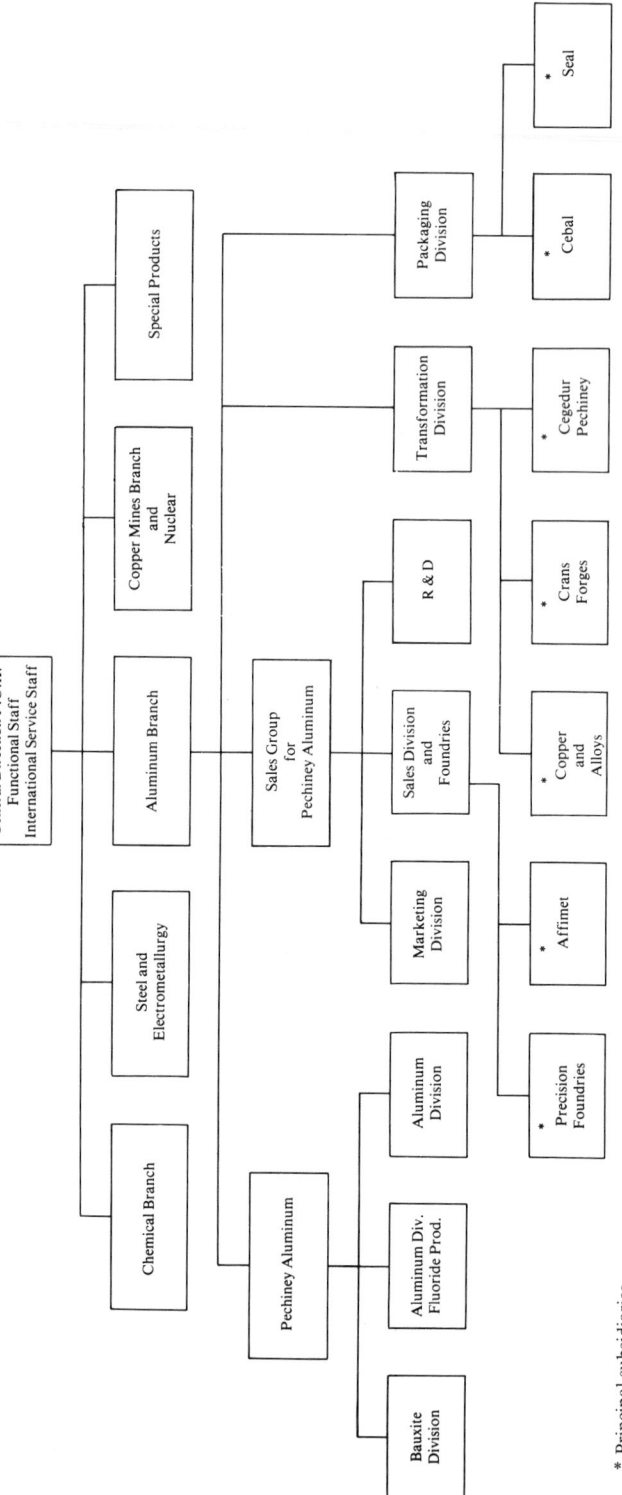

* Principal subsidiaries.

The Cebal subsidiary was part of the packaging division of the Aluminum Branch of Pechiney (see Exhibit 2). Turnover had grown dramatically from FF25 million in 1968 to FF400 million in 1974. Of the FF400 million, FF60.4 million represented non-French sales. The company's product line included aluminum containers, easy-open cans, collapsible tubes and aluminum caps and closures.

The analysis of capital budgeting proposals at P.U.K.

The analysis of investment projects at P.U.K. was intimately linked to the long-range planning process. Essentially, each business sector was analyzed in terms of its strategic strengths and weaknesses. In this regard, competition, current and potential market share, technological capabilities, as well as numerous other factors were considered. The P.U.K. management then evaluated both the current and expected profitability of each of its principal sectors and subsectors of activity.

The primary measure of profitability used in this analysis was the return on gross assets employed. The return on gross assets was defined as the ratio of the industrial margin (earnings before interest and taxes minus an allowance for straight-line depreciation) of a given sector to the gross assets (fixed assets plus inventory) employed by that sector.[2]

The profitability and strategic analysis outlined above was designed to identify development objectives. Essentially, development objectives were outlines of investment (or disinvestment) projects all of which would warrant completion if there were no limitation on the availability of investment funds.

After development objectives were identified, the implied total need for funds was calculated. At the same time, the expected total sources of funds was determined. If the implied uses exceeded the estimated sources of funds, as had always been the case at P.U.K., then it was necessary to modify the development objectives. A long-range plan was completed when the expected uses of funds were equal to the expected sources of funds.

The inclusion of specific development objectives in the P.U.K. long-range plan did not mean that the underlying projects were already approved. Each individual investment project had to be analyzed in great detail before corporate capital would be released for expenditure.

Actually, the analysis of individual investment projects was divided into three related parts. First, each proposal was evaluated on the strategic level. At issue was how the project matched with the strategic strengths and weaknesses of the group.

---

[2] Generally, gross assets were valued on a historical cost basis. However, in analyzing the return on gross assets of each sector, the ratio was recomputed using both price-level adjusted and replacement values for gross assets.

The second step in the analysis of individual capital expenditure proposals entailed the preparation of detailed operating budgets including funds flow forecasts, income statements and balance sheets. It was at this stage that the profitability of the individual project was measured.

The measure of profitability of capital investment proposals used at P.U.K. was the expected internal rate of return. The internal rate of return was defined by P.U.K. as the discount rate which, when applied to the expected net after-local-taxes operating cash flow (before financial flows), resulted in the present value of those flows equaling the total investment in the project. Thus, the internal rate of return was that discount rate at which the *net* present value of the project was zero.

Ordinarily, the profitability of the project was measured using several different plausible variations. A variation might entail making a different assumption about the price expectations for a new product, or locating the new plant at a different site. Changing the assumptions underlying the project also allowed management to identify the sensitivity of the profitability estimates to certain key variables.

The reason behind using several variations and testing the sensitivity of the project to changes in certain variables was to specify the risk in the project.

The final step in analyzing individual investment projects was to outline a tentative financing plan. That is, for most major projects, the probable sources and cost of finance for the project were identified.

The three parts to the analysis of individual projects comprised the "investment file." The completed investment file was submitted to the appropriate manager for approval.

The setting of investment return objectives at P.U.K.

In order to achieve its overall profitability goals, the P.U.K. management believed that each individual investment project had to meet certain profitability criteria, chief among which was a minimum internal rate of return.

The process of determining the minimum required internal rate of return for all projects at P.U.K. involved several steps. First, it was necessary to calculate the cost of equity capital, the cost of debt capital, and therefore the overall cost of capital for the entire P.U.K. group. The cost of equity capital for P.U.K. was estimated to be roughly 11 percent. The aftertax cost of debt for P.U.K. was estimated at approximately 4.5 percent.

The overall cost of capital was calculated as a weighted average of the cost of equity and the cost of debt capital.[3] P.U.K. used the current relative

---

[3] See the Appendix for a more complete description of the method used by P.U.K. to compute the cost of capital for the group.

book values of shareholders' equity and long- and medium-term debt to weight the cost of each. The overall cost of capital for P.U.K. was estimated to be roughly 9 percent after taxes.

The minimum required internal rate of return for individual projects was initially set equal to the estimated overall cost of capital. However, the P.U.K. management noted three reasons why this rule was not optimal. First, there were a number of investment projects which were absolutely necessary but which would not earn a positive return for the company (e.g., pollution control equipment). Second, despite the best efforts of the management groups submitting the projects for approval, the P.U.K. staff believed it was inevitable that all the costs of the projects would not be taken into consideration.

Finally, in order to take into account the riskiness of the new project, the P.U.K. staff believed that the minimum required rate of return should be higher than the estimated cost of capital. The risks envisioned in this regard included uncertainty about the general economic and political situation as well as uncertainty about the particular market for which the new product was being produced.

Thus, in order to take into account these three items, the minimum required rate of return was set at a level of 15 percent as compared to the estimated cost of capital of 9 percent.

THE BROWN/CEBAL PROJECT

Under the terms of the proposed venture, Cebal would own 51 percent of the project and Brown, 49 percent. Essentially, Brown would provide the expertise necessary to build and put into operation the can plant. For this contribution, Brown would be paid a royalty by the newly formed company.

The new plant would be managed by Cebal which would receive a management fee equal to one half of the royalties paid to Brown.

The cans produced by the new plant would be sold to the Italian Division of Byron, Ltd. Under the terms of the proposed contract with Byron, Ltd., Byron–Italy would agree to purchase virtually the entire output of the new plant for the first five years of production beginning in 1977. The price to be paid by Byron, Ltd. would be linked to an index of the cost elements of production. (See Exhibit 3 for a resume of the contract with Byron, Ltd.)

Canned beer was first introduced by Byron, Ltd. in Italy in 1973, having been sold only in bottled form prior to that time. Byron, Ltd. was just finishing the construction of its first canning plant, located at Varese near Milano in the north of Italy. It was to this new plant that Brown/Cebal would sell its production. Byron–Italy, which had been importing its cans from Austria and Belgium, was primarily interested in having its can requirements met by a plant near the canning facilities.

EXHIBIT 3
Summary of the principal clauses of the proposed contract between Brown (Wilson)/Cebal and Byron, Ltd.

1. **Duration of the contract:** Five years (then annual renewal by tacit agreement).
2. **Minimum and maximum quantities:** To be sold by the supplier and purchased by the customer:

First year	50–110 million units
Second year	120–180 million units
Third year and following	150–200 million units

3. **Sales forecasts:** They will be established by Byron, Ltd. three months in advance and revised each month.
4. **Sales price:** (delivered to the customer's factory): 80 lire
5. **Sales price indexing:**
   a. The standards for materials consumed by each physical unit (metal, ink, energy, etc. . .) and the standard costs per unit will be communicated to Price Waterhouse by Brown/Cebal as soon as the contract is signed (for aluminium cans for tin cans).
      Category 1—Basic raw materials: metal, paint, ink, etc. . .
      Category 2—Salaries and social charges.
      Category 3—Other cost elements: packaging, energy, tooling, maintenance, taxes, royalties.
   b. All changes in unit consumption of materials and all changes in standard unit costs (in lira) will bring about, after verification by Price Waterhouse, a change in the sales price (for the cost components listed in categories 1, 2, and 3). The sales price is subject to revision every two months.
   c. Each increase in the standard costs for Categories 1 and 2 will be increased an additional 25 percent to cover the costs such as depreciation, leasing, research and development, profits and their eventual modificatiion, these cost factors being considered as fixed in the framework of the contract.
6. **Payment terms:** Thirty days from the billing date; a discount of 1 percent for payment in the week following the billing day. All payments will be made in lire.
7. **Inventory:** Three weeks of finished products at the Brown/Cebal factory.
8. **Sales to third parties:** Brown/Cebal will be able to sell to other customers, even competitors of Byron, Ltd., after having satisfied the contract.
9. **Responsibility:** The seller and the buyer will be "excused" for not satisfying their respective obligations in case of extreme outside conditions. Such conditions are fire, floods, strikes, acts of God, and so forth.
10. **Arbitration:** All litigation will be submitted to an international commercial court and to arbitrators following the laws in practice.

Byron–Italy had been the first European subsidiary to substitute the two-piece can for bottles. Should the new venture be successful, Brown/Cebal would be in an excellent position to win further can supply contracts from Byron, Ltd.'s other European subsidiaries. Similarly, Brown/Cebal might also win contracts from other beverage producers who might switch from one-way bottles to two-piece cans.

One important aspect of the proposed new venture was the expected sources of supply of the aluminum necessary to manufacture the cans. Essentially, Brown/Cebal would purchase its aluminum requirements from the market supplier offering the most advantageous terms, which might or might not be P.U.K.'s Aluminum Division, Cégédur Pechiney. However, if Cégédur Pechiney's price was competitive, then Brown/Cebal would purchase as much of its aluminum needs as Cégédur Pechiney wished to provide. At current and predicted prices, it was expected that Cégédur Pechiney would supply roughly 75 percent of Brown/Cebal's raw material requirements.[4]

In return for the preferential treatment of Cégédur Pechiney, the Brown Company had required that Cégédur Pechiney act as a supplier of last resort to the Brown/Cebal project. Thus, if a worldwide shortage of aluminum developed or if other suppliers refused to supply aluminum to Brown/Cebal, Cégédur Pechiney would have to supply the aluminum. On the other hand, if there occurred a world glut of aluminum, the price to be paid by Brown/Cebal for the aluminum purchased from Pechiney was subject to certain minimums.

The expected total investment in the Brown/Cebal project was FF86 million for the first production line and FF106 million for a second production line, assuming an 8.4 percent per year increase in plant and equipment costs due to inflation. (See Exhibit 4 for a schedule showing the timing of investment outlays for the Brown/Cebal project). The second line would begin production in 1980 should Bryon, Ltd.'s requirements exceed the capacity of the first line and/or should new markets open up for the Brown/Cebal product. Indeed, both events were expected to take place.

The proposed financing plan for this investment relied on six primary sources of funds:

1. *Equity capital:* FF24 million in 1975–1976 (51 percent to be provided by Cebal).
2. *Stockholder loans:* FF22.4 million from 1976 to 1979, then FF24.8 million in 1979; terms—interest rate of 12 percent and repayable in 1980–1981 (51 percent to be provided by Cebal).
3. *Long-term loans:* FF8 million at 12.0 percent interest in 1975–1976 for the building of the factory; FF20.8 million in 1978–1979 for the equipment for the second production line, assuming it is not leased.
4. *Leasing:* FF53.9 million worth of equipment beginning in 1976 from a leasing company that would be formed by Cebal and Brown, and that would purchase the equipment and then lease it to the Italian operation. The purchase would be financed completely by parent company guaranteed long-term debt. The ownership of the separate leasing company would be divided between Brown and Cebal in the same proportions as the project, i.e., 49 percent–51 percent. Payments to the leasing company would be denominated in U.S. dollars.

---

[4] Pechiney Cégédur would make a reasonable profit at the current and expected prices and costs. Pechiney Cégédur had adequate capacity to meet the needs of the Brown/Cebal project.

EXHIBIT 4
Sources and uses of funds by Italian aluminum can subsidiary (FF millions)

	1975	1976	1977	1978	1979	1980	1981	1982	1983	1984	Total
Sources:											
Equity from parents	11.2	12.8	0	0	0	0	0	0	0	0	24.0
Loans from parents	0	6.4	9.6	6.4	24.8	0	0	0	0	0	47.2
Lease agreement	0	53.9	0	0	0	0	0	0	0	0	53.9
Other long-term loans	3.2	4.8	4.8	4.8	16.0	0	0	0	0	0	28.8
Bank loans	0	14.4	4.8	0	0	0	0	0	0	0	19.2
Credit from suppliers	0	.8	0	4.0	2.4	6.4	6.4	3.2	2.2	2.4	32.6
Accrued taxes	0	0	0	0	0	7.3	21.1	9.6	5.3	10.8	54.1
Cash flow from operations	(.3)	(4.8)	(11.2)	12.5	22.3	37.0	65.5	81.0	91.3	99.8	417.0
Total sources	14.1	88.3	8.0	27.7	65.5	50.7	93.0	93.8	98.8	113.0	676.8
Uses:											
Investment in fixed assets	10.8	73.8	1.1	23.1	59.9	2.7	2.8	4.5	6.5	6.9	192.1
Start-up costs	2.7	8.3	0	.8	0	0	0	0	0	0	11.0
Increase in inventories	0	1.6	4.0	4.8	2.9	6.4	9.0	4.5	2.1	2.4	37.7
Increase in accounts receivable	0	0	2.4	2.4	1.4	3.2	4.0	2.2	1.1	1.2	17.9
Repayment of borrowings:											
Shareholder loans	0	0	0	0	0	28.8	18.4	0	0	0	47.2
Other medium and long term	0	0	.3	.8	.8	1.3	2.9	2.9	2.9	16.9	28.8
Supplier loan	0	0	0	0	0	1.1	19.3	2.5	2.5	2.5	27.9
Bank loan	0	0	0	0	0	0	19.2	0	0	0	19.2
Dividends to parents	0	0	0	0	0	9.7	17.4	77.2	83.7	83.1	295.0
	13.5	83.7	7.8	31.1	65.0	53.2	93.0	93.8	98.8	113.0	676.8
Investment in liquid assets	.6	4.6	.2	(3.4)	.5	(2.5)	0	0	0	0	0
Total uses	14.1	88.3	8.0	27.7	65.5	50.7	93.0	93.8	98.8	113.0	676.8

5. *Local borrowing:* The working capital needs of the company would be met with short-term debt in Italy at an interest rate of 20 percent. It was forecast that local bank borrowing would reach FF19 million by year-end 1977.
6. *Internally generated funds:* Beginning in 1978, the project was expected to show a positive and increasing cash flow.
(See Exhibit 4 for a table showing the financing plan for the project.)

In presenting the Brown/Cebal project for approval, the Cebal financial analysis staff had stressed the low amount of investment required by Cebal. The investment proposal included the following statement:

> Cebal, as a 51 percent shareholder, must invest FF43.9 million for the first production line and FF97.9 million total for the two lines.
>
> However, given the proposed financing plan, the actual funds put in by Cebal will be much smaller than that. Recourse will be made to long-term debt and to leasing.
>
> Therefore, Cebal's actual investment in the first production line will be only FF5.71 million in 1975, FF9.79 million in 1976, and FF4.90 million in 1977. The total investment for these three years will be roughly FF20.8 million, comprised of FF12.24 million equity, and FF8.56 million in shareholders' loans to be repaid starting in 1980. The second production line will only require a FF15.9 million investment in 1978 and 1979.
>
> Thus, it is only for FF20.8 million that we are making a capital appropriation request.

In making forecasts of the income statements and funds flows for the can manufacturing plant, the Cebal management had evaluated three alternative projects. The first was the most likely and involved manufacturing two-piece aluminum cans in Italy as described previously.

The second project evaluated was different only in that the cans were to be made out of tin rather than aluminum. This was a feasible alternative in that tin could be substituted for aluminum on the same machines and Byron, Ltd. was willing to accept tin cans. However, this alternative was not as attractive because the added benefit of purchasing aluminum from Pechiney Cégédur would be lost.

The final option studied by the Cebal management entailed building the plant in France, some 500 kilometers from the proposed Italian location. This alternative had the advantage of avoiding an investment in Italy, but concurrently had the disadvantage of removing the plant from its primary market. The potential market for cans in France was considered to be less than in Italy. Further, Byron–Italy was hesitant to have its can requirements met by a plant so far away. Finally, transportation costs were high relative to the value of the product.

The first and most attractive option of manufacturing aluminum cans in Italy was expected to show accounting profits beginning in 1978. (See

EXHIBIT 5
Operating forecasts for Italian aluminum can alternative (FF millions)

	1975	1976	1977	1978	1979	1980	1981	1982	1983	1984
Millions of units	0	0	60	140	170	245	330	360	360	360
Number of production lines	0	0	1	1	1	2	2	2	2	2
Net sales	0	0	45.3	113.6	147.6	227.6	328.1	383.1	409.9	438.6
Cash manufacturing costs	0	0	31.2	68.4	88.2	138.0	193.6	226.7	242.6	259.5
Other cash costs	0	0	4.1	4.8	6.0	7.0	8.1	9.5	10.2	10.9
Industrial margin before leasing	0	0	10.0	40.4	53.4	82.6	126.3	146.8	157.1	168.1
Leasing expense	0	2.6	12.3	12.3	12.3	12.3	12.3	12.3	12.3	0
Industrial margin	0	(2.6)	(2.3)	28.1	41.1	70.4	114.0	134.5	144.8	168.1
Brown royalties	0	0	2.3	5.7	5.9	9.1	9.8	11.5	8.2	8.8
Cebal management fee	0	0	1.1	2.8	3.0	4.6	4.9	5.7	4.1	4.4
Interest costs:										
Stockholder loans	0	.2	1.3	1.9	2.3	5.3	2.1	0	0	0
Other loans	.3	2.0	4.2	5.1	7.7	7.0	7.6	2.6	2.2	1.0
Profit before depreciation and taxes	(.3)	(4.8)	(11.2)	12.6	22.3	44.3	89.4	114.7	130.3	153.9
Depreciation expense	0	0	3.6	5.2	10.4	13.9	18.6	18.4	19.0	18.6
Amortization of start-up expense	0	0	2.2	2.1	2.2	2.2	2.2	0	0	0
Profit before taxes	(.3)	(4.8)	(17.0)	5.2	9.7	28.2	68.7	96.3	111.3	135.3
Taxes*	0	0)	0	0	0	7.3	24.0	33.7	39.0	54.1
Profit after taxes	(.3)	(4.8)	(17.0)	5.2	9.7	20.9	44.7	62.6	72.3	81.2
Noncash charges	0	0	5.8	7.3	12.6	16.1	20.8	18.4	19.0	18.6
Cash flow from operations	(.3)	(4.8)	(11.2)	12.5	22.3	37.0	65.5	81	91.3	99.8

* 35 percent rate until 1984 when it increases to 40 percent.

EXHIBIT 5 (*continued*)
Major assumptions underlying income statement projections

1. **Inflation**—All items leading up to the industrial margin have been adjusted to take into account the expected inflation of 8.4 percent per year over the period in question. All other items are set by contract or by accounting principles and will not be impacted by inflation.
2. **Reference money**—$1 = FF4.75 and 100 lire = FF0.71. The line items for each year have been converted from lire to FF on the basis of the 100 lire/FF0.71 exchange rate.
3. **Sales price estimates**—The initial price is 80 lire per can (79.20 lire after deducting the 1 percent discount given for payment within 10 days). In constant prices, the price per can has been assumed to fall 10 percent in 1982 when the contract with Byron, Ltd. is up for renewal. The revenues have been converted to current FF as per item 1 above.
4. **Sales volume estimates**—It is assumed that, beginning in 1980, sales will begin to be made outside Italy: 1980 (10%); 1981 (20%); 1982 to 1984 (25%).
5. **Materials costs and scrap**—These figures are based on current prices and assume that Cégédur Pechiney supplies 75 percent of the aluminum for the can frames and 100 percent for the can tops. Alcoa will supply the remaining 25 percent for the can frames.
6. **Transportation cost**—Estimated at FF0.29 per 100 cans in Italy and FF3.92 per 100 cans for sales outside of Italy.
7. **Direct manufacturing costs**—The assumed operating efficiencies are as follows:

1977, June	40 percent
1977, December	55
1978, May	65
1978, October	70
1979, September	75

8. **Financial costs**—12 percent for medium-term loans in Italy and 20 percent for short-term loans in Italy.
9. **Leasing costs**—The contract duration is seven years with an interest rate of 15 percent, and is denominated in $U.S. The annual payment in lire has been determined by multiplying the annual payment in $U.S. times the 667 lire/$U.S.1 exchange rate.
10. **Depreciation schedules**—All straight line:

Buildings	20 years
Installation	7 years
Tools and replacement parts	3 years
Start-up costs	5 years

Exhibit 5 for the projected income statement for Brown/Cebal and an outline of the major assumptions underlying the forecasts.) The alternative projects were also expected to show profits in 1978, though initial losses were higher and subsequent profits lower.

The return on the total funds actually invested by the 51 percent shareholder, Cebal, was estimated at 33 percent for the proposed Italian aluminum can option. The funds flows projections upon which this calculation was based included as cash outflows the subscriptions to equity and debt by Cebal, which financed the initial losses and the investment. The management fee, the interest on the loans and the expected dividends comprised the inflows to Cebal. (See Exhibit 6 for a table showing the forecasted inflows and outflows and the underlying assumptions upon which this calculation was based. Exhibit 7 shows pro forma balance sheets for the subsidiary.)

EXHIBIT 6
Cash flow analysis of Italian aluminum can project (FF millions)

	1975	1976	1977	1978	1979	1980	1981	1982	1983	1984	Total
Investment in form of:											
Loan	0	(3.2)	(4.9)	(3.3)	(12.6)	0	0	0	0	0	(24.0)
Equity	(5.6)	(6.6)	0	0	0	0	0	0	0	0	(12.2)
Interest income on loan	0	0.1	0.7	1.0	1.2	2.7	1.0	0	0	0	6.7
Management fee	0	0	1.1	2.8	3.0	4.6	4.9	5.7	4.1	4.4	30.6
French tax on interest and management fee*	0	0	(.9)	(1.9)	(2.1)	(3.7)	(2.9)	(2.9)	(2.0)	(2.2)	(18.6)
Dividends from subsidiary	0	0	0	0	0	4.9	8.9	39.4	42.7	42.4	138.3
French tax on dividends†	0	0	0	0	0	(1.7)	(3.1)	(13.8)	(14.9)	(14.8)	(48.3)
Loan repayment by subsidiary	0	0	0	0	0	15.0	9.0	0	0	0	24.0
Residual value‡	0	0	0	0	0	0	0	0	0	15.0	15.0
Annual aftertax cash flows to Cebal	(5.6)	(9.7)	(4.0)	(1.4)	(10.5)	21.8	17.8	28.4	29.9	44.8	111.5

Internal rate of return = 33%
Net present value at 15% = FF27.7 million
Payback = period 6

* Interest and the management fee would be taxed at a 50 percent rate.
† Dividends would be taxed at a 35 percent rate.
‡ Residual value was estimated equal to Cebal's share of the book value at year-end 1984, adjusted for any taxes on liquidation dividends [.51 × FF27.3 million (−).35 (.51 × FF27.3 million (−) FF24 million)]. Exhibit 6 shows a pro forma balance sheet for year-end 1984, with book value = FF27.3 million.

EXHIBIT 7
Projected balance sheets for Italian aluminum can subsidiary (FF millions)

	1975		1979		1984
Assets:					
Cash and marketable securities		0.6		2.5	0
Accounts receivable		0		6.2	17.9
Inventory		0		13.3	37.7
Total current		0.6		22.1	55.6
Gross fixed assets	10.8		114.8		138.2
Less: Accumulated depreciation	0		19.2		107.7
Net fixed assets		10.8		95.6	30.6
Capitalized start-up costs		2.7		4.4	0
		14.1		122.1	86.1
Liabilities and net worth:					
Accounts payable		0		12.0	4.7
Accrued taxes		0		0	54.1
Bank loan		0		19.2	0
Total current		0		31.2	58.8
Shareholder loan		0		47.2	0
Other medium- and long-term loan		3.2		26.9	0
Shareholders equity		10.9		16.8	27.3
		14.1		122.1	86.1

The estimated return of 33 percent resulted in part from the significant extent to which the subsidiary would raise its own finance from sources other than the parent. If the return were calculated on the basis of the total cash flows of the project before any financing arrangements, the return would be 22 percent. (See Exhibit 8.)

Finally, the profitability of the project at the level of the entire aluminum sector was analyzed. This calculation was based on a marketing study recently completed within the aluminum sector which found that the expected, integrated internal rate of return on new investment projects for manufacturing aluminum beverage cans was on the order of 17 percent.[5] The integrated return was calculated for the complete investment project, starting with the supply of raw aluminum and ending with the sale of the final product, aluminum cans. The marketing study referred to predicted a decline in profitability over time due to product pricing pressures. These pressures would be absent from the specific Brown/Cebal project for the first years due to the contract with Byron, Ltd.

All of the measures of profitability for the Brown/Cebal project exceeded minimum investment return objectives set by the P.U.K. management.

---

[5] This figure refers not to this project in particular, but to other similar projects facing the aluminum sector.

EXHIBIT 8

Analysis of total cash flows before any financing arrangements—Italian aluminum can project (FF millions)

	1975	1976	1977	1978	1979	1980	1981	1982	1983	1984	Total
Industrial margin before leasing*	0	0	10.0	40.4	53.4	82.6	126.3	146.8	157.1	168.1	
Brown royalties*	0	0	2.3	5.7	5.9	9.1	9.8	11.5	8.2	8.8	
Cebal management fee*	0	0	1.1	2.8	3.0	4.6	4.9	5.7	4.1	4.4	
Depreciation expense*	0	0	3.6	5.2	10.4	13.9	18.6	18.4	19.0	18.6	
Imputed depreciation leased equipment	0	0	7.7	7.7	7.7	7.7	7.7	7.7	7.7	0	0
Amortization of start-up expense*	0	0	2.2	2.1	2.2	2.2	2.2	0	0	0	0
Profit before taxes	0	0	(6.9)	16.9	24.2	45.1	83.1	103.5	118.1	136.3	
Italian taxes	0	0	0	3.5	8.5	15.8	29.1	36.2	41.3	54.5	
French taxes on dividends	0	0	0	0	0	3.4	6.1	27.0	29.3	29.1	
Profit after taxes	0	0	(6.9)	13.4	15.7	25.9	47.9	40.3	47.5	52.7	
Noncash charges	0	0	13.5	15.0	20.3	23.8	28.5	26.1	26.7	18.6	
Cash flow from operations	0	0	6.6	28.4	36.0	49.7	76.4	66.4	74.2	71.3	

* See Exhibit 5.

	1975	1976	1977	1978	1979	1980	1981	1982	1983	1984	Total
Investment in fixed assets	(10.8)	(73.8)	(1.1)	(23.1)	(59.9)	(2.7)	(2.8)	(4.5)	(6.5)	(6.9)	(192.1)
Start-up costs	(2.7)	(8.3)	0	0	0	0	0	0	0	0	(11.0)
Increase in inventories	0	(1.6)	(4.0)	(4.8)	(2.9)	(6.4)	(9.0)	(4.5)	(2.1)	(2.4)	(37.7)
Increase in accounts receivable	0	0	(2.4)	(2.4)	(1.4)	(3.2)	(4.0)	(2.2)	(1.1)	(1.2)	(17.9)
Increase in accounts payable	0	0.8	4.8	4.0	2.4	5.3	(12.9)	0.7	(0.3)	(0.1)	4.7
Increase in accrued taxes	0	0	0	7.7	3.9	9.0	13.6	8.0	3.4	14.6	59.8
Cash flow from operations	0	0	6.6	28.4	36.0	49.7	76.4	66.4	74.2	71.3	
Total cash flow	(13.5)	(82.9)	3.9	9.8	(21.9)	51.7	61.3	63.9	67.6	75.3	

Internal rate of return, ignoring any terminal value = 21 percent.
Internal rate of return, assuming terminal value equals net book value in 1985 = 22 percent.
Payback period = Year 6.

The analysis of the project extended beyond the numerical calculations of expected profitability. The Cebal management had identified three major sources of risk in the project. First, there was the risk that the price of tin would decline relative to aluminum. This possibility was believed to be unlikely, and the project showed a reasonable return even if it were to occur and tin were substituted for aluminum.

The second risk identified by the Cebal management was the possibility of some form of prohibitive legislation on no-deposit packaging (i.e., cans, one-way bottles). Management believed that prohibition of such containers would not occur in the near future, though some form of tax or deposit might be imposed. By agreement, Cebal would be able to pass on any producer tax to Byron, Ltd.

The final and most important risk was potential deterioration in the economic and political situation in Italy. This concern was addressed by the Cebal management:

The situation in Italy

With the political instability, lack of Government, deteriorated economic and social situation, the deficit in the balance of payments and the commercial trade balance, heavy foreign debt, high union demands present at the end of 1974, Italy gives all indication of being a country and an economy which should not attract investments.

However, are Italy and its 50 million people irretrievably destined to anarchy, and is the proposed Brown/Cebal investment destined to failure? Let's be straight-forward. The risk cannot be eliminated, but the concrete risks can be analyzed and reduced.

1. The most serious risk is without a doubt the strike risk. But for our project, assuming three shift operations, salaries represent only 10 percent of sales, and the number of workers is only 88 for each line; a policy of "high salary" should reduce the strike risk without penalizing the profits too much. Byron, Ltd. has been subject to only one day of strike in Italy since January 1974 (the national strike).

   The projected operating results have been established by including, in addition to paid vacation, an allowance for one week of strike per year.
2. The risk of devaluation is also serious. The contract with Byron, Ltd. substantially reduces the risk by indexing raw materials costs which are paid for in foreign exchange by Brown/Cebal.

   This risk remains however for the leasing contract made in dollars; a 10 percent devaluation of the lire would reduce the annual profit FF800-thousand during the life of this contract.
3. The risk of nationalization does not appear very big for a factory of 100 to 150 people.

Are the risks resulting from the Italian environment so much higher than the risks that would be run with the same investment in France?

By 1977, the date of the starting up of the factory (located, moreover, in an industrial region in the northeast of Italy, considered as socially calm), won't

Italy have found again an acceptable financial and economic appearance? Can one think that a situation such as that of 1974 will prolong itself another three years, while Italy belongs to the European community, while its interests are not isolated from those of Germany, France, and the United States?

The assured sale of the production for five years to a customer with a solid international reputation and position counterbalances in our opinion the risk of locating in Italy.

Furthermore, the opportunity to earn a 33 percent return on the funds supplied by Cebal on this project as well as on future possible projects with Byron, Ltd., seems highly attractive; and does not even include the benefits to Cégédur Pechiney.

APPENDIX: COST OF CAPITAL

P.U.K. obtains funds from borrowing and from increasing its stockholder's equity. This money has a cost. It is not difficult to determine the cost for debt; it is the rate of interest. Concerning equity funds, we will indicate the possible approaches for realistically estimating their cost, that is the "interest" for the stockholders.

The cost of capital for P.U.K. is the weighted average of these two rates of interest (on debt and on equity). It is the average interest rate which must be obtained on long-term capital available to us.

Cost of debt

The correct cost to take into account is that of future debt and not the average cost of current debt.

The gross cost of future debt can be estimated at 9 percent (that is 4.5 percent after taxes at a 50 percent tax rate).

Cost of equity

Method 1. The only serious studies of the cost of equity funds over a long period were made for the financial market in the United States. These studies established that, on average, the return on an investment in the stock market (dividends and capital gains) was between 7 and 8 percent before inflation. These statistics have led to the following formula:

Current interest rate of the common stock market = 7 to 8 percent

+ Rate of inflation

The current rate of inflation being exceptionally high, the inflation rate to be used in the formula is around 4 to 5 percent. Thus, the cost of equity funds runs from 11 to 13 percent for the average company.

Method 2. One can use a discounting formula by assuming that the stockholder discounts a series of dividends and the resale price (terminal value) of his shares. However, the resale price will depend on the series of future dividends.

In this way one reaches the conclusion that the price of a share today is equal to the discounted value of an infinite series of dividends, these dividends increasing at the same rate as reinvested profits. This reasoning leads to the following mathematical formula.

$$\text{Rate of interest of equity funds} = D/P + g$$

where:

D = Dividend per share
P = Price of the share
g = Rate of increase of the dividend per share

This formula verifies the hypotheses that the stockholder expects, on the one hand, a certain annual return from his investment (dividend), and on the other hand, an increase in this return due to the future return on retained earnings. (This formula is however not valid for "growth stocks.")

Application to the case of P.U.K. The relationship (in percent) of the dividend/price of the stock has moved from less than 3 percent in 1963 (2.8 percent for the Pechiney shares and 1.8 percent for the Ugine Kuhlmann shares) to 5.7 percent in 1973 (taking 140 Francs as the average price). This evolution is without a doubt due on the one hand to the acceleration of inflation, and on the other hand to anticipation of smaller dividend increases today than 10 years ago.

The average increase of the dividend over the 1963–70 period was 7 percent per year (for Pechiney as well as for Ugine Kuhlmann). In 1972 and 1973 the dividend was not changed because of the particularly difficult economic situation.

One can presume that the stockholder expects a renewed annual progression of the dividend from 5 to 6 percent, this increase being lower than that experienced in the past, but slightly higher than the long-term rate of inflation (4 to 5 percent).

Application of the formula gives an interest rate for equity funds of between *11 and 12 percent* after taxes. We use the lowest estimate (11 percent) as the cost of equity funds because it seems the most realistic over the long term, even if the probable actual cost is around 13 percent given the level of the stock price and inflation.

Cost of capital

The cost of capital is the weighted average of the interest rates for debt and for equity funds. For the weighting coefficients two approaches can be used.

Method 1. The respective weighting of the debt and the equity can be taken from the 1972 P.U.K. consolidated balance sheet.

$$\text{Cost of capital} = \frac{re \times SE + i(1 - t)D}{SE + D}$$

where

re = cost of equity funds $\qquad\qquad$ = 11%

SE = shareholders' equity + minority interest $\quad$ = 7 261 MF

i = gross cost of debt $\qquad\qquad$ = 9%

t = tax rate for the totality of the consolidated = 0.40
companies

D = consolidated medium- and long-term debt = 5 181 MF

One obtains a cost of capital equal to 8.7 percent.

Method 2. Instead of using the consolidated net shareholders' equity as the weighting coefficient for equity funds, one can use current stockmarket value and the current cost of equity funds (13 percent).

$$\text{Cost of capital} = \frac{re \times mv + i(1 - t)D}{mv + D}$$

re = current rate of interest on equity funds $\qquad$ = 13%

mv = stockmarket value (on the basis of an average
stockmarket price ex dividend of Fr. 140) + minority
interest and annual dividends $\qquad\qquad$ = 4 845 MF

The other factors remain unchanged.

The cost of capital evaluated by this method is equal to 9.1 percent. We retain 9 percent as the cost of the capital. The stockmarket capitalization is lower than the consolidated net position, which reflects the current poor return on equity funds. This shows that improving the stockmarket price of the shares depends closely on an improvement in profits. Therefore, it is necessary to establish return on investment objectives which are as ambitious as possible.

────◄CASE IV-3►────

AB Thorsten (A)

────••◄∞►••────

This case deals with an investment proposal made by Anders Ekstrom, president of AB Thorsten, a firm engaged in the production and sale of chemicals, with headquarters in Stockholm, Sweden. This proposal was made to the management of Roget S.A., in Brussels, Belgium. AB Thorsten is a 100 percent-owned subsidiary of Roget S.A.[1]

Summary of operations: Roget S.A.

Roget S.A. is one of the largest industrial companies in Belgium. Founded 40 years ago, the company originally produced a line of simple products for sale in Belgium. Today it has expanded to produce 208 complex chemical products in 21 factories.

André Juvet, president of Roget, states that the organization of the company (Exhibit 1) is the result of careful planning.

> Until five years ago, we were organized with one large manufacturing division here in Belgium, and one large sales division. One department of the sales division was devoted to export sales. However, exports grew so fast, and domestic markets became so complex, that we created three main product divisions, each with its own manufacturing plants and sales organizations. In addition, we have created foreign subsidiaries to take over the business in certain areas. For example, in Industrial Chemicals we have two subsidiaries—one in the United Kingdom and one in Sweden which serves all Scandinavia. At the same time, the domestic department of the Industrial Chemicals Division exports to the rest of Europe. The United Kingdom and Sweden account for 9 percent and 5 percent of sales in that division, but 14 percent added to total sales is very important.
>
> Another thing we achieve in the new organization is individual profit responsibility of all executives at all levels. Mr. Gillot is responsible for profits for all industrial chemicals, Mr. Lambert is responsible for profits from domestic operations [manufacturing and sales] and export sales to countries where we do not have subsidiaries or factories, and Mr. Ekstrom is responsible for profits in Scandinavia. We also utilize a rather liberal bonus system to reward executives at each level, based on the profits of their divisions.

Copyright © 1969 by l'Institut pour l'Etude des Méthodes de Direction de l'Entreprise (IMEDE), Lausanne, Switzerland. Names of people and places have been disguised. Authors of this case are Professor Gordon Shillinglaw, Columbia University, and Professor Charles E. Summer, University of Washington. Reproduced by permission.

[1] The letters AB and S.A. are the equivalent designations in Sweden and Belgium of "Corp." or "Inc." in the United States and "Ltd." in the United Kingdom.

EXHIBIT 1
Organization chart

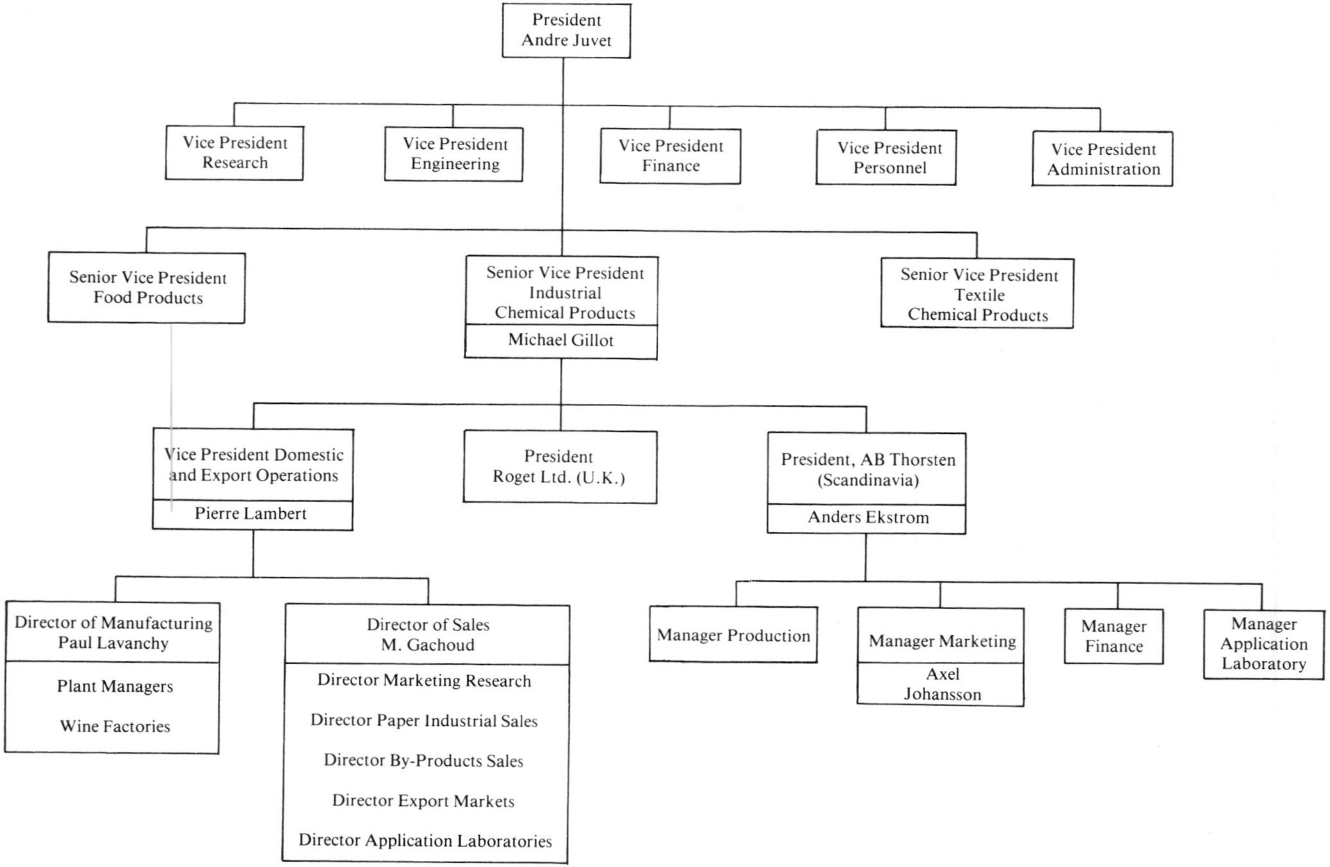

This, together with a policy of promotion from within, helps stimulate managers in Roget to a degree not enjoyed by some of our competitors. It also helps to keep men in an industry where experience is of great importance. Most of our executives have been in the starch chemicals business all of their lives. It is a complex business, and we feel that it takes many years to learn it.

We have developed certain policies—rules of the game—which govern relationships with our subsidiary company presidents. These are intended to maintain efficiency of the whole Roget complex, while at the same time to give subsidiary managers autonomy to run their own businesses. For example a subsidiary manager can determine what existing Roget products he wants to sell in his part of the world market. Export Sales will quote him the same price as they quote agents in all countries. He is free to bargain, and if he doesn't like the price he needn't sell the product. Second, we encourage subsidiaries to propose to division management in Brussels the development of new products. If these are judged feasible we manufacture them in Belgium for supply to world markets. Third, the subsidiary president can build his own manufacturing plants if he can justify the investment in his own market."

Company background: AB Thorsten

AB Thorsten was purchased by Roget S.A. eight years ago. Since that time the same four men have constituted Thorsten's Board of Directors: Ekstrom; Michael Gillot, senior vice president in charge of Roget's industrial chemical products division; Ingve Norgren, a Swedish banker; and Ove Svensen, a Stockholm industrialist. Swedish corporation law requires any company incorporated in Sweden to have Swedish directors, and the Roget management felt fortunate in finding two men as prominent as Norgren and Svensen to serve on the Thorsten board.

During the first four years of Roget's ownership, Thorsten's sales fluctuated between Skr5 and 7 million, but hit a low at the end of that period.[2] The board of AB Thorsten decided at that time that the company was in serious trouble, and that the only alternative to selling the company was to hire a totally different management to overhaul and streamline the entire company operation.

On advice of the Swedish directors, Anders Ekstrom, a 38-year-old graduate of the Royal Institute of Technology, was hired. He had had 16 years of experience in production engineering for a large machinery company, as marketing manager of a British subsidiary in Sweden, and as division manager responsible for profits in a large paper company.

Ekstrom has been president of AB Thorsten for the past four years. In that time, sales have increased to Skr 20 million and profits have reached

---

[2] In round numbers, the Skr is approximately equivalent to U.S. 20 cents, or 10 Belgian francs (BFr). To avoid confusion, all monetary figures in this case series are stated in Swedish kroner, even though some of the actual transactions are made in Belgian francs.

levels that Roget's management finds highly satisfactory. Both Ekstrom and Norgren (a director) attribute this performance to: (*a*) increase in industrial activity in Scandinavia; (*b*) changes in production methods, marketing strategy, and organization structure made by Ekstrom; (*c*) the hiring of competent staff; and (*d*) Ekstrom's own ambition and hard work. To these reasons the case writer also adds Ekstrom's knowledge of modern planning techniques—rather sophisticated market research methods, financial planning by use of discounted cash flows and incremental analysis, and, as Ekstrom puts it, "all those things my former company had learned from the American companies."

Ekstrom says that at the time he joined Thorsten, he knew it was a risk. "I like the challenge of building a company. If I do a good job here I will have the confidence of Norgren and Svenson as well as of the Roget management in Brussels. Deep down inside, succeeding in this situation will teach me things that will make me more competent as a top executive. So I chose this job even though I had at the time (and still have) offers from other companies."

Initial proposal for manufacture of XL–4

Two years ago, Ekstrom informed the Thorsten board of directors that he proposed to study the feasibility of constructing a factory in Sweden for the manufacture of XL–4, a product used in paper converting. He explained that he and his customer engineers had discovered a new way of helping large paper mills convert their machines at little cost so that they could use XL–4 instead of competitors' products. Large paper mill customers would be able to realize dramatic savings in material handling and storage costs and to shorten drying time substantially. In his judgment, Thorsten could develop a market in Sweden almost as big as Roget's present worldwide market for XL–4. XL–4 was then being produced in Roget's domestic division at the rate of 600 tons a year, but none of this was going to Sweden.

"At that meeting," Ekstrom states, "Mr. Gillot and the other directors seemed enthusiatic. Gillot said, 'Of course—go ahead with your study and when you have a proposed plan, with the final return on investment, send it in and we will consider it thoroughly.'

"During the next six months, we did the analysis. My market research department estimated the total potential in Sweden at 800 tons of XL–4 per year. We interviewed important customers and conducted trials in the factories of three big companies which proved that with the introductiin of our machine designs the large cost saving would indeed materialize. We determined that if we could sell the product for Skr1,850 per ton, we could capture one half of the market within a three-year period, or 400 tons a year.

"At the same time, I called the head of the Corporate Engineering Division in Brussels [see Exhibit 1] asking his help in designing a plant to produce

400 tons per year, and in estimating the cost of the investment. This is a routine thing. The central staff divisions are advisory and always comply with requests for help. He assigned a project manager and four other engineers to work on the design of factory and machinery, and to estimate the cost. At the same time I assigned three men from my staff to work on the project. In three months this joint task group reported that the necessary plant could be built for Skr700,000.

"All of this we summarized in a pro forma calculation [Exhibits 2 through 5]. This calculation, together with a complete written explanation, was mailed 18 months ago to Mr. Gillot. I felt rather excited, as did most of my staff. We all know that introduction of new products is one of the keys to continued growth and profitability. The yield of this investment (15 percent) was well above the minimum 8 percent established as a guideline for new investment by the Roget vice president of finance. We also knew that it was a *good* analysis, done by modern tools of management. In the covering letter, I asked that it be put on the agenda for the next board meeting."

The minutes of the next board meeting held in Stockholm three weeks later show on the agenda "A Proposal for Investment in Sweden" to be presented by Mr. Ekstrom, using a series of charts (Exhibits 1 through 5). The minutes also quote his remarks as he explained the proposal to other directors:

> You will see from the summary table (Exhibit 2) that this project is profitable. On an initial outlay of Skr700,000 for equipment and Skr56,000 for working capital, we get a rate of return of 15 percent and a present value of Skr246,000.
>
> Let me explain some of the figures underlying this summary table. My second chart [Exhibit 3] summarizes the operating cash flows that we expect to get from the XL–4 project. The sales forecast for the first seven years is shown in column (2). The forecast was not extended beyond seven years because our engineers estimate that the technology of starch manufacture will improve gradually, so that major plant renovations will become economical at about the end of the seventh year. Actually, we see no reason why this particular product, XL–4, will decline in demand after seven years.
>
> The estimated variable cost of Skr1,000 per ton shown in column (3) is our estimate of the full operating cost of manufacturing XL–4 in Sweden, including out-of-pocket fixed costs such as plant management salaries, but excluding depreciation. These fixed costs must of course be included because they are incremental to the decision.
>
> As column (4) shows, we feel certain that we can enter the market initially with a selling price of Skr2,000 a ton, but full market penetration will require a price reduction to Skr1,850 at the beginning of the second year.
>
> The variable profit resulting from these figures is shown in columns (5) and (6). Column (7) then lists the market development and promotion expenditures that are needed to launch the product and achieve the forecasted sales levels. Column (8) contains the net operating cash flows before tax, based on figures in the preceding columns.

EXHIBIT 2
Proposal for manufacture of XL–4 in Sweden, financial summary (all figures in Skr)

Year	Description	Aftertax cash flows*	Present value at 8 percent
	Equipment	−700,000	
	Working capital	− 56,000	
	Total	−756,000	−756,000
1	Cash operating profit	105,000	
	Working capital	− 2,000	
	Total	103,000	95,000
2	Cash operating profit	160,000	
	Working capital	− 7,000	
	Total	153,000	131,000
3	Cash operating profit	215,000	171,000
4	Cash operating profit	215,000	158,000
5	Cash operating profit	215,000	146,000
6	Cash operating profit	145,000	91,000
7	Cash operating profit	145,000	
	Recovery value of equipment and working capital	+215,000	
	Total	+360,000	210,000
	Grand Total	+650,000	246,000
	Net present value	Skr. 246,000	
	Payback period (before tax).....	4 years	
	Internal rate of return..........	15 percent	

* From Exhibits 3, 4 and 5.

The cost of the plant can be written off for tax purposes over a five-year period, at the rate of 20 percent of original cost each year. Subtracting this amount from the before-tax cash flow yields the taxable income figures summarized in column (9). The tax in column (10) is then subtracted from the before-tax cash flow to yield the after tax cash flow in column (11).

A proposal of this kind also requires some investment in working capital. My third chart [Exhibit 4] summarizes our estimates on this element. We'll need about Skr80,000 to start with, but some of this can be deducted immediately from our income taxes. Swedish law permits us to deduct 60 percent of the cost of inventories from taxable income. For this reason, we can get an immediate reduction of Skr24,000 in the taxes we have to pay on our other income in Sweden. This is shown in column (5). The net investment of working capital is thus only Skr56,000, the figure we show in column (6).

We'll need small additional amounts of working capital in the next two years, and these amounts are also shown in column (6). Altogether, our working capital requirements will add up to Skr65,000 by the end of our second full year of operations.

EXHIBIT 3
Estimated operating cash flows from manufacture and sales of XL–4 in Sweden

(1)	(2)	(3)	(4)	(5)	(6)	(7)	(8)	(9)	(10)	(11)
	Sales (in tons)	Variable costs per ton	Sales price per ton	Variable profit margin per ton (4) – (3)	Total variable profit margin (2) × (5)	Promotion costs	Profit contribution (6) – (7)	Tax depreciation	Tax 50 percent of (8) – (9)	Net cash flow after tax (8) – (10)
Year		——(Skr per ton)——			——————(figures in Skr 000)——————					
1	200	1,000	2,000	1,000	200	130	70	140	(35)	105
2	300	1,000	1,850	850	255	75	180	140	20	160
3	400	1,000	1,850	850	340	50	290	140	75	215
4	400	1,000	1,850	850	340	50	290	140	75	215
5	400	1,000	1,850	850	340	50	290	140	75	215
6	400	1,000	1,850	850	340	50	290	—	145	145
7	400	1,000	1,850	850	340	50	290	—	145	145
Total	2,500				2,155	455	1,700	700	500	1,200

EXHIBIT 4
Estimated working capital required for manufacture and sale of XL–4 in Sweden* (Skr 000)

	(1)	(2)	(3)	(4)	(5)	(6)
				Change	*Tax credit*	*Net*
		Other current	*Working*	*from*	*(30% of*	*funds*
	Inventory	*assets less*	*capital*	*previous*	*change*	*required*
	at cost	*current liabilities*	*(1) + (2)*	*year*	*in (1))*	*(4) − (5)*
Year 0	80	0	80	+80	24	56
Year 1	90	−5	85	+ 5	3	2
Year 2	100	−5	95	+10	3	7
Year 3						
and later.........	100	−5	95	0	0	0
Total	100	−5	95	95	30	65

* These figures are in addition to the estimated cost of Skr 700,000

Now let's look at one last chart [Exhibit 5]. Seven years is a very conservative estimate of the life of the product. If we limit the analysis to seven years, we'll be overlooking the value of our assets at the end of that time. At the very worst, the plant itself should be worth Skr300,000 after seven years. We'd have to pay tax on that, of course, because the plant would be fully depreciated, but this would still leave us with Skr150,000 for the plant.

The working capital should be fully recoverable, too. After paying the deferred tax on inventories, we'd still get Skr65,000 back on that. The total value at the end of seven years would thus be Skr215,000."

Mr. Ekstrom ended this opening presentation by saying, "Gentlemen, it seems clear from these figures that we can justify this investment in Sweden on the basis of sales to the Swedish market. The group vice president for finance has laid down the policy that any new investment should yield at least 8 percent. This particular proposal shows a return of 15 percent. My management and I strongly recommend this project." (The Thorsten vice presidents for production, sales, and finance had been called into the board meeting to be present when this proposal was made.)

Ekstrom told the casewriter that while he was making this proposal he was sure that it would be accepted.

EXHIBIT 5
Estimated end-of-life value of Swedish assets

Plant	Skr300,000	
Less tax on gain if sold at this price	150,000	
Net value of plant		Skr150,000
Working capital	Skr 95,000	
Less payment of deferred tax on special inventory reserves	30,000	
Net value of working capital		65,000
Net value of Swedish assets after 7 years.....................		Skr215,000

APPENDIX

Present value tables

Present value of $1 $P = \$1 \; \dfrac{1}{(1 + i)^n}$

Number of periods	1%	2%	2½%	3%	3½%	4%	4½%	5%	6%	8%
1	.990	.980	.976	.971	.966	.962	.957	.952	.943	.926
2	.980	.961	.952	.943	.934	.925	.916	.907	.890	.857
3	.971	.942	.929	.915	.902	.889	.876	.864	.840	.794
4	.961	.924	.906	.888	.871	.855	.839	.823	.792	.735
5	.951	.906	.884	.863	.842	.822	.802	.784	.747	.681
6	.942	.888	.862	.837	.814	.790	.768	.746	.705	.630
7	.933	.871	.841	.813	.786	.760	.735	.711	.665	.583
8	.923	.853	.821	.789	.759	.731	.703	.667	.627	.540
9	.914	.837	.801	.766	.734	.703	.673	.645	.592	.500
10	.905	.820	.781	.744	.709	.676	.644	.614	.558	.433
11	.896	.804	.762	.722	.685	.650·	.616	.585	.527	.428
12	.887	.788	.744	.701	.662	.625	.590	.557	.497	.397
13	.879	.773	.725	.681	.639	.601	.564	.530	.469	.368
14	.870	.758	.708	.661	.618	.577	.540	.505	.442	.340
15	.861	.743	.690	.642	.597	.555	.517	.481	.417	.315
16	.853	.728	.674	.623	.577	.534	.494	.458	.394	.292
17	.844	.714	.657	.605	.557	.513	.473	.436	.371	.270
18	.836	.700	.641	.587	.538	.494	.453	.416	.350	.250
19	.828	.686	.626	.570	.520	.475	.433	.396	.331	.232
20	.820	.673	.610	.554	.503	.456	.415	.377	.312	.215
21	.811	.660	.595	.538	.486	.439	.397	.359	.294	.199
22	.803	.647	.581	.522	.469	.422	.380	.342	.278	.184
23	.795	.634	.567	.507	.453	.406	.363	.326	.262	.170
24	.788	.622	.553	.492	.438	.390	.348	.310	.247	.158
25	.780	.610	.539	.478	.423	.375	.333	.295	.233	.146
26	.772	.598	.526	.464	.409	.361	.318	.281	.220	.135
27	.764	.586	.513	.450	.395	.347	.305	.268	.207	.125
28	.757	.574	.501	.437	.382	.333	.292	.255	.196	.116
29	.749	.563	.489	.424	.369	.321	.279	.243	.185	.107
30	.742	.552	.477	.412	.356	.308	.267	.231	.174	.099
31	.735	.541	.465	.400	.344	.296	.256	.220	.164	.092
32	.727	.531	.454	.388	.333	.285	.244	.210	.155	.085
33	.720	.520	.443	.377	.321	.274	.234	.200	.146	.079
34	.713	.510	.432	.366	.310	.264	.224	.190	.138	.073
35	.706	.500	.421	.355	.300	.253	.214	.181	.130	.068
36	.699	.490	.411	.345	.290	.244	.205	.173	.123	.063
37	.692	.481	.401	.335	.280	.234	.196	.164	.116	.058
38	.685	.471	.391	.325	.271	.225	.188	.157	.109	.054
39	.678	.462	.382	.316	.261	.217	.180	.149	.103	.050
40	.672	.453	.372	.307	.253	.208	.172	.142	.097	.046
41	.665	.444	.363	.298	.244	.200	.165	.135	.092	.043
42	.658	.435	.354	.289	.236	.193	.157	.129	.087	.039
43	.652	.427	.346	.281	.228	.185	.151	.123	.082	.037
44	.645	.418	.337	.272	.220	.178	.144	.117	.077	.034
45	.639	.410	.329	.264	.213	.171	.138	.111	.073	.031
46	.633	.402	.321	.257	.205	.165	.132	.106	.069	.029
47	.626	.394	.313	.249	.199	.158	.126	.101	.065	.027
48	.620	.387	.306	.242	.192	.152	.121	.096	.061	.025
49	.614	.379	.298	.235	.185	.146	.116	.092	.058	.023
50	.608	.372	.291	.228	.179	.141	.111	.087	.054	.021

10%	12%	14%	16%	18%	20%	25%	30%	40%	50%	Number of periods
.909	.893	.877	.862	.847	.833	.800	.769	.714	.667	1
.826	.797	.769	.743	.718	.694	.640	.592	.510	.444	2
.751	.712	.675	.641	.609	.579	.512	.455	.364	.296	3
.683	.636	.592	.552	.516	.482	.410	.350	.260	.198	4
.621	.567	.519	.476	.437	.402	.328	.269	.186	.132	5
.564	.507	.456	.410	.370	.335	.262	.207	.133	.088	6
.513	.452	.400	.354	.314	.279	.210	.159	.095	.059	7
.467	.404	.351	.305	.266	.233	.168	.123	.068	.039	8
.424	.361	.308	.263	.225	.194	.134	.094	.048	.026	9
.386	.322	.270	.227	.191	.162	.107	.073	.035	.017	10
.350	.287	.237	.195	.162	.135	.086	.056	.025	.012	11
.319	.257	.208	.168	.137	.112	.069	.043	.018	.008	12
.290	.229	.182	.145	.116	.093	.055	.033	.013	.005	13
.263	.205	.160	.125	.099	.073	.044	.025	.009	.003	14
.239	.183	.140	.108	.084	.065	.035	.020	.006	.002	15
.218	.163	.123	.093	.071	.054	.028	.015	.005	.002	16
.198	.146	.108	.080	.060	.045	.023	.012	.003	.001	17
.180	.130	.095	.069	.051	.038	.018	.009	.002	.001	18
.164	.116	.083	.060	.043	.031	.014	.007	.002	.000	19
.149	.104	.073	.051	.037	.026	.012	.005	.001	.000	20
.135	.093	.064	.044	.031	.022	.009	.004	.001	.000	21
.123	.083	.056	.038	.026	.018	.007	.003	.001	.000	22
.112	.074	.049	.033	.022	.015	.006	.002	.000	.000	23
.102	.066	.043	.028	.019	.013	.005	.002	.000	.000	24
.092	.059	.038	.024	.016	.010	.004	.001	.000	.000	25
.084	.053	.033	.021	.014	.009	.003	.001	.000	.000	26
.076	.047	.029	.018	.011	.007	.002	.001	.000	.000	27
.069	.042	.026	.016	.010	.006	.002	.001	.000	.000	28
.063	.037	.022	.014	.008	.005	.002	.000	.000	.000	29
.057	.033	.020	.012	.007	.004	.001	.000	.000	.000	30
.052	.030	.017	.010	.006	.004	.001	.000	.000	.000	31
.047	.027	.015	.009	.005	.003	.001	.000	.000	.000	32
.043	.024	.013	.007	.004	.002	.001	.000	.000	.000	33
.039	.021	.012	.006	.004	.002	.001	.000	.000	.000	34
.036	.019	.010	.006	.003	.002	.000	.000	.000	.000	35
.032	.017	.009	.005	.003	.001	.000	.000	.000	.000	36
.029	.015	.008	.004	.002	.001	.000	.000	.000	.000	37
.027	.013	.007	.004	.002	.001	.000	.000	.000	.000	38
.024	.012	.006	.003	.002	.001	.000	.000	.000	.000	39
.022	.011	.005	.003	.001	.001	.000	.000	.000	.000	40
.020	.010	.005	.002	.001	.001	.000	.000	.000	.000	41
.018	.009	.004	.002	.001	.000	.000	.000	.000	.000	42
.017	.008	.004	.002	.001	.000	.000	.000	.000	.000	43
.015	.007	.003	.001	.001	.000	.000	.000	.000	.000	44
.014	.006	.003	.001	.001	.000	.000	.000	.000	.000	45
.012	.005	.002	.001	.000	.000	.000	.000	.000	.000	46
.011	.005	.002	.001	.000	.000	.000	.000	.000	.000	47
.010	.004	.002	.001	.000	.000	.000	.000	.000	.000	48
.009	.004	.002	.001	.000	.000	.000	.000	.000	.000	49
.009	.003	.001	.001	.000	.000	.000	.000	.000	.000	50

Present value of $1 per period
$$P = \$1 \left[\frac{1 - \dfrac{1}{(1 + i)^n}}{j} \right]$$

Number of periods	1%	2%	2½%	3%	3½%	4%	4½%	5%	6%	8%
1	0.990	0.980	0.976	0.971	0.966	0.962	0.957	0.952	0.943	0.926
2	1.970	1.942	1.927	1.913	1.900	1.886	1.873	1.859	1.833	1.783
3	2.941	2.884	2.856	2.829	2.802	2.775	2.749	2.723	2.673	2.577
4	3.902	3.808	3.762	3.717	3.673	3.630	3.588	3.546	3.465	3.312
5	4.853	4.713	4.646	4,580	4.515	4.452	4.390	4.329	4.212	3.993
6	5.795	5.601	5.508	5.417	5.329	5.242	5.158	5.076	4.917	4.623
7	6.728	6.472	6.349	6.230	6.115	6.002	5.893	5.786	5.582	5.206
8	7.652	7.325	7.170	7.020	6.874	6.733	6.596	6.463	6.210	5.747
9	8.566	8.162	7.971	7.786	7.608	7.435	7.269	7.108	6.802	6.247
10	9.471	8.983	8.752	8.530	8.317	8.111	7.913	7.722	7.360	6.710
11	10.368	9.787	9.514	9.253	9.002	8.760	8.529	8.306	7.887	7.139
12	11.255	10.575	10.258	9.954	9.663	9.385	9.119	8.863	8.384	7.536
13	12.134	11.348	10.983	10.635	10.303	9.986	9.683	9.394	8.853	7.904
14	13.004	12.106	11.691	11.296	10.921	10.563	10.223	9.899	9.295	8.244
15	13.865	12.849	12.381	11.938	11.517	11.118	10.740	10.380	9.712	8.559
16	14.718	13.578	13.055	12.561	12.094	11.652	11.234	10.838	10.106	8.851
17	15.562	14.292	13.712	13.166	12.651	12.166	11.707	11.274	10.477	9.122
18	16.398	14.992	14.353	13.754	13.190	12.659	12.160	11.690	10.828	9.372
19	17.226	15.678	14.979	14.324	13.710	13.134	12.593	12.085	11.158	9.604
20	18.046	16.351	15.589	14.877	14.212	13.590	13.008	12.462	11.470	9.818
21	18.857	17.011	16.185	15.415	14.698	14.029	13.405	12.821	11.764	10.017
22	19.660	17.658	16.765	15.937	15.167	14.451	13.784	13.163	12.042	10.201
23	20.456	18.292	17.332	16.444	15.620	14.857	14.148	13.489	12.303	10.371
24	21.243	18.914	17.885	16.936	16.058	15.247	14.495	13.799	12.550	10.529
25	22.023	19.523	18.424	17.413	16.482	15.622	14.828	14.094	12.783	10.675
26	22.795	20.121	18.951	17.877	16.890	15.983	15.147	14.375	13.003	10.810
27	23.560	20.707	19.464	18.327	17.285	16.330	15.451	14.643	13.211	10.935
28	24.316	21.281	19.965	18.764	17.667	16.663	15.743	14.898	13.406	11.051
29	25.066	21.844	20.454	19.188	18.036	16.984	16.022	15.141	13.591	11.158
30	25.808	22.396	20.930	19.600	18.392	17.292	16.289	15.372	13.765	11.258
31	26.542	22.938	21.395	20.000	18.736	17.588	16.544	15.593	13.929	11.350
32	27.270	23.468	21.849	20.389	19.069	17.874	16.789	15.803	14.084	11.435
33	27.990	23.989	22.292	20.766	19.390	18.148	17.023	16.003	14.230	11.514
34	28.703	24.499	22.724	21.132	19.701	18.411	17.247	16.193	14.368	11.587
35	29.409	24.999	23.145	21.487	20.001	18.665	17.461	16.374	14.498	11.655
36	30.108	25.489	23.556	21.832	20.290	18.908	17.666	16.547	14.621	11.717
37	30.800	25.969	23.957	22.167	20.571	19.143	17.862	16.711	14.737	11.775
38	31.485	26.441	24.349	22.492	20.841	19.368	18.050	16.868	14.846	11.829
39	32.163	26.903	24.730	22.808	21.102	19.584	18.230	17.017	14.949	11.879
40	32.835	27.355	25.103	23.115	21.355	19.793	18.402	17.159	15.046	11.925
41	33.500	27.799	25.466	23.412	21.599	19.993	18.566	17.294	15.138	11.967
42	34.158	28.235	25.821	23.701	21.835	20.186	18.724	17.423	15.225	12.007
43	34.810	28.662	26.166	23.982	22.063	20.371	18.874	17.546	15.306	12.043
44	35.455	29.030	26.504	24.254	22.283	20.549	19.018	17.663	15.383	12.077
45	36.095	29.490	26.833	24.519	22.495	20.720	19.156	17.774	15.456	12.108
46	36.727	29.892	27.154	24.775	22.701	20.885	19.288	17.880	15.524	12.137
47	37.354	30.287	27.467	25.025	22.899	21.043	19.415	17.981	15.589	12.164
48	37.974	30.673	27.773	25.267	23.091	21.195	19.536	18.077	15.650	12.189
49	38.588	31.052	28.071	25.502	23.277	21.341	19.651	18.169	15.708	12.212
50	39.196	31.424	28.362	25.730	23.456	21.482	19.762	18.256	15.762	12.233

10%	12%	14%	16%	18%	20%	25%	30%	40%	50%	Number of periods
0.909	0.893	0.877	0.862	0.847	0.833	0.800	0.769	0.714	0.667	1
1.736	1.690	1.647	1.605	1.566	1.528	1.440	1.361	1.244	1.111	2
2.487	2.402	2.322	2.246	2.174	2.106	1.952	1.816	1.589	1.407	3
3.170	3.037	2.914	2.798	2.690	2.589	2.362	2.166	1.849	1.605	4
3.791	3.605	3.433	3.274	3.127	2.991	2.689	2.436	2.035	1.737	5
4.355	4.111	3.889	3.685	3.498	3.326	2.951	2.643	2.168	1.824	6
4.868	4.564	4.288	4.039	3.812	3.605	3.161	2.802	2.263	1.883	7
5.335	4.968	4.639	4.344	4.078	3.837	3.329	2.925	2.331	1.922	8
5.759	5.328	4.946	4.607	4.303	4.031	3.463	3.019	2.379	1.948	9
6.145	5.650	5.216	4.833	4.494	4.192	3.571	3.092	2.414	1.965	10
6.495	5.938	5.453	5.029	4.656	4.327	3.656	3.147	2.438	1.977	11
6.814	6.194	5.660	5.197	4.793	4.439	3.725	3.190	2.456	1.985	12
7.103	6.424	5.842	5.342	4.910	4.533	3.780	3.223	2.469	1.990	13
7.367	6.628	6.002	5.468	5.008	4.611	3.824	3.249	2.478	1.993	14
7.606	6.811	6.142	5.575	5.092	4.675	3.859	3.268	2.484	1.995	15
7.824	6.974	6.265	5.668	5.162	4.730	3.887	3.283	2.489	1.997	16
8.022	7.120	6.373	5.749	5.222	4.775	3.910	3.295	2.492	1.998	17
8.201	7.250	6.467	5.818	5.273	4.812	3.928	3.304	2.494	1.999	18
8.365	7.366	6.550	5.877	5.316	4.843	3.942	3.311	2.496	1.999	19
8.514	7.469	6.623	5.929	5.353	4.870	3.954	3.316	2.497	1.999	20
8.649	7.562	6.687	5.973	5.384	4.891	3.963	3.320	2.498	2.000	21
8.772	7.645	6.743	6.011	5.410	4.909	3.970	3.323	2.498	2.000	22
8.883	7.718	6.792	6.044	5.432	4.925	3.976	3.325	2.499	2.000	23
8.985	7.784	6.835	6.073	5.451	4.937	3.981	3.327	2.499	2.000	24
9.077	7.843	6.873	6.097	5.467	4.948	3.985	3.329	2.499	2.000	25
9.161	7.896	6.906	6.118	5.480	4.956	3.988	3.330	2.500	2.000	26
9.237	7.943	6.935	6.136	5.492	4.964	3.990	3.331	2.500	2.000	27
9.307	7.984	6.961	6.152	5.502	4.970	3.992	3.331	2.500	2.000	28
9.370	8.022	6.983	6.166	5.510	4.975	3.994	3.332	2.500	2.000	29
9.427	8.055	7.003	6.177	5.517	4.979	3.995	3.332	2.500	2.000	30
9.479	8.085	7.020	6.187	5.523	4.982	3.996	3.332	2.500	2.000	31
9.526	8.112	7.035	6.196	5.528	4.985	3.997	3.333	2.500	2.000	32
9.569	8.135	7.048	6.203	5.532	4.988	3.997	3.333	2.500	2.000	33
9.609	8.157	7.060	6.210	5.536	4.980	3.998	3.333	2.500	2.000	34
9.644	8.176	7.070	6.215	5.539	4.992	3.998	3.333	2.500	2.000	35
9.677	8.192	7.079	6.220	5.541	4.993	3.999	3.333	2.500	2.000	36
9,706	8.208	7.087	6.224	5.543	4.994	3.999	3.333	2.500	2.000	37
9.733	8.221	7.094	6.228	5.545	4.995	3.999	3.333	2.500	2.000	38
9.757	8.233	7.100	6.231	5.547	4.996	3.999	3.333	2.500	2.000	39
9.779	8.244	7.105	6.233	5.548	4.997	3.999	3.333	2.500	2.000	40
9.799	8.253	7.110	6.236	5.549	4.997	4.000	3.333	2.500	2.000	41
9.817	8.262	7.114	6.238	5.550	4.998	4.000	3.333	2.500	2.000	42
9.834	8.270	1.117	6.239	5.551	4.998	4.000	3.333	2.500	2.000	43
9.349	8.276	7.120	6.241	5.552	4.998	4.000	3.333	2.500	2.000	44
9.863	8.283	7.123	6.242	5.552	4.999	4.000	3.333	2.500	2.000	45
9.875	8.288	7.126	6.243	5.553	4.999	4.000	3.333	2.500	2.000	46
9.887	8.293	7.128	6.244	5.553	4.999	4.000	3.333	2.500	2.000	47
9.897	8.297	7.130	6.245	5.554	4.999	4.000	3.333	2.500	2.000	48
9.906	8.301	7.131	6.246	5.554	4.999	4.000	3.333	2.500	2.000	49
9.915	8.304	7.133	6.246	5.554	4.999	4.000	3.333	2.500	2.000	50

Index and source of cases

The cases published in this book are listed below in alphabetical order, together with their authors or supervisors and the institutions with which they were associated when they wrote them. Unless otherwise indicated, the copyright on all cases is held by the President and Fellows of Harvard College. No case included herein may be reproduced, in whole or in part, without the written permission of the copyright holder.

442

DATE DUE

Lewis and Clark College - Watzek Library

HF5635 .C32   wmain
/Case problems in management accounting

3 5209 00339 7136

LEWIS
PO